Springer Texts in Business and Economics

Springer Texts in Business and Economics (STBE) delivers high-quality instructional content for undergraduates and graduates in all areas of Business/Management Science and Economics. The series is comprised of self-contained books with a broad and comprehensive coverage that are suitable for class as well as for individual self-study. All texts are authored by established experts in their fields and offer a solid methodological background, often accompanied by problems and exercises.

Hamilton Galindo Gil • Alexis Montecinos Bravo •
Marco Antonio Ortiz Sosa

Dynamic Stochastic General Equilibrium Models

Real Business Cycles Models: Closed and Open Economy

Springer

Hamilton Galindo Gil
Department of Finance and Economics
Cleveland State University
Cleveland, OH, USA

Marco Antonio Ortiz Sosa
Department of Economics
University of the Pacific
Lima, Peru

Alexis Montecinos Bravo
Department of Finance
Sawyer Business School - Suffolk University
Boston, MA, USA

Universidad Adolfo Ibáñez
Business School
Santiago, Chile

ISSN 2192-4333 ISSN 2192-4341 (electronic)
Springer Texts in Business and Economics
ISBN 978-3-031-58104-5 ISBN 978-3-031-58105-2 (eBook)
https://doi.org/10.1007/978-3-031-58105-2

This Springer imprint is published by the registered company Springer Nature Switzerland AG
The registered company address is: Gewerbestrasse 11, 6330 Cham, Switzerland

To Jesus Christ: my God, my Savior, my Lord,
. . . my everything

Hamilton Galindo Gil

To Catita, Agustincito, and Loreto, the engine of my life.

Alexis Montecinos Bravo

To my beloved Niome, Mochi, and Cani.

Marco Antonio Ortiz Sosa

Preface

This book aims to guide the student step by step in developing and solving a DSGE (*Dynamic Stochastic General Equilibrium*) model—not only from the technical and conceptual aspects but also through the simulation process of each model. Excellent books in the literature address different aspects of DSGE models. However, due to the richness of the topic and the limited space, these books do not take a step-by-step approach to building DSGE models, making it difficult for students to dive into this area. This book attempts to fill this gap to some extent.

Three features of this book are worth highlighting. First, it attempts to perform all the algebra associated with each model. For instance, the optimization problem of each agent is carried out step by step, in the same way as the calculation of steady-state and the log-linearization of the model. Likewise, the solution method of undetermined coefficients and that of Blanchard and Kahn are developed with special detail. The purpose of all these steps is to allow students to understand each stage of the construction model process.

The second feature is that each model developed in each chapter has been placed in Dynare. In addition, some m-files have been built for certain specific tasks, such as model comparison. These codes allow students to replicate exactly what they find in the chapter. This generates *learning by doing* approach throughout the book.

The third characteristic is that the models considered are toy models in the closed and open economy. This allows the student to learn the basic lessons and understand the fundamental relationships of the variables. All of this will prepare the student to deal with more complex models.

Who Should Read This Book?

This book is intended for advanced undergraduate, master's degrees in economics or finance, or even applied mathematics. It also could be used as a complement to a basic course of business cycles at the doctoral level. We also hope this book could be useful for researchers in academia or central banks that use these models daily to prepare forecasts or simulations of aggregate variables.

Programs

Every chapter is accompanied by a set of codes (mod-files and m-files) that the reader can use to replicate the model developed in every chapter. These codes are available on the following webpage:

https://academic.csuohio.edu/galindogil-hamilton/book-rbc-english/

Cleveland, OH, USA — Hamilton Galindo Gil
Boston, MA, USA — Alexis Montecinos Bravo
Lima, Peru — Marco Antonio Ortiz Sosa

Acknowledgements

This book would not have been possible without the support and encouragement of many friends and colleagues. My profound gratitude goes to Jesus Christ, my God, for His guidance, love, and mercy and for making this project possible. I would like to express my deeply felt gratitude to my wife, Jenny, for her profound love and patience—she is a huge blessing to me. Special thanks to Cesar Ramos Huarachi, my research assistant, for his brilliant proofreading and book review. I am sure that any PhD program would be fortunate to have him. I am also highly indebted to Alexis Montecinos and Marco Ortiz, my coauthors, for making this project better and better. I especially thank Cleveland State University for providing a great environment to work on this book.

Hamilton Galindo Gil

I'm truly grateful for the trust and collaboration of my co-authors, Hamilton Galindo and Alexis Montecinos, in undertaking this project. A special acknowledgment goes to my dedicated research assistant, Javier Ayala, whose exceptional contributions have undeniably elevated the quality of our work. I also want to express my heartfelt thanks to Universidad del Pacifico for providing a supportive and fertile environment that has greatly contributed to the success of our project. Last but certainly not least, I'm indebted to my family for their unwavering support and encouragement throughout this journey.

Marco Antonio Ortiz Sosa

I embarked on this book project during my time pursuing a PhD in finance at MIT. It became evident to me that there was a significant gap between intermediate macroeconomics and the more advanced concepts in the field. This need was further emphasized during my tenure as a visiting professor at MIT, where I conducted research and witnessed the challenges faced by first-year PhD students in grasping foundational macroeconomics courses. The journey of bridging this gap through the creation of this book was incredibly rigorous and demanding, a collaborative effort shared with my coauthors.

Throughout this endeavor, I received invaluable support from various individuals. I extend my sincere gratitude to my coauthors for their unwavering support, patience, and commitment to quality, which laid the groundwork for the final product. My children, Catita and Agustincito, have been my constant motivation and the driving force behind everything I do. Without them, nothing would be possible. I want to thank my brother, Marcelo, who from heaven is always protecting me and giving me energy.

I am immensely thankful for the enduring support of my dear friends Carlos Jara, Pablo Gracia, Christian Belmar, Marcelo Farr, and Alejandro Inzunza, who have consistently believed in my ideas and entrusted me with their unwavering confidence. Special acknowledgment goes to Symnetics Chile and Pharu Analytics for their support during the creation of this book.

Lastly, but most importantly, I want to express my profound gratitude to my beloved wife, Loreto, who has been my rock, my pillar of strength, and the foundation of my entire life. Without her, everything I do would lack purpose and meaning.

Alexis Montecinos Bravo

Contents

1 An Overview of RBC Models 1
1.1 Introduction 1
1.2 Business Cycles 2
1.2.1 Definition 2
1.2.2 Stylized Facts 3
1.2.2.1 Characterization of the Stylized Facts 3
1.2.2.2 Stylized Facts in the United States 4
1.3 Historical Perspective of the RBC Theory 23
1.3.1 Overview of Schools of Economic Thought 23
1.3.2 The Historical Development of the RBC School 26
1.3.2.1 Research on the State of the Art of RBC Models 31
1.3.2.2 Research Related to the Labor Market 39
1.3.2.3 Investigations Related to Fiscal Policy 41
1.3.2.4 Research Associated with Money 48
1.3.2.5 Research Associated with Investment Shock 53
1.4 Theoretical Foundations of RBC Models 54
1.4.1 Main Assumptions 54
1.4.2 Steps to Develop an RBC Model 56
1.5 Codes 58

2 Dynare Foundations: Solving and Simulating DSGE Models 59
2.1 Introduction 59
2.2 What Is Dynare? 60
2.3 Structure of .mod File 61
2.3.1 The Preamble 61
2.3.2 The Model 64
2.3.3 Initials Values 65
2.3.4 Stationary State 66
2.3.5 Dynare and LaTeX 67
2.3.6 Definition of *Shocks* 68
2.3.7 Model Evaluation: Blanchard and Kahn Conditions 69

2.3.8 Computation of the Stochastic Solution 69
2.3.9 Simulation and HP Filter 72
2.3.10 Sensitivity Analysis 73
2.3.11 Ways to Write the Model in Dynare 74
2.4 Long and Plosser (1983)'s Model: Application in Dynare 75
2.4.1 Long and Plosser (1983)'s Model 75
2.4.2 Preamble 76
2.4.3 Model 81
2.4.4 Initial Values 83
2.4.5 Steady State 85
2.4.6 Definition of *Shock* 86
2.4.7 Model Evaluation 86
2.4.8 Solution 88
2.4.9 Impulse-Response Function (IRF) 93
2.4.10 Sensitivity Analysis 95
2.4.11 Simulation of Endogenous Variables 96
2.4.12 Calculation of Moments 100
2.4.13 HP Filter 100
2.5 Codes 102
2.6 Summary 103

3 RBC Model with Analytical Solution 105
3.1 Introduction 105
3.2 Model Construction 105
3.2.1 Utility Function 106
3.2.2 Households 108
3.2.3 Firms 111
3.2.4 Market Equilibrium and Definition of *shock* 114
3.2.5 Principal Equations 115
3.3 Calibration 115
3.4 Steady State 116
3.5 Linearization vs. Log-Linearization 121
3.5.1 Linearization (Variable in Levels) 122
3.5.2 Linearization (Logarithmic Variables) or Log-Linearization 126
3.6 Solution of Linear System 135
3.6.1 Analytical Method 136
3.6.2 Blanchard and Kahn Method 139
3.7 Time Series Representation 156
3.8 Impulse-Response Functions 159
3.9 Simulation of Endogenous Variables 170
3.10 Cyclic Component of Simulated Variables 171
3.11 Calculation of Theoretical Moments 172
3.12 Comparison of the Theoretical Model with the Data 174
3.13 Codes 175

4 RBC Model with Constant Labor 177
4.1 Introduction 177
4.2 Model Building 178
4.2.1 Households 178
4.2.2 Firms 182
4.2.3 Market Equilibrium and *Shock* Definition 182
4.2.4 Main Equations 183
4.3 Calibration 184
4.4 Steady State 184
4.5 Log-Linearization 187
4.5.1 Substitution and Income Effect of the Interest Rate 192
4.6 Solution of Linear System 200
4.6.1 Method of Undetermined Coefficients 200
4.6.2 Analysis of Elasticities 203
4.7 Representation of Time Series 207
4.7.1 Capital Time Series 208
4.7.2 Production Time Series 208
4.7.3 Consumption Time Series 209
4.7.4 Time Series of Gross Real Interest Rate 209
4.7.5 Inversion Time Series 210
4.8 Impulse-Response Functions 210
4.9 Simulation of the Endogenous Variables 218
4.10 Cyclic Component of Simulated Variables 220
4.11 Computation of Theoretical Moments 221
4.12 Comparison of the Theoretical Model with the Empirical Data 224
4.13 Summary 225
4.14 Codes 226

5 RBC Model with Variable Labor Supply 229
5.1 Introduction 229
5.2 Model Elements 230
5.2.1 Model Construction 230
5.2.1.1 Households 230
5.2.1.2 Firms 234
5.2.1.3 Market Equilibrium and Definition of Shock 235
5.2.1.4 System of Principal Equations 235
5.2.2 Calibration 235
5.2.3 Stationary State 236
5.2.4 Log-Linearization 240
5.2.5 Solution of the Linear System 246
5.2.5.1 Method of Undetermined Coefficients 246
5.2.5.2 Solution Obtained from Dynare 257
5.3 Model Solution Analysis 259
5.3.1 Analysis of the Coefficients of the Solution 259
5.3.1.1 Effects of δ 259

5.3.1.2 Effects of γ_n 264
5.3.1.3 Effects of ϕ 270
5.3.2 Impulse-Response Functions 274
5.3.2.1 How Does the Economy React to a Shock of Productivity? 275
5.3.3 Comparison of the Theoretical Model with the Data 275
5.3.3.1 Does the Shock Need to be Significant for the Model to Replicate the Data? 275
5.3.3.2 Does the Labor Supply Need to Be Very Elastic for the Model to Replicate the Data? 277
5.4 Summary 280
5.5 Codes 281

6 RBC Model with Shock to Investment and Variable Use of Capital 287
6.1 Introduction 287
6.2 Standard RBC Model and the Investment Shock 288
6.2.1 System of Principal Equations 289
6.2.2 Model Solution 290
6.2.3 Impulse-Response Functions 291
6.2.4 Comparison of the Model with the Data 295
6.3 Extended RBC Model: Inclusion of Shock to Investment and Variable Use of Capital 297
6.3.1 Model Elements 297
6.3.1.1 Households 297
6.3.1.2 Firms 303
6.3.1.3 Market Equilibrium and Definition of Shock 304
6.3.1.4 System of Principal Equations 304
6.3.1.5 Calibration 304
6.3.1.6 Stationary State 306
6.3.1.7 Model Solution 310
6.3.2 Solution Analysis 311
6.3.2.1 Impulse-Response Functions 311
6.3.2.2 Comparison of the Theoretical Model with the Data 319
6.4 Summary 320
6.5 Codes 321

7 Small Open Economy RBC 323
7.1 Introduction 323
7.2 Empirics 324
7.2.1 Construction of the Macroeconomic Series 324
7.2.2 Detrending Techniques for Extraction of the Cyclical Component 328
7.2.2.1 Log-Quadratic Detrending 329
7.3 Model Elements 334
7.3.1 Two-Period Small Open Economy Model 335

7.3.2 Introducing Stochasticity into the Infinite Horizon Model ... 340
7.4 Building the Model ... 341
7.4.1 Households ... 343
7.4.2 Firms ... 346
7.4.3 The External Sector ... 347
7.4.4 Market Equilibrium and *Shock* Definition ... 347
7.4.5 System of Main Equations ... 348
7.5 Parametrization ... 348
7.6 Steady State ... 350
7.6.1 Model Solution ... 353
7.7 Impulse-Response Functions ... 355
7.7.1 Impulse-Response Functions to Total Factor Productivity Shock ... 355
7.7.2 Impulse-Response Functions to External Interest Rate Shock ... 362
7.7.3 Comparison of the Model with the Data ... 364
7.8 Summary ... 365
7.9 Codes ... 366

8 Nontradable Goods in a Small Open Economy RBC ... 367
8.1 Introduction ... 367
8.2 Empirics ... 368
8.2.1 Construction of the Macroeconomic Series ... 368
8.2.2 Business Cycle Properties ... 369
8.3 Model Elements ... 372
8.4 Building the Model ... 373
8.4.1 Households ... 373
8.4.2 Firms ... 380
8.4.3 Market Clearing and Shock Definitions ... 382
8.4.4 Expressing Variables at Import Prices ... 383
8.4.5 External Sector ... 387
8.4.6 Parametrization ... 387
8.4.7 Steady State ... 387
8.4.8 Model Solution ... 392
8.5 Impulse-Response Analysis ... 393
8.5.1 Impulse-Response Functions to Terms of Trade Shock ... 393
8.5.2 Impulse-Response Functions to Productivity Shock Across Sectors ... 396
8.5.3 Comparison of Data and Theoretical Moments ... 397
8.6 Summary ... 399
8.7 Codes ... 399

A Dynamic Optimization 401
A.1 Introduction 401
A.2 Fundamentals of Real Analysis 401
A.2.1 What Mathematical Concepts Do We Need? 401
A.2.2 Concepts (Part I): Spaces 402
A.2.2.1 Vectorial Space 402
A.2.2.2 Metric Space 404
A.2.2.3 Normed (Vector) Space 405
A.2.2.4 Complete Space 405
A.2.3 Concepts (Part II): Contractions 406
A.2.3.1 Contraction (Contractive Application) 406
A.2.3.2 Blackwell's Conditions 407
A.2.4 Concepts (Part III): Fixed Point 407
A.2.4.1 What Is a Fixed Point? 407
A.2.4.2 Contractive Application Theorem 407
A.3 Dynamic Programming 408
A.3.1 Outlook 408
A.3.1.1 What Kind of Problem Do We Want to Solve? .. 408
A.3.1.2 Function Valor 410
A.3.1.3 Bellman Equation 410
A.3.1.4 Functional Problem 411
A.3.1.5 From SP to FP 411
A.3.2 Details 412
A.3.2.1 Optimality Principle 413
A.3.2.2 Method to Solve the FP 423
A.3.2.3 Differential Calculus Method to Solve the PF 430
A.3.3 Applications 438
A.3.3.1 Growth with Human Capital 438
A.3.3.2 Hercowitz and Sampson (1991) Model 444
References 445

Index 453

List of Figures

Fig. 1.1	Cyclical component of GDP per capita (1988.3–2016.4)	7
Fig. 1.2	HE-1| Annual growth rate of real GDP per capita (1930–2015)	8
Fig. 1.3	HE-2| Annual growth rate of the real capital stock per capita (1930–2015)	9
Fig. 1.4	HE-3| Rate of return on capital by the industrial sector (1987–2014)	9
Fig. 1.5	HE-4| Capital Stock Ratio (real)/GDP (real)	11
Fig. 1.6	HE-5| Participation of factors in the National Income (1948–2014)	12
Fig. 1.7	Long-run relationships between GDP, consumption, investment, and government purchases	12
Fig. 1.8	GDP, consumption, and investment (1954.1–2015.4)	15
Fig. 1.9	Real quarterly (net) capital *stock* (1954.1–2015.4)	16
Fig. 1.10	Macroeconomic series (1954.1–2015.4)	18
Fig. 1.11	US real GDP and trend component (1954.1–2015.4)	19
Fig. 1.12	Cyclical component of the economic series for the United States (1954.1–2015.4)	20
Fig. 1.13	Cyclical component of the economic series for the United States (1954.1–2015.4)	21
Fig. 1.14	Correlation between GDP (cyclical component) and labor productivity (cyclical component) (1954.1–2015.4)	22
Fig. 1.15	Historical development of schools in macroeconomics	23
Fig. 1.16	Steps to develop an RBC model	56
Fig. 2.1	Dynare as a Matlab preprocessor	61
Fig. 2.2	Structure of the .mod file	62
Fig. 2.3	Nonlinear and linear models	65
Fig. 2.4	Structure M	79
Fig. 2.5	Structure oo_	86
Fig. 2.6	oo_.steady_state	86
Fig. 2.7	Decision rules (oo_.dr)	88
Fig. 2.8	oo_.dr.eigval	88

Fig. 2.9 Impulse-response function (oo_.irfs) 93
Fig. 2.10 Consumption impulse-response function (oo_.irfs.cc_e) 94
Fig. 2.11 Impulse-response function (Dynare graph) 94
Fig. 2.12 Impulse-response function (Matlab plot) 95
Fig. 2.13 Sensitivity analysis: Persistence of the productivity shock ρ 97
Fig. 2.14 Structure oo_ (simulation) 98
Fig. 2.15 Simulation of the exogenous variable 99
Fig. 2.16 Simulation of the endogenous variable 99
Fig. 2.17 Six simulations of capital and output 100
Fig. 2.18 Cyclical and trend components of capital 102
Fig. 3.1 Long and Plosser model (1983, 1989) 106
Fig. 3.2 Steps of the Blanchard and Kahn method 140
Fig. 3.3 Policy function 156
Fig. 3.4 Impulse-response function 160
Fig. 3.5 Firm response to productivity *shock* ($t = 1$) 161
Fig. 3.6 Household response to *productivity shock* ($t = 1$) 163
Fig. 3.7 Equilibrium in the labor market ($t = 1$) 164
Fig. 3.8 Equilibrium at $t = 1$ 164
Fig. 3.9 Firms' response to productivity *shock* (t = 2) 166
Fig. 3.10 Household response to the *productivity shock* (t = 2) 167
Fig. 3.11 Equilibrium at $t = 2$ 168
Fig. 3.12 Firm response to productivity *shock* (t = 3) 169
Fig. 3.13 Household response to the *productivity shock* (t = 3) 170
Fig. 3.14 Simulation (first alternative) 171
Fig. 3.15 Simulation (second alternative) 172
Fig. 3.16 Trend 173
Fig. 3.17 Cycle 173
Fig. 3.18 Distribution of the standard deviation 174
Fig. 4.1 Scheme of the constant labor supply model 178
Fig. 4.2 Elasticities (coefficients of the solution) 207
Fig. 4.3 Effect on the production function 213
Fig. 4.4 Effect on capital demand 213
Fig. 4.5 Effect on the supply and demand of capital 214
Fig. 4.6 Impulse-response function of log-linear macroeconomic variables 216
Fig. 4.7 Impulse-response function of macroeconomic variables in levels 217
Fig. 4.8 Impulse-response function (comparison of variables log-linear vs. in levels) 219
Fig. 4.9 Simulation of log-linear macroeconomic variables 221
Fig. 4.10 Application of the HP filter to the simulated variables 222
Fig. 4.11 Distributions of the standard deviation of the theoretical model ... 224
Fig. 5.1 Effects of δ on capital ratios 260
Fig. 5.2 Effects of δ on the coefficients of consumption and investment 261

Fig. 5.3 Effects of δ on the product and interest rate coefficients 262
Fig. 5.4 Effects of δ on the labor and salary coefficients 264
Fig. 5.5 Elasticity of labor supply 265
Fig. 5.6 Effects of γ_n on the labor and salary coefficients 266
Fig. 5.7 Effects of γ_n on the coefficients of consumption and investment 267
Fig. 5.8 Effects of γ_n on the product and interest rate coefficients 268
Fig. 5.9 Effects of γ_n on capital coefficients 270
Fig. 5.10 Effects of ϕ on capital coefficients 271
Fig. 5.11 Effects of ϕ on the consumption and investment coefficients 271
Fig. 5.12 Effects of ϕ on the product and interest rate coefficients 272
Fig. 5.13 Effects of ϕ on the labor and salary coefficients 272
Fig. 5.14 Campbell (1994) with variable work: *productivity shock*. 274
Fig. 5.15 Elasticity of substitution of consumption ($1/\gamma$) 283
Fig. 5.16 Size (σ_ϵ) of productivity shock 283
Fig. 5.17 Persistence (ϕ) of productivity shock 284
Fig. 5.18 Labor supply elasticity ($1/\gamma_n$) 284
Fig. 5.19 Depreciation rate (δ) 285
Fig. 5.20 Comparison between the model of Long and Plosser (1983) and Campbell (1994) with variable work 285
Fig. 6.1 Campbell (1994) model with investment shock 293
Fig. 6.2 Campbell (1994) model with investment shock 294
Fig. 6.3 Scheme of the Greenwood et al. (1988) model 298
Fig. 6.4 Variable depreciation: dependent on the use of capital 300
Fig. 6.5 Effects of the investment shock in the capital services market 315
Fig. 6.6 Effects of the investment shock in the supply of capital and the labor market 316
Fig. 6.7 Greenwood et al. (1988)-*shock* to investment 317
Fig. 6.8 Variable utilization model (Greenwood et al., 1988) vs. fixed use model (Campbell, 1994) 318
Fig. 7.1 Canada GDP per capita (in logs) and trend component (1961–2021) 330
Fig. 7.2 Canada GDP per capita (in logs), consumption and investment (1961–2021) 330
Fig. 7.3 Canada GDP per capita (in logs), trade balance to GDP ratio, and current account to output ratio (1961–2021) 331
Fig. 7.4 Map of indifference curves 336
Fig. 7.5 Effects of a productivity shock ($v_t^e = 1.29$) 355
Fig. 7.6 Impact response of trade balance to productivity shock $v_t^e = 1.29$ 357
Fig. 7.7 Effects of the *shock* to productivity. Capital adjustment costs (ϕ) 360

Fig. 7.8 Effects of the *shock* to productivity. Persistence of the shock (ρ) 361
Fig. 7.9 Effects of an external interest rate shock ($v_t^n = 1.29$) 362
Fig. 8.1 Series of Chile 370
Fig. 8.2 Effects of a terms of trade shock 394
Fig. 8.3 Effects of a terms of trade shock on capital allocations 395
Fig. 8.4 Effects of a terms of trade shock 396
Fig. 8.5 Effects of a productivity shock across sectors 397
Fig. 8.6 Effects of a productivity shock across sectors 398
Fig. A.1 From SP to FP and its solution process 412
Fig. A.2 Three main theorems in dynamic programming (and their relationship with their hypotheses and propositions) 413
Fig. A.3 Solution of a system of nonlinear equations (see the function "system_na.m") 444

List of Tables

Table 1.1 Dates of economic cycles in the United States (1854–2009) 6
Table 1.2 Descriptive statistics of the cyclical component of the series for the United States (1954.1–2015.4) 10
Table 1.3 Historical development of RBC models 32
Table 1.4 Historical development of RBC models (continued) 33
Table 1.5 Historical development of RBC models (continued) 34
Table 1.6 State of the art 40
Table 1.7 RBC models with fiscal variables 49
Table 1.8 RBC models with fiscal variables (continued) 50
Table 1.9 Codes in Matlab and Dynare 58
Table 2.1 Files created by Dynare 60
Table 2.2 Variables created by Dynare 60
Table 2.3 Examples of declaration of endogenous variables 62
Table 2.4 Endogenous variable declaration examples 63
Table 2.5 Parameter declaration examples 64
Table 2.6 Initial values (nonlinear and linear model) 66
Table 2.7 Definition of *shock* 69
Table 2.8 Options in stoch_simul 71
Table 2.9 Options in stoch_simul (continued) 73
Table 2.10 Macro-language vs. Matlab for sensitivity analysis 74
Table 2.11 Four ways to write a model in Dynare 74
Table 2.12 Agent optimization problem 75
Table 2.13 System of nonlinear equations of the model (Long and Plosser, 1983) 75
Table 2.14 System of linear equations of the model (Long and Plosser, 1983) 76
Table 2.15 System of log-linear equations of the model (Long and Plosser, 1983) 76
Table 2.16 Calibration 77
Table 2.17 Steady state 77

Table 2.18 Declaration of endogenous variables 78
Table 2.19 Parameter declaration 79
Table 2.20 Declaration of parameter values 79
Table 2.21 Nonlinear model declaration 81
Table 2.22 Linear model declaration 82
Table 2.23 Declaration of initial values 83
Table 2.24 The Resid command: results 84
Table 2.25 Steady State 85
Table 2.26 Clash definition 86
Table 2.27 Eigenvalues 87
Table 2.28 Policy and state function 89
Table 2.29 Theoretical moments 101
Table 2.30 Theoretical moments (HP filter) 102
Table 2.31 Codes in Matlab and Dynare 103
Table 3.1 Effect of impatience on discount factor 109
Table 3.2 Nonlinear system of equations of the model 115
Table 3.3 Calibration 116
Table 3.4 Steady state 121
Table 3.5 Linear system of equations of the model (Long and Plosser 1983) 126
Table 3.6 Log-linear equations 135
Table 3.7 Policy and state functions (model solution) 156
Table 3.8 Time series representation 158
Table 3.9 Comparison of the cyclical behavior of the theoretical model with the empirical data 175
Table 3.10 Codes in Matlab and Dynare 175
Table 4.1 Nonlinear system of equations of the model 183
Table 4.2 Calibration (base values) 184
Table 4.3 Stationary state 187
Table 4.4 Log-linear equations 190
Table 4.5 Log-linear equations (reduced system) 191
Table 4.6 Coefficients (elasticities) of the linear model solution 204
Table 4.7 Special cases 207
Table 4.8 Construction of the capital impulse-response function 212
Table 4.9 Values of the impulse-response function (log-linear variables) 215
Table 4.10 Log-linear capital simulation 219
Table 4.11 Simulation of productivity and capital (log-linear) 220
Table 4.12 Simulation of log-linear macroeconomic variables 220
Table 4.13 Comparison of the cyclical behavior of the theoretical model with the empirical data 225
Table 4.14 Codes in Matlab and Dynare 227
Table 5.1 Elasticity of substitution 234
Table 5.2 System of principal nonlinear equations 236
Table 5.3 Calibration 236

Table 5.4 System of principal nonlinear equations in steady state 237
Table 5.5 Steady State 240
Table 5.6 Log-linear system of equations 246
Table 5.7 Value of $\eta_{kk_{1,2}}$ 253
Table 5.8 Policy and state functions 257
Table 5.9 Policy and state functions (from Dynare) 257
Table 5.10 Policy and state functions (xx = logx) 258
Table 5.11 Comparison of the cyclical behavior of the theoretical model with the empirical data 276
Table 5.12 Comparison of the cyclical behavior of the theoretical model with the empirical data 278
Table 5.13 Comparison of the cyclical behavior of the theoretical model with the empirical data 278
Table 5.14 Codes in Matlab and Dynare 282
Table 6.1 *Shock* to investment vs. shock to productivity 288
Table 6.2 System of principal nonlinear equations (Campbell 1994 model with *investment shock*) 289
Table 6.3 Policy and state function 290
Table 6.4 Comparison of the cyclical behavior of the theoretical model with the empirical data 296
Table 6.5 System of principal nonlinear equations 305
Table 6.6 Calibration 305
Table 6.7 System of principal nonlinear equations 306
Table 6.8 Steady state 310
Table 6.9 Policy and state function (model 1 ($\gamma = 1$)) 312
Table 6.10 Policy and state function (model 2 ($\gamma = 2$)) 313
Table 6.11 Comparison of the cyclical behavior of the theoretical model with the empirical data 320
Table 6.12 Codes in Matlab and Dynare 322
Table 7.1 Stylized facts of global macroeconomic fluctuations 325
Table 7.2 Variables included in the study 326
Table 7.3 Log-quadratic detrending (1990–2020) 332
Table 7.4 HP filtering (1990–2020) 333
Table 7.5 First differences (1990–2020) 334
Table 7.6 Net financial assets 342
Table 7.7 Nonlinear system of equations on the model 349
Table 7.8 Parametrization 350
Table 7.9 Steady state 351
Table 7.10 Policy and state functions 354
Table 7.11 Model generated moments for alternative model economies 360
Table 7.12 Moments generated across models 361
Table 7.13 Comparison of the cyclical behavior of the theoretic model with the empirical data 364
Table 7.14 Codes in Matlab and Dynare 366
Table 8.1 Variables included in the study 368

Table 8.2 Business cycle properties (1980–2020) 371
Table 8.3 Supply of households to firms 374
Table 8.4 Household equations 379
Table 8.5 Firms equations 382
Table 8.6 Rest of the model 388
Table 8.7 Parametrization 389
Table 8.8 Comparison of the cyclical behavior of the theoretic model with the empirical data 398
Table 8.9 Codes in Matlab and Dynare 400

Chapter 1
An Overview of RBC Models

1.1 Introduction

This chapter aims to provide an overview of the development of the Real Business Cycles (RBC) school since its inception in the 1980s. To do this, the chapter is divided into three parts.

In the first part, two essential aspects of the business cycle are described: on the one hand, a clear definition of the business cycle is enunciated and, on the other hand, its main characteristics, known as the stylized facts.

The second part develops a historical perspective of RBC models through two complementary approaches. The first briefly describes the evolution of economic schools since the Great Depression. This description allows us to locate the historical context in which the RBC school began to develop its main ideas. The second approach describes the development of the RBC school through the categorization of the research of this school. For example, the investigations that have tried to explain this school's state of the art in the 1980s and 1990s are analyzed. Finally, we explore studies on the labor market, fiscal policy, the money market, and investment shocks.

In the last part, the RBC models' main assumptions have been described, as well as the steps for the construction, solution, and simulation of these models.

Supplementary Information The online version contains supplementary material available at (https://doi.org/10.1007/978-3-031-58105-2_1).

H. Galindo Gil et al., *Dynamic Stochastic General Equilibrium Models*, Springer Texts in Business and Economics, https://doi.org/10.1007/978-3-031-58105-2_1

1.2 Business Cycles

Snowdon and Vane (2005) indicate that the primary goal of macroeconomics is to analyze and understand the determinants of the aggregate economic series, such as the gross domestic product (GDP), unemployment, inflation, and international transactions (both in the real and financial sectors). In particular, macroeconomics studies the determinants and impacts of fluctuations in economic activity in the short term (business cycles) and the determinants of the long-term path of economic activity (economic growth).

With this goal, many schools of economic thought have tried to provide explanations of the behavior of aggregate economic series throughout history. For instance, the so-called Keynesian school attempted to explain the high unemployment of the early 1930s due to "insufficient" aggregate demand. On the other hand, the Neoclassical Synthesis supported the existence of an inverse relationship between unemployment and inflation (Phillips curve), which could serve as a framework to analyze economic policies. Likewise, monetarists emphasized the money market as the primary variable to explain business cycles. All these and subsequent schools of economic thought (New Classical Economics, the Real Business Cycles school, New Keynesian Economics, and the recent New Neoclassical Synthesis) have built their theoretical frameworks to explain the behavior of aggregate variables.

Given this set of theories, the following question arises: what aspects should be considered to evaluate a theory in macroeconomics? Greenwald et al. (1988) suggest that the theory's ability to explain the main features and "stylized facts" of macroeconomic instability should be considered. This idea is in line with that previously indicated by Kaldor (1961), who suggests that any model's minimum requirement is to explain the characteristics of economic processes as they are observed in reality. Applying these requirements to business cycle theory, Abel and Bernanke (2001) suggests that in order for a business cycle theory to be successful, it must explain the cyclical behavior of a **wide range** of main economic variables. Furthermore, these authors state a reasonable consensus on the basic stylized facts of business cycles.

From an empirical point of view, Snowdon and Vane (2005) suggest that to explain economic cycles, the statistical properties between the comovements of the cyclical component of the aggregate variables and the cyclical component of GDP must be identified. As a result, two relevant questions emerge for studying business cycles: What is the definition of business cycles? What are the stylized facts of business cycles? The first question is addressed in the next section and the second in the subsequent one.

1.2.1 Definition

The classic definition of business cycles was proposed by Burns and Mitchell (1946): they state, "the business cycle is a type of fluctuation of the aggregate economic activities of the countries that organize their work mainly in corporate business." In addition, these authors consider that three characteristics define the economic cycle: the first is that the said cycle consists of a **phase of expansion**, experienced at the same time by various economic activities, followed by a recession phase (contraction), and a subsequent recovery, which is part of the expansion phase of the next cycle.

The second characteristic is that the business cycle is **recurring**; that is, it repeatedly occurs in the economies and is **nonperiodic**. This characteristic implies that the business cycles vary in length and do not occur at predictable intervals. The third characteristic is that the duration of a cycle varies from a period greater than one year to 10 or 20 years.

To these considerations of the cycle, Lucas (1977) contributed to its characterization in two aspects:

- Concerning the qualitative behavior of comovements between series, business cycles are **all the same**.
- This suggests the possibility of a unified explanation of business cycles within a framework of **general laws** that govern the market economy.

Finally, Long and Plosser (1983) indicate that the term "business cycle" refers to the joint temporal behavior of many economic variables such as price, output, employment, consumption, and investment. At least two empirical regularities can describe this behavior. The first refers to the cyclical component of each variable, that is, the deviations of the variable with respect to its trend. The second refers to the joint movement of various economic activities, such as, for example, the product in different economic sectors.

1.2.2 Stylized Facts

The term "stylized facts" is used in different fields of economic science. For instance, it is used in economic growth, business cycles, and economic development (Arroyo Abad and Khalifa 2015). Furthermore, this term is attributed to Kaldor (1957) and essentially represents the empirical regularities observed in the statistical properties of time series economic variables (Snowdon and Vane 2005).

1.2.2.1 Characterization of the Stylized Facts

Usually, the stylized facts of economic cycles are characterized or described through four criteria: variability, direction, persistence, and temporality. These criteria are associated with particular statistics. Thus, for example, variability is measured by variance, direction by correlation (usually with GDP), persistence by autocorrelation, and temporality by dynamic correlations with respect to GDP.

- **Variability (variance)**
  Measured by the variance or standard deviation (sd) of the variable. The normalized standard deviation is also considered, which is the division between the "sd" of the variable and the "sd" of the GDP.
- **Direction (correlation)**
  They are the comovements of the variables in relation to GDP.

corr(x,GDP)> 0	corr(x,GDP)=0	corr(x,GDP)< 0
procyclical	acyclic	countercyclical

- **Persistence (1st-order autocorrelation)**
  Persistence indicates that if a point of the variable "X" is taken above the trend, what is the probability that in the next period that variable will remain above that reference point?
- **Temporality (dynamic correlations)**
  It contemplates if the variable is lagging behind, coincides with, or is ahead of the GDP.

Leading	Lagging	Coincidence
If the variable moves ahead of GDP	If the variable moves behind GDP	If the variable moves at the same time as GDP

It is important to mention that to obtain the cyclical component of the macroeconomic variables, a method must be used that allows each component to be separated from the trend component of the variable. In the existing literature, various methods (filters) perform this work with their advantages and disadvantages. Throughout the book, the Hodrick and Prescott filter (HP filter) will be used due to its simplicity and because it has usually been used by the RBC school.[1]

1.2.2.2 Stylized Facts in the United States

[A] Business Cycle The National Bureau of Economic Research (NBER) has determined a set of dates that allow identifying the beginning and end of an economic cycle (see Table 1.1). This historical account dates back to 1854.

[1] In addition to the HP filter, there are other approaches developed by Baxter and King (1999), Woitek (1998) and Christiano and Fitzgerald (1999). For a better detail of the HP filter and that of Baxter and King, see DeJong and Dave (2007, ch. 3).

To determine the dates that define an economic cycle, the NBER examines a set of macroeconomic indicators (GDP, employment, income, and sectoral variables). That is, this institution conceives economic activity from a holistic view.

Also, NBER considers an expansion to be a period from the lowest point of economic activity to the next highest point. Similarly, a contraction (recession) starts from the peak of economic activity and ends at the trough. It should be added that for this agency, a recession is not defined as the reduction of real GDP in two consecutive quarters, but rather that said institution conceives that a recession is the significant reduction of economic activity in the vast majority of economic sectors, which could last several months. This contraction should be seen in real GDP, real income, employment, industrial production, and wholesale and retail sales.[2]

Table 1.1 shows the 33 business cycles identified by NBER. Each is associated with its start and end date according to the two approaches used to measure the business cycle length. The first of these approaches counts the number of months between two peaks in economic activity. The second approach counts the number of months between two minimum points of economic activity.

Three conclusions can be drawn from Table 1.1. The first is that between 1854 and 2009, the US economy has experienced 33 cycles. Dividing the sample into three segments, two before World War II and one after, we have the following: the United States, between 1854 and 1919, has experienced 16 cycles; between 1919 and 1945, that is, between the First and Second World War, there are six cycles, and between 1945 and 2009 (post-World War II), there are 11 cycles.

The second conclusion is that the average time that a cycle lasts is approximately five years in the entire sample. However, the cycles before the Second World War lasted about four years, while after that, their duration rose to 6.

Finally, the third conclusion is that the average expansion time is approximately three years, and the contraction time is one and a half years for the 33 cycles. However, these numbers change when we consider World War II as the turning point in the sample. Before this world conflict, the expansion lasted 2.4 years, while after this, the expansion doubled, reaching up to approximately five years. Similarly, with the time of the contraction, before the Second World War, the recession lasted about two years, while after this event, the recession reached approximately one year.

Figure 1.1 illustrates the last two business cycles of the US economy since 1988, as determined by the NBER. It can be seen that both approaches to measuring the business cycles described above consider approximately the same number of months that a business cycle lasts. Likewise, from mid-2007 to 2016, a cycle has not been completed.

[B] Stylized Facts Related to Economic Growth In the existing literature on economic growth, there is a large set of stylized facts. These empirical regularities usually encompass the behavior of accounting for the growth of physical capital, the

---

[2] For more detail, see http://www.nber.org/cycles/cyclesmain.html. In particular, see http://www.nber.org/cycles/sept2010.html.

Table 1.1 Dates of economic cycles in the United States (1854–2009)

Month year				Duration (months)		
Maximum point (MP)		Minimum point (mp)		PM a PM	pm a pm	Cycle
		December	1854			
June	1857	December	1858		48	Cycle 1
October	1860	June	1861	40	30	Cycle 2
April	1865	December	1867	54	78	Cycle 3
June	1869	December	1870	50	36	Cycle 4
October	1873	March	1879	52	99	Cycle 5
March	1882	May	1885	101	74	Cycle 6
March	1887	April	1888	60	35	Cycle 7
July	1890	May	1891	40	37	Cycle 8
January	1893	June	1894	30	37	Cycle 9
December	1895	June	1897	35	36	Cycle 10
June	1899	December	1900	42	42	Cycle 11
September	1902	August	1904	39	44	Cycle 12
May	1907	June	1908	56	46	Cycle 13
January	1910	January	1912	32	43	Cycle 14
January	1913	December	1914	36	35	Cycle 15
August	1918	March	1919	67	51	Cycle 16
January	1920	July	1921	17	28	Cycle 17
May	1923	July	1924	40	36	Cycle 18
October	1926	November	1927	41	40	Cycle 19
August	1929	March	1933	34	64	Cycle 20
May	1937	June	1938	93	63	Cycle 21
February	1945	October	1945	93	88	Cycle 22
November	1948	October	1949	45	48	Cycle 23
July	1953	May	1954	56	55	Cycle 24
August	1957	April	1958	49	47	Cycle 25
April	1960	February	1961	32	34	Cycle 26
December	1969	November	1970	116	117	Cycle 27
November	1973	March	1975	47	52	Cycle 28
January	1980	July	1980	74	64	Cycle 29
July	1981	November	1982	18	28	Cycle 30
July	1990	March	1991	108	100	Cycle 31
March	2001	November	2001	128	128	Cycle 32
December	2007	June	2009	81	91	Cycle 33

Source: NBER (National Bureau Economics Research) [hacer un update]

proportion of factors in national income, and human capital, among other relevant variables (Jones 2016). Within these facts, there are the so-called classics proposed

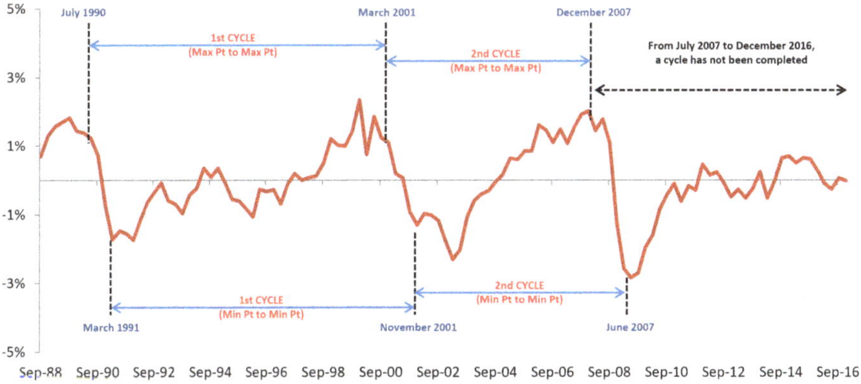

Fig. 1.1 Cyclical component of GDP per capita (1988.3–2016.4). This series has been obtained by applying the HP filter to GDP per capita with a smoothing parameter $\lambda = 1600$ (Source: U.S. Bureau of Economic Analysis, "Table 1.1 Real Gross Domestic Product, Chained Dollars" (GDP in billions of US$ of 2009). In addition, the population has been obtained from "Table 7.1. Selected Per Capita Product and Income Series in Current and Chained Dollars")

by Kaldor (1961) and Kaldor (1963), who, in his/her opinion, suggested six stylized facts,[3] which are described below:

HE-1: Per capita production grows over time and its growth rate is not decreasing.
HE-2: Physical capital per capita grows over time.
HE-3: The rate of return on capital is relatively constant.
HE-4: The capital-output ratio is relatively constant: $K_t/Y_t = constant$.
HE-5: The shares of labor and physical capital in national production are relatively constant: $\frac{r_t K_t}{Y_t} = constant$ and $\frac{w_t L_t}{Y_t} = constant$.
HE-6: The growth rate of GDP per capita is different between countries.

HE-1 Kaldor's first stylized fact concerns the per capita growth rate of GDP. Looking at the data between 1930 and 2015, it can be inferred that the average annual growth rate of real GDP per capita is 2.2%. From the analysis sample, it can be seen that, between the early 1930s and the mid-1940s, real GDP per capita growth has been very volatile, ranging from about -13% to 17%. This is because this period was characterized by the effects of the economic crisis of 1929 and the Second World War. After this last event, the GDP per capita growth data has shown greater stability. In fact, between 1947 and 2015, the average annual growth rate of real GDP per capita was approximately 1.9% (see Fig. 1.2). In fact, in the mentioned period, the standard deviation of this variable is 2.4%, significantly lower compared to the period 1930–1946 (std. dev. = 10%).

[3] These stylized facts are usually mentioned in books on economic growth. An example of this is the book by Barro et al. (2009).

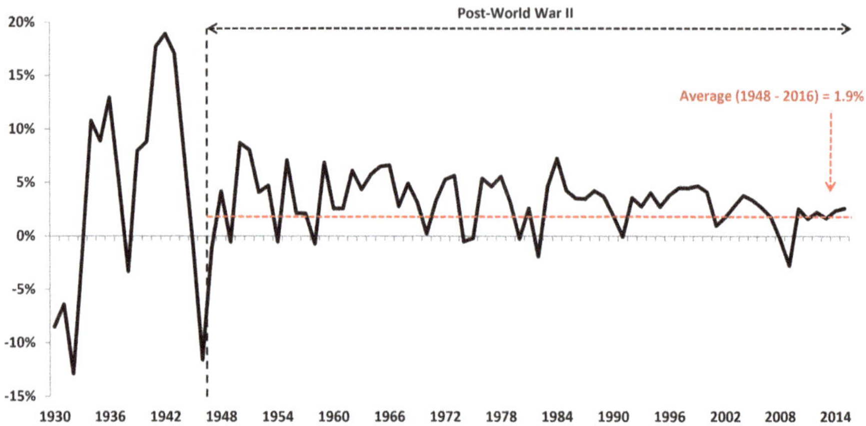

Fig. 1.2 HE-1| Annual growth rate of real GDP per capita (1930–2015). Real GDP is expressed in two ways: the first is in billions of 2009 US$ and the second in quantity index (2009 = 100). In levels, both approaches are different; however, when converted to annual growth rate, both approaches give the same number. To construct the GDP per capita, the real GDP (in billions of US$ of 2009) and the population (in thousands) have been considered (Source: U.S. Bureau of Economic Analysis, "Table 1.1.6. Real Gross Domestic Product, Chained Dollars" (GDP in billions of US$ of 2009). In addition, the population has been obtained from "Table 7.1. Selected Per Capita Product and Income Series in Current and Chained Dollars")

HE-2 Kaldor's second stylized fact refers to the per capita growth rate of physical capital. To analyze this variable, it is necessary to define the *stock* of capital. This section follows Burnside et al. (1996), who define capital stock from a broad perspective (fixed asset components plus durable goods). Under the previous premise, Fig. 1.3 shows the evolution of the growth of capital per capita between 1930 and 2015. A main idea emerges from this figure: just like the GDP growth rate per capita, the per capita capital growth is stable after World War II with an average value of 1.8%. This confirms Kaldor's second stylized fact.

HE-3 Kaldor's third stylized fact indicates that the rate of return on capital is relatively constant. In this context, the Bureau of Labor Statistics (BLS) estimates the rental price of capital, which represents the rental cost of capital (as known in general equilibrium macroeconomic models). Estimated data for this variable are available from 1987 to 2014 with an annual frequency. In addition, the variable is estimated for various levels of the manufacturing and nonmanufacturing industry. However, it is worth mentioning that this estimate is not available for the US economy as a whole.

Observing the data for four industrial sectors (timber, machinery, transport equipment, and electronic equipment), it can be inferred that the capital rental interest rate oscillates, on average, between 12% and 14% during the period between 1987 and 2014 (see Fig. 1.4). If the average of the 18 industrial sectors between 1987 and 2014 is considered, the capital rental interest rate is approximately 13%.

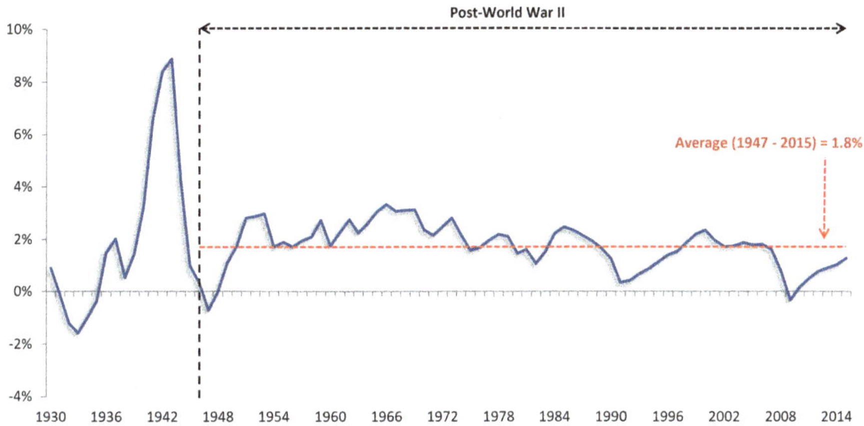

Fig. 1.3 HE-2| Annual growth rate of the real capital stock per capita (1930–2015). The *capital* stock is expressed under the concept of Burnside et al. (1996). The population is expressed in thousands and considers the entire economy (Source: U.S. Bureau of Economic Analysis,"Table 1.2. Chain-Type Quantity Indexes for Net Stock of Fixed Assets and Consumer Durable Goods" (Capital stock). In addition, the population has been obtained from "Table 7.1. Selected Per Capita Product and Income Series in Current and Chained Dollars")

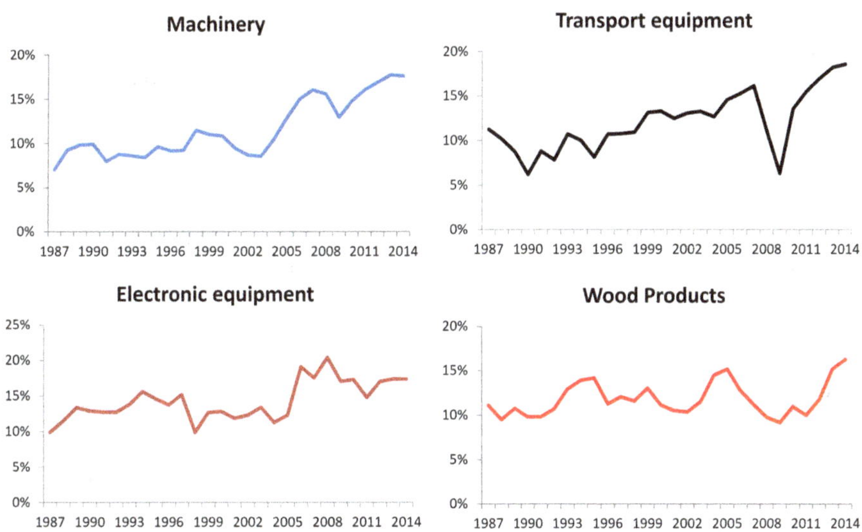

Fig. 1.4 HE-3| Rate of return on capital by the industrial sector (1987–2014) (Source: Bureau of Labor Statistics (BLS), www.bls.gov/mfp)

Kaldor observed that this interest rate is constant over time, which would imply that in a more extended sample of observations, the interest rate shows the behavior of reversion to the mean.

HE-4 To assess whether Kaldor's fourth stylized fact holds up to the present, the capital/output ratio has to be constructed. To do this, first of all, it must be defined what is considered as *stock* of real physical capital. Second, GDP must be obtained in real terms. Finally, proceed to divide both economic aggregates. It should be mentioned that this ratio is constructed with annual variables expressed in real terms.

Capital Stock There are different ways of conceiving the capital stock (Jones 2016). Three approaches are considered in this section. The first explains that the *stock* of capital is only private nonresidential fixed assets, which contain equipment, structures, and intellectual property. The second approach considers that the capital *stock* encompasses not only private nonresidential fixed assets but also government nonresidential fixed assets. The third approach is based on Burnside et al. (1996), who consider that the *stock* of capital is the sum of four components, three related to fixed assets and one to the consumption of durable goods: (1) fixed assets in private equipment and structure, (2) private residential fixed assets, (3) public residential and nonresidential fixed assets, and (4) consumer durables. It should be emphasized that all these concepts are in real terms (quantity index) and can be found in *U.S. Bureau of Economic Analysis, "Table 1.2. Chain-Type Quantity Indexes for Net Stock of Fixed Assets and Consumer Durable Goods"*.

With the previous definitions of the *stock* of capital and the real GDP, the capital/output ratio is constructed, which is shown in Fig. 1.5. Two essential ideas emerge from this graph: the first is that the capital/output ratio has been relatively constant since the Second World War (1947–2015), which is consistent with Kaldor's suggestion. Thus, for example, the ratio (considering that the *stock* of capital is only nonresidential private fixed assets) is close to one. Under the second capital approach, this ratio is 2.2, and under Burnside et al. (1996) conception, the capital stock is six times the real GDP. The second idea is that among the three capital approaches, the first allows for obtaining a much more stable capital/output ratio compared to the other two. This is verified when comparing the sample standard deviations between the years 1947 and 2015:

Table 1.2 Descriptive statistics of the cyclical component of the series for the United States (1954.1–2015.4)

Variable	Volatility (est. dev. %)	Relative volatility	Autocorrelation	Correlation with GDP
GDP	1.52	1	0.85	1
Consumption	0.81	0.53	0.88	0.82
Investment	5.95	3.91	0.83	0.93
Stock of capital	0.26	0.17	0.96	0.08
Hours	1.86	1.23	0.91	0.87
Employment	1.56	1.03	0.93	0.8
Real wage	0.96	0.63	0.69	0.22
Productivity	0.94	0.62	0.79	−0.1

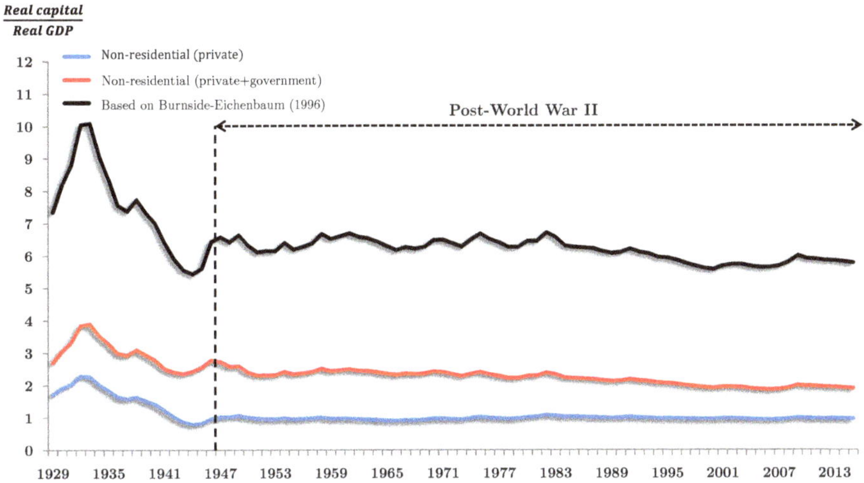

Fig. 1.5 HE-4| Capital Stock Ratio (real)/GDP (real). GDP and the *stock* of capital are expressed in real terms (quantity index, 2009 = 100) (Source: U.S. Bureau of Economic Analysis, "Table 1.2. Chain-Type Quantity Indexes for Net Stock of Fixed Assets and Consumer Durable Goods" (*Stock* de Capital) y "Table 1.1.3. Real Gross Domestic Product, Quantity Indexes" (GDP))

$$\sigma_{\text{Approach-1}}(=4\%) < \sigma_{\text{Approach-2}}(=21\%) < \sigma_{\text{Approach-3}}(=32\%)$$

However, a better interpretation of the degree of burden than that suggested by the standard deviation is the coefficient of variation (CV = standard deviation/mean), which expresses the standard deviation as a percentage of the mean. For the correct application of this statistic, it is required that all the values of the series be positive, which is true for this case. The coefficient of variation is shown below:

$$CV_{\text{Approach-1}}(=4\%) < CV_{\text{Approach-3}}(=5\%) < CV_{\text{Approach-2}}(=10\%)$$

This statistic suggests that the first and third approaches are very similar in terms of variability; however, both are far removed from the variability of the second approach.

HE-5 This stylized fact refers to the share of labor and capital in national income. Figure 1.6 shows that the share of both factors in national income has been relatively stable. For example, in the case of capital, the average share between 1948 and 2014 was 33.7%. For work, this is equal to 66.3%. These values are important because, as you will see in the course of the book, the Cobb-Douglas production function suggests that the capital share is constant and equal to the exponent of capital in the production function. Under the standard calibration process in RBC models, it can be considered that the said exponent is equal to 33.7%, which is observed in the data.

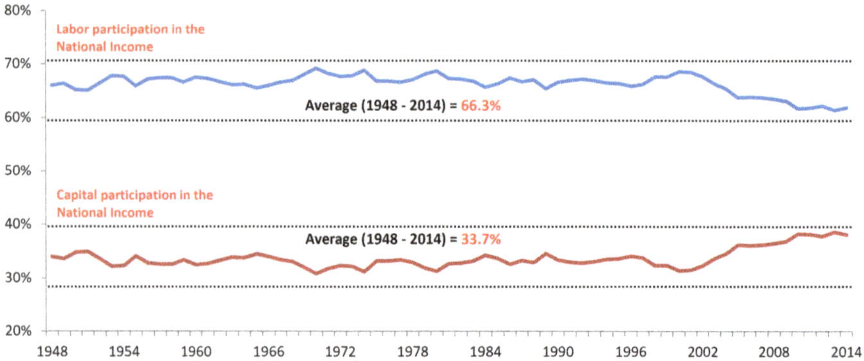

Fig. 1.6 HE-5| Participation of factors in the National Income (1948–2014). GDP and the *stock* of capital are expressed in real terms (quantity index, 2009 = 100) (Source: Bureau of Labor Statistics, Multifactor Productivity Trends, "Private Business Sector" (www.bls.gov/mfp/mprdload.htm, Historical Series))

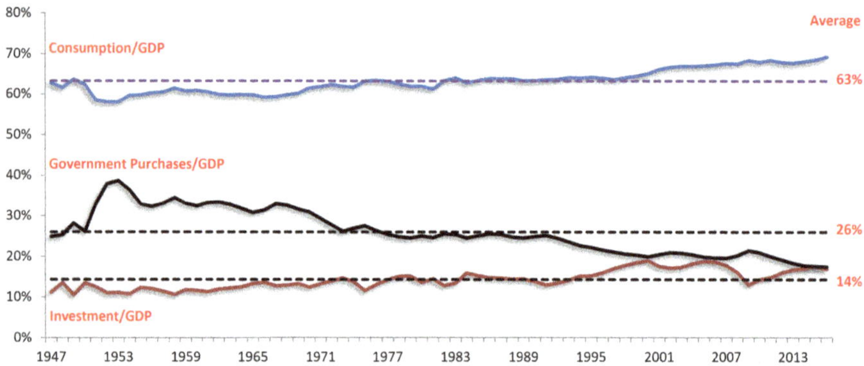

Fig. 1.7 Long-run relationships between GDP, consumption, investment, and government purchases (Source: Bureau of Economic Analysis, "Table 1.1.6. Real Gross Domestic Product, Chained Dollars")

In addition to Kaldor's stylized facts, in the existing literature, there is a set of long-run relationships between GDP, consumption, and investment (Stock and Watson 1999), called "**balanced growth relationships**." These are important because they serve as input in the calibration process of the RBC models, especially in the steady-state relationships.

Figure 1.7 shows the consumption-GDP, investment-GDP, and government purchases-GDP ratios. It can be seen that the average value of each ratio between 1947 and 2016 is 63%, 14%, and 26%, respectively. An important feature of the evolution of these ratios is that the government's share has slowly declined over time. On the other hand, consumption and investment have gained participation in the GDP. However, these ratios show certain stability for the same time window.

[C] Business Cycle Stylized Facts One of the main references regarding business cycle stylized facts is the research by Stock and Watson (1999)[4] under the title "*Business Cycle Fluctuations in US Macroeconomic Time Series*." In this article, the authors examine the cyclical properties of 71 quarterly economic variables, which are grouped into eight categories: sectoral employment, national accounts, aggregate employment, productivity, and capacity utilization, prices and wages, asset prices, monetary aggregates, leading indicators, and international products.

These authors' sample period of analysis corresponds to the data after the Second World War (1947–1995). This is mainly due to two reasons: the first is that the US economy is very different before World War II in terms of technology, institutions, production of goods, and services, among other characteristics. The second is due to the quality of the data before this world conflict occurred, which could generate problems of comparability of the variables throughout the entire sample. Moreover, the authors use this period to show the variables' evolution graphically. Still, in calculating the statistics (standard deviation, correlation [dynamic], and autocorrelation), they focus on the postwar period between the United States and Korea. They thus consider the data between 1954 and 1995.

Another important aspect is that Stock and Watson used the Baxter and King (1993) filter (*band-pass filter*) to obtain the cyclical component of the 71 variables. Stock and Watson (1999) suggest that an ideal filter preserves the cyclic component and eliminates the other fluctuations (high and low frequencies). However, as DeJong and Dave (2011) (Chap. 3) point out, the ideal filter cannot be implemented because it requires an infinite number of observations of the series prior to applying the filter. In the case of the Baxter and King filter, which approximates the ideal filter, the cyclical component has a periodicity of between six quarters and eight years. The advantage of this filter is that it essentially eliminates high-frequency (less than six quarters) and low-frequency (greater than eight years) fluctuations. In contrast to this filter, the one proposed by Hodrick and Prescott (1981) does not prevent high-frequency fluctuations from being part of the cyclic component.

It should be mentioned that throughout this book, the filter used is that of Hodrick and Prescott. This is because research at the RBC school has primarily used this methodology. Furthermore, and despite its weaknesses, this filter is still used in the existing literature due to its simplicity.

This section will show the stylized facts of eight real variables: GDP, consumption, investment, capital stock, total hours, employment, real wages, and (labor)

[4] Another essential reference is the work from Kydland and Prescott (1990). These authors showed the cyclical regularities of a set of real and nominal variables. The analysis sample corresponds to data after the war between the United States and Korea (1950–1953), from 1954 to 1989. The main difference concerning Stock and Watson's research is that Kydland and Prescott used the Hodrick and Prescott filter to obtain the cyclical component of the variables. Another investigation with emphasis on the stylized facts in the cyclical component of the variables related to the labor market is that of Kydland (1995).

productivity. These variables are found in logarithms and quarterly frequency (they are not expressed in per capita terms).

[C.1] Construction of the Macroeconomic Series Before obtaining the cyclical component of each variable and calculating the statistics, it is necessary to define each of the variables and identify the sources of information. The following paragraphs detail how each variable is constructed (when necessary) and the source, which is usually the Economic Analysis Agency (BEA).

Gross Domestic Product (GDP) and Consumption The GDP is in real terms (billions of US$ of 2009). On the other hand, consumption is calculated as the sum (in real terms) of the consumption of nondurable goods and the consumption of services:

$$\text{Real consumption} = \frac{C_{bnd}}{IP_{ND}} + \frac{C_{services}}{IP_S} \tag{1.1}$$

where C_{bnd} is personal consumption spending on nondurable goods and $C_{services}$ is personal consumption spending on services. Furthermore, these expenditure components are in nominal terms, and to transform them into real terms, it is necessary to deflate them by the respective price index. In this way, the consumption of nondurable goods is deflated by the price index of nondurable goods (IP_{ND}). The same procedure is applied for services whose price index is IP_S. It is worth mentioning that each price index must be divided by 100.

Investment It is calculated as the sum of real private investment and consumption of durable goods (in real terms):

$$\text{Real investment} = Inv_{pr} + \frac{C_{bd}}{IP_{bd}} \tag{1.2}$$

where Inv_{pr} is gross domestic private investment (in real terms) and C_{bd} is consumption of durable goods (in nominal terms), which is deflated by the durable goods' price index (IP_{db}). Like consumption, each price index is divided by 100.

Figure 1.8 shows the evolution of GDP, consumption, and investment, all in real terms and natural logarithms. From the evolution of these three variables, it can be seen that investment is more volatile than GDP and consumption. It is necessary to mention that the sample considered for the graphs and statistics comprises between the first quarter of 1954 and the fourth quarter of 2015. The war period between the United States and Korea is not considered, as Stock and Watson (1999) did.

Capital Stock As mentioned in the previous lines, this section considers Burnside and Eichenbaum (1996) concept of capital *stock*. The available data of the said *stock* are in annual frequency. However, it is necessary to "extrapolate" these data to a quarterly frequency to calculate the statistics of the cyclical component. For

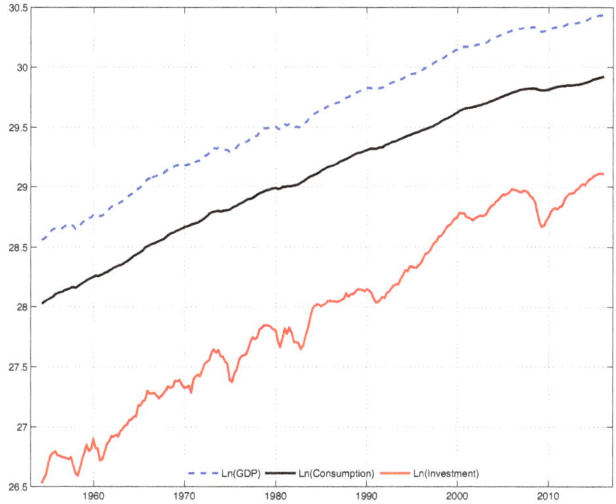

Fig. 1.8 GDP, consumption, and investment (1954.1–2015.4). The variables are in natural logarithms with a quarterly frequency. Consumption considers nondurable goods and services. The investment includes private investment and consumption of durable goods (Source: Bureau of Economic Analysis, "Table 1.1.6. Real Gross Domestic Product, Chained Dollars" (GDP-Private investment); "Table 2.3.5. Personal Consumption Expenditures by Major Type of Product"; "Table 2.3.4. Price Indexes for Personal Consumption Expenditures by Major Type of Product")

example, to calculate the dynamic correlation with GDP or investment, since these variables are in quarterly frequency, capital must be in the same frequency. In this context, Levy and Chen (1994) suggest four methods of constructing a quarterly real (net) capital stock series.

The first method is a linear interpolation of the annual series. The idea is to construct the quarterly values along a segment that connects two consecutive yearly observations. Formally:

$$K_{i,j} = K_{i-1} + k_j \quad i = 1948, 1849, ...2015 \text{ (years)} \quad j = 1, 2, 3, 4 \text{ (quarters)} \tag{1.3}$$

In Eq. (1.3), $K_{i,j}$ represents the *stock* of capital for quarter "j" of year "i." For example, $K_{1948.1}$ is the *stock* of capital for the first quarter of 1948. Also, K_{i-1} is the *stock* for the previous year that, in this example, it would represent the *stock* of capital for 1947. On the other hand, k_j is the factor of *stock* of additional capital per quarter, which is calculated as follows:

$$k_j = \frac{K_i - K_{i-1}}{4} \cdot j \tag{1.4}$$

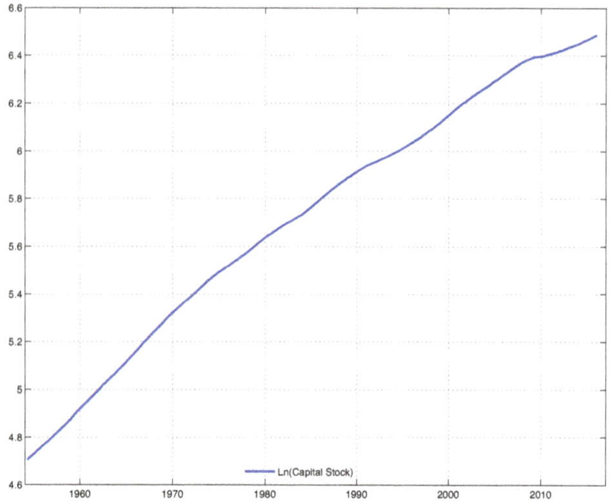

Fig. 1.9 Real quarterly (net) capital *stock* (1954.1–2015.4). The quarterly series has been obtained by the linear interpolation method, considering the capital *stock* of 1947 as the starting point (Source: Bureau of Economic Analysis, "Table 1.2. Chain-Type Quantity Indexes for Net Stock of Fixed Assets and Consumer Durable Goods")

Because it is linear interpolation, the arithmetic ratio is simply the difference of two consecutive annual capital stocks divided by the number of quarters (points). Under this assumption, the calculation of the *stock* of capital for the first quarter will be equal to the *stock* of the initial capital (from the previous year) plus the said arithmetic ratio. For the second quarter, it will be the *stock* of the initial capital (from the previous year) plus twice the arithmetic ratio and so on until reaching the *stock* of the final capital (annual). This calculation logic is reflected in Eq. (1.4). It should be noted that this method is used in this chapter to "build" the quarterly net capital stock series (see Fig. 1.9).

The second method uses the relationship between the capital *stock*, depreciation, and (real) investment, reflected in the capital equation of motion to estimate the depreciation rate (assumed to be constant throughout the year, but intertemporally distinct). Then, based on this depreciation rate and the quarterly investment (which is available), the quarterly capital *stock* is estimated. This exercise is carried out each year. The method follows these steps: first, the law of movement of capital is written for each quarter of a specific year (Eqs. (1.5) to (1.8)).

$$K_{i,1} = (1 - \delta_i)K_{i-1} + I_{i,1} \tag{1.5}$$

$$K_{i,2} = (1 - \delta_i)K_{i,1} + I_{i,2} \tag{1.6}$$

$$K_{i,3} = (1 - \delta_i)K_{i,2} + I_{i,3} \tag{1.7}$$

$$K_{i,4} = (1 - \delta_i)K_{i,3} + I_{i,4} \tag{1.8}$$

where $K_{i,4}$ is the *capital* stock for the next year (K_i) and K_{i-1} is the *capital* stock of the previous year. After defining the quarterly equations, the second step is to recursively replace Eq. (1.5) into (1.6), the latter into (1.7), and finally the latter into (1.8). This recursive substitution allows obtaining a fourth-degree equation where the variable is the depreciation rate, which can be solved by some method of nonlinear equations such as "Newton's method." Finally, as a third step, once the depreciation rate is known, it is replaced in Eqs. (1.5) to (1.8) and the quarterly capital *stock* is obtained. This procedure must be carried out for each year so that the quarterly time series of the *stock* of capital can be obtained.

The third method suggests that, instead of estimating the depreciation rate, the quarterly depreciation amount should be estimated directly by linear interpolation of the annual depreciation series. Given this calculation, the quarterly capital stock is calculated under the "capital movement equation" (given that the quarterly real investment is known). Finally, the fourth method assumes that the quarterly depreciation is simply the annual depreciation divided by four. With this, in a similar way to the third method, the quarterly capital stock is calculated.

Total Hours and Employment Total hours worked and employment (jobs) are obtained from the database of Valerie Ramey. She has compiled quarterly employment data based on the Bureau of Labor Statistics (BLS) information. Ramey has two main aggregates of the series of hours worked: the total of the economy and the business sector that does not include farming (*nonfarm business [all persons]*). For calculating the statistics, this last concept of "hours worked" will be taken into account. This variable is found every quarter, but at an annualized level; it considers the total hours worked in a year. The calculation form is as follows:

$$\text{Hours}_t = UE_t * UH_t * [52 \text{ weeks/year}]/1000 \tag{1.9}$$

where Hours_t is the number of hours "annual" of quarter "t." For its calculation, the average number of jobs (jobs) during the quarter (UE_t) is multiplied by the average weekly hours worked during the quarter (UH_t). This number is multiplied by the number of weeks in a year (52). Concerning employment, similarly to total hours worked, the business sector that does not include farming (*nonfarm business [all persons]*) is considered.

Real Wage and Productivity (Labor) The real wage, as well as the number of hours worked and employment, is calculated for the business sector that does not include cultivation. Also, it represents actual hourly compensation as an index 2009 =100. On the other hand, (labor) productivity is calculated as the ratio between real GDP and the total number of hours. Figure 1.10 shows the evolution of the natural logarithm of the variables associated with the labor market.

[C.2] Separation of the Cyclical Component of the Variables To extract the cyclical component of the eight macroeconomic variables, the filter of Hodrick and Prescott (1981) is used. Figure 1.11 shows the trend component of real GDP. Its cyclical component is the difference between the value of the variable in levels (real GDP) and the trend component (obtained by the HP filter).

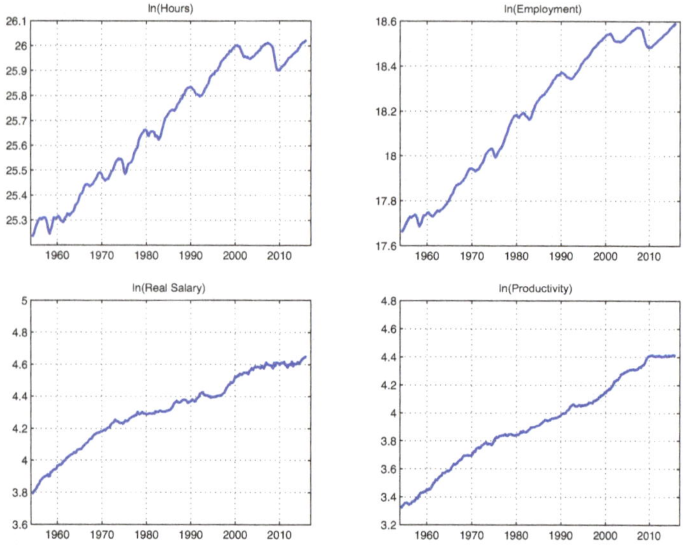

Fig. 1.10 Macroeconomic series (1954.1–2015.4). The total number of hours (billions of hours worked) and employment (millions of jobs) correspond to the sector *nonfarm business (all persons)*. The real salary (index 2009 = 100) is the real compensation per hour. Productivity (labor) is the ratio between real GDP and total hours worked (productivity = GDP/H). All variables are in logarithms (Source: The total hours and employment have been obtained from the data of Valerie Ramey (http://econweb.ucsd.edu/~vramey/). The real wage is obtained from *Federal Reserve Bank of St. Louis*, "Nonfarm Business Sector: Real Compensation Per Hour, Index 2009 = 100, Quarterly, Seasonally Adjusted")

Figures 1.12 and 1.13 show the cyclical component of the eight variables and compare them with the cyclical component of GDP. The idea of this first comparison is to understand the volatility of the variables and their movements with the GDP. Some observations emerge from this graphical analysis:

[Obs1] The cyclical component of GDP seems to be less volatile during the second half of the 1980s,[5] the entire decade of the 1990s, and part of the first five years of the new millennium. This phenomenon is called "The Great Moderation" and was coined by Stock and Watson (2002). These authors found that the volatility of the annual GDP growth rate between 1960 and 2001 (std. dev. = 2.3%) is greater than the volatility between 1990 and 2001 (std. dev. = 1.5%). One of his/her main findings was that the reduction in volatility was found in the rate of GDP growth and throughout the entire economy. In other words, the growth of

[5] McConnell and Perez-Quiros (2000) were the ones who found the first indication of this "moderation," but they only indicated that the reduction in volatility was focused on the production of durable goods. Likewise, these authors found that the structural break in which volatility began to moderate was in the first quarter of 1984. Stock and Watson (2002) confirmed this finding with certain differences.

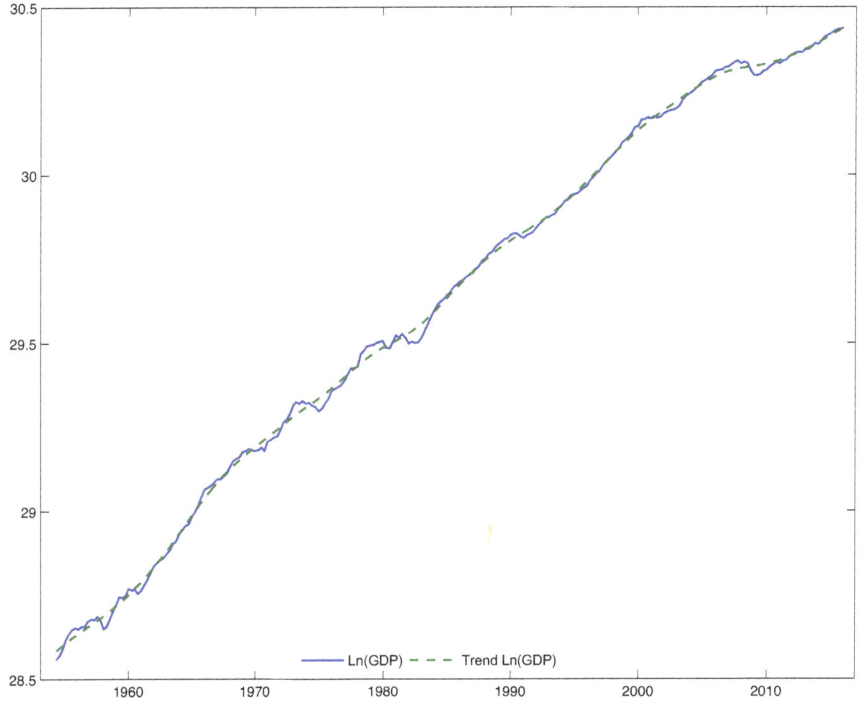

Fig. 1.11 US real GDP and trend component (1954.1–2015.4). The trend component has been obtained by applying the HP filter to the variables in logarithm (per capita) with the smoothing parameter $\lambda = 1600$

employment, consumption, and sectoral GDP also showed a significant reduction in their volatility in the same period. These findings initiated a body of research to explain the sources of this "moderation" (e.g., Davis and Kahn 2008).

[Obs2] Consumption appears to be less volatile than GDP but seems to be strongly (positively) correlated with output.

[Obs3] Investment seems to be more volatile than GDP. In addition, it is more volatile than consumption. Between observations 2 and 3, it is concluded that $\sigma_{\text{investment}} > \sigma_{\text{GDP}} > \sigma_{\text{consumption}}$, where σ_x represents volatility.

[Obs4] The *stock* of capital seems to have very little volatility compared to GDP and also appears to have little correlation with output.

[Obs5] Total hours seem to be a bit more volatile than GDP and have a high correlation with output.

[Obs6] Employment appears to be as volatile as GDP and to have a positive correlation with this variable. Also, employment is almost as volatile as the number of hours.

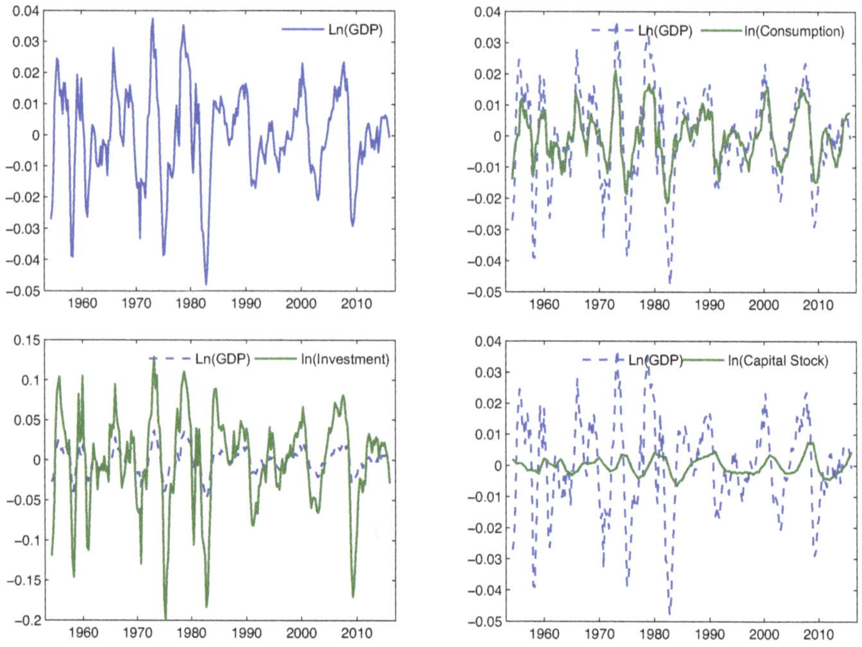

Fig. 1.12 Cyclical component of the economic series for the United States (1954.1–2015.4). The cyclical component has been obtained by applying the HP filter to the variables in logarithm (per capita) with the smoothing parameter $\lambda = 1600$

[Obs7] Real wage volatility seems to have increased over time. Furthermore, between 1954 and mid-1980, the volatility of real wages appears to be much less than that of GDP. However, from the second half of 1980 to 2015, the volatility of real wages and GDP are very close.

[Obs8] Labor productivity appears to have lower volatility than GDP.

[C.3] Calculation of the Statistics Table 1.2 summarizes the main statistics of the cyclical component of the macroeconomic variables, which complements what is observed graphically. Some conclusions can be drawn from these calculations.

First of all, investment shows greater volatility (5.5%) than the other variables. Likewise, it can be seen that its volatility is greater than that of GDP (1.52%), and, in turn, this is greater than that of consumption (0.81%). On the other hand, the variable that has less volatility is the *stock* of capital (0.26%); that is, this variable is more stable than the others. Regarding the labor market variables, it is observed that total hours worked and employment have volatility very close to that of GDP. However, employment has less volatility than the number of hours worked (1.56% vs. 1.86%). This suggests that the business cycle manifests itself in the labor market, as Cooley and Prescott (1995) mention.

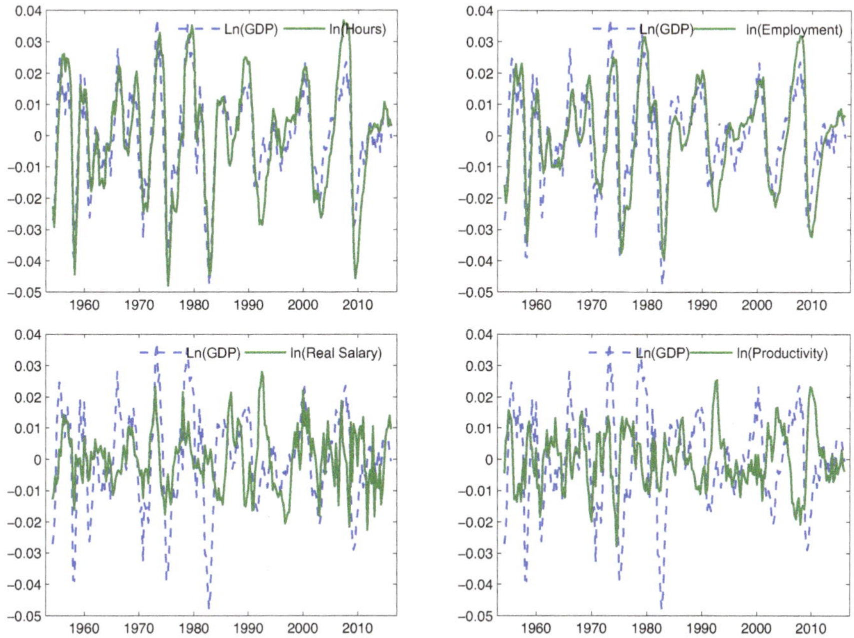

Fig. 1.13 Cyclical component of the economic series for the United States (1954.1–2015.4). The cyclical component has been obtained by applying the HP filter to the variables in logarithm (per capita) with the smoothing parameter $\lambda = 1600$

When comparing the volatility of the real salary with that of the hours worked and employment, it is concluded that the real salary is less volatile than these variables; even the volatility of the real salary represents 50% of the volatility of the total hours and the 60% of employment. In RBC models, this stylized fact could be (partially) captured under the assumption of a highly elastic labor supply. However, as we will see in Chapter 6 (Hansen 1985), microeconomic data suggest that such elasticity is low. Given this, Hansen (1985) developed an extension of the basic RBC model with which he/she partially overcame this weakness.

Second, the volatility of an investment is approximately four times that of GDP, and that of capital is 0.17 times that of GDP. This suggests that although investment can be highly volatile due to the behavior of investors, the accumulated capital stock behaves smoothly over time. Moreover, the volatility of an investment is 22.8 times that of capital.

Third, although the *stock* of capital has low volatility, this variable has a high persistence reflected in its autocorrelation (0.96). In general, all the variables, except real wages and productivity, show persistence levels above 0.8. Even hours worked and employment exceed 90% autocorrelation. It should be noted that real wages and productivity show similar volatilities (0.96% vs. 0.94%) and relatively close autocorrelations (0.69 and 0.79).

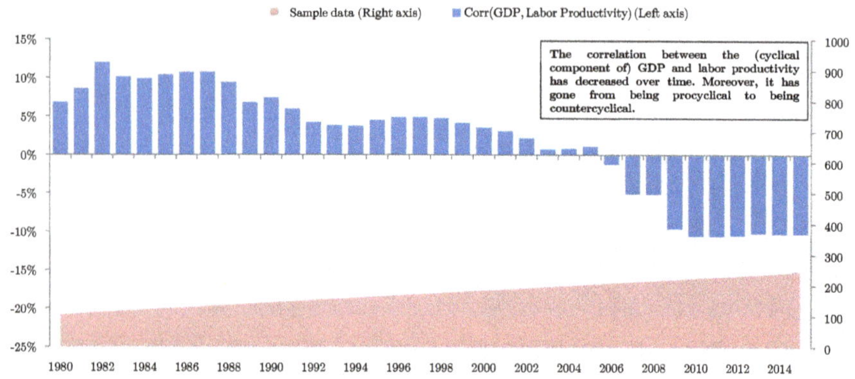

Fig. 1.14 Correlation between GDP (cyclical component) and labor productivity (cyclical component) (1954.1–2015.4)

Fourth, it is observed that consumption, investment, hours worked, and employment are highly procyclical (correlation with GDP greater than 0.8). On the other hand, it is appreciated that the *stock* of capital is eventually acyclic since it presents a correlation with the GDP close to zero (0.08). Likewise, the real wage is slightly procyclical (correlation with GDP of 0.22).

In fifth place, it is observed that the correlation between GDP and labor productivity is negative (−0.1); that is, this suggests that productivity is countercyclical. In the first instance, this result seems counterintuitive, since RBC models have usually considered labor productivity to be procyclical. However, recent studies suggest that the correlation between GDP and labor productivity has declined and has even become negative. The first study to show this "new" feature of the US business cycle was conducted by Stiroh (2009), under the title "*Volatility Accounting: As Production Perspective on Increased Economic Stability*." This research started an academic discussion about the possible factors that explain this behavior (for example, Gali and van Rens (2010) and Fernald and Wang (2016)).

Figure 1.14 shows the correlation of the cyclical component of real GDP with the cyclical component of labor productivity. Each correlation value is calculated from the first quarter of 1954 to the fourth quarter of the year shown on the horizontal axis. For example, the value of 7% that appears in 1980 (first blue bar) has been calculated considering the sample from 1954.1 to 1980.4. Similarly, the value associated with 1982 (greater than 10%) has been calculated with the 1954.1–1982.4 sample.

This figure clearly shows how the correlation between both variables has decreased over time. This behavior can be separated into four stages: the first is in the 1980s when said correlation reached an average value of 10%. The second stage is in the 1990s, in which the said correlation showed a first reduction (average value of 5%) but maintained the procyclical behavior. The third stage takes place in the first five years of the new millennium where the correlation reaches values close to zero (2% on average). Finally, the last stage between 2006 and 2015 shows that the correlation maintains negative levels; that is, labor productivity presents a countercyclical behavior.

1.3 Historical Perspective of the RBC Theory

1.3.1 Overview of Schools of Economic Thought

Figure 1.15 outlines the evolution of macroeconomic theory from a historical point of view. This figure is not exhaustive in considering all currents of economic thought; however, it presents an overview of economic schools.

At least three momentous economic crises have marked the twentieth century and the beginning of the twenty-first century. The first manifested itself in 1929 with the New York Stock Exchange crash, whose effects were global and persistent. This crisis was called the Great Depression. This event had at least two important impacts: the first is that it showed the weakness of the neoclassical school to explain this phenomenon. Likewise, the said school could not provide a solution to this crisis. The second effect is that the Keynesian school emerged as an alternative to explain this crisis and propose some economic policies to mitigate its effects.

The Keynesian School originated with Keynes' General Theory in 1936. In this research, Keynes offered an interpretation of the Great Depression and a solid theoretical framework with a strong argument for state intervention in the economy.

One of Keynes' central ideas was that the market economy is inherently unstable. The said instability causes situations where the level of activity falls below full employment without the market being able to recover independently. This situation produces a level of unemployment that, according to Keynes, has an involuntary character, reflecting an insufficient level of demand. Since the market does not guarantee a return to equilibrium, Keynes suggests that economic policy can correct this aggregate instability to bring the economy to full employment. This contrasts with the fundamental pillar of the neoclassical paradigm: "the automatic tendency towards full employment."

Other important ideas in the Keynesian revolution are as follows: [1] the dependence of the level of activity and the level of employment on effective demand; [2] the crucial role that expectations play in a world of uncertainty (*animal spirits*); [3] the conception of markets as rigid and imperfect mechanisms, so there is no

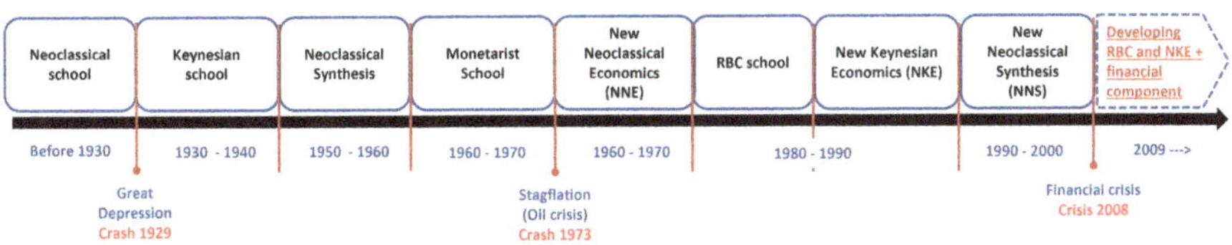

Fig. 1.15 Historical development of schools in macroeconomics

continuous emptying of them; and [4] the essential role assigned to economic policy, aimed at influencing effective demand of the economy. Some of these elements were operationalized, in a certain sense, in the IS-LM model elaborated by Hicks (1937), Hansen (1949), and Hansen (1953). Keynes' main ideas and the IS-LM model formed the basis for what is known as "The Neoclassical Synthesis," which dominated economic theory during the 1950s and 1960s.

The Neoclassical Synthesis, a term proposed by Samuelson (1955), reconciled the neoclassical approach with the Keynesian approach. Between 1950 and 1970, the idea that the neoclassical model was relevant for microeconomic issues and the analysis of economic growth, while the Keynesian model was the most suitable for short-term analysis was accepted in academia. It should be noted that the Neoclassical Synthesis has three main elements: the IS-LM model for a closed economy, the IS-LM model for an open economy, and the Phillips curve. This school of thought dominated macroeconomic theory between 1950 and 1970 until the second crisis of the twentieth century.

The second crisis of the twentieth century was associated with the oil price. In 1973, OPEC (Organization of Petroleum Exporting Countries) decided to restrict oil exports to countries that supported Israel in the war called Yom Kippur, which took place in October 1973. This decision affected the United States and some European countries. The restriction in the production increased its price. Since the industrialized countries of that time depended heavily on oil, they were forced to reduce their production of goods, which finally increased prices. High unemployment and high inflation, a joint phenomenon known as stagflation, was the characteristic of this crisis.

This crisis exposed at least two main weaknesses of the Neoclassical Synthesis. The first weakness was in the *theoretical field* and referred to the fact that this school could not explain stagflation. This is because the Phillips curve only considered an inverse relationship between unemployment and inflation; however, in the crisis of 1970, it was observed that both increased. The second weakness is in the *methodological field*, which mentions that the said school did not consider rational expectations in its modeling (Criticism of Lucas). All this led to a distrust of the economic policy recommendations of the Keynesian synthesis and gave rise to the resurgence of neoclassical ideas under a new approach called new classical economics (NEC), led by Robert Lucas.

The novelty of the NEC was that this school proposed a new way of doing macroeconomics. The NEC argued that macroeconomic models were built from the behavior of rational agents, which optimized their decisions in a stochastic and dynamic environment. This was contrary to the Neoclassical Synthesis approach, where there was no optimization, and the models were usually static. Furthermore, the NEC assumes that the models are Walrasian because the markets were in equilibrium at all times. These models incorporate an aggregate supply based on two orthodox microeconomic assumptions: the rational decisions made by workers and firms in terms of their optimizing behavior and, second, that the labor supply and the level of production of firms depend on relative prices (Lucas 1972, 1973). Likewise, the NEC in its modeling considers rational expectations and thus overcomes Lucas' criticism.

On the other hand, the NEC rests on three sets of assumptions, mainly. The first is concerning the behavior of *agents*: they are assumed to be rational in the sense that they optimize their utility/profit function subject to certain constraints. In addition, it uses the representative agent assumption and assumes that agents are not carried away by the monetary illusion; that is, they make their decisions based on real variables. Also, expectations are rational because all available information is used and no systematic errors are made. Finally, the information is not always complete. It is used optimally and is not asymmetrical, eliminating the problems of adverse selection or moral hazard.

The second set of assumptions is regarding the characteristics of the *markets*: it is assumed that there is perfect competition in all markets and that markets are continually clear given price flexibility. The third set of assumptions refers to the *methodological* issues: the models must have a strict microeconomic foundation, and the expectations must be introduced in a way that is consistent with the model (rational expectations). In addition, the models must be dynamic and general equilibrium and must overcome the Lucas critique.

This new way of doing macroeconomics and its main assumptions led to the New Classical Economics becoming the main macroeconomic approach during the 1970s.

In the early 1980s, a branch of the NEC called real business cycle (RBC) models emerged. Unlike the NEC, which considered that the main driver of business cycles was a *nominal (monetary) shock*, the RBC school considered that the main driver should be a *real shock*. With this main difference, but under the same assumptions as to the NEC school, the RBC school gained prominence in the 1980s and the first half of the 1990s due to its ability to replicate the stylized facts of the North American economy. Although their evolution will be described in greater detail in the next section, two important ideas are worth underlining: the first is that RBC models have become a starting point for various models (theories) that *do not* consider real (or technological) shock as the main driving mechanism, and the second idea is that RBC models are used as laboratories for policy analysis, in line with what was proposed by Lucas (1980).

In the 1980s and 1990s, parallel to the RBC models, a Keynesian approach was developed with new microeconomic elements. This school is known as New Keynesian Economics and emphasizes monopolistic competition and costly price adjustment. As Goodfriend and King (1997) point out, three generations of NEK models can be distinguished: the first introduces rational expectations in price/wage modeling (Taylor 1980; Gordon 1982). The second generation goes from investigating wage stickiness to investigating price stickiness. Furthermore, firms are modeled in monopolistic competition and are used to explain the effects of money on output when price rigidities exist. The best way to introduce dynamic pricing models into the monopolistic competition formulation in the third generation of NEK models is evaluated. The *state-dependent* approach was attractive because of its microeconomic foundations; however, it was challenging to fit it into a macroeconomic model. An alternative was to use the *time-dependent* approach developed by Calvo (1983). The advantage of this approach is that its incorporation in the macroeconomic models did not present difficulties.

In the mid-1990s, a consensus emerged between the RBC and NEK models. This consensus is known as the New Neoclassical Synthesis (NSN) (Goodfriend and King 1997). On the one hand, the NSN is based on the RBC models by incorporating intertemporal optimization and rational expectations within dynamic macroeconomic models; on the other hand, the NSN takes elements of the NEK such as monopolistic competition costly price adjustment (price stickiness). The main model of the NSN is summarized in three equations: the dynamic IS, the Phillips curve, and the monetary policy rule. The NSN has dominated the way of doing macroeconomics until today. However, the financial crisis of 2008 caused some assumptions of the NSN to be rethought, which are currently being evaluated.

The third crisis occurred in the early years of the twenty-first century and finally materialized in 2008. This is known as the 2008 financial crisis. The origin of this crisis is found in the collapse of the housing bubble in the United States in 2006 and then sparked a *subprime* mortgage crisis. The effects of this crisis became global in 2008, and this caused, in turn, an international liquidity crisis. Faced with this crisis, the NSN model was limited because international interest rates were at very low levels (close to zero), which prevented using the Taylor rule to encourage the economy. One of the main challenges to these models was the absence of the financial sector. Elements of the financial system are currently being incorporated into the NEK and RBC models. The idea is to evaluate the performance of these models in explaining financial crises and to evaluate alternative policies that smooth the economic cycle.

1.3.2 The Historical Development of the RBC School

The 1980s and the first half of the 1990s witnessed the development of the real business cycle theory. The initial model proposed by Kydland and Prescott (1982) was extended in several directions. These directions include the study of money, the labor market, public spending, financial assets, imperfect competition, and the open economy in the theoretical framework proposed by the RBC school. The objective of all these investigations was to increase the understanding of how these variables help explain the business cycle. To understand how the main ideas of this school of economic thought have evolved, it is necessary to study chronologically the different investigations associated with real business cycles, which together provide a holistic view of the RBC school.

In 1981 a new technique emerged to separate the cyclical component from the trend of a variable. This technique was proposed by Hodrick and Prescott (1981), who conducted an empirical study of cycles for the United States after World War II. These authors proposed a methodology to separate the cycle and the trend of a series, known as the HP filter. Under this methodology, Hodrick and Prescott found empirical regularities of the cycles (volatility, comovements, and persistence).

Kydland and Prescott published research in 1982 in which they used the neoclassical growth theory with some modifications to study business cycles. One of the main modifications was the assumption that capital construction takes several periods and not just one, as was the assumption of the neoclassical growth model. This assumption is fundamental to explaining the aggregate fluctuations because it behaves as a transmission mechanism with persistence over several periods. In addition, the authors considered modifying the utility function to be temporally non-separable, which indicates a high intertemporal substitution of leisure. In this context, productivity *shocks* are the only variable that explains business fluctuations.

Under the assumptions of their model, Kydland and Prescott were successful in replicating several features observed in US macroeconomic series after World War II. For example, the model suggests that the investment's standard deviation is 6.45%, while the data indicates that it is 5.1%. It is worth mentioning that these authors used the HP filter to separate the trend cycle of main macroeconomic variables from both the data and the model. With this model and its results, these authors began the theory of real economic cycles.

According to Rebelo (2005), three revolutionary ideas emerged from the Kydland and Prescott (1982) research: the first is that business cycles can be studied using dynamic general equilibrium models. The second is that these authors unified the theory of **economic growth** and that of **economic cycles**. In addition, business cycle models must be consistent with empirical regularities of long-term growth. Finally, in their research Kydland and Prescott gave importance to quantitative analysis when comparing the properties of the model with stylized facts.

The contribution of Kydland and Prescott (1982) could at least be summarized in two groups. On the one hand, the assumptions that they considered in their proposal were sufficient to approach the stylized facts of the economic cycles of the United States. On the other hand, its influence on future research, not only those that emphasize the supply side (or real variables) as driving mechanisms (productivity), but also those that consider that the main cause of fluctuations, is on the demand and nominal variables side.

In line with the above, the *main assumptions* considered by Kydland and Prescott (1982) and which have later formed part of the RBC models are as follows: (1) agents respond optimally to economic events all the time; (2) output fluctuations come from real sources, that is, business cycles are a consequence of *exogenous* change in productivity; (3) work fluctuates due to the intertemporal substitution of leisure (or work); (4) the product is persistent due to the effect of the *internal propagation mechanism—capital accumulation*—and (5) investment is more volatile than consumption because agents prefer to smooth their consumption and transfer any transitory movement in their income to savings (investment).

Also, the research that grew out of the Kydland and Prescott (1982) study was called "RBC models" due to the emphasis on the role of "*real shock*." These models have become a starting point for several theories that **do not consider** technological change (*shock*) as the main driving mechanism. For example, the New Keynesian

Economics (NEK) models in their basic three-equation model (dynamic IS, Phillips curve, and the monetary policy rule) consider three *shocks* (demand, productivity, and policy), each associated with each equation. An additional contribution is that RBC models can be used as *laboratories* for policy analysis in line with what was proposed by Lucas (1980).

Long and Plosser (1983) published an investigation that sought to explain the joint movements of the economic variables of the various productive sectors such as agriculture, mining, construction, etc. To do this, they proposed a model based on two groups of hypotheses: the hypothesis of preferences (families) and those of production possibilities (companies). In particular, the objective of these authors was to evaluate the ability of these hypotheses to explain the behavior of the economic cycle (at the aggregate and sectoral level).

Usually, when hypotheses about preferences are studied, emphasis is placed on their intra-temporal implication (static approach), which indicates that in the face of an unexpected increase in wealth, the consumer increases his/her demand for consumption **current** of goods and leisure. In addition to this, Long and Plosser, in their research, highlight that these hypotheses also have intertemporal implications (dynamic approach), which suggest that the same wealth *shock* encourages the consumer to increase his/her consumption demand **future** of goods (including leisure). The main implication of the latter is that consumption (of different goods) as a time series presents comovements and persistence.

Although the preference hypotheses help to describe the comovement and persistence of consumption, they fail to explain why these characteristics are due. This is related to the fact that price movements are required for consumption (demand) to find its counterpart on the side of production (supply). That is why, to better understand the cyclical movements of the variables, the hypotheses of production possibilities must be considered. In this respect, Long and Plosser (1983) assumes a neoclassical production function (described in Chapter 3). Furthermore, they assume that all goods are perishable, in other words, that all goods available at the beginning of the current period are *new units* produced at the beginning of this period. In practical terms, the depreciation rate is assumed to be equal to one.

The main conclusion of Long and Plosser (1983) was that the time series properties derived from the model show a certain approximation to those found in the data. Also, the authors acknowledge that this model does not capture all the empirical regularities due, in part, to the full depreciation assumption; however, this model is a good starting point (*benchmark*) to evaluate the inclusion of other factors such as money, fiscal policy, etc.

In 1985, two landmark investigations emerged at the RBC school. The first is the Hansen model, and the second is the Mehra and Prescott model.

One of the main criticisms of the Kydland and Prescott (1982) model was that the model did not capture the high volatility of hours worked and the low volatility of real wages. This criticism, in part, is based on the fact that the model of Kydland and Prescott (1982) considered that there is no unemployment and that the volatility of working hours is only because the worker adjusts his/her number of working hours. However, Hansen (1985) found that the data suggest that 55% of the variance of "total working hours" is explained by the number of workers entering and leaving the labor market, and only 20% is explained by the working hours of each individual. This led Hansen to postulate the main assumption of his/her model: "the individual decides to work a fixed number of hours or not to work," that is, work is *indivisible*. The main result of Hansen's model is that it explains the high volatility of employment compared to wages, without requiring a high elasticity of substitution of leisure, which is consistent with the data.

On the other hand, Mehra and Prescott (1985) published an investigation in which they wondered if the RBC model could capture two stylized facts of the financial series: the first corresponds to the historical average of the real return of risky assets (SP500), the which is 6.98% for the period 1889–1978, and the second is the same empirical moment for the risk-free real return on assets (*treasure bill*), which is 0.8% for the same period. Based on these data, the risk premium is 6.18% on average. The results of these authors' model suggest that the RBC model can capture the qualitative characteristics of the relationships between financial and macroeconomic series, but not their quantitative characteristics. The authors indicate that the maximum risk premium that the model can generate is 0.35%. This result opened an essential line of research that has sought to solve this enigma.

Until now, the RBC models had emphasized the *shock* of productivity, that is, the *shock* on the supply side. However, Keynesian thought suggested that economic fluctuations were primarily due to movements in investment. With this in mind, Greenwood et al. (1988) introduced two features to the standard RBC model. The first is that physical capital is considered and its services through a utilization rate. It not only considers, for example, a computer (capital good) but also the number of hours that this good is used, which is known as the utilization rate. One impact of such a rate is that capital depreciates more quickly. The second is that the *shock* considered is not productivity, but one associated with the marginal efficiency of the investment. The main conclusion of this model is that the *shock* to investment under the described mechanism could be an essential element to explain business cycles.

On the other hand, Cooley and Hansen (1989) studied the role of money in economic fluctuations. To do this, the authors used the standard RBC model, to which they incorporated the money through a *cash-in-advance* constraint. With this model, the authors attempted to estimate the welfare costs caused by the inflation tax and studied the effects of anticipated inflation on the characteristics of the economic series. The main conclusion is that in the short term, money does correlate with the product; however, the characteristics of the business cycles of an economy with high and low inflation are similar. This suggests that under the model's assumptions, money does not help to explain business cycles better.

Benhabib et al. (1991) considered household production in an RBC model to assess whether this extension could help strengthen the quantitative performance of the model. The result was that this model better captures the empirical moments of business cycles. For example, the Hansen (1985) model obtained the value of 1.29 for the GDP standard deviation, while the Benhabib et al. (1991) recorded 1.71, which is closer to that suggested by the data (1.74). Likewise, Hansen's model (1985) overestimated the investment's standard deviation (3.14 of the model vs. 2.82

of the data). In contrast, the model of Benhabib et al. (1991) infers that the standard deviation of investment is equal to 2.73, much closer to the data.

One of the main criticisms of the RBC models is that they do not capture the low correlation between the number of working hours and the real wage. The data suggest that this correlation is very close to zero, while the RBC (divisible/indivisible work) models indicate close to 0.951/0.915, respectively. Given this deficiency of the model, Christiano and Eichenbaum (1992b),[6] they published an investigation where when considering public consumption in the Hansen (1985) model, it is obtained that the model captures this correlation a little better (between 0.5 and 0.7). Government consumption influences the economy in two ways: the first is that part of public consumption is considered within the household consumption basket. The second is that public spending behaves like a *shock* that has a permanent and transitory component. An interesting feature of this research is that it does not use the *calibration* like the standard RBC models, but instead, the authors use an econometric technique (generalized method of moments [GMM]) to estimate the eight structural parameters, leaving only three under the calibration approach.

On the other hand, Baxter and King (1993) published a study that evaluated the macroeconomic effects of fiscal policy in an RBC model. Although the objective was not to assess whether fiscal policy is a source of business cycles, his/her research is relevant to understanding the short- and long-term effects of temporary and permanent government spending. In this model, the government influences families through transfers and the utility function. Capital and government spending are assumed to increase the consumer's level of utility, but not their marginal utility. In addition, the influence of the government on the companies is obtained through the government capital that acts as a factor in the production function. This is because companies need public goods such as roads, highways, etc., which influence their production.

One of the main assumptions of RBC models is that all markets (goods and factors) have a perfectly competitive structure, which suggests that price equals marginal cost. However, the data suggest that the price eventually is greater than the marginal cost, that is, that the *markup* ($\mu = \frac{p_t}{cmg_t}$) is greater than one. Under this and other empirical facts, Rotemberg and Woodford (1993) published an article where they introduced the structure of monopolistic competition in an RBC model. In this scenario, the authors analyzed how this new market structure could influence the transmission of the *shock* of productivity, especially through its influence on labor demand. Furthermore, under this structure, the analysis of a *shock* to the *markup* could provide a new driving mechanism to explain the cycles.

[6] A previous investigation by these authors is found in 1988, in which they question Prescott (1986)'s assertion that "theory comes before measurement." Christiano and Eichenbaum's main argument is that the RBC models do not capture the Dunlop-Tarshis observation, which indicates that the correlation between the number of hours worked and the real wage is close to zero. Under this argument, the authors conclude that the *shock* of productivity cannot be the only source of economic fluctuations after the Second World War.

Cogley and Nason (1995) published an investigation in which they evaluated the ability of the standard RBC model to capture two stylized facts of the dynamics of the gross national product (GNP) in the United States: the first is that GNP is positively autocorrelated in the short run and negatively (but slightly) in the long run, and the second is that GNP appears to have a significant *trend reversal* component, which has a hump-shaped moving average representation. The results of this investigation suggest that the standard RBC model needs a strong exogenous factor to replicate both stylized facts. This is because most RBC models have a weak internal propagation mechanism. Furthermore, these authors indicate that RBC models that consider lags or job adjustment costs partially capture both stylized facts. However, they still rely on large transient *shocks* (which is implausible) to replicate the impulse response found in the data.

The criticism of RBC models, suggested by Cogley and Nason (1995), is supported by Rotemberg and Woodford (1996) when they publish research in which they show that the standard RBC model has two empirical weaknesses. The first is that the model suggests that the variance of the product is very small compared to what is observed. The second is that the comovements between output, consumption, and working hours have the same direction in the data, which the model does not capture. To improve the model's ability to capture these stylized facts, the authors perform a sensitivity analysis of the value of three parameters (elasticity of labor supply, the intertemporal elasticity of substitution, and the capital share of output). The result of this effort is that the model improves the volatility of the product, but there is no more significant effect on the comovements of the variables in question.

Given the main criticisms of Cogley and Nason (1995) and Rotemberg and Woodford (1996), Burnside et al. (1996) analyze the importance of the utilization rate of capital as a transmission mechanism to evaluate the possibility of strengthening the internal mechanism of propagation of the RBC models. The results indicate that this variable is important in quantitative terms to propagate the effects of a productivity *shock*. A natural result of this is that the *shock* needed to capture the empirical regularities of the business cycle is significantly less than standard RBC models.

The following three Tables 1.3, 1.4, and 1.5 show the chronological development of the investigations in the RBC school. These tables are not exhaustive in terms of all the investigations carried out between 1980 and 1996, but they are referential as they try to point out the main investigations.

1.3.2.1 Research on the State of the Art of RBC Models

This section describes a set of investigations that have attempted to summarize RBC models' state of the art over time.

The first researchers who tried to summarize the development of the RBC theory were King, Plosser, and Rebelo, who in 1988 published two papers in the *Journal of Monetary Economics*. The first described the theoretical framework of the RBC

Table 1.3 Historical development of RBC models

Author	Year	Description
Hodrick and Prescott	1981	**Title:** *Post-War U.S. Business Cycles: An Empirical Investigation.* **Topic:** They proposed a method of decomposition of a series. **Contribution:** The objective of this method is to separate the cyclical and trend components of a macroeconomic series. It is known as a HP filter.
Kydland and Prescott	1982	**Title:** *Time to Build and Aggregate Fluctuations.* **Topic:** Use of the neoclassical growth model to explain business cycles. **Contribution:** The main contribution was to explain economic cycles using the neoclassical economic growth model with two variants: the first is that it takes more than one period to build capital and the second is that the consumer faces a temporal inseparable utility function. With this investigation, the RBC school begins.
Long and Plosser	1983	**Title:** *Real Business Cycles.* **Topic:** RBC model with several economic sectors. **Contribution:** It was shown that a simple RBC model can explain some stylized facts of business cycles. These authors coined the name “RBC models” to denote all models that emphasize the productivity *shock* as the main source of the business cycle.
Hansen	1985	**Title:** *Indivisible Labor and the Business Cycle.* **Topic:** RBC model with indivisible work. **Contribution:** With this model, the criticism that RBC models require that the elasticity of substitution of labor be high is overcome, which is not what is observed by the data. This model became the standard RBC model.
Mehra and Prescott	1985	**Title:** *The Equity Premium: A Puzzle.* **Topic:** RBC model with risk premium. **Contribution:** We evaluated whether the RBC model with financial variables can explain the stylized fact of the risk premium. They found that the model explains their behavior qualitatively, but not quantitatively. This result opened a long-term line of research.

Table 1.4 Historical development of RBC models (continued)

Author	Year	Description
Greenwood et al.	1988	**Title:** *Investment, Capacity Utilization, and the Real Business Cycle.* **Topic:** RBC model with variable capital utilization and *shock* to the marginal efficiency of investment (EMgI). **Contribution:** There were two: [1] to evaluate from a Keynesian approach the source of the economic cycles (*shock* to the EMgI) and [2] to propose a new transmission mechanism (the variable utilization of capital). This work initiated an important line of research. Currently, RBC models usually consider variable capital utilization as a main element in the model.
Cooley and Hansen	1989	**Title:** *The Inflation Tax in a Real Business Cycle Model.* **Topic:** RBC model with money. **Contribution:** It is evaluated whether money (money supply rule) affects the nature and amplitude of economic cycles. Under the assumptions of the research, the authors found that money does not provide a further explanation of the cycles.
Mendoza	1991	**Title:** *Real Business Cycle in a Small Open Economy.* **Topic:** RBC model with open economy. **Contribution:** It is evaluated whether the RBC model could explain the typical stylized facts of an open economy. In particular, the author finds that the positive correlation between saving and investment is explained by the persistence of the *shock* of productivity. It is worth mentioning that the behavior of the economy was analyzed in the face of two shocks: productivity and external interest rate.
Benhabib et al.	1991	**Title:** *Homework in Macroeconomics: Household Production and Aggregate Fluctuations.* **Topic:** RBC model with home production. **Contribution:** By introducing household production and the labor used in the said production in an RBC model, the model better captures the empirical moments of the macroeconomic variables.
Christiano and Eichenbaum	1992a	**Title:** *Current Real-Business Cycle Theories and Aggregate Labor-Market Fluctuations.* **Topic:** RBC model with government consumption. **Contribution:** Strengthened the RBC model to better capture the low correlation between working hours and real wages. To do this, the authors introduced public spending in Hansen (1985)'s RBC model.

Table 1.5 Historical development of RBC models (continued)

Author	Year	Description
Baxter and King	1993	**Title:** *Fiscal Policy in General Equilibrium.* **Topic:** RBC model with fiscal policy. **Contribution:** They evaluated the real short- and long-term effects of fiscal policy in an RBC model. The main difference is that in this model a *shock* of productivity is not considered, but rather a *shock* to public investment and public spending.
Rotemberg and Woodford	1993	**Title:** *Dynamic General Equilibrium Models with Imperfectly Competitive Product Markets.* **Topic:** RBC model with imperfect competition. **Contribution:** The authors considered a market structure of monopolistic competition in contrast to the assumption of standard RBC models (perfect competition). The authors analyze the role that this structure could have in transmitting *shocks* and as a source of fluctuations through disturbances of the *markup*.
Cogley and Nason	1995	**Title:** *Output Dynamics in Real-Business-Cycle Models.* **Topic:** Criticism of the RBC model. **Contribution:** The authors show that RBC models have a weak internal transmission mechanism that prevents them from capturing two stylized facts of the product (autocorrelation and trend reversal). Although this problem can be overcome with some assumptions in the labor market, they still depend on large transient *shocks*, which is implausible in the data.
Rotemberg and Woodford	1996	**Title:** *Real-Business-Cycle Models and Forecastable Movements in Output, Hours, and Consumption.* **Topic:** Criticism of the RBC model. **Contribution:** The authors make evident the weakness of the RBC models in capturing the variance of the product and the positive correlation between consumption, product, and work shown in the data.
Burnside and Eichenbaum	1996	**Title:** *Factor-Hoarding and the Propagation of Business-Cycle Shocks.* **Topic:** RBC model with capacity utilization (capital and labor). **Contribution:** Given the criticisms of Cogley and Nason (1995) and Rotemberg and Woodford (1996), these authors propose a transmission mechanism (capacity utilization) that strengthens the internal mechanism of RBC models. With this, the modified model better captures what is observed in the data without the need to resort to large *shocks* of productivity.

models and the solution method of these models; the second described the main lines of research that emerged from the standard RBC model.[7]

In their first research, King, Plosser, and Rebelo considered that the theoretical framework for studying real business cycles is the neoclassical model of growth augmented by job choices. Under this approach, they study the effects on the economic cycle of a *shock* of productivity. The main conclusion that emerges from this research is that the neoclassical model of growth (augmented with labor) can replicate some stylized facts of business cycles only when there is a highly persistent technological *shock*. In particular, the model captures two groups of stylized facts: the first is that it shows the procyclical behavior of employment, consumption, and investment. The second is that the model generates the observed *ranking* of the relative volatility of investment, output, and consumption ($var_{\text{investment}} > var_{\text{output}} > var_{\text{consumption}}$).

However, the model is limited in generating other stylized facts. One of them, which is extremely important to characterize the business cycle, is the serial correlation of output (first-order autocorrelation: 0.96 in the data [1948.I–1986.IV]). The model requires a high persistence of productivity to generate a strong serial correlation of output (when the persistence of the *shock* is equal to 0.9, it produces the first-order autocorrelation of the output of 0.93; however, when the first is equal to zero, the autocorrelation is 0.03).

In their second investigation, King, Plosser, and Rebelo outline some new study directions within the theoretical framework of RBC models. One of these new directions is to consider that the growth path could have a stochastic component, that is, that it could have a unit root. This differs from the usual analysis of RBC models because the growth path is considered to be exogenous and deterministic in these models. The second line of research allows the long-run growth rate to be the endogenous result of technology. This clearly contrasts with the usual assumption in standard RBC models: the long-run growth rate is exogenously determined by the growth rate of labor-increasing technical change, which is assumed to be a calibrated parameter.

The third line of research mentioned by these authors is the inclusion of distorting taxes, imperfect competition, and other elements that produce a suboptimal equilibrium. In this case, the authors focus on the methods to include such elements in the RBC model. Finally, the fourth line of research refers to heterogeneous agents, which contrasts with the "representative agent" assumption in RBC models. This line of research responds that empirical evidence suggests that families are different due to different variables. Furthermore, Heckman (1984) indicates that the most appropriate way to study the labor market is the assumption of heterogeneity among agents.

Stadler (1994) published an investigation that summarizes and evaluates the theory of real business cycles. One of his/her main conclusions is that the RBC

[7] These authors published a technical appendix after several years (2002) in the journal *Computational Economics*.

theory has changed the way of looking at business cycles. This theory suggests that distortions are not needed to obtain macroeconomic fluctuations; that is, an efficient economy with complete markets could show fluctuations if technological change is stochastic. This statement opens a whole line of research on business cycles. Another conclusion is that there are still some challenges that the RBC theory has not overcome. One is the difficulty of these models capturing the stylized facts very closely. Another difficulty is that they cannot satisfactorily explain the dynamics of the product, which is associated with another weakness: a weak transmission mechanism. Rouwenhorst (1991) indicates that the fluctuations produced in the Kydland and Prescott (1982) model are essentially due to the stochastic behavior of productivity. The role of the capital "time to build" transmission mechanism is small, which was expected to be important in propagating the initial impulse.

An additional difficulty is that the assumption of a "representative agent" is questionable due to microeconomic data. As Stoker (1993) points out, data at the microeconomic level suggest the existence of heterogeneity between households and firms. For example, differences can be found between the size of families or companies. Likewise, there are differences between companies according to what type of factors are labor-intensive (some capital-intensive and others labor-intensive). Finally, Stadler (1994) suggests that, despite the challenges that the CBR theory faces, its long-term contribution lies in the fact that it has proposed new methods of macroeconomic research and evaluation of economic policies.

Cooley and Prescott (1995) published a book that brings together different important themes of the RBC school. As the author points out, the goal of this book is to provide an organized exposition of the main ideas and methods of RBC models. The themes addressed in the book are the following: an investigation oriented to economic growth and the business cycle, which provides the point of reference throughout the book, a set of investigations that describe the extensions of the RBC model (heterogeneous agents, money, domestic production, imperfect competition, asset prices, and open economy), and two methodological investigations, one of them oriented to the solution of the model in an environment of competitive equilibrium and the other oriented to the solution in suboptimal economies. Finally, the author includes an investigation on non-Walrasian economies and another on policy analysis in RBC models.

In the same spirit as Cooley and Prescott (1995), Hartley et al. (1998) present a collection of articles that, in their opinion, define and show the development of the RBC school, on the one hand, and express its main criticisms, on the other hand. As the authors point out, the book's goal is to balance research that is in favor of the RBC school and research that criticizes it. When comparing this collection with the book by Cooley and Prescott (1995), two main differences are observed: the first is that the collection by Hartley et al. (1998) has a greater extension than that of Cooley and Prescott (1995), so much so that Hartley et al. (1998) considers 31 investigations, while Cooley and Prescott (1995) 12. The second important difference is that Hartley et al. (1998) do take stock of research in the field of RBC models; in other words, among his/her 31 articles, at least 11 of them are critical. This differs from the work of Cooley and Prescott (1995), which does not include any criticism, since the objective of this author was only to show the ideas and methods of the RBC school in an organized way.

It is important to underline that the work of Hartley et al. (1998) is organized into five categories: the first contains a body of research on the fundamentals of modeling real business cycles. For example, this first research is the article by Kydland and Prescott (1982), which started the RBC school. The second category contains the main extensions of the RBC models. In this respect, Cooley and Prescott (1995)'s work is more exhaustive because it includes more extensions. For example, in Cooley and Prescott (1995), one can find the RBC model with an open economy or financial assets absent in Hartley et al. (1998). The third category contains research that criticizes the calibration method of RBC models. The fourth category refers to research on how to evaluate RBC models. It should be noted that this category is the largest in the book, which is not surprising given the debate that arose over the "unconventional" way of evaluating RBC models pioneered by Kydland and Prescott (1982), that is, the comparison between the theoretical moments (from the simulation of the model) and the empirical moments, which contrasts with the usual econometrics. The fifth category refers to the Solow residual, and the last one describes how to obtain the cyclical component of the aggregate variables. Reading both books provides a comprehensive overview of the strengths and weaknesses of RBC models.

King and Rebelo (1999) wrote an article in the *Handbook of Macroeconomics*,[8] which they titled "*Reanimation of real business cycles*." At least three ideas can be extracted from this article: the first is that the authors adopt the main weakness of RBC models and suggest a way to overcome this weakness. The second idea is that the authors show that the main criticisms or problems faced by the RBC models could have been successful results. Finally, the authors suggest new lines of research in RBC models, which indicates that this research program is still in force.

Regarding the first idea, the authors state that the main weakness of RBC models is that they require large technology shocks (significant standard deviation and persistence) to produce business cycles close to reality. However, these technology shocks are not as large or as persistent in the data as the model requires. Given this weakness, the authors propose considering an important amplifying mechanism: the variable use of capital. By introducing this component into an RBC model, it could reproduce the observed business cycles with little *shock* of productivity, as the empirical evidence indicates.

Regarding the second idea, the authors argue that three main criticisms have been resolved in favor of RBC models. The first criticism is the sensitivity of the model results to parameterization. As the authors point out, the RBC model is resistant to different values of the parameters; for example, the model results are satisfactory

[8] The goal of the *Handbook of Macroeconomics*, as stated on its very pages, is to provide a review of the literature on the current state of knowledge in macroeconomics. Topics reviewed include the theory of economic growth and business cycles and the consequences of fiscal and monetary policy. Currently, there are two *handbooks*: the first was published in 1999 (edited by John B. Taylor and Michael Woodford) and the last in 2016 (edited by John B. Taylor and Harald Uhlig).

even in the case of a small labor supply elasticity at the individual (family) level but high at the aggregate level. The second criticism is the limitation of the model to produce a realistic behavior of prices. This has been overcome by including nominal variables (money supply, prices, etc.) in the RBC model. For example, this can be seen in Cooley and Hansen (1989). Finally, the third criticism is about the assumption of large technological *shocks*. As indicated in the previous paragraph, the authors recognize this weakness, which can be overcome when the variable use of capital is added to the standard RBC model.

The third idea that emerges from the research by King and Rebelo (1999) is that the RBC model research program is still in force due to the new lines of research that have emerged. For example, the study of a multisectoral model is still pending. The usual way of studying business cycles in RBC models has been under a single-sector model; however, by considering various sectors, one could better understand the relationship between those sectors and how the variable utilization of capital behaves in each sector. In this field, there are previous investigations such as those made by Long and Plosser (1983). However, they have not been fully exploited, considering variable capital utilization and more realistic technological *shocks*. Another line of research is the consideration of heterogeneous agents. In principle, its introduction in the RBC model could enrich the labor market dynamics, bringing the model closer to reality.

In 2005, Rebelo published an article in which he/she briefly reviews the contribution of RBC models to the understanding of business cycles and describes *in detail* the main open issues in the existing literature. This research complements the study by King and Rebelo (1999) in a meaningful way by emphasizing future lines of research.

According to Rebelo (2005), two issues that still require further investigation, within the framework of RBC models, are, on the one hand, the explanation of the behavior of the prices of financial assets and, on the other hand, the understanding of the Great Depression. Regarding the former, the pioneering work of Mehra and Prescott (1985) showed that the RBC model was capable of capturing the qualitative characteristics of the risk premium, but failed to replicate its *quantitative* characteristics. This weakness of the model is known as the "risk premium puzzle" (*equity premium puzzle*). These findings started a line of research active to this day. One of the proposals to overcome this weakness was elaborated by Boldrin et al. (2001), who introduced habit formation in an RBC model. The result was that the model still maintained the weakness found by Mehra and Prescott (1985). Another effort in the same direction was that of Boldrin et al. (2001), who, under the assumption that the production of consumer and investment goods is carried out in different sectors and that there are frictions in the movement of capital and labor between sectors, obtained results for the behavior of the risk premium that is closer to what is observed in the data. However, this line of research demands further study.

The second topic that demands further investigation, in light of the RBC models, is the Great Depression. In particular, the challenge presented by RBC models is to explain what caused the Great Depression. As Rebelo (2005) points out, there is a set of investigations in this field to date. However, it is still an open topic in the

RBC school because the Great Depression was caused by the combination of several adverse shocks and inadequate economic policies.

In addition to these two major research topics, the author mentions other open lines of research: one of them is the study of *shocks* alternative to productivity (oil, fiscal, and technological change specific to investment). Another line is the monetary model, that is, the extension of the RBC model to include nominal and real frictions, which in practice are NEK models. In addition to the above, Rebelo (2005) indicates that considering models with multiple equilibria in the spirit of Farmer (1997) is still an issue that requires further study.

Table 1.6 briefly describes, from a historical perspective, the research that has tried to provide the state of art of the RBC school over time.

1.3.2.2 Research Related to the Labor Market

Kydland (1995) states that the behavior of the labor market plays a vital role in understanding business cycles. That is why one of the main aspects in evaluating RBC models is their ability to replicate the stylized facts of the labor market. In particular, the US economy shows two important stylized facts: the first is that hours worked are more volatile than real wages; the second is that the correlation between hours worked and real wages is close to zero. In addition, microeconometric studies suggest that the labor supply elasticity is small. The main investigations that have tried to capture these stylized facts are described below.

One of the main criticisms of the Kydland and Prescott (1982) model was the assumption that the elasticity of labor supply is significant, which is not supported by the data. In their research, Kydland and Prescott (1982) focused on the *intensive margin* component of labor supply, which is measured as the average number of hours worked. These authors assumed that the movement of "added work hours" is essentially due to the adjustment of hours worked by the employee. However, Hansen (1985) considers that the variation in aggregate working hours is mainly due to the entry and exit of individuals in the labor market, that is, the *extensive margin* component of the job offer. Under this assumption, Hansen (1985) manages to obtain a labor supply elasticity that is more in line with the microeconomic data.

Christiano and Eichenbaum (1992b) indicate that the Kydland and Prescott (1982) and Hansen (1985) models fail to replicate the two main stylized facts of the labor market: (1) hours worked are more volatile than real wages, and (2) the correlation between hours worked and real wages is close to zero. Given this, Christiano and Eichenbaum (1992b) propose a model in which public spending plays an important role in private consumption. Under the assumption that public consumption is an imperfect substitute for private consumption, these authors indicate that an increase in government spending produces a negative wealth effect, which induces families to reduce their demand for leisure and, therefore, to increase their job offers. With this specification, the authors find that the model is closer to the data.

Table 1.6 State of the art

Author	Year	Description
King et al.	1988a	**Title:** *Production, Growth and Business Cycles - I. The Basic Neoclassical Model.* **Topic:** Theoretical framework and solution methods of RBC models. **Contribution:** On the one hand, they argue that the extended neoclassical growth model (endogenously incorporating the consumption-investment decision and the leisure-work decision) has the capacity to replicate the characteristics of some aggregate variables. On the other hand, they state that the conclusions of the model require that the *shocks* of productivity be persistent.
King et al.	1988b	**Title:** *Production, Growth and Business Cycles - II. New Directions.* **Topic:** New lines of research in RBC models. **Contribution:** They list and explain the lines of investigation pending in the models.
Stadler	1994	**Title:** *Real Business Cycles.* **Topic:** Summarizes and evaluates the RBC theory. **Contribution:** Describe the standard RBC model, then mention the main extensions, and, finally, mention the criticisms.
Cooley and Prescott	1995	**Title:** *Frontiers of Business Cycle Research.* **Topic:** Development of RBC models. **Contribution:** It shows in an organized way the development of the main ideas and methods of the RBC models. The book is a compendium of research within the framework of RBC theory.
Hartley et al.	1998	**Title:** *Real Business Cycles - A Reader.* **Topic:** Balance between the research that supports the RBC models and those that criticize them. **Contribution:** It brings together 31 articles, which not only show the development of the RBC school, but also its main weaknesses and the research that supports it.
King and Rebelo	1999	**Title:** *Resuscitating Real Business Cycles.* **Topic:** RBC model with *modifications* that overcomes initial criticism and future lines of research. **Contribution:** At least three ideas are rescued. The first is that the inclusion of variable capital utilization helps to obtain a better performance of the model with a more realistic *shock* of productivity. The second is that the RBC models have overcome three important criticisms and the last idea is that there are still lines of research in these models.
Rebelo	2005	**Title:** *Real Business Cycle Models: Past, Present, and Future.* **Topic:** Emphasis on the lines of research pending in the RBC models. **Contribution:** Briefly reviews the contribution of the RBC models and explains in detail the pending lines of research.

Another effort to improve the quantitative performance of the RBC model in the labor market was carried out by Benhabib et al. (1991). These authors proposed including in the modeling the production of the sector that works at home (not the market) due to its high participation in the national product (20% to 50%), according to Eisner (1988). The main idea of this model is that agents also obtain utility when they consume what is produced by this sector and those who work in this sector obtain disutility, as observed in the market. Under this premise, the authors find that there are incentives for an individual to move from working at home (nonmarket) to working in the market. The effect of this is that the labor supply could increase in a similar way to the public spending *shock* of Christiano and Eichenbaum (1992b). With this specification, the authors find that the model is closer to the data.

1.3.2.3 Investigations Related to Fiscal Policy

In this section, two sets of investigations are described. The first set, from the empirical point of view, has pointed out the relationship that exists between the fiscal variables (taxes, spending, and deficit) and the macroeconomic variables (product, consumption, investment, employment, and real wages). The second, from a theoretical point of view, has raised various RBC models with the public sector. The objective of this is to evaluate the capacity of these models to capture empirical evidence. From all these efforts it is concluded, as Cooper (1998) points out, that there is *no* role for fiscal policy in the standard RBC model, which considers complete markets and the absence of externalities. For the fiscal sector to gain an important role in modeling, it is necessary to consider some *different assumptions* to those proposed by the RBC school.

[A] Empirical Evidence In the existing literature, at least two sets of empirical investigations can be distinguished. The first set relates the public spending *shock* as a consequence of military events rather than macroeconomic events (Hall and Mishkin 1980; Hall 1986; Barro 1983; Rotemberg and Woodford 1992; Ramey and Shapiro 1998) and usually use linear regression models or the "narrative approach"[9] to identify the *shock* of fiscal spending. The second set emphasizes that public spending responds to macroeconomic events and uses the structural autoregressive

[9] The narrative approach consists of reviewing various historical sources such as the presidential address, the president's economic report, and reports from congressional meetings to identify the motivation for each legislated tax/public spending change. The idea of this method is to separate the changes in legislated fiscal variables into those that legitimately respond to changes in macroeconomic variables from those that respond to other motivations (for example, political motivations). For a better description of this method, see Romer and Romer (2010).

vector (SVAR) approach[10] to identify the fiscal *shock*. In this section, we will focus on this last set of investigations.

Using the VAR approach, various studies have found that the fiscal policy *shock* (defined as government purchases) has positive effects on output, hours worked, consumption, and real wages (Fatás and Mihov 2001; Blanchard and Perotti 2002; Perotti 2005; Galí et al. 2007; Pappa 2009). Mountford and Uhlig (2009) find that anticipated public spending *shock* has positive effects on output and consumption, but they are small.

Fatás and Mihov (2001), based on research by Blanchard and Perotti (1999),[11] studied the effect of public spending *shock* on consumption, investment, and employment. In their initial VAR model, they found that the positive *shock* of public spending increases real GDP. In a second model, in which they included the components of consumption (total consumption, consumption of durable goods, consumption of nondurable goods, and consumption of services), they observed that total consumption and all its components react positively to the *shock* of public spending. This suggests that consumption is procyclical. By carrying out the same exercise with investment and its components, the authors conclude that total investment contracts slightly in the first six quarters and then reacts positively to the *shock*, until returning to trend after three yearsİn addition, it is observed that the driver of investment behavior is residential investment, which always remains above the trend until the third year. From these exercises, the authors infer that consumption and investment react positively to public spending *shock*.

By evaluating the impacts of the fiscal *shock* on labor market variables, the authors conclude that employment increases after the *shock*, but that real wages change marginally. Given this last result, the authors indicate that the real wage reaction of the economy is not robust enough to different nominal wage specifications and deflation methods (Burnside et al. 2000), for which they prefer to analyze the response of the real wages in the manufacturing sector, which is robust. Under

---

[10] VAR (or SVAR) models have become one of the most widely used econometric tools in macroeconometrics. This is because this technique can describe the relationships in reduced form between the aggregate variables without imposing a priori on economic theory. However, when you want to analyze the economic *structural* relationships between variables, you need some form of identification, which is usually based on economic theory. Chudik and Fidora (2011) point out that in the existing literature, there are at least four approaches to impose *identification constraints* of *shock*: the first is to place the variables (Cholesky decomposition) recursively; the second is to impose "zero" constraints on the system of linear equations. These constraints are a set of variables that are not affected by the *shock* of interest for a certain period of time. The third approach is the decomposition into permanent and temporary components. The fourth way of imposing identification constraints is sign constraints. This alternative consists of indicating the sign that the structural impulse-response function must have for a number of periods after the *shock*. As Chudik and Fidora (2011) indicate, the basic idea behind this method is to be able to identify the structural *shock* by checking if the corresponding sign of its impulse-response function is in accordance with economic theory.

[11] It should be noted that this research was later published in 2002 in *"The Quarterly Journal of Economics,"* which is described in the next paragraph.

this change of variable, the authors find that real wages (in the manufacturing sector) respond positively (and significantly) to the *shock* of public spending.

Fatás and Mihov (2001), in a further step, contrast their empirical results with the RBC model. The objective of this contrast is to evaluate if the RBC model with a government sector has the capacity to capture the empirical behavior of consumption and employment in the face of a *shock* of public spending. What these authors find is that the model is not capable of replicating the procyclical behavior of consumption. Furthermore, the RBC model predicts that consumption should contract.

Blanchard and Perotti (2002) analyzed the effect of a *shock* of public spending and taxes on output. The main conclusion of this study is that output increases when faced with a positive *shock* of public spending and falls when faced with an increase in taxes. This result is consistent with what is suggested by RBC models that introduce public spending as a *shock*. At a further level of analysis, the authors assess the impact of fiscal *shocks* on GDP components. The results indicate that private consumption reacts positively to the *shock* of public spending and that investment contracts; that is, they find that consumption is procyclical. When observing the results of the RBC models that include fiscal policy, it is found that they are not consistent with the observed behavior of consumption, but that they do capture the reduction in investment.

It should be mentioned that the research by Fatás and Mihov (2001) and Blanchard and Perotti (2002) have some similarities, but also some differences. First, in both studies the fiscal *shock* generates a positive output response with a fiscal multiplier greater than one in Fatás and Mihov (2001) and very close to one in Blanchard and Perotti (2002). Second, both investigations find that consumption increases significantly in the face of a fiscal *shock*. Third, there is an important difference in the behavior of the investment. Fatás and Mihov (2001) indicate that the public spending *shock* generates a marginally positive investment response, while Blanchard and Perotti (2002) find that this response is negative and significant.

Galí et al. (2007) confirm previous evidence on the macroeconomic effects of the public spending *shock*. In particular, they find similar results for product and consumption. In the case of investment, their results are in line with what was found *qualitatively* by Blanchard and Perotti (2002) (reduction of investment), but quantitatively said response is insignificant. In addition, they find that the real wage and the number of hours worked increase persistently in the face of the fiscal *shock*.

Given this evidence, the authors suggest a NEK model that considers a heterogeneous component in families. The main assumption is that two types of families subsist in the economy: Ricardian and non-Ricardian. The first type of family has a standard behavior in macroeconomic models (intertemporal optimization); the second type of family only consumes their labor income and cannot transfer resources intertemporally. Under this assumption and those corresponding to the NEK models (monopolistic competition and price stickiness), the model generates an increase in consumption in response to the *shock* of public spending.

The aforementioned research has emphasized *standard* constraints for identifying *shocks*, such as Cholesky decomposition or "zero" constraints. Unlike these investigations, Mountford and Uhlig (2009) studied the effects of fiscal policy *shocks* from a different perspective. The novelty of this research is the use of "sign constraints" in a VAR model to identify fiscal policy *shocks*. As these authors point out, the identification of these *shocks* is difficult due to three factors. In the first place, there is difficulty in discerning whether the movement of fiscal variables is due to the *shock* of fiscal policy or simply to the response to other *shocks* such as monetary or productivity. The second is that it is not clear what is meant by fiscal *shock*, which can be an increase (expected or unexpected) in public spending, or a tax cut, among other variables. This contrasts with the *shock* of monetary policy, which is clearly understood as the unexpected increase in the interest rate. The third factor is that the announcement and implementation of the fiscal policy must be taken into account. This is important because the announcement can cause movements in the macroeconomic variables without the need for the fiscal variables to show any previous movement.

One of the main conclusions of this study is that an anticipated *shock* of public spending[12] has a weak positive effect on output, the interest rate, and consumption; that is, consumption is procyclical. Furthermore, the effects of this *shock* are stronger than the *shock* of *unanticipated* public spending. In general terms, these results are in line with previous empirical investigations.

Using the same econometric technique (SVAR with sign restrictions), Pappa (2009) focused on studying the effects of the fiscal *shock* on the labor market. What is new about this study is that the author used the results of the DSGE models with fiscal *shock* to then use the predicted "signs" as constraints on the identification of fiscal *shocks* in a model SVAR. In particular, the author proposes an RBC model with the fiscal sector in line with Finn (1998) and an alternative NEK model to find the effect of the fiscal *shock* on macroeconomic variables. The result of this is that, in both models, output and the fiscal deficit increase in the face of a positive *shock* of public consumption. This result is used by the author to identify the fiscal *shock* in his/her SVAR model. The empirical result of this econometric model is that real wages and employment respond positively (and significantly) to public consumption *shock*. One conclusion that emerges from this research is that the empirical evidence on the (positive) response of the real wage is not captured by the RBC model (which predicts a reduction in the real wage), but by the NEK model.

[B] Theoretical Models Ramey (2016) suggests that the existing literature on public spending has usually sought to answer two main questions: (1) Do the theoretical DSGE models (RBC and NEK) capture the stylized facts of fiscal policy? (2) What are the fiscal multipliers? In this section we are going to focus on the first question and, in particular, on how RBC models have tried to capture the empirical evidence of fiscal variables.[13]

[12] It is assumed that the announcement of the fiscal *shock* is made today but its implementation is within a year.

[13] To see a detailed review of the literature on fiscal multipliers, see Ramey (2011, 2016).

Before describing some RBC models that include the government sector, it is important to mention that usually the variables that describe public spending have been introduced in RBC models as *shocks*. This is because the question that has been sought to be answered in these investigations is about what are the impacts of government spending on output volatility. Under this premise, government spending has been modeled as an exogenous stochastic process, usually AR(1), like the *shock* of productivity. It is in this scenario where the RBC models have served as a theoretical framework to evaluate different fiscal policies (government spending). However, as Stadler (1994) points out, given the assumptions of the RBC models (representative agent and absence of nominal and real frictions), it has been difficult for these models to stand as a "conceptually complete framework" for the analysis of fiscal policies.

In addition to the above, King and Rebelo (2000) indicate that another disadvantage of considering public spending as a *shock* in RBC models is that the model cannot replicate the comovements of macroeconomic variables. For example, when it is considered that the only *shock* of the model is public spending, financed by lump-sum taxes, it is obtained that consumption is countercyclical, which is inconsistent with the data. This is because the negative wealth effect produced by public spending induces the family to reduce its consumption, but encourages it to increase the hours worked and, therefore, the aggregate product. That is, an increase in public spending financed with lump-sum taxes (in the current period or in the future) reduces the wealth of families due to the present (or expected) increase in taxes, which ultimately encourages families to reduce their consumption.

Hall and Mishkin (1980) and Barro (1981, 1987) analyzed the impact of government consumption on output, employment, and the real interest rate. In both cases the authors used the standard neoclassical growth model. Four conclusions can be drawn from these studies: first, a temporary or persistent increase in public consumption should increase output and hours worked. The second is that Hall and Mishkin (1980) suggests that the effects on employment and output of a temporary increase in public consumption are greater when it is temporary than when it is permanent. The third conclusion is that the fiscal multiplier (of public consumption) is less than one (in steady state); that is, $\Delta Y/\Delta G < 1$. The fourth conclusion is that the interest rate reacts differently depending on whether the change in public consumption is temporary or permanent. In the first case (temporary change), the interest rate responds positively, while in the second case (permanent) it practically does not change (Barro 1981, 1987).

These findings were contrasted by Aiyagari et al. (1992), who used a standard *modified* neoclassical growth model that included a variable labor supply and a government sector, that is, an RBC model with the public sector. In addition, the authors made two main assumptions: the first is that government consumption is financed by lump-sum taxes, and the second is that the utility function is additively separable in public and private consumption. Under all these assumptions, the model provides four conclusions. The first is that similar to Hall and Mishkin (1980) and Barro (1981, 1987), output and employment respond positively to the increase in public consumption. The second is that a persistent change in public consumption has *stronger* effects on employment and output than a temporary change. This clearly contradicts what was suggested by Hall and Mishkin (1980).

The third conclusion is that the fiscal multiplier (of public consumption) is *greater than one* (in steady state) if the change in public consumption is permanent; that is, $\Delta Y/\Delta G > 1$ (if ΔG is permanent). The fourth conclusion is that the interest rate reacts positively regardless of the persistence of the change in public consumption. However, the persistence of the latter determines the magnitude of the interest rate response: the greater the persistence, the greater the interest rate response.

Baxter and King (1993) address three relevant questions in fiscal policy: what are the macroeconomic effects of temporary/permanent government purchases? How do the effects of government purchases change under different financing decisions? And what are the macroeconomic effects if government purchases increase the *stock* of public capital? To answer these questions, the authors introduce fiscal variables in families and companies in the theoretical framework of a standard RBC model. In the case of households, it is assumed that government spending and the *stock* of public capital provide utility, but do not affect marginal utility. On the other hand, in the case of companies, it is assumed that the *stock* of public capital is a factor of production and that it does affect the productivity of the factors of production (*stock* of private capital and labor). Likewise, it is considered that, like the *stock* of private capital, public capital follows a law of movement of capital accumulation. This law considers the same depreciation rate of private capital and the way to increase public capital is through government investment.

The main results of the model can be summarized in three groups. The first contains the impacts of the increase in government purchases. In this case, the model predicts that output will respond positively to a temporary or permanent *shock* from government purchases. In contrast, consumption in both scenarios contracts, resulting in a negative correlation between GDP and consumption. This result is not consistent with what is observed in the data. On the other hand, real wages contract and work increases regardless of the persistence of the fiscal *shock* (temporary or permanent). The real wage contraction clearly differs from the empirical evidence.

The second group of results is about how the decision or the form of financing of the government could change the impacts of the fiscal *shock*. When comparing two financing alternatives (lump-sum taxes vs. distortionary taxes), it is observed that the model predicts a reduction in output when taxes are proportional (distortionary). Moreover, the negative impact is not only observed in the product, but also in consumption, investment, and work. Therefore, the authors conclude that the form of financing does influence the impacts of the fiscal *shock*.

The third set of results is about the effects of the public capital *shock*. The model suggests that output and labor respond positively, while consumption contracts for the first six years and then shows a positive response for the remaining periods until it returns to a steady state.

Ludvigson (1996) studies the macroeconomic effects of government debt. The usual analysis of the impact of the fiscal *shock* is that the current increase in public spending (government purchases) will be financed by lump-sum taxes in the future. This expected increase in taxes has a negative wealth effect today, inducing families to reduce their consumption and savings (= investment, in a closed economy). However, Ludvigson (1996) suggests that if the reduction of distortionary taxes (positive fiscal *shock*) is financed by public debt issuance, then the said fiscal *shock* could induce an increase in consumption and investment. The rationale behind this result is that families see a current reduction in taxes, but expect them to increase in the future to pay today's public debt. This expected increase in the tax rate reduces the future interest rate. This is because the tax rate affects the demand for capital (because it is proportional to income). Given this interest rate reduction, families increase their consumption/investment today due to the substitution effect, which reinforces the initial increase due to the tax reduction today.

In addition, Ludvigson (1996) points out that this effect on consumption and investment depends on the elasticity of the labor supply and the degree of persistence of public debt. This is so true that as the labor supply tends to be more elastic and public debt tends to be more persistent, the response of consumption to debt issuance is strengthened.

Finn (1998), unlike previous research, separates public spending into two components: purchase of final goods and labor compensation (from the public sector). Previous investigations have focused their analysis on the first component; however, labor compensation has a relevant participation in public spending (59% on average between 1950.1 and 1993.4). In addition, as Finn (1998) points out, theoretically the *shock* to the purchase of public sector goods has different effects on the business cycle than the *shock* to public labor compensation. Under these premises, the author develops an RBC model, from which a main result emerges: government spending is not an important source of economic fluctuations. This is observed when evaluating the model with only a productivity *shock* compared to the model that, in addition to the productivity *shock*, contains the fiscal *shock*. In particular, the simulation indicates that the fiscal *shock* adds 0.02% to the standard deviation of output.

Fatás and Mihov (2001) use an RBC model with a government sector similar to that of Ludvigson (1996). The objective of these authors is to assess whether the RBC model, under different fiscal scenarios, could capture the positive correlation between GDP and consumption in the presence of public spending *shock*, as suggested by empirical evidence. For this, the authors evaluate the model in four scenarios: (1) increase in public spending financed by taxes (lump sum), (2) increase in public spending financed by taxes (distorting), (3) reduction of the tax (distorting) financed by debt, and (4) increase in public spending financed by debt.

Under these scenarios, at least two results are important to mention: the first is that in the four fiscal scenarios of consumption contracts, this reveals the difficulty of the model in capturing the observed behavior of consumption in the face of a fiscal *shock*. The second result is that output increases in all cases, except when public spending is financed by distortionary taxes, which captures to a certain degree what is suggested by the empirical evidence.

Table 1.7 describes chronologically some research on the empirical evidence of fiscal variables and their effects on macroeconomic variables. Likewise, Table 1.8 shows the evolution of the different RBC models that have included the government sector to try to capture the empirical evidence mentioned in Table 1.7.

1.3.2.4 Research Associated with Money

In this section, two sets of investigations are described. The first set refers to empirical research, which suggests that the *shock* of monetary policy has effects on output and price. The second set summarizes the different RBC models that have tried to capture this observed behavior in the data. One conclusion that emerges from all this research is that the RBC model needs other assumptions, such as nominal and real frictions, to capture the effects of the monetary *shock* on real variables.

[A] Empirical Evidence In the existing literature there is a vast body of research suggesting that the monetary *shock* (or monetary policy *shock*) has output and price effects (Friedman and Schwartz 1963; Romer and Romer 1989; Bernanke and Blinder 1992; Shapiro 1994; Leeper 1997; Christiano and Fitzgerald 1999; Faust and Henderson 2004; Bernanke et al. 2005; Smets and Wouters 2007; Coibion 2012; Ahmadi and Uhlig 2015). It is generally a consensus in the empirical literature that a contractionary monetary policy shock (reduction in the growth rate of the money supply) has (important) negative effects on output. In the case of the price response, the literature is not conclusive. What is expected is that in the face of a contractive monetary policy *shock*, the price will fall (due to a reduction in demand); however, what is observed, in some specifications,[14] is that in the short run the price increases. Eichenbaum (1992) called this empirical fact "the price puzzle" (*Price Puzzle*).

On the other hand, Christiano and Eichenbaum (1992a,b) indicate that a positive monetary *shock* (increase in the growth rate of the money supply) reduces the interest rate, but increases output, employment, and money—actual salary.

In addition to the above, Christiano and Fitzgerald (1999) highlight two important issues: the first refers to the *identification* of the *shock* of monetary policy and the second to the *evaluation of the model* that seeks to capture the empirical evidence.

Regarding the first, it is important to differentiate between two components of the *monetary policy actions*: the first component is the response to nonmonetary behaviors in the economy, and the second is the monetary *shock* itself. This separation is important because before building any DSGE model (with money) it is necessary to know how the economy reacts after a monetary *shock*. To identify the monetary *shock*, the existing literature suggests three strategies. The first is to

[14] For example, Christiano and Fitzgerald (1999) under their econometric specification (SVAR) find the price increases (price puzzle), but with small magnitude. In contrast, Smets and Wouters (2007), under an estimated DSGE, finds that the price decreases (absence of the price puzzle).

Table 1.7 RBC models with fiscal variables

Author	Year	Description
Empirical researches		
Fatas and Mihov	2001	**Title:** *The Effects of Fiscal Policy on Consumption and Employment: Theory and Evidence.* **Topic:** They study the effect of the *shock* of public spending on consumption, investment, and employment. **Contribution:** They find that before a *shock* of public spending, employment, real wages (in the manufacturing sector), the product, and the components of consumption (durable goods, nondurable goods, and services) respond positively. The investment response in the short term is negative, but it expands in the medium term.
Blanchard and Perotti	2002	**Title:** *An Empirical Characterization of the Dynamic Effects of Changes in Government Spending and Taxes on Output.* **Topic:** They analyze the effect of the *shock* of public spending and taxes on the product. **Contribution:** They find that before a *shock* of positive public spending (or *shock* of negative taxes), GDP increases. Furthermore, under a public spending *shock* consumption increases and investment contracts (marginally).
Gali et al.	2007	**Title:** *Understanding the Effects of Government Spending on Consumption.* **Topic:** They analyze the effect of the *shock* of public spending on macroeconomic variables and propose a NEK model that captures the empirical evidence. **Contribution:** They find that consumption and output increase when faced with a *shock* of public spending. In contrast, investment contracts (significantly). In addition, they propose a NEK model with Ricardian and non-Ricardian families that allows capturing the empirical effects of the *shock* of public spending.
Pappa	2009	**Title:** *The Effects of Fiscal Shocks on Employment and the Real Wage.* **Topic:** Analysis of the impact of public spending on employment and wages. **Contribution:** It uses the DSGE models (RBC and NEK) to determine sign constraints, which it uses in an SVAR model. Under this last model, he/she obtains that real wages and employment increase with the increase in public consumption. The proposed RBC model fails to capture this empirical evidence, while the NEK model succeeds.

Table 1.8 RBC models with fiscal variables (continued)

Author	Year	Description
Theoretical investigations		
Aiyagari et al.	1992	**Title:** *The Output, Employment, and Interest Rate Effects of Government Consumption.* **Topic:** They analyze the effects of temporary/permanent government consumption under an RBC model. **Contribution:** Pioneers in using an RBC model to analyze the effects of government consumption. Previous studies used the standard growth model (without extensions). The model captures the positive response of GDP to the fiscal *shock* (regardless of the persistence of the *shock*). In addition, the interest rate increases.
Baxter and King	1993	**Title:** *Fiscal Policy in General Equilibrium.* **Topic:** Evaluates the macroeconomic effects of fiscal spending, the type of financing, and public investment in an RBC model. **Contribution:** The model fails to capture the observed increase in consumption and suggests that the type of financing does affect the response of the product. Furthermore, it indicates that a public capital *shock* increases output and employment.
Ludvigson	1996	**Title:** *The Macroeconomic Effects of Government Debt in Stochastic Growth Model.* **Topic:** Study the macroeconomic effects of public debt in an RBC model. **Contribution:** Analyze the effects of a positive fiscal *shock* (reduction of distortionary taxes) financed by debt. This is different from the standard way to analyze the fiscal *shock* ($\uparrow$ government spending financed by lump-sum taxes). In this scenario, the model predicts an increase in output and consumption, which is consistent with the data.
Finn	1998	**Title:** *Cyclical Effects of Government's Employment and Goods Purchases.* **Topic:** Under an RBC model, study whether the public spending *shock* helps explain the business cycle. **Contribution:** Difference between two components of public spending (consumption vs. compensation). The usual models have studied the first component leaving aside the second. Under an RBC model that considers the two components, it is concluded that the *shock* of public spending does not help to explain business cycles.
Fatas and Mihov	2001	**Title:** *The Effects of Fiscal Policy on Consumption and Employment: Theory and Evidence.* **Topic:** Study four fiscal scenarios in an RBC model. **Contribution:** The main conclusion is that in the four fiscal scenarios consumption contracted in contrast to what was predicted by the data.

assume that the monetary authority responds to the state of the economy through a *feedback rule*, and all those monetary policy movements that do not follow this rule are classified as *shock monetary*. RBC models with a monetary sector usually follow this way of identifying the monetary *shock*. The second strategy is to search the data for any sign of exogenous monetary policy. The third is to identify the *shock* of monetary policy by assuming that this *shock* does not affect economic activity in the long run.

The second important issue is the evaluation of the models. Unlike the usual way of evaluating RBC models, in which the statistics of the theoretical model are compared with those observed in the data, in this case the impulse-response functions observed in the data are compared with what is obtained from the model. This allows discriminating which models (and under which assumptions) are closer to reality.

[B] Theoretical Models Cooper (1998) points out that any model that includes monetary policy faces two dilemmas. The first dilemma is that the model must have the capacity to generate a demand for money. The second is that the model must consider a source of non-neutrality (real effects of money). Although RBC models have tried to include these two elements to capture the real effects of the monetary *shock* observed in the empirical evidence, the result is that these models predict such an effect to be small (which is inconsistent with the data). This represents a major limitation of RBC models, which has been overcome by New Keynesian Economics (NEK) models. The NEK models manage to obtain the influence of money in the short term and its effects on the business cycle under two main assumptions: monopolistic competition (real friction) and price stickiness (nominal friction).

In this section, the theoretical investigations (RBC models with money) are categorized, according to the way in which each of them has modeled the demand for money. Under this premise, in the existing literature it can be distinguished that RBC models have usually considered three ways of obtaining a demand for money: *cash in advance* constraint, real balances in the utility function, and liquidity effects. The first form indicates that money is required to buy goods, the second indicates that real balances provide direct utility to the consumer, and the third indicates that the money may be required to save transaction costs associated with the purchase of goods. This section describes the first two ways to obtain a demand for money.

[B1] *Cash in Advance* Constraint The theoretical foundation of the *cash in advance* constraint was developed by Lucas and Stokey (1983, 1987) and Svensson (1985). Likewise, the empirical application has been developed by various authors including Eichenbaum and Singleton (1986), Cooley and Hansen (1989, 1991, 1992), Greenwood and Huffman (1987), and Christiano (1991). In this section, two such investigations are described: that of Eichenbaum and Singleton (1986) and that of Cooley and Hansen (1989). This is because the first investigation was an initial effort to assess whether RBC models with money have the ability to capture empirical evidence. The second investigation is chosen because it represents a significant contribution to the study of money within the framework of RBC models.

Eichenbaum and Singleton (1986) assessed whether monetary policy *shocks* were important in determining economic activity during the post-World War II period. For this, they were based on two models: the first is a monetary model; that is, a constraint of *cash in advance* is considered to determine the demand for money and a monetary rule is devised to represent the supply of money. The second is an RBC (no money market) model. It is worth mentioning that both models are similar in the representation of the agents (family and company) and in the consideration of the parameters. The only difference is the monetary component. Likewise, both models consider the two main assumptions of Long and Plosser (1983), logarithmic utility and total depreciation, but under the assumption that work is fixed. The main result is that the equilibrium expressions are similar in both models, which suggests that money does not play a role in explaining the cycles. Furthermore, under a bivariate VAR (money and output growth) formulation, the authors find that an exogenous monetary *shock* is not an important source of output variation in the postwar period (1949–1983).

Although the work of Eichenbaum and Singleton (1986) is important in showing the weak influence of money in RBC models to explain cycles, these authors did not follow the standard evaluation of RBC models: comparing the theoretical moments (produced by the model) with the empirical moments (produced by the data), but instead relied on a VAR model and Granger causality.

Unlike them, Cooley and Hansen (1989) follow the standard RBC model evaluation process. In particular, these authors add to Hansen (1985) model the money market similar to Eichenbaum and Singleton (1986). In this model, the main mechanism for transmitting money is the inflation tax; that is, an increase in money (monetary supply) produces inflation and this behaves like a tax by reducing the purchasing power of consumers, which ultimately affects their consumption and investment and their work/leisure decisions; in other words, it affects the real variables. The main result of the model is that the characteristics of the cycles of an economy with high inflation are similar to those of an economy with low inflation. Money does not play a relevant role in explaining business cycles.

[B2] Real Balances in the Utility Function Farmer (1997) developed an RBC model where the way to obtain the demand for money is by assuming that real balances provide utility to families (utility function with real balances). In addition, another of the main differences of this model, compared to the RBC models that have considered money, is that the utility function does not follow the standard form of temporal separability.[15] This is because the author seeks to capture two observed

[15] The utility function proposed by Farmer (1997) is:

$$U(C, M/P, L) = \frac{(F_1(C, M/P))^{1-\rho}}{1-\rho} - (F_2(C, M/P))^{1-\rho} V(L).$$

effects of money. On the one hand, the marginal utility of money is small (direct effect); on the other hand, the complementarity of money with other *commodities* (consumption and labor supply) is high (indirect effect).

One of the main implications of this type of utility function is that in steady-state equilibrium not only can there be a unique solution, but that for a set of values of the parameters, the solution is indeterminate. That is, near the path of balanced growth, there is a continuum of rational expectations equilibria.[16] The author emphasizes that the indeterminacy of the steady-state equilibrium allows the model to capture the main dynamic characteristics of the data in the United States.

1.3.2.5 Research Associated with Investment Shock

One of the main criticisms of RBC models is that their ability to replicate the stylized facts of business cycles rests on the fact that the productivity *shock* must be significant and persistent, which is not supported by empirical evidence. Given this, various authors have studied alternative *shocks* that would have the potential to explain business cycles. Among them, the main one is the specific technological change to the investment. This *stock* indicates that more units of capital could be produced with one unit of investment due to the existence of a specific investment technology. This is different from the orthodox approach which indicates that with one unit of investment one unit of new capital is produced, which can be observed in the equation of movement of capital.

One of the first efforts to consider investment fluctuations as a possible source of business cycles was made by Greenwood, Hercowitz, and Huffman in 1988. Unlike standard RBC models, these authors introduced an investment shock. 6n, which reflects the Keynesian view of investment fluctuations, which are important in explaining the cycle. In this model, the transmission mechanism is the variable capital utilization rate. The simulation results of this model indicate that the *shock* to investment and the transmission mechanism mentioned may be important elements in the explanation of business cycles.

In the 1990s, Greenwood, Hercowitz, and Krusell produced two complementary investigations on the role of investment-specific technological change. The first was published in 1997 and focused on the long-term effects of this type of technological change. The main conclusion of this research was that this technological change explains about 60% of the growth of output per man-hour after World War II. In addition, in this research, these authors showed empirical evidence about the existence of this *shock*. In particular, these authors observed two behaviors in the data: the first is that in the long term, the relative price of equipment has decreased significantly while the investment in equipment/gross national product (GNP) ratio

[16] The case that Farmer studies is a set of equilibria in a steady state (indeterminacy), but all of them are stable, in contrast, for example, to the Ramsey model where there are two steady-state equilibria, but only one is stable.

has increased. The second behavior is that in the short term there is a negative correlation between the price of the equipment and the investment in equipment or GNP. The first observation suggests that investment-specific technological change could be a source of economic growth, while the second suggests that such technological change could be a source of economic fluctuation.

The second investigation was published in 2000 and its study focus was the short-term effects of the same type of technological change. In this research, the authors used the same RBC model from 1997 with some modifications. One of them is that the equipment utilization rate is endogenous and has an important role in the transmission of *shocks* in the short term. The main conclusion of this research is that the *shock* specific to investment explains around 30% of the variability of the gross national product. The authors indicate that this result is significant since the investment in the new equipment is only 7%.

In line with the above, various investigations have highlighted the importance of investment-specific technological change in explaining the economic cycle (Fisher 2006; Smets and Wouters 2007; Justiniano and Primiceri 2008). However, when this *shock* is introduced into the DSGE models, it is found that it produces a negative correlation between consumption and investment, which is contrary to the data (Guerrieri et al. 2010). This represents the main weakness of this type of *shock* and is one of the main challenges of DSGE models.

1.4 Theoretical Foundations of RBC Models

This section describes the main assumptions of RBC models and the steps to develop such a model.

1.4.1 Main Assumptions

General assumptions. These assumptions focus essentially on the type of economy, the type of market, and the agents that participate in the model.

- Usually, RBC models assume a closed economy, which implies that investment is equal to saving. However, several authors have extended the model to the open economy (Mendoza 1991, 1995).
- The markets for factors and final goods are perfectly competitive. However, Rotemberg and Woodford (1993) evaluated the implications of the RBC model under the assumption of monopolistic competition in the goods market.
- Two types of agents are assumed: families and firms. When considering the government, it is considered through its budget constraint. Likewise, the monetary authority is expressed by its budgetary restriction and by a monetary policy rule.

- The only source of uncertainty comes from the supply side (*shock* of productivity).
- The only good produced is used for consumption and investment.

Representative Agent It is assumed that all families in the economy are identical and that they can be represented by a typical family. Similarly, it is assumed that there is a representative company. This way of simplifying the economy avoids aggregation problems.

Optimization It is assumed that the representative family and firm optimize an explicit objective function subject to resource and technology constraints, respectively.

Impulse and Transmission Mechanisms Based on Frisch (1933) and Slutsky (1937), RBC models differentiate two types of mechanisms: **impulse** and **propagation**.

- The **drive mechanism** causes a variable to deviate from its steady state.
- The **propagation mechanism** amplifies the effects of the impulse shock on the endogenous variables. It makes these variables deviate from their steady-state values.

The main drive mechanism in RBC models is the ***shock* to productivity** and the main propagation mechanism is the **elasticity of substitution of leisure**. In the RBC literature at least four types of propagation mechanisms can be observed:

- **Smoothing of consumption:** a temporary (positive) *shock* on the economy would strongly affect savings. In a closed economy, investment is equal to saving; therefore, the investment will increase allowing a greater *stock* of capital in the following period. Given his/her participation in the production function, he/she would raise output in the said period (**weak mechanism**).
- **Investment lags:** a *shock* today can affect investment in the future (Kydland and Prescott 1982) increasing future output (**most used mechanism**).
- **Intertemporal elasticity of substitution:** a change in wages increases the amount of work supplied, and the effect on output is positive (**most used mechanism**).
- **Accumulation of inventories:** firms accumulate inventories to face unexpected variations in demand (**mechanism not consistent with empirical evidence**).

Rational Expectations It is assumed that the agents present in the economy have rational expectations in order to overcome the "Lucas critique."

General Equilibrium The RBC theory maintains the Walras approach (general equilibrium) in a context of perfect competition (flexible prices) where agents are price takers and there is a continuum of market equilibriums, symmetric information, complete markets, and absence of friction.

Dynamic Consider an intertemporal analysis, where the decisions of the agents are made intertemporally.

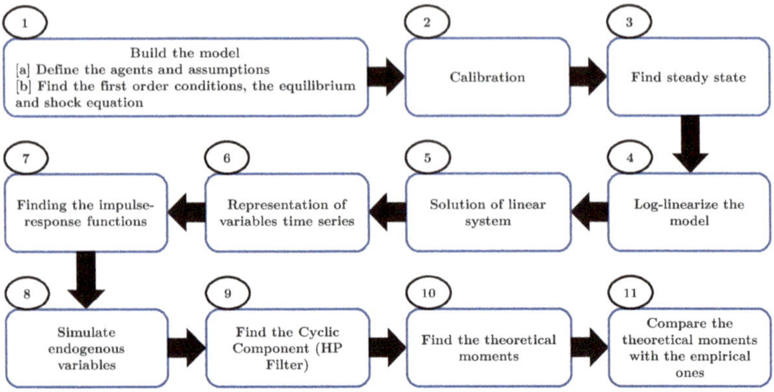

Fig. 1.16 Steps to develop an RBC model

1.4.2 Steps to Develop an RBC Model

In this section, the steps or stages that must be followed in the development of an RBC model and in general in any DSGE model are described in a practical way. Figure 1.16 outlines the 11 steps.

[1] Build the Model In this stage the main assumptions of the model are defined, which include at least [a] the type of economy (open or closed), [b] agents in the economy (family, companies, government, and monetary authority), [c] the rules of behavior of each agent (objective function of maximization and the restrictions), [d] assumptions about the market of factors and goods (perfect competition or monopoly competition or some combination of both), and [e] the type of *shock* (productivity, fiscal, monetary, and international interest rate, among others).

[2] Find First-Order Conditions, Equilibrium, and *Shock* In this stage we proceed to solve the optimization problem of each agent. For example, the family usually maximizes its expected, discounted utility function, subject to its budget constraint. Solving this optimization problem gives Euler's equation and the job offer. In the same way we proceed with the company, which maximizes its profit function subject to the available technology (production function). From this optimization, the demand for labor and capital is obtained. In addition to these equations, it is necessary to explicitly indicate the market equilibrium equations. For example, it is usual to consider the equilibrium in the goods market ($c_t + i_t = y_t$). Finally, the behavior of the *shock* must also be made explicit; that is, indicate if it has an AR(1) behavior. This entire set of equations represents a nonlinear system. It is important to mention that the number of equations must be equal to the number of variables for the system to be well defined.

[3] Calibration Here a value is assigned to each parameter. If the model is fully calibrated, then all parameters have an assigned value based on other investigations.

At this stage, in a practical way, a list of the parameters with their assigned values and the investigations from which these values have been extracted could be drawn up.

[4] Find the Steady State To find the steady state it is necessary to take the system of equations from the second stage. To this system all temporality is eliminated; that is, in all the equations the following change of variable is made: $x_t = x_{t+1} = x_{ss}$, where x_{ss} represents the steady-state value of the variable "x." Likewise, the expectations operator is eliminated in those equations where it is present. For example, when considering Euler's equation $c_t^{-1} = \beta E_t c_{t+1}^{-1} R_{t+1}$. In a steady state, expectations are eliminated, leaving $c_t^{-1} = \beta c_{t+1}^{-1} R_{t+1}$, and if we also apply the previous principle of eliminating temporality, Euler's equation in steady state would be $c_{ss}^{-1} = \beta c_{ss}^{-1} R_{ss}$. The objective of this stage is to find the steady-state value of each variable in the system x_{ss} depending on the set of parameters, which have been previously calibrated. For example, from the Euler equation in steady state it follows that the real interest rate in steady state depends on the discount factor $R_{ss} = \frac{1}{\beta}$.

[5] Log-Linearize the Model The nonlinear system of equations described in the second stage requires to be linearized to apply the mathematical methods of solving the system of linear equations. In general terms, linearization consists of approximating a nonlinear equation by means of the Taylor expansion of the first order. At this stage, the model can be linearized considering the variables in levels or considering the variables in logarithms. The latter is called log-linearization. In both cases, the linearization is performed around the stationary state of each variable.

[6] Solution of the Linear System The solution of the linear system consists in finding the functions of policies, that is, the control variables as a function of the state variables and exogenous variables. In the existing literature, there are several ways to solve the system of stochastic difference equations. DeJong and Dave (2011) suggest that at least four methods are usual: the Blanchard and Kahn (1980) method, the Sims (2002) method, the Klein (2000) method, and the Uhlig (1999) method of undetermined coefficients. To find the solution of the system, a *software* such as Matlab is usually used because the system of equations is large. In some cases, such as the Long and Plosser (1983) model, in its single-sector version, it could have an analytical solution. The solution of the system is important because, based on it, the following steps will be obtained (impulse-response function, simulation of the variables, cyclical component of each variable, and the theoretical moments).

[7] Find the Impulse-Response Function In this stage, the impulse-response function of each variable of the model is calculated before the *shock* previously defined in the model. Three elements must be observed in the response of each variable: the magnitude, the sign, and the number of periods that the variable takes to return to its stationary state. This is important because the impulse-response function of the model is usually compared with what is observed in the data. To obtain the impulse-response function, each variable is expressed in its ARMA(p,q) time series form. For this, the solution of each variable obtained in the previous stage is used.

[8] Simulate the Endogenous Variables By having each variable expressed in its ARMA(p,q) form, it allows simulations of each variable to be carried out assuming that the error of the *shock* equation is a series with a normal distribution with mean zero and constant variance. Usually, the number of periods considered in the simulation is the same as that available in the data. For example, if the available sample with which the empirical moments are calculated includes 120 quarterly data, then this same number is considered for the simulation of the series in the model. Another aspect is the *number of times* the series will be simulated. In the existing literature, it is not clear the number of times that should be simulated; however, a number close to 100 could be considered. For example, Hansen (1985) simulated the series 100 times as did Cooley and Prescott (1995, Ch. 1), while Cooley and Hansen (1989) used 50 simulations.

[9] Find the Cyclical Component In stages 7 and 8 the variables have been considered in levels; that is, each variable contains its trend and cyclical component. However, in order to assess whether the RBC model has the capacity to replicate the stylized facts of the economic cycle, the cyclical component of each variable must be extracted, and then its theoretical moments must be calculated. In the existing literature there are several methods to extract the cyclical component of the variables. The most widely used in the RBC school is the Hodrick and Prescott (1981) filter.

[10] Find the Theoretical Moments In this stage, the theoretical moments of the cyclical component of each variable are calculated. Usually these theoretical moments are four: standard deviation, autocorrelation, correlation with GDP, and dynamic correlations.

[11] Compare the Theoretical Moments with the Empirical Ones Here the theoretical moments provided by the model are compared with those found in the data. The objective of this stage is to evaluate if the model is capable of capturing the stylized facts of the economy.

1.5 Codes

Table 1.9 indicates the code used in this chapter.

Table 1.9 Codes in Matlab and Dynare

Codes	Description
Aggregate_stylized_facts.m	This *m-file* plots the macroeconomic variables in levels and finds the cyclical component using the HP filter. In addition, it calculates the statistics of the cyclical component.

Chapter 2
Dynare Foundations: Solving and Simulating DSGE Models

2.1 Introduction

DSGE models can be summarized in a set of nonlinear difference equations. This system requires numerical methods to approximate the solution—a tedious and perhaps inefficient task without a specialized computational *software*.

In this context, Matlab is a *software* that has implemented tools for optimizing and solving nonlinear difference equations using a matrix approach. These characteristics make this *software* an important candidate for the solution and simulation of DSGE models. However, adapting the model to the Matlab language requires to have an advanced level of programming in that language, which complicates the use of the *software*.

In this scenario, many economists with a background in mathematics and computer science have tried to build programs based on *Matlab* that facilitate the solution of DSGE models. From these efforts, Dynare has emerged. It is a preprocessor that allows us to translate a DSGE model into *Matlab* language[1] making it easy to solve and simulate DSGE models.

This chapter aims to understand the main Dynare commands used to perform each step in the building, solution, and simulation of a DSGE model. To do this, this chapter is divided into three parts.

In the first part, we describe the commands to transfer the DSGE model to the Dynare environment. We also explain the necessary commands to solve and simulate the model. In the second part, we show how to use Dynare to solve a basic RBC model (Long and Plosser, 1983, 's model). Finally, the codes used in this chapter are described in the last section.

[1] This chapter is based on the Dynare manual available on its website "www.dynare.org." Also, on this webpage, you will find this *toolbox* ready to download and different illustrative examples.

H. Galindo Gil et al., *Dynamic Stochastic General Equilibrium Models*, Springer Texts in Business and Economics, https://doi.org/10.1007/978-3-031-58105-2_2

Table 2.1 Files created by Dynare

3 intermediate files created by Dynare		
filename.m	filename_dynamic.m	filename_static.m
Contains [1] variable declarations and [2] calculation tasks	Contains the equations of the dynamic model; that is, it considers the leads and lags of the variables	Contains the long-term static model, i.e., the equations without time

Table 2.2 Variables created by Dynare

3 main variables (structure) created by Dynare		
M_	options_	oo_
Contains various model information. For example, the mod file name and variable names	Contains the values of various options used by Dynare during the calculation	Contains various results of the calculation. For example, the impulse-response function and simulations

2.2 What Is Dynare?

Dynare is a preprocessor and collector for Matlab routines that acts as a *toolbox*. The main objective of Dynare is to solve, simulate, and estimate different nonlinear models with *forward looking* variables, among which are the DSGE and OLG (overlapping generations) models.

The main input of this *toolbox* is a file with the extension ".mod," where you write the model and the statements that you want Dynare to execute (solve, estimate, etc.). To create this file, open a notepad and save it with the extension mod. In this context, how is Dynare invoked? After creating the .mod file "`example.mod`," the following is placed in the Matlab *prompt*:

≫ `dynare` example

The command **`dynare`** starts the preprocessor[2] (Dynare) on the .mod file and executes the instructions included in this file ("example.mod"). For instance, considering a generic name for the .mod file "filename.mod," the preprocessor creates three intermediate files shown in Table 2.1.

Dynare will perform the calculation tasks by executing the file "**filename.m**." Furthermore, Dynare will provide many results, of which three are main variables shown in the *Matlab workspace* (see Table 2.2). Dynare saves these three variables in the current working folder (*current folder*) with the name: "**filename_results.mat**."

Figure 2.1 shows how Dynare works with Matlab. We first write down our DSGE model on a mod file very similar to what we have in our notebook. Then, Dynare will transform the .mod file in Matlab language, creating three m-files that all contain a different version of the model. Now Matlab plays a key role. It uses, for instance, the

[2] A preprocessor is a program that processes input data (the mod file) to produce output used as input in another program, such as Matlab.

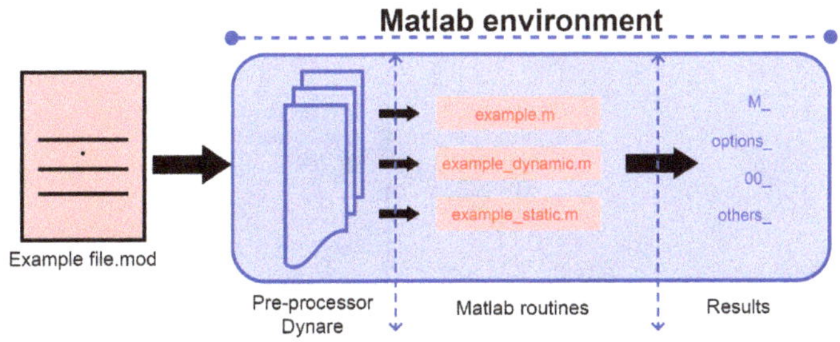

Fig. 2.1 Dynare as a Matlab preprocessor

m-file example.m to solve the model. As a result, three main variables are created: M_, oo_, and options_. We then use these variables to analyze the model, such as plotting the impulse-response functions using the oo_ variable.

2.3 Structure of .mod File

The file that contains the model (.mod), which Dynare will use, has a structure of six main blocks (Fig. 2.2). The first block is the preamble, in which the endogenous and exogenous variables and the model parameters are specified. The second is the model itself. The equations are written in this block in a nonlinear or linear (or log-linear) fashion. The third is the specification of the initial values, which define the starting point for Dynare to calculate the system's steady state. The fourth is the calculation of the steady state. The fifth corresponds to the definition of the variance or standard deviation of the shocks; finally, the sixth block contains the calculation of the model solution, the simulations, the calculation of the moments, and the construction of the impulse-response functions.[3]

It is important to mention that in addition to these six blocks, other commands can be added depending on the required tasks; for example, if we want to do a sensitivity analysis of the parameters, we can add commands that perform this task. The six blocks mentioned above are the fundamental parts every mod file must have.

2.3.1 The Preamble

The variables (endogenous and exogenous) and the parameters (and their values) are specified in the preamble. Three commands will tell Dynare which variables

[3] The fact that Dynare is a preprocessor implies that the statements in the mod file are "translated" into the Matlab language; however, it is not a *m.file*, and therefore we cannot execute it in parts.

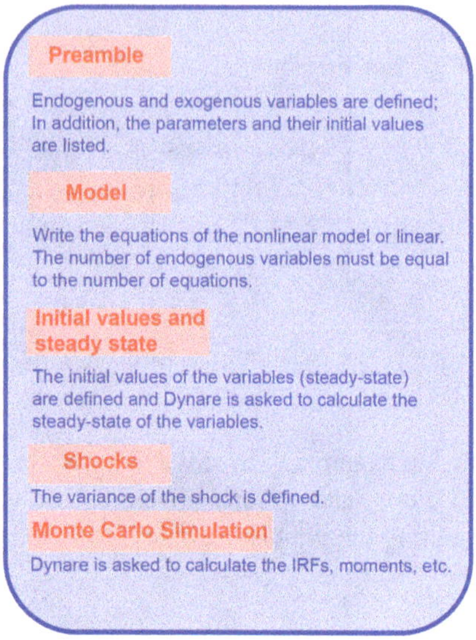

Fig. 2.2 Structure of the .mod file

Table 2.3 Examples of declaration of endogenous variables

Example 1	Example 2	Example 3
var	var	var
y	y \$y_t\$	y \$y_t\$ (long_name = 'Output')
c	c \$c_t\$	c \$c_t\$ (long_name = 'Consumption')
k;	k \$k_t\$;	k \$k_t\$ (long_name = 'Capital');

are from the model and which are the parameters: variables (*var* and *varexo*) and parameters (*parameters*).

Declaration of endogenous variables

```
var variable_name1 $latex_name1$ (long_name= 'name');
```

The **var** command declares endogenous variables and has three components: The first refers to the variable name that will be used throughout the .mod file (`variable_name1`); the second indicates the name that this variable will take in the LaTeX file (\$latex_name1\$); and the third is an option (which has to be in parentheses) that allows you to write the long name of the variable (long_name= 'name'). Table 2.3 illustrates the use of this code.

Table 2.4 Endogenous variable declaration examples

Example 1	Example 2	Example 3
varexo e	varexo e e_t	varexo e e_t (long_name = 'productivity shock')

Declaration of exogenous variables

```
varexo variable_name1 $latex_name1$ (long_name=
'name');
```

The command **varexo** declares exogenous variables (shocks) and, in the same way as endogenous variables, has three components: The first refers to the name of the variable that will be used throughout the .mod file (`variable_name1`); the second indicates the name that this variable will take in the LaTeX file ($latex_name1$); and the third is an option (which has to be in parentheses) that allows you to write the long name of the variable (long_name= 'name').

It is worth mentioning that in a stochastic model, productivity (a_t) usually has an autoregressive behavior in the following form:

$$a_{t+1} = \rho a_t + \epsilon_t$$

where ϵ_t is the stochastic component with a normal distribution with zero mean and constant variance. To Dynare, a_t is an endogenous variable, and since ϵ_t is white noise, it is considered an exogenous variable. Therefore, under the commands declared in code 2, this exogenous variable could be written to Dynare in three ways (see Table 2.4).

Parameters

```
parameters parameter_name1 $latex_name1$ (long_name=
'name1')
   parameter_name2 $latex_name2$ (long_name= 'name2');
```

The *parameters* command declares the parameters to be used in the model. Not only those referring to the behavior equations (functions) of the agents (for instance, the utility function) but also the initial values, which are usually the steady state values, and the parameters associated with the shocks. In addition, in this block, the values corresponding to each parameter must be assigned (calibration). Table 2.5 describes three examples of the declaration of parameters and the assignment of their values.

Table 2.5 Parameter declaration examples

Example 1	Example 2	Example 3
Parameters	Parameters	Parameters
beta	beta $ \ beta$	beta $ \ beta$ (long_name = 'Frisch elasticity')
delta;	delta $ \ delta$;	delta $ \ delta$ (long_name = 'Depreciation');
beta=0.99;	beta=0.99;	beta=0.99;
delta=0.22;	delta=0.99;	delta=0.99;

2.3.2 *The Model*

The model (a system of nonlinear equations) is declared in Dynare by means of the block *model;... end;*.

Model Statement

```
    model(options); equation1; equation2;...;equationN;
end;
```

This block details the main equations of the model. You can write the (nonlinear) model in Dynare as it is on the *paper* and to do so, enter the equations in the environment `model; – – – end;`

Code
model;
equation1;
equation2;
...
equationN;
end;

It must be taken into account that the number of equations must be equal to the number of endogenous variables. If the model that is written in Dynare is linearized (either with variables in levels or variables in logarithms), then it is written: **model(linear)** (Fig. 2.3).

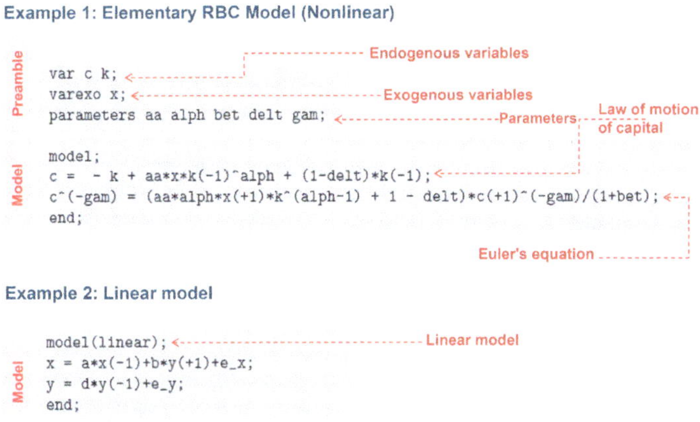

Fig. 2.3 Nonlinear and linear models

2.3.3 *Initials Values*

Within this block, the initial values of each of the endogenous variables are placed, which are generally the steady state values calculated by the user. These values are used by Dynare as a starting point for the calculation of the steady state. It is important to mention that when the model is in log-linear form, the steady state values of the variables (in log deviations) are equal to zero; therefore, the initial values are equal to zero, too.

Declaration of initial values

```
initval;
variable_name1 = value1;
⋮
variable_nameN = valueN;
end;
```

Table 2.6 describes two examples of initial values.

Note that the variable ch is equal to "$lnc_t - lnc_{ss}$"; that is, it is the deviation of the variable in logarithm with respect to its steady state, which, by construction, in steady state is equal to zero.

The initial values are what Dynare will use in the "filename_static.mod" to calculate the steady state. Dynare needs a starting point for this calculation because the solution method is successive approximations (Newton's method).

Table 2.6 Initial values (nonlinear and linear model)

Code	Example (nonlinear)	Example (log-linear)
initval;	`initval;`	`initval;`
variable_name1 = value1;	`c = 0.5;`	`ch = 0`
variable_name2 = value2;	`k = 0.1;`	`kh = 0`
...	...	...
variable_nameN = valueN;	`y = 0.8;`	`yh = 0`
end;	`end;`	`end;`

2.3.4 Stationary State

Dynare has two ways of considering the steady state of the model. The first is that Dynare itself calculates the steady state. To do this, Dynare uses Newton's method to solve nonlinear equations. The second is to provide Dynare with a *Matlab* file (*m-file*) containing the steady state.

Newton's method, also known as Newton–Raphson's method, is a technique aimed at solving nonlinear equations. This technique finds the solution through successive iterations from a starting point. The goal of this technique is to find the values of the variable "x" that make the function (or equation) zero; that is, look for the roots of the function:

$$f(x) = 0$$

The technique starts with a starting point x_0 and approximates the next value of "x" by means:

$$x_1 = x_0 - \frac{f(x_0)}{f'(x_0)} \xrightarrow{\text{Generalizing}} x_{n+1} = x_n - \frac{f(x_n)}{f'(x_n)}$$

This, applied to the calculation of the steady state of the model, is obtained, for example, for the production function:

$$y_t = a_t k_t^{\alpha} h_t^{1-\alpha}$$

We define $f(x)$, where $x = [y_t, a_t, k_t, h_t]$

$$f(x) = y_t - a_t k_t^{\alpha} h_t^{1-\alpha} = 0$$

The goal is to find the solution; that is, the steady state ($x_t = x_{t+1}$). To see greater detail of the method, review Kelley (2003).

(Method 1) Using Newton's method

```
steady;
```

For Dynare to calculate the steady state using Newton's method, the command **steady** is placed after the model block. To do this, it considers the values indicated in the `initval` section as the starting point. Dynare applies Newton's method to the static model (the .mod model without lags and leads) to find the steady state.

Saving the steady state

```
oo_.steady_state;
```

The steady state computed by `steady` is stored in "oo_.steady_state." It is worth mentioning that the order in which the steady state values appear is the same as the endogenous variables declared in section `var`.

(Method 2) Using a file containing the steady state

In this second method, there are two options:

- **"Steady state" block in the .mod:** In this case, each variable is defined according to the deep parameters. The code is:
  ```
  steady_state_model; r = 1/beta; k = delta*beta;...;
  end;
  ```
  The *m-file* in which Dynare will save the steady states is "ModName_steadystate2.m" where "ModName" is the name of the ".mod" file. This block is placed after the *parameters* block.
- ***m-file* containing the "steady state":** In this case, you can build a Matlab function that calculates the steady states. This requires doing a bit more programming in an *m-file*.

2.3.5 Dynare and LaTeX

In Dynare, there is a possibility to translate the model equations to LaTeX format. To do this, two codes are used depending on what type of model you want to translate into LaTeX language:

Dynamic model in LaTeX

```
write_latex_dynamic_model;
```

This code writes each model equation in LaTeX format and saves it to a ".tex" file depending on the name of the ".mod" file. For example, if the mod file is named "campbell.mod," the LaTeX file will be "campbell_dynamic.tex," which contains the list of all dynamic equations. It is worth mentioning that if the parameters and variables have names declared in version LaTeX, the ".tex" file will use them.

Static model in LaTeX

```
write_latex_static_model;
```

This code allows you to save the model equations, in their static version, in a ".tex" file. The static version means that lags and delays have been removed from the equations. In the same way as the code for the dynamic model, the static version is stored in "campbell_static.tex" (when the model in Dynare is named "campbell.mod").

It is worth mentioning that these codes (dynamic or static equations) are written after the block *model*.

2.3.6 Definition of Shocks

In this block, the temporary *shocks* of the model are defined (*shock* of productivity, public spending, etc.). In Dynare, exogenous (shock) variables take random values that follow a normal distribution with zero mean and constant variance. In the .mod file, the variance must be specified.

Definition of *shocks*

To define the variance or standard deviation of the *shock*, there are two ways:

Alternative 1	Alternative 2
`shocks;`	`shocks;`
`var variable_name` = valor_variance;	`var variable_name`;
`end;`	`stderr` valor_standard_deviation;
	`end;`

Table 2.7 Definition of *shock*

Alternative 1	Alternative 2
`shocks;`	`shocks;`
`var e = 0.5;`	`var e;`
`end;`	`stderr` $0.5^{1/2}$`;`
	`end;`

Table 2.7 describes an example of the implementation of the *shock* block code.

2.3.7 Model Evaluation: Blanchard and Kahn Conditions

Dynare has the ability to compute the eigenvalues of the linearized model around the values assigned in the `initval` block, which are usually the steady states. In particular, if the number of eigenvalues with modulus greater than one is equal to the number of variables *forward looking*, then the system of linearized equations has a unique solution. Chapter 3 details these criteria and the solution method of Blanchard and Kahn (1980).

Model Evaluation

```
check;
```

This command calculates the eigenvalues and stores them in the global variable "oo_.dr.eigval." Dynare also has another command that provides various model health tests and prints a message if a problem is detected: `model_diagnostics;`.

2.3.8 Computation of the Stochastic Solution

Dynare uses the code `stoch_simul` to obtain the policy and state (transition) functions of the model.

Model Simulation

```
stoch_simul (options);
```

This command solves the stochastic model (or rational expectations model) using the perturbation method.[4] It is worth mentioning that in the process of solving the system of equations, Dynare uses the generalized Schur decomposition method (or QZ decomposition). What this method does is decompose a matrix into three multiplicative matrices: $A = QUQ^{-1}$. The Schur decomposition maintains the same spirit as the Jordan decomposition (see Chap. 3 for more details).

Impulse-Response Functions (IRFs)

All econometric or statistical exercises require to communicate results in a simple and transparent way. For multi-equation (and, potentially, nonlinear) models, reporting parameters seldom meet the above objective. This is why macroeconomists use **impulse-response functions** (IRFs).

An impulse-response function gives us a profile of responses over a time horizon (say, 2 years for quarterly data) by applying an impulse or *shock*, hence its name. This function is usually a nonlinear combination of various parameters present in the model.

In formal terms, let x_t be the endogenous variable of interest (for example, output) and ε be the *shock* of interest (for example, a technological *shock*), and the IRF is defined as

$$IRF_{\tau}^{x,\varepsilon} = \frac{\partial x_{t+\tau}}{\partial \varepsilon_t} \tag{2.1}$$

In other words, it is the response in period τ of applying the *shock* ε in period t.

As we mentioned, the IRFs are usually nonlinear expressions of the model parameters. Therefore, they are usually presented graphically, with the x axis showing the horizon of interest over which the response is to be evaluated, and the y axis showing the response of the endogenous variable to the *shock* .

As the student will learn later, macroeconomists have a particular interest in having the IRFs in their DSGE model resemble the IRFs present in the data. This is because the IRFs deliver a very useful set of information to the

(continued)

[4] This method builds Taylor series approximations to the solution of the DSGE model around its deterministic steady state. This method has been used in physics and in other natural sciences; in economics, it was popularized by Judd and Guu (1993). It has gained popularity in economics in the last two decades due to three reasons:

•It is suitable. The perturbation method finds an approximate solution that is local; that is, it is well suited around the point where the Taylor expansion is taken.

•The result is intuitive and easily interpretable.

•Thanks to the development of *software* such as Dynare and Dynare++, the perturbation method for higher degrees of expansion is easy to calculate and does not require familiarity with numerical methods.

econometrician. They allow us to compare the magnitude of the response of different variables with respect to the *shocks*, the persistence of the responses, and their direction, among other objects of interest.

Strictly speaking, the IRFs are usually obtained by estimating the structural vector autoregressive (VAR) model and are sensitive to the economic or statistical assumptions imposed by the econometrician in order to identify them. Despite the above, in this book, we will take the IRF as external data that we are interested in replicating, postponing the discussion of its estimation.

Within the options of `stoch_simul` you can ask Dynare to perform specific operations such as finding the impulse responses, estimating the parameters, etc. For example:

stoch_simul(order=1;irf=30)

This statement tells Dynare to linearize the system of nonlinear equations (written in the `model` block) by means of a first-order Taylor approximation, which is computed around the steady state (order = 1). He/she then uses those approximations to compute the impulse-response function and various descriptive statistics (moments, variance decomposition, correlation coefficients, and autocorrelation). Also, this statement tells Dynare to compute the impulse-response function with 30 periods (irf = 30). The IRF is calculated as the difference between the trajectory of the variable before a shock (at $t = 1$) and its steady state. Dynare plots the IRF for only 12 variables (Table 2.8).

The "stoch_simul" code provides the policy and state functions (also known as decision rules), whose coefficients are stored in "oo_.dr" (**dr** is a shorthand for *decision rules*). It is worth mentioning that the policy function, in Dynare, has the following structure:

Table 2.8 Options in stoch_simul

[1] Solution of the model	
order = integer	Give the order of the Taylor approximation. Available values are 1, 2 y 3 (*default* = 2). **Example:** $stoch\_simul(order = 1);$
loglinear	Convert all variables to log-linear. Therefore, we have to ensure that the steady states are strictly positive. All results (IRF, moments, policy function, etc.) consider the variables to be log-linear. **Example:** $stoch\_simul(loglinear);$
[2] Impulse-Response Function (IFR)	
irf = integer	Number of periods for the calculation of the IRF (*default* = 40). IRFs are stored in "oo_.irfs". **Example:** $stoch\_simul(order = 1, irf = 30);$
irf_shocks = (name of the exogenous variable)	Calculates the IRF for the requested exogenous variable. It is used when there are multiple shocks in the model. **Example:** $stoch\_simul(order = 1, irf\_shocks = (e));$

$$y_t = y_{ss} + Ax_t + Bu_t$$

where: y_{ss} is the vector of the steady state of the variables:

- **oo_.dr.ys:** Stores the steady states y_{ss}, whose order is similar to how the variables have been declared in the `var` block.
- **oo_.dr.ghx:** Stores array "A." The rows correspond to all the endogenous variables (in order as listed in "oo_.dr.order_var"), while the columns correspond to the state variables.
- **oo_.dr.ghu:** Stores array "B." The rows correspond to all the endogenous variables (in order as listed in "oo_.dr.order_var"), while the columns correspond to the exogenous variables.

2.3.9 *Simulation and HP Filter*

From the solution of the system of nonlinear equations, the time series behavior of each of the endogenous variables can be obtained. For example, the state function of capital might suggest that capital behaves like an AR(2); or from the policy function of the product, it can be deduced that the product behaves like an ARMA(2,1). The way to obtain the time series of each variable will be described in detail in Chaps. 3 and 4. By having the time series representation, a simulation of the variable can be carried out. For this, two inputs are important: the number of periods (months, quarters, or years) that we want to simulate the variable and the number of simulation times; for example, you might want to simulate the same variable 30 times.

To perform this simulation in Dynare, two commands are used in "stoch_simul": `periods` and `simul_replic`. Both are described in Table 2.9. On the other hand, if you want Dynare to plot some simulated variable, you can write, after "stoch_simul," the code "rplot name_variable," and Dynare will display the plot.

Furthermore, suppose you want to evaluate the ability of the model to capture the behavior of the economic cycle. In that case, it is necessary to calculate the theoretical moments of the cyclical component of each variable coming from the model. In this sense, it is necessary to apply a filter that allows the cycle to be separated from the trend. For this task, Dynare has the HP filter, whose code is: `hp_filter = integer`, which is placed inside "stoch_simul." The " `integer`" reflects the smoothing parameter, which varies in value depending on the frequency (monthly, quarterly, or yearly). The choice of the parameter lies in the frequency in which the model parameters have been calibrated; for example, if all model parameters (depreciation rate, utility discount factor, etc.) have been calibrated quarterly, then the smoothing parameter in the HP filter should be quarterly. Table 2.9 describes in greater detail what was mentioned above.

Table 2.9 Options in stoch_simul (continued)

[3] Simulation of endogenous variables	
periods = integer	Indicates the number of periods to be used in the simulation of each endogenous variable (only perform **one** simulation). This simulation is saved in the global array *oo_.endo_simul*. Under this option, the empirical moments will be calculated instead of the theoretical ones. **Example:** $stoch\_simul(order = 1, periods = 300);$
simul_replic = integer	This option allows you to simulate the variables the number of times indicated in the "integer." This option is always accompanied by the "*periods*" option. **Example:** $stoch\_simul(order = 1, periods = 300, simul\_replic = 150);$. This example indicates that the variables must be simulated 150 times for 300 periods each. It is worth mentioning that these simulations are not considered to calculate the empirical moments; also, they are saved in "ModName_simul." The *default* value is one.
rplot name_variable	Plot the simulated variables, which are stored in "oo_.endo_simul." This command is placed after "stoch_simul," in which it is necessary to put *periods*. **Example:** stoch_simul(order = 1, periods=150); rplot c;
[4] HP filter	
hp_filter = integer	Use the HP filter with λ = integer (monthly:14400 ;quarterly:1600; yearly:100) to calculate moments. **Example:** $stoch\_simul(order = 1, hp\_filter = 1600);$

2.3.10 Sensitivity Analysis

It is usual to carry out a sensitivity analysis of the model, which consists in solving and simulating the model when a parameter value is changed. For example, it is useful to compare the IRFs of the model for two different values of the shock persistence parameter. To perform this type of task, Dynare provides an option via "macro" commands. This Dynare macro-language provides a set of macro commands, which can be inserted into the ".mod" file. The main tasks that this macro-language performs are: including a file in the .mod, the substitution of expressions, conditional structures (if), and loops (for).

Loops (*loops*) are emphasized in this subsection because they help to perform sensitivity analysis. Table 2.10 shows a comparison of the Dynare macro-language and the *Matlab* code. Both produce the same; however, the main difference between them is that the vector containing the parameter values will not appear in the Matlab environment when we run the macro-language, while the Matlab code will successively replace the parameter values, displaying the last value in Matlab's *workspace*, and save the array of parameter values. It is worth mentioning that these codes are written after the "stoch_simul."

Table 2.10 Macro-language vs. Matlab for sensitivity analysis

Macro-language	Matlab
rhos = [0.8, 0.9, 1];	rhos = [0.8, 0.9, 1];
@♯for i in 1:3	for i = 1:length(rhos)
rho = rhos(@i);	rho = rhos(i);
stoch_simul(order=1);	stoch_simul(order=1);
save oo_ = oo_;	save oo_ = oo_;
@♯endfor	end

Table 2.11 Four ways to write a model in Dynare

Model (.mod)	Description
Long_Plosser_Dynare_linear_log.mod (mod1)	This .mod contains the log-linear equations. It should be noted that the steady state value of each log-linear variable is equal to zero.
Long_Plosser_Dynare_linear_niv.mod (mod2)	This .mod contains the linear equations but with the variables in levels.
Long_Plosser_Dynare_nonlinear_log.mod (mod3)	This .mod contains the nonlinear equations and with the variables in logarithms.
Long_Plosser_Dynare_nonlinear_niv.mod (mod4)	This .mod contains the nonlinear equations and with the variables in levels.

2.3.11 Ways to Write the Model in Dynare

An advantage of Dynare is that the same model can be written in different forms. You can first write the nonlinear model and wait for Dynare to linearize it, or write the linearized model directly on the mod file. Second, the variable can be entered in levels or in logarithms. This is important because when Dynare linearizes the system or the user writes the linearized system, the coefficients of the policy and state functions will be read as elasticities. In the next section, the model of Long and Plosser (1983) will be used to illustrate the commands described above. To that end, four ways of writing this model in Dynare will be considered. The objective of the latter is to see the differences between them in terms of the solution, the impulse-response function, and the moments.

Table 2.11 describes the four .mod files that reflect the four different ways to enter or write a model into Dynare. As mentioned previously, all four files contain the same model.

Table 2.12 Agent optimization problem

Households	Firms
$\underset{\{c_t,h_t,k_{t+1}\}_{t=0}^{\infty}}{\text{Max}} \quad E_0 \sum_{t=0}^{\infty} \beta^t \left[ln(c_t) + \theta ln(1-h_t)\right]$	$\underset{\{k_t,l_t\}_{t=0}^{\infty}}{\text{Max}} \quad \pi_t = y_t - [w_t h_t + r_t k_t]$
$c_t + i_t = w_t h_t + r_t k_t + \pi_t \; k_{t+1} = i_t$	$y_t = a_t k_t^{1-\alpha} h_t^{\alpha}$

Table 2.13 System of nonlinear equations of the model (Long and Plosser, 1983)

Agent	Equations	Description
Household	$\frac{1}{c_t} = \beta E_t\left[\frac{1}{c_{t+1}} r_{t+1}\right]$	Euler's equation
	$k_{t+1} = i_t$	Law of motion of capital
	$\frac{\theta}{1-h_t} = \frac{w_t}{c_t}$	Labor supply
Firm	$y_t = a_t k_t^{1-\alpha} h_t^{\alpha}$	Production function
	$r_t = (1-\alpha)\frac{y_t}{k_t}$	Capital demand
	$w_t = \alpha \frac{y_t}{h_t}$	Labor demand
Equilibrium	$y_t = c_t + i_t$	Goods market equilibrium
Shock	$lna_t = \phi lna_{t-1} + \epsilon_t$	Productivity shock

2.4 Long and Plosser (1983)'s Model: Application in Dynare

2.4.1 Long and Plosser (1983)'s Model

To apply the Dynare codes described above in the solution and simulation of a general equilibrium model, in this section the model of Long and Plosser (1983) will be used, which is described in detail in Chap. 3. In addition, it is necessary to mention that this model has two important assumptions: The first is that capital depreciates completely in each period, and the second is that utility is logarithmic in consumption and leisure. Table 2.12 describes the optimization problem for the household and the firm.

In each optimization problem, first-order conditions are obtained that reflect the behavior of each agent. Together, these behavior rules make up a system of stochastic nonlinear equations, which are described in Table 2.13.

These nonlinearities make their solution difficult. The usual way to reduce the complexity of this system of equations is to obtain a first-order approximation by means of the Taylor expansion, which is called linearization. As mentioned in Chap. 3, there are two ways to linearize the system of equations. The first is considering the variable in levels, and the second is considering the variable in logarithm. Table 2.14 shows the equations after linearizing the model considering the variables in levels, where for the case of consumption we have: $\widetilde{c}_t = c_t - c_{ss}$.

On the other hand, Table 2.15 shows the linearized equations considering the variables in logarithms. In this approach, the change of variable, for example for consumption, follows the form: $\widehat{c}_t = lnc_t - lnc_{ss}$.

Table 2.16 shows the values that the parameters of the model take, which are based on King et al. (2002). It is worth mentioning that these parameters have

Table 2.14 System of linear equations of the model (Long and Plosser, 1983)

Agent	Equations	Description
Household	$\widetilde{c}_t = \beta E_t(r_{ss}\widetilde{c}_{t+1} - c_{ss}\widetilde{r}_{t+1})$	Equation from Euler
	$\widetilde{k}_{t+1} = \widetilde{i}_t$	Law of movement of capital
	$\widetilde{w}_t = \frac{w_{ss}}{(1-h_{ss})}\widetilde{h}_t + \frac{\theta}{1-h_{ss}}\widetilde{c}_t$	Labor supply
Firm	$\widetilde{y}_t = \frac{y_{ss}}{a_{ss}}\widetilde{a}_t + (1-\alpha)\frac{y_{ss}}{k_{ss}}\widetilde{k}_t + \alpha\frac{y_{ss}}{a_{ss}}\widetilde{h}_t$	Production function
	$\frac{y_{ss}}{k_{ss}}\widetilde{k}_t = \widetilde{y}_t - \frac{k_{ss}}{1-\alpha}\widetilde{r}_t$	Capital demand
	$\widetilde{w}_t = \left(\frac{\alpha}{h_{ss}}\right)\widetilde{y}_t - \left(\frac{\alpha y_{ss}}{h_{ss}^2}\right)\widetilde{h}_t$	Labor demand
Equilibrium	$\widetilde{y}_t = \widetilde{c}_t + \widetilde{i}_t$	Goods market equilibrium
Shock	$\widetilde{a}_t = \phi\widetilde{a}_{t-1} + \epsilon_t$	Productivity shock

Table 2.15 System of log-linear equations of the model (Long and Plosser, 1983)

Log-linear equations	Description
[1] $\widehat{c}_t = E_t\left[\widehat{c}_{t+1} - \widehat{r}_{t+1}\right]$	Equation of Euler
[2] $\widehat{k}_{t+1} = \widehat{i}_t$	Law of movement of capital
[3] $\frac{h_{ss}}{1-h_{ss}}\widehat{h}_t = \widehat{w}_t - \widehat{c}_t$	Labor supply
[4] $\widehat{y}_t = \widehat{a}_t + (1-\alpha)\widehat{k}_t + \alpha\widehat{h}_t$	Production function
[5] $\widehat{r}_t = \widehat{y}_t - \widehat{k}_t$	Capital demand
[6] $\widehat{w}_t = \widehat{y}_t - \widehat{h}_t$	Labor demand
[7] $\widehat{y}_t = \frac{c_{ss}}{y_{ss}}\widehat{c}_t + \frac{i_{ss}}{y_{ss}}\widehat{i}_t$	Goods market equilibrium
[8] $\widehat{a}_t = \phi\widehat{a}_{t-1} + \epsilon_t$	Productivity shock

Note: To directly obtain the solution of the model with Dynare, you can use the file "Long_Plosser_Dynare_nolinear_log.mod"

been obtained considering that the data is quarterly. Therefore, each period in the model, both in the simulation and in the impulse-response function, is understood as a quarter.

Table 2.17 mentions the steady state of each variable. To calculate this long-term equilibrium, it is assumed that the variable is the same, regardless of the temporality; that is, $x_t = x_{t+1}$. In this sense, all the lags and advances present in the system of equations that reflect the model disappear. It is in this scenario that the steady state for each variable is calculated, which ultimately depends on the model parameters. The detail of how each expression was arrived at is found in Chap. 3.

2.4.2 *Preamble*

Definition of endogenous variables Table 2.18 describes the declaration of endogenous variables in each of the .mod files, and four conclusions can be drawn

Table 2.16 Calibration

Parameter	Remark
$\alpha = 0.667$	Long-run share of labor in national income
$\theta = 3.968$	Calibrated so that the steady state work is equal to 20%
$\rho = 0.979$	Shock persistence
$\beta = 0.984$	Discount factor
$\sigma_e = 0.0072$	Standard deviation of the productivity shock

Table 2.17 Steady state

Steady state (recursive form)	Steady state (parametric form)
$r_{ss} = \frac{1}{\beta}$	$= \frac{1}{\beta}$
$h_{ss} = \frac{\alpha}{\theta(1-\beta(1-\alpha))+\alpha}$	$= \frac{\alpha}{\theta(1-\beta(1-\alpha))+\alpha}$
$a_{ss} = 1$	$= 1$
$k_{ss} = h_{ss}\left[\frac{1}{\beta(1-\alpha)}\right]^{-1/\alpha}$	$= \left[\frac{alpha}{\theta(1-\beta(1-\alpha))+\alpha}\right]\left[\beta(1-\alpha)\right]^{1/\alpha}$
$i_{ss} = k_{ss}$	$= \left[\frac{\alpha}{\theta(1-\beta(1-\alpha))+\alpha}\right]\left[\beta(1-\alpha)\right]^{1/\alpha}$
$y_{ss} = k_{ss}\left[\frac{1}{\beta(1-\alpha)}\right]$	$= \left[\frac{\alpha}{\theta(1-\beta(1-\alpha))+\alpha}\right]\left[\beta(1-\alpha)\right]^{\frac{1}{\alpha}-1}$
$c_{ss} = k_{ss}\left[\frac{1}{\beta(1-\alpha)} - 1\right]$	$= \left[\frac{\alpha}{\theta(1-\beta(1-\alpha))+\alpha}\right]\left[\beta(1-\alpha)\right]^{1/\alpha}\left[\frac{1}{\beta(1-\alpha)} - 1\right]$
$w_{ss} = \alpha\frac{y_{ss}}{h_{ss}}$	$= \alpha\left[\beta(1-\alpha)\right]^{\frac{1}{\alpha}-1}$

Note: Steady states calculation is in Long_Plosser.m (Sect. 3.2) (see Chap. 3).

from it. The first is that in [mod1] each declared variable is the variable that appears in the nonlinear model. For example "c" represents the consumption in period "t."

The second is that in [mod2] each declared variable represents the natural logarithm of the variable. For example "cc" is equal to "lnc_t." It is worth mentioning that [mod1] and [mod2] contain the nonlinear model. The third is that in [mod3] each variable declared represents the deviation of the variable with respect to its steady state. For example, "ct" is equal to "$c_t - c_{ss}$." It is worth mentioning that "ct" is a way of representing $\widetilde{c}_t$, as it appears in the level linearized model (see Table 2.14).

In addition, a fourth conclusion is that in [mod4] each variable declared represents the deviation of the logarithm of the variable with respect to the logarithm of its steady state. For example "ch" is equal to "$lnc_t - lnc_{ss}$." As in [mod3], "ch" is a way to represent $\widehat{c}_t$, as it appears in the log-linearized model (see Table 2.15).

Also, it is important to mention that the number of declared variables is the same as the number of equations to write in the `model` block. Finally, productivity in Dynare is declared as an endogenous variable, and it is the shock ϵ_t that is declared as exogenous.

Definition of exogenous variables The only exogenous variable is the disturbance (error) of productivity ϵ_t. The way of entering it in the .mod file is similar between the four versions.

varexo e e_t (long_name = 'Productivity shock');

Table 2.18 Declaration of endogenous variables

Nonlinear model		Linear model	
Variable in levels	Variable in logarithm	Variable in levels	Variable in logarithm
(mod1)	(mod2)	(mod3)	(mod4)
var	var	var	var
c	cc	ct	ch
i	ii	it	ih
y	yy	yt	yh
k	kk	kt	kh
h	hh	ht	hh
r	rr	rt	rh
w	ww	wt	wh
a	aa	at	ah
;	;	;	;

where: \$e_t\$ is the name that the variable will take in LATEX,[5] and (long_name = 'Productivity shock') is the "long" name that is assigned to the variable.

Parameter definition Table 2.19 describes the parameter definition, which is similar in all four .mod files. It is worth mentioning that not only the parameters associated with the equations are indicated, such as the production function, for example, but also the steady state values are defined as parameters.

After defining the parameters, it is necessary to indicate to Dynare the values of each one (calibration), including the steady state values. This is important because, in the linear model, the value of the steady state of some variables usually appears multiplicatively or additively and also because these steady states are placed in the block of initial values. Table 2.20 describes how to enter parameter values in Dynare. These codes are written after the parameter block and before the model block.

Where Does Dynare Store Information About Variables and Parameters? Dynare, after reading the .mod file, creates a variable in Matlab's *workspace*: M_, in which it stores model information. Under Matlab's categorization of variables, this variable is a **structure**; that is, it can contain other variables, such as numeric (arrays and vectors), logical, and string (text); it may even contain another structure.

In Fig. 2.4 it is observed that the variable M_ contains a wide set of other variables. This section mentions those in which Dynare saves the name of the variables and the parameters of the model. It is worth mentioning that since these Matlab variables store text (names), then under the Matlab typology, they are "string (char)" variables:

---

[5] LATEX format is a free source *software* designed to write texts with high typographic quality. It is a very flexible tool due to the number of options it has, especially to include mathematical expressions (equations, regression tables, optimization problems) in an elegant and simple way.

Table 2.19 Parameter declaration

Parameters	
theta	$ \theta$ (long_name = 'weight of leisure in utility function')
beta	$ \beta$ (long_name = 'discount factor')
alpha	$ \alpha$ (long_name = 'labour share of national income')
rho	$ \rho$ (long_name = 'shock persistence')
sigma_ee	$ \sigma_e$ (long_name = 'std shock offset')
y_ss	
c_ss	
i_ss	
w_ss	
r_ss	
k_ss	
h_ss	
a_ss	
;	

Note: This parameter declaration belongs to Mod1

Table 2.20 Declaration of parameter values

For (mod1) to (mod4)
h_ss=0.2;
beta=0.984;
alpha=0.667;
rho=0.979;
sigma_ee=0.0072;
theta=alpha*(1-h_ss)/(h_ss*(1-beta*(1-alpha)));
r_ss=1/beta;
a_ss=1;
k_ss=h_ss*(1/(beta*(1-alpha)))^(-1/alpha);
i_ss=k_ss;
y_ss=k_ss*(1/(beta*(1-alpha)));
c_ss=k_ss*(1/(beta*(1-alpha))-1);
w_ss=alpha*y_ss/h_ss;

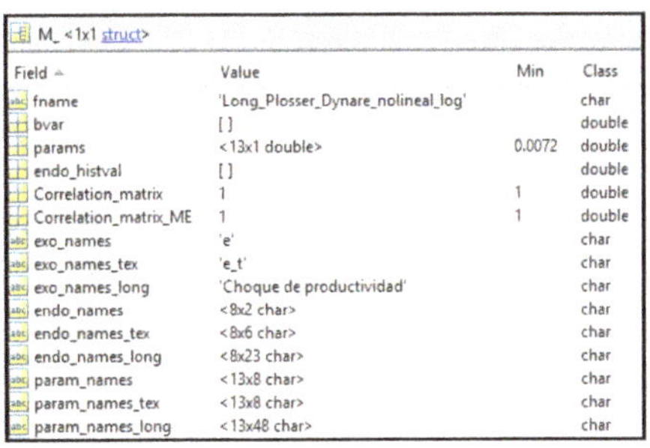

M_ <1x1 struct>

Field	Value	Min	Class
fname	'Long_Plosser_Dynare_nolineal_log'		char
bvar	[ ]		double
params	<13x1 double>	0.0072	double
endo_histval	[ ]		double
Correlation_matrix	1	1	double
Correlation_matrix_ME	1	1	double
exo_names	'e'		char
exo_names_tex	'e_t'		char
exo_names_long	'Choque de productividad'		char
endo_names	<8x2 char>		char
endo_names_tex	<8x6 char>		char
endo_names_long	<8x23 char>		char
param_names	<13x8 char>		char
param_names_tex	<13x8 char>		char
param_names_long	<13x48 char>		char

Fig. 2.4 Structure M_. (**Note:** This structure M_ is obtained from the file "Long_Plosser_Dynare_nolinear_log.mod")

- **Variable associated with model name:** "fname" is a variable that contains the name of the .mod file.
- **Variables associated with the exogenous variable:** In this case there are three variables. The first is "exo_names," which contains the name of the exogenous variable; the second is "exo_names_tex," which contains the name that the variable will take in LaTeX format; and finally "exo_names_long," which contains the long names of the exogenous variables.
- **Variables associated with the endogenous variable:** As in the case of the exogenous variable, there are also three variables for the endogenous variable. The first is "endo_names," which contains the names of the endogenous variables; the second is "endo_names_tex," which includes the name that the variables will take in LaTeX format; finally, "endo_names_long" contains said extended names of the endogenous variables.
- **Variables associated with the parameters:** In this case there are four variables. One of them is "params," which contains the values of the parameters (in the same order as they were written in the `parameters` block in the .mod). The remaining three variables are associated with the names of the parameters: The first is "param_names," which contains the names of the parameters; the second is "param_names_tex," which includes the name that the parameters will take in LaTeX format; and finally "param_names_long," which contains the long names of the parameters.

It is worth mentioning that to extract a variable found within the structure M_ it is enough to write in the Matlab *Command Window*: "M_.VariableName." For example, if you want to extract the name of the .mod file, you would type the following:

≫ M_.fname

This will show:

ans =
Long_Plosser_Dynare_nonlinear_log

It may be necessary to extract the long version of the endogenous variable names. In this case, the following is written in the Matlab *Command Window*:

≫ M_.endo_names_long

This will show:

ans =
Ln Consumption
Ln Investment
Ln Product
Ln Capital
Ln Work
Ln Real interest rate
Ln Real wage
Productivity

It is important to mention that one of the variables that has the structure M_ is Sigma_e. This is a special Dynare variable, and you cannot use this name to define another variable in the .mod file (for example, the standard deviation of *shock*). Sigma_e is the variance–covariance matrix of the stochastic shock and is written as an upper or lower triangular matrix. For example, for the nonlinear model with variables in logarithm (mod2), Sigma_e = 0.00005184, which corresponds to the variance of the *shock*. Since in the .mod file, we define the standard deviation of the shock as sigma_ee = 0.0072, then the variance is 0.00005184, which Dynare calculates and saves in Sigma_e (variable of the structure M_).

2.4.3 Model

Table 2.21 mentions how to write the nonlinear model in Dynare considering the variables in levels or in logarithms. The main takeaways from this table, which are applied to any model, are the following:

- **Definition of time:** It is important to mention how Dynare considers "time." First of all, when you write a variable in Dynare in the current period "t," just write down the variable without any time label. For example, current consumption in our model (c_t) is written in the mod file as "c." If you want to write a variable ahead by one period, you write "c(+1)" in the .mod file, which represents c_{t+1} in our model.
- **Control variables:** Dynare considers control variables to be written in "t," and variables accompanied by (+1) are *forward looking*. In this case, it is not necessary to write the expectations because Dynare understands that any variable written in (+1) is always accompanied by the expectations operator E_t. For example, the Euler equation described in Table 2.21 does not carry the expectation operator.

Table 2.21 Nonlinear model declaration

Variables in levels (mod1)	Variables in logarithms (mod2)
model;	model;
1/c=beta*(1/c(+1))*(r(+1));	1/exp(cc)=beta*(1/exp(cc(+1)))*(exp(rr(+1)));
k=i;	exp(kk)=exp(ii);
theta/(1-h)=w/c;	theta/(1-exp(hh))=exp(ww)/exp(cc);
y=a*((k(-1))^(1-alpha))*h^(alpha);	exp(yy)=exp(yy)*((exp(kk(-1)))^(1-alpha))*exp(hh)^(alpha);
r=(1-alpha)*y/k(-1);	exp(rr)=(1-alpha)*exp(yy)/exp(kk(-1));
w=(alpha)*y/h;	exp(ww)=(alpha)*exp(yy)/exp(hh);
y=c+i;	exp(yy)=exp(cc)+exp(ii);
ln(a)=rho*ln(a(-1))+e;	aa=rho*aa(-1)+e;
end;	end;

- **State variable:** It is important to mention that capital, in this model, is a state variable. That is, in "t" capital is already determined. So, the capital in period "t+1" is k_{t+1} in our model, which is determined at "t." Therefore, when we write that in Dynare, "k" must be placed to represent k_{t+1}, and when k_t appears in an equation, it must be written in Dynare as "k(−1)." This can be seen in the capital demand and production function in Table 2.21. For example, the production function is $y_t = a_t k_t^{\alpha-1} h_t^{\alpha}$ in our model, which is written in Dynare as y=a*((k(−1))^(1-alpha))*h^(alpha).

Additionally, some specific conclusions can be drawn from Table 2.21:

- **Nonlinear model with variables in levels (mod1):** In this case, the variable that represents consumption is "c," which is similar for the other variables. The equations are written the same way as on the *paper*; that is, they are the nonlinear first-order relations that arise from the optimization. When Dynare is asked to perform the linearization, it will create the variable $x = x - x_{ss}$.
- **Nonlinear model with logarithmic variables (mod2):** In this case, Dynare defines the variable "ln x" as "xx." This is done in order to consider the variables in logarithms. So, in each equation of the nonlinear system, instead of writing "x," we rewrite that variable as "exp(ln x)," which yields the same "x." But we know that "xx = ln x," so "exp(ln x)" becomes "exp(xx)." This last expression is what is written in Dynare for each variable. When Dynare is asked to perform the linearization, it will create the variable $xx = xx - xx_{ss} = lnx - lnx_{ss}$.

Regarding the linear version of the model, Table 2.22 shows the two alternatives to linearize the model: in levels (mod3) or in logarithms (mod4). It is worth mentioning that this linearization is previously done by the user, and then the linearized model is written in Dynare. In this case, Dynare will no longer apply the first-order Taylor approximation on the model. This is different from the two previous models where the user wrote the nonlinear model and only changed the nature of the variable (linear or logarithmic). From Table 2.22 some considerations can be deduced:

Table 2.22 Linear model declaration

Variables in levels (mod3)	Variables in logarithms (mod4)
model(linear);	model(linear);
ct=beta*(r_ss*ct(+1)-c_ss*rt(+1));	ch=ch(+1)-rh(+1);
kt=it;	(h_ss/(1-h_ss))*hh=wh-ch;
wt=(w_ss/(1-h_ss))*ht+(theta/(1-h_ss))*ct;	kh=ih;
yt=(y_ss/a_ss)*at+(1-alpha)*(y_ss/k_ss)*kt(-1) +alpha*(y_ss/h_ss)*ht;	yh=ah+(1-alpha) *kh(-1)+alpha*hh;
(y_ss/k_ss)*kt(-1)=yt-(k_ss/(1-alpha))*rt;	rh=yh-kh(-1);
wt=(alpha/h_ss)*yt-((alpha*y_ss)/(h_ss)^2)*ht;	wh=yh-hh;
yt=ct+it;	yh=(c_ss/y_ss)*ch+(i_ss/y_ss)*ih;
at=rho*at(-1)+e;	ah=rho*ah(-1)+e;
end;	end;

Table 2.23 Declaration of initial values

Nonlinear model				Linear model			
Variables in levels		Variables in logarithms		Variables in levels		Variables in logarithm	
(mod1)		(mod2)		(mod3)		(mod4)	
initval;		initval;		initval;		initval;	
h	=h_ss;	hh	=log(h_ss);	ht	=0;	hh	=0;
k	=k_ss;	kk	=log(k_ss);	kt	=0;	kh	=0;
i	=i_ss;	ii	=log(i_ss);	it	=0;	ih	=0;
c	=c_ss;	cc	=log(c_ss);	ct	=0;	ch	=0;
w	=w_ss;	ww	=log(w_ss);	wt	=0;	wh	=0;
r	=r_ss;	rr	=log(r_ss);	rt	=0;	rh	=0;
y	=y_ss;	yy	=log(y_ss);	yt	=0;	yh	=0;
a	=a_ss;	aa	=log(a_ss);	at	=0;	ah	=0;
end;		end;		end;		end;	

- **Linear model:** When you want to write a linearized model in Dynare, you must place the option `linear` in the block `model`. This is done as follows: `model (linear); . . . end.`
- **Linear model with variable in levels (mod3):** In this case, the variable $xt = x - x_{ss}$ has been defined. This variable is the one that represents the variable $\widetilde{x}_t$ of Table 2.14.
- **Linear model with variable in logarithm (mod4):** In this case, the variable $xh = lnx - lnx_{ss}$ has been defined. This variable is the one represented by the variable $\widehat{x}_t$ of Table 2.15.

An important difference in the equations between the nonlinear and the linearized model is that in the latter the steady state values are present in the equations.

2.4.4 *Initial Values*

The initial values are important because they are the starting point that Dynare uses to calculate the steady state through successive approximations. Usually, we first calculate the steady state manually and then enter it in the initial values block. Table 2.23 contains the way to enter the initial values in Dynare according to the type of model we are using. The following conclusions can be drawn from this table:

- **Nonlinear model with variables in levels:** In this way of writing the model, the initial value of each variable is the steady state previously defined in the parameter block "`parameters` " and then calculated (see Table 2.20).
- **Nonlinear model with variables in logarithm:** Because the variable that has been defined is the logarithm of itself (xx = ln x), then "xx =

$lnisplacedintheinitialvaluesx_{ss}$." It is worth mentioning that in Matlab the natural logarithm (ln) is expressed as "log."

- **Linear model with variables in levels:** Given that the defined variable is "$xt = x - x_{ss}$," then in the block of initial values it is placed: $xt = x_{ss} - x_{ss}$, so $xt = 0$.
- **Linear model with logarithmic variables:** Similarly to the previous case, since the defined variable is "$xh = lnx - lnx_{ss}$," then the steady state is "$xh = lnx_{ss} - lnx_{ss}$," and, consequently, $xh = 0$, this being the value that is placed in the block of initial values for all variables.

Resid This command, placed after the initial values block, calculates the residual in each equation when each variable is replaced by its initial value; that is, put the initial values in each equation and compute the remainder between the expression on the right minus the expression on the left. For example, for the production function:

$$F = y_t - a_t k_t^{1-\alpha} h_t^{\alpha}$$

In steady state:

$$F = y - ak^{1-\alpha} h^{\alpha}$$

What Dynare does is plug the initial values into this equation and compute the remainder (F). If this remainder is zero, it means that the initial values entered are exactly correct; that is, we have correctly calculated the steady state. It may be that the residual is different from zero, which indicates that we have made a mistake in the calculation of the steady state, and still, Dynare finds the true value of the steady state. This is because Dynare needs a starting point close to the true value of the steady state and with that start to iterate. After calculating the steady state, Dynare will display these values in Matlab's *prompt*, which is found in Table 2.24.

In addition, Table 2.24, which corresponds to the nonlinear model with variables in logarithm, indicates that the initial values (calculated steady state) considered are exactly the correct steady states of the model; therefore, the remainder of each equation is equal to zero. If we have not placed the initial values correctly, Dynare will show that the residual is different from zero in some equations, which gives us information to detect in which variable we have not calculated the steady state

Table 2.24 The Resid command: results

Residuals of the static equations:
Equation number 1 : 0
Equation number 2 : 0
Equation number 3 : 0
Equation number 4 : 0
Equation number 5 : 0
Equation number 6 : 0
Equation number 7 : 0
Equation number 8 : 0

Table 2.25 Steady State

Nonlinear model				Linear model			
Variables in levels		Variables in logarithms		Variables in levels		Variables in logarithm	
(mod1)		(mod2)		(mod3)		(mod4)	
c	0.0770361	cc	−2.56348	ct	0	ch	0
i	0.037545	ii	−3.28221	it	0	ih	0
y	0.114581	yy	−2.16647	yt	0	yh	0
k	0.037545	kk	−3.28221	kt	0	kh	0
h	0.2	hh	−1.60944	ht	0	hh	0
r	1.01626	rr	0.0161294	rt	0	rh	0
w	0.382128	ww	−0.962	wt	0	wh	0
a	1	aa	0	at	0	ah	0

correctly. If the residual is very large, it means that the initial values are very different or very far from the steady state and Dynare could stop the process because it could not find the steady state from the given initial point.

2.4.5 *Steady State*

Table 2.25 shows the results of applying the command `steady;`. Some conclusions can be drawn from this table:

- **Nonlinear model with variables in logarithms (mod2):** Let us remember that in this model the variables are expressed in logarithms. For example, the log of consumption is represented by "cc"; that is, $cc = lnc$. Then in steady state $cc_{ss} = lnc_{ss}$. Considering that $cc_{ss} = -2.56348$, then $c_{ss} = exp(-2.56348) = 0.0770361$. The same is done with the other variables.
- **Linear model:** In the case of the linear model with variables in levels (mod3), it is known that each variable is expressed as the difference between its level and its steady state. For example, for consumption, we have $ct = c - c_{ss}$. Evaluating the variable in steady state we have: $ct_{ss} = c_{ss} - c_{ss} = 0$. In a similar way, we have the linear model with variables in logarithm (mod4). For example, for consumption, we have $ch = lnc - lnc_{ss}$. When evaluating this variable in steady state: $ch_{ss} = c_{ss} - c_{ss} = 0$.

Where Does Dynare Store the Steady States?

Dynare creates a structure variable (similar to M_) called oo_, in which it saves the simulations, the steady state, the moments of the endogenous variables (mean, variance, and autocorrelation), and the impulse-response function of each variable. Figure 2.5 shows all the variables that have the oo_ structure.

In particular, the variable that contains the steady states calculated by Dynare is "oo_.steady_state" (see Fig. 2.6).

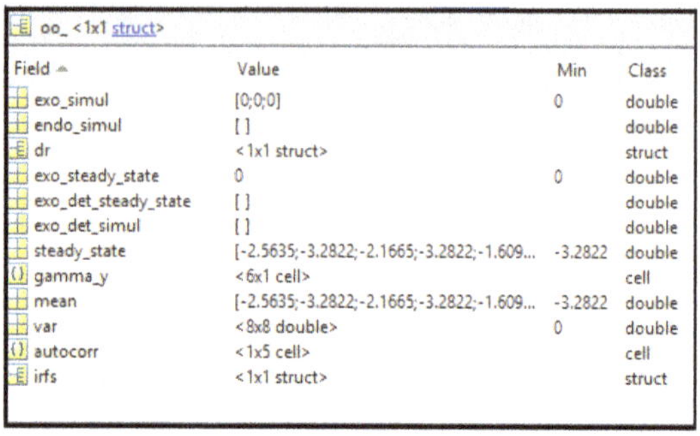

Fig. 2.5 Structure oo_. (**Note:** This oo_ structure is obtained from the file "Long_Plosser_Dynare_nolinear_log.mod")

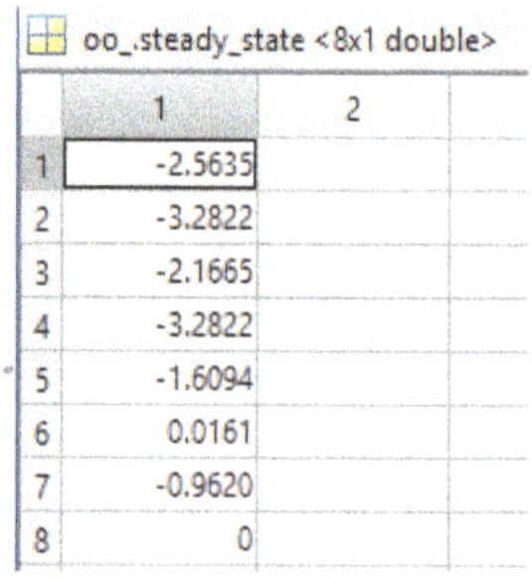

Fig. 2.6 oo_.steady_state. (**Note:** This variable oo_.steady_state is obtained from the file "Long_Plosser_Dynare_nolinear_log.mod")

Table 2.26 Clash definition

```
shock;
var e = (sigma_ee)^2;
end;
```

2.4.6 *Definition of* Shock

For all four .mod files the shock is defined similarly. Table 2.26 shows how the variance of the productivity *shock* is written in Dynare.

2.4.7 *Model Evaluation*

To evaluate the model, the code `check;` is placed. The result of this command is the vector of eigenvalues of matrix F. This matrix is obtained by writing the model (a system of linear equations) in state-space form. Equation (2.2) reflects the state-space version of the model. Chapter 3 describes how this equation is obtained in greater detail.

$$\begin{bmatrix} X_{t+1} \\ E_t Y_{t+1} \end{bmatrix} = F \begin{bmatrix} X_t \\ Y_t \end{bmatrix} + G V_{t+1} \tag{2.2}$$

Table 2.27 Eigenvalues

Nonlinear Model					
Variables in levels (mod1)			Variables in logarithms (mod2)		
Module	Real	Imaginary	Module	Real	Imaginary
0.333	0.333	0	0.333	0.333	0
0.979	0.979	0	0.979	0.979	0
3,052	3,052	0	3,052	3,052	0
Low	−Low	0	9.84E+15	−9.84E+15	0
There are two eigenvalues greater than 1 in modulo for 2 variables *forward looking* The range condition is checked			There are two eigenvalues greater than 1 in modulo for 2 variables *forward looking* The range condition is checked		
Linear Model					
Variables in levels (mod3)			Variables in logarithms (mod4)		
Module	Real	Imaginary	Module	Real	Imaginary
0.333	0.333	0	0.333	0.333	0
0.979	0.979	0	0.979	0.979	0
3,052	3,052	0	3,052	3,052	0
4.59E+17	4.59E+17	0	Inf	−Inf	0
There are two eigenvalues greater than 1 in modulo for 2 variables *forward looking* The range condition is checked			There are two eigenvalues greater than 1 in modulo for 2 variables *forward looking* The range condition is checked		

In Table 2.27 the vector of eigenvalues of each model is written; in addition, Dynare displays a message indicating whether the model satisfies the Blanchard and Kahn condition. For example, in mod1 it is observed that there are four eigenvalues whose modules are: 0.333, 0.979, 3.052, and ∞. Of these four modules, two are greater than one. On the other hand, the model has two variables *forward looking* c_{t+1} and r_{t+1}. Therefore, the Blanchard and Kahn condition is fulfilled, which indicates that if the number of eigenvalues whose modulus is greater than one is equal to the number of variables *forward looking*, then the system has a unique solution. This is the message that Dynare prints on the screen.

Where Does Dynare Store the Vector of Eigenvalues?

Inside the oo_ structure that Dynare creates when processing the model is the oo_.dr structure. This structure stores two important variables: the eigenvalues and the decision rule; that is, the solution of the model. Figure 2.7 shows the variables contained in oo_.dr.

Figure 2.8 shows the variable oo_.dr.eigval, which contains the vector of eigenvalues.

oo_.dr <1x1 struct>

Field	Value	Min	Class
eigval	[0.3330 + 0.0000i;0.9790 + 0.0000i;3.051...	0.3330	double (co...
order_var	[2;3;5;7;4;8;1;6]	1	double
inv_order_var	[7;1;2;5;3;8;4;6]	1	double
kstate	<4x4 double>	0	double
transition_auxiliary_vari...	[ ]		double
ys	[-2.5635;-3.2822;-2.1665;-3.2822;-1.609...	-3.2822	double
ghx	<8x2 double>	-0.6670	double
ghu	[1.0000;1.0000;2.5432e-14;1.0000;1.0000...	2.5432...	double
state_var	[4 8]	4	double
gx	[0.3330 0.9790;-0.6670 0.9790]	-0.6670	double
Gy	[0.3330 0.9790;0 0.9790]	0	double

Fig. 2.7 Decision rules (oo_.dr). (**Note:** This oo_.dr structure is obtained from the file "Long_Plosser_Dynare_nolinear_log.mod")

oo_.dr.eigval <4x1 complex double>

	1	2	3
1	0.3330		
2	0.9790		
3	3.0518		
4	-9.8365e+15		
5			

Fig. 2.8 oo_.dr.eigval. (**Note:** This vector oo_.dr.eigval is obtained from the file "Long_Plosser_Dynare_nolinear_log.mod")

2.4.8 Solution

Table 2.28 shows the model solution (policy and state function) for the four .mod files. It is worth mentioning that the code used to obtain the solution is

$$stoch\_simul(order = 1, irf = 40);$$

where: "order = 1" indicates that the model should be approximated by the first-order Taylor expansion. This option does not work when in the model block it has been specified that the model is linear by means of "`model(linear)`." Some observations emerge from Table 2.28:

- **Nonlinear model with variable levels (mod1):** For consumption "c," the solution is as follows:

$$c = 0.077 + 0.683k(-1) + 0.075a(-1) + 0.077\epsilon$$

  Since Dynare has been asked to linearize the system (`order=1`), which gives a system of equations like Table 2.14, then the state variable k(−1) and exogenous a(-1) are expressed as deviations from their steady state. That is: $k(-1) = k_t - k_{ss}$ and $a(-1) = a_{t-1} - a_{ss}$; then:

Table 2.28 Policy and state function

Nonlinear model: variables in levels (mod1)								
	c	i	y	k	h	r	w	a
Constant	0.077	0.038	0.115	0.038	0.2	1.016	0.382	1
k(−1)	0.683	0.333	1.016	0.333	0	−18.054	3.389	0
a(−1)	0.075	0.037	0.112	0.037	0	0.995	0.374	0.979
e	0.077	0.038	0.115	0.038	0	1.016	0.382	1
Nonlinear model: variables in logarithm (mod2)								
	cc	ii	yy	kk	hh	rr	ww	aa
Constant	−2.563	−3.282	−2.166	−3.282	−1.609	0.016	−0.962	0
kk(−1)	0.333	0.333	0.333	0.333	0	−0.667	0.333	0
aa(−1)	0.979	0.979	0.979	0.979	0	0.979	0.979	0.979
e	1	1	1	1	0	1	1	1
Linear model: variables in levels (mod3)								
	ct	it	yt	kt	ht	rt	wt	at
kt(−1)	0.683	0.333	1.016	0.333	0	−18.054	3.389	0
at(−1)	0.075	0.037	0.112	0.037	0	0.995	0.374	0.979
e	0.077	0.038	0.115	0.038	0	1.016	0.382	1
Linear model: variables in logarithm (mod4)								
	ch	ih	yh	kh	hh	rh	wh	ah
kh(−1)	0.333	0.333	0.333	0.333	0	−0.667	0.333	0
ah(−1)	0.979	0.979	0.979	0.979	0	0.979	0.979	0.979
e	1	1	1	1	0	1	1	1

This table has been built based on what Dynare shows in the Matlab *prompt*, maintaining the (initial) order of the variables that appear in the .mod

$$c_t = 0.077 + 0.683(k_t - k_{ss}) + 0.075(a_{t-1} - a_{ss}) + 0.077\epsilon_t$$

It is worth mentioning that the constant 0.077 is the steady state value of consumption.

$$(c_t - 0.077) = 0.683(k_t - k_{ss}) + 0.075(a_{t-1} - a_{ss}) + 0.077\epsilon_t$$

Factoring 0.077 from $(a_{t-1} - a_{ss})$ and e_t, we have

$$(c_t - 0.077) = 0.683(k_t - k_{ss}) + 0.077(0.979(a_{t-1} - a_{ss}) + e_t)$$

It is known that in the nonlinear model, the productivity equation is $lna_t = \rho lna_{t-1} + \epsilon_t$. However, when we ask Dynare to linearize the system, this equation is transformed into $\widetilde{a}_t = 0.979\widetilde{a}_{t-1} + e_t$, where $\widetilde{a}_t = a_t - a_{ss}$. Therefore, substituting this expression in the previous equation:

$$\underbrace{(c_t - 0.077)}_{\widetilde{c}_t} = 0.683\widetilde{k}_t + 0.077\widetilde{a}_t$$

$$\widetilde{c}_t = 0.683\widetilde{k}_t + 0.077\widetilde{a}_t$$

This is the consumption policy function (expressed in deviations from its steady state): $\widetilde{c}_t = F(\widetilde{k}_t, \widetilde{a}_t)$. The coefficients are read as follows: A one unit increase in $\widetilde{k}_t$ (holding everything else constant) produces an increase of $\widetilde{c}_t$ by 0.683 units; that is, if capital today is one unit away from its steady state, consumption is 0.683 units away from its steady state. These coefficients allow calculating in units the deviation of the variables with respect to their stationary state; however, a more appropriate measure would be to consider said deviation in percentage terms. To do this, the following can be done:

$$\begin{aligned}
(c_t - 0.077) &= 0.683(k_t - k_{ss}) + 0.077(a_t - a_{ss}) + \epsilon_t \\
\frac{(c_t - 0.077)}{c_{ss}}c_{ss} &= 0.683\frac{(k_t - k_{ss})}{k_{ss}}k_{ss} + 0.077\frac{(a_t - a_{ss})}{a_{ss}}a_{ss} + \epsilon_t \\
\widehat{c}_t c_{ss} &= 0.683\widehat{k}_t k_{ss} + 0.077\widehat{a}_t a_{ss} + \epsilon_t \\
\widehat{c}_t c_{ss} &= 0.683k_{ss}\widehat{k}_t + 0.077a_{ss}\widehat{a}_t + \epsilon_t \\
\widehat{c}_t 0.077 &= 0.683 * 0.0375\widehat{k}_t + 0.077 * 1\widehat{a}_t + \epsilon_t \\
\widehat{c}_t 0.077 &= 0.0256\widehat{k}_t + 0.077\widehat{a}_t + \epsilon_t \qquad (2.3)
\end{aligned}$$

From equation (2.3), the variable $\widehat{x}_t$ is read as the deviation **percentage** of the variable with respect to its steady state. So: a 1% increase in $\widehat{k}_t$, that is, that capital is increasing by 1% with respect to its steady state and produces an increase of (0.0256/0.077)*1% = 0.333% of $\widehat{c}_t$; in other words, consumption deviates above its steady state by 0.333%.

- **Nonlinear model with variables in logarithms (mod2):** In this case, for example, the solution for consumption is

$$cc = -2.563 + 0.333kk(-1) + 0.979aa(-1) + e$$

Considering that Dynare has performed the linearization taking into account that each variable is expressed in logarithm, then $cc_t = lnc_t$, but the state variable and the exogenous variable are expressed as $kk(-1) = lnk_t - lnk_{ss}$ and $aa(-1) = lna_{t-1} - lna_{ss}$.

$$lnc_t = -2.563 + 0.333(lnk_t - lnk_{ss}) + 0.979ln(lna_{t-1} - lna_{ss}) + e_t$$

The constant in this equation corresponds to the steady state of the variable; that is, $lnc_{ss} = -2.563$, and then: $c_{ss} = exp(-2.563) = 0.077$, which coincides with what was calculated in the first model (mod1). Plugging this into the previous equation:

$$
\begin{aligned}
lnc_t &= -2.563 + 0.333(lnk_t - lnk_{ss}) + 0.979(lna_{t-1} - lna_{ss}) + e_t \\
lnc_t - lnc_{ss} &= 0.333(lnk_t - lnk_{ss}) + 0.979(lna_{t-1} - lna_{ss}) + e_t \\
\widehat{c}_t &= 0.333\widehat{k}_t + \underbrace{0.979\widehat{a}_{t-1} + e_t}_{\widehat{a}_t} \\
\widehat{c}_t &= 0.333\widehat{k}_t + \widehat{a}_t
\end{aligned} \tag{2.4}
$$

In this case, the coefficients are elasticities; that is, if capital increases by 1% with respect to its steady state (keeping everything else constant), consumption increases by 0.333% with respect to its steady state.

- **Linear model:** Regarding the linear model, it can be seen that it has the same coefficients as in the nonlinear model, which was linearized by Dynare. The main difference is that when we introduce a linear model in Dynare, the steady state is zero; therefore, no intercept appears in the equations of the linear model (mod3 and mod4).

From the above, two conclusions are important to mention: The first is that it is preferable that in the policy functions, each variable is expressed in percentage deviations with respect to the steady state; that is, variables in logarithms are preferred. This is because the solution coefficients are understood as elasticities allowing a simple reading of the impulse-response function. The second conclusion is that the policy and state function coefficients will be the same if we put the nonlinear or linearized model into Dynare. For example, the nonlinear model (mod1) and the linear model (mod3) have the same coefficients for variables in levels. Similarly, for variables in logarithm (mod2 and mod4).

Where Does Dynare Store the Coefficients of the Policy and State Function? Dynare stores the policy and state function in several variables inside the "oo_.dr" structure. There are some considerations to capture the coefficients of these functions correctly.

[1] Variable order The initial variable order, as written in the .mod file, is as follows: c, i, y, k, h, r, w, a. So, consumption comes first, investment comes second, and so on for the other variables. However, when Dynare solves the system, it reorders these variables, saving the new order to "oo_.dr.oder_var." This variable returns a vector of numbers that contains the new position of the variables: 2, 3, 5, 7, 4, 8, 1, 6. This means that the variable that was at initial position 2 (which is the inversion) now it is in the first place. For instance, consumption was initially in the first position, but now it appears in position 7. This is important because the coefficients of the solution correspond to this new order. Then the reordered variable vector is

$$
\begin{array}{cccccc}
\text{Initial position} & & & & & \text{Reordered position} \\
\begin{matrix}1\\2\\3\\4\\5\\6\\7\\8\end{matrix} & \begin{bmatrix}c\\i\\y\\k\\h\\r\\w\\a\end{bmatrix} & \longrightarrow & \begin{bmatrix}i\\y\\h\\w\\k\\a\\c\\r\end{bmatrix} & \begin{matrix}2\\3\\5\\7\\4\\8\\1\\6\end{matrix}
\end{array}
$$

[2] Policy and state functions as a system of equations. Let be the vector of rearranged endogenous variables Y_t, the vector of steady state values Y_{ss}, the matrix containing the coefficients of the state variables "ghx," the vector of the state variables X_t, and the vector containing the coefficients associated with the error "ghu." So, the system of equations representing the policy and state functions is

$$Y_t = Y_{ss} + ghx * X_t + ghu * U_t$$

Writing this system in its extensive form:

$$
\begin{bmatrix} i \\ y \\ h \\ w \\ k \\ a \\ c \\ r \end{bmatrix} = \begin{bmatrix} i_{ss} \\ y_{ss} \\ h_{ss} \\ w_{ss} \\ k_{ss} \\ a_{ss} \\ c_{ss} \\ r_{ss} \end{bmatrix} + \begin{bmatrix} \eta_{ik} & \eta_{ia} \\ \eta_{yk} & \eta_{ya} \\ \eta_{hk} & \eta_{ha} \\ \eta_{wk} & \eta_{wa} \\ \eta_{kk} & \eta_{ka} \\ \eta_{ak} & \eta_{aa} \\ \eta_{ck} & \eta_{ca} \\ \eta_{rk} & \eta_{ra} \end{bmatrix} * \begin{bmatrix} k(-1) \\ a(-1) \end{bmatrix} + \begin{bmatrix} \eta_{iu} \\ \eta_{yu} \\ \eta_{hu} \\ \eta_{wu} \\ \eta_{ku} \\ \eta_{au} \\ \eta_{cu} \\ \eta_{ru} \end{bmatrix} * e
$$

For example, the investment policy equation is

$$i = i_{ss} + \eta_{ik} k(-1) + \eta_{ia} a(-1) + \eta_{iu} e$$

So, for mod2, in Table 2.28, we have

$$i = -3.282 + 0.333k(-1) + 0.979a(-1) + 1e$$

[3] Coefficients of these functions in oo_.dr. The steady state vector is found in "oo_.dr.ys," which maintains the initial order of the variables. The new order only applies to the array associated with the status and error variables stored respectively in "oo_.dr.ghx" and "oo_.dr.ghu."

oo_.irfs <1x1 struct>

Field	Value	Min	Class
cc_e	<1x40 double>	0.0048	double
ii_e	<1x40 double>	0.0048	double
yy_e	<1x40 double>	0.0048	double
kk_e	<1x40 double>	0.0048	double
hh_e	<1x40 double>	0	double
rr_e	<1x40 double>	-1.983...	double
ww_e	<1x40 double>	0.0048	double
aa_e	<1x40 double>	0.0031	double

Fig. 2.9 Impulse-response function (oo_.irfs). (**Note:** This impulse-response function is obtained from the file "Long_Plosser_Dynare_nolinear_log.mod")

$$\text{oo\_.dr.ys} = \begin{bmatrix} -2.563 \\ -3.282 \\ -2.166 \\ -3.282 \\ -1.609 \\ 0.016 \\ -0.962 \\ 0 \end{bmatrix} \quad \text{oo\_.dr.ghx} = \begin{bmatrix} 0.333 & 0.979 \\ 0.333 & 0.979 \\ 3.09E-15 & 1.03E-14 \\ 0.333 & 0.979 \\ 0.333 & 0.979 \\ 0 & 0.979 \\ 0.333 & 0.979 \\ -0.667 & 0.979 \end{bmatrix}$$

$$\text{oo\_.dr.ghu} = \begin{bmatrix} 1 \\ 1 \\ 2.54E-14 \\ 1 \\ 1 \\ 1 \\ 1 \\ 1 \end{bmatrix}$$

2.4.9 Impulse-Response Function (IRF)

As mentioned previously, the oo_ structure also contains the impulse-response function of the model. Since all endogenous variables are required to respond to the impulse, then Dynare creates another structure called "irfs," in which it stores the impulse-response function of each variable, as can be seen in Fig. 2.9.

For example, if only the consumption impulse-response function is required, click on the variable "oo_.irfs.cc_e." As shown in Fig. 2.10, the variable "oo_.irfs.cc_e" contains a vector of 40 periods, which was defined in `stoch_simul` when it put "irf=40."

oo_.irfs.cc_e <1x40 double>

	1	2	3	4	5	6	7	8	9	10	11
1	0.0072	0.0094	0.0100	0.0101	0.0100	0.0098	0.0096	0.0094	0.0092	0.0090	0.0088

Fig. 2.10 Consumption impulse-response function (oo_.irfs.cc_e). (**Note:** This impulse-response function is obtained from the file "Long_Plosser_Dynare_nolinear_log.mod")

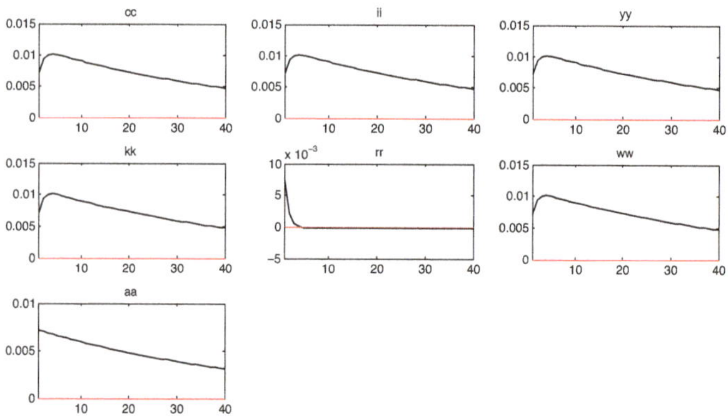

Fig. 2.11 Impulse-response function (Dynare graph). (**Note:** This impulse-response plot is obtained from the file "Long_Plosser_Dynare_nolinear_log.mod")

Dynare also plots each of the variables found in the "oo_.irfs" structure; however, the graph is essentially basic in the sense that the lines are not modified and, furthermore, it does not consider the names of the variables in their extended version. This can be seen in Fig. 2.11.

Figure 2.11 could be improved if a code is built in Matlab that is fed from the .mod file and that graphs with the extended names of the variables and aesthetic modifications in the graph. This is done in the code "irfs_nolinear_log.m," and you can see the result in Fig. 2.12.

Description of the code First, the .mod file is run (line 1 of the code):

dynare Long_Plosser_Dynare_nonlinear_log.mod;

Then an array containing all the impulse-response functions (IRF) is defined in line 2 of the code. Third, a cell array containing the variable names (*names*) is defined. Finally, a loop is built to plot each impulse-response function with the appropriate variable name and the appropriate line size (lines 4 through 9 of the code). The last two commands of this code segment place the sheet where the graph is saved in landscape orientation (`orient landscape`) and then save it in pdf extension (line 11).

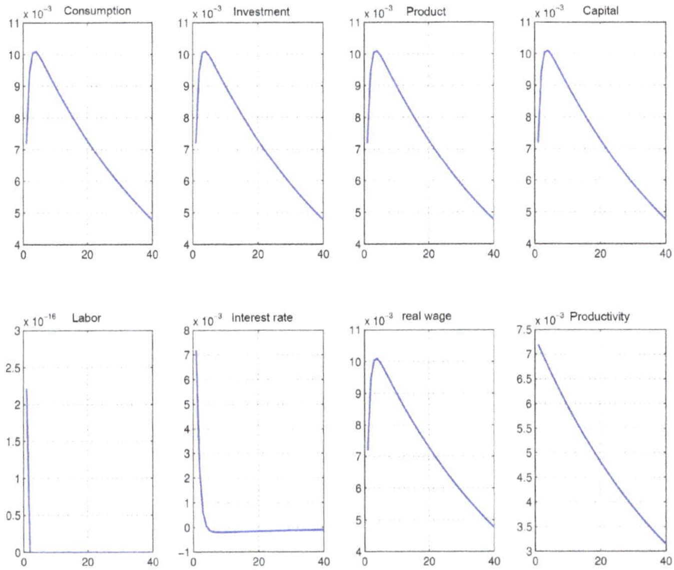

Fig. 2.12 Impulse-response function (Matlab plot). (**Note:** This impulse-response plot is obtained from the file "ifrs_nolinear_log.m")

2.4.10 *Sensitivity Analysis*

The Fig. 2.13 shows the impulse-response function for three values of the persistence of the productivity *shock*. It can be seen that the greater the persistence of the *shock*, the greater the reaction of each endogenous variable (except the interest rate and labor, which remain at their steady state value). In addition, it can be seen that the variables take more time to return to their steady state. This graph is obtained by writing the following codes in the .mod file after writing `stoch_simul`.

```
% Valores del parametro
rhos = [0.5 0.7 0.9];
for j= 1:size(rhos,2)
rho = rhos(j);
stoch_simul(order=1, irf=40, nograph, nomoments,nofunctions);
oo_sen{j} = oo_;
end;
% Grafica
name = {'Consumo', ...
    'Inversion','Produccion','Capital','Trabajo','Tasa de ...
    interes real', 'Salario', 'Productividad'};
field_name = fieldnames(oo_sen{1}.irfs); time = 1:40;
    for j=1:size(name,2)
        subplot(2,4,j)
        plot(time,oo_sen{1}.irfs.(field_name{j}),...
```

```
14                time,oo_sen{2}.irfs.(field_name{j}),'--',...
15                time,oo_sen{3}.irfs.(field_name{j}),'-.',
16                'LineWidth', 1.5)
17            title(name{j});
18            grid;
19        end;
20        legend('\rho=0.5', '\rho=0.7', '\rho=0.9');
21    orient landscape
22    saveas(gcf,'analisis_sensibilidad','pdf');
```

Code description This code has two parts. The first consists of saving the simulation of the model before each value of the productivity persistence. To do this, a vector of persistence values is defined (line 2), and then `stoch_simul` is applied to the three values, and each result (oo_) is stored in a cell vector (oo_sen).

The second part of the code is to plot the impulse-response function under the three values of the parameter. To obtain this graph, first, the name of the variables is defined, whose order is described at the beginning of the .mod file. Second, the names of the structure "oo_sen{1}.irfs" (line 9) are extracted (as a cell vector). The utility of this is that it will serve to make loops with structures. Third, a loop is built to plot the impulse response of each variable to the three persistence values. Line 13 is of special importance: The code "oo_sen{1}.irfs.(field_name{j})" for j=1 is "oo_sen{1} .irfs.cc_e." For j=2 it is "oo_sen{1}.irfs.ii_e" and so on. In this, you can see the usefulness of the "field" of a structure variable. Finally, the code `orient` indicates the orientation of the sheet in which the graph will be saved, and the code `saveas` indicates the name and extension with which the graph will be saved (usually, it is saved in pdf or eps for its usefulness in LaTeX).

2.4.11 Simulation of Endogenous Variables

After Dynare finds the solution of the linearized system, the ARMA(p,q) time series representation of the endogenous variables can be obtained. For example, from Table 2.28 for the capital of the nonlinear model with variables in logarithm, we have

$$
\begin{aligned}
kk_{t+1} &= kk_{ss} + \eta_{kk} kk_t + \eta_{ka} aa_{t-1} + \epsilon_t \\
kk_{t+1} - kk_{ss} &= \eta_{kk} kk_t + \eta_{ka} aa_{t-1} + \epsilon_t \\
(lnk_{t+1} - lnk_{ss}) &= \eta_{kk}(lnk_t - lnk_{ss}) + \eta_{ka}(lna_{t-1} - lna_{ss}) + \epsilon_t \\
\widehat{k}_{t+1} &= \eta_{kk}\widehat{k}_t + \eta_{ka}\widehat{a}_{t-1} + \epsilon_t \\
\widehat{k}_{t+1} &= 0.333\widehat{k}_t + \underbrace{0.979\widehat{a}_{t-1} + \epsilon_t}_{\widehat{a}_t}
\end{aligned}
$$

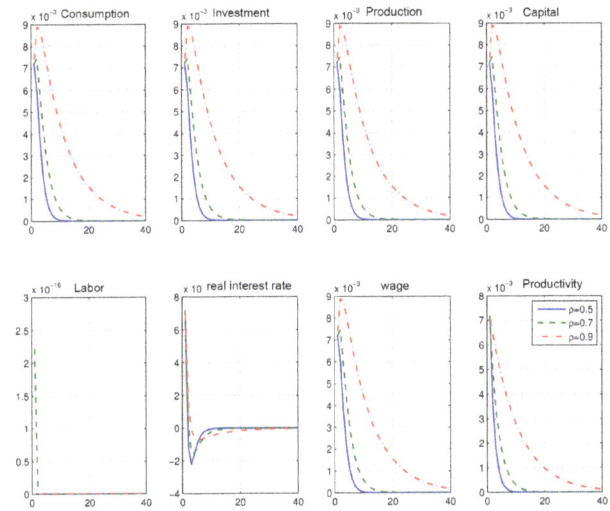

Fig. 2.13 Sensitivity analysis: Persistence of the productivity shock ρ. (**Note:** This impulse-response graph is obtained from the file "Long_Plosser_Dynare_nolineal_log.mod")

$$\widehat{k}_{t+1} = 0.333\widehat{k}_t + \widehat{a}_t$$
$$(1 - 0.333L)\widehat{k}_{t+1} = \widehat{a}_t \tag{2.5}$$

Considering that productivity, which behaves like an AR(1), can be expressed in its MA(∞) form, thus:

$$\begin{aligned} aa_t &= \phi aa_{t-1} + \epsilon_t \\ (1 - \phi L)aa_t &= \epsilon_t \\ aa_t &= \frac{\epsilon_t}{1 - \phi L} \\ \text{Given} &: a_{ss} = 1 \\ lna_t - lna_{ss} &= \frac{\epsilon_t}{1 - \phi L} \\ \widehat{a}_t &= \frac{\epsilon_t}{1 - \phi L} \end{aligned} \tag{2.6}$$

Introducing the equation (2.6) in the equation (2.5), we have that capital behaves like an AR(2):

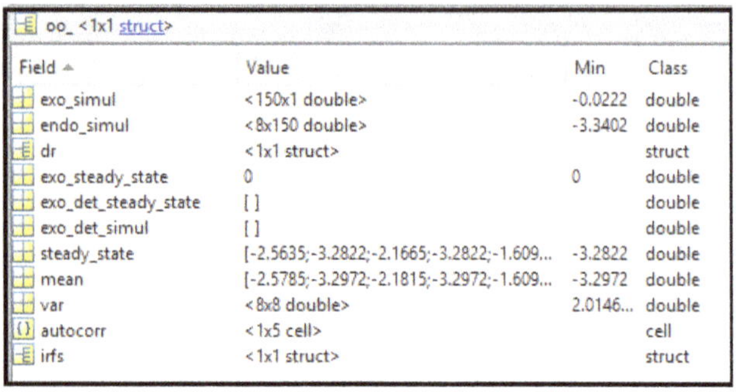

oo_ <1x1 struct>

Field	Value	Min	Class
exo_simul	<150x1 double>	-0.0222	double
endo_simul	<8x150 double>	-3.3402	double
dr	<1x1 struct>		struct
exo_steady_state	0	0	double
exo_det_steady_state	[]		double
exo_det_simul	[]		double
steady_state	[-2.5635;-3.2822;-2.1665;-3.2822;-1.609...	-3.2822	double
mean	[-2.5785;-3.2972;-2.1815;-3.2972;-1.609...	-3.2972	double
var	<8x8 double>	2.0146...	double
autocorr	<1x5 cell>		cell
irfs	<1x1 struct>		struct

Fig. 2.14 Structure oo_ (simulation). (**Note:** This structure is obtained from "Long_Plosser_Dynare_nolineal_log.mod")

$$
\begin{aligned}
(1 - 0.333L)\widehat{k}_{t+1} &= \widehat{a}_t \\
(1 - 0.333L)\widehat{k}_{t+1} &= \frac{\epsilon_t}{1 - \phi L} \\
\widehat{k}_{t+1} &= \frac{\epsilon_t}{(1 - 0.333L)(1 - \phi L)}
\end{aligned}
\tag{2.7}
$$

Given that we have the time series expression for each variable, Dynare could simulate the behavior of each variable assuming a random behavior $N(0, \sigma_e^2)$ for the error ϵ. For Dynare to perform this task, it is enough to indicate in the `stoch_simul` the number of periods (`periods`) that we want the variable to have. For example:

```
stoch_simul(order=1, periods = 150)
```

Three results can be emphasized about this code: Firstly, the simulated variables are stored in the oo_ structure, in particular in the variables "exo_simul" and "endo_simul" (see Fig. 2.14). The first variable contains the simulated exogenous variable; that is, the error ϵ_t that is distributed as a normal with zero mean and constant variance σ_e^2 (see Fig. 2.15). The second (endo_simul) contains the simulation of all the endogenous variables (in this case, there are eight). Each row represents the simulation of a variable, and the number of columns is the number of periods defined in stoch_simul (see Fig. 2.16).

The above shows **a** simulation for each endogenous variable. However, if someone wants to perform, for example, 300 simulations for each variable considering 150 periods, it is necessary not only to use `periods = 150` but also `simul_replic = 300`. The result of these `stoch_simul` options is a binary file with the following name: "NombreMod_simul." One disadvantage of this file is that it cannot be opened directly in Matlab or any other program. To read this file, a

Fig. 2.15 Simulation of the exogenous variable. (**Note:** This structure is obtained from "Long_Plosser_Dynare_nolineal_log.mod")

oo_.exo_simul <150x1 double>

	1	2
1	-2.8711e-04	
2	-0.0076	
3	-0.0019	
4	0.0058	
5	0.0044	
6	-0.0066	
7	-0.0126	
8	0.0018	
9	0.0039	
10	0.0027	
11	-0.0110	
12	-0.0162	

oo_.endo_simul <8x150 double>

	1	2	3	4	5	6	7	8	9	10
1	-2.5638	-2.5715	-2.5752	-2.5697	-2.5632	-2.5679	-2.5816	-2.5827	-2.5778	-2.5727
2	-3.2825	-3.2902	-3.2939	-3.2884	-3.2820	-3.2866	-3.3003	-3.3014	-3.2966	-3.2914
3	-2.1668	-2.1745	-2.1782	-2.1727	-2.1662	-2.1709	-2.1846	-2.1857	-2.1808	-2.1757
4	-3.2825	-3.2902	-3.2939	-3.2884	-3.2820	-3.2866	-3.3003	-3.3014	-3.2966	-3.2914
5	-1.6094	-1.6094	-1.6094	-1.6094	-1.6094	-1.6094	-1.6094	-1.6094	-1.6094	-1.6094
6	0.0158	0.0084	0.0124	0.0216	0.0226	0.0115	0.0024	0.0151	0.0210	0.0213
7	-0.9623	-0.9700	-0.9737	-0.9682	-0.9618	-0.9664	-0.9801	-0.9812	-0.9763	-0.9712
8	-2.8711e-04	-0.0079	-0.0090	-0.0023	0.0023	-0.0045	-0.0166	-0.0132	-0.0080	-0.0044
9										

Fig. 2.16 Simulation of the endogenous variable. (**Note:** This structure is obtained from "Long_Plosser_Dynare_nolineal_log.mod")

function created by Johannes Pfeifer[6] will be used, which can be downloaded from the Web. The steps to apply this function are described below:

- First of all, the function "get_simul_replications.m" has to be present in the directory where the .mod file is located.
- In the mod file, after the command `stoch_simul` the following should be placed:

  ```
  [sim_array]=get_simul_replications(M_,options_);
  y_sim=squeeze(sim_array(strmatch('y',M_.endo_names,'exact'),:,:));
  k_sim=squeeze(sim_array(strmatch('k',M_.endo_names,'exact'),:,:));
  ```

  The first line calls the function "get_simul_replications.m" to convert the binary file into a Matlab array variable called "sim_array," which is stored in the *workspace*. The second line creates the variable "y_sim," which contains the simulation of production; that is, it contains the 300 simulations (rows) of 100 periods (columns). This same line of code can be applied to each variable. The result is a matrix, per variable, of 300 rows with 100 columns. The third line, the code, is the same as the second, only for capital.

  Figure 2.17 shows six simulations of the set of 300 for capital and output.

[6] https://github.com/JohannesPfeifer/DSGE_mod/blob/master/Hansen_1985/get_simul_replications.m

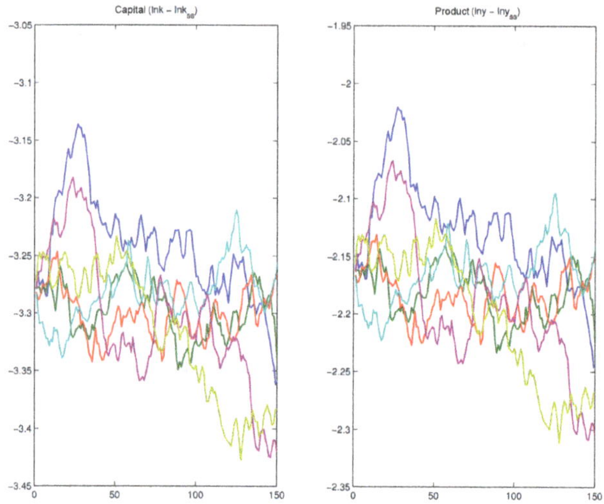

Fig. 2.17 Six simulations of capital and output. (**Note:** This structure is obtained from "Long_Plosser_Dynare_nolineal_log.mod" and the code "simulacion_filtrohp.m")

2.4.12 Calculation of Moments

Table 2.29 shows the moments calculated by Dynare for the four ways of writing the model in Dynare. A first observation is that the moments are similar when the variables have the same nature; that is, if the variables are in levels, then it does not matter if the model written in Dynare was nonlinear or linearized since the moments are similar. The same is concluded for the variables in logarithms. A second observation is that the moments between the model with the variables in levels and the model with the variables in logarithms are different, which is consistent with what is expected.

Where Does Dynare Store the Moments?

Dynare stores the mean, variance–covariance matrix, and autocorrelations within the oo_ structure. As you can see in Fig. 2.14, the average is stored in the variable "mean," the covariance matrix in the variable "var," and the autocorrelation matrix in "autocorr."

2.4.13 HP Filter

Table 2.29 shows the moments of the endogenous variables. However, it does not show the moments of their cyclical component, which is necessary to compare with the stylized facts and evaluate the model's explanatory power. To obtain the

Table 2.29 Theoretical moments

Nonlinear Model							
Variables in levels				Variables in logarithms			
Variable	Mean	Des. Std.	Variance	Variable	Mean	Des. Est.	Variance
c	0.077	0.004	0	cc	−2.564	0.053	0.0028
i	0.038	0.002	0	ii	−3.282	0.053	0.0028
y	0.115	0.006	0	yy	−2.167	0.053	0.0028
k	0.038	0.002	0	kk	−3.282	0.053	0.0028
h	0.200	0	0	hh	−1.609	0	0
r	1.016	0.008	0.0001	rr	0.016	0.008	0.0001
w	0.382	0.020	0.0004	w w	−0.962	0.053	0.0028
a	1	0.035	0.0012	aa	0	0.035	0.0012
Linear model							
Variables in levels				Variables in logarithms			
Variable	Mean	Des. Std.	Variance	Variable	Mean	Des. Est.	Variance
ct	0.077	0.004	0	ch	−2.564	0.053	0.0028
it	0.038	0.002	0	ih	−3.282	0.053	0.0028
yt	0.115	0.006	0	yh	−2.167	0.053	0.0028
kt	0.038	0.002	0	kh	−3.282	0.053	0.0028
ht	0.200	0	0	hh	−1.609	0	0
rt	1.016	0.008	0.0001	rh	0.016	0.008	0.0001
wt	0.382	0.020	0.0004	wh	−0.962	0.053	0.0028
at	1	0.035	0.0012	ah	0	0.035	0.0012

cyclical component, a filter must be applied; that is, a technique that breaks down the variable into its two components: trend and cycle. The HP filter is usually applied to accomplish this task, which Dynare has enabled as an option of stoch_simul. The code to use the HP filter is as follows:

stoch_simul(order=1, hp_filter= lambda)

where "lambda" is equal to 1600 for quarterly data (for more details, see Table 2.9). This code gives the moments of the cyclical component in Matlab's *command window*, shown in Table 2.30. It is worth mentioning that Dynare does not display the cyclical component as a time series.

Given the disadvantage that Dynare does not calculate the cyclical component of the series, Matlab has a function called "hpfilter.m," which provides the trend and cyclical component of the series. The use of this function is shown below:

```
[trend_k,cycle_k] =hpfilter(kk_sim(:,1),1600);
```

The "hpfilter.m" function requires two inputs. The first is the series or set of series to which you want to apply the filter; in this case, it is the first capital simulation "kk_sim(:,1)." The second is the smoothing parameter, which depends on the frequency of the data (which is reflected in the calibration). The parameter takes the value of 14400 for monthly data, 1600 for quarterly data, and 100 for

Table 2.30 Theoretical moments (HP filter)

Theoretical moments (HP filter, λ=1600)			
Variable	Mean	Des. Est.	Variance
cc	−2.5635	0.0126	0.0002
ii	−3.2822	0.0126	0.0002
yy	−2.1665	0.0126	0.0002
kk	−3.2822	0.0126	0.0002
hh	−1.6094	0.0000	0.0000
rr	0.0161	0.0072	0.0001
ww	−0.962	0.0126	0.0002
aa	0.000	0.0094	0.0001

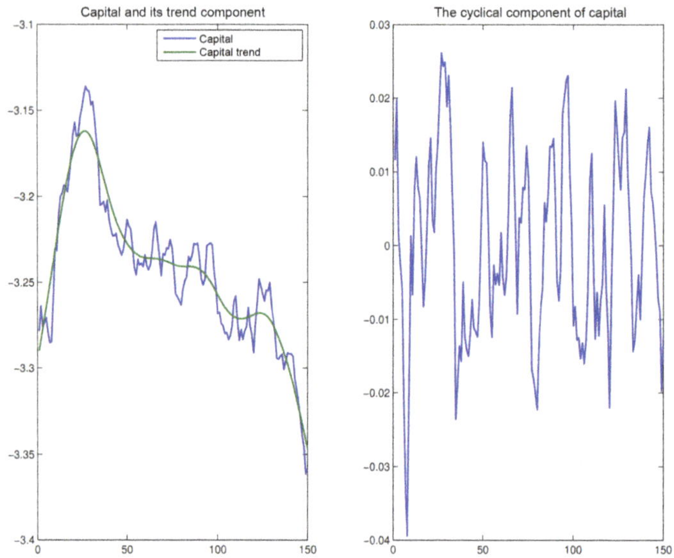

Fig. 2.18 Cyclical and trend components of capital. (**Note:** This structure is obtained from "Long_Plosser_Dynare_nolineal_log.mod" and the code "simulacion_filtrohp.m")

annual data. In this particular case, we are considering quarterly data; therefore, 1600 is placed.

Likewise, this function delivers two results: The first is the trend component of the series (trend_k), and the second is the cyclical component (cycle_k). Figure 2.18 shows the cyclical and trend components of the capital derived from the application of the HP filter.

2.5 Codes

Table 2.31 indicates the codes used in this chapter.

Table 2.31 Codes in Matlab and Dynare

Codes	Description
Matlab	
irfs_nonlinear_log.m	This *m-file* illustrates that the graphs for the impulse-response function obtained from Dynare can be improved through Matlab codes
simulation_hpfilter.m	This *m-file* applies the HP filter to the simulated series of the model
aux_irfs_nonlinear_log.m	This *m-file* plots the impulse-response functions via a loop
aux_analysis_sensitivity.m	This *m-file* describes the code that can be written at the end of a .mod file to perform sensitivity analysis, that is, to obtain the impulse-response functions for different values of the parameters
Dynare	
Long_Plosser_Dynare_nolinear_niv.mod	This .mod contains the nonlinear equations with the variables in levels of Long and Plosser (1983)'s model
Long_Plosser_Dynare_nolinear_log.mod	This .mod contains the nonlinear equations with the variables in logarithms of Long and Plosser (1983)'s model. This code is used in Chapters 2 and 3. In Chapter 2, this code is used to instantiate Dynare commands. Chapter 3 uses it to obtain the solution of the model and the IRFs
Long_Plosser_Dynare_linear_niv.mod	Considers the linear model with the variables in levels of Long and Plosser (1983)'s model
Long_Plosser_Dynare_linear_log.mod	Considers the linear model with the variables in logarithm of Long and Plosser (1983)'s model

2.6 Summary

Unlike the conventional macroeconomic models, the system of nonlinear equations that describes the behavior of the endogenous variables of the DSGE models rarely has an analytical solution. Given that, a natural question is whether any *software* equips the profession with computational tools that facilitate the solution of these models without requiring high programming knowledge.

In this chapter, we have introduced *Dynare*, a preprocessor associated with Matlab that provides a set of computational tools to solve DSGE models. The main advantage of using Dynare is that it does not require the user to have advanced knowledge of the programming language underlying Matlab, which makes it highly accessible.

We start explaining the structure of the .mod file and the files created by Dynare. We then describe step by step how to introduce the nonlinear equations that describe the DSGE model into a .mod file, how to calculate the initial values of the model, and how to obtain the steady state. Likewise, we detail how to evaluate the model with the Blanchard–Kahn method, calculate the solution (policy and state function), and simulate the model when we have an aggregate *shock*. We complement this analysis by explaining how to perform the sensitivity analysis of the model.

Finally, to illustrate these steps, we use the Long and Plosser (1983)'s model as an example. In particular, we have paid attention to how to enter the lines of code in each step, the *outputs* that Dynare gives us, and their location in the *workspace*. Finally, the codes (*m-file* and *mod-file*) used in this chapter are described to facilitate the replication of the model by the reader.

Chapter 3
RBC Model with Analytical Solution

3.1 Introduction

The goal of this chapter is to illustrate in depth each of the steps in the construction of an RBC model. With this end in mind, studying a simple model (*toy model*) is an advantage. To do this, this chapter is based on the model developed by Long and Plosser (1983) and Plosser (1989).

The model proposed by Long and Plosser (1983) seeks to capture the dynamics of various economic sectors and their behaviors among themselves in the face of a productivity *shock*. On the other hand, the model proposed by Plosser (1989) is a single-sector model. Both models have two underlying assumptions. The first is that goods are assumed to be perishable and last for a single period; that is, the capital is fully depreciated. The second assumes that preferences are additive and are expressed as the logarithm of consumption and the logarithm of leisure.

These two assumptions have important effects on the solution of the model. First, it allows the model to be solved analytically; that is, an exact solution to *hand and paper* can be found. The second is that the labor policy function suggests that this variable does not react to capital nor the *shock* of productivity; that is, it always remains in a steady state. This is because the effect of the interest rate on consumption is zero, which means the substitution and income effects perfectly offset each other.

3.2 Model Construction

This model is based on the work of Long and Plosser (1983) and Plosser (1989) and has an analytical solution; that is, it can be solved directly by means of algebraic operations. This is due to two assumptions: total depreciation and logarithmic utility (in consumption and leisure). In addition, the model assumes that there are two

H. Galindo Gil et al., *Dynamic Stochastic General Equilibrium Models*, Springer Texts in Business and Economics, https://doi.org/10.1007/978-3-031-58105-2_3

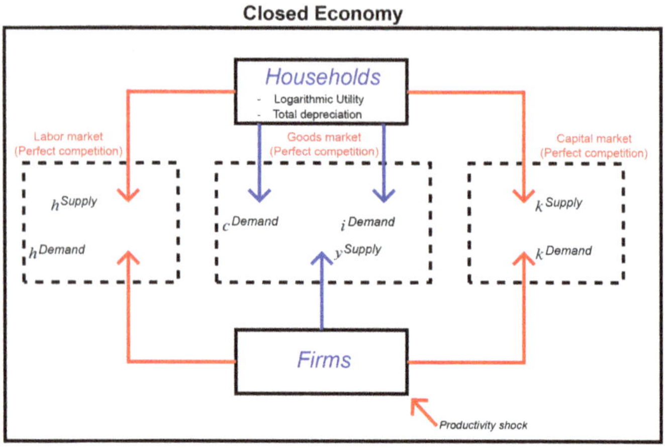

Fig. 3.1 Long and Plosser model (1983, 1989)

economic agents in the economy (households and firms), of which the households own the capital and the firms develop in an environment of perfect competition, both in the goods market and in that of factors.

On the other hand, the economy is assumed to be closed, which implies that saving equals investment. Finally, in this economy, the only source of uncertainty comes from the supply side, where, in particular, a productivity *shock* is assumed. Figure 3.1 outlines the interaction between households, firms, and the markets in which they participate.

3.2.1 Utility Function

Before describing the model in detail, it is important to understand the role of the utility function in the construction of the general equilibrium model. King et al. (1988a) impose two restrictions on preferences (utility function) that allow the steady state to be compatible with an optimal competitive equilibrium:

- The intertemporal substitution elasticity of consumption must be invariant at the scale of consumption.
- The income and substitution effects associated with growth in labor productivity should not alter labor supply.

The utility function that satisfies these two restrictions is:

$$u(c,l) = \begin{cases} \left[\frac{1}{1-\sigma}c^{1-\sigma}\right]v(l), & \text{si } \sigma > 0 \text{ y } \sigma \neq 1 \\ ln(c) + v(l), & \text{si } \sigma = 1 \end{cases}$$

where c is consumption, and l is leisure; σ is the elasticity of substitution of consumption (consumption is scale-invariant) and $v(l)$ is a function of leisure. According to King et al. (1988a), a particular case of this utility function is when $v(l) = \theta ln(l)$:

$$u(c, l) = ln(c) + \theta ln(l) \tag{3.1}$$

In addition, other utility functions appear in the literature on RBC models, in which it is considered that l_t is leisure, h_t is work, and that the following relationship holds between them: $l_t + h_t = 1$, where the time available by the household, which is usually 24 hours, has been normalized to 1. Other usual utility functions in the existing literature are mentioned below:

- Hansen (1985):

$$u(c_t, l_t) = ln(c_t) + Bl_t \tag{3.2}$$

- Greenwood et al. (1988):

$$u(c_t, h_t) = \frac{1}{1-\gamma}\left[\left(c_t - \frac{h_t^{1+\theta}}{1+\theta}\right)^{1-\gamma} - 1\right] \tag{3.3}$$

- Campbell (1994): fixed labor (used in Chap. 4)

$$u(c_t, h_t) = \frac{c_t^{1-\gamma}}{1-\gamma} \tag{3.4}$$

- Campbell (1994): variable labor (used in Chap. 5)

$$u(c_t, h_t) = ln(c_t) + \theta\frac{(1-h_t)^{1-\gamma_n}}{1-\gamma_n} \tag{3.5}$$

- Long and Plosser (1983) and Plosser (1989):

$$u(c_t, h_t) = ln(c_t) + \theta ln(1 - h_t) \tag{3.6}$$

The utility function of equation (3.6) is obtained by considering $\gamma_n = 1$ in the utility function (3.5). This is the utility function that Long and Plosser (1983) consider in their model. Two ideas stand out: the first is that θ is the share of leisure in all the time available to the representative household. The second is that each utility function has a different level of **Frisch elasticity**[1] and the elasticity of intertemporal substitution of consumption (ESI_c).

3.2.2 Households

One of the main assumptions of the RBC models is that the households present in the economy are all identical. In other words, their preferences and restrictions are similar. This assumption makes it possible to analyze the behavior of the households through the study of a representative agent (a household that represents all of them) and allows for the aggregation of the households in a simple way. In the Long and Plosser model, the representative agent assumption is considered, which maximizes a discounted utility function:

$$\underset{\{c_t,h_t,k_{t+1}\}_{t=0}^{\infty}}{\text{Max}} \quad E_0 \sum_{t=0}^{\infty} \beta^t u(c_t, h_t) \tag{3.7}$$

where c_t is the consumption of the period t and β is the discount factor, which is expressed as follows:

$$\beta = \frac{1}{1+\rho}$$

Here, ρ reflects the impatience of the representative agent. The more impatient the household, the larger ρ will be; therefore, β will be smaller. That is, the individual values future utilities less. For instance, $\rho = 0$ means that the household is totally patient and, therefore, $\beta = 1$, indicating that the household places the same value on utility today as tomorrow's utility. This analysis is better appreciated in Table 3.1 considering that the present value of the utility function is expressed as follows:

$$\sum_{t=0}^{\infty} \beta^t u(c_t, h_t) = u(c_0, h_0) + \beta u(c_1, h_1) + \beta^2 u(c_2, h_2) + \beta^3 u(c_3, h_3) \ldots$$

Considering the functional form of the instantaneous utility function according to equation (3.6), the objective function to be maximized would be:

$$\underset{\{c_t,h_t,k_{t+1}\}_{t=0}^{\infty}}{\text{Max}} \quad E_0 \sum_{t=0}^{\infty} \beta^t \left(ln(c_t) + \theta ln(1-h_t)\right)$$

[1] The Frisch elasticity is the elasticity of labor supply holding the income effect constant. This elasticity will be analyzed in greater detail in Chap. 5.

Table 3.1 Effect of impatience on discount factor

Impatience ρ	Effect on β	$\sum_{t=0}^{\infty} \beta^t u(c_t, h_t)$	Value
Zero impatience $\rho = 0$	$\beta = 1$	$u(c_0, h_0) + u(c_1, h_1) + u(c_2, h_2) + \ldots$	The household gives the same value to utility over time
Little impatience $\rho = 1$	$\beta = 1/2$	$u(c_0, h_0) + \frac{1}{2}u(c_1, h_1) + \frac{1}{4}u(c_2, h_2) + \ldots$	The household gives more value to the utility today than in the future: the value to the utility today is 1, while the value to the utility at $t = 1$ is 0.5, and at $t = 2$ it is 0.25
Greater impatience $\rho = 2$	$\beta = 1/3$	$u(c_0, h_0) + \frac{1}{3}u(c_1, h_1) + \frac{1}{9}u(c_2, h_2) + \ldots$	The household gives more value to today's utility than in the future: the value to today's utility is 1, while tomorrow's utility is valued at 0.33, and in "$t = 2$" it is 0.11
Total impatience $\rho = \infty$	$\beta = 0$	$u(c_0, h_0) + 0u(c_1, h_1) + 0u(c_2, h_2) + \ldots$	The individual only values the current consumption. He/she does not value anything to consume in the future

The maximization of this objective function is subject to two constraints: the budget constraint and the law of motion of capital, which are described below.

Budget constraint On the one hand, the household receives its income from renting capital k_t to firms at a real interest rate r_t. In addition, households are part of the labor market where they offer labor h_t at a real wage w_t. Both revenues are observed in each period and are equal to $r_t k_t + w_t h_t$.

On the other hand, the household allocates its income to consumer goods c_t and savings which, in a closed economy, equals investment i_t. Therefore, joining income and expenses, the budget constraint of the representative household is:

$$c_t + i_t = r_t k_t + w_t h_t \tag{3.8}$$

Law of movement of capital From national accounts, it is known that net investment is equal to gross investment minus depreciation:

$$\mathrm{I}_{\text{net}} = \mathrm{I}_{\text{gross}} - \text{Depreciation} \tag{3.9}$$

$$k_{t+1} - k_t = i_t - \delta k_t$$

$$k_{t+1} = (1 - \delta)k_t + i_t \tag{3.10}$$

Equation (3.10) is known as the law of motion of capital, which describes the behavior of the *stock* of capital. It is worth mentioning that this equation assumes that the *stock* of capital depreciates by a percentage δ (usually 2.5% quarterly) in each period. However, Long and Plosser (1983) assumed that the depreciation rate is full ($\delta = 1$), that is, that the capital in each period is fully depreciated in that same period in such a way that there is no capital left for the next (this under the assumption that all *commodities* are perishable). Although the assumption is highly unrealistic, it helps to remove certain nonlinearities from the system of equations. With this assumption in mind, equation (3.10) becomes:

$$k_{t+1} = i_t \tag{3.11}$$

The capital in $t+1$ is the investment made in "t." Since there is no *stock* of capital, capital becomes a flow and is always equal to new goods in each period. Introducing equation (3.11) in the budget constraint, equation (3.8), we have:

$$c_t + k_{t+1} = r_t k_t + w_t h_t \tag{3.12}$$

So, the optimization problem of the household is:

$$\underset{\{c_t, h_t, k_{t+1}\}_{t=0}^{\infty}}{\text{Max}} \quad E_0 \sum_{t=0}^{\infty} \beta^t \left(ln(c_t) + \theta ln(1 - h_t) \right)$$

subject to:

$$c_t + k_{t+1} = r_t k_t + w_t h_t$$

Building the Lagrange function:

$$\mathcal{L} = E_0 \sum_{t=0}^{\infty} \beta^t \left[u(c_t, h_t) + \lambda_t \left(r_t k_t + w_t h_t - (c_t + k_{t+1}) \right) \right]$$

where the extended version of the Lagrange function can be expressed as follows:

$$\begin{aligned}
\mathcal{L} = E_0 \Big\{ & \beta^0 \left[u(c_0, h_0) + \lambda_0 \left(r_0 k_0 + w_0 h_0 - (c_0 + k_1) \right) \right] + \\
& \beta^1 \left[u(c_1, h_1) + \lambda_1 \left(r_1 k_1 + w_1 h_1 - (c_1 + k_2) \right) \right] + \\
& \beta^2 \left[u(c_2, h_2) + \lambda_2 \left(r_2 k_2 + w_2 h_2 - (c_2 + k_3) \right) \right] + \\
& \beta^3 \left[u(c_3, h_3) + \lambda_3 \left(r_3 k_3 + w_3 h_3 - (c_3 + k_4) \right) \right] + \\
& \beta^4 \left[u(c_4, h_4) + \lambda_4 \left(r_4 k_4 + w_4 h_4 - (c_4 + k_5) \right) \right] + \\
& \ldots + \\
& \beta^t \left[u(c_t, h_t) + \lambda_t \left(r_t k_t + w_t h_t - (c_t + k_{t+1}) \right) \right] + \\
& \beta^{t+1} \left[u(c_{t+1}, h_{t+1}) + \lambda_{t+1} \left(r_{t+1} k_{t+1} + w_{t+1} h_{t+1} - (c_{t+1} + k_{t+2}) \right) \right] +
\end{aligned}$$

$$\ldots +$$
$$\ldots \Big\}$$

The first-order conditions, in period "t," are:

$$\frac{\partial \mathcal{L}}{\partial c_t} = 0 \Longrightarrow E_0 \Big\{ \beta^t \big[u_{c_t} + \lambda_t(-1) \big] \Big\} = 0$$

$$u_{c_t} = \lambda_t \tag{3.13}$$

$$\frac{\partial \mathcal{L}}{\partial h_t} = 0 \Longrightarrow E_0 \Big\{ \beta^t \big[u_{h_t} + \lambda_t(w_t) \big] \Big\} = 0$$

$$u_{h_t} = -\lambda_t w_t \tag{3.14}$$

Substituting equation (3.13) in equation (3.14), the labor supply is obtained:

$$\begin{aligned} u_{h_t} &= -\lambda_t w_t \\ -\frac{\theta}{1-h_t} &= -\frac{1}{c_t} w_t \\ \frac{\theta}{1-h_t} &= \frac{w_t}{c_t} \end{aligned} \tag{3.15}$$

On the other hand, the first-order condition with respect to capital k_{t+1} is:

$$\frac{\partial \mathcal{L}}{\partial k_{t+1}} = 0 \Longrightarrow E_0 \Big\{ \beta^t \big[\lambda_t(-1) \big] + \beta^{t+1} \big[\lambda_{t+1}(r_{t+1}) \big] \Big\} = 0$$

$$\lambda_t = \beta E_t \lambda_{t+1}(r_{t+1}) \tag{3.16}$$

Substituting equation (3.13) into equation (3.16) we get the Euler equation:

$$\begin{aligned} u_{c_t} &= \beta E_t u_{c_{t+1}}(r_{t+1}) \\ \frac{1}{c_t} &= \beta E_t \frac{1}{c_{t+1}}(r_{t+1}) \end{aligned} \tag{3.17}$$

3.2.3 Firms

Production function It is assumed that there is only one final good in the economy and it is produced by a neoclassical production function $f(a_t, k_t, h_t)$.

The Cobb-Douglas production function meets the characteristics of a neoclassical function and describes a country's production reasonably well:

$$y_t = f(a_t, k_t, h_t) = a_t k_t^{1-\alpha} h_t^{\alpha} \tag{3.18}$$

where k_t is the default capital *stock* (chosen in period "t−1") and h_t is the labor input. Also, the variable a_t refers to productivity, which is assumed to behave stochastically and is expressed by AR(1).

An important feature of the Cobb-Douglas function is that the share of each factor in total income is constant and equal to the exponents of each factor in the production function. As is known in perfect competition (a key assumption in RBC models), the rental of capital is equal to the marginal productivity of capital; that is: $r_t = (1-\alpha)\frac{y_t}{k_t}$. Similarly for work: $w_t = \alpha\frac{y_t}{h_t}$.

The income destined for the payment of capital and labor is $r_t k_t$ and $w_t h_t$, respectively. Considering that production represents all the income of a country, then the fraction of the income allocated to the payment of capital with respect to the total income is $r_t k_t / y_t$:

$$\frac{r_t k_t}{y_t} = (1-\alpha)\frac{y_t}{k_t}\frac{k_t}{y_t} = (1-\alpha) \tag{3.19}$$

In the same way, calculating the proportion of the total income oriented to the payment of work:

$$\frac{w_t h_t}{y_t} = \alpha\frac{y_t}{h_t}\frac{h_t}{y_t} = \alpha \tag{3.20}$$

Equations (3.19) and (3.20) indicate that capital's income share is equal to "1 − α," and labor's income share is "α." Both parameters are constant and equal to the exponents of the factors in the production function. This suggests that the value of "α" could be obtained through the national accounts, which would be, in terms of the RBC models, a calibration of the parameter α. Chapter 1 shows that the average share of labor in national income between 1948 and 2014 for the North American economy is equal to 66.3%. This suggests that α could take that value.

Characteristics of the neoclassical production function

For a production function $f(a_t, k_t, h_t)$ to be considered neoclassical, it must have three characteristics (Barro et al. 2009):

1. **Constant returns to scale:** the function $f(a_t, k_t, h_t)$ must show constant returns to scale; that is, if we multiply capital and labor by a constant λ, the product is multiplied by that same constant.

(continued)

$$f(a_t, \lambda k_t, \lambda h_t) = \lambda f(a_t, k_t, h_t) \tag{3.21}$$

2. **Positive and diminishing returns:** The neoclassical production function exhibit positive and diminishing marginal productivity for each production factor.

$$\text{Increasing returns}: \frac{\partial f(\cdot)}{\partial k_t} > 0, \quad \frac{\partial f(\cdot)}{\partial h_t} > 0$$

$$\text{Diminishing returns}: \frac{\partial^2 f(\cdot)}{\partial k_t^2} < 0, \quad \frac{\partial^2 f(\cdot)}{\partial h_t^2} < 0$$

3. **Inada conditions:** These conditions state that the marginal product of capital approaches infinity as capital approaches zero and approaches zero as capital approaches infinity. The same condition holds for labor. In mathematical terms, these conditions are expressed as:

$$\text{Capital}: \operatorname*{Lim}_{k_t \to 0}\left(\frac{\partial f(\cdot)}{\partial k_t}\right) = \infty, \quad \operatorname*{Lim}_{k_t \to \infty}\left(\frac{\partial f(\cdot)}{\partial k_t}\right) = 0$$

$$\text{Labor}: \operatorname*{Lim}_{h_t \to 0}\left(\frac{\partial f(\cdot)}{\partial h_t}\right) = \infty, \quad \operatorname*{Lim}_{h_t \to \infty}\left(\frac{\partial f(\cdot)}{\partial h_t}\right) = 0$$

Optimization Firms operate in a context of perfect competition in the goods market and the factor market (labor and capital). They maximize their profit function considering their technology, which is assumed to have the Cobb-Douglas functional form. In this model, firms decide how much capital to rent and how much labor (in hours) to hire. Therefore, the two optimization variables are capital k_t and labor h_t.

$$\operatorname*{Max}_{\{k_t, h_t\}_{t=0}^{\infty}} \Pi_t = y_t - (r_t k_t + w_t h_t)$$

Subject to production function:

$$y_t = a_t k_t^{1-\alpha} h_t^{\alpha} \tag{3.22}$$

It is worth mentioning that since the firm does not face a dynamic constraint, it maximizes profits at each moment. Therefore, the optimization problem is static. To solve this problem, we introduce the production function in the objective function:

$$\operatorname*{Max}_{\{k_t, h_t\}_{t=0}^{\infty}} \Pi_t = a_t k_t^{1-\alpha} h_t^{\alpha} - (r_t k_t + w_t h_t) \tag{3.23}$$

Deriving this expression, equation (3.23), with respect to capital k_t:

$$\frac{\partial \Pi}{\partial k_t} = 0 \Longrightarrow \frac{\partial (a_t k_t^{1-\alpha} h_t^{\alpha} - r_t k_t)}{\partial k_t} = 0 \Longrightarrow (1-\alpha) a_t {k_t}^{-\alpha} {h_t}^{\alpha} - r_t = 0$$

From this first-order condition, the demand for capital is obtained:

$$r_t = (1-\alpha) a_t \left[\frac{h_t}{k_t} \right]^{\alpha}$$

$$r_t = (1-\alpha) a_t \left[\frac{h_t^{\alpha}}{k_t^{\alpha}} \right]$$

$$r_t = (1-\alpha) a_t h_t^{\alpha} k_t^{-\alpha} \frac{k_t}{k_t}$$

$$r_t = (1-\alpha) a_t h_t^{\alpha} k_t^{1-\alpha} \frac{1}{k_t}$$

$$r_t = (1-\alpha) \frac{y_t}{k_t} \tag{3.24}$$

Differentiating equation (3.23) with respect to work h_t:

$$\frac{\partial \Pi}{\partial h_t} = 0 \Longrightarrow \frac{\partial (a_t k_t^{1-\alpha} h_t^{\alpha} - r_t k_t - w_t h_t)}{\partial h_t} = 0 \Longrightarrow \alpha a_t {k_t}^{1-\alpha} {h_t}^{\alpha-1} - w_t = 0$$

From this first-order condition we obtain the labor demand:

$$w_t = \alpha a_t \left[\frac{k_t}{h_t} \right]^{1-\alpha}$$

$$w_t = \alpha a_t \left[\frac{k_t^{1-\alpha}}{h_t^{1-\alpha}} \right]$$

$$w_t = \alpha a_t \frac{k_t^{1-\alpha} h_t^{\alpha}}{h_t}$$

$$w_t = \alpha \frac{y_t}{h_t} \tag{3.25}$$

3.2.4 *Market Equilibrium and Definition of shock*

To close the model, it is necessary to define the equilibrium in the goods market:

$$y_t = c_t + i_t \tag{3.26}$$

Table 3.2 Nonlinear system of equations of the model

Agent	Equations	Description
Household	$\frac{1}{c_t} = \beta E_t\left[\frac{1}{c_{t+1}} r_{t+1}\right]$	Euler equation
	$k_{t+1} = i_t$	Law of movement of capital
	$\frac{\theta}{1-h_t} = \frac{w_t}{c_t}$	Labor supply
Firm	$y_t = a_t k_t^{1-\alpha} h_t^{\alpha}$	Production function
	$r_t = (1-\alpha)\frac{y_t}{k_t}$	Capital demand
	$w_t = \alpha \frac{y_t}{h_t}$	Labor demand
Equilibrium	$y_t = c_t + i_t$	Goods market equilibrium
Shock	$lna_t = \phi lna_{t-1} + \epsilon_t$	Productivity *shock*

In addition, it is necessary to define the behavior of productivity:

$$lna_t = \phi lna_{t-1} + \epsilon_t \tag{3.27}$$

It is worth mentioning that the *shock* of productivity ϵ_t behaves like a normal distribution with zero mean and constant variance: $\epsilon_t \sim N(0, \sigma_\epsilon^2)$.

3.2.5 *Principal Equations*

The main equations of the model are summarized in Table 3.2:

It is important to mention that the system of equations is made up of the following:

(1) the capital market: the supply of capital represented by the law of movement of capital and the demand for capital;
(2) the labor market: labor supply and labor demand;
(3) the goods market: the supply of goods represented by the production function, the demand for consumption represented by the Euler equation, and the investment demand which is represented by the law of movement of capital. Likewise, this market requires that its equilibrium be made explicit through the equation $y_t = c_t + i_t$; and finally,
(4) the *shock* of productivity. All these equations are described in Table 3.2. Likewise, it is important to verify that the number of variables equals the number of equations. In this case, there are eight variables (y_t, c_t, i_t, k_t, h_t, r_t, w_t, and a_t) and eight equations.

3.3 Calibration

Calibration can be understood as a way of *estimation by simulation* (Hoover 1995). This procedure consists of assigning values to the model parameters and then comparing the main characteristics of the simulated variables of the calibrated

Table 3.3 Calibration

Parameter	Remark
$\alpha = 0.667$	Long-run share of labor in national income
$\theta = 3.968$	Calibrated so that the steady-state work is equal to 20%
$\phi = 0.979$	Persistence of the *shock*
$\beta = 0.984$	Discount factor
$\sigma_e = 0.0072$	Standard deviation of the *shock* of productivity

model with those from the data. In this chapter, as in Chap. 2, the calibration is based on King and Rebelo (1999), whose values are shown in Table 3.3.

As Cooley and Prescott (1995) mention, since the underlying structure of RBC models is a neoclassical growth model, the choice of parameter values (calibration) and functional forms (for example, utility function and the law of movement of capital) should ensure that the economic model shows balanced growth.[2]

3.4 Steady State

The steady state is known as a long-run equilibrium where $\Delta x_t = 0$ (for all model variables) and the productivity *shock* (ε_t) takes its average value ($= 0$). Furthermore, given the productivity equation of motion, its steady-state value is $a = 1$. Likewise, expectations disappear; therefore, it is known as a non-stochastic solution. The goal is to find the steady-state value as a function of the model parameters. To this end, it is important to consider the following three criteria. First, place all the model equations in a steady state; that is, eliminate temporality and expectations. Second, use the variables that only depend on the model parameters to find the steady state of the other variables. Third, try to solve the system of equations in terms of ratios; for example, instead of searching for the value of k_{ss} (steady-state capital), one could search for the value of the ratio y_{ss}/k_{ss}. It is worth mentioning that finding the steady state is a previous step to model log-linearization. For Euler's equation, we have the following:

[2] Balanced growth (*balanced growth*) is understood as the situation in which all sectors of an economy growing at the same constant rate. This is similar to the definition of "steady-state growth" (*steady-state growth*), which indicates the situation in which output, capital, labor, and consumption change at the same rate. Since the growth rate of capital depends on savings, steady-state growth requires that the savings function be stable: borrowing policy can promote stability by keeping the interest rate constant. If the growth rate is equal to zero, then the economy is said to be in a steady state (*stationary state or steady state*). The latter is a theoretical state of the economy in which exactly what is produced is consumed and replaces what is consumed at the end of the period. Another way to understand it is when an economy has a constant population size and *stock* of capital; that is, the investment is only made to maintain the existing *stock* of capital; in other words, its *steady-state growth* is equal to zero (Lau et al. 2002).

$$
\begin{aligned}
\frac{1}{c_t} &= \beta E_t \frac{1}{c_{t+1}} r_{t+1} \\
\frac{1}{c_{ss}} &= \beta E_t \frac{1}{c_{ss}} r_{ss} \\
1 &= \beta r_{ss} \\
r_{ss} &= \frac{1}{\beta}
\end{aligned} \tag{3.28}
$$

In the same way for the law of motion of capital:

$$
\begin{aligned}
k_{t+1} &= i_t \\
k_{ss} &= i_{ss}
\end{aligned} \tag{3.29}
$$

For the labor supply:

$$
\begin{aligned}
\frac{\theta}{1-h_t} &= \frac{w_t}{c_t} \\
\frac{\theta}{1-h_{ss}} &= \frac{w_{ss}}{c_{ss}}
\end{aligned} \tag{3.30}
$$

for the production function:

$$
\begin{aligned}
y_t &= a_t k_t^{1-\alpha} h_t^{\alpha} \\
y_{ss} &= a_{ss} k_{ss}^{1-\alpha} h_{ss}^{\alpha}
\end{aligned} \tag{3.31}
$$

For the demand for capital:

$$
\begin{aligned}
r_t &= (1-\alpha)\frac{y_t}{k_t} \\
r_{ss} &= (1-\alpha)\frac{y_{ss}}{k_{ss}}
\end{aligned} \tag{3.32}
$$

Considering equation (3.28) in equation (3.32), we have the ratio $\frac{y_{ss}}{k_{ss}}$ as a function of model parameters:

$$
\begin{aligned}
r_{ss} &= (1-\alpha)\frac{y_{ss}}{k_{ss}} \\
\frac{1}{\beta} &= (1-\alpha)\frac{y_{ss}}{k_{ss}} \\
\frac{y_{ss}}{k_{ss}} &= \frac{1}{\beta(1-\alpha)}
\end{aligned} \tag{3.33}
$$

It is a good strategy to find ratios, especially when the denominator is capital. This allows each variable to depend on capital in a steady state, which, by finding its value, allows finding the values of the remaining variables.

For labor demand:

$$w_t = \alpha \frac{y_t}{h_t}$$

$$w_{ss} = \alpha \frac{y_{ss}}{h_{ss}} \tag{3.34}$$

For the equilibrium equation in the goods market:

$$y_t = c_t + i_t$$

$$y_{ss} = c_{ss} + i_{ss} \tag{3.35}$$

But from equation (3.29) it is known that: $k_{ss} = i_{ss}$. Then considering this equality in equation (3.35), we have:

$$\begin{aligned} y_{ss} &= c_{ss} + i_{ss} \\ y_{ss} &= c_{ss} + k_{ss} \\ \frac{y_{ss}}{k_{ss}} &= \frac{c_{ss}}{k_{ss}} + 1 \\ \frac{c_{ss}}{k_{ss}} &= \frac{y_{ss}}{k_{ss}} - 1 \\ \frac{c_{ss}}{k_{ss}} &= \frac{1}{\beta(1-\alpha)} - 1 \end{aligned} \tag{3.36}$$

Finally, for the productivity behavior equation:

$$\begin{aligned} lna_t &= \phi lna_{t-1} + \epsilon_t \\ lna_{ss} &= \phi lna_{ss} + \underbrace{\epsilon_{ss}}_{=0(\text{valor de su media})} \\ lna_{ss} &= \phi lna_{ss} \\ ln(a_{ss}) &= ln(a_{ss}^{\phi}) \\ a_{ss} &= a_{ss}^{\phi} \end{aligned} \tag{3.37}$$

Two values of a_{ss} could solve this last equation (3.37): $a_{ss} = 1$ or $a_{ss} = 0$. However, only when $a_{ss} = 1$ does the lna_{ss} exist. Therefore, the correct solution is $a_{ss} = 1$.

In order to find the steady states of the other variables, it is necessary to perform some additional algebraic operations.

Uniting the labor supply, equation (3.30), with the labor demand, equation (3.34), by means of the real wage, we have:

$$\underbrace{\frac{\theta c_{ss}}{1-h_{ss}}}_{\text{labor supply}} = w_{ss} = \underbrace{\alpha\frac{y_{ss}}{h_{ss}}}_{\text{labor demand}} \tag{3.38}$$

Operating on the resulting equation:

$$\begin{aligned}
\frac{\theta c_{ss}}{1-h_{ss}} &= \alpha\frac{y_{ss}}{h_{ss}}\\
\frac{\theta h_{ss}}{1-h_{ss}} &= \alpha\frac{y_{ss}}{c_{ss}}\\
\frac{\theta h_{ss}}{1-h_{ss}} &= \alpha\frac{y_{ss}/k_{ss}}{c_{ss}/k_{ss}}\\
\text{From equations} \quad & (3.33) \text{ and } (3.36):\\
\frac{\theta h_{ss}}{1-h_{ss}} &= \alpha\frac{\frac{1}{\beta(1-\alpha)}}{\frac{1}{\beta(1-\alpha)}-1}\\
\frac{1-h_{ss}}{\theta h_{ss}} &= (\alpha^{-1})\frac{\frac{1}{\beta(1-\alpha)}-1}{\frac{1}{\beta(1-\alpha)}}\\
\frac{1}{h_{ss}}-1 &= \theta(\alpha^{-1})(1-\beta(1-\alpha))\\
\frac{1}{h_{ss}} &= \theta(\alpha^{-1})(1-\beta(1-\alpha))+1\\
h_{ss} &= \frac{\alpha}{\theta(1-\beta(1-\alpha))+\alpha}
\end{aligned} \tag{3.39}$$

Since we already have the value of h_{ss}, then we can find the steady-state capital k_{ss} of the production function (equation (3.31)):

$$\begin{aligned}
y_{ss} &= a_{ss}^{\alpha}k_{ss}^{1-\alpha}h_{ss}^{\alpha}\\
\frac{y_{ss}}{k_{ss}} &= \left[\frac{h_{ss}}{k_{ss}}\right]^{\alpha}\\
\text{From equation } & (3.33):\\
\frac{1}{\beta(1-\alpha)} &= \left[\frac{h_{ss}}{k_{ss}}\right]^{\alpha}\\
\left[\frac{1}{\beta(1-\alpha)}\right]^{1/\alpha} &= \frac{h_{ss}}{k_{ss}}
\end{aligned}$$

$$k_{ss} = h_{ss}\left[\frac{1}{\beta(1-\alpha)}\right]^{-1/\alpha}$$

$$k_{ss} = \left[\frac{\alpha}{\theta(1-\beta(1-\alpha))+\alpha}\right]\left[\beta(1-\alpha)\right]^{1/\alpha} \quad (3.40)$$

Since some variables are expressed as a ratio to capital, then their steady-state value can be found as a function of the steady-state value of capital. From equation (3.33) we find the product y_{ss}:

$$\frac{y_{ss}}{k_{ss}} = \frac{1}{\beta(1-\alpha)}$$

$$y_{ss} = k_{ss}\left[\frac{1}{\beta(1-\alpha)}\right]$$

$$y_{ss} = \left[\frac{\alpha}{\theta(1-\beta(1-\alpha))+\alpha}\right]\left[\beta(1-\alpha)\right]^{\frac{1}{\alpha}-1} \quad (3.41)$$

Doing the same in equation (3.36), the consumption c_{ss} is found:

$$\frac{c_{ss}}{k_{ss}} = \frac{1}{\beta(1-\alpha)} - 1$$

$$c_{ss} = k_{ss}\left[\frac{1}{\beta(1-\alpha)} - 1\right]$$

$$c_{ss} = \left[\frac{\alpha}{\theta(1-\beta(1-\alpha))+\alpha}\right]\left[\beta(1-\alpha)\right]^{1/\alpha}\left[\frac{1}{\beta(1-\alpha)} - 1\right] \quad (3.42)$$

In the labor demand, equation (3.34), substitute y_{ss} and h_{ss} and obtain the steady-state wage w_{ss}:

$$w_{ss} = \alpha\frac{y_{ss}}{h_{ss}}$$

$$w_{ss} = \alpha\frac{\left[\frac{\alpha}{\theta(1-\beta(1-\alpha))+\alpha}\right]\left[\beta(1-\alpha)\right]^{\frac{1}{\alpha}-1}}{\frac{\alpha}{\theta(1-\beta(1-\alpha))+\alpha}}$$

$$w_{ss} = \alpha\left[\beta(1-\alpha)\right]^{\frac{1}{\alpha}-1} \quad (3.43)$$

Table 3.4 summarizes the steady-state expression for each variable in the model.

As mentioned before, this model is based on the King and Rebelo (1999) calibration. In that study the authors assume that the steady-state work h_{ss} is equal to 0.2. Under this premise, the value of the parameter θ is calculated endogenously

Table 3.4 Steady state

Steady-state (recursive form)	Steady state (parametric form)	Values
$r_{ss} = \frac{1}{\beta}$	$= \frac{1}{\beta}$	$r_{ss} = 1.0163$
$h_{ss} = \frac{\alpha}{\theta(1-\beta(1-\alpha))+\alpha}$	$= \frac{\alpha}{\theta(1-\beta(1-\alpha))+\alpha}$	$h_{ss} = 0.2$
$a_{ss} = 1$	$= 1$	$a_{ss} = 1$
$k_{ss} = h_{ss}\left[\frac{1}{\beta(1-\alpha)}\right]^{-1/\alpha}$	$= \left[\frac{alpha}{\theta(1-\beta(1-\alpha))+\alpha}\right]\left[\beta(1-\alpha)\right]^{1/\alpha}$	$k_{ss} = 0.0375$
$i_{ss} = k_{ss}$	$= \left[\frac{\alpha}{\theta(1-\beta(1-\alpha))+\alpha}\right]\left[\beta(1-\alpha)\right]^{1/\alpha}$	$i_{ss} = 0.0375$
$y_{ss} = k_{ss}\left[\frac{1}{\beta(1-\alpha)}\right]$	$= \left[\frac{\alpha}{\theta(1-\beta(1-\alpha))+\alpha}\right]\left[\beta(1-\alpha)\right]^{\frac{1}{\alpha}-1}$	$y_{ss} = 0.1146$
$c_{ss} = k_{ss}\left[\frac{1}{\beta(1-\alpha)} - 1\right]$	$= \left[\frac{\alpha}{\theta(1-\beta(1-\alpha))+\alpha}\right]\left[\beta(1-\alpha)\right]^{1/\alpha}\left[\frac{1}{\beta(1-\alpha)} - 1\right]$	$c_{ss} = 0.077$
$w_{ss} = \alpha\frac{y_{ss}}{h_{ss}}$	$= \alpha\left[\beta(1-\alpha)\right]^{\frac{1}{\alpha}-1}$	$w_{ss} = 0.3821$

Note: The calculation of the steady states is found in Long_Plosser_SteadyState.m

from the steady-state expression of work, which is derived from the model. So, under this consideration, we have:

$$h_{ss} = \frac{\alpha}{\theta\underbrace{(1-\beta(1-\alpha))}_{\eta}+\alpha}$$

$$h_{ss} = \frac{\alpha}{\theta\eta+\alpha}$$

$$\text{Clearing}\theta \; :$$

$$\theta\eta+\alpha = \frac{\alpha}{h_{ss}}$$

$$\theta\eta = \alpha(\frac{1}{h_{ss}} - 1)$$

$$\theta = \alpha\left(\frac{1-h_{ss}}{\eta h_{ss}}\right) \tag{3.44}$$

3.5 Linearization vs. Log-Linearization

An important step in the model solution process is to linearize or log-linearize the equations of the system. Strictly speaking, the linearization technique is unique; what differs is the nature of the variable, which in one case is considered in levels and in another case in logarithms. In practical terms, the first linearization will be called variable in levels and the second log-linearization variable in logarithms. In both cases, each equation of the model is approximated by means of the first-order Taylor expansion (DeJong and Dave 2011).

3.5.1 Linearization (Variable in Levels)

Step 1 The first step consists of ordering each equation of the system in such a way that the right side of the equation is equal to zero. Then, the left side of the equation needs to be renamed as a function that depends on the variables that appear in the equation. For example, let the following expression be an equation of the model:

$$\alpha x_t y_t = \beta y_t + \theta z_t \tag{3.45}$$

The terms are ordered on the left side:

$$\alpha x_t y_t - \beta y_t - \theta z_t = 0 \tag{3.46}$$

Finally, we rename the equation as a function:

$$F(x_t, y_t, z_t) = \alpha x_t y_t - \beta y_t - \theta z_t = 0 \tag{3.47}$$

Step 2 The second step is to approximate the function (3.47) by means of a first-order Taylor expansion around the steady state.

$$\begin{aligned} F(x_t, y_t, z_t) &= \alpha x_t y_t - \beta y_t - \theta z_t = 0 \\ F(x_t, y_t, z_t) &\approx F(\cdot)|_{ss} + \frac{\partial F}{\partial x_t}|_{ss}(x_t - x_{ss}) + \frac{\partial F}{\partial y_t}|_{ss}(y_t - y_{ss}) \\ &\quad + \frac{\partial F}{\partial z_t}|_{ss}(z_t - z_{ss}) \end{aligned} \tag{3.48}$$

Considering that $F(\cdot)|_{ss} = 0$ and performing a change of variable: $\widetilde{x}_t = x_t - x_{ss}$, where $\widetilde{x}_t$ is the deviation of the variable (in levels) with respect to its steady state. Applying this change of variable to equation (3.48), we have:

$$\begin{aligned} F(x_t, y_t, z_t) &\approx F(\cdot)|_{ss} + \frac{\partial F}{\partial x_t}|_{ss}(x_t - x_{ss}) + \frac{\partial F}{\partial y_t}|_{ss}(y_t - y_{ss}) + \frac{\partial F}{\partial z_t}|_{ss}(z_t - z_{ss}) \\ F(x_t, y_t, z_t) &\approx 0 + \frac{\partial F}{\partial x_t}|_{ss}(\widetilde{x}_t) + \frac{\partial F}{\partial y_t}|_{ss}(\widetilde{y}_t) + \frac{\partial F}{\partial z_t}|_{ss}(\widetilde{z}_t) \\ F(x_t, y_t, z_t) &\approx (\alpha y_{ss})\widetilde{x}_t + (-\beta)\widetilde{y}_t + (-\theta)\widetilde{z}_t \\ \text{but} &: \; F(x_t, y_t, z_t) = 0\,, \text{ so} \ldots \\ 0 = F(x_t, y_t, z_t) &\approx (\alpha y_{ss})\widetilde{x}_t + (-\beta)\widetilde{y}_t + (-\theta)\widetilde{z}_t \end{aligned}$$

$$
\begin{aligned}
0 &= (\alpha y_{ss})\widetilde{x}_t + (-\beta)\widetilde{y}_t + (-\theta)\widetilde{z}_t \\
\alpha y_{ss}\widetilde{x}_t &= \beta\widetilde{y}_t + \theta\widetilde{z}_t
\end{aligned} \tag{3.49}
$$

Equation (3.49) is the linear version of equation (3.46). Applying this technique to each equation of the nonlinear system, the linear system with the variables in levels will be obtained. For the case of Euler's equation, we have:

$$
F(c_t, c_{t+1}, r_{t+1}) = \frac{1}{c_t} - \beta E_t \frac{r_{t+1}}{c_{t+1}} = 0
$$

Extracting expectations :

$$
\begin{aligned}
E_t F(c_t, c_{t+1}, r_{t+1}) &= E_t\left(\frac{1}{c_t} - \beta\frac{r_{t+1}}{c_{t+1}}\right) = 0 \\
F(c_t, c_{t+1}, r_{t+1}) &\approx F(\cdot)|_{ss} + \frac{\partial F}{\partial c_t}|_{ss}(c_t - c_{ss}) + \frac{\partial F}{\partial c_{t+1}}|_{ss}(c_{t+1} - c_{ss}) + \\
&\quad \frac{\partial F}{\partial r_{t+1}}|_{ss}(r_{t+1} - r_{ss}) \\
F(c_t, c_{t+1}, r_{t+1}) &\approx 0 + \left(-\frac{1}{c_{ss}^2}\right)\widetilde{c}_t + \left(\beta\frac{r_{ss}}{c_{ss}^2}\right)\widetilde{c}_{t+1} + \left(-\frac{\beta}{c_{ss}}\right)\widetilde{r}_{t+1} \\
0 &= E_t\left[\left(-\frac{1}{c_{ss}^2}\right)\widetilde{c}_t + \left(\beta\frac{r_{ss}}{c_{ss}^2}\right)\widetilde{c}_{t+1} + \left(-\frac{\beta}{c_{ss}}\right)\widetilde{r}_{t+1}\right] \\
0 &= \left(-\frac{1}{c_{ss}^2}\right)\widetilde{c}_t + E_t\left[\left(\beta\frac{r_{ss}}{c_{ss}^2}\right)\widetilde{c}_{t+1} + \left(-\frac{\beta}{c_{ss}}\right)\widetilde{r}_{t+1}\right] \\
\left(\frac{1}{c_{ss}^2}\right)\widetilde{c}_t &= E_t\left[\left(\beta\frac{r_{ss}}{c_{ss}^2}\right)\widetilde{c}_{t+1} + \left(-\frac{\beta}{c_{ss}}\right)\widetilde{r}_{t+1}\right] \\
\widetilde{c}_t &= \beta E_t(r_{ss}\widetilde{c}_{t+1} - c_{ss}\widetilde{r}_{t+1})
\end{aligned} \tag{3.50}
$$

Doing the same linearization procedure for the law of movement of capital:

$$
\begin{aligned}
F(k_{t+1}, i_t) &= k_{t+1} - i_t = 0 \\
F(k_{t+1}, i_t) &\approx F(\cdot)|_{ss} + \frac{\partial F}{\partial k_{t+1}}|_{ss}(k_{t+1} - k_{ss}) + \frac{\partial F}{\partial i_t}|_{ss}(i_t - i_{ss}) \\
F(k_{t+1}, i_t) &\approx 0 + (1)\widetilde{k}_{t+1} + (-1)\widetilde{i}_t \\
0 &= \widetilde{k}_{t+1} + (-1)\widetilde{i}_t \\
\widetilde{k}_{t+1} &= \widetilde{i}_t
\end{aligned} \tag{3.51}
$$

For the labor supply, the linearized equation would be:

$$
\begin{aligned}
F(h_t, w_t, c_t) &= \frac{\theta}{1-h_t} - \frac{w_t}{c_t} = 0 \\
F(h_t, w_t, c_t) &\approx F(\cdot)|_{ss} + \frac{\partial F}{\partial h_t}|_{ss}(h_t - h_{ss}) + \frac{\partial F}{\partial w_t}|_{ss}(w_t - w_{ss}) + \frac{\partial F}{\partial c_t}|_{ss}(c_t - c_{ss}) \\
F(h_t, w_t, c_t) &\approx 0 + \frac{\theta}{(1-h_{ss})^2}\widetilde{h}_t + \frac{-1}{c_{ss}}\widetilde{w}_t + \frac{w_{ss}}{c_{ss}^2}\widetilde{c}_t \\
0 &= \frac{\theta}{(1-h_{ss})^2}\widetilde{h}_t - \frac{1}{c_{ss}}\widetilde{w}_t + \frac{w_{ss}}{c_{ss}^2}\widetilde{c}_t \\
\frac{1}{c_{ss}}\widetilde{w}_t &= \frac{\theta}{(1-h_{ss})^2}\widetilde{h}_t + \frac{w_{ss}}{c_{ss}^2}\widetilde{c}_t \\
\widetilde{w}_t &= \frac{w_{ss}}{(1-h_{ss})}\widetilde{h}_t + \frac{\theta}{1-h_{ss}}\widetilde{c}_t
\end{aligned}
\tag{3.52}
$$

Similarly for the production function:

$$
\begin{aligned}
F(y_t, a_t, k_t, h_t) &= y_t - a_t k_t^{1-\alpha} h_t^{\alpha} = 0 \\
F(y_t, a_t, k_t, h_t) &\approx F(\cdot)|_{ss} + \frac{\partial F}{\partial y_t}|_{ss}(y_t - y_{ss}) + \frac{\partial F}{\partial a_t}|_{ss}(a_t - a_{ss}) + \frac{\partial F}{\partial k_t}|_{ss}(k_t - k_{ss}) \\
&\quad + \frac{\partial F}{\partial h_t}|_{ss}(h_t - h_{ss}) \\
F(y_t, a_t, k_t, h_t) &\approx 0 + (\widetilde{y}_t) + (-k_{ss}^{1-\alpha} h_{ss}^{\alpha})(\widetilde{a}_t) + (-(1-\alpha)a_{ss}k_{ss}^{-\alpha}h_{ss}^{\alpha})(\widetilde{k}_t) \\
&\quad + (-\alpha a_{ss} k_{ss}^{1-\alpha} h_{ss}^{\alpha-1})(\widetilde{h}_t) \\
0 &= \widetilde{y}_t - \frac{y_{ss}}{a_{ss}}\widetilde{a}_t - (1-\alpha)\frac{y_{ss}}{k_{ss}}\widetilde{k}_t - \alpha\frac{y_{ss}}{h_{ss}}\widetilde{h}_t \\
\widetilde{y}_t &= \frac{y_{ss}}{a_{ss}}\widetilde{a}_t + (1-\alpha)\frac{y_{ss}}{k_{ss}}\widetilde{k}_t + \alpha\frac{y_{ss}}{h_{ss}}\widetilde{h}_t
\end{aligned}
\tag{3.53}
$$

Doing the same for capital demand:

$$
\begin{aligned}
F(r_t, y_t, k_t) &= r_t - (1-\alpha)\frac{y_t}{k_t} = 0 \\
F(r_t, y_t, k_t) &\approx F(\cdot)|_{ss} + \frac{\partial F}{\partial r_t}|_{ss}(r_t - r_{ss}) + \frac{\partial F}{\partial y_t}|_{ss}(y_t - y_{ss}) + \frac{\partial F}{\partial k_t}|_{ss}(k_t - k_{ss}) \\
F(r_t, y_t, k_t) &\approx 0 + (1)\widetilde{r}_t + \frac{-(1-\alpha)}{k_{ss}}\widetilde{y}_t + \frac{(1-\alpha)y_{ss}}{k_{ss}^2}\widetilde{k}_t \\
0 &= (1)\widetilde{r}_t + \frac{-(1-\alpha)}{k_{ss}}\widetilde{y}_t + \frac{(1-\alpha)y_{ss}}{k_{ss}^2}\widetilde{k}_t \\
\frac{y_{ss}}{k_{ss}}\widetilde{k}_t &= \widetilde{y}_t - \frac{k_{ss}}{1-\alpha}\widetilde{r}_t
\end{aligned}
\tag{3.54}
$$

In the same way for the labor demand:

$$F(w_t, y_t, h_t) = w_t - \alpha \frac{y_t}{h_t} = 0$$

$$F(w_t, y_t, h_t) \approx F(\cdot)|_{ss} + \frac{\partial F}{\partial w_t}|_{ss}(w_t - w_{ss}) + \frac{\partial F}{\partial y_t}|_{ss}(y_t - y_{ss}) + \frac{\partial F}{\partial h_t}|_{ss}(h_t - h_{ss})$$

$$F(w_t, y_t, h_t) \approx 0 + (1)\widetilde{w}_t + \left(\frac{-\alpha}{h_{ss}}\right)\widetilde{y}_t + \left(\frac{\alpha y_{ss}}{h_{ss}^2}\right)\widetilde{h}_t$$

$$0 = \widetilde{w}_t - \left(\frac{\alpha}{h_{ss}}\right)\widetilde{y}_t + \left(\frac{\alpha y_{ss}}{h_{ss}^2}\right)\widetilde{h}_t$$

$$\widetilde{w}_t = \left(\frac{\alpha}{h_{ss}}\right)\widetilde{y}_t - \left(\frac{\alpha y_{ss}}{h_{ss}^2}\right)\widetilde{h}_t \tag{3.55}$$

For the equilibrium equation in the goods market:

$$F(y_t, c_t, i_t) = y_t - c_t - i_t = 0$$

$$F(y_t, c_t, i_t) \approx F(\cdot)|_{ss} + \frac{\partial F}{\partial y_t}|_{ss}(y_t - y_{ss}) + \frac{\partial F}{\partial c_t}|_{ss}(c_t - c_{ss}) + \frac{\partial F}{\partial i_t}|_{ss}(i_t - i_{ss})$$

$$F(y_t, c_t, i_t) \approx 0 + (1)\widetilde{y}_t + (-1)\widetilde{c}_t + (-1)\widetilde{i}_t$$

$$\widetilde{y}_t = \widetilde{c}_t + \widetilde{i}_t \tag{3.56}$$

Finally for the productivity *shock*:

$$F(a_t, a_{t-1}, \epsilon_t) = lna_t - \phi lna_{t-1} - \epsilon_t = 0$$

$$F(a_t, a_{t-1}, \epsilon_t) \approx F(\cdot)|_{ss} + \frac{\partial F}{\partial a_t}|_{ss}(a_t - a_{ss}) + \frac{\partial F}{\partial a_{t-1}}|_{ss}(a_{t-1} - a_{ss}) + \frac{\partial F}{\partial \epsilon_t}|_{ss}(\epsilon_t - \epsilon_{ss})$$

Considering : $\epsilon_{ss} = 0$

$$F(a_t, a_{t-1}, \epsilon_t) \approx 0 + \frac{1}{a_{ss}}\widetilde{a}_t + \left(-\frac{\phi}{a_{ss}}\right)\widetilde{a}_{t-1} + (-1)\epsilon_t$$

$$0 = \frac{1}{a_{ss}}\widetilde{a}_t + \left(-\frac{\phi}{a_{ss}}\right)\widetilde{a}_{t-1} + (-1)\epsilon_t$$

$$\frac{1}{a_{ss}}\widetilde{a}_t = \left(\frac{\phi}{a_{ss}}\right)\widetilde{a}_{t-1} + \epsilon_t$$

Given that : $a_{ss} = 1$

$$\widetilde{a}_t = \phi\widetilde{a}_{t-1} + \epsilon_t \tag{3.57}$$

Table 3.5 Linear system of equations of the model (Long and Plosser 1983)

Agent	Equations	Description
Household	$\widetilde{c}_t = \beta E_t(r_{ss}\widetilde{c}_{t+1} - c_{ss}\widetilde{r}_{t+1})$	Equation from Euler
	$\widetilde{k}_{t+1} = \widetilde{i}_t$	Law of movement of capital
	$\widetilde{w}_t = \frac{w_{ss}}{(1-h_{ss})}\widetilde{h}_t + \frac{\theta}{1-h_{ss}}\widetilde{c}_t$	Labor Supply
Firm	$\widetilde{y}_t = \frac{y_{ss}}{a_{ss}}\widetilde{a}_t + (1-\alpha)\frac{y_{ss}}{k_{ss}}\widetilde{k}_t + \alpha\frac{y_{ss}}{a_{ss}}\widetilde{h}_t$	Production function
	$\frac{y_{ss}}{k_{ss}}\widetilde{k}_t = \widetilde{y}_t - \frac{k_{ss}}{1-\alpha}\widetilde{r}_t$	Capital demand
	$\widetilde{w}_t = \left(\frac{\alpha}{h_{ss}}\right)\widetilde{y}_t - \left(\frac{\alpha y_{ss}}{h_{ss}^2}\right)\widetilde{h}_t$	Labor demand
Equilibrium	$\widetilde{y}_t = \widetilde{c}_t + \widetilde{i}_t$	Goods market equilibrium
Shock	$\widetilde{a}_t = \phi\widetilde{a}_{t-1} + \epsilon_t$	Productivity *Shock*

Table 3.5 summarizes the linearized equations of the model.

3.5.2 *Linearization (Logarithmic Variables) or Log-Linearization*

It is usual to consider the log-linearization of the model because the transformed variables are expressed as the percentage deviation from their steady state. Namely:

$$\widehat{x_t} = ln(x_t) - ln(x_{ss})$$

In that context, the coefficients of the solution of the linear system are interpreted as elasticities. This technique was initially proposed by King et al. (1991) and Campbell (1994).

To log-linearize the nonlinear system two ways can be applied. The first alternative is following the same path described in the previous section but with a twist. The standard form suggests that the terms of the equation are moved to the left-hand side and then renamed by a function (depending on the variables of the equation), to finally apply an approximation of this function by means of the first-order Taylor expansion. The variant is that first, you have to apply the logarithm to both sides of each equation and then try to express each variable in logarithms. For example, if the consumption c_t is in levels, and we want to express it in logarithms, the following can be done: e^{lnc_t}.

The second alternative is proposed by Uhlig (1995), which is much more practical. Uhlig (1995)'s proposal consists of replacing each of the variables by its log deviation ($x_t = x_{ss}e^{\widehat{x_t}}$) and then considering three approximation properties, which are mentioned later.

It is worth mentioning that, for the model of this chapter in particular, both ways of log-linearizing do not represent a difference in effort. Uhlig (1995)'s proposal gains greater importance in terms of practicality as the model becomes more complex. For example, the model from Chap. 5 forward can be log-linearized quickly and with little effort by means of the Uhlig technique compared to the standard path.

Standard method Due to the assumptions of the model of Long and Plosser (1983), some equations will not require a first-order Taylor approximation because it would be easy to obtain these equations expressed in log deviations. In these cases, it will be sufficient to write the equation in logarithms and subtract the equation in the steady state. These equations are the following: the law of movement of capital, the production function, the capital demand, the labor demand, and productivity. However, it is required to apply the Taylor expansion for the Euler equation, the labor supply, and the equilibrium equation of the goods market. Clearly, as the model becomes more complex, the application of the Taylor expansion will be more required.

For Euler's equation, we have the following: first, we take logarithms on both sides of equation (equation (3.58)), and then we take all the elements of this equation to the left side and rename it as a function of the endogenous variables that appear in this equation. In this particular case, the function is $f(lnr_{t+1}, lnc_{t+1}, lnc_t)$.

$$\frac{1}{c_t} = \beta E_t \frac{r_{t+1}}{c_{t+1}}$$

$$ln\left[\frac{1}{c_t}\right] = E_t ln\left[\beta \frac{r_{t+1}}{c_{t+1}}\right] \tag{3.58}$$

$$-lnc_t = E_t[ln\beta + lnr_{t+1} - lnc_{t+1}]$$

$$E_t[ln\beta + lnr_{t+1} - lnc_{t+1}] + lnc_t = 0$$

$$F(lnr_{t+1}, lnc_{t+1}, lnc_t) = E_t[ln\beta + lnr_{t+1} - lnc_{t+1} + lnc_t] = 0$$

$$F(lnr_{t+1}, lnc_{t+1}, lnc_t) = 0 \tag{3.59}$$

The next step is to approximate the function "$F(\cdot)$" by means of a first-order Taylor expansion:

$$F(lnr_{t+1}, lnc_{t+1}, lnc_t) \approx E_t\big[F(\cdot)|_{ss} + \frac{\partial F}{\partial lnr_{t+1}}|_{ss}(lnr_{t+1} - lnr_{ss}) + \frac{\partial F}{\partial lnc_{t+1}}|_{ss}(lnc_{t+1} - lnc_{ss}) + \frac{\partial F}{\partial lnc_t}|_{ss}(lnc_t - lnc_{ss})\big]$$

$$F(y_t, c_t, i_t) \approx E_t\big[0 + (1)(lnr_{t+1} - lnr_{ss}) + (-1)(lnc_{t+1} - lnc_{ss}) + (1)(lnc_t - lnc_{ss})\big]$$

$$F(y_t, c_t, i_t) \approx E_t\big[\widehat{r}_{t+1} - \widehat{c}_{t+1} + \widehat{c}_t\big]$$

$$\widehat{c}_t = E_t\big[\widehat{c}_{t+1} - \widehat{r}_{t+1}\big] \tag{3.60}$$

With respect to the law of motion of capital, we proceed in the same way as in the Euler equation, except that it is not necessary to apply the Taylor approximation:

$$
\begin{aligned}
k_{t+1} &= i_t \\
lnk_{t+1} &= lni_t \\
lnk_{ss} &= lni_{ss} \\
lnk_{t+1} - lnk_{ss} &= lni_t - lni_{ss} \\
\widehat{k}_{t+1} &= \widehat{i}_t
\end{aligned}
\tag{3.61}
$$

In the case of the labor supply:

$$\frac{\theta}{1-h_t} = \frac{w_t}{c_t}$$

$$ln\frac{\theta}{1-h_t} = ln\frac{w_t}{c_t}$$

$$ln\theta - ln(1-h_t) = lnw_t - lnc_t \tag{3.62}$$

$$ln\theta - ln(1-h_{ss}) = lnw_{ss} - lnc_{ss} \tag{3.63}$$

$$(3.62)\text{–}(3.63):$$

$$-ln(1-h_t) + ln(1-h_{ss}) = lnw_t - lnc_t - lnw_{ss} + lnc_{ss}$$

$$\text{Ordering}:$$

$$-ln(1-h_t) + ln(1-h_{ss}) = (lnw_t - lnw_{ss}) - (lnc_t - lnc_{ss})$$

$$-ln(1-h_t) + ln(1-h_{ss}) = \widehat{w}_t - \widehat{c}_t \tag{3.64}$$

For equation (3.64) to be fully log-linearized, we need to express labor as its log deviation from its steady state. To do this, the following will be done:

$$ln(1-h_t) = ln(1-e^{lnh_t})$$

This expression is approximated by means of the first-order Taylor expansion:

$$g(lnh_t) = ln(1-e^{lnh_t}) \approx g(\cdot)|_{ss} + \frac{\partial g}{\partial lnh_t}|_{ss}(lnh_t - lnh_{ss})$$

$$ln(1-e^{lnh_t}) \approx ln(1-e^{lnh_{ss}}) + \left[\frac{-e^{lnh_t}}{1-e^{lnh_t}}\right](lnh_t - lnh_{ss})$$

$$ln(1-e^{lnh_t}) \approx ln(1-h_{ss}) - \left[\frac{h_{ss}}{1-h_{ss}}\right](lnh_t - lnh_{ss})$$

$$ln(1 - e^{lnh_t}) \approx ln(1 - h_{ss}) - \left[\frac{h_{ss}}{1 - h_{ss}}\right]\widehat{h}_t \tag{3.65}$$

Replacing equation (3.65) in (3.64), the log-linear expression of the labor supply is obtained:

$$\begin{aligned} -ln(1 - h_t) + ln(1 - h_{ss}) &= \widehat{w}_t - \widehat{c}_t \\ -ln(1 - h_{ss}) + \left[\frac{h_{ss}}{1 - h_{ss}}\right]\widehat{h}_t + ln(1 - h_{ss}) &= \widehat{w}_t - \widehat{c}_t \\ \left[\frac{h_{ss}}{1 - h_{ss}}\right]\widehat{h}_t &= \widehat{w}_t - \widehat{c}_t \end{aligned} \tag{3.66}$$

To obtain the log-linear form of the production function, it is enough to apply the logarithm to the production function and then evaluate it in its steady state, to finally subtract both equations:

$$y_t = a_t k_t^{1-\alpha} h_t^{\alpha}$$

$$lny_t = lna_t + (1 - \alpha)lnk_t + \alpha h_t \tag{3.67}$$

$$lny_{ss} = lna_{ss} + (1 - \alpha)lnk_{ss} + \alpha h_{ss} \tag{3.68}$$

(3.67)–(3.68) :

$$lny_t - lny_{ss} = lna_t - lna_{ss} + (1 - \alpha)lnk_t - (1 - \alpha)lnk_{ss} + \alpha h_t - \alpha h_{ss}$$

$$\widehat{y}_t = \widehat{a}_t + (1 - \alpha)\widehat{k}_t + \alpha\widehat{h}_t \tag{3.69}$$

The labor demand follows the same steps as the production function:

$$w_t = \alpha\frac{y_t}{h_t}$$

$$lnw_t = ln\alpha + lny_t - lnh_t \tag{3.70}$$

$$lnw_{ss} = ln\alpha + lny_{ss} - lnh_{ss} \tag{3.71}$$

(3.70)–(3.71) :

$$lnw_t - lnw_{ss} = lny_t - lny_{ss} - lnh_t + lnh_{ss}$$

$$\widehat{w}_t = \widehat{y}_t - \widehat{h}_t \tag{3.72}$$

With respect to the demand for capital, we obtain:

$$r_t = (1 - \alpha)\frac{y_t}{k_t}$$

$$lnr_t = ln(1 - \alpha) + lny_t - lnk_t \tag{3.73}$$

$$lnr_{ss} = ln(1-\alpha) + lny_{ss} - lnk_{ss} \tag{3.74}$$

$$(3.73)\text{–}(3.74) :$$

$$lnr_t - lnr_{ss} = lny_t - lny_{ss} - lnk_t + lnk_{ss}$$

$$\widehat{r_t} = \widehat{y_t} - \widehat{k_t} \tag{3.75}$$

For the market equilibrium equation, we have:

$$y_t = c_t + i_t$$

$$lny_t = ln(c_t + i_t)$$

$$lny_t - ln(c_t + i_t) = 0 \tag{3.76}$$

Since we want the variables to be expressed in logarithms, the following trick is made: each variable x_t is expressed as e^{lnx_t}. Applying this artifice to equation (3.76):

$$lny_t - ln(c_t + i_t) = 0$$

$$lny_t - ln(e^{lnc_t} + e^{lni_t}) = 0$$

$$F(y_t, c_t, i_t) = lny_t - ln(e^{lnc_t} + e^{lni_t}) = 0 \tag{3.77}$$

Approximating $F(y_t, c_t, i_t)$ by means of the first-order Taylor expansion, we have:

$$F(y_t, c_t, i_t) \approx F(\cdot)|_{ss} + \frac{\partial F}{\partial lny_t}|_{ss}(lny_t - lny_{ss}) + \frac{\partial F}{\partial lnc_t}|_{ss}(lnc_t - lnc_{ss})$$

$$+ \frac{\partial F}{\partial lni_t}|_{ss}(lni_t - lni_{ss})$$

$$F(y_t, c_t, i_t) \approx 0 + (1)(lny_t - lny_{ss}) + \frac{-e^{lnc_{ss}}}{e^{lnc_{ss}} + e^{lni_{ss}}}(lnc_t - lnc_{ss})$$

$$+ \frac{-e^{lni_{ss}}}{e^{lnc_{ss}} + e^{lni_{ss}}}(lni_t - lni_{ss})$$

$$\approx \widehat{y_t} - \frac{c_{ss}}{c_{ss} + i_{ss}}\widehat{c_t} - \frac{i_{ss}}{c_{ss} + i_{ss}}\widehat{i_t}$$

$$\approx \widehat{y_t} - \frac{c_{ss}}{y_{ss}}\widehat{c_t} - \frac{i_{ss}}{y_{ss}}\widehat{i_t}$$

$$\widehat{y_t} \approx \frac{c_{ss}}{y_{ss}}\widehat{c_t} + \frac{i_{ss}}{y_{ss}}\widehat{i_t} \tag{3.78}$$

Finally, for the productivity equation:

$$lna_t = \phi lna_{t-1} + \epsilon_t$$

$$\text{We know } : lna_{ss} = 0$$

$$lna_t - lna_{ss} = \phi lna_{t-1} - \phi lna_{ss} + \epsilon_t$$

$$\widehat{a_t} = \phi \widehat{a}_{t-1} + \epsilon_t \tag{3.79}$$

Uhlig (1995) method $\widehat{x_t}$ is defined as the log deviation of the variable x_t with respect to its steady-state value (x_{ss}):

$$\widehat{x_t} = ln(x_t) - ln(x_{ss}) \tag{3.80}$$

From the above, we get:

$$x_t = x_{ss}e^{\widehat{x_t}} \tag{3.81}$$

In addition, it is known that for small deviations from the steady state, it is true:

$$\text{1st property} : e^{\widehat{x_t}} \approx 1 + \widehat{x_t} \tag{3.82}$$

This first property is obtained by applying a first-order Taylor approximation, which is explained below.

Taylor approximation (1st order) Approximate the function $f(\widehat{x_t})$ around its steady state $\widehat{x_{ss}}$:

$$f(\widehat{x_t}) \approx f(\widehat{x_{ss}}) + \frac{f'(\widehat{x_{ss}})}{1!}(\widehat{x_t} - \widehat{x_{ss}}) + \frac{f''(\widehat{x_{ss}})}{2!}(\widehat{x_t} - \widehat{x_{ss}})^2 + \ldots$$

Considering a 1st-order approximation:

$$f(\widehat{x_t}) \approx f(\widehat{x_{ss}}) + \frac{f'(\widehat{x_{ss}})}{1!}(\widehat{x_t} - \widehat{x_{ss}})$$

If $f(\widehat{x_t}) = e^{\widehat{x_t}}$, then (knowing that $\widehat{x_{ss}} = 0$, because $\widehat{x_t} = x_t - x_{ss}$):

$$e^{\widehat{x_t}} \approx e^{\widehat{x_{ss}}} + e^{\widehat{x_{ss}}}(\widehat{x_t} - \widehat{x_{ss}})$$

$$e^{\widehat{x_t}} \approx 1 + (\widehat{x_t} - \widehat{x_{ss}})$$

$$e^{\widehat{x_t}} \approx 1 + \widehat{x_t}$$

Two additional properties are important:

$$\text{First property} : \widehat{x_t}\widehat{y_t} \approx 0 \tag{3.83}$$

$$\text{Second property} : E_t[ae^{\widehat{x}_{t+1}}] = E_t[a\widehat{x}_{t+1}] + a \tag{3.84}$$

Applying these properties, we proceed to log-linearize the system described in Table 3.3:

For Euler's equation:

$$\begin{aligned}
c_t^{-1} &= \beta E_t c_{t+1}^{-1} r_{t+1} \\
\left[c_{ss} e^{\widehat{c}_t}\right]^{-1} &= \beta E_t \left[c_{ss} e^{\widehat{c}_{t+1}}\right]^{-1} \left[r_{ss} e^{\widehat{r}_{t+1}}\right] \\
e^{-\widehat{c}_t} &= E_t e^{-\widehat{c}_{t+1}} e^{\widehat{r}_{t+1}} \\
e^{-\widehat{c}_t} &= E_t e^{-\widehat{c}_{t+1}+\widehat{r}_{t+1}} \\
1 - \widehat{c}_t &= E_t \left[1 - \widehat{c}_{t+1} + \widehat{r}_{t+1}\right] \\
\widehat{c}_t &= E_t \left[\widehat{c}_{t+1} - \widehat{r}_{t+1}\right]
\end{aligned} \tag{3.85}$$

The law of movement of capital in its log-linear form would be:

$$\begin{aligned}
k_{t+1} &= i_t \\
k_{ss} e^{\widehat{k}_{t+1}} &= i_{ss} e^{\widehat{i}_t} \\
k_{ss}(1 + \widehat{k}_{t+1}) &= i_{ss}(1 + \widehat{i}_t) \\
k_{ss} + k_{ss}\widehat{k}_{t+1} &= i_{ss} + i_{ss}\widehat{i}_t \\
k_{ss}\widehat{k}_{t+1} &= i_{ss}\widehat{i}_t \\
\text{como} &: k_{ss} = i_{ss} \\
\widehat{k}_{t+1} &= \widehat{i}_t
\end{aligned} \tag{3.86}$$

For the labor supply:

$$\begin{aligned}
\frac{\theta}{1 - h_t} &= \frac{w_t}{c_t} \\
\text{Remembering} &: 1 - h_t = l_t \\
\frac{\theta}{l_t} &= \frac{w_t}{c_t} \\
\frac{\theta}{l_{ss} e^{\widehat{l}_t}} &= \frac{w_{ss} e^{\widehat{w}_t}}{c_{ss} e^{\widehat{c}_t}} \\
e^{-\widehat{l}_t} &= e^{\widehat{w}_t - \widehat{c}_t} \\
1 - \widehat{l}_t &= 1 + \widehat{w}_t - \widehat{c}_t \\
\widehat{l}_t &= \widehat{c}_t - \widehat{w}_t
\end{aligned} \tag{3.87}$$

To finish obtaining the labor supply in its log-linear version, it is necessary to obtain the log-linear relationship between leisure l_t and labor h_t:

$$l_t = 1 - h_t$$

Log-linearizing this expression:

$$\begin{aligned}
l_t &= 1 - h_t \\
l_{ss}e^{\widehat{l_t}} &= 1 - h_{ss}e^{\widehat{h}_t} \\
l_{ss}(1 + \widehat{l}_t) &= 1 - h_{ss}(1 + \widehat{h}_t) \\
l_{ss} + l_{ss}\widehat{l}_t &= 1 - h_{ss} - h_{ss}\widehat{h}_t \\
l_{ss}\widehat{l}_t &= -h_{ss}\widehat{h}_t \\
\widehat{l}_t &= -\frac{h_{ss}}{l_{ss}}\widehat{h}_t \\
\widehat{l}_t &= -\frac{h_{ss}}{1 - h_{ss}}\widehat{h}_t
\end{aligned} \tag{3.88}$$

Inserting (3.88) into (3.87) gives the log-linear labor supply:

$$\begin{aligned}
\widehat{l}_t &= \widehat{c}_t - \widehat{w}_t \\
-\frac{h_{ss}}{1 - h_{ss}}\widehat{h}_t &= \widehat{c}_t - \widehat{w}_t \\
\frac{h_{ss}}{1 - h_{ss}}\widehat{h}_t &= \widehat{w}_t - \widehat{c}_t
\end{aligned} \tag{3.89}$$

Doing the same for the production function:

$$\begin{aligned}
y_t &= a_t k_t^{1-\alpha} h_t^{\alpha} \\
y_{ss}e^{\widehat{y}_t} &= \left[a_{ss}e^{\widehat{a}_t}\right]\left[k_{ss}e^{\widehat{k}_t}\right]^{1-\alpha}\left[h_{ss}e^{\widehat{h}_t}\right]^{\alpha} \\
y_{ss}e^{\widehat{y}_t} &= a_{ss}e^{\widehat{a}_t} k_{ss}^{1-\alpha} e^{(1-\alpha)\widehat{k}_t} h_{ss}^{\alpha} e^{\alpha\widehat{h}_t} \\
e^{\widehat{y}_t} &= e^{\widehat{a}_t + (1-\alpha)\widehat{k}_t + \alpha\widehat{h}_t} \\
1 + \widehat{y}_t &= 1 + \widehat{a}_t + (1 - \alpha)\widehat{k}_t + \alpha\widehat{h}_t \\
\widehat{y}_t &= \widehat{a}_t + (1 - \alpha)\widehat{k}_t + +\alpha\widehat{h}_t
\end{aligned} \tag{3.90}$$

Regarding the demand for capital:

$$\begin{aligned}
r_t &= (1-\alpha)\left(\frac{y_t}{k_t}\right) \\
r_{ss}e^{\widehat{r}_t} &= (1-\alpha)\left(\frac{y_{ss}e^{\widehat{y}_t}}{k_{ss}e^{\widehat{k}_t}}\right) \\
r_{ss}e^{\widehat{r}_t} &= (1-\alpha)\left(\frac{y_{ss}e^{\widehat{y}_t-\widehat{k}_t}}{k_{ss}}\right) \\
e^{\widehat{r}_t} &= e^{\widehat{y}_t-\widehat{k}_t} \\
1+\widehat{r}_t &= 1+\widehat{y}_t-\widehat{k}_t \\
\widehat{r}_t &= \widehat{y}_t-\widehat{k}_t
\end{aligned} \tag{3.91}$$

For the job demand:

$$\begin{aligned}
w_t &= \alpha\frac{y_t}{h_t} \\
w_{ss}e^{\widehat{w}_t} &= \alpha\frac{y_{ss}e^{\widehat{y}_t}}{h_{ss}e^{\widehat{h}_t}} \\
e^{\widehat{w}_t} &= \frac{e^{\widehat{y}_t}}{e^{\widehat{h}_t}} \\
e^{\widehat{w}_t} &= e^{\widehat{y}_t-\widehat{h}_t} \\
1+\widehat{w}_t &= 1+\widehat{y}_t-\widehat{h}_t \\
\widehat{w}_t &= \widehat{y}_t-\widehat{h}_t
\end{aligned} \tag{3.92}$$

Goods market equilibrium:

$$\begin{aligned}
y_t &= c_t+i_t \\
y_{ss}e^{\widehat{y}_t} &= c_{ss}e^{\widehat{c}_t}+i_{ss}e^{\widehat{i}_t} \\
y_{ss}(1+\widehat{y}_t) &= c_{ss}(1+\widehat{c}_t)+i_{ss}(1+\widehat{i}_t) \\
y_{ss}+y_{ss}\widehat{y}_t &= c_{ss}+c_{ss}\widehat{c}_t+i_{ss}+i_{ss}\widehat{i}_t \\
y_{ss}\widehat{y}_t &= c_{ss}\widehat{c}_t+i_{ss}\widehat{i}_t \\
\widehat{y}_t &= \frac{c_{ss}}{y_{ss}}\widehat{c}_t+\frac{i_{ss}}{y_{ss}}\widehat{i}_t
\end{aligned} \tag{3.93}$$

Table 3.6 Log-linear equations

Log-linear equations	Description
[1] $\widehat{c}_t = E_t\left[\widehat{c}_{t+1} - \widehat{r}_{t+1}\right]$	Equation of Euler
[2] $\widehat{k}_{t+1} = \widehat{i}_t$	Law of movement of capital
[3] $\frac{h_{ss}}{1-h_{ss}}\widehat{h}_t = \widehat{w}_t - \widehat{c}_t$	Labor supply
[4] $\widehat{y}_t = \widehat{a}_t + (1-\alpha)\widehat{k}_t + \alpha\widehat{h}_t$	Production function
[5] $\widehat{r}_t = \widehat{y}_t - \widehat{k}_t$	Capital demand
[6] $\widehat{w}_t = \widehat{y}_t - \widehat{h}_t$	Labor demand
[7] $\widehat{y}_t = \frac{c_{ss}}{y_{ss}}\widehat{c}_t + \frac{i_{ss}}{y_{ss}}\widehat{i}_t$	Goods market equilibrium
[8] $\widehat{a}_t = \phi\widehat{a}_{t-1} + \epsilon_t$	*Shock* of productivity

Note: To directly obtain the solution of the model with Dynare, you can use the mod "Long_Plosser_Dynare_linear_log.mod" from Chap. 2

Finally, the productivity equation:

$$
\begin{aligned}
lna_t &= \phi lna_{t-1} + \epsilon_t \\
lna_{ss}e^{\widehat{a}_t} &= \phi lna_{ss}e^{\widehat{a}_{t-1}} + \epsilon_t \\
lna_{ss} + \widehat{a}_t &= \phi lna_{ss} + \phi\widehat{a}_{t-1} + \epsilon_t \\
\widehat{a}_t &= \phi\widehat{a}_{t-1} + \epsilon_t
\end{aligned}
\tag{3.94}
$$

Table 3.6 summarizes the log-linear equations of the model obtained by two alternatives (standard method or Uhlig's approach).

3.6 Solution of Linear System

The solution of the linear system consists in finding the policy functions, that is, the control variables as a function of the state variables and exogenous variables. In this model, the state variable is capital k_t and the exogenous variable is productivity a_t. The idea is to find, for example, for consumption:

$$\widehat{c}_t = \eta_{ck}\widehat{k}_t + \eta_{ca}\widehat{a}_t$$

Similarly, for all endogenous variables: $\widehat{y}_t$, $\widehat{c}_t$, $\widehat{i}_t$, $\widehat{k}_{t+1}$, $\widehat{h}_t$, $\widehat{w}_t$, and $\widehat{r}_t$. In the existing literature, there are several ways to solve the system of stochastic difference equations. DeJong and Dave (2011) suggest that at least four methods are usual: Blanchard and Kahn (1980) method, Sims (2002) method, Klein (2000) method, and Uhlig (1999) method of undetermined coefficients. This chapter focuses on the two most common: the Blanchard and Kahn method and the method of undetermined coefficients. However, before describing and applying both methods, the Long and Plosser model will be solved analytically. This analytical solution is feasible because the nonlinearities disappear due to the two assumptions of the model: total depreciation and log utility.

3.6.1 Analytical Method

In the first place, an attempt is made to reduce the dimension of the system of linear equations by joining some equations. We start with the equilibrium in the labor market (we eliminate $\widehat{w}_t$). From Table 3.4 we join equations [3] and [6]:

$$\frac{h_{ss}}{1-h_{ss}}\widehat{h}_t + \widehat{c}_t = \widehat{y}_t - \widehat{h}_t$$

$$\frac{1}{1-h_{ss}}\widehat{h}_t = \widehat{y}_t - \widehat{c}_t \tag{3.95}$$

Then investment is eliminated $\widehat{i}_t$ by substituting equation [2] in [7]:

$$\widehat{y}_t = \frac{c_{ss}}{y_{ss}}\widehat{c}_t + \frac{i_{ss}}{y_{ss}}\widehat{i}_t$$

$$\widehat{y}_t = \frac{c_{ss}}{y_{ss}}\widehat{c}_t + \frac{i_{ss}}{y_{ss}}\widehat{k}_{t+1} \tag{3.96}$$

Inserting the real interest rate (equation [5]) into the Euler equation (equation [1]):

$$\widehat{c}_t = E_t\left[\widehat{c}_{t+1} - \widehat{r}_{t+1}\right]$$

$$\widehat{c}_t = E_t\left[\widehat{c}_{t+1} - (\widehat{y}_{t+1} - \widehat{k}_{t+1})\right]$$

$$\widehat{c}_t = E_t\left[\widehat{c}_{t+1} - \widehat{y}_{t+1} + \widehat{k}_{t+1}\right] \tag{3.97}$$

But from equation (3.95) it is known that:

$$\frac{1}{1-h_{ss}}\widehat{h}_t = \widehat{y}_t - \widehat{c}_t$$

$$\widehat{c}_t - \widehat{y}_t = -\frac{1}{1-h_{ss}}\widehat{h}_t$$

$$\widehat{c}_{t+1} - \widehat{y}_{t+1} = -\frac{1}{1-h_{ss}}\widehat{h}_{t+1} \tag{3.98}$$

Substituting equation (3.98) into Euler's equation (equation (3.97)):

$$\widehat{c}_t = E_t\left[\widehat{c}_{t+1} - \widehat{y}_{t+1} + \widehat{k}_{t+1}\right]$$

$$\widehat{c}_t = E_t\big[-\frac{1}{1-h_{ss}}\widehat{h}_{t+1} + \widehat{k}_{t+1}\big] \tag{3.99}$$

In addition, from equation (3.96) the capital in "$t + 1$":

$$\begin{aligned} \widehat{y}_t &= \frac{c_{ss}}{y_{ss}}\widehat{c}_t + \frac{i_{ss}}{y_{ss}}\widehat{k}_{t+1} \\ \widehat{k}_{t+1} &= \frac{y_{ss}}{i_{ss}}(\widehat{y}_t - \frac{c_{ss}}{y_{ss}}\widehat{c}_t) \end{aligned} \tag{3.100}$$

This last expression is replaced in the Euler equation (equation (3.99)):

$$\begin{aligned} \widehat{c}_t &= E_t\big[-\frac{1}{1-h_{ss}}\widehat{h}_{t+1} + \widehat{k}_{t+1}\big] \\ \widehat{c}_t &= E_t\big[-\frac{1}{1-h_{ss}}\widehat{h}_{t+1} + \frac{y_{ss}}{i_{ss}}(\widehat{y}_t - \frac{c_{ss}}{y_{ss}}\widehat{c}_t)\big] \\ \widehat{c}_t - \frac{y_{ss}}{i_{ss}}(\widehat{y}_t - \frac{c_{ss}}{i_{ss}}\widehat{c}_t) &= E_t\big[-\frac{1}{1-h_{ss}}\widehat{h}_{t+1}\big] \\ \widehat{c}_t\frac{(c_{ss}+i_{ss})}{i_{ss}} - \frac{y_{ss}}{i_{ss}}\widehat{y}_t &= E_t\big[-\frac{1}{1-h_{ss}}\widehat{h}_{t+1}\big] \\ \widehat{c}_t\frac{y_{ss}}{i_{ss}} - \frac{y_{ss}}{i_{ss}}\widehat{y}_t &= E_t\big[-\frac{1}{1-h_{ss}}\widehat{h}_{t+1}\big] \\ \frac{y_{ss}}{i_{ss}}(\widehat{c}_t - \widehat{y}_t) &= E_t\big[-\frac{1}{1-h_{ss}}\widehat{h}_{t+1}\big] \\ \frac{y_{ss}}{i_{ss}}\left(-\frac{1}{1-h_{ss}}\widehat{h}_t\right) &= E_t\big[-\frac{1}{1-h_{ss}}\widehat{h}_{t+1}\big] \\ \frac{y_{ss}}{i_{ss}}\widehat{h}_t &= E_t\widehat{h}_{t+1} \\ \underbrace{\frac{1}{\beta(1-\alpha)}}_{=\phi_h>1}\widehat{h}_t &= E_t\widehat{h}_{t+1} \end{aligned} \tag{3.101}$$

For a moment let us evaluate equation (3.64) without the expectation operator:

$$\phi_h\widehat{h}_t = \widehat{h}_{t+1} \tag{3.102}$$

Since ϕ_h is greater than one, then this equation is explosive. The only stable solution is when $\widehat{h}_t = 0$. This implies that the model solution for the job is that this variable remains in its steady state: since $\widehat{h}_t = 0$, then, $lnh_t - lnh_{ss} = 0$, which implies that $lnh_t = lnh_{ss}$ and therefore, $h_t = h_{ss}$.

Therefore, the job policy function $\widehat{h}_t$ is $\widehat{h}_t = 0$. Two important conclusions emerge from this last equation. First, it was not necessary to use the method of undetermined coefficients to obtain the solution of $\widehat{h}_t$ and, as we will see later, of the other variables. This is because the two assumptions of the Long and Plosser (1983) model, total depreciation and logarithmic utility, eliminate nonlinearities from the system of equations. This allows the model to be solved directly. Second, the work $\widehat{h}_t$ does not depend on the exogenous variable $\widehat{a}_t$ nor on the state variable $\widehat{k}_t$. This indicates that an increase in productivity does not affect labor directly or indirectly through capital.

To find the solution to the rest of the variables, their behavior equations are reviewed. First, the log-linear production function is reviewed:

$$\begin{aligned}
\widehat{y}_t &= \widehat{a}_t + (1-\alpha)\widehat{k}_t + \alpha\widehat{h}_t \\
\widehat{y}_t &= \widehat{a}_t + (1-\alpha)\widehat{k}_t + 0 \\
\widehat{y}_t &= \widehat{a}_t + \underbrace{(1-\alpha)}_{\eta_{yk}}\widehat{k}_t \\
\widehat{y}_t &= \widehat{a}_t + \eta_{yk}\widehat{k}_t
\end{aligned} \tag{3.103}$$

From the demand for capital we obtain the solution for the real interest rate $\widehat{r}_t$:

$$\begin{aligned}
\widehat{r}_t &= \widehat{y}_t - \widehat{k}_t \\
\text{From equation (3.103)} &: \\
\widehat{r}_t &= \eta_{yk}\widehat{k}_t + \widehat{a}_t - \widehat{k}_t \\
\widehat{r}_t &= \underbrace{(\eta_{yk}-1)}_{\eta_{rk}}\widehat{k}_t + \widehat{a}_t \\
\widehat{r}_t &= \eta_{rk}\widehat{k}_t + \widehat{a}_t
\end{aligned} \tag{3.104}$$

In the labor demand, the real wage $\widehat{w}_t$ is obtained:

$$\begin{aligned}
\widehat{w}_t &= \widehat{y}_t - \widehat{h}_t \\
\text{Of the solution} &: \text{ equation (3.103) y } \widehat{h}_t = 0 \\
\widehat{w}_t &= \eta_{yk}\widehat{k}_t + \widehat{a}_t - 0 \\
\widehat{w}_t &= \eta_{yk}\widehat{k}_t + \widehat{a}_t
\end{aligned} \tag{3.105}$$

Substituting the solution for $\widehat{h}_t$ and $\widehat{w}_t$ in the labor supply, the solution for consumption $\widehat{c}_t$ is found:

$$\frac{h_{ss}}{1-h_{ss}}\widehat{h}_t = \widehat{w}_t - \widehat{c}_t$$

$$
\begin{aligned}
0 &= \widehat{w}_t - \widehat{c}_t \\
\widehat{c}_t &= \widehat{w}_t \\
\widehat{c}_t &= \eta_{yk}\widehat{k}_t + \widehat{a}_t
\end{aligned} \tag{3.106}
$$

From the equilibrium equation in the goods market, the solution for investment is obtained:

$$
\begin{aligned}
\widehat{y}_t &= \frac{c_{ss}}{y_{ss}}\widehat{c}_t + \frac{i_{ss}}{y_{ss}}\widehat{i}_t \\
\widehat{i}_t &= \left(\widehat{y}_t - \frac{c_{ss}}{y_{ss}}\widehat{c}_t\right)\frac{y_{ss}}{i_{ss}} \\
\widehat{i}_t &= \left(\eta_{yk}\widehat{k}_t + \widehat{a}_t - \frac{c_{ss}}{y_{ss}}(\eta_{yk}\widehat{k}_t + \widehat{a}_t)\right)\frac{y_{ss}}{i_{ss}} \\
\widehat{i}_t &= (\eta_{yk}\widehat{k}_t + \widehat{a}_t)(1 - \frac{c_{ss}}{y_{ss}})\frac{y_{ss}}{i_{ss}} \\
\widehat{i}_t &= (\eta_{yk}\widehat{k}_t + \widehat{a}_t)\frac{i_{ss}}{y_{ss}}\frac{y_{ss}}{i_{ss}} \\
\widehat{i}_t &= \eta_{yk}\widehat{k}_t + \widehat{a}_t
\end{aligned} \tag{3.107}
$$

Finally, from the law of movement of capital, the solution for capital is obtained:

$$
\begin{aligned}
\widehat{k}_{t+1} &= \widehat{i}_t \\
\widehat{k}_{t+1} &= \eta_{yk}\widehat{k}_t + \widehat{a}_t
\end{aligned} \tag{3.108}
$$

3.6.2 Blanchard and Kahn Method

The Blanchard and Kahn method solves a system of stochastic difference equations by means of the Jordan decomposition; that is, it tries to split the model or the system into two components. The solution strategy consists of solving the unstable component, from which the policy function is found, and then plugging this policy function into the initial state-space representation to find the equation of state.

In this section, we proceed in two subsections. In the first one, the method is explained in general terms, and, in the second one, the method is applied to the model of Long and Plosser (1983).

Method description Blanchard and Kahn's method can be broken down into seven steps (see Fig. 3.3). The first consists in transforming the system of equations into state-space form. The utility of this representation is that the equations can be written as a first-order difference system. The second step is to obtain an alternate state-space shape, that is, transfer to the right side the matrix of coefficients

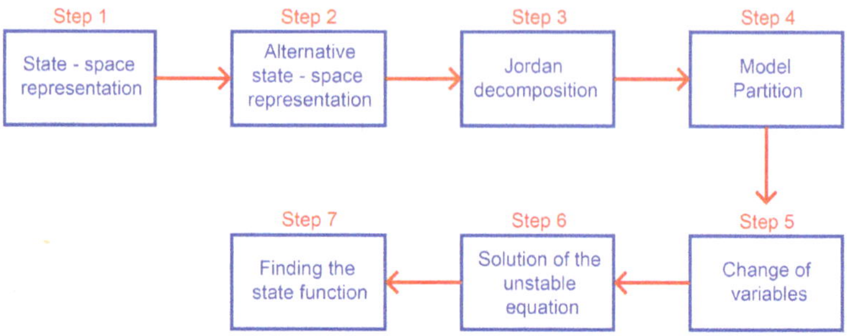

Fig. 3.2 Steps of the Blanchard and Kahn method

associated with the vector on the left of the equation to the right side. The purpose of this is to obtain a system of the following form: $Z_{t+1} = FZ_t + GU_{t+1}$.

The third step is to decompose the system of equations into two parts. For this, the Jordan decomposition is used, which partitions the matrix of coefficients "F" into its associated eigenvalues. The fourth step is to use the Jordan partition to separate the system of equations into an unstable subsystem and a stable subsystem. The unstable nomenclature refers to the equations associated with the unstable eigenvalues (module greater than one) of the matrix "F," and the stable subsystem refers to the equations associated with the stable eigenvalues (module less than one). The fifth step is the change of variable in order to take full advantage of the Jordan decomposition, which simplifies the solution of the model. The sixth step consists in solving the unstable equation by means of the method of *iterated substitution*. The result of this is the *policy function*. Finally, the step is to use the policy function in the alternative state-space model and from there find the *state function* (Fig. 3.2).

Step 1: Generalized State-Space Form

The first step to solving the system of nonlinear equations that represent the model[3] is to put such a system in the state-space form:

$$A\begin{bmatrix} X_{t+1} \\ E_t Y_{t+1} \end{bmatrix} = B\begin{bmatrix} X_t \\ Y_t \end{bmatrix} + CV_{t+1} \tag{3.109}$$

In the representation (3.109), the variable V_{t+1} can be *shocks* iid with mean equal to zero ($E(V_t) = 0$) and zero autocorrelation. Alternatively, V_{t+1} can behave as an AR(1) process, which depends on exogenous *shocks* iid.

In this system of equations, two types of variables can be defined: X_t is the vector of variables *backward looking* (default or state variables). These variables are

[3] It should be mentioned that this system of nonlinear equations is also known as **structural model**. This is because it shows the deep or initial parameters of the model. The reduced model is the one obtained by combining the equations of this initial system; in this case, the parameters are combinations of the deep parameters.

functions only of the known variables in "t," and since they are predetermined, the following holds: $E_t X_{t+1} = X_{t+1}$. An example of this is the capital k_{t+1}, which has been determined in "t"; that is, it is already known in "t"; therefore, $E_t k_{t+1} = k_{t+1}$.

It is worth mentioning that the state variables can be endogenous and exogenous. Usually, the exogenous state variable is productivity because it behaves like an AR(1) and does not depend on any variable in the model. In addition to the above, the second type of variable is the vector of variables *forward looking* (control variables) Y_t.

State variables	Control variables	*Shocks* variables
$X_t = \begin{bmatrix} X_{1t} \\ X_{2t} \\ . \\ . \\ X_{nt} \end{bmatrix}_{nx1}$	$Y_t = \begin{bmatrix} Y_{1t} \\ Y_{2t} \\ . \\ . \\ Y_{mt} \end{bmatrix}_{mx1}$	$V_t = \begin{bmatrix} V_{1t} \\ V_{2t} \\ . \\ . \\ V_{n_v t} \end{bmatrix}_{n_v x1}$

- The number of state variables "n" is equal to the number of endogenous state variables "n_s" plus the number of exogenous state variables "n_v":

$$n = n_s + n_v$$

- The total number of variables "$n + m$" is equal to the total number of equations.

With these considerations, the system (3.72) would be characterized as follows:

$$A_{(n+m)x(n+m)} \begin{bmatrix} X_{t+1} \\ E_t Y_{t+1} \end{bmatrix} = B_{(n+m)x(n+m)} \begin{bmatrix} X_t \\ Y_t \end{bmatrix} + C_{(n+m)xn_v} V_{t+1} \tag{3.110}$$

Step 2: Alternative State-Space Form

$$A \begin{bmatrix} X_{t+1} \\ E_t Y_{t+1} \end{bmatrix} = B \begin{bmatrix} X_t \\ Y_t \end{bmatrix} + C V_{t+1}$$

$$\begin{bmatrix} X_{t+1} \\ E_t Y_{t+1} \end{bmatrix} = \underbrace{A^{-1} B}_{F} \begin{bmatrix} X_t \\ Y_t \end{bmatrix} + \underbrace{A^{-1} C}_{G} V_{t+1}$$

$$\begin{bmatrix} X_{t+1} \\ E_t Y_{t+1} \end{bmatrix} = F \begin{bmatrix} X_t \\ Y_t \end{bmatrix} + G V_{t+1}$$

Step 3: Jordan Decomposition of F

The matrix F can be expressed (by the Jordan decomposition) as follows:

$$F = H J H^{-1} \tag{3.111}$$

$$F = [d_1 ... d_{n+m}] \begin{bmatrix} \lambda_1 & \dots & 0 \\ . & \dots & . \\ . & \dots & . \\ 0 & \dots & \lambda_{n+m} \end{bmatrix} [d_1 ... d_{n+m}]^{-1} \tag{3.112}$$

where H is the matrix of eigenvectors and J is the diagonal matrix of eigenvalues. Also, $\{\lambda_i\}_{i=1}^{n+m}$ are eigenvalues and $\{d_i\}_{i=1}^{n+m}$ are the associated eigenvectors .

Introducing the Jordan decomposition, equation (3.111), in alternate state-space form, we have:

$$\begin{bmatrix} X_{t+1} \\ E_t Y_{t+1} \end{bmatrix} = F \begin{bmatrix} X_t \\ Y_t \end{bmatrix} + G V_{t+1}$$

$$\begin{bmatrix} X_{t+1} \\ E_t Y_{t+1} \end{bmatrix} = H J H^{-1} \begin{bmatrix} X_t \\ Y_t \end{bmatrix} + G V_{t+1}$$

$$H^{-1} \begin{bmatrix} X_{t+1} \\ E_t Y_{t+1} \end{bmatrix} = J H^{-1} \begin{bmatrix} X_t \\ Y_t \end{bmatrix} + H^{-1} G V_{t+1} \tag{3.113}$$

Step 4: Partition the Model

An important step in the Blanchard and Kahn method is that the eigenvalues are ordered in ascending order; this is done in order to identify those eigenvalues that are greater than one in module. Therefore, the ordered eigenvalues, in modulo, are:

$$| \lambda_1 | < | \lambda_2 | < | \lambda_3 | < \dots | \lambda_{n+m} | < \dots$$

Assuming that the eigenvalue array is sorted, "J" can be expressed as follows:

$$J = \begin{bmatrix} J_{1_{nxn}} & 0_{nxm} \\ 0_{mxn} & J_{2_{mxm}} \end{bmatrix}_{(n+m)x(n+m)} \tag{3.114}$$

The matrix "J" has been partitioned into four elements, two of which are important: the first is $J_{1_{nxn}}$, which is a diagonal matrix containing the eigenvalues whose moduli are **minor** to one ($| \lambda | < 1$); the second is $J_{2_{mxm}}$, which is a diagonal matrix containing the eigenvalues whose moduli are **greater** than one ($| \lambda | > 1$).

Based on the partition of the eigenvalue matrix, the eigenvector matrix and its inverse matrix are also partitioned:

Matrix of eigenvectors	Inverse of the matrix of eigenvectors
$H = \begin{bmatrix} H_{11_{nxn}} & H_{12_{nxm}} \\ H_{21_{mxn}} & H_{22_{mxm}} \end{bmatrix}_{(n+m)x(n+m)}$	$H^{-1} = \begin{bmatrix} \widetilde{H}_{11_{nxn}} & \widetilde{H}_{12_{nxm}} \\ \widetilde{H}_{21_{mxn}} & \widetilde{H}_{22_{mxm}} \end{bmatrix}_{(n+m)x(n+m)}$

Considering the partition of matrices in equation (3.114):

$$H^{-1}\begin{bmatrix} X_{t+1} \\ E_t Y_{t+1} \end{bmatrix} = JH^{-1}\begin{bmatrix} X_t \\ Y_t \end{bmatrix} + H^{-1}GV_{t+1}$$

$$\begin{bmatrix} \widetilde{H}_{11} & \widetilde{H}_{12} \\ \widetilde{H}_{21} & \widetilde{H}_{22} \end{bmatrix}\begin{bmatrix} X_{t+1} \\ E_t Y_{t+1} \end{bmatrix} = J\begin{bmatrix} \widetilde{H}_{11} & \widetilde{H}_{12} \\ \widetilde{H}_{21} & \widetilde{H}_{22} \end{bmatrix}\begin{bmatrix} X_t \\ Y_t \end{bmatrix} + \begin{bmatrix} \widetilde{H}_{11} & \widetilde{H}_{12} \\ \widetilde{H}_{21} & \widetilde{H}_{22} \end{bmatrix} GV_{t+1}$$

Furthermore, considering that $G = \begin{bmatrix} G1_{nxn_v} \\ G2_{mxn_v} \end{bmatrix}$

$$\begin{bmatrix} \widetilde{H}_{11} & \widetilde{H}_{12} \\ \widetilde{H}_{21} & \widetilde{H}_{22} \end{bmatrix}\begin{bmatrix} X_{t+1} \\ E_t Y_{t+1} \end{bmatrix} = J\begin{bmatrix} \widetilde{H}_{11} & \widetilde{H}_{12} \\ \widetilde{H}_{21} & \widetilde{H}_{22} \end{bmatrix}\begin{bmatrix} X_t \\ Y_t \end{bmatrix} + \begin{bmatrix} \widetilde{H}_{11} & \widetilde{H}_{12} \\ \widetilde{H}_{21} & \widetilde{H}_{22} \end{bmatrix}\begin{bmatrix} G_1 \\ G_2 \end{bmatrix} V_{t+1} \tag{3.115}$$

Step 5: Change of Variable
In equation (3.114) two new variables $\widetilde{X}_t$ and $\widetilde{Y}_t$ can be defined:

$$\begin{bmatrix} \widetilde{H}_{11} & \widetilde{H}_{12} \\ \widetilde{H}_{21} & \widetilde{H}_{22} \end{bmatrix}\begin{bmatrix} X_t \\ Y_t \end{bmatrix} = \begin{bmatrix} \widetilde{X}_t \\ \widetilde{Y}_t \end{bmatrix} \tag{3.116}$$

In addition, it is considered:

$$\begin{bmatrix} \widetilde{H}_{11} & \widetilde{H}_{12} \\ \widetilde{H}_{21} & \widetilde{H}_{22} \end{bmatrix}\begin{bmatrix} G_1 \\ G_2 \end{bmatrix} = \begin{bmatrix} \widetilde{G}_1 \\ \widetilde{G}_2 \end{bmatrix} \tag{3.117}$$

Introducing the two new variables in equation (3.116) and the new vector $\widetilde{G}$, we have:

$$\begin{bmatrix} \widetilde{H}_{11} & \widetilde{H}_{12} \\ \widetilde{H}_{21} & \widetilde{H}_{22} \end{bmatrix}\begin{bmatrix} X_{t+1} \\ E_t Y_{t+1} \end{bmatrix} = J\begin{bmatrix} \widetilde{H}_{11} & \widetilde{H}_{12} \\ \widetilde{H}_{21} & \widetilde{H}_{22} \end{bmatrix}\begin{bmatrix} X_t \\ Y_t \end{bmatrix} + \begin{bmatrix} \widetilde{H}_{11} & \widetilde{H}_{12} \\ \widetilde{H}_{21} & \widetilde{H}_{22} \end{bmatrix}\begin{bmatrix} G_1 \\ G_2 \end{bmatrix} V_{t+1}$$

$$\begin{bmatrix} \widetilde{X}_{t+1} \\ E_t \widetilde{Y}_{t+1} \end{bmatrix} = J\begin{bmatrix} \widetilde{X}_t \\ \widetilde{Y}_t \end{bmatrix} + \begin{bmatrix} \widetilde{G}_1 \\ \widetilde{G}_2 \end{bmatrix} V_{t+1}$$

$$\begin{bmatrix} \widetilde{X}_{t+1} \\ E_t \widetilde{Y}_{t+1} \end{bmatrix} = \begin{bmatrix} J_1 & 0 \\ 0 & J_2 \end{bmatrix}\begin{bmatrix} \widetilde{X}_t \\ \widetilde{Y}_t \end{bmatrix} + \begin{bmatrix} \widetilde{G}_1 \\ \widetilde{G}_2 \end{bmatrix} V_{t+1} \tag{3.118}$$

Introducing the two new variables in equation (3.116) and the new vector $\widetilde{G}$, we have:

Stable equation

$$\widetilde{X}_{t+1} = J_1 \widetilde{X}_t + \widetilde{G}_1 V_{t+1} \tag{3.119}$$

Unstable equation

$$E_t \widetilde{Y}_{t+1} = J_2 \widetilde{Y}_t + \widetilde{G}_2 V_{t+1} \tag{3.120}$$

The advantage of this decoupling is that each equation can be solved separately.

Step 7: Solving the Unstable Equation (Finding the Policy Function)
Equation (3.120) is a stochastic difference equation with first-order rational expectations. To obtain the solution of this type of equation, the technique of *repeated substitution* is usually applied:

$$E_t\widetilde{Y}_{t+1} = J_2\widetilde{Y}_t + \widetilde{G}_2 V_{t+1}$$

Rearranging the terms and considering that J_2 is a diagonal matrix $(m \times m)$, whose elements are greater than one, we have:

$$\begin{aligned} J_2\widetilde{Y}_t &= E_t\widetilde{Y}_{t+1} - \widetilde{G}_2 V_{t+1} \\ \widetilde{Y}_t &= \underbrace{J_2^{-1}}_{=P_1} E_t\widetilde{Y}_{t+1} - \underbrace{J_2^{-1}\widetilde{G}_2}_{=P_2} V_{t+1} \\ \widetilde{Y}_t &= P_1 E_t\widetilde{Y}_{t+1} - P_2 V_{t+1} \end{aligned} \tag{3.121}$$

where P_1 is a diagonal matrix, whose elements are greater than one. The solution of equation (3.121) is obtained by applying the method of repeated substitution. This technique works as follows: since this equation holds in all periods under rational expectations, then equation (3.121) can be moved forward one period and the expectation operator applied on "t":

$$\begin{aligned} \widetilde{Y}_{t+1} &= P_1 E_t\widetilde{Y}_{t+1} - P_2 V_{t+1} \\ \widetilde{Y}_{t+1} &= P_1 E_t\widetilde{Y}_{t+2} - P_2 V_{t+2} \\ E_t\widetilde{Y}_{t+1} &= P_1 E_t\widetilde{Y}_{t+2} - P_2 E_t V_{t+2} \end{aligned} \tag{3.122}$$

Equation (3.122) is replaced in (3.121) and the following is obtained:

$$\begin{aligned} \widetilde{Y}_t &= P_1 E_t\widetilde{Y}_{t+1} - P_2 V_{t+1} \\ \widetilde{Y}_t &= P_1\left[P_1 E_t\widetilde{Y}_{t+2} - P_2 E_t V_{t+2}\right] - P_2 V_{t+1} \\ \widetilde{Y}_t &= P_1^2 E_t\widetilde{Y}_{t+2} - P_1 P_2 E_t V_{t+2} - P_2 V_{t+1} \end{aligned} \tag{3.123}$$

Moving forward two periods in equation (3.123) and applying expectations on "t," we have:

$$\begin{aligned} \widetilde{Y}_{t+2} &= P_1 E_t\widetilde{Y}_{t+3} - P_2 V_{t+3} \\ E_t\widetilde{Y}_{t+2} &= P_1 E_t\widetilde{Y}_{t+3} - P_2 E_t V_{t+3} \end{aligned} \tag{3.124}$$

Again, substituting equation (3.124) into (3.123), we get:

$$\widetilde{Y}_t = P_1^2\left[P_1 E_t \widetilde{Y}_{t+3} - P_2 E_t V_{t+3}\right] - P_1 P_2 E_t V_{t+2} - P_2 V_{t+1}$$

$$\widetilde{Y}_t = P_1^3 E_t \widetilde{Y}_{t+3} - P_1^2 P_2 E_t V_{t+3} - P_1 P_2 E_t V_{t+2} - P_2 V_{t+1} \tag{3.125}$$

Generalizing equation (3.125) for "n" periods, we have:

$$\begin{aligned}\widetilde{Y}_t &= P_1^n E_t \widetilde{Y}_{t+n} - P_1^{n-1} P_2 E_t V_{t+n} - P_1^{n-2} P_2 E_t V_{t+(n-1)} \\ &\quad - P_1^{n-3} P_2 E_t V_{t+(n-2)} \ldots - P_1 P_2 E_t V_{t+2} - P_2 V_{t+1}\end{aligned} \tag{3.126}$$

In compact form:

$$\widetilde{Y}_t = P_1^n E_t \widetilde{Y}_{t+n} - \sum_{j=2}^{n} P_1^{j-1} P_2 E_t V_{t+j} - P_2 V_{t+1} \tag{3.127}$$

Considering $n \to \infty$:

$$\widetilde{Y}_t = \underset{n\to\infty}{\mathrm{Lim}}\left\{P_1^n E_t \widetilde{Y}_{t+n}\right\} - \underset{n\to\infty}{\mathrm{Lim}} \sum_{j=2}^{n} P_1^{j-1} P_2 E_t V_{t+j} - \underset{n\to\infty}{\mathrm{Lim}}\, P_2 V_{t+1}$$

$$\widetilde{Y}_t = \underset{n\to\infty}{\mathrm{Lim}}\left\{P_1^n E_t \widetilde{Y}_{t+n}\right\} - \sum_{j=2}^{\infty} P_1^{j-1} P_2 E_t V_{t+j} - P_2 V_{t+1} \tag{3.128}$$

The first term of equation (3.128), $\underset{n\to\infty}{\mathrm{Lim}}\left\{P_1^n E_t \widetilde{Y}_{t+n}\right\}$, is equal to zero. This is because the diagonal matrix P_1^n has values less than one, which tend to zero as "n" grows. Furthermore, from an optimization point of view, the fact that this term is equal to zero reflects the transversality condition that is imposed on the solution of this difference equation. From an economic point of view, it makes sense to assume that the expected value of the variable in a very distant time has no influence on the variable today. The following shows the convergence to zero of the matrix P_1^n when n tends to infinity:

$$\begin{aligned}P_1^n &= (J_2^{-1})^n \\ &= \begin{bmatrix} 1/\lambda_{i,1} & & & & \\ & 1/\lambda_{i,1} & & & \\ & & 1/\lambda_{i,1} & & \\ & & & \cdots & \\ & & & & 1/\lambda_{i,m} \end{bmatrix}^n\end{aligned}$$

$$= \begin{bmatrix} 1/\lambda_{i,1} & & & & \\ & 1/\lambda_{i,1}^{n} & & & \\ & & 1/\lambda_{i,1}^{n} & & \\ & & & \cdots & \\ & & & & 1/\lambda_{i,m}^{n} \end{bmatrix}$$

Applying limit with "n" that tends to infinity:

$$\underset{n\to\infty}{\text{Lim}}\, P_1^n = \begin{bmatrix} \underset{n\to\infty}{\text{Lim}}\, 1/\lambda_{i,1} & & & & \\ & \underset{n\to\infty}{\text{Lim}}\, 1/\lambda_{i,1}^{n} & & & \\ & & \underset{n\to\infty}{\text{Lim}}\, 1/\lambda_{i,1}^{n} & & \\ & & & \cdots & \\ & & & & \underset{n\to\infty}{\text{Lim}}\, 1/\lambda_{i,m}^{n} \end{bmatrix}$$

$$\underset{n\to\infty}{\text{Lim}}\, P_1^n = [0]_{mxm}$$

$$\text{So}: \ \underset{n\to\infty}{\text{Lim}} \left\{ P_1^n E_t \widetilde{Y}_{t+n} \right\} = 0 \tag{3.129}$$

Considering the result of equation (3.129), equation (3.128) would be:

$$\widetilde{Y}_t = -\sum_{j=2}^{\infty} P_1^{j-1} P_2 E_t V_{t+j} - P_2 V_{t+1} \tag{3.130}$$

Furthermore, it is known that the variable V_t is distributed as a normal with zero mean and constant variance; that is, $V_t \sim N(0, \sigma_v^2)$. This distribution is maintained for each period; that is, it holds: $V_t \sim N(0, \sigma_v^2)$, $V_{t+1} \sim N(0, \sigma_v^2), \cdots, V_{t+n} \sim N(0, \sigma_v^2)$, where the conditional mean of the variable is always equal to zero: $E_t V_{t+n} = 0$ when $j = 1, 2, 3, \ldots$. Under this premise, then $E_t V_{t+j} = 0$. Replacing this expression in equation (3.92) we have:

$$\widetilde{Y}_t = -\sum_{j=2}^{\infty} P_1^{j-1} P_2 \underbrace{E_t V_{t+j}}_{=0} - P_2 V_{t+1}$$

$$\widetilde{Y}_t = -P_2 V_{t+1} \tag{3.131}$$

Applying the expectation operator in t to equation (3.131), we obtain:

$$\widetilde{Y}_t = -P_2 V_{t+1}$$

$$E_t \widetilde{Y}_t = -P_2 E_t V_{t+1}$$

$$\text{We know}: \ E_t V_{t+1} = 0$$

$$\text{Then :}$$
$$E_t\widetilde{Y}_t = 0$$
$$\text{Therefore :}$$
$$\widetilde{Y}_t = 0 \tag{3.132}$$

From equation (3.116) that reflects the change of variable:

$$\widetilde{H}_{21}X_t + \widetilde{H}_{22}Y_t = \widetilde{Y}_t$$
$$\widetilde{H}_{21}X_t + \widetilde{H}_{22}Y_t = 0$$
$$\widetilde{H}_{22}Y_t = -\widetilde{H}_{21}X_t$$
$$\text{Policy function} = Y_t = -\widetilde{H}_{22}^{-1}\widetilde{H}_{21}X_t \tag{3.133}$$

Equation (3.133) represents the policy function because the control variables (represented by the vector Y_t) are a function of the state variables (represented by the vector X_t).

Step 8: In the Initial System (Finding the State Function)
Rewriting the alternative state-space representation:

$$\begin{bmatrix} X_{t+1} \\ E_tY_{t+1} \end{bmatrix} = F\begin{bmatrix} X_t \\ Y_t \end{bmatrix} + GV_{t+1}$$

$$\begin{bmatrix} X_{t+1} \\ E_tY_{t+1} \end{bmatrix} = \begin{bmatrix} F_{11} & F_{12} \\ F_{21} & F_{22} \end{bmatrix}\begin{bmatrix} X_t \\ Y_t \end{bmatrix} + \begin{bmatrix} G_1 \\ G_2 \end{bmatrix} V_{t+1}$$

The equation for the first variable (the state variable) is:

$$X_{t+1} = F_{11}X_t + F_{12}Y_t + G_1V_{t+1} \tag{3.134}$$

This equation depends on the control variable; however, from the policy function, equation (3.133), the relationship between Y_t and X_t is known. Substituting this relation in equation (3.134):

$$X_{t+1} = F_{11}X_t + F_{12}(-\widetilde{H}_{22}^{-1}\widetilde{H}_{21}X_t) + G_1V_{t+1}$$
$$\text{State equation : } X_{t+1} = (F_{11} - F_{12}\widetilde{H}_{22}^{-1}\widetilde{H}_{21})X_t + G_1V_{t+1} \tag{3.135}$$

Equation (3.135) is the equation of state. With it, the model is solved.

Application of the method In the application of the Long and Plosser model, the same steps will be followed to maintain the common thread of the solution method. Before applying the method, it is necessary to reduce the number of equations and, therefore, the number of variables. The purpose of this is to prevent any zero-filled row from appearing on either side (matrix A or B) of the state-space representation. If, for example, a row of zeros appears in matrix A, then the matrix A would not be invertible. This would make it impossible to apply the Blanchard and Kahn method. Then starting from the system of linear equations (with variables in logarithm) of Table 3.6, some algebraic artifices described below are performed.

First, the real wage w_t is eliminated when considering the equilibrium in the labor market; that is, the labor supply (equation [3] of Table 3.6) is equalized with the labor demand (equation [6] of Table 3.6). The resulting equation is shown below:

$$\begin{aligned}
\text{Labor supply}: & \frac{h_{ss}}{1-h_{ss}}\widehat{h}_t = \widehat{w}_t - \widehat{c}_t \\
\text{Labor demand}: & \widehat{w}_t = \widehat{y}_t - \widehat{h}_t \\
\text{Equilibrium}: & \frac{h_{ss}}{1-h_{ss}}\widehat{h}_t + \widehat{c}_t = \widehat{w}_t = \widehat{y}_t - \widehat{h}_t \\
: & \frac{h_{ss}}{1-h_{ss}}\widehat{h}_t + \widehat{c}_t = \widehat{y}_t - \widehat{h}_t \\
: & \frac{1}{1-h_{ss}}\widehat{h}_t = \widehat{y}_t - \widehat{c}_t
\end{aligned} \tag{3.136}$$

Equation [5] of Table 3.6, which represents the demand for capital, can be inserted into equation [1] (Euler's equation) by means of the interest rate:

$$\begin{aligned}
\text{Capital demand}: & \widehat{r}_t = \widehat{y}_t - \widehat{k}_t \\
\text{Euler's equation}: & \widehat{c}_t = E_t\left[\widehat{c}_{t+1} - \widehat{r}_{t+1}\right] \\
\widehat{r}_{t+1}\text{in Euler's equation}: & \widehat{c}_t = E_t\left[\widehat{c}_{t+1} - \widehat{y}_{t+1} + \widehat{k}_{t+1}\right]
\end{aligned} \tag{3.137}$$

Finally, equation [2] is plugged into the budget constraint (equation [7]):

$$\begin{aligned}
\text{Law of movement of capital}: & \widehat{k}_{t+1} = \widehat{i}_t \\
\text{Budget constraint}: & \widehat{y}_t = \frac{c_{ss}}{y_{ss}}\widehat{c}_t + \frac{i_{ss}}{y_{ss}}\widehat{i}_t \\
: & \widehat{y}_t = \frac{c_{ss}}{y_{ss}}\widehat{c}_t + \frac{i_{ss}}{y_{ss}}\widehat{k}_{t+1}
\end{aligned} \tag{3.138}$$

So far we have a set of five equations with five variables because we have eliminated three variables ($\widehat{r}_t$, $\widehat{i}_t$ and $\widehat{w}_t$). However, the system could still be summarized a little more. Solving the job $\widehat{h}_t$ from equation (3.100) and introducing this expression in the production function (equation [4] of Table 3.6), we have :

$$\text{Equilibrium (labor market)}: \widehat{h}_t = (1-h_{ss})(\widehat{y}_t - \widehat{c}_t)$$

$$
\begin{aligned}
\text{Production function} &: \widehat{y}_t = \widehat{a}_t + (1-\alpha)\widehat{k}_t + \alpha\widehat{h}_t \\
&: \widehat{y}_t = \widehat{a}_t + (1-\alpha)\widehat{k}_t + \alpha(1-h_{ss})(\widehat{y}_t - \widehat{c}_t) \\
&: (1-\alpha(1-h_{ss}))\widehat{y}_t = \widehat{a}_t + (1-\alpha)\widehat{k}_t \\
&\quad -\alpha(1-h_{ss})\widehat{c}_t
\end{aligned} \tag{3.139}
$$

With this last equation and having eliminated the work $\widehat{h}_t$ and its corresponding equation, the system becomes four equations with four variables: $\widehat{c}_t$, $\widehat{y}_t$, $\widehat{k}_t$ y $\widehat{a}_t$.

$$
\text{E1} : \widehat{c}_t = E_t\left[\widehat{c}_{t+1} - \widehat{y}_{t+1} + \widehat{k}_{t+1}\right] \tag{3.140}
$$

$$
\text{E2} : \widehat{y}_t = \frac{c_{ss}}{y_{ss}}\widehat{c}_t + \frac{i_{ss}}{y_{ss}}\widehat{k}_{t+1} \tag{3.141}
$$

$$
\text{E3} : (1-\alpha(1-h_{ss}))\widehat{y}_t = \widehat{a}_t + (1-\alpha)\widehat{k}_t - \alpha(1-h_{ss})\widehat{c}_t \tag{3.142}
$$

$$
\text{E4} : \widehat{a}_t = \phi\widehat{a}_{t-1} + \epsilon_t \tag{3.143}
$$

At this level, one can try to write the system of four equations in state-space form. To do this, the control variables ($\widehat{c}_t$ and $\widehat{y}_t$) and the state variables ($\widehat{k}_t$ and $\widehat{a}_t$) are defined. The first two variables have the expectation operator associated with them, which is why they are considered *forward looking* or control variables. It is worth mentioning that although the capital in "t+1" has the expectation operator associated, this is still a state variable because $\widehat{k}_{t+1}$ is determined in "t." So $E_t\widehat{k}_{t+1}$ is equal to $\widehat{k}_{t+1}$ (without expectations).

The following equation expresses the generic way of writing the system in the state-space form:

$$
A\begin{bmatrix} X_{t+1} \\ E_tY_{t+1} \end{bmatrix} = B\begin{bmatrix} X_t \\ Y_t \end{bmatrix} + CV_{t+1}
$$

where in this particular case $X_t = [\widehat{k}_t \quad \widehat{a}_t]^t$ and $Y_t = [\widehat{y}_t \quad \widehat{c}_t]^t$. Under this premise, the system is written in state-space form:

$$
\begin{bmatrix} -1 & 0 & -1 & 1 \\ -i_{ss}/y_{ss} & 0 & 0 & 0 \\ 0 & 0 & 0 & 0 \\ 0 & 1 & 0 & 0 \end{bmatrix} \begin{bmatrix} \widehat{k}_{t+1} \\ \widehat{a}_{t+1} \\ E_t\widehat{c}_{t+1} \\ E_t\widehat{y}_{t+1} \end{bmatrix} = \dots \tag{3.144}
$$

The state-space representation stopped because the matrix "A" has a line filled with zeros. This makes it impossible to find the inverse of this matrix and, therefore, to find a solution to the system. All this suggests that the model can be further summarized.

Solve the production $\widehat{y}_t$ from equation (3.142) and plug it into equations (3.140) and (3.141). This eliminates a variable ($\widehat{y}_t$) and an equation (3.142):

$$\text{From E3}: \widehat{y}_t = \frac{1}{1-\alpha(1-h_{ss})}(\widehat{a}_t + (1-\alpha)\widehat{k}_t - \alpha(1-h_{ss})\widehat{c}_t) \tag{3.145}$$

$$\text{(3.145) in E2}: \frac{1}{1-\alpha(1-h_{ss})}(\widehat{a}_t + (1-\alpha)\widehat{k}_t - \alpha(1-h_{ss})\widehat{c}_t) = \frac{c_{ss}}{y_{ss}}\widehat{c}_t + \frac{i_{ss}}{y_{ss}}\widehat{k}_{t+1}$$

$$: n_c\widehat{c}_t + n_k\widehat{k}_{t+1} = \widehat{a}_t + (1-\alpha)\widehat{k}_t \tag{3.146}$$

where $n_c = \frac{c_{ss}}{y_{ss}}(1-\alpha(1-h_{ss})) + \alpha(1-h_{ss})$ y $n_k = \frac{i_{ss}}{y_{ss}}(1-\alpha(1-h_{ss}))$. Replacing equation (3.145) in E1 we have:

$$\text{E1}: \widehat{c}_t = E_t\left[\widehat{c}_{t+1} - \widehat{y}_{t+1} + \widehat{k}_{t+1}\right] \tag{3.147}$$

$$: \widehat{c}_t = E_t\Big[\widehat{c}_{t+1} - [\widehat{a}_{t+1} + (1-\alpha)\widehat{k}_{t+1} - \alpha(1-h_{ss})\widehat{c}_{t+1}]\underbrace{\frac{1}{1-\alpha(1-h_{ss})}}_{n_y} + \widehat{k}_{t+1}\Big]$$

$$: \widehat{c}_t = E_t\left[(1+\alpha(1-h_{ss})n_y)\widehat{c}_{t+1} - n_y\widehat{a}_{t+1} + (1-(1-\alpha)n_y)\widehat{k}_{t+1}\right] \tag{3.148}$$

Finally, the system is composed of three equations with three variables—$\widehat{c}_t$, $\widehat{k}_t$ and $\widehat{a}_t$:

$$\begin{aligned} \text{E1}^*: \widehat{c}_t &= E_t\big[(1+\alpha(1-h_{ss})n_y)\widehat{c}_{t+1} - n_y\widehat{a}_{t+1} \\ &\quad + (1-(1-\alpha)n_y)\widehat{k}_{t+1}\big] \end{aligned} \tag{3.149}$$

$$\text{E2}^*: n_c\widehat{c}_t + n_k\widehat{k}_{t+1} = \widehat{a}_t + (1-\alpha)\widehat{k}_t \tag{3.150}$$

$$\text{E3}^*: \widehat{a}_t = \phi\widehat{a}_{t-1} + \epsilon_t \tag{3.151}$$

Considering that the only variable *forward looking* is consumption and that there are two state variables—capital and productivity—we proceed to write this system in the state-space form:

$$\begin{bmatrix} -(1-(1-\alpha)n_y) & n_y & -(1+\alpha(1-h_{ss})n_y) \\ n_k & 0 & 0 \\ 0 & 1 & 0 \end{bmatrix} \begin{bmatrix} \widehat{k}_{t+1} \\ \widehat{a}_{t+1} \\ E_t\widehat{c}_{t+1} \end{bmatrix} =$$

$$\begin{bmatrix} 0 & 0 & -1 \\ (1-\alpha) & 1 & -n_c \\ 0 & \phi & 0 \end{bmatrix} \begin{bmatrix} \widehat{k}_t \\ \widehat{a}_t \\ E_t\widehat{c}_t \end{bmatrix} + \begin{bmatrix} 0 \\ 0 \\ 1 \end{bmatrix} \epsilon_{t+1} \tag{3.152}$$

In this case, each matrix (A and B) does not have rows filled with zeros, so the inverse of A could be found. Next, the steps described above in the Blanchard and

Kahn methodology are followed, but this time applied to the model of Long and Plosser (1983).

Step 1: State-Space Form
In general terms, the state-space form for this model would be:

$$A\begin{bmatrix}\widehat{k}_{t+1}\\ \widehat{a}_{t+1}\\ E_t\widehat{c}_{t+1}\end{bmatrix}=B\begin{bmatrix}\widehat{k}_{t}\\ \widehat{a}_{t}\\ \widehat{c}_{t}\end{bmatrix}+C\epsilon_{t+1} \tag{3.153}$$

However, for this model, the matrices A, B, and C have their own values depending on the parameters:

$$\begin{bmatrix}-(1-(1-\alpha)n_y) & n_y & -(1+\alpha(1-h_{ss})n_y)\\ n_k & 0 & 0\\ 0 & 1 & 0\end{bmatrix}\begin{bmatrix}\widehat{k}_{t+1}\\ \widehat{a}_{t+1}\\ E_t\widehat{c}_{t+1}\end{bmatrix}=$$

$$\begin{bmatrix}0 & 0 & -1\\ (1-\alpha) & 1 & -n_c\\ 0 & \phi & 0\end{bmatrix}\begin{bmatrix}\widehat{k}_{t}\\ \widehat{a}_{t}\\ E_t\widehat{c}_{t}\end{bmatrix}+\begin{bmatrix}0\\0\\1\end{bmatrix}\epsilon_{t+1} \tag{3.154}$$

Replacing the parameter values, equation (3.154) would be:

$$\begin{bmatrix}-0.2860 & 2.14416 & -2.1441\\ 0.1528 & 0 & 0\\ 0 & 1 & 0\end{bmatrix}\begin{bmatrix}\widehat{k}_{t+1}\\ \widehat{a}_{t+1}\\ E_t\widehat{c}_{t+1}\end{bmatrix}=$$

$$\begin{bmatrix}0 & 0 & -1\\ 0.333 & 1 & -0.8472\\ 0 & 0.979 & 0\end{bmatrix}\begin{bmatrix}\widehat{k}_{t}\\ \widehat{a}_{t}\\ \widehat{c}_{t}\end{bmatrix}+\begin{bmatrix}0\\0\\1\end{bmatrix}\epsilon_{t+1} \tag{3.155}$$

Step 2: Alternate State-Space Form
Equation (3.155) is multiplied by the inverse of matrix A in order to obtain the alternative space state form:

$$\begin{bmatrix}\widehat{k}_{t+1}\\ \widehat{a}_{t+1}\\ E_t\widehat{c}_{t+1}\end{bmatrix}=\begin{bmatrix}2.1789 & 6.5434 & -5.5434\\ 0 & 0.9790 & 0\\ -0.2907 & 0.1061 & 1.2059\end{bmatrix}\begin{bmatrix}\widehat{k}_{t}\\ \widehat{a}_{t}\\ \widehat{c}_{t}\end{bmatrix}+\begin{bmatrix}0\\1\\1\end{bmatrix}\epsilon_{t+1} \tag{3.156}$$

where the matrix accompanying the vector $[\widehat{k}_t, \widehat{a}_t, \widehat{c}_t]^t$ is the matrix "F" and the vector [0,1,1] t is the vector "G." It is worth mentioning that the inverse of matrix A is represented by the following matrix:

$$A^{-1} = \begin{bmatrix} 0 & 6.5434 & 0 \\ 0 & 0 & 1.0000 \\ -0.4664 & -0.8729 & 1.0000 \end{bmatrix}$$

Step 3: Jordan Decomposition of F
By applying the Jordan decomposition of the matrix F, the following is obtained:

$$J = \begin{bmatrix} 0.333 & 0 & 0 \\ 0 & 0.979 & 0 \\ 0 & 0 & 3.0518 \end{bmatrix} \tag{3.157}$$

In matrix J it can be seen that it has two eigenvalues with a modulus less than one and an eigenvalue with a modulus greater than one. The Blanchard and Kahn condition for the system to have a unique solution indicates that the number of eigenvalues with modulus greater than one must be equal to the number of variables *forward looking*. Since consumption is the only variable *forward looking*, then the Blanchard and Kahn condition holds for this model.

Step 4: Partition the Model
Partitioning the matrix of eigenvalues, we have J_1 that contains those stable eigenvalues.

$$J_1 = \begin{bmatrix} 0.333 & 0 \\ 0 & 0.979 \end{bmatrix} \tag{3.158}$$

On the other hand, J_2 contains the only unstable eigenvalue:

$$J_2 = 3.0518 \tag{3.159}$$

Also, considering the matrix inverse of H and its partitioned matrices:

$$H^{-1} = \begin{bmatrix} 0.3384 & -3.7805 & 2.1490 \\ 0 & 2.3860 & 0 \\ 0.6873 & 2.0640 & -2.0640 \end{bmatrix} \quad H^{-1} = \begin{bmatrix} \widetilde{H}_{11_{nxn}} & \widetilde{H}_{12_{nxm}} \\ \widetilde{H}_{21_{mxn}} & \widetilde{H}_{22_{mxm}} \end{bmatrix}$$

where each partitioned array is:

$$\widetilde{H}_{11} = \begin{bmatrix} 0.3384 & -3.7805 \\ 0 & 2.3860 \end{bmatrix} \quad \widetilde{H}_{12} = \begin{bmatrix} 2.1490 \\ 0 \end{bmatrix} \quad \widetilde{H}_{21} = \begin{bmatrix} 0.6873 & 2.0640 \end{bmatrix}$$
$$\widetilde{H}_{22} = \begin{bmatrix} -2.0640 \end{bmatrix}$$

Step 5: Change of Variable
In line with equation (3.116) we have:

$$\begin{bmatrix} \widetilde{H}_{11} & \widetilde{H}_{12} \\ \widetilde{H}_{21} & \widetilde{H}_{22} \end{bmatrix} \begin{bmatrix} X_t \\ Y_t \end{bmatrix} = \begin{bmatrix} \widetilde{X}_t \\ \widetilde{Y}_t \end{bmatrix}$$

Applying to the model parameters:

$$\begin{bmatrix} 0.3384 & -3.7805 & 2.1490 \\ 0 & 2.3860 & 0 \\ 0.6873 & 2.0640 & -2.0640 \end{bmatrix} \begin{bmatrix} \widehat{k}_t \\ \widehat{a}_t \\ \widehat{c}_t \end{bmatrix} = \begin{bmatrix} \widetilde{\widetilde{k}}_t \\ \widetilde{\widetilde{a}}_t \\ \widetilde{\widetilde{c}}_t \end{bmatrix} \tag{3.160}$$

Similarly with equation (3.117):

$$\begin{bmatrix} \widetilde{H}_{11} & \widetilde{H}_{12} \\ \widetilde{H}_{21} & \widetilde{H}_{22} \end{bmatrix} \begin{bmatrix} G_1 \\ G_2 \end{bmatrix} = \begin{bmatrix} \widetilde{G}_1 \\ \widetilde{G}_2 \end{bmatrix}$$

We apply it to the model parameters:

$$\begin{bmatrix} 0.3384 & -3.7805 & 2.1490 \\ 0 & 2.3860 & 0 \\ 0.6873 & 2.0640 & -2.0640 \end{bmatrix} \begin{bmatrix} 0 \\ 1 \\ 1 \end{bmatrix} = \begin{bmatrix} \widetilde{G}_1 \\ \widetilde{G}_2 \end{bmatrix} \tag{3.161}$$

Therefore, the system with the change of variable would be:

$$\begin{bmatrix} \widetilde{\widetilde{k}}_{t+1} \\ \widetilde{\widetilde{a}}_{t+1} \\ E_t\widetilde{\widetilde{c}}_{t+1} \end{bmatrix} = \begin{bmatrix} J_1 & 0 \\ 0 & J_2 \end{bmatrix} \begin{bmatrix} \widetilde{\widetilde{k}}_t \\ \widetilde{\widetilde{a}}_t \\ \widetilde{\widetilde{c}}_t \end{bmatrix} + \begin{bmatrix} \widetilde{G}_1 \\ \widetilde{G}_2 \end{bmatrix} \epsilon_{t+1}$$

$$\begin{bmatrix} \widetilde{\widetilde{k}}_{t+1} \\ \widetilde{\widetilde{a}}_{t+1} \\ E_t\widetilde{\widetilde{c}}_{t+1} \end{bmatrix} = \begin{bmatrix} 0.3330 & 0 & 0 \\ 0 & 0.9790 & 0 \\ 0 & 0 & 3.0518 \end{bmatrix} \begin{bmatrix} \widetilde{\widetilde{k}}_t \\ \widetilde{\widetilde{a}}_t \\ \widetilde{\widetilde{c}}_t \end{bmatrix} + \begin{bmatrix} -1.6316 \\ 2.3860 \\ 0 \end{bmatrix} \epsilon_{t+1} \tag{3.162}$$

Step 6: Decoupling the Equations
From equation (3.118), two subsystems could be obtained; that is, the system can be decoupled:

Stable equation

$$\widetilde{X}_{t+1} = J_1\widetilde{X}_t + \widetilde{G}_1 V_{t+1}$$

$$\begin{bmatrix} \widetilde{\widetilde{k}}_{t+1} \\ \widetilde{\widetilde{a}}_{t+1} \end{bmatrix} = \begin{bmatrix} 0.3330 & 0 \\ 0 & 0.9790 \end{bmatrix} \begin{bmatrix} \widetilde{\widetilde{k}}_t \\ \widetilde{\widetilde{a}}_t \end{bmatrix} + \begin{bmatrix} -1.6316 \\ 2.3860 \end{bmatrix} \epsilon_{t+1} \tag{3.163}$$

Unstable equation

$$E_t\widetilde{Y}_{t+1} = J_2\widetilde{Y}_t + \widetilde{G}_2 V_{t+1}$$

$$E_t\widetilde{\widetilde{c}}_{t+1} = 3.0518\widetilde{\widetilde{c}}_t + 0\epsilon_{t+1} \tag{3.164}$$

Step 7: Solving the Unstable Equation (Finding the Policy Function)
Solving equation (3.164) we have:

$$\widetilde{\widehat{c_t}} = 0 \tag{3.165}$$

In addition, it is known from the change of variable (equation (3.160)) that:

$$\widetilde{\widehat{c_t}} = 0.6873\widehat{k_t} + 2.064\widehat{a_t} - 2.064\widehat{c_t} \tag{3.166}$$

Therefore, combining equation (3.165) and (3.166):

$$\widehat{c_t} = \frac{0.6873}{2.064}\widehat{k_t} + \frac{2.064}{2.064}\widehat{a_t}$$

$$\widehat{c_t} = 0.333\widehat{k_t} + \widehat{a_t} \tag{3.167}$$

Equation (3.167) represents the policy function for consumption.

Step 8: In the Initial System (Finding the State Function)
The following equation is the alternative state-space representation (equation (3.156)) mentioned above:

$$\begin{bmatrix} \widehat{k}_{t+1} \\ \widehat{a}_{t+1} \\ E_t\widehat{c}_{t+1} \end{bmatrix} = \begin{bmatrix} 2.1789 & 6.5434 & -5.5434 \\ 0 & 0.9790 & 0 \\ -0.2907 & 0.1061 & 1.2059 \end{bmatrix} \begin{bmatrix} \widehat{k_t} \\ \widehat{a_t} \\ \widehat{c_t} \end{bmatrix} + \begin{bmatrix} 0 \\ 1 \\ 1 \end{bmatrix} \epsilon_{t+1}$$

From this equation, we can obtain the equations for the state variables. For example, for $\widehat{k}_{t+1}$ we have:

$$\widehat{k_t} = 2.1789\widehat{k_t} + 6.5434\widehat{a_t} - 5.5434\widehat{c_t} \tag{3.168}$$

Replacing the policy equation (equation (3.167)) we have:

$$\widehat{k}_{t+1} = 2.1789\widehat{k_t} + 6.5434\widehat{a_t} - 5.5434(0.333\widehat{k_t} + \widehat{a_t})$$

$$\widehat{k}_{t+1} = 0.333\widehat{k_t} + \widehat{a_t} \tag{3.169}$$

This equation represents the equation of state. The same is done with the second variable, which shows the evolution of productivity:

$$\widehat{a}_{t+1} = 0.9790\widehat{a_t} + \epsilon_{t+1} \tag{3.170}$$

With the policy function for consumption and the state function, the decision rules for the other variables could be obtained. From Table 3.6, which contains the log-linear equations, equation [2] can be extracted:

$$\widehat{i}_t = \widehat{k}_{t+1}$$
$$\widehat{i}_t = 0.333\widehat{k}_t + \widehat{a}_t \tag{3.171}$$

Equation (3.171) represents the policy function (solution) for the investment $\widehat{i}_t$. From equation [7] of the same table, the solution for production can be obtained (equation (3.172)):

$$\widehat{y}_t = \frac{c_{ss}}{y_{ss}}\widehat{c}_t + \frac{i_{ss}}{y_{ss}}\widehat{i}_t$$
$$\widehat{y}_t = \frac{c_{ss}}{y_{ss}}(0.333\widehat{k}_t + \widehat{a}_t) + \frac{i_{ss}}{y_{ss}}(0.333\widehat{k}_t + \widehat{a}_t)$$
$$\widehat{y}_t = \underbrace{(\frac{c_{ss}}{y_{ss}} + \frac{i_{ss}}{y_{ss}})}_{=1}(0.333\widehat{k}_t + \widehat{a}_t)$$
$$\widehat{y}_t = 0.333\widehat{k}_t + \widehat{a}_t \tag{3.172}$$

In the same way for the interest rate (equation [5] of Table 3.6):

$$\widehat{r}_t = \widehat{y}_t - \widehat{k}_t$$
$$\widehat{r}_t = (0.333\widehat{k}_t + \widehat{a}_t) - \widehat{k}_t$$
$$\widehat{r}_t = -0.667\widehat{k}_t + \widehat{a}_t \tag{3.173}$$

For the job $\widehat{h}_t$, equation [4] is used to obtain its solution:

$$\widehat{y}_t = \widehat{a}_t + \underbrace{(1-\alpha)}_{=0.333}\widehat{k}_t + \alpha\widehat{h}_t$$
$$0.333\widehat{k}_t + \widehat{a}_t = \widehat{a}_t + 0.333\widehat{k}_t + \alpha\widehat{h}_t$$
$$0 = \alpha\widehat{h}_t$$
$$\widehat{h}_t = 0 \tag{3.174}$$

Finally, from equation [3] we obtain the solution for the real wage $\widehat{w}_t$:

$$\frac{h_{ss}}{1-h_{ss}}\widehat{h}_t = \widehat{w}_t - \widehat{c}_t$$
$$0 = \widehat{w}_t - (0.333\widehat{k}_t + \widehat{a}_t)$$
$$\widehat{w}_t = 0.333\widehat{k}_t + \widehat{a}_t \tag{3.175}$$

Equations (3.167) and (3.169) to (3.175) represent the solution of the system of log-linear equations, which are similar to those obtained analytically (Table 3.7).

Table 3.7 Policy and state functions (model solution)

Policy functions	Coefficients (elasticities)	Values
[1] $\widehat{h}_t = 0$		
[2] $\widehat{y}_t = \eta_{yk}\widehat{k}_t + \widehat{a}_t$	$\eta_{yk} = 1 - \alpha$	$\eta_{yk} = 0.333$
[3] $\widehat{r}_t = \eta_{rk}\widehat{k}_t + \widehat{a}_t$	$\eta_{rk} = \eta_{yk} - 1$	$\eta_{rk} = 0.667$
[4] $\widehat{w}_t = \eta_{yk}\widehat{k}_t + \widehat{a}_t$		
[5] $\widehat{c}_t = \eta_{yk}\widehat{k}_t + \widehat{a}_t$		
[6] $\widehat{i}_t = \eta_{yk}\widehat{k}_t + \widehat{a}_t$		
[7] $\widehat{k}_{t+1} = \eta_{yk}\widehat{k}_t + \widehat{a}_t$		

Fig. 3.3 Policy function

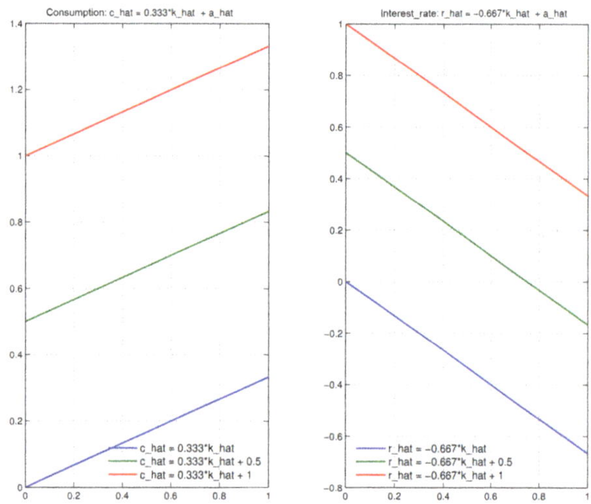

In Fig. 3.3 the function of consumption policy and interest rate is plotted. The relationship between these variables and capital is linear because the approximation of the solution has been restricted to the first-order Taylor expansion.

3.7 Time Series Representation

The policy and state functions are useful for finding the time series representation of each variable. First, productivity must be expressed in its MA(∞) form and then it is necessary to find the time series representation of the state variable k_t in its MA(∞) form. The MA(∞) representation allows obtaining both variables based on the error ϵ_t. Finally, because the other variables are a function of productivity and capital, then the time series representation of each of them can be obtained by simply substituting the MA(∞) form of productivity and of capital in each policy function. The described procedure is shown below.

$$\begin{aligned}\widehat{a}_t &= \phi\widehat{a}_{t-1} + \epsilon_t \\ (1-\phi L)\widehat{a}_t &= \epsilon_t \\ \widehat{a}_t &= \frac{\epsilon_t}{1-\phi L}\end{aligned} \tag{3.176}$$

Following the same procedure for capital and considering the representation (3.176):

$$\begin{aligned}\widehat{k}_{t+1} &= \eta_{yk}\widehat{k}_t + \widehat{a}_t \\ (1-\eta_{yk}L)\widehat{k}_{t+1} &= \widehat{a}_t \\ (1-\eta_{yk}L)\widehat{k}_{t+1} &= \frac{\epsilon_t}{1-\phi L} \\ \widehat{k}_{t+1} &= \frac{\epsilon_t}{(1-\eta_{yk}L)(1-\phi L)}\end{aligned} \tag{3.177}$$

Equation (3.177) indicates that capital behaves like an AR(2):

$$\begin{aligned}(1-(\eta_{yk}+\phi)L + \eta_{yk}\phi L^2)\widehat{k}_{t+1} &= \epsilon_t \\ \widehat{k}_{t+1} - (\eta_{yk}+\phi)\widehat{k}_t + \eta_{yk}\phi\widehat{k}_{t-1} &= \epsilon_t \\ \widehat{k}_{t+1} &= \eta_{yk}+\phi)\widehat{k}_t - \eta_{yk}\phi\widehat{k}_{t-1} + \epsilon_t\end{aligned} \tag{3.178}$$

From Table 3.7 it can be seen that output, consumption, investment, and wages have the same policy function, which is the same as that of capital:

$$\widehat{y}_t = \widehat{c}_t = \widehat{i}_t = \widehat{w}_t = \widehat{k}_{t+1} = \eta_{yk}\widehat{k}_t + \widehat{a}_t$$

Therefore, these variables also behave like an AR(2), the same time series representation of capital and even the same coefficients associated with each component of the time series. On the other hand, the interest rate policy function is different from the other variables in its coefficient associated with capital:

$$\begin{aligned}\widehat{r}_t &= \eta_{rk}\widehat{k}_t + \widehat{a}_t \\ \text{where}: \eta_{rk} &= \eta_{yk} - 1 \\ \widehat{r}_t &= (\eta_{yk}-1)\widehat{k}_t + \widehat{a}_t\end{aligned}$$

$$\widehat{r}_t = \underbrace{\eta_{yk}\widehat{k}_t + \widehat{a}_t}_{=\widehat{k}_{t+1}} - \widehat{k}_t$$

$$\widehat{r}_t = \widehat{k}_{t+1} - \widehat{k}_t$$

$$\widehat{r}_t = \frac{\epsilon_t}{(1-\eta_{yk}L)(1-\phi L)} - \frac{\epsilon_{t-1}}{(1-\eta_{yk}L)(1-\phi L)}$$

$$\widehat{r}_t = \frac{\epsilon_t - \epsilon_{t-1}}{(1-\eta_{yk}L)(1-\phi L)}$$

$$\widehat{r}_t = \frac{(1-L)\epsilon_t}{(1-\eta_{yk}L)(1-\phi L)} \tag{3.179}$$

Equation (3.179) suggests that the interest rate behaves like an ARMA(2,1), as can be seen in the following equation:

$$\widehat{r}_t = \frac{(1-L)\epsilon_t}{(1-\eta_{yk}L)(1-\phi L)}$$

$$(1-(\eta_{yk}+\phi)L + \eta_{yk}\phi L^2)\widehat{r}_t = \epsilon_t - \epsilon_{t-1}$$

$$\widehat{k}_{t+1} - (\eta_{yk}+\phi)\widehat{r}_{t-1} + \eta_{yk}\phi\widehat{r}_{t-2} = \epsilon_t - \epsilon_{t-1}$$

$$\widehat{r}_t = (\eta_{yk}+\phi)\widehat{r}_{t-1} - \eta_{yk}\phi\widehat{r}_{t-2} + \epsilon_t - \epsilon_{t-1} \tag{3.180}$$

It is worth mentioning that, like the other endogenous variables, the interest rate maintains the coefficients of the autoregressive component of order 2 that capital presents. A summary of the time series representation of the model variables is shown in Table 3.8.

So far, the solution of the model has been found, which are decision rules that describe the optimal consumption, work, and investment of the representative agent. These rules depend on the (default) capital stock and productivity. To show the effect of the *shock* of productivity in these decisions, productivity could be replaced by its representation MA(∞). From equation (3.176) the moving average version of productivity can be obtained:

Table 3.8 Time series representation

Variable	Time series
$\widehat{y}_t$	AR(2)
$\widehat{c}_t$	AR(2)
$\widehat{i}_t$	AR(2)
$\widehat{k}_t$	AR(2)
$\widehat{h}_t$	AR(2)
$\widehat{w}_t$	AR(2)
$\widehat{r}_t$	AR(2)
$\widehat{a}_t$	AR(1)

$$\widehat{a}_t = \frac{\epsilon_t}{1 - \phi L}$$

$$\widehat{a}_t = \epsilon_t + \phi\epsilon_{t-1} + \phi^2\epsilon_{t-2} + \phi^3\epsilon_{t-3} + \ldots$$

Introducing this expression in the solution, for example, of the product (equation (3.172)):

$$\widehat{y}_t = 0.333\widehat{k}_t + \widehat{a}_t$$

$$\widehat{y}_t = 0.333\widehat{k}_t + \epsilon_t + \phi\epsilon_{t-1} + \phi^2\epsilon_{t-2} + \phi^3\epsilon_{t-3} + \ldots$$

In compact form :

$$\widehat{y}_t = 0.333\widehat{k}_t + \sum_{j=0}^{\infty} \phi^j \epsilon_{t-j}$$

This last equation suggests that today's product depends on the *stock* of capital accumulated up to today (which was determined in the previous period) and on the accumulation of *shocks* on productivity (positive or negative).

3.8 Impulse-Response Functions

The impulse-response function represents the temporary behavior of each endogenous variable before the realization of a *shock*. It is important to note that each element of this function is an equilibrium. For example, each value of the consumption impulse-response function reflects the equilibrium in the goods market in each period. Similarly, the wage impulse-response function reflects the equilibrium in each period of the labor market.

Figure 3.4 illustrates the reactions of the variables to a positive *shock* of productivity in the period "t = 1." To understand why each variable behaves as shown in the Fig. 3.4, the behavior of the variables (of the model in general) will be analyzed from "t = 0" to "t = 4."

Period $t = 0$ In this period, the economy is in a steady state; that is, it is in long-term equilibrium. In such an equilibrium, all variables are equal to their steady-state value:

$$\widehat{r}_0 = \widehat{y}_0 = \widehat{c}_0 = \widehat{w}_0 = \widehat{h}_0 = \widehat{i}_0 = \widehat{k}_0 = \widehat{a}_0 = 0$$

Furthermore, the capital in the period "t = 1" is equal to the investment in "t = 0":

$$\widehat{k}_1 = \widehat{i}_0 = 0$$

From the above, we conclude that the capital in the period "t = 0" and "t = 1" is equal to zero (it is in its steady state):

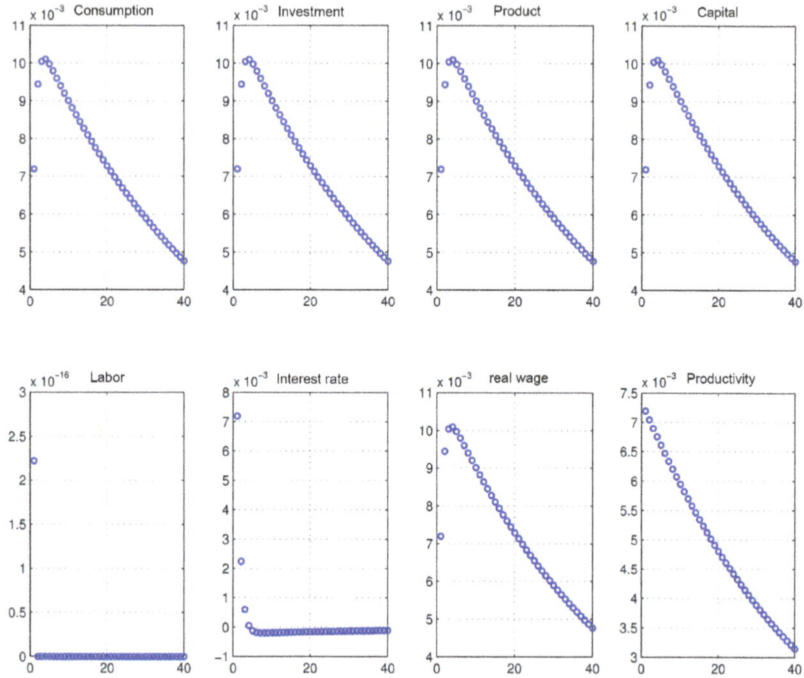

Fig. 3.4 Impulse-response function. (**Note:** This impulse-response graph is obtained from the file "irfs_nolineal_log.m")

$$\widehat{k}_1 = \widehat{k}_0 = 0$$

Period $t = 1$ In this period the *shock* occurs, which takes the value of its standard deviation $\sigma_\epsilon = 0.0072$:

$$\widehat{a}_1 = \phi \underbrace{\widehat{a}_0}_{=0} + \underbrace{\epsilon_1}_{=\sigma_\epsilon}$$

$$\widehat{a}_1 = \sigma_\epsilon \tag{3.181}$$

Reactions of firms The increase in productivity positively influences the product, which in turn increases the demand for factors.

$$\uparrow \widehat{a}_1 \rightarrow \uparrow \widehat{y}_1 \rightarrow \uparrow Pmg\widehat{k}_1(D_{k_1}) \wedge \uparrow Pmg\widehat{h}_1(D_{h_1})$$

First, the direct effect of increased productivity is on the production function:

$$\widehat{y}_1 = \underbrace{\widehat{a}_1}_{=\sigma_\epsilon} + (1-\alpha) \underbrace{\widehat{k}_1}_{=0} + \alpha \widehat{h}_1$$

$$\widehat{y}_1 = \sigma_\epsilon + \alpha \widehat{h}_1 \tag{3.182}$$

Equation (3.182) suggests that output at "t = 1" is greater than at "t = 0" even though work is equal to zero. Second, this increase in production generates an increase in the marginal productivity of capital and labor; that is, it encourages a greater demand for these factors by the firm.

$$\begin{aligned} \text{Labor demand} : \widehat{w}_1 &= \widehat{y}_1 - \widehat{h}_1 \\ : \widehat{w}_1 &= \sigma_\epsilon + \alpha \widehat{h}_1 - \widehat{h}_1 \end{aligned} \tag{3.183}$$

Therefore, since $\widehat{y}_1 > \widehat{y}_0$, then the labor demand increases (see Fig. 3.5). Third, the demand for capital expands:

$$\begin{aligned} \text{Capital demand} : \widehat{r}_1 &= \widehat{y}_1 - \underbrace{\widehat{k}_1}_{=0} \\ : \widehat{r}_1 &= \widehat{y}_1 = \sigma_\epsilon + \alpha \widehat{h}_1 \end{aligned} \tag{3.184}$$

Reactions of the household The representative household is indirectly affected by the *shock* of productivity through the factor market. Faced with this change in conditions, the household responds by adjusting its labor and capital supply curve.

First, since the supply of capital at "t = 1" has been determined at "t = 0," which is equal to zero, that is, capital remains in the steady state, the equilibrium in the capital market at "t = 1" is determined at point "B" of Fig. 3.5. The increase in the interest rate ($\widehat{r}_1 > \widehat{r}_0$) produces two effects on consumption. The first is known as the substitution effect, which indicates that an increase in the expected interest rate in the following period reduces consumption in the current period and increases consumption in the following period. This is because the consumer has the

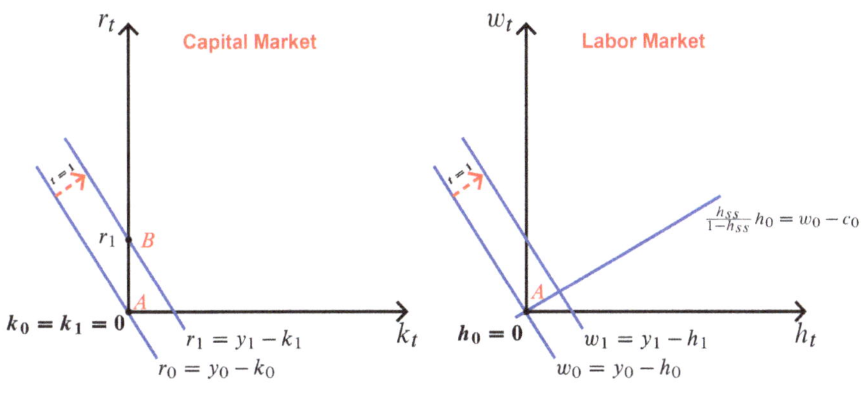

Fig. 3.5 Firm response to productivity *shock* ($t = 1$)

willingness to substitute consumption intertemporally if the incentive (the interest rate) is getting stronger. It is worth mentioning that by “increase” we mean that the variable is above its steady state; that is, $\widehat{r}_t > 0$. When this happens, the substitution effect suggests that consumption $\widehat{c}_{t-1}$ is reduced. On the other hand, if $\widehat{r}_t < 0$, the consumption $\widehat{c}_{t-1}$ increases.

The analysis of the substitution effect is carried out using the Euler equation. When analyzing this equation in $t = 0$ we have:

$$\widehat{c}_0 = E_t[\widehat{c}_1 - \widehat{r}_1]$$

In this case, an increase of $\widehat{r}_1$ would produce a decrease of $\widehat{c}_0$ and an increase of $\widehat{c}_1$; however, since at $t = 0$ the economy is in steady state, the only effect that remains is the increase in consumption at “$t = 1$.” That is, $\widehat{c}_1 = \widehat{r}_1$ (**effect 0**).

Since the household is stopped at “t = 1,” it is necessary to analyze the substitution effect in this period:

$$\widehat{c}_1 = E_t[\widehat{c}_2 - \widehat{r}_2]$$

This equation suggests that if the next period’s interest rate increases, that is, $\widehat{r}_2 > 0$, then today’s consumption $\widehat{c}_1$ decreases. As will be seen later, effectively at “t = 2” we have $\widehat{r}_2 > 0$ and, therefore, the substitution effect indicates that $\widehat{c}_1$ decreases (**effect 1**).

The second effect of the interest rate is known as the “wealth effect” or “income effect,” which indicates that the consumer feels richer because the rental cost of capital (interest rate) has increased and so has their income. To analyze this effect it is necessary to use the budget constraint (in levels) at “t = 1”:

$$c_1 + i_1 = w_t h_1 + r_1 k_1$$

Given the increase in the interest rate at “t = 1,” the household could allocate these resources to greater consumption $\widehat{c}_1$ and investment $\widehat{i}_1$ (**effect 2**). So far these two effects are opposed, so the natural question is: which effect is dominant? In this model, both effects cancel each other out because the intertemporal elasticity of substitution is equal to one. As will be shown in Chap. 4, the dominance of the substitution effect over the income effect depends on the elasticity of substitution. Therefore, there is no movement in consumption in this way, only because of the substitution effect at “t = 0” that produces an increase in consumption at “t = 1” (**effect 0**).

Figure 3.6 shows the reaction of the household through the labor supply, leading the equilibrium at “t = 1” to point “B.” The question that arises is, then, to what extent does the household reduce its labor supply, if we assume that h_1 is the final equilibrium? If this is so, it must be fulfilled that the wage w_1 must balance the labor supply and demand:

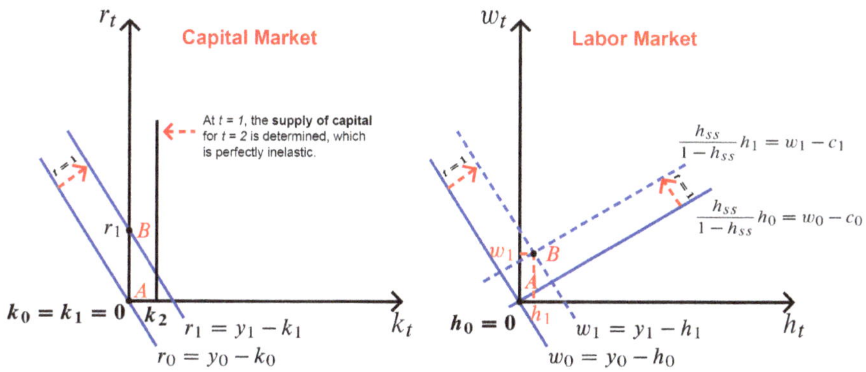

Fig. 3.6 Household response to *productivity shock* ($t = 1$)

$$\underbrace{\frac{h_{ss}}{1-h_{ss}}\widehat{h}_1 + \widehat{c}_1}_{\text{labor supply}} = \widehat{w}_1 = \underbrace{\widehat{y}_1 - \widehat{h}_1}_{\text{labor demand}} \tag{3.185}$$

Working on both sides of (3.185), we have:

$$\frac{h_{ss}}{1-h_{ss}}\widehat{h}_1 = \widehat{y}_1 - \widehat{c}_1 \tag{3.186}$$

But it is known that:

$$\widehat{c}_1 = \widehat{r}_1 = \widehat{y}_1 = \sigma_\epsilon + \alpha\widehat{h}_1$$

So substituting this expression into equation (3.186):

$$\frac{h_{ss}}{1-h_{ss}}\widehat{h}_1 = 0 \tag{3.187}$$

Therefore, the equilibrium work at "t = 1" is equal to zero; that is, it is equal to its steady-state value: $\widehat{h}_1 = 0$. Therefore, what really happens with the labor supply is that it is successively reduced until it reaches point "C" (see Fig. 3.7).

Therefore, to summarize the equilibrium values of the variables, we have the following: $\widehat{a}_1 = \sigma_\epsilon$, then $\widehat{h}_1 = 0$ and $\widehat{y}_1 = \widehat{w}_1 = \widehat{c}_1 = \widehat{r}_1 = \sigma_\epsilon$.

Also, $\widehat{k}_1 = 0$ and $\widehat{i}_1 = \widehat{k}_2$. To find the value of $\widehat{k}_2$, the goods market equilibrium equation is used:

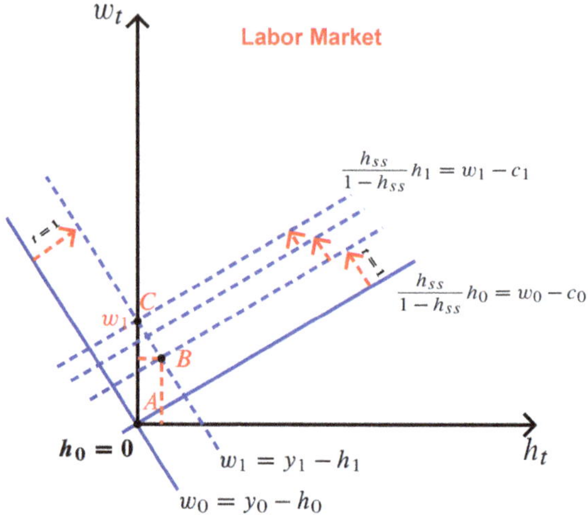

Fig. 3.7 Equilibrium in the labor market ($t = 1$)

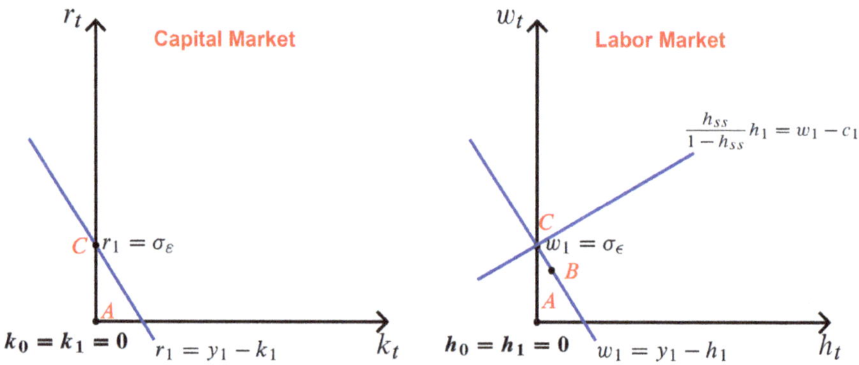

Fig. 3.8 Equilibrium at $t = 1$

$$\begin{aligned}
\underbrace{\widehat{y_1}}_{=\widehat{c_1}} &= \frac{c_{ss}}{y_{ss}}\widehat{c_1} + \frac{i_{ss}}{y_{ss}}\widehat{i_1} \\
(1 - \frac{c_{ss}}{y_{ss}})\widehat{c_1} &= \frac{i_{ss}}{y_{ss}}\widehat{i_1} \\
\frac{i_{ss}}{y_{ss}}\widehat{c_1} &= \frac{i_{ss}}{y_{ss}}\widehat{i_1} \\
\widehat{c_1} &= \widehat{i_1}
\end{aligned} \tag{3.188}$$

Since $\widehat{c_1} = \sigma_\epsilon$, then $\widehat{i_1} = \sigma_\epsilon$ and therefore $\widehat{k_2} = \sigma_\epsilon$. Figure 3.8 indicates the final equilibrium in the period "t= 1" in the factor market.

Period $t = 2$ In this period even the effect of productivity can be seen, although with less force. Equation (3.189) indicates that productivity in this period $\widehat{a_2}$ is lower than in the previous period $\widehat{a_1}$:

$$\widehat{a}_2 = \phi \underbrace{\widehat{a}_1}_{=\sigma_\epsilon} + \underbrace{\epsilon_2}_{=0}$$

$$\widehat{a}_2 = \phi\sigma_\epsilon \tag{3.189}$$

It is worth mentioning that the *shock* considered in this model is temporary; that is, its realization is in a single period and is equal to its standard deviation: $\epsilon_1 = \sigma_\epsilon$. In the following periods, the *shock* is equal to its steady state; that is: $\epsilon_2 = \epsilon_3 = \epsilon_4 = \ldots = 0$. In addition, by obtaining the MA(∞) representation of productivity, the effects of the *shock* of productivity on productivity in the following periods can be analyzed:

$$\widehat{a}_t = \epsilon_t + \phi\epsilon_{t-1} + \phi^2\epsilon_{t-2} + \phi^3\epsilon_{t-3} + \phi^4\epsilon_{t-4} + \ldots \tag{3.190}$$

When calculating the variation of productivity in "t" before a *shock* in the same period, we have:

$$\frac{\Delta\widehat{a}_t}{\Delta\epsilon_t} = 1$$

Considering that $\Delta\epsilon_t = \sigma_\epsilon$, then $\Delta\widehat{a}_t = \sigma_\epsilon$, and also if it is known that the variation of productivity is with respect to its steady state ($= 0$), then $\widehat{a}_t = \sigma_\epsilon$. In the same way, the impact of the *shock* is calculated at "t+1," "t+2," and so on, and we have the following:

$$\widehat{a}_{t+1} = \phi\sigma_\epsilon, \quad \widehat{a}_{t+2} = \phi^2\sigma_\epsilon, \quad \widehat{a}_{t+3} = \phi^3\sigma_\epsilon \ldots$$

This result is important and suggests two central ideas: the first is that since $\phi < 1$, then the impact of the *shock* is diluted or diminishes over time. The second idea is that the magnitude of the impact depends on the value of the persistence parameter ϕ. If this parameter is small, then the effect will quickly disappear over time.

Firms' reactions As mentioned before, the first impact of the *shock* of productivity is on the production function:

$$\begin{aligned}
\widehat{y}_2 &= \widehat{a}_2 + (1-\alpha)\widehat{k}_2 + \alpha\widehat{h}_2 \\
\widehat{y}_2 &= \phi\sigma_\epsilon + (1-\alpha)\sigma_\epsilon + \alpha\widehat{h}_2 \\
\widehat{y}_2 &= (\phi + (1-\alpha))\sigma_\epsilon + \alpha\widehat{h}_2, \qquad \phi = 0.979, \quad \alpha = 0.667 \\
\widehat{y}_2 &= 1.312\sigma_\epsilon + \alpha\widehat{h}_2
\end{aligned} \tag{3.191}$$

From the equilibrium results in period "t = 1," it is known that $\widehat{y}_1 = \sigma_\epsilon$. Then, given $\widehat{h}_2$, in equation (3.191) it is observed that coefficient (1.312) that multiplies σ_ϵ in $\widehat{y}_2$ is greater than that associated with $\widehat{y}_1$ (1). This suggests that: $\widehat{y}_2 > \widehat{y}_1 > 0$. The increase in product due to higher productivity encourages the firm to expand its demand for labor and capital as seen in the Fig. 3.9.

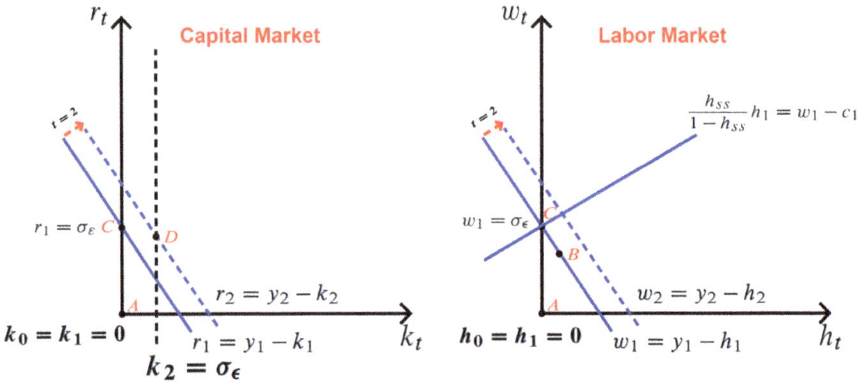

Fig. 3.9 Firms' response to productivity *shock* (t = 2)

By substituting the value of the product in the demand for capital, the following is obtained:

$$\begin{aligned}\widehat{r_2} &= \widehat{y_2} - \widehat{k_2}\\ \widehat{r_2} &= (\phi + (1-\alpha))\sigma_\epsilon + \alpha\widehat{h_2} - (\sigma_\epsilon)\\ \widehat{r_2} &= \underbrace{(\phi - \alpha)}_{0.312}\sigma_\epsilon + \alpha\widehat{h_2}\end{aligned} \tag{3.192}$$

It is known that the equilibrium interest rate in period "t = 1" is $\widehat{r_1} = \sigma_\epsilon$. So when comparing this result with equation (3.192) it follows that $\widehat{r_2} < \widehat{r_1}$. This indicates that the demand for capital in period "t = 2" has not expanded enough to increase the interest rate above $\widehat{r_1}$. It is worth mentioning that, although the interest rate is lower than the previous period, it is still higher than the steady state and, therefore, it continues to produce an incentive to substitute today's consumption for tomorrow (negative substitution effect on today's consumption), and it continues to generate positive income for the household (positive income effect), although to a **lesser extent** than in period "t = 1."

Household reactions The income effect can be seen in the budget constraint (in levels):

$$c_2 + i_2 = w_2 h_2 + r_2 k_2$$

where the income side increases due to the increase in the interest rate with respect to its steady state. It is worth mentioning that this increase is less than in the previous period. This causes consumption and investment to increase at "t = 2," but to a lesser extent (with respect to the previous period). On the other hand, the substitution effect suggests that consumption in "t = 2" should also increase and consumption in period "t = 1" should decrease:

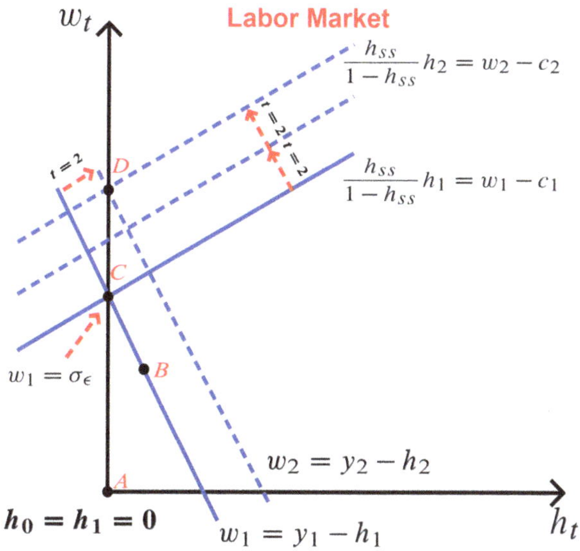

Fig. 3.10 Household response to the *productivity shock* (t = 2)

$$\widehat{c}_1 = E_t[\widehat{c}_2 - \widehat{r}_2] \tag{3.193}$$

Therefore, given the increase in consumption due to the effects of the interest rate, the household feels that they have enough resources to sacrifice leisure. This leads to the reduction of labor supply in the period "t = 2" to the level at which labor remains at its steady-state value (see Fig. 3.10).

After the firm and the household have reacted to the effects of *shock* on productivity, which materialized in period 1, the following equilibrium values of the variables are obtained in period 2: $\widehat{a}_2 = \phi\sigma_\epsilon$; then $\widehat{h}_2 = 0$ and $\widehat{y}_2 = \widehat{w}_2 = \widehat{c}_2 = (\phi + 1 - \alpha)\sigma_\epsilon$. Furthermore, $\widehat{r}_2 = (\phi - \alpha)\sigma_\epsilon$. In the same way as in period 1, we can conclude that under the budget constraint, the investment is equal consumption at the equilibrium:

$$\widehat{c}_2 = \widehat{i}_2$$

Likewise, by the law of movement of capital it is known that: $\widehat{k}_3 = \widehat{i}_2$. Therefore, the equilibrium values of all the variables are:

$$\widehat{y}_2 = \widehat{w}_2 = \widehat{c}_2 = \widehat{i}_2 = \widehat{k}_3 = (\phi + 1 - \alpha)\sigma_\epsilon, \quad \widehat{a}_2 = \phi\sigma_\epsilon, \quad \widehat{h}_2 = 0$$

Figure 3.11 shows the equilibrium in the factor market in the second period.

Period $t = 3$ In this period, the effects of the *shock* on productivity still persist, although with less impact.

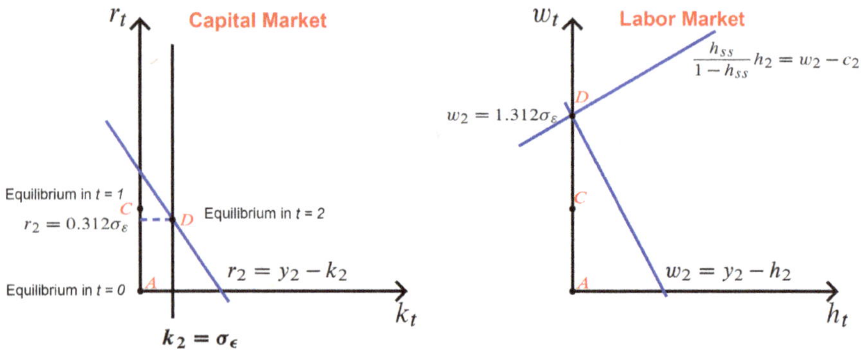

Fig. 3.11 Equilibrium at $t = 2$

$$\widehat{a}_3 = \phi \underbrace{\widehat{a}_2}_{=\phi\sigma_\epsilon} + \underbrace{\epsilon_3}_{=0}$$

$$\widehat{a}_3 = \phi^2 \sigma_\epsilon \tag{3.194}$$

From equation (3.194) it can be inferred that $\widehat{a}_3 = \phi^2\sigma_\epsilon$ and is less than $\widehat{a}_2 = \phi\sigma_\epsilon$. Therefore, the impact on output will be positive, but less than in period "t = 2."

Reactions of the firm Given that the capital stock has been increasing between periods 2 and 3 (going from $\widehat{k}_2 = \sigma_\epsilon$ to $\widehat{k}_3 = 1.312\sigma_\epsilon$) and also that the effects of the *shock* that materialized in the first period still persist, to a lesser extent, in the third period. All this leads the product to increase in this period, as shown below:

$$\widehat{y}_3 = \widehat{a}_3 + (1-\alpha)\widehat{k}_3 + \alpha\widehat{h}_3$$

$$\widehat{y}_3 = \phi^2\sigma_\epsilon + (1-\alpha)(1+\phi-\alpha)\sigma_\epsilon + \alpha\widehat{h}_3$$

$$\widehat{y}_3 = \underbrace{(\phi^2 + (1-\alpha)(1+\phi-\alpha))}_{=1.3953}\sigma_\epsilon + \alpha\widehat{h}_3$$

$$\widehat{y}_3 = 1.3953\sigma_\epsilon + \alpha\widehat{h}_3 \tag{3.195}$$

Comparing with the product of the period "t = 2," we have the following:

$$1.3953\sigma_\epsilon + \alpha\widehat{h}_3 = \widehat{y}_3 > \widehat{y}_2 = 1.312\sigma_\epsilon$$

Given the increase in product, the firm expands its demand for capital and labor as in previous periods, as shown in Fig. 3.12.

By substituting the value of the product in the demand for capital, the following is obtained:

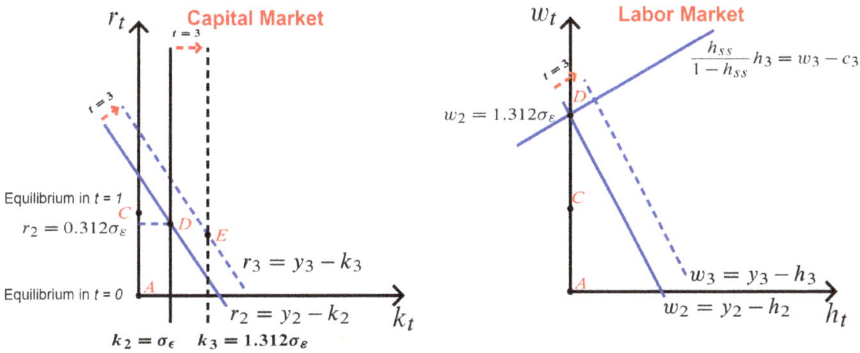

Fig. 3.12 Firm response to productivity *shock* (t = 3)

$$
\begin{aligned}
\widehat{r}_3 &= \widehat{y}_3 - \widehat{k}_3 \\
\widehat{r}_3 &= 1.3953\sigma_\epsilon + \alpha\widehat{h}_3 - 1.312\sigma_\epsilon \\
\widehat{r}_3 &= 0.0833\sigma_\epsilon + \alpha\widehat{h}_3
\end{aligned}
\tag{3.196}
$$

When comparing the equilibrium value of the interest rate in the period "t = 1," equation (3.192) with equation (3.196), it is observed that the interest rate in period 3 has been significantly reduced: the coefficient of σ_ϵ in the interest rate demand equation went from 31.2% in the second period to 8.33% in the third (equation 3.196). This is due to two effects: on the one hand, the influence of the *shock* on productivity is diluted over time and the expansion of the *stock* of capital is less; that is, it increases but at a slower rate.

Reactions of the household Faced with a scenario of greater demand for labor and capital on the part of firms, although to a lesser extent than in the previous period, household income still remains positive—it is that is—above the steady state because the interest rate (albeit small) is still positive. Likewise, real wages remain on the rise. All this implies that the household experiences a lower income effect than the previous period but that it allows consumption, leisure, and investment to increase. The increase in leisure translates into a reduction in the labor supply until equilibrium is reached at "E" (see Fig. 3.13).

On the other hand, the substitution effect implies a reduction in consumption in the second period, but an increase in the current period. It is worth mentioning that since the interest rate in this period is already very close to zero, the substitution effect is small.

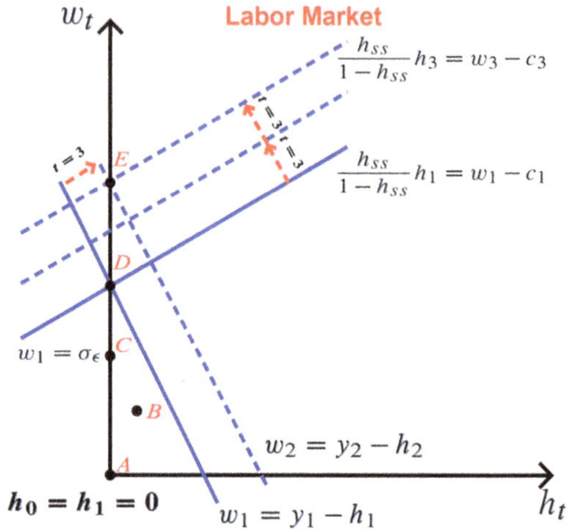

Fig. 3.13 Household response to the *productivity shock* (t = 3)

The equilibrium values of all the variables are:

$$\widehat{y}_3 = \widehat{w}_3 = \widehat{c}_3 = \widehat{i}_3 = \widehat{k}_4 = (\phi^2 + (1-\alpha)(1+\phi-\alpha))\sigma_\epsilon, \quad \widehat{a}_3 = \phi^2\sigma_\epsilon, \quad \widehat{h}_3 = 0$$

In the following periods, the effect of the productivity *shock* will practically disappear, which will lead to the demand for capital increasing marginally in the face of an expansion in the supply of capital. This will cause the interest rate to become negative; that is, it is below its steady state. Given this situation, due to the substitution effect, the household will increase its consumption today, avoiding transferring present consumption to the future. The increase in present consumption implies less investment today, which ultimately translates into a reduction in the *stock* of capital in subsequent periods. This reduction in the supply of capital on the household side will continue until capital returns to a steady state. This behavior will lead to all the variables of the economy returning to a steady state in a period of time.

3.9 Simulation of Endogenous Variables

As indicated in Chap. 2, the simulation of the endogenous variables can be carried out in two ways: the first is by indicating to Dynare within "stoch_simul" the number of periods to be simulated. The disadvantage of this path is that only one simulation can be done. The second is to use two Dynare options (periods and replica number). The first option indicates the number of periods and the second the number of times you want to run the simulation. The disadvantage of this method is that Dynare creates a binary file, which is difficult to read in Matlab. However, Johannes Pfeifer has created a Matlab function that solves this problem (see Chap. 2 for more details).

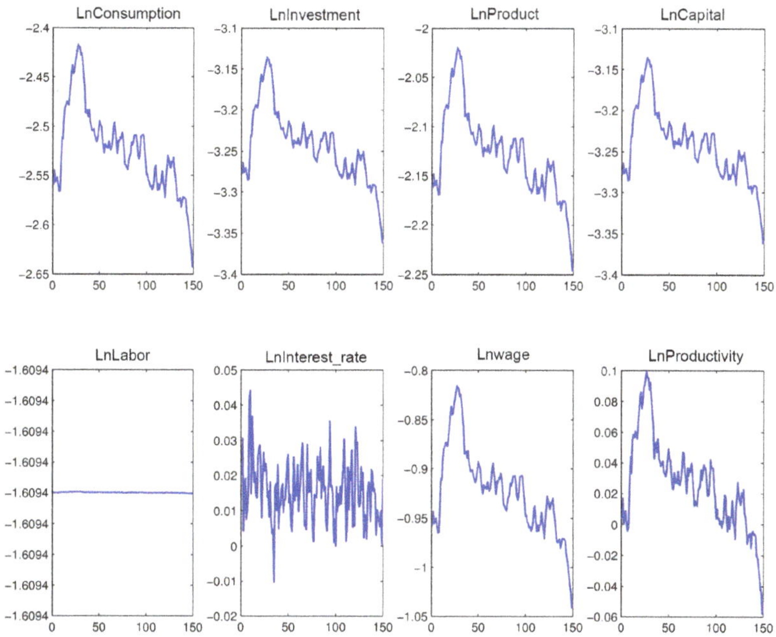

Fig. 3.14 Simulation (first alternative)

Figure 3.14 shows the simulation using the first option. It is worth mentioning that for this simulation the code "Long_Plosser.m" (See Section 5 of the m-file) is used. Likewise, Fig. 3.15 shows the tenth simulation of the variables by means of the second option.

As can be seen, in both simulation alternatives, the endogenous variables (in logarithm) behave according to the time series representation derived from the solution (see Table 3.8).

3.10 Cyclic Component of Simulated Variables

Simulated series (100 times with 150 periods) are used to calculate the cyclical component. The steps are as follows: first, the HP filter is applied to each simulation of the variables; for example, given that the production has been simulated 100 times, then there are 100 series and the HP filter is applied to each series in such a way that 100 cyclical components and 100 trends are obtained. They are related to the same variable—production. Second, we proceed to graph the trend and cyclical component of one of the 100 simulations. In this case, simulation 10 has been graphed (see Fig. 3.16).

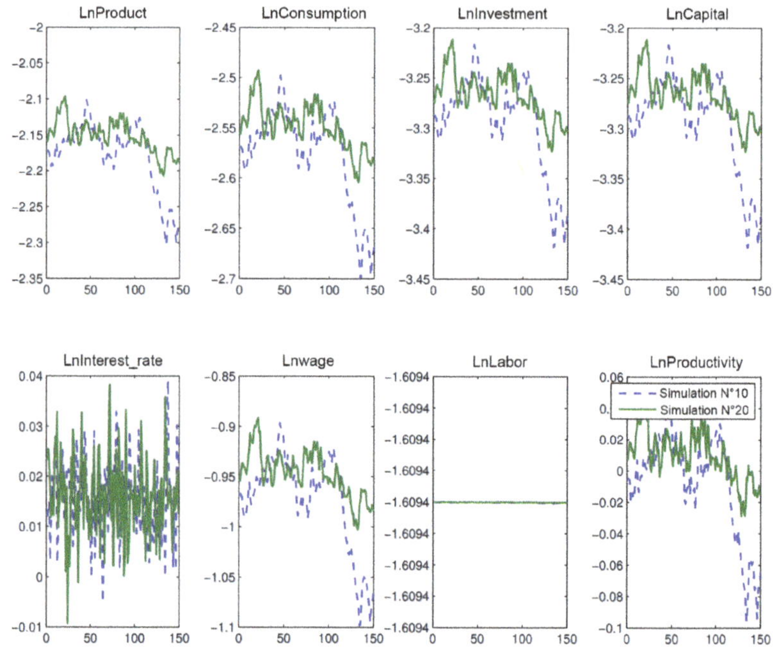

Fig. 3.15 Simulation (second alternative)

Figure 3.16 shows the trend component of each endogenous variable (corresponding to the tenth simulation). As can be seen, the trend is the smoothed series that passes through the middle of the entire series. It should be emphasized that the work has no trend; the line that fluctuates around the variable has the same value on the "Y" axis; therefore, it has no trend or cyclical component.

Figure 3.17 shows the cyclic component for each variable (from the tenth simulation). This component is obtained from the difference between the variable and its trend. As a result, the average value of the cyclical component is equal to zero. It is worth mentioning that Figs. 3.16 and 3.17 are obtained from the code "Long_Plosser.m" (See Section 4 of the m-file).

3.11 Calculation of Theoretical Moments

In this section, the 100 simulations from the previous section will be taken to calculate the distribution of each moment, especially the standard deviation. For the calculation of the moments of the cyclic component of the variables, the code "Long_Plosser.m" (See Section 5 of the m-file) is used.

The model assumes that the error ϵ_t is distributed as a normal $(0.\sigma_\epsilon)$. Then, each of the variables is also distributed as a normal, with its own mean and standard

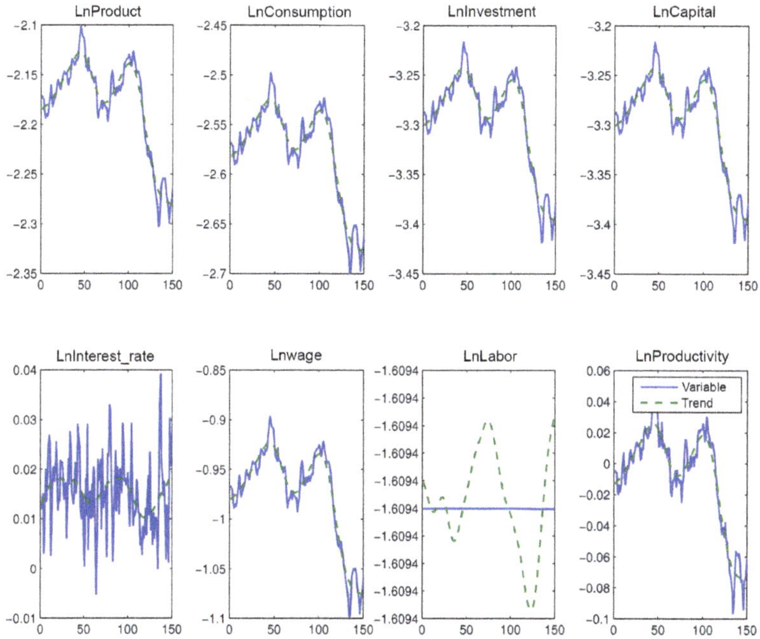

Fig. 3.16 Trend

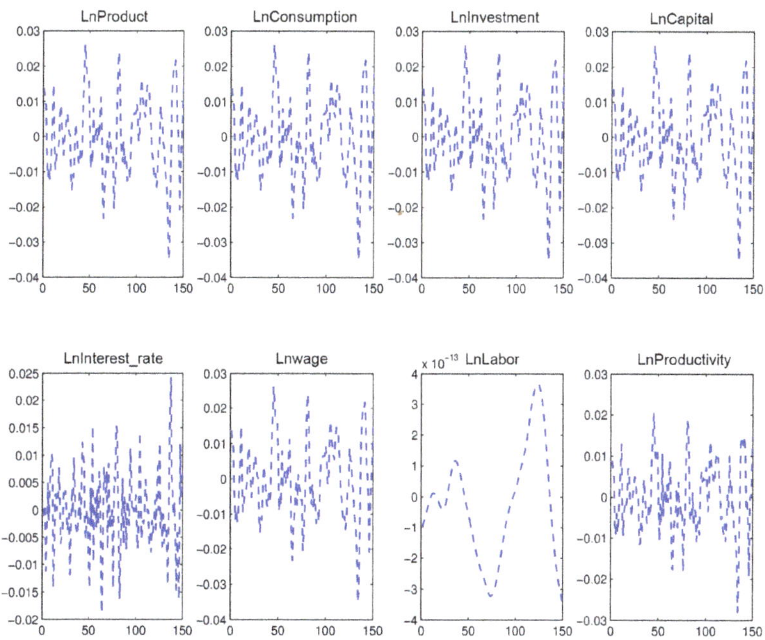

Fig. 3.17 Cycle

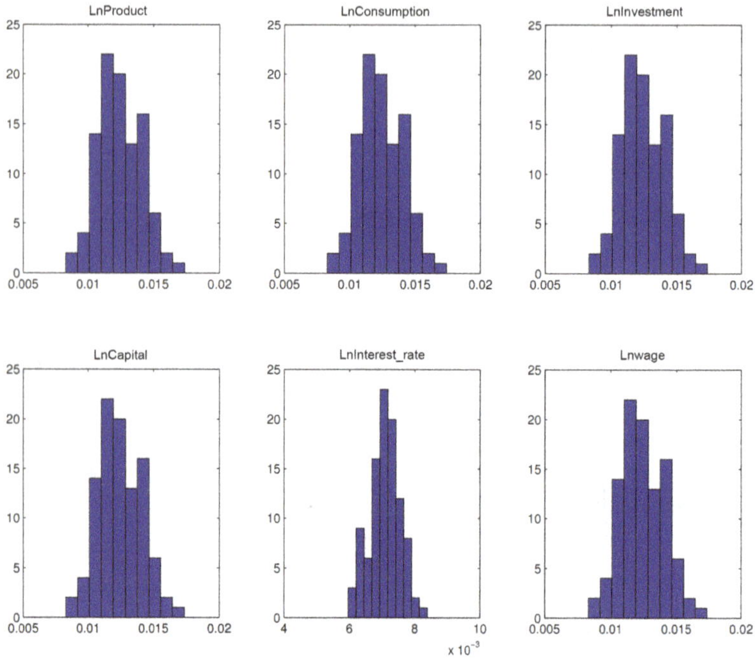

Fig. 3.18 Distribution of the standard deviation

deviation. Figure 3.18 shows the standard deviation of each simulated variable (100 times). The standard deviation value of each variable produced by the model is the mean or median of each distribution. For example, the mean of the standard deviation distribution of the log product is 0.0124. Similarly, for the logarithm of consumption, it is 0.0124.

3.12 Comparison of the Theoretical Model with the Data

A key test that evaluates the power of the model to capture reality is to compare the theoretical moments (provided by the model) with the empirical moments (found in the data). Table 3.9 shows the moments obtained from the model compared to those obtained from the data. It should be noted that the theoretical moments are obtained using the file "Long_Plosser_Dynare_nolineal_log.mod," which considers the HP filter.

Two conclusions can be drawn from Table 3.9: the first is that Long and Plosser's model is very far from replicating reality. This was to be expected given the assumptions considered. The second is that the model can be strengthened in several directions; for example, the assumption of total depreciation can be raised or a utility function can be assumed that allows obtaining an elasticity of substitution different from one.

3.13 Codes

In Table 3.10 the codes used in this chapter are indicated.

Table 3.9 Comparison of the cyclical behavior of the theoretical model with the empirical data

	US empirical data		Theoretical model	
Variable	Std.	Corr. with product (t)	Std.	Corr. with product (t)
Product	1.72	1	0.0126 (0.0017)	1
Consumption	1.27	0.83	0.0126 (0.0017)	1
Investment	8.24	0.91	0.0126 (0.0017)	1
Capital	5.34	0.9	0.0126 (0.0017)	1
Labor	1.59	0.86	0 (0)	
Wage	0.757	0.68	0.0126 (0.0017)	1
Interest rate			0.0072 (0.00045)	0.2841

Note: The empirical values have been taken from Cooley and Prescott (1995), which have been calculated under the sample period from 1954.I to 1991.III, while the theoretical values have been obtained from a 100-fold simulation considering a period of 150 quarters. The values shown in the theoretical model are the average values of each distribution. These values are obtained from the file "Long_Plosser_Dynare_nolinear_log.mod"

Table 3.10 Codes in Matlab and Dynare

Codes	Description
Matlab	
Long_Plosser.m	This m-file calculates the steady state and the coefficients of the model solution and applies the HP filter to the simulated variables (100 times with 150 periods). In addition, the theoretical moments of the cyclic component are calculated
Long_Plosser_BlanchardKahn.m	This m-file seeks to follow step by step the application of the Blachard and Kahn method to the Long and Plosser model
ifrs_nolinear_log.m	This m-file plots the impulse-response function of the Long and Plosser model, which is described in the mod file described below
Dynare	
Long_Plosser_Dynare_nolinear_log.mod	This .mod contains the nonlinear equations with the variables in logarithms of the Long and Plosser (1983, 1989) model

Chapter 4
RBC Model with Constant Labor

4.1 Introduction

The main objective of this chapter is to understand in detail the process of building and solving a model of real business cycles. Additionally, it is important to understand how the simulation of the variables is constructed and how the impulse-response function is obtained. For these purposes, in this chapter, one of the models proposed by Campbell (1994) is analyzed in detail.

The base model proposed by Campbell (1994) is a stationary model (without trend) but with nonzero growth in the steady state. This model is an extension of the stochastic growth model, which allows tracking the dynamic effects of any random event (*shock*).

However, the solution of the stochastic model is difficult to characterize, mainly because of the nonlinearities that emerge from the model itself, which are derived from the interaction between multiplicative elements (function Cobb-Douglas production model) and additive elements (law of movement of capital). A special case is the model proposed by Long and Plosser (1983), described in Chap. 3. In this model, the nonlinearities disappear due to the unrealistic assumption that the depreciation is total; that is, the depreciation rate is equal to one ($\delta = 1$) and that, furthermore, the utility function is logarithmic ($u(c_t, h_t) = lnc_t + \theta ln(1 - h_t)$). In this case, the model becomes linear and can be solved analytically; in the others, an "approximate solution" is required.

In line with the above, Campbell (1994) mentions that a typical *paper* in the RBC literature outlines the model and then moves directly to the discussion of solution properties without specifying how this solution has been arrived at. The above does not allow the reader to understand the process to obtain the said solution properties, nor the solution itself.

Given this, the author proposes a simple analytical approach to the stochastic growth model, whose log-linear version can be solved analytically to show the solution mechanism in the most accurate way, ás transparent as possible. In order to

H. Galindo Gil et al., *Dynamic Stochastic General Equilibrium Models*, Springer Texts in Business and Economics, https://doi.org/10.1007/978-3-031-58105-2_4

illustrate the solution method, Campbell (1994) applies it to four models: (1) model with fixed labor supply, (2) model with variable labor supply and with function with an additively separable utility function, (3) a model with variable labor supply and a nonadditively separable utility function, and (4) the second extended model with a *shock* of public spending.

This chapter focuses on the first model (constant or fixed labor supply), leaving the model with variable labor supply for the next chapter.

4.2 Model Building

This model is made up of households and firms in a closed economy environment, in which there is only one good. On the one hand, households have permanent jobs; that is, all households are employed. On the other hand, households own the capital and therefore demand goods to invest, which in turn creates a supply of capital. Likewise, households demand consumer goods.

On the other hand, firms have the technology to produce the only good in the economy based on capital. Therefore, firms demand capital. Figure 4.1 outlines the model.

4.2.1 Households

In this model, it is assumed that the economy is populated by a set of identical households that have infinite life. The representative household seeks to maximize its discounted utility function:

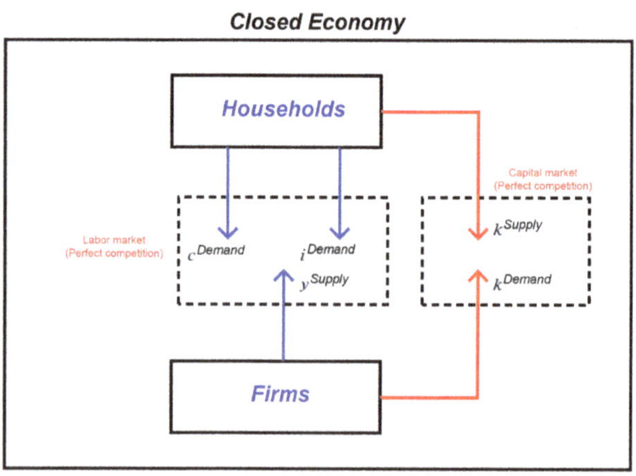

Fig. 4.1 Scheme of the constant labor supply model

$$\underset{\{c_t,k_{t+1}\}_{t=0}^{\infty}}{\text{Max}} \; E_0 \sum_{t=0}^{\infty} \beta^t u(c_t) \tag{4.1}$$

where c_t is the consumption of the period t and β is the discount factor. In addition, the instant utility function is described by the following functional form:

$$u(c_t) = \frac{c_t^{1-\gamma}}{1-\gamma} \tag{4.2}$$

Utility Function Properties
The prior utility function has a risk aversion coefficient equal to γ and elasticity of intertemporal substitution (of consumption) $\sigma = 1/\gamma$
Computation of $EIS^c_{t+1,t}(\sigma)$:

$$u_{c_t} = c_t^{-\gamma}$$

$$TMgSI^c_{t+1,t} = -E_t\left[\frac{u_{c_t}}{\beta u_{ct+1}}\right] = -E_t\left[\frac{c_t^{\gamma}}{\beta c_{t+1}^{\gamma}}\right]$$

$$EIS^c_{t+1,t} = \frac{\partial ln(\frac{c_{t+1}}{c_t})}{\partial ln(TMgSI^c_{t+1,t})} = \frac{TMgSI^c_{t+1,t}}{\frac{c_{t+1}}{c_t}} \frac{1}{\frac{\partial TMgSI^c_{t+1,t}}{\partial\left(\frac{c_{t+1}}{c_t}\right)}} = \frac{1}{\gamma}$$

The elasticity of intertemporal substitution (EIS) of consumption (σ) is understood as the household's willingness to substitute consumption today ($\downarrow c_t$) for consumption tomorrow ($\uparrow c_{t+1}$). When the said elasticity is said to be strong (σ is large), it is understood that the consumer is willing to reduce his/her consumption today by a greater amount.

On the other hand, it is assumed that the household owns the physical capital (k_t), whose accumulation dynamics is represented by the law of movement of capital:

$$k_{t+1} = (1-\delta)k_t + i_t \tag{4.3}$$

The said capital (k_t) is rented to firms at a real interest rate r_t. This positive flow ($r_t k_t$) represents the household's income, which is distributed between consumption (c_t) and investment (i_t). This equivalence of flows, for each period of time, is represented in the budget constraint:

$$c_t + i_t = r_t k_t \tag{4.4}$$

Optimization Problem

The optimization problem of the representative household is the following:

$$\underset{\{c_t, k_{t+1}\}_{t=0}^{\infty}}{\text{Max}} \quad E_0 \sum_{t=0}^{\infty} \beta^t \frac{c_t^{1-\gamma}}{1-\gamma}$$

subject to budget constraint:

$$c_t + k_{t+1} - (1-\delta)k_t = r_t k_t$$

where the investment (i_t) has been replaced by its expression derived from the law of movement of capital (Eq. 4.3). Also, it is worth mentioning that the control variables in this optimization problem are: c_t and k_{t+1}.

The household optimization problem can be written as a Lagrange function:

$$\mathcal{L} = E_0 \sum_{t=0}^{\infty} \beta^t \left[u(c_t) + \lambda_t \left(r_t k_t - (c_t + k_{t+1} - (1-\delta)k_t) \right) \right]$$

where, similarly to Chap. 3 (Long and Plosser (1983) model), the extended version of the Lagrange function can be expressed as follows:

$$\begin{aligned}
\mathcal{L} = E_0 \Big\{ & \beta^0 \left[u(c_0) + \lambda_0 \left(r_0 k_0 - (c_0 + k_1 - (1-\delta)k_0) \right) \right] + \\
& \beta^1 \left[u(c_1) + \lambda_1 \left(r_1 k_1 - (c_1 + k_2 - (1-\delta)k_1) \right) \right] + \\
& \beta^2 \left[u(c_2) + \lambda_2 \left(r_2 k_2 - (c_2 + k_3 - (1-\delta)k_2) \right) \right] + \\
& \beta^3 \left[u(c_3) + \lambda_3 \left(r_3 k_3 - (c_3 + k_4 - (1-\delta)k_3) \right) \right] + \\
& \beta^4 \left[u(c_4) + \lambda_4 \left(r_4 k_4 - (c_4 + k_5 - (1-\delta)k_4) \right) \right] + \\
& \ldots + \\
& \beta^t \left[u(c_t) + \lambda_t \left(r_t k_t - (c_t + k_{t+1} - (1-\delta)k_t) \right) \right] + \\
& \beta^{t+1} \left[u(c_{t+1}) + \lambda_{t+1} \left(r_{t+1} k_{t+1} - (c_{t+1} + k_{t+2} - (1-\delta)k_{t+1}) \right) \right] + \\
& \ldots + \\
& \ldots \Big\}
\end{aligned}$$

The first-order conditions, in period "t," are:

$$\frac{\partial \mathcal{L}}{\partial c_t} = 0 \Longrightarrow E_0 \left\{ \beta^t \left[u_{c_t} + \lambda_t(-1) \right] \right\} = 0$$

$$u_{c_t} = \lambda_t \tag{4.5}$$

$$\frac{\partial \mathcal{L}}{\partial k_{t+1}} = 0 \Longrightarrow E_0 \left\{ \beta^t \left[\lambda_t(-1) \right] + \beta^{t+1} \left[\lambda_{t+1}(r_{t+1} + (1 - \delta)) \right] \right\} = 0$$

$$\lambda_t = \beta E_t \lambda_{t+1}(r_{t+1} + (1 - \delta)) \tag{4.6}$$

Substituting Eq. (4.5) into Eq. (4.6) we get the Euler equation:

$$\begin{aligned} u_{c_t} &= \beta E_t u_{c_{t+1}}(r_{t+1} + (1 - \delta)) \\ c_t^{-\gamma} &= \beta E_t c_{t+1}^{-\gamma}(r_{t+1} + (1 - \delta)) \end{aligned} \tag{4.7}$$

In line with Campbell (1994), the variable R_t is defined as the one-period investment gross interest rate, which is equal to the interest rate net real interest (r_t) plus the non-depreciated capital $(1 - \delta)$. In the period "t+1," this relationship is expressed as follows:

$$R_{t+1} = r_{t+1} + (1 - \delta) \tag{4.8}$$

Considering the previous expression, the Euler equation would have the following form:

$$c_t^{-\gamma} = \beta E_t c_{t+1}^{-\gamma} R_{t+1} \tag{4.9}$$

Euler's equation expresses a marginal benefit/cost comparison of consuming one unit of the good. On the one hand, there is the marginal cost of not consuming an additional unit of the good, which is expressed by the marginal utility u_{c_t} and, on the other hand, there is the marginal benefit of not consuming the said unit of the good at "t," which in the next period "$t + 1$" becomes $1(1 + r_{t+1} - \delta)$ units of good. This is because there is an interest rate and a depreciation rate. The marginal utility provided by this additional unit at "t+1" is $u_{c_{t+1}} R_{t+1}$. However, to compare it with the marginal cost in "t," it is necessary to bring it to present value by means of the discount factor "β." Therefore, the marginal benefit at "t" is equal to $\beta u_{c_{t+1}}(R_{t+1})$. This is observed in the following equation:

$$\underbrace{u_{c_t}}_{\text{marginal cost}} = \underbrace{\beta E_t u_{c_{t+1}}(r_{t+1} + (1 - \delta))}_{\text{marginal benefit}}$$

Therefore, Euler's equation indicates that the household is willing to sacrifice consumption today until the marginal cost of not consuming a unit of the good today is equal to the marginal benefit of the said unit of the good brought to present value.

4.2.2 Firms

It is assumed that firms develop in a context of perfect competition both in the market for goods and in the market for factors of production. In this scenario, the representative firm maximizes its profit function subject to its technology (production function). This optimization problem is described as follows:

$$\underset{\{k_t\}_{t=0}^{\infty}}{\text{Max}}\ \Pi_t = y_t - r_t k_t$$

Subject to the production function:

$$y_t = a_t^{\alpha} k_t^{1-\alpha} \tag{4.10}$$

The production function only depends on the productivity a_t and the capital k_t because the work h_t is assumed to be constant (fixed). Also, because the firm does not make intertemporal decisions, its optimization problem is performed for each of the periods. Therefore, the optimization problem can be performed on t and extend the result for the following periods.

Introducing the production function in the objective function and differentiating the latter with respect to the only control variable (k_t), the following expression is obtained:

$$\frac{\partial \Pi}{\partial k_t} = 0 \Longrightarrow \frac{\partial (a_t^{\alpha} k_t^{1-\alpha} - r_t k_t)}{\partial k_t} = 0 \Longrightarrow (1-\alpha)\left[\frac{a_t}{k_t}\right]^{\alpha} - r_t = 0$$

From this first-order condition, the demand for capital is obtained:

$$r_t = (1-\alpha)\left[\frac{a_t}{k_t}\right]^{\alpha} \tag{4.11}$$

4.2.3 Market Equilibrium and Shock Definition

To complete the model described above, it is necessary to specify two additional equations. The first describes equilibrium in the goods market; that is, everything that is produced in the economy must find its counterpart in the different components of aggregate spending. The second specifies the behavior of productivity. With respect to the latter, it is usually assumed that it is stationary in the mean and that it has a constant variance. The standard way to represent it is assuming that productivity follows an autoregressive process of order one.

In this particular model, it is assumed that there is no government spending ($g_t = 0$) and that the economy is small and closed. Therefore, the whole production will have two possible destinations: consumption (c_t) and investment (i_t). In that sense, the equilibrium condition is described by the following equation:

$$y_t = c_t + i_t \tag{4.12}$$

On the other hand, productivity follows a stationary behavior AR(1), in which the *shock* is represented by the white noise ϵ_t, which has a distribution function normal with zero mean and constant variance $[N(0, \sigma_\epsilon^2)]$. In a steady state, it is assumed that the said white noise takes the value of its mean. Likewise, when it is said that the economy has suffered a "*shock*" at $t = 0$, it means that in that period the white noise (ϵ_t) has ceased to be zero and has taken, only in that period, some value proportional to its standard deviation ($n\sigma_\epsilon$). Usually, n is considered to be equal to one. Equation (4.13) describes the behavior of productivity:

$$lna_t = \phi lna_{t-1} + \epsilon_t \tag{4.13}$$

It should be noted that the logarithm of productivity behaves like an AR(1) and not productivity itself. This is important because it allows the steady-state productivity to be equal to one, which avoids any division by zero.

4.2.4 Main Equations

The main equations of the model are summarized in Table 4.1.

This set of equations represents a system of nonlinear and stochastic difference equations. To solve this system, as usual in the literature, it is transformed into a system of linear equations. This is because the mathematical techniques for solving linear systems are widely known. The solution of the linear system will then be an approximation of the solution of the nonlinear system. It is worth mentioning that a previous step to the linearization of the system of equations is the assignment of values to the parameters (calibration) and the calculation of the steady state.

Table 4.1 Nonlinear system of equations of the model

Equations	Description
$c_t^{-\gamma} = \beta E_t c_{t+1}^{-\gamma} R_{t+1}$	Euler's equation
$y_t = a_t^\alpha k_t^{1-\alpha}$	Production function
$r_t = (1-\alpha)\left[\frac{a_t}{k_t}\right]^\alpha$	Capital demand
$R_t = r_t + (1-\delta)$	R_t is the real (gross) interest rate
	r_t is the real (net) interest rate that considers depreciation
$y_t = c_t + i_t$	Goods market equilibrium
$k_{t+1} = (1-\delta)k_t + i_t$	Law of motion of capital
$lna_t = \phi lna_{t-1} + \epsilon_t$	*Productivity shock*

Note: These 7 equations can be written directly in a "mod" in Dynare to get the model solution and IRFs

4.3 Calibration

Calibration is an empirical methodology, which consists of assigning a value to the parameters of the general equilibrium model based on a variety of sources. According to Heer and Maussner (2009), the most common sources are the following:

1. The use of the average of the level of economic variables of time series or the average of the ratios of the said variables
2. The econometric estimate of an equation
3. The reference to econometric studies based on microeconomic or macroeconomic data
4. The adjustment of the parameters so that the model replicates certain empirical facts such as second moments of the data or impulse-response of a structural VAR

The way to evaluate the power of the model to capture reality is by comparing the values of the second moments and the impulse-response functions with the values obtained empirically. Table 4.2 indicates the values of the model parameters, which are based on Campbell (1994).

4.4 Steady State

For the calculation of the stationary state, it is considered that the variable x_t remains constant. Then, in the stationary state, $x_t = x_{t+1} = x_{ss}$. This last condition applies to all endogenous variables. Furthermore, in the steady state the *shock* ϵ_{ss} takes its average value, which is equal to zero.

For Euler's equation we have the following:

$$c_t^{-\gamma} = \beta E_t c_{t+1}^{-\gamma} R_{t+1}$$

$$c_{ss}^{-\gamma} = \beta c_{ss}^{-\gamma} R_{ss}$$

Table 4.2 Calibration (base values)

Parameter	Name	Annual calculation
$\alpha = 0.667$	$(1 - \alpha)$ is the share of capital in the product	
$\delta = 0.025$	Depreciation rate	10% annual
$ln(R_{ss}) = 0.015$, implies $R_{ss} = 1.015$ and hence $\beta = 0.9852$	Steady-state gross real interest rate	6.184% annual: $(1+0.015)^4-1$
$\sigma = 0.2$	Consumption elasticity of intertemporal substitution	
$\phi = 0.95$	Persistence of the *shock*	
$\sigma_\epsilon = 1$	Standard deviation of the *shock*	

$$1 = \beta R_{ss}$$
$$R_{ss} = \frac{1}{\beta} \tag{4.14}$$

For the production function:

$$y_t = a_t^{\alpha} k_t^{1-\alpha}$$
$$y_{ss} = a_{ss}^{\alpha} k_{ss}^{1-\alpha} \tag{4.15}$$

For the demand for capital:

$$r_t = (1-\alpha)\left[\frac{a_t}{k_t}\right]^{\alpha}$$
$$r_{ss} = (1-\alpha)\left[\frac{a_{ss}}{k_{ss}}\right]^{\alpha} \tag{4.16}$$

From the gross interest rate equation:

$$R_t = r_t + (1-\delta)$$
$$R_{ss} = r_{ss} + (1-\delta) \tag{4.17}$$

by Eq. (4.14):

$$\frac{1}{\beta} = r_{ss} + (1-\delta)$$
$$r_{ss} = \frac{1}{\beta} - (1-\delta) \tag{4.18}$$

For the equilibrium equation in the goods market:

$$y_t = c_t + i_t$$
$$y_{ss} = c_{ss} + i_{ss} \tag{4.19}$$

In the same way for the law of motion of capital:

$$k_t = (1-\delta)k_t + i_t$$
$$k_{ss} = (1-\delta)k_{ss} + i_{ss}$$
$$i_{ss} = \delta k_{ss} \tag{4.20}$$

Finally, for the productivity behavior equation:

$$
\begin{aligned}
lna_t &= \phi lna_{t-1} + \epsilon_t \\
lna_{ss} &= \phi lna_{ss} + \underbrace{\epsilon_{ss}}_{=0\text{(value of its mean)}} \\
lna_{ss} &= \phi lna_{ss} \\
ln(a_{ss}) &= ln(a_{ss}^{\phi}) \\
a_{ss} &= a_{ss}^{\phi}
\end{aligned} \tag{4.21}
$$

As in the Long and Plosser (1983) model, two values of a_{ss} could solve this last Eq. (4.21): $a_{ss} = 1$ or $a_{ss} = 0$. However, only when $a_{ss} = 1$ does the lna_{ss} exist. Therefore, the correct solution is $a_{ss} = 1$. The advantage of considering the productivity *shock* equation in logarithms is that it prevents steady-state productivity from being zero. This is important because it prevents any number or variable divided by zero from being found in the steady-state equations and in the log-linear equations.

So far we have found the steady-state value of the gross interest rate R_{ss}, the net interest rate r_{ss}, and the productivity a_{ss}; however, to find the steady state for the other variables, some additional algebraic operations have to be performed. From Eq. (4.16) we have:

$$
r_{ss} = (1-\alpha)\left[\frac{a_{ss}}{k_{ss}}\right]^{\alpha}
$$

Since the value of r_{ss} is already known from Eq. (4.18) and of a_{ss}, then the value of capital k_{ss} can be known:

$$
r_{ss} = (1-\alpha)\left[\frac{a_{ss}}{k_{ss}}\right]^{\alpha}
$$

$$
k_{ss} = a_{ss}\left[\frac{r_{ss}}{(1-\alpha)}\right]^{-\frac{1}{\alpha}} \tag{4.22}
$$

Since k_{ss} is already known, then the value of the product y_{ss}, of the investment i_{ss}, and of the consumption c_{ss} can be found:

$$
y_{ss} = a_{ss}^{\alpha} k_{ss}^{1-\alpha}, \quad \text{from Eq. (4.15)} \tag{4.23}
$$

$$
i_{ss} = \delta k_{ss}, \quad \text{from Eq. (4.20)} \tag{4.24}
$$

$$
c_{ss} = y_{ss} - i_{ss}, \quad \text{from Eq. (4.19)} \tag{4.25}
$$

Table 4.3 summarizes the steady-state expression for each model variable.

Table 4.3 Stationary state

Steady state (recursive form)	Steady state (parametric form)
$R_{ss} = \frac{1}{\beta}$	$= \frac{1}{\beta}$
$r_{ss} = R_{ss} - (1-\delta)$	$= \frac{1}{\beta} - (1-\delta)$
$a_{ss} = 1$	$= 1$
$k_{ss} = a_{ss}\left[\frac{r_{ss}}{(1-\alpha)}\right]^{-\frac{1}{\alpha}}$	$= \left[\frac{\frac{1}{\beta}-(1-\delta)}{1-\alpha}\right]^{-\frac{1}{\alpha}}$
$y_{ss} = a_{ss}^{\alpha} k_{ss}^{1-\alpha}$	$= \left[\frac{\frac{1}{\beta}-(1-\delta)}{1-\alpha}\right]^{-\frac{(1-\alpha)}{\alpha}}$
$i_{ss} = \delta k_{ss}$	$= \delta\left[\frac{\frac{1}{\beta}-(1-\delta)}{1-\alpha}\right]^{-\frac{1}{\alpha}}$
$c_{ss} = y_{ss} - i_{ss}$	$= \left[\frac{\frac{1}{\beta}+\alpha\delta-1}{1-\alpha}\right]\left[\frac{\frac{1}{\beta}-(1-\delta)}{1-\alpha}\right]^{-\frac{1}{\alpha}}$

Note: Computation of steady states can be found in Campbell_Lfijo.m (Sect. 4.1)

4.5 Log-Linearization

The system of equations that describes the model of Campbell (1994) is nonlinear. This characteristic of the model makes it difficult to find the solution. A standard way of dealing with this difficulty is to log-linearize each equation, that is, to transform a nonlinear equation to a linear equation in terms of the log deviation of the variable with respect to its steady state. Furthermore, for small deviations from the steady state, the log deviation of a variable has an important economic interpretation: it is approximately equal to the deviation, in percentage, of the stationary state (Uhlig 1995).

The advantage of applying log-linearization is that it converts the nonlinear system into a linear one, to which the standard mathematical methods for solving such systems can be applied (Blanchard and Kahn 1980).

First, the variable is defined in log deviations:

$$\widehat{x}_t = lnx_t - lnx_{ss} \tag{4.26}$$

Second, clearing the variable x_t from Eq. (4.26) we have:

$$x_t = x_{ss}e^{\widehat{x}_t} \tag{4.27}$$

Third, a first-order Taylor approximation of $e^{\widehat{x}_t}$ is made with respect to the steady state, in which $\widehat{x}_t = 0$; that is, $x_t = x_{ss}$:

$$e^{\widehat{x}_t}\Big|_{\widehat{x}_t=0} \cong e^{\widehat{x}_t=0} + e^{\widehat{x}_t=0}(\widehat{x}_t - 0)$$

$$
\begin{aligned}
e^{\widehat{x}_t}\Big|_{\widehat{x}_t=0} &\cong 1+\widehat{x}_t \\
e^{\widehat{x}_t} &\cong 1+\widehat{x}_t
\end{aligned} \tag{4.28}
$$

This last equation is replaced in Eq. (4.27):

$$
x_t = x_{ss}e^{\widehat{x}_t} \cong x_{ss}(1+\widehat{x}_t) \tag{4.29}
$$

From Eq. (4.29), we obtain $\widehat{x}_t$:

$$
\widehat{x}_t \cong \frac{x_t - x_{ss}}{x_{ss}} \tag{4.30}
$$

Therefore, the variable in log deviations is approximately equal to the deviation, in percent, from the steady state. From a practical point of view, we can replace each variable by its log-linear expression and then apply the first-order approximation according to Eq. (4.28).

The log-linearized Euler's equation is given by

$$
\begin{aligned}
c_t^{-\gamma} &= \beta E_t c_{t+1}^{-\gamma} R_{t+1} \\
\left[c_{ss}e^{\widehat{c}_t}\right]^{-\gamma} &= \beta E_t\left[c_{ss}e^{\widehat{c}_{t+1}}\right]^{-\gamma}\left[R_{ss}e^{\widehat{R}_{t+1}}\right] \\
e^{-\gamma\widehat{c}_t} &= E_t e^{-\gamma\widehat{c}_{t+1}} e^{\widehat{R}_{t+1}} \\
e^{-\gamma\widehat{c}_t} &= E_t e^{-\gamma\widehat{c}_{t+1}+\widehat{R}_{t+1}} \\
1-\gamma\widehat{c}_t &= E_t\left[1-\gamma\widehat{c}_{t+1}+\widehat{R}_{t+1}\right] \\
\widehat{c}_t &= E_t\left[\widehat{c}_{t+1}-\frac{1}{\gamma}\widehat{R}_{t+1}\right]
\end{aligned} \tag{4.31}
$$

Doing the same for the production function:

$$
\begin{aligned}
y_t &= a_t^{\alpha} k_t^{1-\alpha} \\
y_{ss}e^{\widehat{y}_t} &= \left[a_{ss}e^{\widehat{a}_t}\right]^{\alpha}\left[k_{ss}e^{\widehat{k}_t}\right]^{1-\alpha} \\
y_{ss}e^{\widehat{y}_t} &= a_{ss}^{\alpha}e^{\alpha\widehat{a}_t}k_{ss}^{1-\alpha}e^{(1-\alpha)\widehat{k}_t} \\
e^{\widehat{y}_t} &= e^{\alpha\widehat{a}_t+(1-\alpha)\widehat{k}_t} \\
1+\widehat{y}_t &= 1+\alpha\widehat{a}_t+(1-\alpha)\widehat{k}_t \\
\widehat{y}_t &= \alpha\widehat{a}_t+(1-\alpha)\widehat{k}_t
\end{aligned} \tag{4.32}
$$

Regarding the capital demand:

$$\begin{aligned}
r_t &= (1-\alpha)\left(\frac{a_t}{k_t}\right)^{\alpha} \\
r_{ss}e^{\widehat{r}_t} &= (1-\alpha)\left(\frac{a_{ss}e^{\widehat{a}_t}}{k_{ss}e^{\widehat{k}_t}}\right)^{\alpha} \\
r_{ss}e^{\widehat{r}_t} &= (1-\alpha)\left(\frac{a_{ss}}{k_{ss}}\right)^{\alpha}\left(\frac{e^{\widehat{a}_t}}{e^{\widehat{k}_t}}\right)^{\alpha} \\
r_{ss}e^{\widehat{r}_t} &= (1-\alpha)\left(\frac{a_{ss}}{k_{ss}}\right)^{\alpha}(e^{\alpha(\widehat{a}_t-\widehat{k}_t)}) \\
e^{\widehat{r}_t} &= e^{\alpha(\widehat{a}_t-\widehat{k}_t)} \\
1+\widehat{r}_t &= 1+\alpha(\widehat{a}_t-\widehat{k}_t) \\
\widehat{r}_t &= \alpha(\widehat{a}_t-\widehat{k}_t)
\end{aligned} \tag{4.33}$$

In the case of the gross interest rate, its log-linear form is obtained as follows:

$$\begin{aligned}
R_t &= r_t + (1-\delta) \\
R_{ss}e^{\widehat{R}_t} &= r_{ss}e^{\widehat{r}_t} \\
R_{ss}(1+\widehat{R}_t) &= r_{ss}(1+\widehat{r}_t) \\
\widehat{R}_t &= \frac{r_{ss}}{R_{ss}}\widehat{r}_t
\end{aligned} \tag{4.34}$$

In goods market equilibrium:

$$\begin{aligned}
y_t &= c_t + i_t \\
y_{ss}e^{\widehat{y}_t} &= c_{ss}e^{\widehat{c}_t} + i_{ss}e^{\widehat{i}_t} \\
y_{ss}(1+\widehat{y}_t) &= c_{ss}(1+\widehat{c}_t) + i_{ss}(1+\widehat{i}_t) \\
y_{ss} + y_{ss}\widehat{y}_t &= c_{ss} + c_{ss}\widehat{c}_t + i_{ss} + i_{ss}\widehat{i}_t \\
y_{ss}\widehat{y}_t &= c_{ss}\widehat{c}_t + i_{ss}\widehat{i}_t \\
\widehat{y}_t &= \frac{c_{ss}}{y_{ss}}\widehat{c}_t + \frac{i_{ss}}{y_{ss}}\widehat{i}_t
\end{aligned} \tag{4.35}$$

The law of movement of capital in its log-linear form would be:

$$\begin{aligned}
k_{t+1} &= (1-\delta)k_t + i_t \\
k_{ss}e^{\widehat{k}_{t+1}} &= (1-\delta)k_{ss}e^{\widehat{k}_t} + i_{ss}e^{\widehat{i}_t} \\
k_{ss}(1+\widehat{k}_{t+1}) &= (1-\delta)k_{ss}(1+\widehat{k}_t) + i_{ss}(1+\widehat{i}_t)
\end{aligned}$$

$$
\begin{aligned}
k_{ss} + k_{ss}\widehat{k}_{t+1} &= (1-\delta)k_{ss} + (1-\delta)k_{ss}\widehat{k}_t + i_{ss} + i_{ss}\widehat{i}_t \\
k_{ss}\widehat{k}_{t+1} &= (1-\delta)k_{ss}\widehat{k}_t + i_{ss}\widehat{i}_t \\
\widehat{k}_{t+1} &= (1-\delta)\widehat{k}_t + \frac{i_{ss}}{k_{ss}}\widehat{i}_t
\end{aligned} \tag{4.36}
$$

Finally, the productivity equation is:

$$
\begin{aligned}
lna_t &= \phi lna_{t-1} + \epsilon_t \\
lna_{ss}e^{\widehat{a}_t} &= \phi lna_{ss}e^{\widehat{a}_{t-1}} + \epsilon_t \\
lna_{ss} + \widehat{a}_t &= \phi lna_{ss} + \phi\widehat{a}_{t-1} + \epsilon_t \\
\widehat{a}_t &= \phi\widehat{a}_{t-1} + \epsilon_t
\end{aligned} \tag{4.37}
$$

Table 4.4 summarizes the log-linear equations of the model.

The number of equations in Table 4.4 can be reduced to five. To do so, the equilibrium equation of the goods market (Eq. 4.5) is introduced in the equation on the movement of capital (Eq. 4.6). The variable that connects these two equations is the investment. First, we write investment on the left side of Eq. 4.5:

$$
\widehat{i}_t = \left[\widehat{y}_t - \frac{c_{ss}}{y_{ss}}\widehat{c}_t\right]\frac{y_{ss}}{i_{ss}}
$$

Second, this equation is inserted into the law of motion of capital:

$$
\widehat{k}_{t+1} = (1-\delta)\widehat{k}_t + \frac{i_{ss}}{k_{ss}}\left(\left[\widehat{y}_t - \frac{c_{ss}}{y_{ss}}\widehat{c}_t\right]\frac{y_{ss}}{i_{ss}}\right)
$$

In addition, the equation of the production function (y_t) is introduced:

Table 4.4 Log-linear equations

Log-linear equations	Description
1. $\widehat{c}_t = E_t\left[\widehat{c}_{t+1} - \frac{1}{\gamma}\widehat{R}_{t+1}\right]$	Euler's equation
2. $\widehat{y}_t = \alpha\widehat{a}_t + (1-\alpha)\widehat{k}_t$	Production function
3. $\widehat{r}_t = \alpha[\widehat{a}_t - \widehat{k}_t]$	Capital demand
4. $\widehat{R}_t = \frac{r_{ss}}{R_{ss}}\widehat{r}_t$	Gross interest rate
5. $\widehat{y}_t = \frac{c_{ss}}{y_{ss}}\widehat{c}_t + \frac{i_{ss}}{y_{ss}}\widehat{i}_t$	Equilibrium in the goods market
6. $\widehat{k}_{t+1} = (1-\delta)\widehat{k}_t + \frac{i_{ss}}{k_{ss}}\widehat{i}_t$	Law of movement of capital
7. $\widehat{a}_t = \phi\widehat{a}_{t-1} + \epsilon_t$	Productivity *shock*

Note: To directly obtain the solution of the model with Dynare, you can use the mod "Campbell_Lfijo_Dynare.mod"

Table 4.5 Log-linear equations (reduced system)

Log-linear equations
1. $\widehat{c}_t = E_t\left[\widehat{c}_{t+1} - \frac{1}{\gamma}\widehat{R}_{t+1}\right]$
2. $\widehat{y}_t = \alpha\widehat{a}_t + (1-\alpha)\widehat{k}_t$
3. $\widehat{R}_t = \lambda_3[\widehat{a}_t - \widehat{k}_t]$
4. $\widehat{k}_{t+1} = \lambda_1\widehat{k}_t + \lambda_2\widehat{a}_t + (1-\lambda_1-\lambda_2)\widehat{c}_t$
5. $\widehat{a}_t = \phi\widehat{a}_{t-1} + \epsilon_t$

$$\widehat{k}_{t+1} = (1-\delta)\widehat{k}_t + \frac{i_{ss}}{k_{ss}}\left(\left[\left(\alpha\widehat{a}_t + (1-\alpha)\widehat{k}_t\right) - \frac{c_{ss}}{y_{ss}}\widehat{c}_t\right]\frac{y_{ss}}{i_{ss}}\right)$$

Putting the algebraic terms in order, we have:

$$\widehat{k}_{t+1} = \underbrace{\left[(1-\delta) + \delta(1-\alpha)\frac{y_{ss}}{i_{ss}}\right]}_{\lambda_1}\widehat{k}_t + \underbrace{\delta\alpha\frac{y_{ss}}{i_{ss}}}_{\lambda_2}\widehat{a}_t - \delta\frac{c_{ss}}{i_{ss}}\widehat{c}_t \tag{4.38}$$

From the coefficients of Eq. (4.38) it is shown that:

$$-\delta\frac{c_{ss}}{i_{ss}} = 1 - \lambda_1 - \lambda_2$$

Therefore, the final equation is:

$$\widehat{k}_{t+1} = \lambda_1\widehat{k}_t + \lambda_2\widehat{a}_t + (1-\lambda_1-\lambda_2)\widehat{c}_t \tag{4.39}$$

On the other hand, Eq. (4.3) (demand for capital) is plugged into Eq. (4.4) (gross interest rate):

$$\widehat{R}_t = \alpha\frac{r_{ss}}{R_{ss}}\widehat{r}_t$$

$$\widehat{R}_t = \alpha\frac{r_{ss}}{R_{ss}}[\widehat{a}_t - \widehat{k}_t]$$

$$\widehat{R}_t = \lambda_3[\widehat{a}_t - \widehat{k}_t] \tag{4.40}$$

where, in the previous equation, the coefficient λ_3 has been defined:

$$\lambda_3 = \alpha\frac{r_{ss}}{R_{ss}}$$

Table 4.5 summarizes the five main log-linear equations of Campbell (1994) fixed work model.

4.5.1 Substitution and Income Effect of the Interest Rate

Before solving the log-linear system, it is important to analyze the impact of the real interest rate on consumption. To approach this analysis it is very useful to use the log-linear equations.

Consumer theory suggests that when the price (p_t) of a good (q_t) changes, there are two effects on the consumer: first, the price of q_t relative to other products changes, and second, due to the change in p_t, the consumer's real income also changes. The change in optimal consumption as a result of a change in price contains both effects.

The substitution effect is the effect obtained only by the change in relative prices, keeping real income constant, while the income effect is the effect obtained only by the change in real income.

The interest rate represents the relative price of the basket in period "t+1" (c_{t+1}) with respect to today (c_t). Therefore, a change in the interest rate will produce two effects: substitution and income.

Substitution Effect (ES) An increase in the real interest rate makes tomorrow's consumption c_{t+1} relatively less expensive compared to today's consumption c_t. This is because saving is more profitable to reach the same amount of consumption tomorrow; that is, the consumer needs to sacrifice less consumption today. Therefore, the substitution effect is summarized as follows:

$$\uparrow R_t \xrightarrow{\text{Substitution Effect}} \downarrow c_t \text{ y } \uparrow c_{t+1}$$

It is worth mentioning that the Euler equation reflects the substitution effect of consumption. In addition, σ is EIS:

$$\widehat{c_t} = E_t\left[\widehat{c_{t+1}} - \frac{1}{\gamma}\widehat{R_{t+1}}\right]$$

The magnitude of the substitution effect is controlled by σ. The larger σ, the larger the substitution effect; namely:

$$\uparrow R_t \xrightarrow{\text{Substitution effect}} \downarrow\downarrow c_t \text{ y } \uparrow\uparrow c_{t+1}$$

Income Effect (IE) An increase in the interest rate produces an income effect. If the consumer has assets (bonds or savings), an increase in the interest rate produces higher profits for those assets and, consequently, higher income. This effect tends to increase consumption in all periods:

$$\uparrow R_t \xrightarrow{\text{Income effect}} \uparrow c_t \text{ y } \uparrow c_{t+1}$$

It is worth mentioning that the budget constraint reflects the income effect:

$$c_t + i_t = r_t k_t$$

An increase in the interest rate produces two effects:				
SE →	$\downarrow c_t$	y	$\uparrow c_{t+1}$	(Euler's equation)
IE →	$\uparrow c_t$	y	$\uparrow c_{t+1}$	(Budget constraint)
	– – –		– – –	
TE →	Depends on EIS σ	y	$\uparrow c_{t+1}$	

Total Effect (TE) To observe the final effect of the interest rate on consumption, we will rely on the budget constraint and the Euler equation (of the variables in levels):

$$c_t + i_t = r_k k_t \tag{4.41}$$

$$\text{but it is known}: \quad k_{t+1} = (1-\delta)k_t + i_t$$

$$\text{clearing } i_t: \quad i_t = k_{t+1} - (1-\delta)k_t \tag{4.42}$$

$$\text{(4.42) en (4.41)}:$$

$$c_t + k_{t+1} - (1-\delta)k_t = r_k k_t$$

$$c_t + k_{t+1} = \underbrace{(r_k + (1-\delta))}_{R_t} k_t$$

$$c_t + k_{t+1} = R_t k_t \tag{4.43}$$

As is known, the income of the representative household in "t" is $R_t k_t$, which is summarized in A_t. Likewise for the income at "t+1": $R_{t+1}k_{t+1} = A_{t+1}$. Rewriting Eq. (4.43) in terms of income, we have:

$$c_t + k_{t+1} = R_t k_t$$

$$c_t + \frac{R_{t+1}k_{t+1}}{R_{t+1}} = R_t k_t$$

$$c_t + \frac{A_{t+1}}{R_{t+1}} = A_t \tag{4.44}$$

Equation (4.44) is a difference equation, which can be solved by iterating forward. By mathematical induction, we do the following:

$$A_t = c_t + \frac{A_{t+1}}{R_{t+1}} \tag{4.45}$$

$$A_{t+1} = c_{t+1} + \frac{A_{t+2}}{R_{t+2}} \tag{4.46}$$

$$A_{t+2} = c_{t+2} + \frac{A_{t+3}}{R_{t+3}} \tag{4.47}$$

Then Eq. (4.47) is replaced in (4.46):

$$A_{t+1} = c_{t+1} + \frac{A_{t+2}}{R_{t+2}}$$

$$A_{t+1} = c_{t+1} + \frac{1}{R_{t+2}}(c_{t+2} + \frac{A_{t+3}}{R_{t+3}})$$

$$A_{t+1} = c_{t+1} + \frac{c_{t+2}}{R_{t+2}} + \frac{A_{t+3}}{R_{t+2}R_{t+3}} \tag{4.48}$$

Equation (4.48) is replaced in (4.45):

$$A_t = c_t + \frac{A_{t+1}}{R_{t+1}}$$

$$A_t = c_t + \frac{1}{R_{t+1}}(c_{t+1} + \frac{c_{t+2}}{R_{t+2}} + \frac{A_{t+3}}{R_{t+2}R_{t+3}})$$

$$A_t = c_t + + \frac{c_{t+1}}{R_{t+1}} + \frac{c_{t+2}}{R_{t+1}R_{t+2}} + \frac{A_{t+3}}{R_{t+1}R_{t+2}R_{t+3}} \tag{4.49}$$

Dividing the entire Eq. (4.49) by R_t to make a simpler generalization (in summation):

$$\frac{A_t}{R_t} = \frac{c_t}{R_t} + \frac{c_{t+1}}{R_t R_{t+1}} + \frac{c_{t+2}}{R_t R_{t+1} R_{t+2}} + \frac{A_{t+3}}{R_t R_{t+1} R_{t+2} R_{t+3}}$$

summarizing : in a summation...

$$\frac{A_t}{R_t} = \sum_{s=0}^{2} \frac{c_{t+s}}{\prod_{j=0}^{s} R_{t+j}} + \frac{A_{t+3}}{\prod_{j=0}^{3} R_{t+j}} \tag{4.50}$$

generalizing for "n" :

$$\frac{A_t}{R_t} = \sum_{s=0}^{n} \frac{c_{t+s}}{\prod_{j=0}^{s} R_{t+j}} + \frac{A_{t+(n+1)}}{\prod_{j=0}^{n+1} R_{t+j}}$$

applying **Limit** when : $n \to \infty$

$$\frac{A_t}{R_t} = \sum_{s=0}^{\infty} \frac{c_{t+s}}{\prod_{j=0}^{s} R_{t+j}} + \underbrace{\mathrm{Lim}_{n\to\infty} \frac{A_{t+(n+1)}}{\prod_{j=0}^{n+1} R_{t+j}}}_{=0(\text{by transversality})}$$

$$\frac{A_t}{R_t} = \sum_{s=0}^{\infty} \frac{c_{t+s}}{\prod_{j=0}^{s} R_{t+j}} \tag{4.51}$$

To find the relationship of the interest rate with today's consumption, it is necessary to find the relationship of c_{t+s} with current consumption c_t. For this, the Euler equation is used (abstracting the expectation operator) for "t," "$t+1$," and "$t+2$":

$$c_t^{-\gamma} = \beta c_{t+1}^{-\gamma} R_{t+1}$$
$$c_{t+1}^{-\gamma} = \beta c_{t+2}^{-\gamma} R_{t+2}$$
$$c_{t+2}^{-\gamma} = \beta c_{t+3}^{-\gamma} R_{t+3}$$

Multiplying these equations, we get:

$$c_t^{-\gamma} c_{t+1}^{-\gamma} c_{t+2}^{-\gamma} = \beta^3 c_{t+1}^{-\gamma} R_{t+1} c_{t+2}^{-\gamma} R_{t+2} c_{t+3}^{-\gamma} R_{t+3}$$
$$c_t^{-\gamma} = \beta^3 c_{t+3}^{-\gamma} \frac{R_t}{R_t} R_{t+1} R_{t+2} R_{t+3}$$
$$c_t^{-\gamma} = \beta^3 \frac{c_{t+3}^{-\gamma}}{R_t} \prod_{j=0}^{3} R_{t+j}$$

generalizing for "s" :

$$c_t^{-\gamma} = \beta^s \frac{c_{t+s}^{-\gamma}}{R_t} \prod_{j=0}^{s} R_{t+j}$$
$$\left(\frac{c_{t+s}}{c_t}\right)^{-\gamma} = \frac{R_t}{\beta^s \prod_{j=0}^{s} R_{t+j}}$$

clearing c_{t+s} :

$$c_{t+s} = \left[\frac{R_t}{\beta^s \prod_{j=0}^{s} R_{t+j}}\right]^{-\frac{1}{\gamma}} c_t \tag{4.52}$$

Plugging Eq. (4.52) into Eq. (4.51):

$$\frac{A_t}{R_t} = \sum_{s=0}^{\infty} \frac{\left[\frac{R_t}{\beta^s \prod_{j=0}^{s} R_{t+j}}\right]^{\frac{-1}{\gamma}} c_t}{\prod_{j=0}^{s} R_{t+j}}$$

$$\frac{A_t}{R_t} = \sum_{s=0}^{\infty} \beta^{\frac{s}{\gamma}} [\prod_{j=0}^{s} R_{t+j}]^{\frac{1}{\gamma}-1} c_t R_t^{-1/\gamma}$$

$$\frac{A_t}{R_t} = c_t \left[\sum_{s=0}^{\infty} \beta^{\frac{s}{\gamma}} [\prod_{j=0}^{s} R_{t+j}]^{\frac{1}{\gamma}-1} R_t^{-1/\gamma}\right] \tag{4.53}$$

Simplified Case To analyze the effect of the interest rate on today's consumption c_t, it is assumed that the interest rate is the same in all periods; that is, $R_t = R_{t+1} = R_{t+2} = ... = R_{t+j} = R$. Introducing this assumption in the producer of Eq. (4.53), then:

$$\prod_{j=0}^{s} R_{t+j} = R_{s+1}$$

Replacing the previous expression in Eq. (4.53) we have:

$$\frac{A_t}{R} = c_t \left[\sum_{s=0}^{\infty} \beta^{\frac{s}{\gamma}} \left[R^{s+1}\right]^{\frac{1}{\gamma}-1} R^{-1/\gamma}\right]$$

$$\frac{A_t}{R} = c_t \left[\sum_{s=0}^{\infty} \beta^{\frac{s}{\gamma}} R^{(s+1)\frac{1}{\gamma}-1} R^{-1/\gamma}\right]$$

$$\frac{A_t}{R} = c_t \left[\sum_{s=0}^{\infty} \beta^{\frac{s}{\gamma}} R^{(s(\frac{1}{\gamma}-1)+\frac{1}{\gamma}-1} R^{-1/\gamma}\right]$$

$$\frac{A_t}{R} = c_t \left[\sum_{s=0}^{\infty} \beta^{\frac{s}{\gamma}} R^{(s(\frac{1}{\gamma}-1)} R^{-1}\right]$$

$$A_t = c_t \left[\sum_{s=0}^{\infty} \beta^{\frac{s}{\gamma}} R^{(s(\frac{1}{\gamma}-1)}\right]$$

$$A_t = c_t \left[\sum_{s=0}^{\infty} \left(\beta^{\frac{1}{\gamma}} R^{\frac{1}{\gamma}-1}\right)^{s}\right] \tag{4.54}$$

By geometric progression of $\sum_{s=0}^{\infty}\left(\beta^{\frac{1}{\gamma}} R^{\frac{1}{\gamma}-1}\right)^{s}$ we have that:

$$\sum_{s=0}^{\infty}\left(\beta^{\frac{1}{\gamma}} R^{\frac{1}{\gamma}-1}\right)^{s} = 1+\left(\beta^{\frac{1}{\gamma}} R^{\frac{1}{\gamma}-1}\right)+\left(\beta^{\frac{1}{\gamma}} R^{\frac{1}{\gamma}-1}\right)^{2}+\left(\beta^{\frac{1}{\gamma}} R^{\frac{1}{\gamma}-1}\right)^{3}\ldots$$

$$\sum_{s=0}^{\infty}\left(\beta^{\frac{1}{\gamma}} R^{\frac{1}{\gamma}-1}\right)^{s} = \frac{1}{1-\beta^{\frac{1}{\gamma}} R^{\frac{1}{\gamma}-1}} \tag{4.55}$$

Substituting the expression (4.55) into Eq. (4.54):

$$A_t = c_t\left[\frac{1}{1-\beta^{\frac{1}{\gamma}} R^{\frac{1}{\gamma}-1}}\right]$$

$$c_t = A_t\left[1-\beta^{\frac{1}{\gamma}} R^{\frac{1}{\gamma}-1}\right] \tag{4.56}$$

Applying logarithm to Eq. (4.56):

$$ln(A_t) = ln(c_t) + ln\left[1-\beta^{\frac{1}{\gamma}} R^{\frac{1}{\gamma}-1}\right] \tag{4.57}$$

Applying the first-order Taylor approximation to $ln\left[1-\beta^{\frac{1}{\gamma}} R^{\frac{1}{\gamma}-1}\right]$ must:

$$ln\left[1-\beta^{\frac{1}{\gamma}} R^{\frac{1}{\gamma}-1}\right] \approx -\beta^{\frac{1}{\gamma}} R^{\frac{1}{\gamma}-1} \tag{4.58}$$

Replacing (4.58) in (4.57):

$$ln(A_t) = ln(c_t) + \beta^{\frac{1}{\gamma}} R^{\frac{1}{\gamma}-1} \tag{4.59}$$

Taking differential to Eq. (4.59) and considering that A_t does not change and, furthermore, $\frac{1}{\gamma} = \sigma$ (EIS), then:

$$\Delta ln(c_t) = -(\sigma-1)\beta^{\sigma} R^{\sigma}\Delta R$$

$$\frac{\Delta ln(c_t)}{\Delta R} = -(\sigma-1)\beta^{\sigma} R^{\sigma} \tag{4.60}$$

Equation (4.60) reflects the final effect on today's consumption as a movement in the real interest rate. An important conclusion is that the **final effect** depends on the elasticity of intertemporal substitution of consumption (σ). The following expression shows the final effect on consumption depending on the value of the EIS:

$$\sigma < 1 \longrightarrow \frac{\Delta ln(c_t)}{\Delta R} > 0 \longrightarrow \uparrow c_t$$
$$\sigma = 1 \longrightarrow \frac{\Delta ln(c_t)}{\Delta R} = 0 \longrightarrow \text{R does not affect consumption}$$
$$\sigma > 1 \longrightarrow \frac{\Delta ln(c_t)}{\Delta R} < 0 \longrightarrow \downarrow c_t$$

General Case Considering Eq. (4.53) and developing it, we have:

$$\frac{A_t}{R_t} = c_t \left[\sum_{s=0}^{\infty} \beta^{\frac{s}{\gamma}} [\prod_{j=0}^{s} R_{t+j}]^{\frac{1}{\gamma}-1} R_t^{-1/\gamma} \right]$$
$$\frac{A_t}{R_t^{1-1/\gamma}} = c_t \left[\sum_{s=0}^{\infty} \beta^{\frac{s}{\gamma}} [\prod_{j=0}^{s} R_{t+j}]^{\frac{1}{\gamma}-1} \right]$$

being explicit in the sum:

$$\frac{A_t}{R_t^{1-1/\gamma}} =$$

$$c_t \left[1 + \underbrace{\beta^{\frac{1}{\gamma}} (R_t R_{t+1})^{\frac{1}{\gamma}-1} + \beta^{\frac{2}{\gamma}} (R_t R_{t+1} R_{t+2})^{\frac{1}{\gamma}-1} + \beta^{\frac{3}{\gamma}} (R_t R_{t+1} R_{t+2} R_{t+3})^{\frac{1}{\gamma}-1} ...}_{N_t} \right]$$

$$A_t = c_t R_t^{1-1/\gamma} [1 + N_t]$$
$$A_t = c_t R_t^{1-1/\gamma} + c_t R_t^{1-1/\gamma} N_t \tag{4.61}$$

Differentiating Eq. (4.61) with respect to R_{t+1} and considering that R_j $(j \neq 1)$ does not depend on R_{t+1}:

$$\frac{\Delta A_t}{\Delta R_{t+1}} = R_t^{1-1/\gamma} \frac{\Delta c_t}{\Delta R_{t+1}} + \frac{\Delta c_t}{\Delta R_{t+1}} R_t^{1-1/\gamma} N_t + c_t R_t^{1-1/\gamma} \frac{\Delta N_t}{\Delta R_{t+1}} \tag{4.62}$$

Expanding the differential: $\frac{\Delta N_t}{\Delta R_{t+1}}$,

$$\frac{\Delta N_t}{\Delta R_{t+1}} = (\frac{1}{\gamma} - 1)\beta^{\frac{1}{\gamma}} (R_t R_{t+1})^{\frac{1}{\gamma}-2} R_t + (\frac{1}{\gamma} - 1)\beta^{\frac{2}{\gamma}} (R_t R_{t+1} R_{t+2})^{\frac{1}{\gamma}-2} R_t R_{t+2} +$$
$$(\frac{1}{\gamma} - 1)\beta^{\frac{3}{\gamma}} (R_t R_{t+1} R_{t+2} R_{t+3})^{\frac{1}{\gamma}-2} R_t R_{t+2} R_{t+3} + ...$$

multiplying and dividing by R_{t+1}

$$
\begin{aligned}
&= \frac{1}{R_{t+1}}\Big[(\frac{1}{\gamma}-1)\beta^{\frac{1}{\gamma}}(R_tR_{t+1})^{\frac{1}{\gamma}-2}R_tR_{t+1}+\\
&(\frac{1}{\gamma}-1)\beta^{\frac{2}{\gamma}}(R_tR_{t+1}R_{t+2})^{\frac{1}{\gamma}-2}R_tR_{t+1}R_{t+2}+\\
&(\frac{1}{\gamma}-1)\beta^{\frac{3}{\gamma}}(R_tR_{t+1}R_{t+2}R_{t+3})^{\frac{1}{\gamma}-2}R_tR_{t+1}R_{t+2}R_{t+3}+...\Big]\\
&= \frac{1}{R_{t+1}}(\frac{1}{\gamma}-1)\Big[\beta^{\frac{1}{\gamma}}(R_tR_{t+1})^{\frac{1}{\gamma}-1}+\beta^{\frac{2}{\gamma}}(R_tR_{t+1}R_{t+2})^{\frac{1}{\gamma}-1}+\\
&\beta^{\frac{3}{\gamma}}(R_tR_{t+1}R_{t+2}R_{t+3})^{\frac{1}{\gamma}-1}+...\Big]\\
&= \frac{1}{R_{t+1}}(\frac{1}{\gamma}-1)N_t\\
&= (\frac{1}{\gamma}-1)\frac{N_t}{R_{t+1}} \qquad (4.63)
\end{aligned}
$$

Plugging Eq. (4.63) into Eq. (4.62):

$$
\begin{aligned}
\frac{\Delta A_t}{\Delta R_{t+1}} &= R_t^{1-1/\gamma}\frac{\Delta c_t}{\Delta R_{t+1}}+\frac{\Delta c_t}{\Delta R_{t+1}}R_t^{1-1/\gamma}N_t+c_tR_t^{1-1/\gamma}\frac{\Delta N_t}{\Delta R_{t+1}}\\
\frac{\Delta A_t}{\Delta R_{t+1}} &= R_t^{1-1/\gamma}\frac{\Delta c_t}{\Delta R_{t+1}}+\frac{\Delta c_t}{\Delta R_{t+1}}R_t^{1-1/\gamma}N_t+c_tR_t^{1-1/\gamma}(\frac{1}{\gamma}-1)\frac{N_t}{R_{t+1}}\\
\Delta A_t &= R_t^{1-1/\gamma}\Delta c_t+\Delta c_tR_t^{1-1/\gamma}N_t+\Delta R_{t+1}c_tR_t^{1-1/\gamma}(\frac{1}{\gamma}-1)\frac{N_t}{R_{t+1}} \qquad (4.64)
\end{aligned}
$$

It is known that $\Delta A_t = 0$, so:

$$
\begin{aligned}
0 &= R_t^{1-1/\gamma}\Delta c_t+\Delta c_tR_t^{1-1/\gamma}N_t+\Delta R_{t+1}c_tR_t^{1-1/\gamma}(\frac{1}{\gamma}-1)\frac{N_t}{R_{t+1}}\\
0 &= R_t^{1-1/\gamma}\big[\Delta c_t+\Delta c_tN_t+(\frac{1}{\gamma}-1)c_tN_t\frac{\Delta R_{t+1}}{R_{t+1}}\big]\\
0 &= \Delta c_t+\Delta c_tN_t+(\frac{1}{\gamma}-1)c_tN_t\frac{\Delta R_{t+1}}{R_{t+1}}\\
0 &= \Delta c_t[1+N_t]+(\frac{1}{\gamma}-1)c_tN_t\frac{\Delta R_{t+1}}{R_{t+1}}
\end{aligned}
$$

Algebraically ordering the terms, we have:

$$
-\Delta c_t[1+N_t] = (\frac{1}{\gamma}-1)c_tN_t\frac{\Delta R_{t+1}}{R_{t+1}}
$$

$$-\frac{\Delta c_t}{c_t}\frac{[1+N_t]}{N_t} = (\frac{1}{\gamma}-1)\frac{\Delta R_{t+1}}{R_{t+1}}$$
$$\frac{\Delta c_t}{c_t} = -(\frac{1}{\gamma}-1)\frac{N_t}{1+N_t}\frac{\Delta R_{t+1}}{R_{t+1}} \tag{4.65}$$

From Eq. (4.65) it can be concluded that the impact of the next period's interest rate on today's consumption is governed by the consumption elasticity of substitution ($\frac{1}{\gamma} = \sigma$), as observed in the simplified case.

4.6 Solution of Linear System

In Chaps. 1 and 3 it was pointed out that in the existing literature, there are various methods for solving systems of linear equations. In Chap. 3, the Blanchard and Kahn (1980) method was illustrated, and given the nature of the Long and Plosser (1983) model, the solution could also be obtained analytically. In this chapter, the method of undetermined coefficients of Uhlig (1999) will be used in order to have an overview of the different solution methods.

4.6.1 Method of Undetermined Coefficients

The method of undetermined coefficients seeks that the control variables are a function of the state variables ($\widehat{k}_t$) and the exogenous variable ($\widehat{a}_t$). That is, in the same way as the Blanchard and Kahn method, this method looks for the policy function and the state function.

When analyzing whether each log-linear equation is found as a function of capital ($\widehat{k}_t$) and productivity ($\widehat{a}_t$), the table shows (Table 4.5) that Eq. (4.2) (production function) and Eq. (4.3) (demand for capital considering the interest rate is raw) depend on these variables. Also, Eq. (4.5) describes productivity.

By introducing the demand for capital in Euler's equation, this equation would be a function of capital and productivity:

$$\widehat{c}_t = E_t(\widehat{c}_{t+1} - \sigma\lambda_3(\widehat{a}_{t+1} - \widehat{k}_{t+1})) \tag{4.66}$$

On the other hand, the law of motion of capital contains the state variable and the *shock*:

$$\widehat{k}_{t+1} = \lambda_1\widehat{k}_t + \lambda_2\widehat{a}_t + (1-\lambda_1-\lambda_2)\widehat{c}_t \tag{4.67}$$

Therefore, if we find the $\widehat{c}_t$ and $\widehat{k}_{t+1}$ in terms of $(\widehat{k}_t, \widehat{a}_t)$, the system would be solved. To do this, under the method of undetermined coefficients, the following solution is proposed:

$$\widehat{c}_t = \eta_{ck}\widehat{k}_t + \eta_{ca}\widehat{a}_t \tag{4.68}$$

$$\widehat{k}_{t+1} = \eta_{kk}\widehat{k}_t + \eta_{ka}\widehat{a}_t \tag{4.69}$$

In this context, the problem lies in finding the values of the coefficients: η_{ck}, η_{ca}, η_{kk}, η_{ka}. To this end, the analysis will be performed in five steps:

(1) Euler's equation. By substituting the proposed solution in Euler's equation (4.66), an expression for the coefficients η_{ca} and η_{ck}:

$$\eta_{ca} = \frac{\eta_{ka}(\sigma\lambda_3 + \eta_{ck}) - \phi\sigma\lambda_3}{1-\phi} \rightarrow \eta_{ca} = f(\eta_{ka}, \eta_{ck}) \tag{4.70}$$

$$\eta_{ck} = \frac{\eta_{kk}\sigma\lambda_3}{1-\eta_{kk}} \rightarrow \eta_{ck} = f(\eta_{kk}) \tag{4.71}$$

(2) Equation of capital. By substituting the proposed solution in the equation of movement of capital (4.67), an expression for the coefficients is obtained η_{kk} and η_{ka}:

$$\eta_{kk} = \lambda_1 + (1-\lambda_1-\lambda_2)\eta_{ck} \rightarrow \eta_{kk} = f(\eta_{ck}) \tag{4.72}$$

$$\eta_{ka} = \lambda_2 + (1-\lambda_1-\lambda_2)\eta_{ca} \rightarrow \eta_{ka} = f(\eta_{ca}) \tag{4.73}$$

(3) First coefficient. To find η_{ck}, we choose (4.71) and (4.72):
$\eta_{ck} = f(\eta_{kk})$:

$$\eta_{ck} = \frac{\eta_{kk}\sigma\lambda_3}{1-\eta_{kk}} \tag{4.74}$$

$\eta_{kk} = f(\eta_{ck})$:

$$\eta_{kk} = \lambda_1 + (1-\lambda_1-\lambda_2)\eta_{ck} \tag{4.75}$$

(4) Finding η_{ck}. Equation (4.75) is replaced in (4.74), from which we obtain:

$$Q_2\eta_{ck}^2 + Q_1\eta_{ck} + Q_0 = 0 \tag{4.76}$$

where, first of all, the two roots of this equation represent the two values that η_{ck} can take. Second, the value of this coefficient allows us to obtain the value of the remaining three and, finally, the values of Q_i are:

$$Q_2 = 1 - \lambda_1 - \lambda_2$$

$$Q_1 = \lambda_1 - 1 + \sigma\lambda_3(1-\lambda_1-\lambda_2)$$

$$Q_0 = \lambda_1\sigma\lambda_3$$

Solving Eq. (4.76) yields the two values of η_{ck}:

$$\eta_{ck1} = \frac{-Q_1 + \sqrt{Q_1^2 - 4Q_2Q_0}}{2Q_2}$$

$$\eta_{ck2} = \frac{-Q_1 - \sqrt{Q_1^2 - 4Q_2Q_0}}{2Q_2}$$

The sign of η_{ck} that must be chosen is positive because this allows η_{kk} to be less than one, which indicates that the capital equation is stable (not explosive). To do this, the sign of each Q_i is evaluated:

- $Q_2 < 0$ (porque $\lambda_1 > 1$ y $\lambda_2 > 0$)
- $Q_0 > 0$
- $Q_1 > 0$ ($Q_1 = \lambda_1 - 1 + Q_2Q_0/\lambda_1$)

From the above, it is shown that η_{ck2} has a positive sign; therefore, this root is chosen. This allows us to obtain the two coefficients η_{ck} and η_{kk}:

$$\eta_{ck} = \frac{-Q_1 - \sqrt{Q_1^2 - 4Q_2Q_0}}{2Q_2} \tag{4.77}$$

$$\eta_{kk} = \lambda_1 + (1 - \lambda_1 - \lambda_2)\eta_{ck} \tag{4.78}$$

(5) **Remaining coefficients.** To find the two remaining coefficients η_{ca} and η_{ka}, we choose Eqs. (4.70) and (4.73):

$$\eta_{ka} = \lambda_2 + (1 - \lambda_1 - \lambda_2)\eta_{ca} \rightarrow \eta_{ka} = f(\eta_{ca})$$

$$\eta_{ca} = \frac{\eta_{ka}(\sigma\lambda_3 + \eta_{ck}) - \phi\sigma\lambda_3}{1 - \phi} \rightarrow \eta_{ca} = f(\eta_{ka}, \eta_{ck})$$

η_{ka} and η_{ca}:

$$\eta_{ca} = \frac{-\eta_{ck}\lambda_2 + \sigma\lambda_3(\phi - \lambda_2)}{\phi - 1 + (1 - \lambda_1 - \lambda_2)(\eta_{ck} + \sigma\lambda_3)}$$

$$\eta_{ka} = \lambda_2 + (1 - \lambda_1 - \lambda_2)\eta_{ca}$$

With the parameters calibrated for the base model, it is obtained that: $\eta_{ck} = 0.3253$, $\eta_{ca} = 0.2643$, $\eta_{kk} = 0.9841$, and $\eta_{ka} = 0.0551$. Finally, the solution of the model for each of the endogenous variables are:

Solution for consumption:

$$\widehat{c}_t = \eta_{ck}\widehat{k}_t + \eta_{ca}\widehat{a}_t \tag{4.79}$$

Solution for capital:

$$\widehat{k}_{t+1} = \eta_{kk}\widehat{k}_t + \eta_{ka}\widehat{a}_t \tag{4.80}$$

Solution for the product:

$$\widehat{y}_t = (1-\alpha)\widehat{k}_t + \alpha\widehat{a}_t \tag{4.81}$$

Investment solution:

$$\widehat{y}_t = \frac{c_{ss}}{y_{ss}}\widehat{c}_t + \frac{i_{ss}}{y_{ss}}\widehat{i}_t$$

$$\widehat{i}_t = \frac{y_{ss}}{i_{ss}}\left(\widehat{y}_t - \frac{c_{ss}}{y_{ss}}\widehat{c}_t\right)$$

Replacing (4.79) and (4.81):

$$\begin{aligned}\widehat{i}_t &= \frac{y_{ss}}{i_{ss}}(1-\alpha-\frac{c_{ss}}{y_{ss}}\eta_{ck})\widehat{k}_t + \\ &\frac{y_{ss}}{i_{ss}}(\alpha-\frac{c_{ss}}{y_{ss}}\eta_{ca})\widehat{a}_t\end{aligned} \tag{4.82}$$

Solution (net interest rate):

$$\widehat{r}_t = \alpha(\widehat{a}_t - \widehat{k}_t) \tag{4.83}$$

Solution (gross interest rate):

$$\widehat{R}_t = \alpha\frac{r_{ss}}{R_{ss}}(\widehat{a}_t - \widehat{k}_t) \tag{4.84}$$

4.6.2 Analysis of Elasticities

The coefficients of the solution of each one of the variables represent elasticities. This is because the variables are expressed in logarithms. For example, in the case of consumption we have:

$$\widehat{c}_t = \eta_{ck}\widehat{k}_t + \eta_{ca}\widehat{a}_t$$

Given that $\widehat{c}_t = ln(\frac{c_t}{c_{ss}})$ and similarly for the other variables, we have:

$$\begin{aligned}ln(\frac{c_t}{c_{ss}}) &= \eta_{ck}ln(\frac{k_t}{k_{ss}}) + \eta_{ca}ln(\frac{a_t}{a_{ss}})\\ ln(c_t) - ln(c_{ss}) &= \eta_{ck}(ln(k_t) - ln(k_{ss})) + \eta_{ca}(ln(a_t) - ln(a_{ss}))\\ ln(c_t) &= -[ln(c_{ss}) + ln(k_{ss}) + ln(a_{ss})] + \eta_{ck}ln(k_t) + \eta_{ca}ln(a_t)\end{aligned}$$

Taking differential with respect to capital (k_t):

Table 4.6 Coefficients (elasticities) of the linear model solution

Elasticity	Expression	Value
Elasticity of consumption to capital: η_{ck}	$\eta_{ck} = \frac{-Q_1-\sqrt{Q_1^2-4Q_2Q_0}}{2Q_2}$	0.3253
Elasticity of consumption to productivity: η_{ca}	$\eta_{ca} = \frac{-\eta_{ck}\lambda_2+\sigma\lambda_3(\phi-\lambda_2)}{\phi-1+(1-\lambda_1-\lambda_2)(\eta_{ck}+\sigma\lambda_3)}$	0.2643
Elasticity of $t+1$ capital to the t capital: η_{kk}	$\eta_{kk} = \lambda_1 + (1-\lambda_1-\lambda_2)\eta_{ck}$	0.9841
Elasticity of tomorrow's capital to productivity: η_{ka}	$\eta_{ka} = \lambda_2 + (1-\lambda_1-\lambda_2)\eta_{ca}$	0.0551

Note: The expression of the elasticities and their values are in "Campbell_Lfijo.m" (Sect. 4.2)

$$\begin{aligned}\Delta ln(c_t) &= \eta_{ck}\Delta ln(k_t)\\ \frac{\Delta c_t}{c_t} &= \eta_{ck}\frac{\Delta k_t}{k_t}\\ \frac{\frac{\Delta c_t}{c_t}}{\frac{\Delta k_t}{k_t}} &= \eta_{ck}\\ \text{Elasticity}_{c_t,k_t} &= \eta_{ck}\end{aligned} \tag{4.85}$$

As can be seen in Eq. (4.85), η_{ck} reflects the elasticity of consumption to a change in capital. In particular, η_{ck} measures the effect of capital ("k_t") on current consumption ("c_t"), keeping productivity constant ("a_t"); that is, if capital increases 1%, consumption increases by η_{ck}%. In this way all the coefficients of the solution of the log-linear system are read. Table 4.6 summarizes the elasticities.

In the analysis of elasticities, two parameters are important: the elasticity of intertemporal substitution of consumption σ and the persistence of the *shock* ϕ. To see how these parameters influence the elasticities, we are going to review each of the elasticities.

Reviewing λ_1, λ_2, and λ_3

$$\begin{aligned}\lambda_1 &= (1-\delta)+\delta(1-\alpha)\frac{y_{ss}}{i_{ss}}\\ &= (1-\delta)+\delta(1-\alpha)\left(\frac{1}{\delta}k_{ss}^{-\alpha}\right)\\ &= (1-\delta)+(1-\alpha)\frac{r_{ss}}{1-\alpha}\\ &= (1-\delta)+(\frac{1}{\beta}-(1-\delta))\\ &= \frac{1}{\beta}\\ \lambda_1 &= F(\beta)\end{aligned} \tag{4.86}$$

$$
\begin{aligned}
\lambda_2 &= \delta\alpha \frac{y_{ss}}{i_{ss}} \\
&= \delta\alpha \left(\frac{1}{\delta} k_{ss}^{-\alpha} \right) \\
&= \alpha \, \frac{r_{ss}}{1-\alpha} \\
&= \frac{\alpha}{1-\alpha} (\frac{1}{\beta} - (1-\delta)) \\
\lambda_2 &= F(\alpha, \beta, \delta)
\end{aligned} \tag{4.87}
$$

$$
\begin{aligned}
\lambda_3 &= \alpha \frac{r_{ss}}{R_{ss}} \\
&= \alpha \frac{\frac{1}{\beta} - (1-\delta)}{\frac{1}{\beta}} \\
&= \alpha(1 - \beta(1-\delta) \\
\lambda_3 &= F(\alpha, \beta, \delta)
\end{aligned} \tag{4.88}
$$

Reviewing Q_0, Q_1, and Q_2

$$
\begin{aligned}
Q_2 &= 1 - \lambda_1 - \lambda_2 \\
&= 1 - (\frac{1}{\beta}) - \frac{\alpha}{1-\alpha} (\frac{1}{\beta} - (1-\delta)) \\
&= -\left[\frac{\frac{1}{\beta} + \alpha\delta - 1}{1-\alpha} \right] \\
Q_2 &= F(\alpha, \beta, \delta)
\end{aligned} \tag{4.89}
$$

$$
\begin{aligned}
Q_1 &= \lambda_1 - 1 + \sigma\lambda_3(1 - \lambda_1 - \lambda_2) \\
&= \underbrace{\lambda_1}_{F(\beta)} - 1 + \sigma \underbrace{\lambda_3(1 - \lambda_1 - \lambda_2)}_{F(\alpha,\beta,\delta)} \\
Q_1 &= F(\sigma^{(+)}\alpha, \beta, \delta)
\end{aligned} \tag{4.90}
$$

$$
\begin{aligned}
Q_0 &= \lambda_1 \sigma \lambda_3 \\
&= \underbrace{\lambda_1}_{F(\beta)} \sigma \underbrace{\lambda_3}_{F(\alpha,\beta,\delta)} \\
Q_0 &= F(\sigma^{(+)}\alpha, \beta, \delta)
\end{aligned} \tag{4.91}
$$

What Parameters Do the Elasticities Depend on (η_{ck} and η_{kk})?
Since Q_2 is negative, the component inside the radical is positive. In that case, σ, which positively affects Q_0 and Q_1, has a positive impact on η_{ck}. On the other hand, Q_1, which is outside the radical, also transfers the positive effect of σ on η_{ck}. It is worth mentioning that η_{ck} does not depend on the persistence of the *shock* (ϕ):

$$\eta_{ck} = \frac{-Q_1 - \sqrt{Q_1^2 - 4Q_2Q_0}}{2Q_2} = F(\sigma^{(+)}\alpha, \beta, \delta) \tag{4.92}$$

From the above, the following observation is concluded:

Observation 1 η_{ck} increases as the EIS (σ) increases.

On the other hand, when analyzing the coefficient η_{kk}, the following is obtained:

$$\begin{aligned}
\eta_{kk} &= \lambda_1 + (1-\lambda_1-\lambda_2)\eta_{ck} \\
&= \underbrace{\lambda_1}_{F(\beta)} + \underbrace{(1-\lambda_1-\lambda_2)}_{=-\delta\frac{c_{ss}}{i_{ss}}} \underbrace{\eta_{ck}}_{F(\sigma^{(+)}\alpha,\beta,\delta)} \\
&= \underbrace{\lambda_1}_{F(\beta)} - \delta\frac{c_{ss}}{i_{ss}} \underbrace{\eta_{ck}}_{F(\sigma^{(+)}\alpha,\beta,\delta)} \\
&= \underbrace{\lambda_1}_{F(\beta)} - \underbrace{\delta\frac{c_{ss}}{i_{ss}}}_{F(\alpha,\beta,\delta)} \underbrace{\eta_{ck}}_{F(\sigma^{(+)}\alpha,\beta,\delta)}
\end{aligned}$$

$$\eta_{kk} = F(\sigma^{(-)}\alpha, \beta, \delta) \tag{4.93}$$

From Eq. (4.93) the following observations are derived:

Observation 2 η_{ck} and η_{kk} do not depend on ϕ.

Observation 3 η_{kk} decreases as the EIS (σ) increases.

What Parameters Do the Elasticities (η_{ca} and η_{ka}) Depend on?

$$\eta_{ca} = \frac{-\eta_{ck}\lambda_2 + \sigma\lambda_3(\phi - \lambda_2)}{\phi - 1 + (1-\lambda_1-\lambda_2)(\eta_{ck} + \sigma\lambda_3)} = F(\phi, \sigma, \alpha, \beta, \delta) \tag{4.94}$$

$$\eta_{ka} = \lambda_2 + (1-\lambda_1-\lambda_2)\eta_{ca} = F(\phi, \sigma, \alpha, \beta, \delta) \tag{4.95}$$

From expression (4.95) it can be seen that η_{ca} has a nonlinear relationship with ϕ and σ. Similarly, it happens for η_{ka} (Fig. 4.2). From the above, the following observations are derived:

Observation 4 η_{ca} increases as ϕ increases for low values of σ ($\sigma \le 1$), but decreases for high values ($\sigma > 1$).

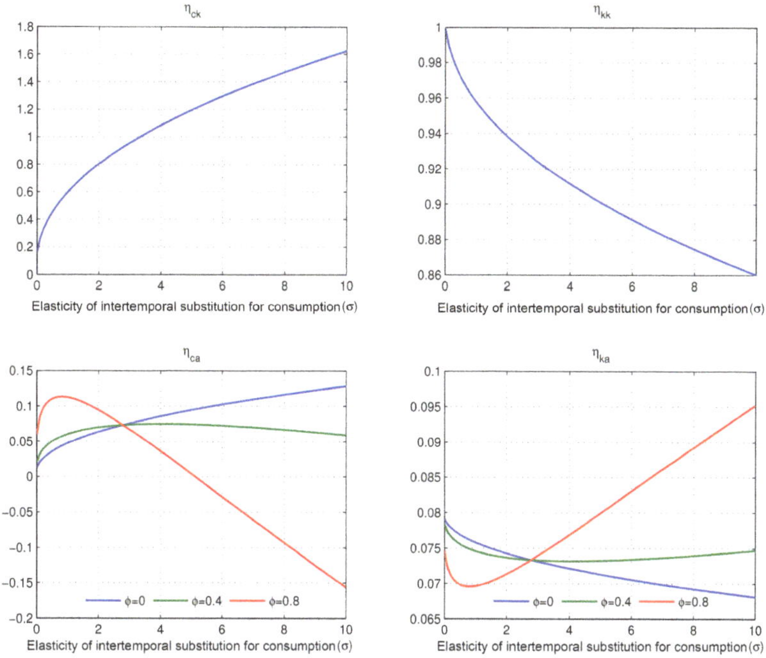

Fig. 4.2 Elasticities (coefficients of the solution) **Note:** It is worth mentioning that these graphics are obtained from the code "Campbell_Lfijo_Sim_Parametros.m"

Table 4.7 Special cases

Case	Value of σ	Utility function	Elasticity	Time series
Case 1	$\sigma = 0$	There is no intertemporal substitution effect	$\eta_{kk} = 1$	$ln(c_t)$ is a *random walk*, and $ln(k_t)$ and $ln(k_t)$ cointegrate with $ln(c_t)$
Case 2	$\sigma = 1$	Logarithmic utility function: $u(c_t) = ln(c_t)$		The substitution effect and the income effect cancel
Case 3	$\sigma = \infty$	Linear utility function: $u(c_t) = c_t$	$\eta_{kk} = 0$, $\eta_{ka} = \phi$	k_t behaves like AR(1), while c_t and y_t behave like ARMA(1,1)

Observation 5 η_{kk} and η_{ka} decrease as the EIS (σ) increases.

Table 4.7 mentions three cases of special interest.

4.7 Representation of Time Series

Because we have the solution of the model, that is, each endogenous variable as a function of the state variable (capital) and the exogenous variable (productivity), also considering that productivity behaves as an AR(1) process, then the time series representation can be found ARMA(p,q) for each variable.

4.7.1 Capital Time Series

From the solution of the model, in particular, from the equation that describes the behavior of capital in $t+1$ as a function of capital in t and productivity, we have the following:

$$\widehat{k}_{t+1} = \eta_{kk}\widehat{k}_t + \eta_{ka}\widehat{a}_t$$

where the coefficients η_{kk} and η_{ka} have been previously found. From this equation, we can find the autoregressive form of capital $(\widehat{k}_{t+1})$:

$$\begin{aligned}(1-\eta_{kk}L)\widehat{k}_{t+1} &= \eta_{ka}\widehat{a}_t \\ \widehat{k}_{t+1} &= \frac{\eta_{ka}}{1-\eta_{kk}L}\widehat{a}_t \qquad (4.96)\\ \text{Also,}\quad \widehat{a}_t &= \phi\widehat{a}_{t-1} + \epsilon_t\end{aligned}$$

whereas $\widehat{a}_t$ can be expressed as:

$$a_t = \frac{\epsilon_t}{1-\phi L} \tag{4.97}$$

Then you have to:

$$\widehat{k}_{t+1} = \frac{\eta_{ka}}{(1-\eta_{kk}L)}\frac{\epsilon_t}{(1-\phi L)} \tag{4.98}$$

The above expression shows that capital behaves like an AR(2): two real roots (ϕ and η_{kk}) and less than 1 (k_{t+1} is stable). The AR(2) expression for capital is:

$$\begin{aligned}\widehat{k}_{t+1} &= \frac{\eta_{ka}}{(1-\eta_{kk}L)}\frac{\epsilon_t}{(1-\phi L)} \\ (1-\eta_{kk}L)(1-\phi L)\widehat{k}_{t+1} &= \eta_{ka}\epsilon_t \\ (1-\eta_{kk}L-\phi L+\eta_{kk}\phi L^2)\widehat{k}_{t+1} &= \eta_{ka}\epsilon_t \\ \widehat{k}_{t+1} - \eta_{kk}\widehat{k}_t - \phi\widehat{k}_t + \eta_{kk}\phi\widehat{k}_{t-1} &= \eta_{ka}\epsilon_t \\ \widehat{k}_{t+1} &= (\phi+\eta_{kk})\widehat{k}_t - \eta_{kk}\phi\widehat{k}_{t-1} + \eta_{ka}\epsilon_t \qquad (4.99)\end{aligned}$$

4.7.2 Production Time Series

In the same way as in the case of capital, to find the time series expression of the product, we start from the solution of the model:

$$\widehat{y}_t = \alpha\widehat{a}_t + (1-\alpha)\widehat{k}_t \tag{4.100}$$

To find the time series model of the product (y_t), the expression for productivity (as a function of the error) and the expression of capital (as a function of productivity). The latter corresponds to Eq. (4.97):

$$
\begin{aligned}
\widehat{y}_t &= \alpha\widehat{a}_t + (1-\alpha)\widehat{k}_t \\
\widehat{y}_t &= \alpha\frac{e_t}{1-\phi L} + (1-\alpha)\frac{\eta_{ka}}{(1-\eta_{kk}L)}\widehat{a}_{t-1} \\
\widehat{y}_t &= \alpha\frac{e_t}{1-\phi L} + (1-\alpha)\frac{\eta_{ka}}{(1-\eta_{kk}L)}\frac{e_{t-1}}{(1-\phi L)} \\
\widehat{y}_t &= \alpha\frac{e_t}{1-\phi L} + (1-\alpha)\frac{\eta_{ka}L}{(1-\eta_{kk}L)}\frac{e_t}{(1-\phi L)}
\end{aligned}
\tag{4.101}
$$

Equation (4.101) suggests that the product behaves like ARMA(2,1):

$$
\widehat{y}_t = \left[\frac{\alpha + [(1-\alpha)\eta_{ka} - \alpha\eta_{kk}]L}{(1-\eta_{kk}L)(1-\phi L)}\right]\epsilon_t \tag{4.102}
$$

$$
\begin{aligned}
(1-\eta_{kk}L)(1-\phi L)\widehat{y}_t &= \big[\alpha + [(1-\alpha)\eta_{ka} - \alpha\eta_{kk}]L\big]\epsilon_t \\
(1-\eta_{kk}L - \phi L + \eta_{kk}\phi L^2)\widehat{y}_t &= \alpha\epsilon_t + [(1-\alpha)\eta_{ka} - \alpha\eta_{kk}]\epsilon_{t-1} \\
\widehat{y}_t - \eta_{kk}\widehat{y}_{t-1} - \phi\widehat{y}_{t-1} + \eta_{kk}\phi\widehat{y}_{t-2} &= \alpha\epsilon_t + [(1-\alpha)\eta_{ka} - \alpha\eta_{kk}]\epsilon_{t-1} \\
\widehat{y}_t = \underbrace{(\eta_{kk}+\phi)\widehat{y}_{t-1} - \eta_{kk}\phi\widehat{y}_{t-2}}_{AR(2)} &+ \underbrace{\alpha\epsilon_t + [(1-\alpha)\eta_{ka} - \alpha\eta_{kk}]\epsilon_{t-1}}_{MA(1)}
\end{aligned}
$$

4.7.3 Consumption Time Series

From the model solution:

$$
\widehat{c}_t = \eta_{ck}\widehat{k}_t + \eta_{ca}\widehat{a}_t
$$

Consumption behaves like a ARMA(2,1):

$$
\widehat{c}_t = \left[\frac{\eta_{ca} + (\eta_{ck}\eta_{ka} - \eta_{ca}\eta_{kk})L}{(1-\eta_{kk}L)(1-\phi L)}\right]\epsilon_t \tag{4.103}
$$

4.7.4 Time Series of Gross Real Interest Rate

From the model solution:

$$
\widehat{R}_{t+1} = \lambda_3(\widehat{a}_{t+1} - \widehat{k}_{t+1})
$$

The interest rate behaves as an ARMA(2,1):

$$\widehat{R}_{t+1} = \lambda_3 \left[\frac{(1 - \eta_{ka} - \eta_{kk} L)}{(1 - \eta_{kk} L)(1 - \phi L)} \right] \epsilon_t \tag{4.104}$$

4.7.5 *Inversion Time Series*

From the solution for the inversion (Eq. 4.82):

$$\begin{aligned}
\widehat{i}_t &= \underbrace{(1 - \alpha - \frac{c_{ss}}{y_{ss}} \eta_{ck})}_{\eta_{ik}} \widehat{k}_t + \underbrace{(\alpha - \frac{c_{ss}}{y_{ss}} \eta_{ca})}_{\eta_{ia}} \widehat{a}_t \\
\widehat{i}_t &= \eta_{ik} \widehat{k}_t + \eta_{ia} \widehat{a}_t \\
\widehat{i}_t &= \eta_{ik} \frac{\eta_{ka}}{(1 - \eta_{kk} L)} \frac{\epsilon_{t-1}}{(1 - \phi L)} + \eta_{ia} \frac{\epsilon_t}{1 - \phi L} \\
\widehat{i}_t &= \left[\eta_{ik} \frac{\eta_{ka} L}{(1 - \eta_{kk} L)} + \eta_{ia} \right] \frac{\epsilon_t}{1 - \phi L} \\
\widehat{i}_t &= \left[\frac{\eta_{ik} \eta_{ka} L + \eta_{ia}(1 - \eta_{kk} L)}{(1 - \eta_{kk} L)} \right] \frac{\epsilon_t}{1 - \phi L} \\
\widehat{i}_t &= \left[\frac{\eta_{ia} + (\eta_{ik} \eta_{ka} - \eta_{ia} \eta_{kk}) L}{(1 - \eta_{kk} L)} \right] \frac{\epsilon_t}{1 - \phi L}
\end{aligned}$$

Therefore, the inversion behaves like an ARMA(2,1):

$$\widehat{i}_t = \left[\frac{\eta_{ia} + (\eta_{ik} \eta_{ka} - \eta_{ia} \eta_{kk}) L}{(1 - \eta_{kk} L)(1 - \phi L)} \right] \epsilon_t \tag{4.105}$$

4.8 Impulse-Response Functions

The construction of the impulse-response function of the endogenous variables requires two stages. In the first, the capital autoregressive form AR(2) is transformed to its moving average version MA(∞). In the second, the impact, in each period, of a temporary *shock* (of a single period) in each endogenous variable is quantified.

First Stage The MA(∞) form of capital is obtained:

$$\begin{aligned}
\widehat{k}_{t+1} &= \underbrace{(\phi + \eta_{kk})}_{\phi_1} \widehat{k}_t + \underbrace{-\eta_{kk} \phi}_{\phi_2} \widehat{k}_{t-1} + \eta_{ka} \epsilon_t \\
\widehat{k}_{t+1} &= \phi_1 \widehat{k}_{t-1} + \phi_2 \widehat{k}_t + \eta_{ka} \epsilon_t
\end{aligned}$$

$$(1 - \phi_1 L - \phi_2 L^2)\widehat{k}_{t+1} = \eta_{ka}\epsilon_t$$

Calculating the roots of AR(2):

$$1 - \phi_1 L - \phi_2 L^2 = 0$$

In factors:

$$(L - y_1)(L - y_2) = 0$$

Factoring y_1 from the first factor and y_2 from the second:

$$y_1\left(\frac{1}{y_1}L - 1\right)y_2\left(\frac{1}{y_2}L - 1\right) = 0$$

The expression reduces to:

$$\left(\underbrace{\frac{1}{y_1}}_{\theta_1} L - 1\right)\left(\underbrace{\frac{1}{y_2}}_{\theta_2} L - 1\right) = 0$$

Multiplying by (-) both terms:

$$(1 - \theta_1 L)(1 - \theta_2 L) = 0$$

So, equivalence of roots:

$$(L - y_1)(L - y_2) = (1 - \theta_1 L)(1 - \theta_2 L) = 0$$

where:

- $\theta_1 = \frac{1}{y_1}$
- $\theta_2 = \frac{1}{y_2}$

Using the equivalence of roots of AR(2):

$$(L - y_1)(L - y_2)\widehat{k}_{t+1} = \eta_{ka}\epsilon_t$$
$$(1 - \theta_1 L)(1 - \theta_2 L)\widehat{k}_{t+1} = \eta_{ka}\epsilon_t$$
$$\widehat{k}_{t+1} = \underbrace{\frac{1}{(1 - \theta_1 L)(1 - \theta_2 L)}}_{\Psi(L)}\eta_{ka}\epsilon_t$$

where:

$$\Psi(L) = 1 + \psi_1 L + \psi_2 L^2 + \psi_3 L^3 + ... + \psi_k L^k + ...$$

$$\psi_k = = \sum_{j=0}^{k} \theta_1^j \theta_2^{k-j}$$

MA(∞) version of capital:

$$\widehat{k}_{t+1} = (1 + \psi_1 L + \psi_2 L^2 + \psi_3 L^3 + ...)\eta_{ka}\epsilon_t \tag{4.106}$$

With this expression, we calculate the impulse-response function. The extended version of Eq. (4.106) is as follows:

$$\widehat{k}_{t+1} = (1 + \psi_1 L + \psi_2 L^2 + \psi_3 L^3 + ...)\eta_{ka}\epsilon_t$$
$$\widehat{k}_{t+1} = \eta_{ka}\epsilon_t + (\psi_1\eta_{ka})\epsilon_{t-1} + (\psi_2\eta_{ka})\epsilon_{t-2} + (\psi_3\eta_{ka})\epsilon_{t-3} + ... \tag{4.107}$$

Second Stage In this stage, the impulse-response function of capital in the face of a *shock* of productivity is calculated. For the calculation of the capital impulse-response function, it is considered that the impulse or *shock* ϵ_t takes place in a single period (period one) and that it takes the value of a standard deviation σ_ϵ, which is assumed to be equal to one; that is, at $t = 1$, $\epsilon_1 = \sigma_\epsilon = 1$. The error ($\epsilon_t$) takes the value of zero during the periods before the *shock* and after the *shock*. Table 4.8 shows the construction of the capital impulse-response function.

At $t = 0$ all variables are in their steady state. The capital at $t = 1$, which is determined at $t = 0$, is also in a steady state, so much so that the law of movement of capital is fulfilled: $k_1 = (1 - \delta)k_0 + i_0$, where $k_1 = k_0 = k_{ss}$. The *shock* of productivity occurs in the period $t = 1$, which produces the following effects:

First Effect (on Firms) An increase in productivity produces an increase in the production function for each level of capital. Capital becomes more productive at

Table 4.8 Construction of the capital impulse-response function

t	ϵ_t	Version MA(∞) of $\widehat{k}_{t+1}$	IRF of $\widehat{k}_{t+1}$
0	$\epsilon_0 = 0$	$\widehat{k}_1 = \eta_{ka} \underbrace{\epsilon_0}_{=0} + (\psi_1\eta_{ka}) \underbrace{\epsilon_{-1}}_{=0} + \ldots$	$\widehat{k}_1 = \eta_{ka}\epsilon_0$
1	$\epsilon_1 = 1$	$\widehat{k}_2 = \eta_{ka} \underbrace{\epsilon_1}_{=1} + (\psi_1\eta_{ka}) \underbrace{\epsilon_0}_{=0} + \ldots$	$\widehat{k}_2 = \eta_{ka}\epsilon_1$
2	$\epsilon_2 = 0$	$\widehat{k}_3 = \eta_{ka} \underbrace{\epsilon_2}_{=0} + (\psi_1\eta_{ka}) \underbrace{\epsilon_1}_{=1} + (\psi_2\eta_{ka}) \underbrace{\epsilon_0}_{=0} + \ldots$	$\widehat{k}_3 = \psi_1\eta_{ka}\epsilon_1$
3	$\epsilon_3 = 0$	$\widehat{k}_4 = \eta_{ka} \underbrace{\epsilon_3}_{=0} + (\psi_1\eta_{ka}) \underbrace{\epsilon_2}_{=0} + (\psi_2\eta_{ka}) \underbrace{\epsilon_1}_{=1} + (\psi_3\eta_{ka}) \underbrace{\epsilon_0}_{=0} + \ldots$	$\widehat{k}_4 = \psi_2\eta_{ka}\epsilon_1$
4	$\epsilon_4 = 0$	$\ldots$	$\widehat{k}_5 = \psi_3\eta_{ka}\epsilon_1$

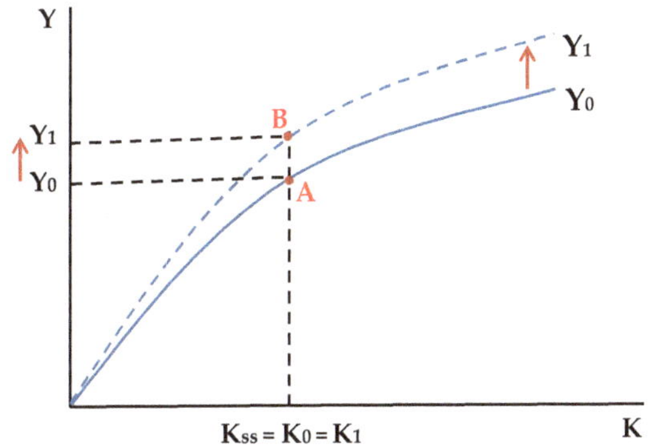

Fig. 4.3 Effect on the production function

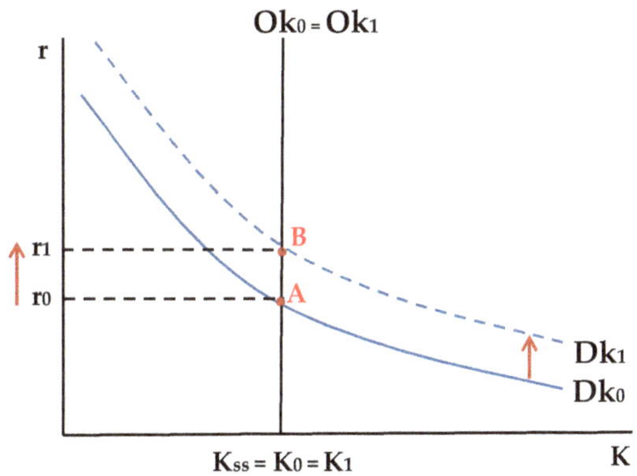

Fig. 4.4 Effect on capital demand

$t = 1$; that is, with the same capital more can be produced. Therefore, the demand for it increases (Fig. 4.3).

Second Effect (on Firms) The increase in capital demand allows the interest rate at $t = 1$ to increase: $\uparrow r_t(r_0 \longrightarrow r_1), \quad r_1 > r_0$. This is because the supply of capital at $t = 1$ remains constant and is not affected by the *shock* of productivity (Fig. 4.4).

Third Effect (on Households) The increase in the real interest rate produces an **income effect** on consumption:

$$\uparrow r_t(r_1 > r_0) \longrightarrow r_1 k_1 > r_0 k_0 \longrightarrow \uparrow c_1$$

Fourth Effect (on Households) The increase in the interest rate encourages saving, which in a closed economy is equal to investment. So, the investment goes from i_0 to i_1 ($i_1 > i_0$). The impact of a greater investment is observed in the increase in the supply of capital in the following period ($t = 2$):

$$k_2 = (1 - \delta)k_1 + i_1$$

So:

$$i_1 > i_0 \longrightarrow k_2 > k_1$$

Fifth Effect (on Firms and Households) The impact of the productivity *shock* is persistent; that is to say, its effects are positive, although they decrease over time. At $t = 2$, the production function increases, which causes the demand for capital to also increase, but to a lesser extent than that observed at $t = 1$. This produces that the real interest rate at $t = 2$ is lower than at $t = 1$ ($r_2 < r_1$); however, it is still greater than the value at $t = 0$.

Then, given that the individual compares his situation in each period with respect to $t = 0$ (steady state), then this higher interest rate ($r_2 > r_0$) produces two effects on consumption:

$$r_2 > r_0 : \text{substitution effect} \longrightarrow \downarrow c_1 \quad \uparrow c_2$$

$$r_2 > r_0 : \text{income effect} \longrightarrow r_2 k_2 > r_1 k_1 \longrightarrow \uparrow c_2$$

Therefore, the final effect of the interest rate on consumption, for small σ, is (Fig. 4.5):

$$\text{EI} > |\text{ES}| \longrightarrow \uparrow c_1 \quad \uparrow c_2$$

Table 4.9 shows the values of the impulse-response function of the endogenous variables of the model. To correctly read these values, remember that these functions correspond to log-linear variables, which, for example, for the product are expressed as follows: $\widehat{y}_t = ln(y_t) - ln(y_{ss})$ or in its reduced form $\widehat{y}_t = ln\left[\frac{y_t}{y_{ss}}\right]$.

In line with the above, according to Table 4.9 the value of the (log-linear) product at $t = 0$ is equal to zero. That is, $\widehat{y}_0 = ln\left[\frac{y_0}{y_{ss}}\right] = 0$. The only solution for this expression is that $\frac{y_0}{y_{ss}} = 1$, which leads to $y_0 = y_{ss}$. This means that when the

Fig. 4.5 Effect on the supply and demand of capital

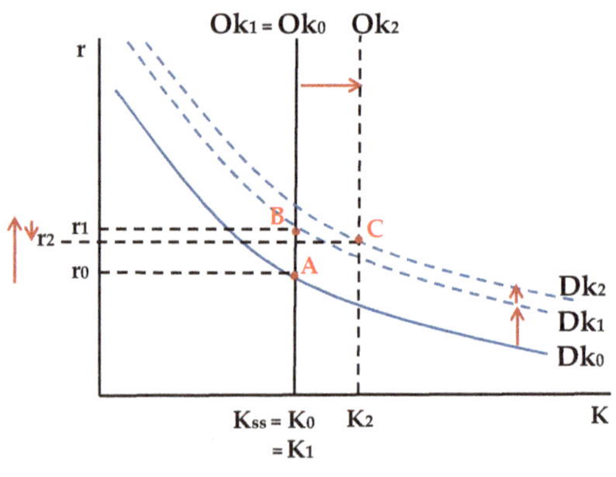

Table 4.9 Values of the impulse-response function (log-linear variables)

t	$\widehat{y}_t$	$\widehat{k}_{t+1}$	$\widehat{c}_t$	$\widehat{i}_t$	$\widehat{R}_t$	$\widehat{a}_t$
0	0	0	0	0	0	0
1	0.667	0.05512	0.26429	2.20468	0.02636	1
2	0.652	0.10660	0.26901	2.11441	0.02359	0.95
3	0.63747	0.15464	0.27321	2.02834	0.02098	0.9025
4	0.62337	0.19943	0.27691	1.94626	0.01852	0.85738
.	.	.	.	.	.	.

Note: Because the *shock* occurs in the first period ($t = 1$), the value of the variables at $t = 0$ is zero. It is worth mentioning that these values are obtained from the code "Campbell_Lfijo.m" (Sect. 4.4)

log-linear variable $\widehat{y}_t$ is at zero, this means that the level variable y_t is in its steady state.

On the other hand, at $t = 1$ the value of the product (log-linear) is equal to 0.667, in which the following is true: $\widehat{y}_1 = 0.667 = ln[\frac{y_1}{y_{ss}}]$. Solving the second equality we have that $\frac{y_1}{y_{ss}} = e^{0.667} \approx 1 + 0.667$. Therefore, $\frac{y_1}{y_{ss}} = 1 + 0.667$, which finally leads to $y_1 = (1 + 0.667)y_{ss}$:

$$\text{At } t = 1 \mapsto \underbrace{\widehat{y}_1 = 0.667}_{\text{log-lineal variable}} \mapsto \underbrace{y_1 = (1 + 0.667)y_{ss}}_{\text{variable in level}}$$

Consequently, the value (0.667) of the impulse-response function at $t = 1$ means that the output variable in levels (y_1) is 66.7% above its steady-state level (y_{ss}).

In Fig. 4.6 and Table 4.9 the following can be observed:

1. At $t = 0$ (before *shock*) all variables remain in their steady state. Therefore, the log-linear variables at $t = 0$ are equal to zero ($\widehat{x}_{ss} = ln(\frac{x_{ss}}{x_{ss}}) = ln(1) = 0$).
2. In the period of the *shock* ($t = 1$), ϵ_1 takes the value of its standard deviation, in this case, equal to 1.
3. The first effect of the *shock* of productivity is an increase in the production function, which increases the marginal productivity of capital $PMgk_t$, that is, the demand for capital in "t" (D_k).
4. The increase in capital demand increases today's interest rate ($\widehat{R}_t$). This is because the supply of capital is perfectly inelastic (vertical) because it is fixed in the previous period $\widehat{k}_t$.
5. $\uparrow \widehat{R}_t \rightarrow$ produces an income effect (IE): $\uparrow (\widehat{R}_t \widehat{k}_t)$.
6. The income effect increases the c_t and i_t.
7. $\uparrow i_t$ expands k_{t+1} (capital supply of "t+1").
8. The above produces a drop in the interest rate at "t+1" ($\downarrow r_{t+1}$), but it is still above its steady state; in other words, it is higher than the interest rate before the *shock* $\widehat{R}_0$, which encourages the household to shift consumption from today "t" to tomorrow̃lullaby "$t + 1$." That is, there is a substitution effect that is governed by the elasticity of substitution of consumption. In order to see this

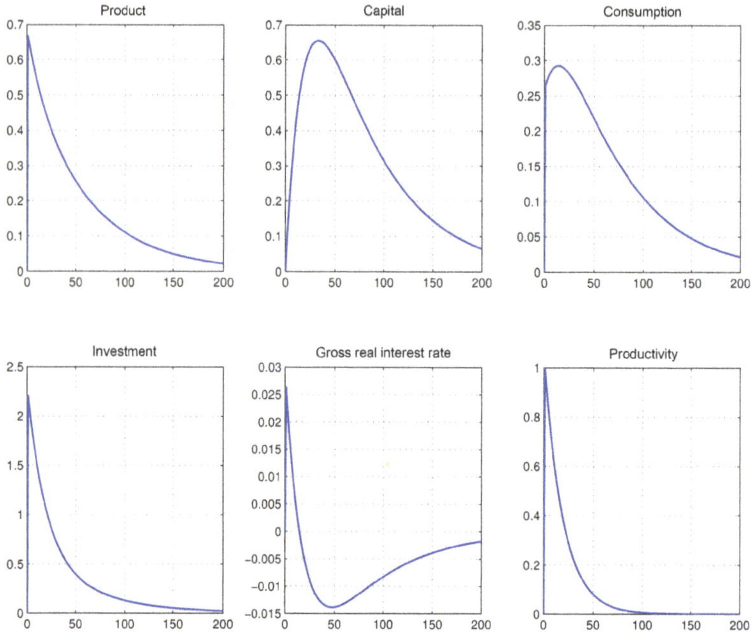

Fig. 4.6 Impulse-response function of log-linear macroeconomic variables **Note:** These impulse-response functions correspond to the log-linear variables, that is to say, to $\widehat{y}_t, \widehat{k}_t, \widehat{c}_t, \widehat{i}_t, \widehat{r}_t$ y $\widehat{a}_t$. It is worth mentioning that these graphics are obtained from the code "Campbell_Lfijo.m" (Sect. 4.4)

relationship, let us review the Euler log-linear equation:

$$\widehat{c}_t = E_t\left[\widehat{c}_{t+1} - \frac{1}{\gamma}\widehat{R}_{t+1}\right]$$

Here it can be seen that if the interest rate of $t + 1$ increases by 1%, then consumption today "t" is reduced by $\frac{1}{\gamma}$ (elasticity of substitution of consumption). All this is the substitution effect produced by the interest rate.

9. $\downarrow \widehat{R}_{t+1}$ (but above the steady state) produces two effects: substitution effect (SE) and income effect (IE).
10. Substitution effect (of the interest rate):

$$\widehat{R}_{t+1} > \widehat{R}_t \rightarrow \downarrow \widehat{c}_t$$

11. Income effect (of the interest rate):

$$\widehat{R}_{t+1} > \widehat{R}_t \rightarrow \uparrow \widehat{c}_{t+1}$$

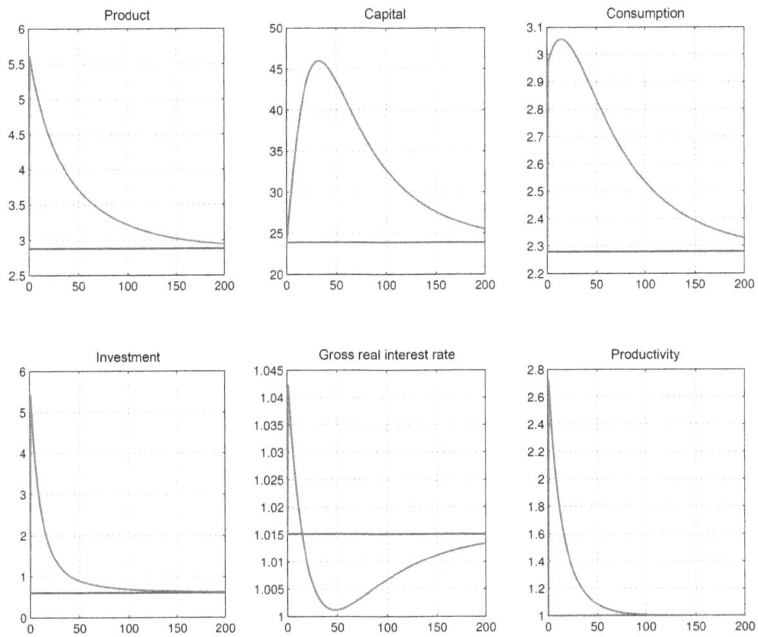

Fig. 4.7 Impulse-response function of macroeconomic variables in levels **Note:** These impulse-response functions correspond to the variables in levels, that is to say, a y_t, k_t, c_t, i_t, R_t, and a_t. It is worth mentioning that this graph is obtained from the code "Campbell_Lfijo.m" (Sect. 4.5)

Some ideas can be concluded from Fig. 4.7. The first is that capital is larger in units than any other variable. For example, the steady-state value of capital is 23.88 units, which is greatly larger than the other variables (the steady-state value of output is 2.87 units). To understand why the *stock* of capital in steady state is large, it is necessary to review the parameters on which it depends:

$$k_{ss} = \left[\frac{\frac{1}{\beta} - (1-\delta)}{1-\alpha}\right]^{-\frac{1}{\alpha}}$$

Applying the sign of the exponent, we have:

$$k_{ss} = \left[\frac{1-\alpha}{\frac{1}{\beta} - (1-\delta)}\right]^{\frac{1}{\alpha}}$$

So, k_{ss} is a function of α, β, and δ. First, the exponent $\frac{1}{\alpha}$ is greater than one because α is less than one ($= 0.667$). The smaller α is, the larger the exponent and the larger the numerator which will increase the k_{ss}. Second, an increase in the depreciation rate reduces k_{ss}, which makes sense since capital is consumed at higher depreciation. For example, if capital is fully depreciated ($\delta = 1$), then $k_{ss} = 0.1880$. Finally, a higher discount rate increases k_{ss}.

The second conclusion is that the investment is very small compared to the capital. This is because in a steady-state investment i_{ss} is equal to a proportion of capital δk_{ss}. Furthermore, δ is equal to 2.5%; that is, the investment in steady state ($= 0.597$) is equal to 2.5% of the capital. A third conclusion is that the values of the impulse-response function of the log-linear variables comply with the following expression:

$$\widehat{y_t} = \frac{c_{ss}}{y_{ss}}\widehat{c_t} + \frac{i_{ss}}{y_{ss}}\widehat{i_t}$$

Then a relationship between the levels of the variables can be obtained (in the impulse-response function of the variables in levels):

$$\begin{aligned}
\widehat{y_t} &= \frac{c_{ss}}{y_{ss}}\widehat{c_t} + \frac{i_{ss}}{y_{ss}}\widehat{i_t} \\
ln\left(\frac{y_t}{y_{ss}}\right) &= \frac{c_{ss}}{y_{ss}}ln\left(\frac{c_t}{c_{ss}}\right) + \frac{i_{ss}}{y_{ss}}ln\left(\frac{i_t}{i_{ss}}\right) \\
ln(y_t) &= (ln(y_t) - \frac{c_{ss}}{y_{ss}}ln(c_{ss}) - \frac{i_{ss}}{y_{ss}}ln(i_{ss})) + \frac{c_{ss}}{y_{ss}}ln(c_t) + \\
&\quad \frac{i_{ss}}{y_{ss}}ln(i_t)
\end{aligned} \tag{4.108}$$

An important conclusion can be drawn from Fig. 4.8 (graph on the right): in the face of a *shock* of productivity, investment reacts strongly, outperforming output and consumption. Moreover, the investment increases a little over 200% of its steady-state value. In addition, the variables take more than 100 periods (quarters) to return to their steady state because the *shock* has a high persistence ($\phi = 0.95$).

4.9 Simulation of the Endogenous Variables

For the simulation of capital, we will use its autoregressive representation AR(2):

$$\widehat{k}_{t+1} = \phi_1\widehat{k}_t + \phi_2\widehat{k}_{t-1} + \eta_{ka}\epsilon_t$$

We will assume that the variable starts at its steady state: $\widehat{k_0} = 0$. Also, it is assumed that the variable in previous periods has been kept in *steady state*, so: $\widehat{k}_{-1} = 0$ (Table 4.10).

For the simulation of the macroeconomic variables such as output, consumption, and investment, we first need the simulated series of productivity $\widehat{a}_t$ and capital

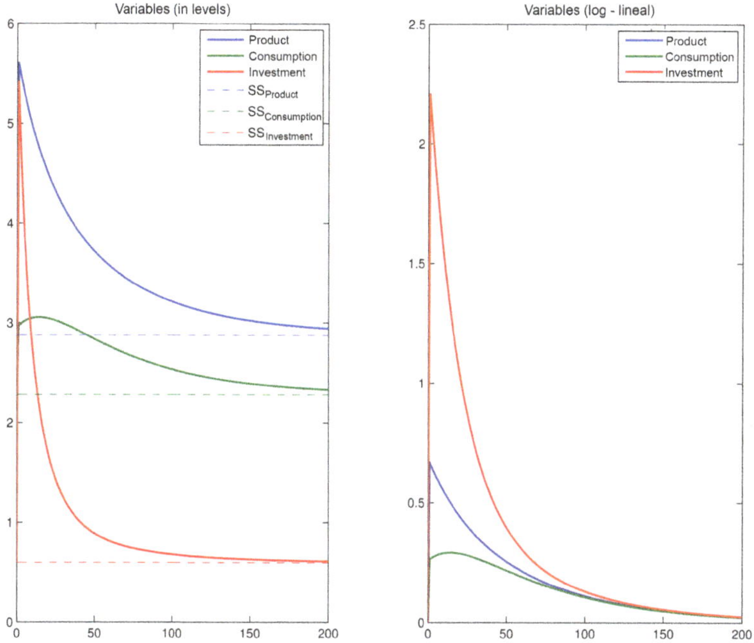

Fig. 4.8 Impulse-response function (comparison of variables log-linear vs. in levels) **Note:** It is worth mentioning that this graph is obtained from the code"Campbell_Lfijo.m" (Sect. 4.5)

Table 4.10 Log-linear capital simulation

t	ϵ_t	AR(2) representation of k_{t+1}
0	$\epsilon_0 = 0$ (steady state)	$\widehat{k}_1 = \phi_1 \widehat{k}_0 + \phi_2 \widehat{k}_{-1} + \eta_{ka} \epsilon_0$
1	$\epsilon_1 =$ random value	$\widehat{k}_2 = \phi_1 \widehat{k}_1 + \phi_2 \widehat{k}_0 + \eta_{ka} \epsilon_1$
2	$\epsilon_2 =$ random value	$\widehat{k}_3 = \phi_1 \widehat{k}_2 + \phi_2 \widehat{k}_1 + \eta_{ka} \epsilon_2$
3	$\epsilon_3 =$ random value	$\widehat{k}_4 = \phi_1 \widehat{k}_3 + \phi_2 \widehat{k}_2 + \eta_{ka} \epsilon_3$
4	$\epsilon_4 =$ random value	$\widehat{k}_5 = \phi_1 \widehat{k}_4 + \phi_2 \widehat{k}_3 + \eta_{ka} \epsilon_4$

$\widehat{k}_t$, which are displayed in Table 4.11. For the latter, the solution of the log-linear equation system is used:

$$
\begin{aligned}
\widehat{a}_t &= \phi \widehat{a}_{t-1} + \epsilon \\
\widehat{k}_{t+1} &= \phi_1 \widehat{k}_t + \phi_2 \widehat{k}_{t-1} + \eta_{ka} \epsilon_t
\end{aligned}
$$

For the simulation of the other macroeconomic variables ($\widehat{y}_t$, $\widehat{c}_t$, $\widehat{i}_t$, and $\widehat{R}_t$), the following solution is used:

$$
\begin{aligned}
\widehat{y}_t &= \alpha \widehat{a}_t + (1 - \alpha \widehat{k}_t) \\
\widehat{c}_t &= \eta_{ck} \widehat{k}_t + \eta_{ca} \widehat{a}_t
\end{aligned}
$$

Table 4.11 Simulation of productivity and capital (log-linear)

t	ϵ_t	$\widehat{a}_t$	$\widehat{k}_{t+1}$
0	$\epsilon_0 = 0$	$\widehat{a}_0 = 0$	$\widehat{k}_1 = 0$
0	$\epsilon_1 =$ random value of N(0,1)	$\widehat{a}_1 = 0.1832$	$\widehat{k}_2 = 0.0101$
0	$\epsilon_2 =$ random value of N(0,1)	$\widehat{a}_2 = -0.8557$	$\widehat{k}_3 = -0.0372$
0	$\epsilon_3 =$ random value of N(0,1)	$\widehat{a}_3 = 0.1363$	$\widehat{k}_4 = -0.0291$
0	$\epsilon_4 =$ random value of N(0,1)	$\widehat{a}_4 = 0.4366$	$\widehat{k}_5 = -0.0046$
.	.	.	.
.	.	.	.

Table 4.12 Simulation of log-linear macroeconomic variables

t	$\widehat{y}_t$	$\widehat{c}_t$	$\widehat{i}_t$	$\widehat{R}_t$
0	$y_0 = \alpha a_0 + (1 - \alpha k_0)$	$c_0 = \eta_{ck} k_0 + \eta_{ca} a_0$	$i_0 = \eta_{ik} k_0 + \eta_{ia} a_0$	$R_0 = \lambda_3(a_0 - k_0)$
1	$y_1 = \alpha a_1 + (1 - \alpha k_1)$	$c_1 = \eta_{ck} k_1 + \eta_{ca} a_1$	$i_1 = \eta_{ik} k_1 + \eta_{ia} a_1$	$R_1 = \lambda_3(a_1 - k_1)$
2	$y_2 = \alpha a_2 + (1 - \alpha k_2)$	$c_2 = \eta_{ck} k_2 + \eta_{ca} a_2$	$i_2 = \eta_{ik} k_2 + \eta_{ia} a_2$	$R_2 = \lambda_3(a_2 - k_2)$
3	$y_3 = \alpha a_3 + (1 - \alpha k_3)$	$c_3 = \eta_{ck} k_3 + \eta_{ca} a_3$	$i_3 = \eta_{ik} k_3 + \eta_{ia} a_3$	$R_3 = \lambda_3(a_3 - k_3)$
4	$y_4 = \alpha a_4 + (1 - \alpha k_4)$	$c_4 = \eta_{ck} k_4 + \eta_{ca} a_4$	$i_4 = \eta_{ik} k_4 + \eta_{ia} a_4$	$R_4 = \lambda_3(a_4 - k_4)$
.	.	.	.	.
.	.	.	.	.

$$\widehat{i}_t = \frac{y_{ss}}{i_{ss}}(1 - \alpha - \frac{c_{ss}}{y_{ss}}\eta_{ck})\widehat{k}_t + \frac{y_{ss}}{i_{ss}}(\alpha - \frac{c_{ss}}{y_{ss}}\eta_{ca})\widehat{a}_t$$

$$\widehat{R}_t = \lambda_3(\widehat{a}_t - \widehat{k}_t)$$

where: $\eta_{ik} = \frac{y_{ss}}{i_{ss}}(1 - \alpha - \frac{c_{ss}}{y_{ss}}\eta_{ck})$ y $\eta_{ia} = \frac{y_{ss}}{i_{ss}}(\alpha - \frac{c_{ss}}{y_{ss}}\eta_{ca})$

The simulation of the variables can take negative values because they are expressed in log deviations from their steady state ($ln(\frac{x_t}{x_{ss}})$). The negative value of the log-linear variable means that the variable in levels is below its steady state (Table 4.12). Also, the log-linear simulated variable is expected to have negative values because its mean is equal to zero. However, the simulated variable in levels has only positive values (Fig. 4.9).

4.10 Cyclic Component of Simulated Variables

To find the cyclical component of the log-linear variables, the Hodrick-Prescott filter (HP filter) is applied. This filter allows the series to be separated into two components: the trend component and the cyclical component. Figure 4.10 shows the cyclical and trend component for each simulated variable.

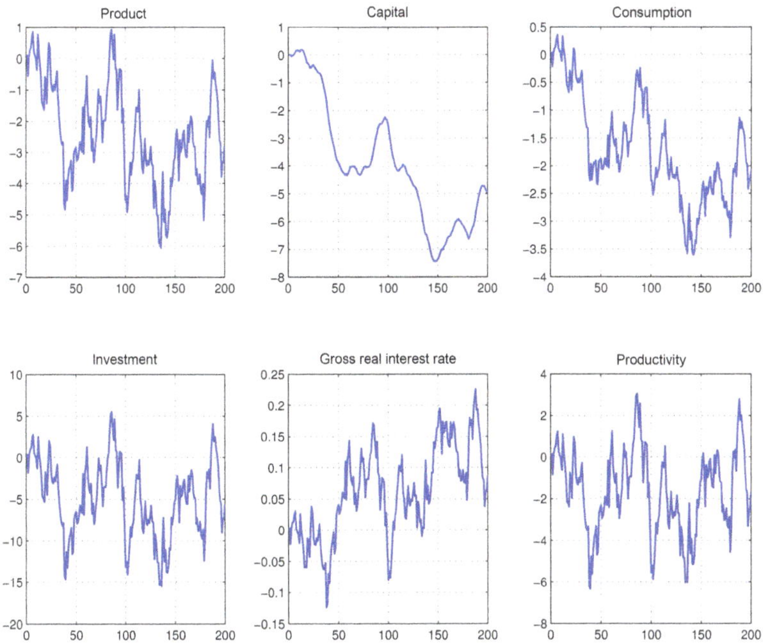

Fig. 4.9 Simulation of log-linear macroeconomic variables **Note:** Capital behaves like AR(2), while output, consumption, investment, and the real interest rate behave like ARMA(2,1). Furthermore, productivity follows an AR(1) process. This graph is obtained from the code "Campbell_Lfijo.m" (Sect. 4.6)

What we are interested in evaluating from the model are the moments of the **cyclical component** of each simulated variable, that is, the variance, the autocorrelation and the correlation with other variables.

4.11 Computation of Theoretical Moments

When simulating the model in Matlab, what is obtained are the theoretical moments for the log-linear variables. What is needed, however, is to return to level variables because the empirical moments correspond to level variables. To calculate the theoretical moments of the variables in levels, the relationship between the log-linear variable and the variable in levels is used:

$$\widehat{x}_t = ln\left(\frac{x_t}{x_{ss}}\right) \tag{4.109}$$

Mean The mean of the log-linear variable is zero. After the algebraic artifices, relation (4.110) is concluded, which indicates that the mean of the logarithm of the variable "x" is equal to the logarithm of the variable in a steady state:

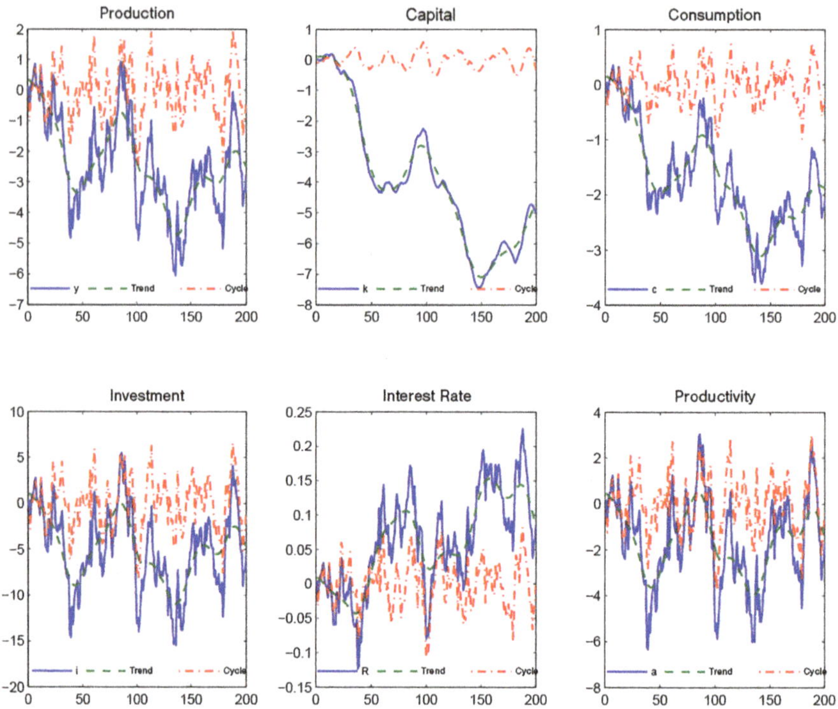

Fig. 4.10 Application of the HP filter to the simulated variables **Note:** Since the calibrated parameters correspond to quarterly data, then each period in this figure is understood as a quarter. This suggests that the HP filter smoothing parameter corresponding to quarterly data ($\lambda = 1600$) should be used. This graph is obtained from the code "Campbell_Lfijo.m" (Sect. 4.7)

$$
\begin{aligned}
\widehat{x}_t &= ln\left(\frac{x_t}{x_{ss}}\right) \\
E\widehat{x}_t &= Eln\left(\frac{x_t}{x_{ss}}\right) \\
\mu_{\widehat{x}_t} &= E(ln(x_t) - ln(x_{ss})) \\
\mu_{\widehat{x}_t} &= E(ln(x_t)) - ln(x_{ss}) \\
\mu_{\widehat{x}_t} &= \mu_{ln(x_t)} - ln(x_{ss}) \\
0 &= \mu_{ln(x_t)} - ln(x_{ss}) \\
\mu_{ln(x_t)} &= ln(x_{ss})
\end{aligned} \tag{4.110}
$$

Variance The variance of the log-linear variable is equal to the variance of the logarithm of the variable in levels (see Eq. 4.111). By default, the standard deviation of both variables is the same:

$$Var(\widehat{x_t}) = Var\left(ln\left(\frac{x_t}{x_{ss}}\right)\right)$$

$$\text{By property}: \; Var(ax+b) = a^2 Var(x)$$

$$Var(\widehat{x_t}) = Var\big(ln(x_t) - ln(x_{ss})\big)$$

$$Var(\widehat{x_t}) = Var\big(ln(x_t)\big)$$

$$\sigma^2_{\widehat{x_t}} = \sigma^2_{ln(x_t)} \tag{4.111}$$

Correlation The correlation between two log-linear variables is equal to the correlation between the logarithm of the said variables in levels:

$$corr(\widehat{x}, \widehat{y}) = \frac{\sum_{i=1}^{N} (\widehat{x_i} - \mu_{\widehat{x_i}})(\widehat{y_i} - \mu_{\widehat{y_i}})}{\sigma_{\widehat{x}} \sigma_{\widehat{y}}}$$

$$\text{Pero}: \; \mu_{\widehat{x_i}} = 0 \text{ y } \mu_{\widehat{x_i}} = 0$$

$$corr(\widehat{x}, \widehat{y}) = \frac{\sum_{i=1}^{N} (\widehat{x_i})(\widehat{y_i})}{\sigma_{\widehat{x}} \sigma_{\widehat{y}}}$$

$$= \frac{\sum_{i=1}^{N} (ln \frac{x_i}{x_{ss}})(ln \frac{y_i}{y_{ss}})}{\sigma_{\widehat{x}} \sigma_{\widehat{y}}}$$

$$= \frac{\sum_{i=1}^{N} (ln(x_i) - lnx_{ss})(ln(y_i) - lny_{ss})}{\sigma_{\widehat{x}} \sigma_{\widehat{y}}}$$

$$= \frac{\sum_{i=1}^{N} (ln(x_i) - \mu_{ln(x_t)})(ln(y_i) - \mu_{ln(y_t)})}{\sigma_{ln(x_t)} \sigma_{ln(y_t)}}$$

$$corr(\widehat{x}, \widehat{y}) = corr(ln(x_t), ln(y_t)) \tag{4.112}$$

From the above, it is concluded that the second moments of the log-linear variables are exactly equal to the second moments of the natural logarithm of the variables in levels. Therefore, we can conclude that the second moments of the cyclical component of the (simulated) log-linear variables are identical to those of the cyclical component of the logarithm of the variables in levels. Then, it is enough to compare the moments (of the cyclical component) obtained by the model (simulation) with the corresponding ones obtained from the data (variables in logarithms).

To make the comparison, the following is done: first, the study period of the macroeconomic variables is set (for example, 1980.Q1 to 2016.Q3). This period is made up of 147 quarters. Second, 500 simulations are performed considering that each variable has a period of 147 quarters. Third, for each simulation, the HP filter is applied and the cyclic component is abstracted. Then, the mean, variance, first-order autocorrelation, and cyclical component correlation are calculated for each simulation. Fifth, a distribution is constructed for the mean, variance, first-order

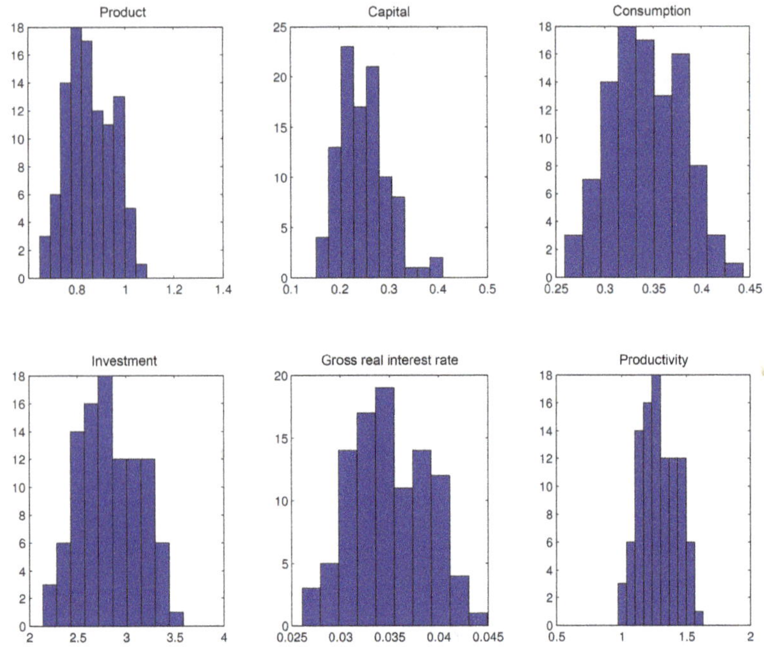

Fig. 4.11 Distributions of the standard deviation of the theoretical model **Note:** These distributions are obtained by simulating the variables 100 times considering a period of 150 quarters. The value taken from each distribution is the average value. This graph is obtained from the code "Campbell_Lfijo_Sim_Variables.m" (Sect. 4.7)

autocorrelation, and correlation. The mean value of each distribution is chosen, and that value represents the value of each second theoretical moment. Finally, these values are compared with the data (Fig. 4.11).

4.12 Comparison of the Theoretical Model with the Empirical Data

Some conclusions can be drawn from Table 4.13. The first is that the data suggest that the volatility of investment is greater than output and consumption, so much so that the standard deviation of investment is 4.8 times the volatility of output and 6.4 times that of consumption. However, the theoretical model does not capture all of these relationships found in the data. In the first place, although it maintains that the volatility of investment is greater than that of consumption, it overestimates the magnitude (the volatility of investment is 8.2 times that of consumption). Second, the volatility for the three variables (product, consumption, and investment) is well below what is observed in the data. On the other hand, a benefit of the model is that

Table 4.13 Comparison of the cyclical behavior of the theoretical model with the empirical data

	US empirical data		Theoretical model	
Variable	DesEst (%)	Corr. with product (t)	DesEst (%)	Corr. with product (t)
Product	1.72	1	0.85 (0.093)	1
Consumption	1.27	0.83	0.34 (0.0382)	0.9874
Investment	8.24	0.91	2.82 (0.3065)	0.9972

Note: The empirical values have been taken from Cooley and Prescott (1995), which have been calculated under the sample period from 1954.I to 1991.III. On the other hand, the theoretical values have been obtained from a simulation of 100 times considering a period of 150 quarters. The values shown in the theoretical model are the average values of each distribution. These values are obtained from the code "Campbell_Lfijo_Sim_Variables.m" (Sect. 4.8)

it captures the correct direction in terms of volatility (γ): $\gamma_{\text{investment}} > \gamma_{\text{product}} > \gamma_{textconsumption}$.

A second conclusion is that the temporal correlation of output with consumption and investment is overvalued by the model. However, this is much closer to the product-investment correlation than the one corresponding to consumption.

4.13 Summary

In this chapter, we have raised the simplifying assumptions about preferences and technology to study an RBC model with constant work. In this context, our objective has been to verify that a model of this nature can replicate the most important stylized facts of the goods market, that is, the properties of consumption C_t, investment I_t, and GDP Y_t.

We begin, as usual, by characterizing the behavior of households, firms, and the competitive equilibrium in the goods market. We proceed to calibrate the model, having to make a decision regarding the value that the elasticity of intertemporal substitution of consumption takes.

We find the steady state of the model and proceed to log-linearize it. We concentrate an important part of this section discussing a fundamental dynamic mechanism in RBC models: the income effect and the substitution effect of the interest rate on aggregate consumption. These effects are reflected (in our model) in a single parameter, θ, the intertemporal elasticity of consumption, which is a very important mechanism to induce persistence in consumption when the economy experiences a *shock*.

With the log-linearized system, we proceed to solve it with the method of the undetermined coefficients of Uhlig. Additionally, we note that log-linearizing the system allows us to interpret the coefficients of each equation as the elasticity of the control variables with respect to the state variables.

Once the model is solved, we proceed to analyze the time series representations of the control and state variables of the model, together with the impulse response functions of each variable of the model when it experiences a *shock* of productivity. The immediate effect on output, investment, and productivity is an increase in each variable, which then decreases monotonically to the steady state; this is because the *shock* is stationary. On the other hand, capital and consumption have an FIR in the form of a "hump," reaching its maximum value after 10–20 periods and then declining monotonically.

The following sections proceed to simulate the endogenous variables of the model, extract their cyclical component, and calculate the theoretical moments of the cyclical component of the simulated series to compare it with its empirical counterpart. By performing this exercise, we can extract two stylized facts: first, the model manages to qualitatively replicate the magnitude of the volatilities, with investment being more volatile than output and consumption less volatile than both. Second, the model predicts that all variables move procyclically with output, which we also observe in the data. However, the model overestimates the degree of procyclicality of investment and output, while underestimating the volatilities of all the variables.

We conclude that although the model *qualitatively* reflects some relevant features of the goods market, *quantitatively* there is still much room for improvement. In the next chapter, we introduce hours worked as a household decision variable and a firm input, with which we are equipped to analyze equilibrium in the labor market.

4.14 Codes

The solution of the model as well as the impulse-response functions and the simulation of the variables have been developed directly in Matlab (by building several *m-file*) and also through Dynare (by building a *mod-file*). The result of both paths is the same, but the advantage of directly building an m-file is that many details can be made explicit in the solution and simulation of the model, which is already programmed in Dynare (Table 4.14).

Table 4.14 Codes in Matlab and Dynare

Codes	Description
Matlab	
Campbell_Lfijo.m	This *m-file* computes the steady state and solution coefficients derived from the method of undetermined coefficients. In addition, it calculates the impulse-response function and performs a simulation of the variables. Finally, apply the HP filter to obtain the trend and cycle of each simulated variable
Campbell_Lfijo_Sim_Parametros.m	This *m-file* simulates the values of the elasticities (coefficients of the solution) as a function of persistence (ϕ) and the EIS of consumption (σ)
Campbell_Lfixed_Sim_Variables.m	This *m-file* simulates 100 times the variables (form ARMA(p,q)) for 150 periods. It is worth mentioning that both parameters can be changed by the user to perform different simulations
Dynare	
Campbell_Lfijo_Dynare_nolinear_log.mod	This mod file contains the nonlinear model with variables in logarithms and is the one used by Dynare to solve the model
Campbell_Lfijo_Dynare_linear_log.mod	This mod file contains the linear model with logarithmic variables and is what Dynare uses to solve the model. It is worth mentioning that both mod files provide the same result in terms of policy and state functions

Chapter 5
RBC Model with Variable Labor Supply

5.1 Introduction

This chapter has two objectives: the first is to extend the model described in Chap. 4 by considering variable labor supply. This extension allows us to understand the labor market's role in economic cycles. The second objective is to compare the performance of the model of Long and Plosser (1983), developed in Chap. 3, with the two models of Campbell (1994): the model with fixed labor supply, developed in Chap. 4, and the model with variable labor supply, developed in this chapter. An advantage of the model in this chapter is that under the assumption of labor substitution elasticity equal to one and full depreciation, the model of Long and Plosser (1983) can be obtained; that is, this last model is a particular case of the more general model described in this chapter.

With these goals in mind, this chapter is split into two sections. In the first, the elements of the model are described; that is, the behavior of households and firms, the market equilibrium, the shock of productivity, and the system of equations that summarizes the model are also specified. Additionally, we show the values that are assigned to the parameters (calibration), the calculation of the steady state, and the log-linearization of the system of equations of the model. Finally, this log-linear system is solved using the method of undetermined coefficients, as explained in Chap. 4.

In the second section, we analyze the model solution. This analysis includes the sensitivity of the coefficients of the solution to different values of the deep parameters of the model. This sensitive-parameter task aims to evaluate how the model solution responds when the parameters change. One conclusion of this task is that the solution coefficients associated with the *stock* of capital are insensitive to the persistence parameter of productivity shock ϕ. Moreover, the impulse-response function is calculated before a shock in productivity. Finally, two analyses are carried out: the first evaluates the need for the shock of productivity to be significant so that the RBC model can replicate the business cycle data, and the second

H. Galindo Gil et al., *Dynamic Stochastic General Equilibrium Models*, Springer Texts in Business and Economics, https://doi.org/10.1007/978-3-031-58105-2_5

evaluates the importance of the elasticity of labor supply to improve the ability of the model to replicate the data.

5.2 Model Elements

5.2.1 Model Construction

5.2.1.1 Households

In this model, it is assumed that identical households with infinite life populate the economy. These households obtain welfare from consuming goods (c_t) and leisure hours (l_t). These preferences are reflected in the following utility function:

$$u(c_t, h_t) = ln(c_t) + \theta \frac{(1 - h_t)^{1-\gamma_n}}{1 - \gamma_n},$$

where θ represents the consumer's valuation of leisure in his/her utility function and γ_n represents the inverse of the labor substitution elasticity, which also represents, as will be seen later, the inverse of the elasticity of labor supply (Frisch elasticity). In addition, the total number of hours available to the household is normalized to one such that the time allocation is consistent with the following constraint:

$$l_t + h_t = 1,$$

where h_t are hours dedicated to work and l_t are hours dedicated to leisure. Since households have rational expectations and are optimizers, they maximize their discounted expected utility function represented by

$$\underset{\{c_t, h_t, k_{t+1}\}_{t=0}^{\infty}}{\text{Max}} \quad E_0 \sum_{t=0}^{\infty} \beta^t \left[ln(c_t) + \theta \frac{(1 - h_t)^{1-\gamma_n}}{1 - \gamma_n} \right]. \tag{5.1}$$

Households must choose the optimal time paths of c_t, h_t, and k_{t+1}. Additionally, the budget constraint of a household is defined by the following expression:

$$c_t + i_t = w_t h_t + r_t k_t, \tag{5.2}$$

where

- i_t is the investment used by the household to accumulate a stock of capital goods that, in turn, will be rented to firms.
- w_t represents the real wages.
- r_t is the capital rental rate paid by firms.

Furthermore, households are supposed to own capital goods in the economy, so they must invest (i_t) to offer capital at "t+1." The equation for movement of capital is

$$k_{t+1} = (1-\delta)k_t + i_t \tag{5.3}$$

Household Optimization Problem
The household optimization problem is summarized in Eq. (5.1) subject to the budget constraint, Eq. (5.2), and the law of motion of capital, Eq. (5.3) :

$$\underset{\{c_t, h_t, k_{t+1}\}_{t=0}^{\infty}}{\text{Max}} \quad E_0 \sum_{t=0}^{\infty} \beta^t \left[ln(c_t) + \theta \frac{(1-h_t)^{1-\gamma_n}}{1-\gamma_n} \right]$$

$$c_t + i_t = w_t h_t + r_t k_t$$

$$k_{t+1} = (1-\delta)k_t + i_t$$

Lagrange Function and First-Order Conditions
Considering the two constraints, it can be concluded that both could become a single constraint. To do this, investment i_t is cleared from the capital equation of motion and introduced into the budget constraint. Thus, the following unique constraint is obtained:

$$c_t + k_{t+1} = w_t h_t + (r_t + (1-\delta))k_t \tag{5.4}$$

Given this unique constraint and objective function, the Lagrange function is defined as follows:

$$\mathcal{L} = E_0 \left\{ \sum_{t=0}^{\infty} \beta^t \left[u(c_t, h_t) + \lambda_t (w_t h_t + r_t k_t - c_t - k_{t+1} + (1-\delta)k_t) \right] \right\}$$

The first-order conditions are the following:

$$\frac{\partial \mathcal{L}}{\partial c_t} = 0 \Longrightarrow \frac{1}{c_t} + \lambda_t(-1) = 0 \tag{5.5}$$

$$\frac{\partial \mathcal{L}}{\partial h_t} = 0 \Longrightarrow \frac{-\theta}{(1-h_t)^{\gamma_n}} + \lambda_t(w_t) = 0 \tag{5.6}$$

$$\frac{\partial \mathcal{L}}{\partial k_{t+1}} = 0 \Longrightarrow E_t \left[\lambda_t(-1) + \beta \lambda_{t+1}(r_{t+1} + (1-\delta)) \right] = 0 \tag{5.7}$$

Intratemporal Condition This is represented by the labor supply, which is obtained from Eqs. (5.5) and (5.6):

$$\theta(1-h_t)^{-\gamma_n} = \frac{w_t}{c_t} \tag{5.8}$$

Intertemporal Condition This is represented by Euler's equation, which indicates the optimal consumption path. This is obtained from (5.5) and (5.7) as follows:

$$\frac{1}{c_t} = \beta E_t \left[\frac{1}{c_{t+1}} [r_{t+1} + (1 - \delta)] \right] \tag{5.9}$$

Equations (5.8) and (5.9) represent the two main behavior equations of the households. One of these equations is labor supply, which is influenced by the parameter γ_n. The inverse of this parameter is known in the literature as the Frisch elasticity of labor supply, as detailed below.

Frisch Elasticity of Labor Supply (FELS) This is the percentage change in labor supply given a percentage change in the real wage holding the marginal utility of consumption constant. In addition, the FELS measures the *substitution effect* that a change in the real wage generates in the labor supply. In other words, it does not consider the *income effect* derived from intratemporal substitution between consumption and leisure. The calculation of the FELS involves three steps, which are described below:

Step 1. The total differentiation of labor supply (5.8) is calculated using Eq. (5.10):

$$\begin{aligned}
\theta(1-h_t)^{-\gamma_n} &= \frac{w_t}{c_t} \\
\text{Applying} &: \text{Full differentiation} \\
\theta(-\gamma_n)(1-h_t)^{-\gamma_n-1}(-\Delta h_t) &= \frac{c_t \Delta w_t - w_t \Delta c_t}{c_t^2} \\
\text{Ordering the terms} &: \\
\theta(1-h_t)^{-\gamma_n} \frac{\gamma_n}{(1-h_t)} \Delta h_t &= \frac{\Delta w_t}{c_t} - \frac{w_t}{c_t} \frac{\Delta c_t}{c_t} \\
\text{For the labor supply} &: \theta(1-h_t)^{-\gamma_n} = \frac{w_t}{c_t} \\
\frac{w_t}{c_t} \frac{\gamma_n}{(1-h_t)} \Delta h_t &= \frac{\Delta w_t}{c_t} - \frac{w_t}{c_t} \frac{\Delta c_t}{c_t} \\
\gamma_n \frac{\Delta h_t}{(1-h_t)} &= \frac{\frac{\Delta w_t}{c_t} - \frac{w_t}{c_t} \frac{\Delta c_t}{c_t}}{\frac{w_t}{c_t}} \\
\gamma_n \frac{\Delta h_t}{(1-h_t)} &= \frac{\Delta w_t}{w_t} - \frac{\Delta c_t}{c_t} \\
\gamma_n \frac{h_t}{h_t} \frac{\Delta h_t}{(1-h_t)} &= \frac{\Delta w_t}{w_t} \left[1 - \frac{\Delta c_t / c_t}{\Delta w_t / w_t} \right] \\
\gamma_n \frac{h_t}{1-h_t} \frac{\Delta h_t}{h_t} &= \frac{\Delta w_t}{w_t} \left[1 - \frac{\Delta c_t / c_t}{\Delta w_t / w_t} \right]
\end{aligned}$$

$$\frac{\Delta h_t/h_t}{\Delta w_t/w_t} = \frac{1}{\gamma_n}\left[\frac{1-h_t}{h_t}\right]\left[1 - \frac{\Delta c_t/c_t}{\Delta w_t/w_t}\right]$$

$$e_t^{hw} = \frac{1}{\gamma_n}\left[\frac{1-h_t}{h_t}\right][1 - e_t^{cw}], \quad (5.10)$$

where e_t^{hw} represents the elasticity of the labor supply with respect to the real wage ($\frac{\Delta h_t/h_t}{\Delta w_t/w_t}$); on the other hand, e_t^{cw} is the elasticity of consumption with respect to the real wage ($\frac{\Delta c_t/c_t}{\Delta w_t/w_t}$).

Step 2. According to the definition of the "Frisch elasticity," the marginal utility of consumption remains constant, which indicates a level of fixed consumption that is invariant to changes in the real wage and, therefore e_t^{cw} would equal zero.

Step 3. Finally, the FELS is represented by the following expression:

$$e_t^{hw} = \frac{1}{\gamma_n}\left[\frac{1-h_t}{h_t}\right] \quad (5.11)$$

As we can observe, FELS (e_t^{hw}) depends inversely on the γ_n. Therefore, γ_n is considered the inverse of Frisch elasticity (FELS).

In the RBC model, a higher Frisch elasticity (low γ_n) further amplifies the productivity shock: a larger labor supply elasticity increases labor and hence production in t.

Intertemporal elasticity of labor substitution The marginal rate of substitution ($TMgS_{1,2}$) indicates the amount of good 1 that one is willing to give up if good 2 is increased by one unit, keeping the utility level constant:

$$TMgS_{1,2} = \frac{\partial x_1}{\partial x_2} = -\frac{UMg_2}{UMg_1}$$

Additionally, the elasticity of substitution ($ES_{1,2}$) measures the ease of substituting one good with another. It also measures the curvature of the indifference curve and, therefore, the substitutability between goods:

$$ES_{1,2} = \frac{\partial ln(x_1/x_2)}{\partial ln(TMgS_{1,2})}$$

It is also worth mentioning that **elasticity of substitution** is observed in two dimensions: intratemporal (between consumption and leisure) and intertemporal (between current and future consumption) (see Table 5.1).

By applying the intertemporal case for labor supply, the intertemporal substitution elasticity of labor (h_t, h_{t+1}) is obtained:

- $TMgSI_{t+1,t}^{h} = -E_t\left[\frac{1}{\beta}\left(\frac{1-h_t}{1-h_{t+1}}\right)^{-\gamma_n}\right]$

Table 5.1 Elasticity of substitution

Intratemporal (c_t, l_t)	Intertemporal (c_t, c_{t+1})
$TMgSI_{c_t,l_t} = -\frac{UMg_l}{UMg_c}$	$TMgSI^c_{t+1,t} = -E_t\left[\frac{UMg_{c_t}}{\beta UMg_{c_{t+1}}}\right]$
$ESI_{c_t,l_t} = \frac{\partial ln(c_1/l_t)}{\partial ln(TMgSI_{c_t,l_t})}$	$ESI^c_{t+1,t} = \frac{\partial ln(c_{t+1}/c_t)}{\partial ln(TMgSI^c_{t+1,t})}$

- $ESI^h_{t+1,t} = -\frac{1}{\gamma_n}E_t\left[\frac{1-h_{t+1}}{h_{t+1}}\right]$

According to the expression of $ESI^h_{t+1,t}$, parameter γ_n can be considered as the inverse of the intertemporal elasticity of labor substitution. In this scenario, **Frisch elasticity** and the $ESI^h_{t+1,t}$ are similar.

5.2.1.2 Firms

In this model, it is assumed that firms operate in a context of perfect competition, both in the market for goods and for factors of production. In this scenario, the representative firm maximizes its profit function, subject to its technology (production function). The firm's optimization problem is described as follows:

$$\underset{\{k_t,h_t\}_{t=0}^{\infty}}{\text{Max}} \quad \Pi_t = y_t - [w_t h_t + r_t k_t]$$

Subject to the production function or available technology

$$y_t = a_t k_t^{\alpha} h_t^{1-\alpha} \tag{5.12}$$

The production function can be introduced into the profit function π_t, which allows the optimization problem to be reduced to an unconstrained one:

$$\underset{\{k_t,h_t\}_{t=0}^{\infty}}{\text{Max}} \quad \Pi_t = a_t k_t^{\alpha} h_t^{1-\alpha} - [w_t h_t + r_t k_t] \tag{5.13}$$

Directly deriving the objective function, Eq. (5.13), with respect to capital k_t and labor h_t, we obtain

$$\frac{\partial \Pi_t}{\partial k_t} = 0 \Longrightarrow a_t \alpha k_t^{\alpha-1} h_t^{1-\alpha} - r_t = 0$$

$$\alpha \frac{a_t k_t^{\alpha} h_t^{1-\alpha}}{k_t} = r_t$$

Capital demand :

$$\alpha \frac{y_t}{k_t} = r_t \tag{5.14}$$

$$\frac{\partial \Pi_t}{\partial h_t} = 0 \Longrightarrow a_t(1-\alpha)k_t^{\alpha}h_t^{-\alpha} - w_t = 0$$

$$(1-\alpha)\frac{a_t k_t^{\alpha} h_t^{1-\alpha}}{h_t} = w_t$$

$$\text{Labor demand :}$$

$$(1-\alpha)\frac{y_t}{h_t} = w_t \tag{5.15}$$

5.2.1.3 Market Equilibrium and Definition of Shock

To complete the model, it is necessary to add two equations. The first is the equilibrium in the goods market, described by the following expression:

$$y_t = c_t + i_t \tag{5.16}$$

The second equation describes the behavior of "productivity," which behaves like an AR(1):

$$ln(a_t) = \phi ln(a_{t-1}) + \epsilon_t, \quad \epsilon_t \sim N(0, \sigma_\epsilon^2) \tag{5.17}$$

Where ϵ is called "*productivity shock*."

5.2.1.4 System of Principal Equations

Table 5.2 shows the equations that describe the optimal behavior of both households and firms. This table also shows the equations of market equilibrium and productivity behavior. This set of equations forms a system that represents the RBC model with variable labor supply, which is in line with Campbell (1994).

5.2.2 *Calibration*

The values of the parameters correspond to the calibration of Campbell (1994), except for the value of θ, which was obtained from Prescott (1986). Table 5.3 shows the values associated with the parameters.

Table 5.2 System of principal nonlinear equations

Equations	Description
$\frac{1}{c_t} = \beta E_t\left[\frac{1}{c_{t+1}}[r_{t+1} + (1-\delta)]\right]$	Euler's equation
$r_t = \alpha\frac{y_t}{k_t}$	Capital demand
$\theta(1-h_t)^{-\gamma_n} = \frac{w_t}{c_t}$	Labor supply
$h_t = (1-\alpha)\frac{y_t}{w_t}$	Labor demand
$y_t = a_t k_t^{\alpha} h_t^{1-\alpha}$	Production function
$y_t = c_t + i_t$	Goods market equilibrium
$k_{t+1} = (1-\delta)k_t + i_t$	Law of motion of capital
$lna_t = \phi lna_{t-1} + \epsilon_t$	Productivity shock

Table 5.3 Calibration

Parameter	Observation
$\alpha = 0.333$	Share of capital in national income
$\gamma_n = 0.25$	Inverse Frisch elasticity (value to simulate)
$\delta = 0.025$	Corresponds to a 10% annual depreciation
$\theta = \frac{\epsilon}{1-\epsilon} = 2$	ϵ Is productive time oriented to nonmarket activities
$\rho = 0.95$	Productivity is stationary
$\beta = 0.984$	Discount factor
$\sigma = 0.01$	Standard deviation of the shock of productivity

5.2.3 Stationary State

The stationary state is known as long-run equilibrium (where $\Delta x_t = 0$ for all variables in the model), and the productivity shock (ε_t) takes its average value (= 0). Furthermore, given the equation of motion of productivity, the steady-state value of productivity is one ($a = 1$). Likewise, expectations disappear; therefore, it is known as a non-stochastic solution. It is worth mentioning that finding the steady state is the previous step before the log-linearization procedure. In Table 5.4, the main equations of the model are presented in their steady-state version.

From *Eq. 8* of Table 5.3, the unique value that solves the expression $lna_{ss} = \phi lna_{ss}$ is $a_{ss} = 1$. Similarly, from *Eq. 2*, we obtain the interest rate in the steady state:

$$r_{ss} = \frac{1}{\beta} - (1-\delta) \tag{5.18}$$

From *Eq. 7*, the investment/capital ratio in steady state is obtained:

$$\frac{i_{ss}}{k_{ss}} = \delta \tag{5.19}$$

Table 5.4 System of principal nonlinear equations in steady state

Equations	Description
[1] $r_{ss} = \alpha \frac{y_{ss}}{k_{ss}}$	Capital demand
[2] $\frac{1}{c_{ss}} = \beta \left[\frac{1}{c_{ss}} [r_{ss} + (1-\delta)] \right]$	Euler's equation
[3] $\theta (1 - h_{ss})^{-\gamma_n} = \frac{w_{ss}}{c_{ss}}$	Labor supply
[4] $h_{ss} = (1-\alpha) \frac{y_{ss}}{w_{ss}}$	Labor demand
[5] $y_{ss} = a_{ss} k_{ss}^{\alpha} h_{ss}^{1-\alpha}$	Production function
[6] $y_{ss} = c_{ss} + i_{ss}$	Goods market equilibrium
[7] $k_{ss} = (1-\delta) k_{ss} + i_{ss}$	Law of motion of capital
[8] $lna_{ss} = \phi lna_{ss} + \epsilon_{\text{mean value}}$	*Shock* of productivity

From *Eq. 1*, which describes the demand for capital, the steady-state output/capital ratio is obtained as follows:

$$\frac{y_{ss}}{k_{ss}} = \frac{r_{ss}}{\alpha} \tag{5.20}$$

From *Eq. 5*, after considering that $a_{ss} = 1$, we obtain

$$\frac{y_{ss}}{k_{ss}} = \left[\frac{h_{ss}}{k_{ss}} \right]^{1-\alpha} \tag{5.21}$$

Because in Eq. (5.20), the value of the ratio y_{ss}/k_{ss} was found, then

$$\frac{h_{ss}}{k_{ss}} = \left[\frac{r_{ss}}{\alpha} \right]^{\frac{1}{1-\alpha}} \tag{5.22}$$

The elements of *Eq. 6* can be divided by the steady-state value of capital (k_{ss}) as follows:

$$\frac{y_{ss}}{k_{ss}} = \frac{c_{ss}}{k_{ss}} + \frac{i_{ss}}{k_{ss}} \tag{5.23}$$

From Eq. (5.19), it is known that the ratio i_{ss}/k_{ss} is equal to δ. Furthermore, using Eq. 5.21, the ratio y_{ss}/k_{ss} is equal to $\frac{r_{ss}}{\alpha}$. Under these values, Eq. (5.23) can be described as follows:

$$\frac{r_{ss}}{\alpha} = \frac{c_{ss}}{k_{ss}} + \delta \tag{5.24}$$

This result allows us to find the ratio c_{ss}/k_{ss}:

$$\frac{c_{ss}}{k_{ss}} = \frac{r_{ss}}{\alpha} - \delta \tag{5.25}$$

On the other hand, by dividing the two sides of the labor demand equation [Eq. 4] by the value of capital in a steady state, we have

$$\frac{h_{ss}}{k_{ss}} = (1-\alpha)\frac{y_{ss}}{w_{ss}k_{ss}} \tag{5.26}$$

The real wage in steady state w_{ss} is cleared from this equation:

$$w_{ss} = (1-\alpha)\frac{\frac{y_{ss}}{k_{ss}}}{\frac{h_{ss}}{k_{ss}}} \tag{5.27}$$

Furthermore, from Eq. (5.22), it is known that the ratio h_{ss}/k_{ss} is a constant and is equal to $\left[\frac{R_{ss}}{\alpha}\right]^{\frac{1}{1-\alpha}}$. Likewise, from Eq. 5.20, we have that the ratio y_{ss}/k_{ss} is equal to $\frac{r_{ss}}{\alpha}$. These two values allow us to obtain the value of the real wage in steady-state w_{ss}:

$$w_{ss} = (1-\alpha)\frac{\frac{r_{ss}}{\alpha}}{\left[\frac{r_{ss}}{\alpha}\right]^{\frac{1}{1-\alpha}}} \tag{5.28}$$

$$w_{ss} = (1-\alpha)\left[\frac{r_{ss}}{\alpha}\right]^{\frac{-\alpha}{1-\alpha}}$$

Finally, in the labor supply [Eq. 3], work in steady state (h_{ss}) and consumption (c_{ss}) are multiplied and divided by k_{ss}:

$$\theta(1-k_{ss}\frac{h_{ss}}{k_{ss}})^{-\gamma_n} = \frac{w_{ss}}{k_{ss}\frac{c_{ss}}{k_{ss}}} \tag{5.29}$$

From this expression, the values of w_{ss}, $\frac{c_{ss}}{k_{ss}}$, and $\frac{h_{ss}}{k_{ss}}$ are determined. For simplicity, it is considered that the ratio $\frac{c_{ss}}{k_{ss}}$ is equal to η_1 and that $\frac{w_{ss}}{\frac{c_{ss}}{k_{ss}}}$ equals η_2. Consequently, we have

$$\theta(1-\eta_1 k_{ss})^{-\gamma_n} = \frac{\eta_2}{k_{ss}} \tag{5.30}$$

This equation is nonlinear in steady-state capital (k_{ss}). If the value of capital that solves this equation is found, then all the values of the variables in the steady state will be found because these variables depend on capital. It is worth mentioning that the nonlinearity of this equation is due to the parameter γ_n (inverse of Frisch elasticity). If the value of this parameter is equal to one, then the nonlinearity disappears, and the value of k_{ss} is equal to $\frac{\eta_2}{\theta+\eta_1\eta_2}$. It is worth mentioning that the fact that γ_n is equal to one means that the work in the utility function is expressed as the $ln(1-h_t)$.

Alternatively, Eq. (5.29) can be expressed nonlinearly at work. This option is better because the steady-state value of work is known to be between zero and one, that is, $h_{ss} \in [0, 1]$. This is important because numerical optimization techniques (approximations) require an initial point. Therefore, Eq. 5.29 is expressed as follows:

$$\theta(1-h_{ss})^{-\gamma_n} = \frac{w_{ss}}{h_{ss}\frac{k_{ss}}{h_{ss}}\frac{c_{ss}}{k_{ss}}} \tag{5.31}$$

Simplifying this expression, we have

$$\theta(1-h_{ss})^{-\gamma_n} = \frac{w_{ss}}{h_{ss}\frac{k_{ss}}{h_{ss}}\frac{c_{ss}}{k_{ss}}}$$

$$\theta\frac{c_{ss}}{k_{ss}}\frac{k_{ss}}{h_{ss}}h_{ss} = w_{ss}(1-h_{ss})^{\gamma_n}$$

Rearranging the terms :

$$\underbrace{\theta\frac{c_{ss}}{k_{ss}}}_{=\gamma_1} h_{ss} = \underbrace{w_{ss}\frac{h_{ss}}{k_{ss}}}_{\gamma_2}(1-h_{ss})^{\gamma_n}$$

$$\gamma_1 h_{ss} = \gamma_2(1-h_{ss})^{\gamma_n} \tag{5.32}$$

Equation (5.32) can be solved using numerical methods. To do this, a function called "trabajo_ss.m" has been built, which solves Eq. (5.32) and, therefore, provides a value of h_{ss}. Given this value, the steady-state values of other variables can be obtained. For instance, from Eq. (5.22), we obtain steady-state capital k_{ss}:

$$\frac{h_{ss}}{k_{ss}} = \left[\frac{r_{ss}}{\alpha}\right]^{\frac{1}{1-\alpha}}$$

$$k_{ss} = h_{ss}\left[\frac{r_{ss}}{\alpha}\right]^{\frac{-1}{1-\alpha}} \tag{5.33}$$

With the value of k_{ss}, the production y_{ss} is obtained from Eq. (5.20):

$$\frac{y_{ss}}{k_{ss}} = \frac{r_{ss}}{\alpha}$$

$$y_{ss} = k_{ss}\frac{r_{ss}}{\alpha} \tag{5.34}$$

Similarly, when considering the value of k_{ss} in Eq. (5.19), the value of the investment in steady state i_{ss} is obtained:

Table 5.5 Steady State

Steady state (recursive form)
$r_{ss} = \frac{1}{\beta} - (1 - \delta)$
$a_{ss} = 1$
$w_{ss} = (1 - \alpha)\left[\frac{r_{ss}}{\alpha}\right]^{\frac{-\alpha}{1-\alpha}}$
$\gamma_1 h_{ss} = \gamma_2 (1 - h_{ss})^{\gamma_n}$
$k_{ss} = h_{ss}\left[\frac{r_{ss}}{\alpha}\right]^{\frac{-1}{1-\alpha}}$
$y_{ss} = k_{ss}\frac{r_{ss}}{\alpha}$
$i_{ss} = \delta k_{ss}$
$c_{ss} = y_{ss} - i_{ss}$

$$\frac{i_{ss}}{k_{ss}} = \delta$$

$$i_{ss} = \delta k_{ss} \tag{5.35}$$

The steady-state consumption c_{ss} can be obtained from Eq. (5.23) because the product and investment (both in the steady state) are known:

$$\frac{y_{ss}}{k_{ss}} = \frac{c_{ss}}{k_{ss}} + \frac{i_{ss}}{k_{ss}}$$

$$c_{ss} = y_{ss} - i_{ss} \tag{5.36}$$

Table 5.5 indicates the expression of the steady state of each variable of the model.

5.2.4 Log-Linearization

In the same way, as in the previous chapters, the model will be log-linearized following the technique of Uhlig (1995). First, variable $\widehat{x_t}$ is defined as the difference between the logarithm of variable "x" and the logarithm of its steady state "x_{ss}" as follows:

$$\widehat{x_t} = lnx_t - lnx_{ss}$$

This expression can be rearranged in such a way that variable x is a function of its steady-state x_{ss} and variable $\widehat{x_t}$:

$$x_t = x_{ss}e^{\widehat{x_t}} \tag{5.37}$$

Then, the expression for "x_t" is substituted into all the nonlinear model equations. Second, Expression (5.37) requires that $e^{\widehat{x_t}}$ to be approximated by a linear function; otherwise, the system of equations would still retain its nonlinear nature. Given this, $e^{\widehat{x_t}}$ is approximated using the first-order Taylor expansion, where the reference point for the approximation is the steady state. By applying the Taylor expansion, $e^{\widehat{x_t}}$ can be expressed as

$$e^{\widehat{x_t}} \approx 1 + \widehat{x_t} \tag{5.38}$$

Considering Properties (5.37) and (5.38), we proceed to log-linearize the system described in Table 5.3:

Capital demand To find the log-linear capital demand, we must first replace each variable x_t by its expression $x_{ss}e^{\widehat{x_t}}$, where $\widehat{x_t}$ is the variable x in the percentage deviation of lnx_t with respect to its steady state (second line). After performing certain algebraic operations, line 4 is reached, where the first-order approximation ($e^x \approx 1 + x$) is applied, and line 5 is obtained. Finally, Eq. (5.39) is the log-linear equation for capital demand:

$$\begin{aligned}
k_t &= \alpha \frac{y_t}{r_t} && \text{Line 1} \\
k_{ss}e^{\widehat{k_t}} &= \alpha \frac{y_{ss}e^{\widehat{y_t}}}{r_{ss}e^{\widehat{r_t}}} && \text{Line 2} \\
e^{\widehat{k_t}} &= \frac{e^{\widehat{y_t}}}{e^{\widehat{r_t}}} && \text{Line 3} \\
e^{\widehat{k_t}} &= e^{\widehat{y_t} - \widehat{r_t}} && \text{Line 4} \\
1 + \widehat{k_t} &= 1 + \widehat{y_t} - \widehat{r_t} && \text{Line 5} \\
\widehat{k_t} &= \widehat{y_t} - \widehat{r_t}
\end{aligned} \tag{5.39}$$

Euler's equation To find the log-linear Euler's equation, we first make a change of variable ($z_{t+1} = r_{t+1} + (1 - \delta)$), which is observed in the second line of Eq. (5.40). This is because to simplify the log-linear transformation of an equation, it is preferable that all variables are in multiplicative form. Second, each variable x_t is replaced by its expression $x_{ss}e^{\widehat{x_t}}$, where $\widehat{x_t}$ is variable x in percentage deviation from lnx_t with respect to its steady state (third line of Eq. (5.40)). After performing some algebraic operations, line 5 is reached, where first-order approximations ($e^{\widehat{x}} \approx 1+\widehat{x}$) and line 6 are obtained. Finally, after eliminating the constant (number one), we arrive at line 7:

$$\frac{1}{c_t} = \beta E_t \left[\frac{1}{c_{t+1}} [R_{t+1} + (1 - \delta)] \right]$$

$$
\begin{aligned}
\frac{1}{c_t} &= \beta E_t\left[\frac{1}{c_{t+1}}[z_{t+1}]\right] \\
\frac{1}{c_{ss}e^{\widehat{c}_t}} &= \beta E_t\left[\frac{1}{c_{ss}e^{\widehat{c}_{t+1}}}[z_{ss}e^{\widehat{z}_{t+1}}]\right] \\
\frac{1}{e^{\widehat{c}_t}} &= E_t\left[\frac{1}{e^{\widehat{c}_{t+1}}}[e^{\widehat{z}_{t+1}}]\right] \\
e^{-\widehat{c}_t} &= E_t\left[e^{\widehat{z}_{t+1}-\widehat{c}_{t+1}}\right] \\
1-\widehat{c}_t &= E_t[1+\widehat{z}_{t+1}-\widehat{c}_{t+1}] \\
-\widehat{c}_t &= E_t[\widehat{z}_{t+1}-\widehat{c}_{t+1}]
\end{aligned}
\tag{5.40}
$$

To characterize Euler's log-linear equation, one must find $\widehat{z}_{t+1}$ as a function of the interest rate in log deviations from its steady-state ($\widehat{r}_{t+1}$).To do so, we must first consider this relationship in the steady state:

$$
Z_{ss} = r_{ss} + (1-\delta) \underbrace{=}_{\text{by the equation (5.18)}} \frac{1}{\beta}
\tag{5.41}
$$

The relationship between $\widehat{z}_{t+1}$ and $\widehat{r}_{t+1}$ is expressed in Eq. (5.42):

$$
\begin{aligned}
z_{t+1} &= r_{t+1} + (1-\delta) \\
Z_{ss}e^{\widehat{z}_{t+1}} &= r_{ss}e^{\widehat{r}_{t+1}} + (1-\delta) \\
Z_{ss}(1+\widehat{z}_{t+1}) &= r_{ss}(1+\widehat{r}_{t+1}) + (1-\delta) \\
Z_{ss} + Z_{ss}\widehat{z}_{t+1} &= r_{ss} + r_{ss}\widehat{r}_{t+1} + (1-\delta)
\end{aligned}
\tag{5.42}
$$

When considering the steady-state relationship of Eq. (5.41) in Eq. (5.42), we have

$$
\begin{aligned}
Z_{ss}\widehat{z}_{t+1} &= r_{ss}\widehat{r}_{t+1} \\
\frac{1}{\beta}\widehat{z}_{t+1} &= r_{ss}\widehat{r}_{t+1} \\
\widehat{z}_{t+1} &= \beta r_{ss}\widehat{r}_{t+1}
\end{aligned}
\tag{5.43}
$$

Then, substituting Eq. (5.43) into Eq. (5.40) yields Euler's log-linear equation:

$$
\begin{aligned}
-\widehat{c}_t &= E_t[\widehat{z}_{t+1}-\widehat{c}_{t+1}] \\
-\widehat{c}_t &= E_t[\beta r_{ss}\widehat{r}_{t+1}-\widehat{c}_{t+1}]
\end{aligned}
\tag{5.44}
$$

Labor supply To obtain the log-linear equation of labor supply, like Euler's equation, a change of variable is made so that all the terms of the equation are multiplied. In this sense, $1-h_t$ is replaced by hh_t (line two of Eq. (5.45)). Similarly, as in the previous equations, each variable x_t is replaced by its expression $x_{ss}e^{\widehat{x_t}}$ (third line of Eq. (5.45)) and the first-order approximation ($e^x \approx 1+\widehat{x}$) (seventh line of Eq. (5.45)):

$$
\begin{aligned}
\theta(1-h_t)^{-\gamma_n} &= \frac{w_t}{c_t} \\
\theta(hh_t)^{-\gamma_n} &= \frac{w_t}{c_t} \\
\theta(hh_{ss}e^{\widehat{hh_t}})^{-\gamma_n} &= \frac{w_{ss}e^{\widehat{w}_t}}{h_{ss}e^{\widehat{c}_t}} \\
\theta hh_{ss}^{-\gamma_n} e^{-\gamma_n \widehat{hh}_t} &= \frac{w_{ss}e^{\widehat{w}_t}}{h_{ss}e^{\widehat{c}_t}} \\
e^{-\gamma_n \widehat{hh}_t} &= \frac{e^{\widehat{w}_t}}{e^{\widehat{c}_t}} \\
e^{-\gamma_n \widehat{hh}_t} &= e^{\widehat{w}_t-\widehat{c}_t} \\
1-\gamma_n \widehat{hh}_t &= 1+\widehat{w}_t-\widehat{c}_t \\
-\gamma_n \widehat{hh}_t &= \widehat{w}_t-\widehat{c}_t
\end{aligned}
\tag{5.45}
$$

To find the log-linear equation of labor supply, it is necessary to find the log-linear version of the change of variable $hh_t = 1-h_t$:

$$
\begin{aligned}
hh_t &= 1-h_t \\
hh_{ss}e^{\widehat{hh}_t} &= 1-h_{ss}e^{\widehat{h}_t} \\
hh_{ss}(1+\widehat{hh}_t) &= 1-h_{ss}(1+\widehat{h}_t) \\
hh_{ss}+hh_{ss}\widehat{hh}_t &= 1-h_{ss}-h_{ss}\widehat{h}_t \\
hh_{ss}\widehat{hh}_t &= -h_{ss}\widehat{h}_t \\
\widehat{hh}_t &= -\frac{h_{ss}}{hh_{ss}}\widehat{h}_t \\
\widehat{hh}_t &= -\frac{h_{ss}}{1-h_{ss}}\widehat{h}_t
\end{aligned}
\tag{5.46}
$$

Substituting Eq. (5.46) into Eq. (5.45), we obtain the log-linear equation of labor supply (Eq. (5.47)):

$$
-\gamma_n \widehat{hh}_t = \widehat{w}_t-\widehat{c}_t
$$

$$
\begin{aligned}
-\gamma_n\left[-\frac{h_{ss}}{1-h_{ss}}\widehat{h}_t\right] &= \widehat{w}_t-\widehat{c}_t \\
\gamma_n\frac{h_{ss}}{1-h_{ss}}\widehat{h}_t &= \widehat{w}_t-\widehat{c}_t
\end{aligned}
\tag{5.47}
$$

Labor demand The log-linear equation of labor demand is described by Eq. (5.48). To do this, in the same way as in the previous equations, each variable x_t was replaced by its expression $x_{ss}e^{\widehat{x}_t}$ (second line of Eq. (5.48)), and the first-order approximation was applied ($e^x \approx 1+x$) (fifth line of Eq. (5.48)):

$$
\begin{aligned}
h_t &= (1-\alpha)\frac{y_t}{w_t} \\
h_{ss}e^{\widehat{h}_t} &= (1-\alpha)\frac{y_{ss}e^{\widehat{y}_t}}{w_{ss}e^{\widehat{w}_t}} \\
e^{\widehat{h}_t} &= \frac{e^{\widehat{y}_t}}{e^{\widehat{w}_t}} \\
e^{\widehat{h}_t} &= e^{\widehat{y}_t-\widehat{w}_t} \\
1+\widehat{h}_t &= 1+\widehat{y}_t-\widehat{w}_t \\
\widehat{h}_t &= \widehat{y}_t-\widehat{w}_t
\end{aligned}
\tag{5.48}
$$

Production function The log-linear production function equation is described by Eq. (5.49). To do this, each variable x_t has been replaced by its expression $x_{ss}e^{\widehat{x}_t}$ (second line of Eq. (5.49)), and the first-order approximation ($e^x \approx 1+x$) (sixth line of Eq. (5.49)):

$$
\begin{aligned}
y_t &= a_t k_t^{\alpha} h_t^{1-\alpha} \\
y_{ss}e^{\widehat{y}_t} &= a_{ss}e^{\widehat{a}_t}[k_{ss}e^{\widehat{k}_t}]^{\alpha}[h_{ss}e^{\widehat{h}_t}]^{1-\alpha} \\
y_{ss}e^{\widehat{y}_t} &= a_{ss}e^{\widehat{a}_t}[k_{ss}^{\alpha}e^{\alpha\widehat{k}_t}][h_{ss}^{1-\alpha}e^{(1-\alpha)\widehat{h}_t}] \\
e^{\widehat{y}_t} &= e^{\widehat{a}_t}[e^{\alpha\widehat{k}_t}][e^{(1-\alpha)\widehat{h}_t}] \\
e^{\widehat{y}_t} &= e^{\widehat{a}_t+\alpha\widehat{k}_t+(1-\alpha)\widehat{h}_t} \\
1+\widehat{y}_t &= 1+\widehat{a}_t+\alpha\widehat{k}_t+(1-\alpha)\widehat{h}_t \\
\widehat{y}_t &= \widehat{a}_t+\alpha\widehat{k}_t+(1-\alpha)\widehat{h}_t
\end{aligned}
\tag{5.49}
$$

Goods market equilibrium As in the previous equations, to obtain the equilibrium condition in the log-linear goods market, each variable x_t must be replaced by its expression $x_{ss}e^{\widehat{x}_t}$ (second line of Eq. (5.50)), and the first-order approximation must be applied ($e^x \approx 1+x$) (third line of Eq. (5.50)):

$$
\begin{aligned}
y_t &= c_t + i_t \\
y_{ss}e^{\widehat{y}_t} &= c_{ss}e^{\widehat{c}_t} + i_{ss}e^{\widehat{i}_t} \\
y_{ss}(1+\widehat{y}_t) &= c_{ss}(1+\widehat{c}_t) + i_{ss}(1+\widehat{i}_t) \\
y_{ss} + y_{ss}\widehat{y}_t &= c_{ss} + c_{ss}\widehat{c}_t + i_{ss} + i_{ss}\widehat{i}_t \\
y_{ss}\widehat{y}_t &= c_{ss}\widehat{c}_t + i_{ss}\widehat{i}_t \\
\widehat{y}_t &= \frac{c_{ss}}{y_{ss}}\widehat{c}_t + \frac{i_{ss}}{y_{ss}}\widehat{i}_t
\end{aligned} \tag{5.50}
$$

Law of motion of capital The log-linear law of motion of capital is expressed in Eq. (5.51). Similar to the previous equations, the transformation of the initial variable k_t by its equivalent in log deviations (line 2 of Eq. (5.51)) is used. Next, we calculate the first-order Taylor approximation of that transformation (line 5 of Eq. (5.51)):

$$
\begin{aligned}
k_{t+1} &= (1-\delta)k_t + i_t \\
k_{ss}e^{\widehat{k}_{t+1}} &= (1-\delta)k_{ss}e^{\widehat{k}_t} + i_{ss}e^{\widehat{i}_t} \\
e^{\widehat{k}_{t+1}} &= (1-\delta)e^{\widehat{k}_t} + \frac{i_{ss}}{k_{ss}}e^{\widehat{i}_t} \\
e^{\widehat{k}_{t+1}} &= (1-\delta)e^{\widehat{k}_t} + \delta e^{\widehat{i}_t} \\
1+\widehat{k}_{t+1} &= (1-\delta)(1+\widehat{k}_t) + \delta(1+\widehat{i}_t) \\
1+\widehat{k}_{t+1} &= (1-\delta) + (1-\delta)\widehat{k}_t + \delta + \delta\widehat{i}_t \\
\widehat{k}_{t+1} &= (1-\delta)\widehat{k}_t + \delta\widehat{i}_t
\end{aligned} \tag{5.51}
$$

Productivity shock Strictly speaking, *productivity shock* is represented by the variable ϵ_t, which has a normal distribution with zero mean and constant variance. Thus, Eq. (5.52) represents the log-linear equation for productivity (not for shock):

$$
\begin{aligned}
lna_t &= \phi lna_{t-1} + \epsilon_t \\
lna_{ss}e^{\widehat{a}_t} &= \phi lna_{ss}e^{\widehat{a}_{t-1}} + \epsilon_t \\
lna_{ss} + \widehat{a}_t &= \phi lna_{ss} + \phi\widehat{a}_{t-1} + \epsilon_t \\
\widehat{a}_t &= \phi\widehat{a}_{t-1} + \epsilon_t
\end{aligned} \tag{5.52}
$$

Table 5.6 summarizes the system of log-linear equations that describe the model.

Table 5.6 Log-linear system of equations

Log-linear equations	Description
$-\widehat{c}_t = E_t[\beta r_{ss}\widehat{r}_{t+1} - \widehat{c}_{t+1}]$	Euler's equation
$\widehat{k}_t = \widehat{y}_t - \widehat{r}_t$	Capital demand
$\gamma_n \frac{h_{ss}}{1-h_{ss}}\widehat{h}_t = \widehat{w}_t - \widehat{c}_t$	Labor supply
$\widehat{h}_t = \widehat{y}_t - \widehat{w}_t$	Labor demand
$\widehat{y}_t = \widehat{a}_t + \alpha\widehat{k}_t + (1-\alpha)\widehat{h}_t$	Production function
$\widehat{y}_t = \frac{c_{ss}}{y_{ss}}\widehat{c}_t + \frac{i_{ss}}{y_{ss}}\widehat{i}_t$	Goods market equilibrium
$\widehat{k}_{t+1} = (1-\delta)\widehat{k}_t + \delta\widehat{i}_t$	Law of movement of capital
$\widehat{a}_t = \phi\widehat{a}_{t-1} + \epsilon_t$	Productivity shock

5.2.5 *Solution of the Linear System*

5.2.5.1 Method of Undetermined Coefficients

In the general equilibrium modeling literature, the methods to find the solution have focused on solving a system of linear (or log-linear) equations. As in the previous chapters, this chapter applies the method of undetermined coefficients. The solution is to place the endogenous variables as functions of the state variables and shock. For instance, for capital, production, and consumption, we have

$$\widehat{k}_{t+1} = \eta_{kk}\widehat{k}_t + \eta_{ka}\widehat{a}_t \tag{5.53}$$

$$\widehat{y}_t = \eta_{yk}\widehat{k}_t + \eta_{ya}\widehat{a}_t \tag{5.54}$$

$$\widehat{c}_t = \eta_{ck}\widehat{k}_t + \eta_{ca}\widehat{a}_t . \tag{5.55}$$

It is worth mentioning that because the system of equations has been log-linearized (see Table 5.4), the variables are expressed as log deviations from their steady state, that is, $\widehat{x}_t = lnx_t - lnx_{ss}$. Furthermore, the coefficients of the solution (e.g., Eqs. (5.53), (5.54), and (5.55)) express elasticity. This elasticity is illustrated as follows: considering Eq. (5.53), if today's capital increases by 1%, then tomorrow's capital increases by η_{kk} %. This is observed in the following expression:

$$\widehat{k}_{t+1} = \eta_{kk}\widehat{k}_t + \eta_{ka}\widehat{a}_t$$

$$\text{Differentiating :}$$

$$\Delta\widehat{k}_{t+1} = \eta_{kk}\Delta\widehat{k}_t + \eta_{ka}\Delta\widehat{a}_t$$

$$\text{Assuming : } \widehat{a}_t \quad \text{remains constant}$$

$$\Delta\widehat{k}_{t+1} = \eta_{kk}\Delta\widehat{k}_t + 0$$

$$\Delta[lnk_{t+1} - lnk_{ss}] = \eta_{kk}\Delta[lnk_t - lnk_{ss}]$$

$$
\begin{aligned}
\Delta[lnk_{t+1}] - 0 &= \eta_{kk}\Delta[lnk_t] - 0 \\
\frac{\Delta k_{t+1}}{k_{t+1}} &= \eta_{kk}\frac{\Delta k_t}{k_t} \\
\frac{\frac{\Delta k_{t+1}}{k_{t+1}}}{\frac{\Delta k_t}{k_t}} &= \eta_{kk} \\
E_{k_{t+1},k_t} &= \eta_{kk}
\end{aligned}
\tag{5.56}
$$

The Expression (5.56) clearly indicates that η_{kk} represents the elasticity of tomorrow's capital to today's capital, holding everything else constant. Therefore, a 1% increase in today's capital increases by η_{kk}% tomorrow's capital, keeping everything else constant. Thus, each coefficient of the model solution is interpreted in that way. It is worth mentioning that, regardless of the solution method of the model, the solution is always described by Eqs. (5.53), (5.54), and (5.55) and the other equations of the endogenous variables that maintain the same shape. The method of undetermined coefficients involves finding the values of the coefficients of the solution as a function of the parameters. When these coefficients are found, the solution is well defined.

Before applying the undetermined coefficients method, the system of equations must be reduced as much as possible. In this eight-equation model, the ideal approach would be to reduce the system to three or four equations. This is the next step that we execute.

[A] Size reduction of system I The system of eight equations described in Table 5.4 can be reduced to five equations. The procedure is as follows:

- First, eliminate the real wage w_t through equilibrium in the labor market.
- Second, eliminate investment $\widehat{i_t}$.
- Third, replace the law of motion of capital in goods market equilibrium.
- Finally, eliminate the real interest rate $\widehat{r_t}$ by introducing the demand for capital into the Euler equation.

Eliminating the real wage w_t The real wage is solved from labor demand.

$$
\begin{aligned}
&\text{Labor demand :} \\
&\qquad \widehat{h_t} = \widehat{y_t} - \widehat{w_t} \\
&\qquad \widehat{w_t} = \widehat{y_t} - \widehat{h_t}
\end{aligned}
\tag{5.57}
$$

Equation (5.57) is introduced into the labor supply, which is described by the following equation:

$$
\gamma_n \frac{h_{ss}}{1-h_{ss}}\widehat{h_t} = \widehat{w_t} - \widehat{c_t} \tag{5.58}
$$

Equating the labor supply with labor demand in real wages, we have

$$\underbrace{\gamma_n\left[\frac{h_{ss}}{1-h_{ss}}\right]}_{=m_1}\widehat{h}_t = \widehat{y}_t - \widehat{h}_t - \widehat{c}_t$$

$$\begin{aligned} m_1\widehat{h}_t &= \widehat{y}_t - \widehat{h}_t - \widehat{c}_t \\ (1+m_1)\widehat{h}_t &= \widehat{y}_t - \widehat{c}_t \end{aligned} \tag{5.59}$$

Eliminating investment i_t Investment is cleared from the law of movement of capital and replaced in the equilibrium of the goods market.

$$\begin{aligned} &\text{Law of movement of capital :} \\ \widehat{k}_{t+1} &= (1-\delta)\widehat{k}_t + \delta\widehat{i}_t \\ \delta\widehat{i}_t &= \widehat{k}_{t+1} - (1-\delta)\widehat{k}_t \\ \widehat{i}_t &= \frac{1}{\delta}[\widehat{k}_{t+1} - (1-\delta)\widehat{k}_t] \end{aligned} \tag{5.60}$$

$$\begin{aligned} &\text{Equilibrium in goods market :} \\ \widehat{y}_t &= \frac{c_{ss}}{y_{ss}}\widehat{c}_t + \frac{i_{ss}}{y_{ss}}\underbrace{\widehat{i}_t}_{\text{Eq. (5.60)}} \\ \widehat{y}_t &= \frac{c_{ss}}{y_{ss}}\widehat{c}_t + \frac{i_{ss}}{y_{ss}}\left[\frac{1}{\delta}[\widehat{k}_{t+1} - (1-\delta)\widehat{k}_t]\right] \end{aligned} \tag{5.61}$$

Eliminating the real interest rate r_t From capital demand, the interest rate is solved and replaced in the Euler equation.

$$\begin{aligned} &\text{Capital Demand :} \\ \widehat{k}_t &= \widehat{y}_t - \widehat{r}_t \\ \widehat{r}_t &= \widehat{y}_t - \widehat{k}_t \end{aligned} \tag{5.62}$$

$$\begin{aligned} &\text{Euler equation :} \\ -\widehat{c}_t &= E_t[\beta r_{ss}\widehat{r}_{t+1} - \widehat{c}_{t+1}] \\ \widehat{c}_t &= E_t[\widehat{c}_{t+1} - \beta r_{ss}\underbrace{\widehat{r}_{t+1}}_{\text{Eq. (5.62)}}] \\ \widehat{c}_t &= E_t[\widehat{c}_{t+1} - \beta r_{ss}[\widehat{y}_{t+1} - \widehat{k}_{t+1}]] \end{aligned} \tag{5.63}$$

With these reductions, the system would be composed of five equations:

$$(1+m_1)\widehat{h}_t = \widehat{y}_t - \widehat{c}_t \tag{5.64}$$

$$\widehat{y}_t = \frac{c_{ss}}{y_{ss}}\widehat{c}_t + \frac{i_{ss}}{y_{ss}}\left[\frac{1}{\delta}[\widehat{k}_{t+1} - (1-\delta)\widehat{k}_t]\right] \tag{5.65}$$

$$\widehat{c}_t = E_t[\widehat{c}_{t+1} - \beta r_{ss}[\widehat{y}_{t+1} - \widehat{k}_{t+1}]] \tag{5.66}$$

Production function :

$$\widehat{y}_t = \widehat{a}_t + \alpha\widehat{k}_t + (1-\alpha)\widehat{h}_t \tag{5.67}$$

Productivity *Shock* :

$$\widehat{a}_t = \phi\widehat{a}_{t-1} + \epsilon_t \tag{5.68}$$

[B] Size reduction of system II The system can be further reduced. From Eq. (5.64), labor $\widehat{h}_t$ is solved and introduced in Eq. (5.67) (production function).

Balance in the labor market :

$$(1+m_1)\widehat{h}_t = \widehat{y}_t - \widehat{c}_t$$

$$\widehat{h}_t = \left[\frac{1}{1+m_1}\right][\widehat{y}_t - \widehat{c}_t] \tag{5.69}$$

Production function :

$$\widehat{y}_t = \widehat{a}_t + \alpha\widehat{k}_t + (1-\alpha)\underbrace{\widehat{h}_t}_{\text{Ecu. (5.69)}}$$

$$\widehat{y}_t = \widehat{a}_t + \alpha\widehat{k}_t + (1-\alpha)\left[\frac{1}{1+m_1}\right][\widehat{y}_t - \widehat{c}_t]$$

$$\left[1 - \frac{1-\alpha}{1+m_1}\right]\widehat{y}_t = \widehat{a}_t + \alpha\widehat{k}_t - \left[\frac{1-\alpha}{1+m_1}\right]\widehat{c}_t$$

$$\left[\frac{m_1+\alpha}{1+m_1}\right]\widehat{y}_t = \widehat{a}_t + \alpha\widehat{k}_t - \left[\frac{1-\alpha}{1+m_1}\right]\widehat{c}_t \tag{5.70}$$

With these additional reductions, the system is composed of four equations:

$$\left[\frac{m_1+\alpha}{1+m_1}\right]\widehat{y}_t = \widehat{a}_t + \alpha\widehat{k}_t - \left[\frac{1-\alpha}{1+m_1}\right]\widehat{c}_t \tag{5.71}$$

$$\widehat{y}_t = \frac{c_{ss}}{y_{ss}}\widehat{c}_t + \frac{i_{ss}}{y_{ss}}\left[\frac{1}{\delta}[\widehat{k}_{t+1} - (1-\delta)\widehat{k}_t]\right] \tag{5.72}$$

$$\widehat{c}_t = E_t[\widehat{c}_{t+1} - \beta r_{ss}[\widehat{y}_{t+1} - \widehat{k}_{t+1}]] \tag{5.73}$$

Productivity shock :

$$\widehat{a}_t = \phi\widehat{a}_{t-1} + \epsilon_t \tag{5.74}$$

[C] Size reduction of system III The previous system of four equations can still be reduced by eliminating one additional equation. To do so, product $\widehat{y}_t$ is cleared from Eq. (5.71) and replaced in Eqs. (5.72) and (5.73):

$$\left[\frac{m_1+\alpha}{1+m_1}\right]\widehat{y}_t = \widehat{a}_t + \alpha\widehat{k}_t - \left[\frac{1-\alpha}{1+m_1}\right]\widehat{c}_t$$

$$\widehat{y}_t = \left[\frac{1+m_1}{m_1+\alpha}\right]\left[\widehat{a}_t + \alpha\widehat{k}_t - \left[\frac{1-\alpha}{1+m_1}\right]\widehat{c}_t\right] \tag{5.75}$$

Equation (5.75) is replaced in the Eq. (5.71):

$$\widehat{y}_t = \frac{c_{ss}}{y_{ss}}\widehat{c}_t + \frac{i_{ss}}{y_{ss}}\left[\frac{1}{\delta}[\widehat{k}_{t+1} - (1-\delta)\widehat{k}_t]\right]$$

$$\left[\frac{1+m_1}{m_1+\alpha}\right]\left[\widehat{a}_t + \alpha\widehat{k}_t - \left[\frac{1-\alpha}{1+m_1}\right]\widehat{c}_t\right] = \frac{c_{ss}}{y_{ss}}\widehat{c}_t + \frac{i_{ss}}{y_{ss}}\left[\frac{1}{\delta}[\widehat{k}_{t+1} - (1-\delta)\widehat{k}_t]\right]$$

$$\left[\frac{1+m_1}{m_1+\alpha}\right]\widehat{a}_t + \alpha\left[\frac{1+m_1}{m_1+\alpha}\right]\widehat{k}_t - \left[\frac{1-\alpha}{m_1+\alpha}\right]\widehat{c}_t = \frac{c_{ss}}{y_{ss}}\widehat{c}_t + \frac{i_{ss}}{y_{ss}\delta}\widehat{k}_{t+1} - \frac{i_{ss}(1-\delta)}{y_{ss}\delta}\widehat{k}_t$$

$$\underbrace{\left[\frac{1+m_1}{m_1+\alpha}\right]}_{m_2}\widehat{a}_t + \widehat{k}_t\underbrace{\left[\frac{\alpha(1+m_1)}{m_1+\alpha} + \frac{i_{ss}(1-\delta)}{y_{ss}\delta}\right]}_{m_3} = \widehat{c}_t\underbrace{\left[\frac{c_{ss}}{y_{ss}} + \frac{1-\alpha}{m_1+\alpha}\right]}_{m_4} + \underbrace{\frac{i_{ss}}{y_{ss}\delta}}_{m_5}\widehat{k}_{t+1}$$

$$m_2\widehat{a}_t + m_3\widehat{k}_t = m_4\widehat{c}_t + m_5\widehat{k}_{t+1}$$

$$m_4\widehat{c}_t = m_2\widehat{a}_t + m_3\widehat{k}_t - m_5\widehat{k}_{t+1} \tag{5.76}$$

Similarly, Eq. (5.75) is introduced into Eq. (5.72):

$$\widehat{c}_t = E_t[\widehat{c}_{t+1} - \beta r_{ss}[\widehat{y}_{t+1} - \widehat{k}_{t+1}]]$$

$$\widehat{c}_t = E_t\left[\widehat{c}_{t+1} - \beta r_{ss}\left[\left[\frac{1+m_1}{m_1+\alpha}\right]\left[\widehat{a}_{t+1} + \alpha\widehat{k}_{t+1} - \left[\frac{1-\alpha}{1+m_1}\right]\widehat{c}_{t+1}\right] - \widehat{k}_{t+1}\right]\right]$$

$$\widehat{c}_t = E_t\left[\widehat{c}_{t+1} - \beta r_{ss}\left[\frac{1+m_1}{m_1+\alpha}\right]\left[\widehat{a}_{t+1} + \alpha\widehat{k}_{t+1} - \left[\frac{1-\alpha}{1+m_1}\right]\widehat{c}_{t+1}\right] - \beta r_{ss}\widehat{k}_{t+1}\right]$$

$$\widehat{c}_t = E_t\left[\left(1 + \beta r_{ss}\frac{1-\alpha}{m_1+\alpha}\right)\widehat{c}_{t+1} - \beta r_{ss}\frac{1+m_1}{m_1+\alpha}\widehat{a}_{t+1} + \left(\beta r_{ss} - \beta r_{ss}\frac{1+m_1}{m_1+\alpha}\right)\widehat{k}_{t+1}\right.$$

$$\widehat{c}_t = E_t\left[\underbrace{\left(1 + \beta r_{ss}\frac{1-\alpha}{m_1+\alpha}\right)}_{n_1}\widehat{c}_{t+1} - \underbrace{\beta r_{ss}\frac{1+m_1}{m_1+\alpha}}_{n_2}\widehat{a}_{t+1} + \underbrace{\left(\beta r_{ss} - \beta r_{ss}\frac{1+m_1}{m_1+\alpha}\alpha\right)}_{n_3}\widehat{k}_{t+1}\right.$$

$$\widehat{c}_t = E_t[n_1\widehat{c}_{t+1} - n_2\widehat{a}_{t+1} + n_3\widehat{k}_{t+1}] \tag{5.77}$$

After the last reduction, the system of equations is represented by the following three equations:

$$m_4\widehat{c}_t = m_2\widehat{a}_t + m_3\widehat{k}_t - m_5\widehat{k}_{t+1} \tag{5.78}$$

$$\widehat{c}_t = E_t[n_1\widehat{c}_{t+1} - n_2\widehat{a}_{t+1} + n_3\widehat{k}_{t+1}] \tag{5.79}$$

$$\widehat{a}_t = \phi\widehat{a}_{t-1} + \epsilon_t \tag{5.80}$$

[D] Application of the undetermined coefficients method The system of equations represented by equations (5.78), (5.79), and (5.80) has three variables: c_t, k_{t+1}, and a_t. One of these variables is exogenous (a_t), while the other two are endogenous (c_t and k_{t+1}). We then propose that endogenous variables have linear solutions in the state variable k_t and the exogenous variable a_t:

$$\widehat{k}_{t+1} = \eta_{kk}\widehat{k}_t + \eta_{ka}\widehat{a}_t \tag{5.81}$$

$$\widehat{c}_t = \eta_{ck}\widehat{k}_t + \eta_{ca}\widehat{a}_t \tag{5.82}$$

Substituting this solution in Eq. (5.78), we have

$$\begin{aligned} m_4\widehat{c}_t &= m_2\widehat{a}_t + m_3\widehat{k}_t - m_5\widehat{k}_{t+1} \\ m_4(\eta_{ck}\widehat{k}_t + \eta_{ca}\widehat{a}_t) &= m_2\widehat{a}_t + m_3\widehat{k}_t - m_5(\eta_{kk}\widehat{k}_t + \eta_{ka}\widehat{a}_t) \\ (m_4\eta_{ck})\widehat{k}_t + (m_4\eta_{ca})\widehat{a}_t &= (m_2 - m_5\eta_{ka})\widehat{a}_t + (m_3 - m_5\eta_{kk})\widehat{k}_t \end{aligned} \tag{5.83}$$

Equating the coefficients of each variable on the right-hand side with its corresponding variable on the left-hand side, we have

$$\text{Capital ratios}:$$

$$m_4\eta_{ck} = m_3 - m_5\eta_{kk} \tag{5.84}$$

$$\text{Coefficients of the productivity}:$$

$$m_4\eta_{ca} = m_2 - m_5\eta_{ka} \tag{5.85}$$

Substituting the solution to Eq. (5.79) results in

$$\begin{aligned} \widehat{c}_t &= E_t[n_1\widehat{c}_{t+1} - n_2\widehat{a}_{t+1} + n_3\widehat{k}_{t+1}] \\ \eta_{ck}\widehat{k}_t + \eta_{ca}\widehat{a}_t &= E_t[n_1(\eta_{ck}\widehat{k}_{t+1} + \eta_{ca}\widehat{a}_{t+1}) - n_2\widehat{a}_{t+1} + \\ &\quad n_3(\eta_{kk}\widehat{k}_t + \eta_{ka}\widehat{a}_t)] \\ (\eta_{ck} - n_3\eta_{kk})\widehat{k}_t + (\eta_{ca} - n_3\eta_{ka})\widehat{a}_t &= E_t[n_1\eta_{ck}\widehat{k}_{t+1} + (n_1\eta_{ca} - n_2)\widehat{a}_{t+1}] \\ \text{Considering that} &: \widehat{a}_t = \phi\widehat{a}_{t-1} + \epsilon_t \\ (\eta_{ck} - n_3\eta_{kk})\widehat{k}_t + (\eta_{ca} - n_3\eta_{ka})\widehat{a}_t &= E_t[n_1\eta_{ck}\widehat{k}_{t+1} + (n_1\eta_{ca} - n_2)(\phi\widehat{a}_t + \epsilon_{t+1})] \\ &= E_t[n_1\eta_{ck}\widehat{k}_{t+1}] + (n_1\eta_{ca} - n_2)E_t[\phi\widehat{a}_t + \epsilon_{t+1}] \end{aligned}$$

$$
\begin{aligned}
&= E_t[n_1\eta_{ck}\widehat{k}_{t+1}] + (n_1\eta_{ca} - n_2)[\phi E_t\widehat{a}_t + \underbrace{E_t\epsilon_{t+1}}_{=0}] \\
\text{Replacing} &: \text{ the solution of } \widehat{k}_{t+1} \\
&= E_t[n_1\eta_{ck}(\eta_{kk}\widehat{k}_t + \eta_{ka}\widehat{a}_t)] + (n_1\eta_{ca} - n_2)\phi\widehat{a}_t \\
&= E_t[n_1\eta_{ck}\eta_{kk}\widehat{k}_t + n_1\eta_{ck}\eta_{ka}\widehat{a}_t] + (n_1\eta_{ca} - n_2)\phi\widehat{a}_t \\
&= (n_1\eta_{ck}\eta_{kk})\widehat{k}_t + (n_1\eta_{ck}\eta_{ka} + (n_1\eta_{ca} - n_2)\phi)\widehat{a}_t \\
(\eta_{ck} - n_3\eta_{kk})\widehat{k}_t + (\eta_{ca} - n_3\eta_{ka})\widehat{a}_t &= (n_1\eta_{ck}\eta_{kk})\widehat{k}_t + (n_1\eta_{ck}\eta_{ka} + \\
&\quad (n_1\eta_{ca} - n_2)\phi)\widehat{a}_t
\end{aligned} \tag{5.86}
$$

From Eq. (5.86), the coefficients for each variable are equalized. For capital, we have

$$
\begin{aligned}
\eta_{ck} - n_3\eta_{kk} &= n_1\eta_{ck}\eta_{kk} \\
\eta_{kk} &= \frac{\eta_{ck}}{n_3 + n_1\eta_{ck}}
\end{aligned} \tag{5.87}
$$

In the case of productivity, equating the coefficients, we have

$$
\begin{aligned}
\eta_{ca} - n_3\eta_{ka} &= n_1\eta_{ck}\eta_{ka} + (n_1\eta_{ca} - n_2)\phi \\
(1 - \phi n_1)\eta_{ca} &= \eta_{ka}(n_1\eta_{ck} + n_3) - \phi n_2
\end{aligned} \tag{5.88}
$$

The method of undetermined coefficients consists of finding the values of the coefficients as a function of the model parameters. In this case, there are four "unknown" coefficients, (η_{ck}, η_{ca}, η_{kk}, and η_{ka}). These four "new" variables require four equations, which are as follows:

$$
\begin{aligned}
&\text{Eq. (5.84)}: \\
&\quad m_4\eta_{ck} = m_3 - m_5\eta_{kk} \\
&\text{Eq. (5.85)}: \\
&\quad m_4\eta_{ca} = m_2 - m_5\eta_{ka} \\
&\text{Eq. (5.87)}: \\
&\quad \eta_{kk} = \frac{\eta_{ck}}{n_3 + n_1\eta_{ck}} \\
&\text{Eq. (5.88)}: \\
&\quad (1 - \phi n_1)\eta_{ca} = \eta_{ka}(n_1\eta_{ck} + n_3) - \phi n_2
\end{aligned}
$$

[D1] Consumption and capital policy functions To solve the system of Eqs. (5.84), (5.85), (5.87), and (5.88), where the variables are the coefficients of the consumption policy function and state function, it is required to reduce the number of equations. First, Eq. (5.84) is solved for η_{ck} and replaced in Eq. (5.87) to determine the value of η_{kk}.

$$\begin{aligned}
&\text{From the equation (5.84) :}\\
m_4\eta_{ck} &= m_3 - m_5\eta_{kk}\\
\eta_{ck} &= \frac{1}{m_4}(m_3 - m_5\eta_{kk}) \qquad (5.89)\\
&\text{From the equation (5.87) :}\\
\eta_{kk} &= \frac{\eta_{ck}}{n_3 + n_1\eta_{ck}}\\
n_3\eta_{kk} + n_1\eta_{ck}\eta_{kk} &= \eta_{ck}\\
n_3\eta_{kk} &= \underbrace{\eta_{ck}}_{\text{Ecu. (5.89)}}(1 - n_1\eta_{kk})\\
n_3\eta_{kk} &= \frac{1}{m_4}(m_3 - m_5\eta_{kk})(1 - n_1\eta_{kk})\\
m_4n_3\eta_{kk} &= (m_3 - m_5\eta_{kk})(1 - n_1\eta_{kk})\\
m_4n_3\eta_{kk} &= m_3 - m_3n_1\eta_{kk} - m_5\eta_{kk} + m_5n_1\eta_{kk}^2
\end{aligned}$$

$$\underbrace{m_5n_1}_{=a}\eta_{kk}^2 + \underbrace{-(m_3n_1 + m_5 + m_4n_3)}_{=b}\eta_{kk} + \underbrace{m_3}_{=c} = 0 \tag{5.90}$$

$$a\eta_{kk}^2 + b\eta_{kk} + c = 0 \tag{5.91}$$

Equation (5.91) has two solutions:

$$\eta_{kk_{1,2}} = \frac{-b \pm \sqrt{b^2 - 4ac}}{2a}$$

Because capital is required to be stationary, then η_{kk} must be less than one in absolute value, that is, $\eta_{kk} \in (-1.1)$ (Table 5.7).

The chosen value of η_{kk} was $\eta_{kk2} = 0.9326$. Given the value of η_{kk}, then η_{ck} can be obtained from Eq. (5.84):

$$\eta_{ck} = \frac{1}{m_4}(m_3 - m_5\eta_{kk}) \tag{5.92}$$

Table 5.7 Value of $\eta_{kk_{1,2}}$

θ	β	δ	γ_n	α	η_{kk_1}	η_{kk_2}
2	0.984	0.025	0.25	0.333	1.0897	0.9326

To determine the value of the coefficient η_{ka}, η_{ca} is cleared from Eq. (5.85) and replaced in Eq. (5.88).

$$\text{From the equation (5.85)}:$$

$$m_4\eta_{ca} = m_2 - m_5\eta_{ka}$$

$$\eta_{ca} = \frac{1}{m_4}(m_2 - m_5\eta_{ka}) \tag{5.93}$$

$$\text{From the equation (5.88)}:$$

$$(1-\phi n_1)\underbrace{\eta_{ca}}_{\text{Ecu. (5.93)}} = \eta_{ka}(n_1\eta_{ck} + n_3) - \phi n_2$$

$$(1-\phi n_1)\left(\frac{1}{m_4}\left(m_2 - m_5\eta_{ka}\right)\right) = \eta_{ka}(n_1\eta_{ck} + n_3) - \phi n_2$$

$$\frac{m_2}{m_4}(1-\phi n_1) - \frac{m_5}{m_4}(1-\phi n_1)\eta_{ka} = \eta_{ka}(n_1\eta_{ck} + n_3) - \phi n_2$$

$$-\eta_{ka}\left[\frac{m_5}{m_4}(1-\phi n_1) + n_1\eta_{ck} + n_3\right] = -\phi n_2 - \frac{m_2}{m_4}(1-\phi n_1)$$

$$\eta_{ka}\left[\frac{m_5}{m_4}(1-\phi n_1) + n_1\eta_{ck} + n_3\right] = \phi n_2 + \frac{m_2}{m_4}(1-\phi n_1)$$

$$\eta_{ka} = \frac{\phi n_2 + \frac{m_2}{m_4}(1-\phi n_1)}{\frac{m_5}{m_4}(1-\phi n_1) + n_1\eta_{ck} + n_3} \tag{5.94}$$

Finally, η_{ca} is obtained from Eq. (5.85):

$$m_4\eta_{ca} = m_2 - m_5\eta_{ka}$$

$$\eta_{ca} = \frac{1}{m_4}(m_2 - m_5\eta_{ka}) \tag{5.95}$$

So far, we have found the values of the coefficients η_{ck}, η_{ca}, η_{kk}, and η_{ka}, which allow defining the consumption solution and of capital, that is, the consumption policy function and the state function of the model:[1]

$$\widehat{k}_{t+1} = \underbrace{\eta_{kk}}_{0.9326}\widehat{k}_t + \underbrace{\eta_{ka}}_{0.1618}\widehat{a}_t \tag{5.96}$$

$$\widehat{c}_t = \underbrace{\eta_{ck}}_{0.5205}\widehat{k}_t + \underbrace{\eta_{ca}}_{0.4945}\widehat{a}_t \tag{5.97}$$

[1] The values of these coefficients and the solution of the other endogenous variables are found in Campbell_Lvariable.m.

[D2] Policy function of the other variables The product policy function is obtained by substituting the consumption solution in Eq. (5.71).

$$\begin{aligned}
&\text{From the equation (5.71)}\ :\\
&\left[\frac{m_1+\alpha}{1+m_1}\right]\widehat{y}_t = \widehat{a}_t + \alpha\widehat{k}_t - \left[\frac{1-\alpha}{1+m_1}\right]\widehat{c}_t\\
&\text{The solution of } \widehat{c}_t \ is\ replaced\ :\\
&\left[\frac{m_1+\alpha}{1+m_1}\right]\widehat{y}_t = \widehat{a}_t + \alpha\widehat{k}_t - \left[\frac{1-\alpha}{1+m_1}\right](\eta_{ck}\widehat{k}_t + \eta_{ca}\widehat{a}_t)\\
&\left[\frac{m_1+\alpha}{1+m_1}\right]\widehat{y}_t = \left(1 - \frac{1-\alpha}{1+m_1}\eta_{ca}\right)\widehat{a}_t + \left(\alpha - \frac{1-\alpha}{1+m_1}\eta_{ck}\right)\widehat{k}_t\\
&\widehat{y}_t = \underbrace{\left[\frac{1+m_1}{m_1+\alpha}\right]\left(1 - \frac{1-\alpha}{1+m_1}\eta_{ca}\right)}_{\eta_{ya}}\widehat{a}_t + \\
&\qquad \underbrace{\left[\frac{1+m_1}{m_1+\alpha}\right]\left(\alpha - \frac{1-\alpha}{1+m_1}\eta_{ck}\right)}_{\eta_{yk}}\widehat{k}_t\\
&\widehat{y}_t = \eta_{ya}\widehat{a}_t + \eta_{yk}\widehat{k}_t
\end{aligned} \tag{5.98}$$

On the other hand, the labor policy function is obtained by substituting the consumption and output solution in Eq. (5.64):

$$\begin{aligned}
&\text{From the equation (5.71)}\ :\\
&(1+m_1)\widehat{h}_t = \widehat{y}_t - \widehat{c}_t\\
&\text{Replacing}\ :\ \text{the solution of } \widehat{c}_t \text{ and } \widehat{y}_t\\
&(1+m_1)\widehat{h}_t = (\eta_{ya}\widehat{a}_t + \eta_{yk}\widehat{k}_t) - (\eta_{ca}\widehat{a}_t + \eta_{ck}\widehat{k}_t)\\
&(1+m_1)\widehat{h}_t = (\eta_{ya} - \eta_{ca})\widehat{a}_t + (\eta_{yk} - \eta_{ck})\widehat{k}_t\\
&\widehat{h}_t = \left(\frac{\eta_{ya} - \eta_{ca}}{1+m_1}\right)\widehat{a}_t + \left(\frac{\eta_{yk} - \eta_{ck}}{1+m_1}\right)\widehat{k}_t\\
&\widehat{h}_t = \eta_{ha}\widehat{a}_t + \eta_{hk}\widehat{k}_t
\end{aligned} \tag{5.99}$$

Furthermore, the real wage is obtained by substituting the product and labor solution in labor demand (Eq. (5.57)).

$$\begin{aligned}
&\text{c(5.57)}\ :\\
&\widehat{w}_t = \widehat{y}_t - \widehat{h}_t
\end{aligned}$$

$$\begin{aligned}
&\text{Replacing : the solution of } \widehat{y}_t \text{ and } \widehat{h}_t \\
&\widehat{w}_t = (\eta_{ya}\widehat{a}_t + \eta_{yk}\widehat{k}_t) - (\eta_{ha}\widehat{a}_t + \eta_{hk}\widehat{k}_t) \\
&\widehat{w}_t = (\eta_{ya} - \eta_{ha})\widehat{a}_t + (\eta_{yk} - \eta_{hk})\widehat{k}_t \\
&\widehat{w}_t = \eta_{wa}\widehat{a}_t + \eta_{wk}\widehat{k}_t
\end{aligned} \tag{5.100}$$

Investment is obtained by substituting the product and consumption solution in the goods market equilibrium equation:

$$\begin{aligned}
\widehat{y}_t &= \frac{c_{ss}}{y_{ss}}\widehat{c}_t + \frac{i_{ss}}{y_{ss}}\widehat{i}_t \\
\widehat{i}_t &= \frac{y_{ss}}{i_{ss}}\left(\widehat{y}_t - \frac{c_{ss}}{y_{ss}}\widehat{c}_t\right) \\
&\text{Replacing : the solution of } \widehat{y}_t \text{ and } \widehat{c}_t \\
\widehat{i}_t &= \frac{y_{ss}}{i_{ss}}((\eta_{ya}\widehat{a}_t + \eta_{yk}\widehat{k}_t) - \frac{c_{ss}}{y_{ss}}(\eta_{ca}\widehat{a}_t + \eta_{ck}\widehat{k}_t)) \\
\widehat{i}_t &= \frac{y_{ss}}{i_{ss}}\left(\left(\eta_{yk} - \frac{c_{ss}}{y_{ss}}\eta_{ck}\right)\widehat{k}_t + \left(\eta_{ya} - \frac{c_{ss}}{y_{ss}}\eta_{ca}\right)\widehat{a}_t\right) \\
\widehat{i}_t &= \frac{y_{ss}}{i_{ss}}\left(\eta_{yk} - \frac{c_{ss}}{y_{ss}}\eta_{ck}\right)\widehat{k}_t + \frac{y_{ss}}{i_{ss}}\left(\eta_{ya} - \frac{c_{ss}}{y_{ss}}\eta_{ca}\right)\widehat{a}_t \\
\widehat{i}_t &= \eta_{ik}\widehat{k}_t + \eta_{ia}\widehat{a}_t
\end{aligned} \tag{5.101}$$

Finally, the real interest rate is obtained by substituting the product and capital solution in the demand for capital.

$$\begin{aligned}
&\text{From the equation (5.62) :} \\
&\widehat{r}_t = \widehat{y}_t - \widehat{k}_t \\
&\text{Replacing : the solution of } \widehat{y}_t \\
&\widehat{r}_t = (\eta_{ya}\widehat{a}_t + \eta_{yk}\widehat{k}_t) - \widehat{k}_t) \\
&\widehat{r}_t = (\eta_{yk} - 1)\widehat{k}_t + \eta_{ya}\widehat{a}_t \\
&\widehat{r}_t = \eta_{rk}\widehat{k}_t + \eta_{ra}\widehat{a}_t
\end{aligned} \tag{5.102}$$

Table 5.8 mentions the solution (policy and state functions) of the log-linear system of equations.

Table 5.8 Policy and state functions

Solution	Coefficients	
$\widehat{k}_t = \eta_{kk}\widehat{k}_t + \eta_{ka}\widehat{a}_t$	$\eta_{kk_{1,2}} = \frac{-b\pm\sqrt{b^2-4ac}}{2a}$	$\eta_{ka} = \frac{\phi n_2+\frac{m_2}{m_4}(1-\phi n_1)}{\frac{m_5}{m_4}(1-\phi n_1)+n_1\eta_{ck}+n_3}$
$\widehat{c}_t = \eta_{ck}\widehat{k}_t + \eta_{ca}\widehat{a}_t$	$\eta_{ck} = \frac{1}{m_4}(m_3 - m_5\eta_{kk})$	$\eta_{ca} = \frac{1}{m_4}(m_2 - m_5\eta_{ka})$
$\widehat{y}_t = \eta_{yk}\widehat{k}_t + \eta_{ya}\widehat{a}_t$	$\eta_{yk} = \left[\frac{1+m_1}{m_1+\alpha}\right](\alpha - \frac{1-\alpha}{1+m_1}\eta_{ck})$	$\eta_{ya} = \left[\frac{1+m_1}{m_1+\alpha}\right](1 - \frac{1-\alpha}{1+m_1}\eta_{ca})$
$\widehat{h}_t = \eta_{hk}\widehat{k}_t + \eta_{ha}\widehat{a}_t$	$\eta_{hk} = \left(\frac{\eta_{yk}-\eta_{ck}}{1+m_1}\right)$	$\eta_{ha} = \left(\frac{\eta_{ya}-\eta_{ca}}{1+m_1}\right)$
$\widehat{w}_t = \eta_{wk}\widehat{k}_t + \eta_{wa}\widehat{a}_t$	$\eta_{wk} = \eta_{yk} - \eta_{hk}$	$\eta_{wa} = \eta_{ya} - \eta_{ha}$
$\widehat{i}_t = \eta_{ik}\widehat{k}_t + \eta_{ia}\widehat{a}_t$	$\eta_{ik} = \frac{y_{ss}}{i_{ss}}(\eta_{yk} - \frac{c_{ss}}{y_{ss}}\eta_{ck})$	$\eta_{ia} = \frac{y_{ss}}{i_{ss}}(\eta_{ya} - \frac{c_{ss}}{y_{ss}}\eta_{ca})$
$\widehat{r}_t = \eta_{rk}\widehat{k}_t + \eta_{ra}\widehat{a}_t$	$\eta_{rk} = \eta_{yk} - 1$	$\eta_{ra} = \eta_{ya}$

Table 5.9 Policy and state functions (from Dynare)

	cc	ii	yy	kk	hh	rr	ww	aa
Constant	−0.1718	−1.5471	0.0535	2.1418	−0.9890	−3.1879	0.6376	0
kk(−1)	0.5205	−1.6972	0.0730	0.9326	−0.3898	−0.9270	0.4628	0
aa(−1)	0.4698	6.1500	1.6159	0.1538	0.9983	1.6159	0.6176	0.95
e	0.4945	6.4737	1.7009	0.1618	1.0508	1.7009	0.6501	1

Note: The results are taken from "Campbell_Lvariable_Dynare_nolineal_log5.mod"

5.2.5.2 Solution Obtained from Dynare

The nonlinear system of equations described in Table 5.2 has been placed in the .mod file "Campbell_Lvariable_Dynare_nolinear_log5." This file, which contains the model, has two characteristics that are worth commenting on: the first is that the variables are in logarithms. The objective of this is that when Dynare linearizes the system, the variable appears in log deviations; that is, $\widehat{x}_t = lnx_t - lnx_{ss}$. It is worth mentioning that under this variable type, Dynare will display the solution (state and policy function) and the impulse-response function in terms of $\widehat{x}_t$. The second feature is that the model written to this file is nonlinear and Dynare has been asked to linearize the system via the "order = 1" command in "stoch_simul." Table 5.9 shows the solution of the model as it is provided by Dynare on the Matlab screen.

To correctly read Table 5.9, the following considerations must be taken into account. First, each column represents the policy function of the header variable. For example, the second column is the consumption policy function, the third column is the investment policy function, and so on. Note that the fourth column is the equation of state.

Second, the endogenous variables in the header of Table 5.9 are expressed in logarithms. For example, the consumption cc is equal to $\ln c_t$, and in the same way

Table 5.10 Policy and state functions (xx = logx)

	$ln(c_t)$	$ln(i_t)$	$ln(y_t)$	$ln(k_{t+1})$	$ln(h_t)$	$ln(r_t)$	$ln(w_t)$	$ln(a_t)$
constant	−0.1718	−1.5471	0.0535	2.1418	−0.9890	−3.1879	0.6376	0
$\widehat{k}_t$	0.5205	−1.6972	0.0730	0.9326	−0.3898	−0.9270	0.4628	0
$\widehat{a}_{t-1}$	0.4698	6.1500	1.6159	0.1538	0.9983	1.6159	0.6176	0.95
e_t	0.4945	6.4737	1.7009	0.1618	1.0508	1.7009	0.6501	1

Note: The results have been obtained from "Campbell_Lvariable_nonlinear_log5.mod"

for the product, $yy = \ln y_t$. In the case of capital "kk," this is equal to the logarithm of the capital at "t+1"; that is, $kk = \ln k_{t+1}$. This is because in the .mod file the capital in "t" has been written as $kk(-1)$; otherwise, Dynare would understand that this variable is a control variable when in fact it is a state variable.

Third, the "constant" in the second row of Table 5.9 represents the logarithm of each of the variables at a steady state. For example, in the consumption equation, we have $-0.1718 = lnc_{ss}$, which in turn allows us to find the steady state of the variable in levels: $c_{ss} = e^{-0.1718} = 0.8421$. Fourth, in the first column of the same table is the state variable and the exogenous variable. The variable $kk(-1)$ is equal to $\widehat{k}_t = lnk_t - lnk_{ss}$; furthermore, $aa(-1) = \widehat{a}_{t-1} = lna_{t-1} - lna_{ss}$ and e represents the shock of productivity ϵ_t. With all these considerations, Table 5.9 is reexpressed, whose results are shown in Table 5.10.

Table 5.10 describes the solution of the log-linear system. The equations are read as follows. For example, in the case of consumption, we have

$$ln(c_t) = -0.1718 + 0.5205\widehat{k}_t + 0.4698\widehat{a}_{t-1} + 0.4945e_t \tag{5.103}$$

It can also be expressed like this:

$$\begin{aligned}
ln(c_t) &= -0.1718 + 0.5205\widehat{k}_t + 0.4698\widehat{a}_{t-1} + 0.4945e_t \\
ln(c_t) &= -0.1718 + 0.5205\widehat{k}_t + 0.4945\left(\frac{0.4698}{0.4945}\widehat{a}_{t-1} + e_t\right) \\
ln(c_t) &= -0.1718 + 0.5205\widehat{k}_t + 0.4945(0.95\widehat{a}_{t-1} + e_t) \\
ln(c_t) &= -0.1718 + 0.5205\widehat{k}_t + 0.4945(\widehat{a}_t) \\
ln(c_t) &= -0.1718 + 0.5205\widehat{k}_t + 0.4945\widehat{a}_t \\
ln(c_t) &= -0.1718 + 0.5205\widehat{k}_t + 0.4945\widehat{a}_t
\end{aligned} \tag{5.104}$$

The constant -0.1718 represents the logarithm of the steady-state consumption $ln(c_{ss})$. Considering the latter in Eq. (5.104), we have

$$\begin{aligned}
ln(c_t) &= -0.1718 + 0.5205\widehat{k}_t + 0.4945\widehat{a}_t \\
ln(c_t) &= ln(c_{ss}) + 0.5205\widehat{k}_t + 0.4945\widehat{a}_t
\end{aligned}$$

$$\begin{aligned} ln(c_t) - ln(c_{ss}) &= 0.5205\widehat{k_t} + 0.4945\widehat{a_t} \\ \widehat{c_t} &= 0.5205\widehat{k_t} + 0.4945\widehat{a_t} \end{aligned} \tag{5.105}$$

The coefficients 0.5205 and 0.4945 represent the elasticity of consumption to capital and productivity, respectively. That is, a 1 percent increase in capital causes consumption to increase by 0.5205 percent.

5.3 Model Solution Analysis

5.3.1 *Analysis of the Coefficients of the Solution*

In the analysis of the coefficients of the solution, it is useful to consider that in the generic solution of the model, the state variable $\widehat{k_t}$ represents the state of the economy in "t," while the variable $\widehat{a_t}$ represents the transitory shock ($\phi < 1$) to which the economy could be subjected at "t."

$$\widehat{x_t} = \eta_{xk} \underbrace{\widehat{k_t}}_{\text{State of the economy}} + \eta_{xa} \underbrace{\widehat{a_t}}_{\text{Transitory shock}}$$

5.3.1.1 Effects of δ

The depreciation rate δ has an important role in the behavior of the coefficients of the model solution (policy and state functions). For example, the investment-equity elasticity η_{ik} changes from negative to positive as δ increases. The different values of $\delta \in [0, 1]$ represent different cases. The extreme case is when δ is equal to one, which corresponds to one of the assumptions of the Long and Plosser (1983) model. This assumption indicates that capital fully depreciates in the same period, causing the capital *stock* to become a flow sustained solely by investment. The latter is observed from the law of movement of capital $\widehat{k_{t+1}} = (1 - \delta)\widehat{k_t} + \delta\widehat{i_t}$, which under $\delta = 1$ becomes $\widehat{k_{t+1}} = \widehat{i_t}$.

[A] Effects on Capital

1. The persistence of capital; that is, its stable coefficient (less than 1) η_{kk2} decreases as the depreciation rate increases (see Fig. 5.1). By increasing the rate of depreciation, the *stock* of the next period will be less. The extreme case is exemplified by the model of Long and Plosser (1983), in which $\delta = 1$; in this case, the *stock* of capital is made up of the flow of investment goods, no capital is accumulated from the previous period, and, therefore, the capital is less. All of this results in capital being very poorly autocorrelated, which can be seen in the decreasing value of η_{kk2} as δ becomes stronger. Given that capital accumulation has a transversal role in the optimal response of the representative agent in all

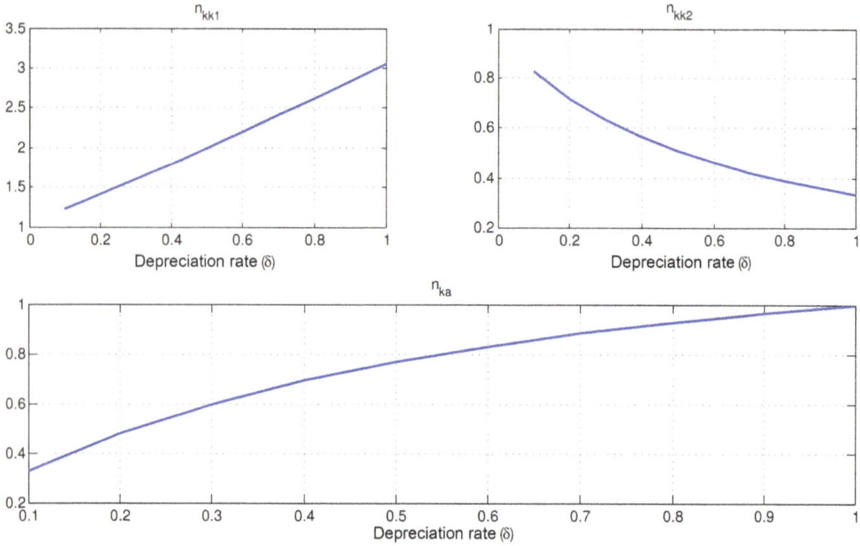

Fig. 5.1 Effects of δ on capital ratios. (**Note:** All the graphs in the "Analysis of the solution coefficients" section are obtained from the *m–file* "Sensitivity_parameters.m")

endogenous variables, then the impact of depreciation will be extended in the decision rule (policy functions) of all variables.

2. The elasticity of capital to productivity η_{ka} becomes stronger as the rate of depreciation increases (see Fig. 5.1). To understand this elasticity, it is important to analyze the law of movement of capital: $\widehat{k}_{t+1} = (1-\delta)\widehat{k}_t + \delta\widehat{i}_t$. This equation suggests that tomorrow's capital is affected by today's *stock* of capital and by investment: each weighted by $(1-\delta)$ and δ. Between these two variables, investment is the one that reacts to a shock of productivity in "t": an increase in $\widehat{a}_t$ raises investment $\widehat{i}_t$, whose elasticity is greater than one (see Fig. 5.2). Therefore, an increase in productivity raises capital by "t+1" through investment; that is, the η_{ka} is positive. On the other hand, an increase in depreciation strengthens the impact of investment on capital at "t+1" ($\widehat{k}_{t+1} = (1-\delta)\widehat{k}_t + \delta\widehat{i}_t$), which suggests that η_{ka} gets stronger as δ increases.

[B] Effects on Consumption and Investment

1. The elasticity of **consumption** to capital η_{ck} decreases as the depreciation rate increases (see Fig. 5.2). In the context of a low depreciation rate, η_{ck} is high because the agent responds by reducing its investment (η_{ik} negative), thus leaving resources for consumption; that is, the representative agent finds it optimal to reduce his/her investment and increase his/her consumption when depreciation is low. However, as δ increases, η_{ck} weakens because the representative agent is willing to allocate more resources to investment because capital depreciates rapidly.

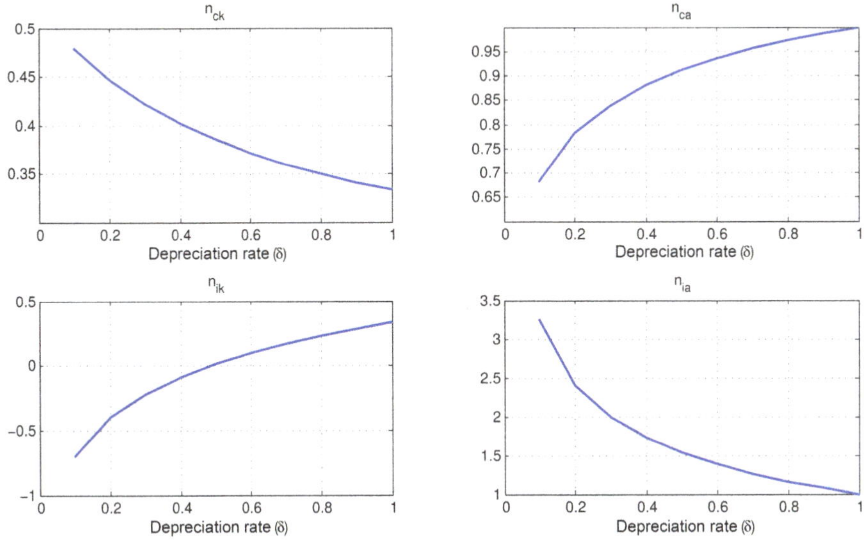

Fig. 5.2 Effects of δ on the coefficients of consumption and investment

2. The elasticity of **investment** to capital η_{ik} changes from negative to positive as the depreciation rate increases (see Fig. 5.2). If the depreciation is small, then not much investment is needed to significantly increase the capital, so the representative agent finds it optimal to reduce his/her investment in the face of an increase in the *stock* of capital in "t," which is reflected in a negative elasticity. However, as δ increases, more investment is required to replace depreciated capital and increase the *stock* of capital, which is reflected in a strengthening of said elasticity η_{ik}. Moreover, this elasticity, which is negative for low levels of depreciation, becomes positive from approximately $\delta = 0.5$.
3. The elasticity of **consumption** to productivity η_{ca} becomes stronger as the depreciation rate increases (see Fig. 5.2). On the other hand, it is observed that the elasticity of **investment** with respect to productivity η_{ia} weakens as the depreciation rate increases (see Fig. 5.2). For small levels of the depreciation rate, the representative agent's response to a transitory shock $\widehat{a}_t$ is to respond strongly in saving (investment) and let consumption react weakly. This is reflected in the high values of η_{ia} and low values of η_{ca} for small values of δ. This makes sense with the theory of the consumer that indicates that the agent prefers to smooth consumption before transient *shocks*. On the other hand, it is observed that a higher depreciation rate encourages the representative agent to allocate the wealth effect, produced by the productivity shock, to increase consumption and reduce investment. This is reflected in the strengthening of η_{ca} and the weakening of η_{ia}. It is worth mentioning that η_{ia} has more volatility than η_{ca}. For values of $\delta \in [0.025 - 1]$, η_{ia} takes values from $[6.47 - 1]$; instead, η_{ca} has more bounded values $[0.49 - 1]$ for the same range of values of δ.

[C] Effects on the Product and the Interest Rate

1. The elasticity of **output** against capital η_{yk} becomes stronger as the depreciation rate increases (see Fig. 5.3). An increase in capital, if we keep labor fixed, increases output through the production function ($\widehat{y}_t = \widehat{a}_t + \alpha\widehat{k}_t + (1 - alpha)\widehat{h}_t$) regardless of the value of δ; which is reflected in the positive sign of η_{yk}. In addition, a higher rate of depreciation reduces the *stock* of capital and, therefore, increases the marginal productivity of capital (due to its decreasing nature in physical capital), which is reflected in the increase in the product-capital elasticity η_{yk} as δ grows (and capital decreases).
2. The elasticity of **output** to productivity η_{ya} weakens as the depreciation rate increases (see Fig. 5.3). The shock of productivity increases output through the production function, which is reflected in the positive sign of η_{ya}. However, this elasticity decreases as δ increases because the increase in depreciation reduces the *stock* of capital, which partially mitigates the effect of productivity. Then, the shock of productivity will have less effect on output as the *stock* of capital is reduced or, equivalently, as δ is increased.
3. The elasticity of the **interest rate** to capital η_{rk} is negative for any value of the depreciation rate and decreases as δ increases (see Fig. 5.3). The sign of this elasticity reflects the demand for capital (negative slope with respect to capital), and the values of this elasticity reflect the equilibrium of the capital market. The correct way to read the values of η_{rk} is as follows: for low values of δ, an increase in the supply of capital (vertical) produces a reduction in the interest rate (provided that keep the demand for capital unchanged). In this scenario, the magnitude of the supply expansion (small or significant) does not matter; in

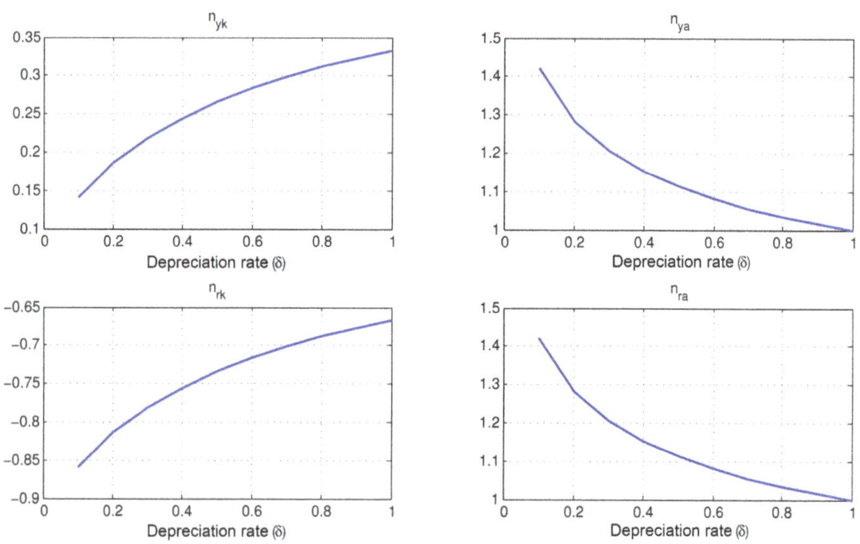

Fig. 5.3 Effects of δ on the product and interest rate coefficients

any case, the interest rate will always be reduced. The latter indicates that the interest rate elasticity – capital η_{rk} has a negative sign. On the other hand, if the rate of depreciation is small, then the expansion of the capital supply will be significant, so it will induce a significant reduction in the interest rate, and this will be reflected in an interest rate elasticity: big capital. However, if the depreciation rate is very high, then the expansion of the capital supply will be small, and, therefore, the interest rate will fall little. This analysis is reflected in the decreasing behavior of η_{rk} before increases of δ.

4. The elasticity of the **interest rate** to productivity η_{ra} weakens as the depreciation rate increases (see Fig. 5.3). In this case, the shock of productivity affects the demand for capital (but not the supply of capital). An increase in productivity encourages the demand for capital and, therefore, increases the real interest rate; that is, the elasticity of the interest rate to productivity η_{ra} is positive as shown in Fig. 5.3 regardless of the value of δ. However, the magnitude of this elasticity depends on the value of δ. When the depreciation rate increases, it reduces the *stock* of capital by "t," which reduces production in that same period and, therefore, causes the demand for capital to contract ($\widehat{r_t} = \widehat{y_t} - \widehat{k_t}$), which partially mitigates the productivity effect. Therefore, the value of η_{ra}, although it remains positive, decreases as δ increases.

[D] Effects on Labor and Wages

1. The elasticity of **labor** to capital η_{hk} is negative and converges to zero as the depreciation rate increases (see Fig. 5.4). The sign of this elasticity is obtained from the following analysis: an increase in capital produces an income effect (which is reflected in the budgetary restriction of the household). Said income effect allows the household to increase its leisure consumption and, thus, reduce its labor supply. As a result, it is observed that an increase in capital entails a reduction in labor via the wealth effect. This inverse relationship is observed in the sign of η_{hk}. On the other hand, if the depreciation rate increases, then the capital *stock* will be smaller and, therefore, the wealth effect will be smaller. Given a weakened wealth effect, then leisure expands but to a lesser extent, and labor supply shrinks to a lesser extent. The extreme case occurs when the wealth effect is zero because the depreciation is total ($\delta = 1$), which means that leisure and work do not react. This is observed in the behavior of η_{hk}.
2. The elasticity of **real wages** to capital η_{wk} decreases as the depreciation rate increases (see Fig. 5.4). This observation merits two comments: first, an increase in capital increases output and thus expands labor demand ($\widehat{h_t} = \widehat{y_t} - \widehat{w_t}$). Under an invariant labor supply, the increase in the demand for labor raises the real wage. Then, it can be deduced that an increase in capital induces an increase in real wages; that is, the real wage-capital elasticity η_{wk} is positive, as can be seen in Fig. 5.4. Second, the depreciation rate influences the *stock* of capital and, consequently, the real wage-capital elasticity η_{wk}. The increase in capital with a higher δ will induce that increase to be smaller and, then, the demand will expand, but to a lesser extent. As a result, the real wage increases but is not as

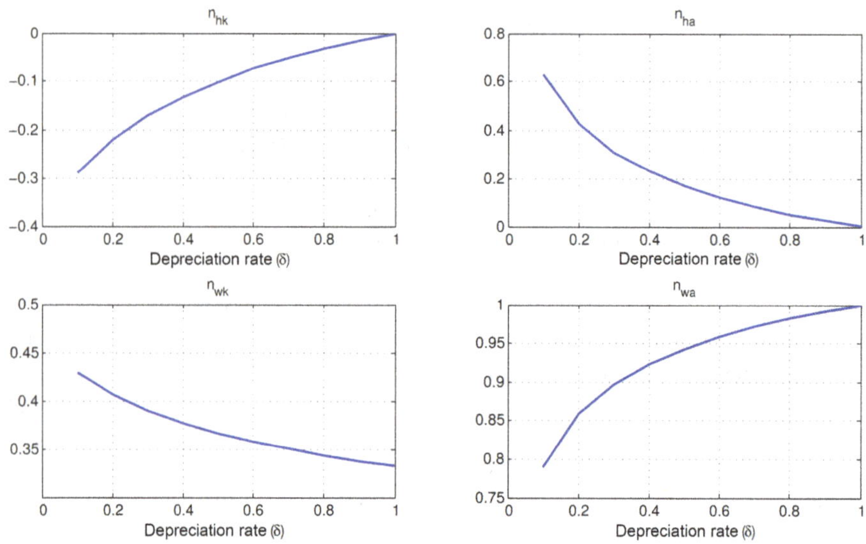

Fig. 5.4 Effects of δ on the labor and salary coefficients

strong as before, which suggests that the real wage-capital elasticity η_{wk} remains positive, but smaller.

3. The elasticity of the **real wage** to productivity η_{wa} becomes stronger as the depreciation rate increases (see Fig. 5.4). Furthermore, the elasticity of **labor** against productivity η_{ha} is positive and converges to zero as the depreciation rate increases (see Fig. 5.4). Productivity shock directly affects labor demand and indirectly labor supply. For a given level of depreciation, it is observed that the shock of productivity increases the demand for labor, and through the increase in consumption, the supply of labor contracts. The result is that equilibrium labor and real wages increase. In this scenario, an increase in depreciation will induce higher consumption because investment is reduced by the increase in depreciation. This additional increase in consumption reduces the labor supply, increases the real wage a little more, and reduces labor. In this new equilibrium, the real wage is higher, and the work is greater than the initial one, but to a lesser extent. In other words, the wage-productivity elasticity has increased, but the labor-productivity elasticity has decreased with a higher depreciation rate.

5.3.1.2 Effects of γ_n

The Frisch elasticity of labor supply ($1/\gamma_n$), also known as the intertemporal elasticity of labor substitution, plays an important role in the transmission of the shock of productivity. As can be seen in Fig. 5.5, the more elastic supply is, then the productivity shock that expands labor demand affects labor to a greater extent and

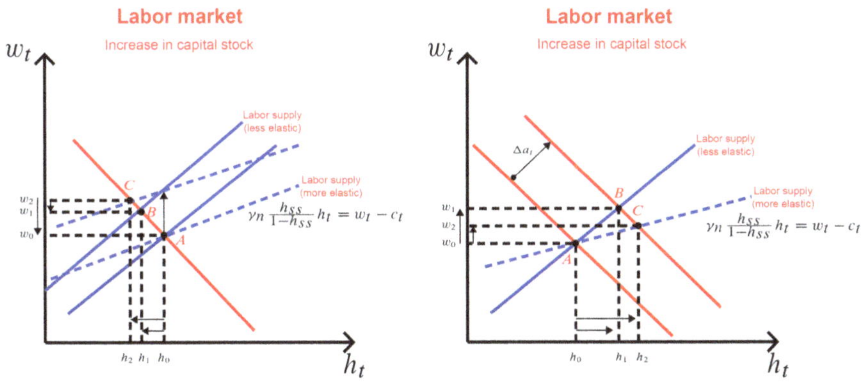

Fig. 5.5 Elasticity of labor supply

to a lesser extent labor: real wage (see Fig. 5.5, graph on the right). This is important because it allows obtaining greater volatility of work compared to salary, which is supported by the data.

This section analyzes the importance of γ_n in the behavior of the coefficients of the policy and state functions. It is worth mentioning that to read the graphs correctly, it is considered that as the horizontal axis approaches zero, the Frisch elasticity increases.

[A] Effects on Work and Salary

1. The elasticity of **labor** to capital η_{hk} is negative and increases as labor supply becomes more elastic (see Fig. 5.6). Furthermore, the elasticity of **real wages** to capital η_{hk} is positive and increases as labor supply becomes more elastic (see Fig. 5.6). As mentioned in previous paragraphs, an increase in capital produces a wealth effect, through an increase in household income, which makes it possible to increase leisure consumption and, as a consequence, reduce labor supply. This reduction, considering that the demand for labor does not move, produces a rise in the real wage and a reduction in employment. Both effects are reflected in the negative sign of η_{hk} and in the positive sign of η_{wk}. In the event that the labor supply is more elastic, then the same increase in capital generates the new equilibrium reflects a greater increase in real wages and a greater reduction in employment; that is, η_{wk} and η_{wk} become stronger as elasticity increases. This is because the consumer is more willing to substitute work today for tomorrow. This arrangement causes tomorrow's leisure to be traded off for more today's leisure and, therefore, a greater reduction in hours worked today (see Fig. 5.5, the graph on the left).
2. The elasticity of **labor** with respect to productivity η_{ha} is positive and increases as labor supply becomes more elastic (see Fig. 5.6). In addition, the elasticity of **real wages** with respect to productivity η_{ha} is positive and decreases as labor supply becomes more elastic (see Fig. 5.6). A temporary increase in productivity directly affects labor demand upward. This expansion is reflected in an increase

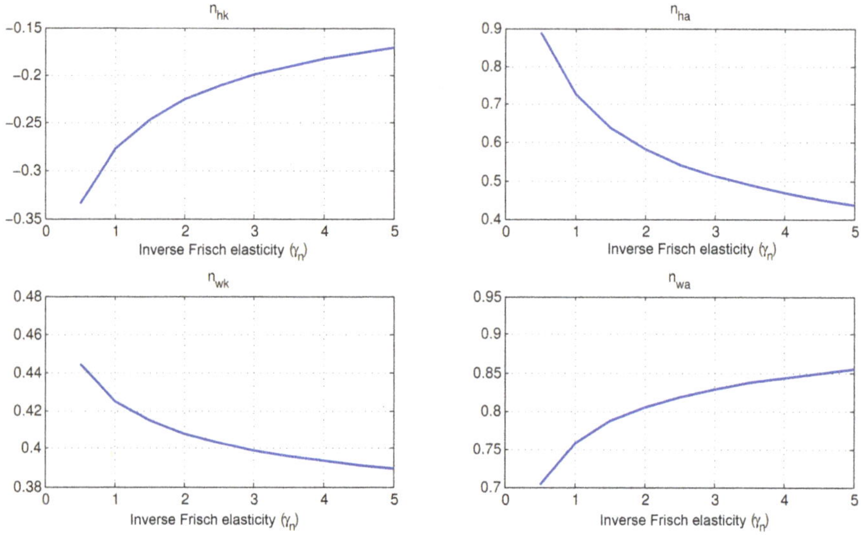

Fig. 5.6 Effects of γ_n on the labor and salary coefficients

in real wages and employment, which justifies the positive sign of η_{ha} and η_{wa}. However, the elasticity of labor supply controls the magnitude of η_{ha} and η_{wa}. In the scenario where the labor supply is very elastic, an increase in productivity will produce that, in the new equilibrium, labor reacts more strongly than wages. This is because households are much more willing to sacrifice leisure today if its price increases ($\uparrow \widehat{w}_t$); therefore, under high elasticity, the household strongly reduces its leisure and strongly increases its number of hours worked (see Fig. 5.5, the graph on the right).

[B] Effects on Consumption and Investment

1. The elasticity of **consumption** to capital η_{ck} is positive and weakens as labor supply becomes more elastic (see Fig. 5.7). An increase in the *stock* of capital in the economy causes households to increase their income by renting capital $(\widehat{r_t k_t})$; on the other hand, the supply of goods is increased by means of the production function. This increase in income leads the household to increase consumption, which is observed in the positive sign of η_{ck}. Also, the magnitude of η_{ck} is affected by the elasticity of labor supply. The increase in capital induces the household to reduce its level of hours worked, which negatively affects income. This effect partially mitigates the initial effect of the capital increase. The stronger the elasticity of labor supply, the stronger will be the reduction in income on the labor side and, therefore, will mitigate the initial increase in capital to a greater extent. The result will be that the consumption-capital elasticity will be lower as γ_n is stronger, as can be seen in Fig. 5.7.

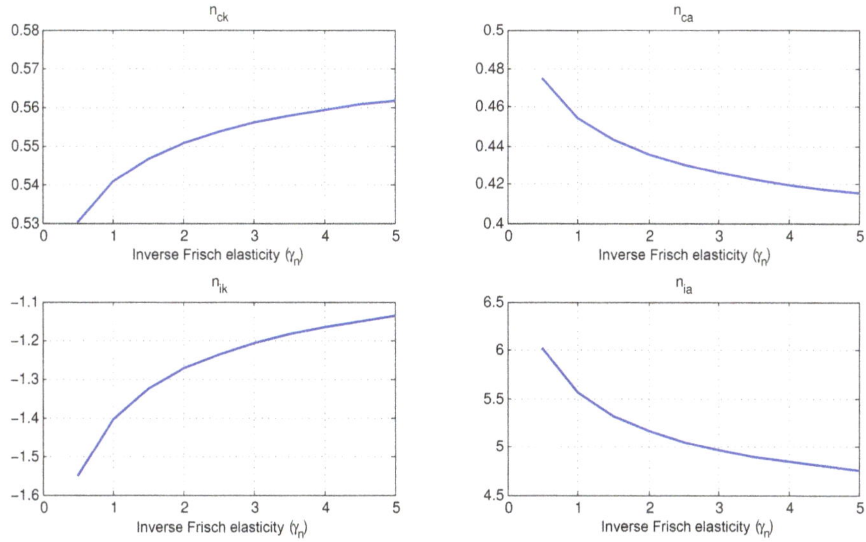

Fig. 5.7 Effects of γ_n on the coefficients of consumption and investment

2. The elasticity of **investment** to capital η_{ik} is negative and becomes stronger as labor supply becomes more elastic (see Fig. 5.7). In the law of movement of capital, there are two control variables: $\widehat{k}_{t+1}$ and $\widehat{i}_t$. Usually, in the optimization, one of these two variables is eliminated since they depend on each other. The law of motion of capital is usually written as $\widehat{k}_{t+1} = (1-\delta)\widehat{k}_t + \delta\widehat{i}_t$; however, this equation can be rewritten as follows: $\delta\widehat{i}_t = \widehat{k}_{t+1} - (1-\delta)\widehat{k}_t$. Under this last form, it is observed that an increase in the *stock* of capital $\widehat{k}_t$ encourages the household to reduce its investment. The greater the elasticity of labor supply, an increase in the *stock* of capital today increases the stock of tomorrow to a lesser extent, which is observed in the behavior of η_{kk}. This effect encourages investment to weaken; thus, as γ_n decreases, η_{ik} becomes stronger.
3. The productivity elasticities of **consumption** η_{ca} and **investment** η_{ia} are positive and become stronger as labor supply becomes more elastic (see Fig. 5.7). A shock of productivity generates a wealth effect, which is oriented toward consumption and savings. As mentioned in the analysis of δ, the representative household finds it optimal to smooth its consumption in the face of transitory *shocks* and transfer a large part of its effect to savings (investment). This household behavior causes consumption and investment to increase, but the latter in greater proportion. This is reflected in the positive sign of η_{ca} and η_{ia} and that η_{ia} is greater than η_{ca} for all values of γ_n (as well as for the values of δ). It is worth mentioning that the magnitude of both elasticities is moderated by the elasticity of labor supply $(1/\gamma_n)$. When said elasticity is greater, then the household reduces strongly its leisure today (i.e., more labor) for greater leisure tomorrow in the face of a shock of productivity. This increase in hours worked induces the household to have

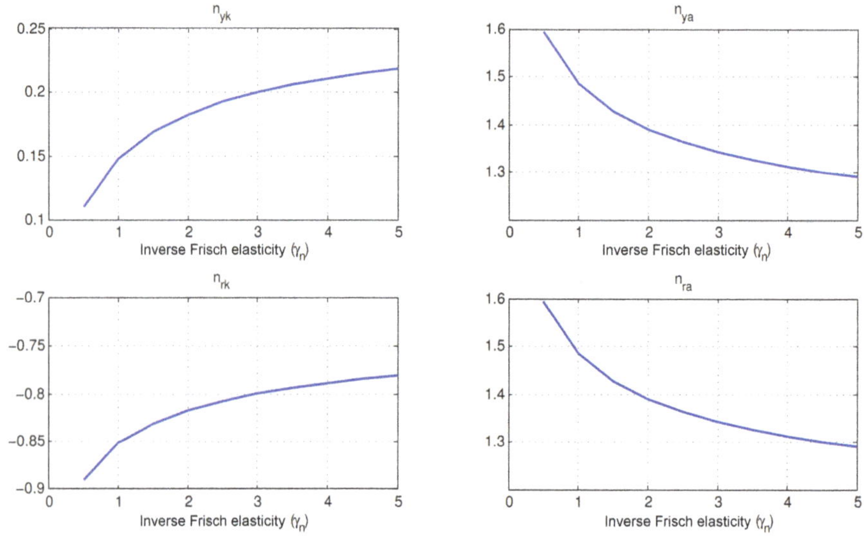

Fig. 5.8 Effects of γ_n on the product and interest rate coefficients

more resources, which are directed to consumption and investment. In the event that the elasticity of labor supply is small, the hours worked will also increase but to a lesser extent, which allows the expansion of consumption and investment to a lesser extent than in the case of a supply elasticity major work.

[C] Effects on Output and the Interest Rate

1. The elasticity of **output** with respect to capital η_{yk} is positive and decreases as labor supply becomes more elastic (see Fig. 5.8). An increase in capital, via the production function, raises output by "t," which is reflected by the positive sign of η_{yk}. On the other hand, the increase in capital raises the income of households, who, feeling more "rich," decide to increase their leisure consumption and reduce their labor supply. This contraction of the labor supply induces a negative effect on the production function, partially mitigating the positive effect of the increase in capital. The magnitude of this negative effect depends on the elasticity of labor supply. If the supply of labor were more elastic, then the equilibrium work would be much less, and, therefore, the negative effect on production would be larger and would more strongly mitigate the initial positive effect of capital. All this is reflected in the fact that η_{yk} would be smaller as the elasticity of labor supply was greater.
2. The elasticity of the **interest rate** with respect to capital η_{rk} is negative and increases as labor supply becomes more elastic (see Fig. 5.8). An increase in the *stock* of capital by "t" means that the supply of capital expands. In this scenario, and under invariant capital demand, the equilibrium interest rate contracts. This behavior is reflected in the negative sign of η_{rk}. A second effect of this increase

in the *stock* of capital is on the demand for capital, which expands by increasing output: capital increases, so it increases output and thus raises the demand for capital. This last movement partially mitigates the initial reduction in the interest rate. One of the parameters that controls the expansion of capital demand is the elasticity of labor supply ($1/\gamma_n$). From the previous paragraph, it is known that η_{yk} is smaller as $1/\gamma_n$ increases. Then, if the elasticity of labor supply is large, the movement in capital demand will be small because η_{yk} is small, and, as a consequence, the mitigating effect on the reduction in the rate of interest will be small. All this indicates that as the elasticity of labor supply is strong, then η_{rk} will also be strong, as can be seen in Fig. 5.8.

3. The elasticity of **output** with respect to productivity η_{ya} is positive and increases as labor supply becomes more elastic (see Fig. 5.8). An increase in productivity parallelly expands the log-linear production function, which suggests the positive sign of η_{ya}. There is an additional effect when considering the elasticity of labor supply γ_n. When the labor supply is more elastic, then the equilibrium number of hours worked is greater than in the case where said supply has less elasticity. This larger increase in labor positively influences the product and thus strengthens η_{ya}.
4. The elasticity of the **interest rate** with respect to productivity η_{ra} is positive and increases as labor supply becomes more elastic (see Fig. 5.8). The positive sign is due to the fact that an increase in productivity stimulates the demand for capital goods, which under a perfectly inelastic supply of capital pushes the real interest rate up. On the other hand, the magnitude of η_{ra} is influenced by γ_n. Under the scenario of a very elastic labor supply, the demand for capital will undergo an additional expansion due to the effect of the increase in labor in the production function. Since γ_n controls this increase in work, then the higher γ_n, the more hours worked, and, therefore, the positive effect on the demand for capital will be greater. This additional movement in the demand for capital further strengthens the increase in the interest rate. Consequently, the higher γ_n, the higher η_{ra}, as shown in Fig. 5.8.

[D] Effects on Capital

1. The elasticity of capital at "t+1" with respect to capital at "t" η_{kk} is positive and decreases as the elasticity of labor supply increases (see Fig. 5.9). From the equation of motion of capital ($\widehat{k_{t+1}} = (1-\delta)\widehat{k_t} + \delta\widehat{i_t}$), it follows that an increase in capital of today can influence capital of tomorrow in two ways: first, directly $(1-\delta)\widehat{k_t}$ and, second, indirectly through investment $\delta\widehat{i_t}$. The effect of this second element on the capital of tomorrow is conditioned to the value of the elasticity of labor supply. As is known from Fig. 5.7, η_{ik} is negative and gets stronger as $1/\gamma_n$ increases. In this scenario, it can be seen that with an increase in the *stock* of capital, the effect of the investment on $\widehat{k_{t+1}}$ partially mitigates the positive effect of $\widehat{k_t}$. Based on all of the above, as $1/\gamma_n$ gets stronger, η_{kk} gets weaker.
2. The elasticity of capital at "t+1" with respect to productivity at "t" η_{ka} is positive and strengthens as the elasticity of labor supply increases (see Fig. 5.9). Productivity shock has a positive impact on investment, as shown in Fig. 5.7, which in turn influences $\widehat{k_{t+1}}$ through the equation of movement of capital.

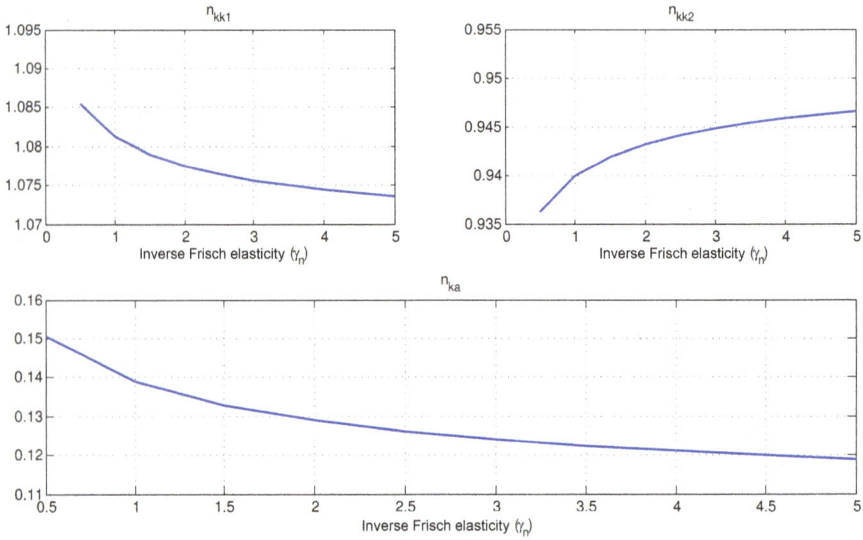

Fig. 5.9 Effects of γ_n on capital coefficients

Figure 5.7 suggests that η_{ia} gets stronger as the elasticity of labor supply increases. Since the investment directly affects tomorrow's capital, then the same behavior of η_{ia} carries over to η_{ka}.

5.3.1.3 Effects of ϕ

The persistence of the productivity shock ϕ is important in the temporary survival of the effects of the initial shock. Given the nature of productivity, which behaves like an AR(1): $\widehat{a}_t = \phi\widehat{a}_{t-1} + \epsilon_t$, high persistence allows $\widehat{a}_t$ remains above its steady state longer, if the shock is positive, which affects the economy longer. There are two extreme cases: on the one hand, persistence equal to zero, which indicates that the shock only lives for one period; on the other hand, persistence equal to one, which indicates that the shock is permanent; that is, the effect of the shock is maintained in all periods. In this section, the effects of persistence on the elasticities of the solution are analyzed considering that the shock is temporary, that is, that $\phi \in [0, 1[$.

One of the first conclusions that emerges from Figs. 5.10, 5.11, 5.12, and 5.13 is that persistence does not affect the elasticities associated with the *stock* of capital $\widehat{k}_t$. For example, η_{kk}, η_{ck}, and η_{ik} remain invariant across values of ϕ. This is because persistence only affects the behavior of productivity, and, therefore, it is expected that this parameter influences the coefficients of the solution associated with productivity $\widehat{a}_t$. For example, η_{ka}, η_{ca}, and η_{ia} show sensitivity to different persistence values.

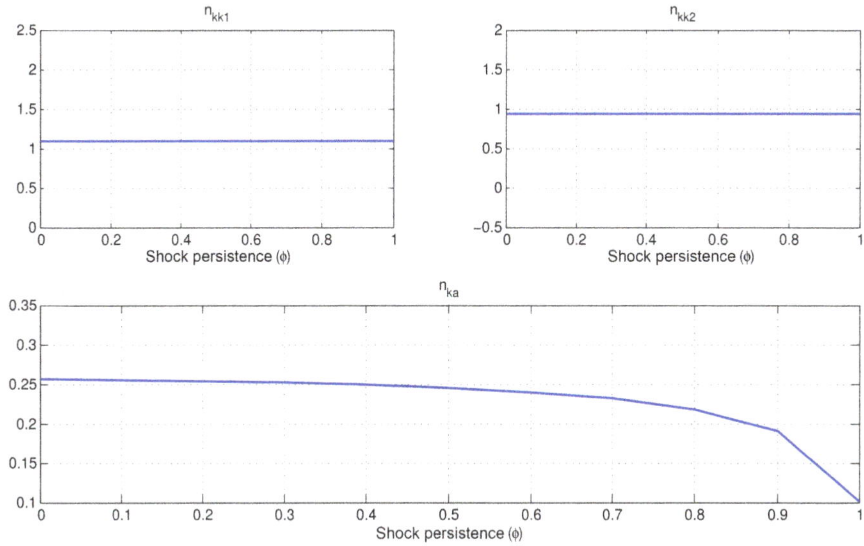

Fig. 5.10 Effects of ϕ on capital coefficients

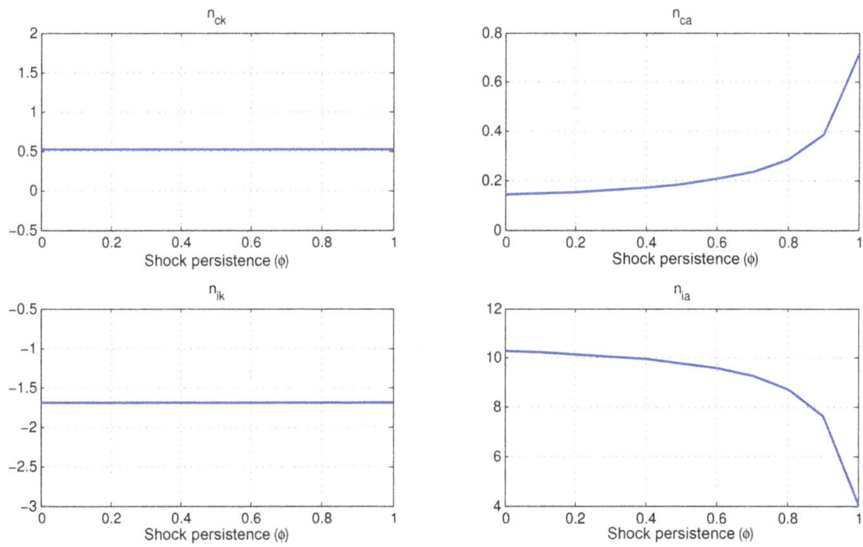

Fig. 5.11 Effects of ϕ on the consumption and investment coefficients

[A] Effects on capital

1. The elasticity of **capital** at "t+1" with respect to productivity η_{ka} is positive and decreases as productivity persistence increases (see Fig. 5.10). A shock of productivity, then, positively influences $\widehat{k}_{t+1}$ through investment. Since productivity shock produces a wealth effect, the representative household decides to increase

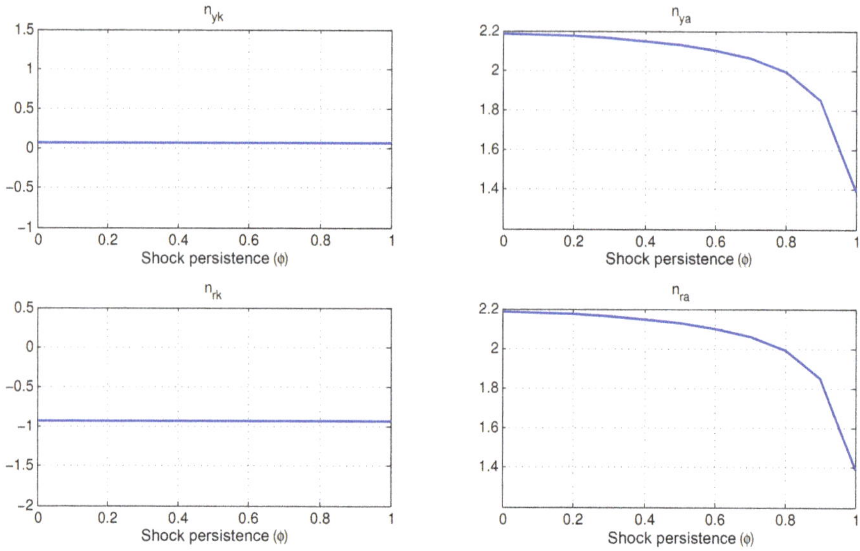

Fig. 5.12 Effects of ϕ on the product and interest rate coefficients

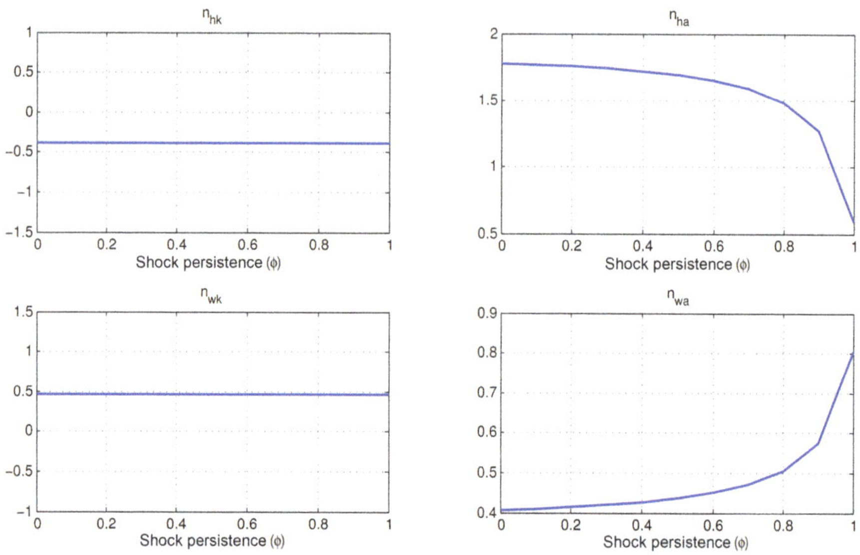

Fig. 5.13 Effects of ϕ on the labor and salary coefficients

consumption and investment, which increases tomorrow's capital. That is why the sign of η_{ka} is positive. On the other hand, the household feels that the shock is more "permanent" as persistence approaches one and consequently decides to increase its consumption more than its investment, which is observed in Fig. 5.11.

This smaller and smaller increase in investment as persistence strengthens causes tomorrow's capital to increase, but under the same pattern, that is, less and less as persistence increases. This behavior is observed in η_{ka}.

[B] Effects on Consumption and Investment

1. The elasticity of **consumption** with respect to productivity η_{ca} is positive and increases as the persistence of productivity increases (see Fig. 5.11). On the contrary, the elasticity of **investment** with respect to productivity η_{ia} is decreasing, although positive as η_{ca} (Fig. 5.11). The shock of productivity produces a wealth effect in the household. This effect is due to the fact that the demand for capital and the demand for labor increase, and, since the household receives income from both factors, then its income level rises. This higher income is destined for consumption and investment, which increase. That is why the elasticities η_{ca} and η_{ia} have the same positive sign. Also, the magnitude of those is influenced by the value of ϕ. As ϕ approaches one, the household perceives that the shock of productivity is more "permanent"; that is, its effects are maintained over time. In this scenario, the household finds it optimal to direct more resources to consumption than to investment because its income pattern has changed almost permanently. Therefore, the elasticity of consumption is high when the persistence of the shock is high, while the elasticity of investment is low in this same scenario. In the event that persistence tends to zero, that is, if the shock lasts only one period and its effects are "temporary," then the household will find it optimal to direct resources to savings (investment) in order to smooth consumption. Therefore, in this scenario, it is observed that the elasticity of consumption is low, while the elasticity of investment is high.

[C] Effects on the Product and Interest Rate

1. The elasticity of **output** with respect to productivity η_{ya} is positive and decreases as productivity persistence increases (see Fig. 5.12). The shock of productivity affects production directly by $\widehat{a}_t$ and indirectly by labor $\widehat{h}_t$. This is observed in the functional form of the production: $\widehat{y}_t = \widehat{a}_t + \alpha \widehat{k}_t + (1-\alpha)\widehat{h}_t$. To understand how ϕ influences η_{ya}, it is necessary to analyze how the work responds to this parameter. It is known, according to Fig. 5.13, that a greater persistence of the shock of productivity induces the household to increase their leisure and reduce work because they feel that productivity has permanent effects. So, as ϕ increases, the household increases its work in the face of a productivity shock, but to a lesser extent. Therefore, as persistence increases, the product increases, but to a lesser extent because work also increases to a lesser extent.
2. The elasticity of the **interest rate** with respect to productivity η_{ya} is positive and decreases as productivity persistence increases (see Fig. 5.12). The productivity shock raises the demand for capital and, under an inelastic supply of capital, increases the equilibrium interest rate. Since capital demand $\widehat{r}_t = \widehat{y}_t - \widehat{k}_t$ depends on output, then the pattern of output movement in the face of productivity shock is fully transferred to the behavior of demand. For example, the previous paragraph indicates that η_{ya} is decreasing as the persistence of productivity increases. This behavior is transferred to the demand for capital which, together

with the supply of capital, allows the interest rate-productivity elasticity to also decrease in ϕ.

[D] Effects on Work and Salary

1. The elasticity of **labor** with respect to productivity is positive and decreases as the persistence of productivity increases (Fig. 5.13). In addition, the elasticity of **salary** with respect to productivity is positive and strengthens as the persistence of productivity increases (see Fig. 5.13). Productivity shock has two effects on the labor market: the first is directly on demand, which expands, and the second goes indirectly on the supply by means of the increase of consumption. On the one hand, demand expands, and, on the other hand, supply contracts.

5.3.2 Impulse-Response Functions

The impulse-response function is the reaction of the endogenous variables to a shock. This reaction has a magnitude and a lifetime. It is worth mentioning that each element of the impulse-response function represents an equilibrium and, therefore, an optimal response of the representative agent. In this section, the shock is considered to be productivity (Fig. 5.14).

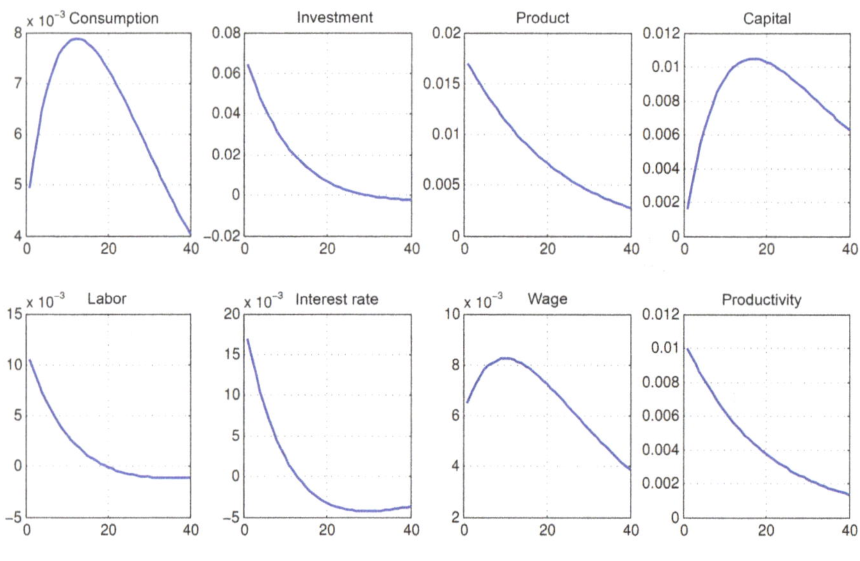

Fig. 5.14 Campbell (1994) with variable work: *productivity shock*. (**Note:** This graph is obtained from the *m–file* "Analisis_sensibilidad_irf.m")

5.3.2.1 How Does the Economy React to a Shock of Productivity?

- The productivity shock occurs at $t = 0$ and in this period ϵ_0 takes the value of its standard deviation $\sigma = 0.763$. This leads to increased productivity ($\uparrow \widehat{a}_t$).
- The increase in productivity has two effects: the first is the increase in the production function $\uparrow \widehat{y}_t = \uparrow \widehat{a}_t + \alpha\widehat{k}_t + (1-\alpha)\widehat{h}_t$ and, the second, the increase in demand in the factor market (of capital and labor).
- In the case of the labor market, the increase in demand raises the real wage and the number of hours of work in equilibrium. It should be noted that as supply is more elastic ($\downarrow \gamma_n$), the impact of the demand movement is greater.
- In the capital goods market, it is observed that the increase in demand is completely transferred to supply. This is because supply is perfectly inelastic (invariant with the interest rate). In addition, this increase in demand raises the interest rate.
- The higher salary ($\uparrow w_t$) and the increase in the interest rate ($\uparrow r_t$) increase the household's income, which leads to increased consumption and investment.

5.3.3 Comparison of the Theoretical Model with the Data

5.3.3.1 Does the Shock Need to be Significant for the Model to Replicate the Data?

The answer to this question a priori is yes. The RBC model generally requires the magnitude of the productivity shock to be significant (around 0.7%). However, this dependence is reduced when the variable use of capital is considered. As King and Rebelo (1999) point out, an RBC model with capital utilization requires a productivity shock of approximately 0.1% to get close to the data. In the following paragraphs, it is described how the magnitude of the shock has implications on the ability of the model to approach the data. In principle, with a shock of 0.4%, the model is very far from the data, while with a shock of 0.7%, the model behaves better, although with certain deficiencies. In addition, it is observed that the correlation of the production with the model's variables and the first-order autocorrelation does not depend on the magnitude of the shock.

Table 5.11 shows three statistics (standard deviation, correlation, and first-order autocorrelation) of the cyclical component of the data and of the model for each variable. The model statistics have been calculated assuming four values of the productivity shock (σ). The idea behind this is to assess whether the model needs a "significant" *shock* to replicate the data. With this in mind, we proceed to describe the conclusions that emerge from this table.

[A] Standard deviation First of all, it is observed that as the shock is stronger (from $\sigma = 0.004$ to 0.015), the standard deviation of the variables increases. For example, the standard deviation of consumption for $\sigma = 0.004$ is equal to 0.31%,

Table 5.11 Comparison of the cyclical behavior of the theoretical model with the empirical data

Variable (x_t)	Standard deviation (%)					Corr(PBI_t, x_t)		Autocorrelation	
	Data	Model				Data	Model	Data	Model
$\sigma =$		0.004	0.007	0.01	0.015		0.004 al 0.015		0.004 al 0.015
Consumption	1.35	0.31	0.54	0.77	1.16	0.88	0.8851	0.80	0.8191
Investment	5.30	3.37	5.9	8.42	12.64	0.80	0.9856	0.87	0.7013
Product	1.81	0.89	1.56	2.22	3.33	1	1	0.84	0.7162
Capital		0.29	0.51	0.73	1.09		0.3915		0.9572
Labor	1.79	0.55	0.96	1.37	2.06	0.88	0.9736	0.88	0.6995
Interest rate	0.30	0.9	1.58	2.26	3.39	-0.35	0.9477	0.60	0.7006
Real wage	0.68	0.38	0.66	0.94	1.41	0.12	0.9423	0.66	0.7826

Nota: The empirical values have been taken from King and Rebelo (1999) and all the variables are in natural logarithms, except the interest rate. The theoretical values have been obtained from a single simulation. These values are obtained from the file "Campbell_Lvariable_nonlinear_log7.mod"

while for $\sigma = 0.015$, it is equal to 1.16%. Second, under a small magnitude of the productivity shock, the model falls far short of what is observed in the data. For $\sigma = 0.004$, the standard deviation of consumption is 0.31%, while the data indicates that said statistic is equal to 1.27%. Similarly, for investment, the model falls short of what is found in the data (3.37% in the model vs. 5.30% in the data). This same behavior is observed in all variables.

Third, the value of $\sigma = 0.007$ has been used by Prescott (1986), a similar value ($\sigma = 0.00712$) by Hansen (1985) and by King and Rebelo (1999) ($\sigma = 0.0072$). Under this magnitude of the shock, the model gets better at approaching the data (compared to $\sigma = 0.004$). For example, the standard deviation of the investment provided by the model is 5.9%, which is closer to the data (5.30%). The same is observed for the product and the real wage. However, the results of the model for consumption, labor, and the interest rate are still far from what was observed. For example, the standard deviation of consumption goes from 0.31% to 0.54% when the shock increases from 0.004 to 0.007, but it is still below the empirical value of 1.35%. The same is observed for work, the model indicates that the standard deviation is 0.96%, while the data suggests that said statistic is equal to 1.79%. Regarding the interest rate, the model strongly overestimates the statistic (1.58% vs 0.30%). Fourth, the value of $\sigma = 0.01$ is considered by Campbell (1994). Under this value, the model overestimates the statistic in four variables: investment, product, interest rate, and real wage. For example, the investment deviation reaches 8.42%, far exceeding what was observed (5.30%). However, it is observed that in consumption and work the model is closer to the data, but still below. For example, the standard deviation of consumption increases from 0.54% to 0.77% when the shock goes from 0.007 to 0.010, but it is even lower than what was observed (1.35%).

Fifth, it is observed that for higher productivity shock ($\sigma = 0.015$), the model results largely overestimate what is found in the data, except for consumption. For example, in the case of investment, the data indicates that its standard deviation is 5.30%, while the model indicates that it is 12.64%. In the same way for the product, since the model suggests that the standard deviation is almost twice that found in the data (3.33% vs. 1.72%). Only in consumption, the model is closer to the data (1.16% in the model vs. 1.35% in the data). Finally, it is important to mention that the impact of the shock on productivity is subject to the values of the parameter of the model.

[B] Correlation with GDP First of all, the correlation of the product with the other variables does not depend on the magnitude of the shock of productivity; therefore, the differences that could be found between what is observed and what is inferred by the model does not correspond to the magnitude of the shock but to the parameterization of the model and the underlying assumptions. Secondly, from Table 5.11, it can be seen that the correlation provided by the model is greater in all the variables with respect to what is suggested by the data. For example, the correlation of output with consumption in the data is 0.88, while the model indicates that it is equal to 0.8851. Similarly for investment, it is 0.80 in the data vs. 0.9856 in the model. This overestimation of the model is observed in the correlation of the product with all the variables.

Third, the data indicate that the interest rate is countercyclical ($corr(y_t, r_t) < 0$); however, the model infers that the interest rate is highly procyclical ($corr(y_t, r_t) = 0.9477$). Fourth, the data suggest that the real wage has a very small correlation with output, although the model suggests that this statistic is very close to one. These two weaknesses of the model in replicating the data are generally transversal to RBC models and represent two main criticisms of this school.

[C] First-order autocorrelation First, first-order autocorrelation, like the correlation of the product with the model variables, does not depend on the magnitude of the productivity shock. Second, the model underestimates the autocorrelation of the product (0.7013 vs. 0.87). This represents one of the main criticisms of the RBC model and has been emphasized by several authors, including Cogley and Nason (1995). Third, the model overestimates the real wage autocorrelation and underestimates the work autocorrelation.

5.3.3.2 Does the Labor Supply Need to Be Very Elastic for the Model to Replicate the Data?

The answer to this question is yes. The RBC model needs a strong transmission mechanism that transfers the effects of the shock to the endogenous variables. In this context, the elasticity of labor supply is positioned as one of the main transmission mechanisms. As can be seen in Tables 5.12 and 5.13, the higher the elasticity of labor supply, the effects of the initial shock are amplified, which influences on the statistics of the model. These statistics are closer to what is observed in the data as labor supply is more elastic. The dependence of the RBC model on the elasticity

Table 5.12 Comparison of the cyclical behavior of the theoretical model with the empirical data

Variable (x_t)	Standard deviation (%)				
	Data	Model			
Frisch elasticity($1/\gamma_n$)=		0.2	1	2	5
Consumption	1.35	0.63	0.7	0.74	0.78
Investment	5.30	6.21	7.25	7.84	8.59
Product	1.81	1.69	1.94	2.08	2.26
Capital		0.54	0.63	0.68	0.74
Work	1.79	0.57	0.95	1.17	1.44
Interest rate	0.30	1.72	1.98	2.12	2.3
Real salary	0.68	1.14	1.04	0.99	0.92

Note: The empirical values have been taken from King and Rebelo (1999) and all the variables are in natural logarithms, except the interest rate. While the theoretical values have been obtained from a single simulation, these values are obtained from the file "Campbell_Lvariable_nonlinear_log8.mod"

Table 5.13 Comparison of the cyclical behavior of the theoretical model with the empirical data

Variable (x_t)	Corr(GDP_t, x_t)					Autocorrelation				
	Datos	Modelo				Datos	Modelo			
$1/\gamma_n$=		0.2	1	2	5		0.2	1	2	5
Consumption	0.88	0.9079	0.897	0.8909	0.8834	0.8	0.8093	0.8142	0.8167	0.8197
Investment	0.8	0.9856	0.9856	0.9856	0.9856	0.87	0.7063	0.704	0.7027	0.7009
Product	1	1	1	1	1	0.84	0.7211	0.7189	0.7176	0.7158
Capital		0.3905	0.3911	0.3913	0.3916		0.9585	0.9579	0.9575	0.9571
Work	0.88	0.973	0.9733	0.9734	0.9736	0.88	0.7045	0.7023	0.7009	0.6991
Interest rate	−0.35	0.9494	0.9485	0.948	0.9476	0.6	0.7054	0.7033	0.702	0.7002
Real salary	0.12	0.9933	0.9776	0.9627	0.9351	0.66	0.7388	0.7553	0.7678	0.7874

Note: The empirical values have been taken from King and Rebelo (1999) and all the variables are in natural logarithms, except the interest rate. The theoretical values have been obtained from a single simulation. These values are obtained from the file "Campbell_Lvariable_nonlinear_log8.mod"

of labor supply was harshly criticized because microeconomic studies indicated that said elasticity is small, which contrasted with what was assumed by the RBC school. However, this criticism was countered by Hansen (1985), who developed an RBC model free from the dependence on a strong elasticity of labor supply. This last model will be studied in detail in the next chapter.

Table 5.12 shows how the standard deviation of each of the variables changes with four Frisch elasticity values, assuming a shock of 0.01. In addition, the statistic obtained from the model is compared with what is observed in the data. The behavior of the standard deviation is described below.

[A] Standard deviation In the first place, it is observed that as labor demand becomes more elastic, the standard deviation of all variables increases, with the exception of real wages, which decreases. Second, the standard deviation of labor and real wages produced by the model gets closer to the data as the elasticity of labor supply increases. For example, the standard deviation of labor goes from 0.57% to 1.44% when the elasticity increases from 0.2 to 5. However, in the case of investment, the model overestimates its standard deviation for all values of said elasticity. The same occurs for the interest rate, where the lowest elasticity value in the table ($\gamma_n = 0.2$) produces a standard deviation of 1.72%, which is well above the observed value (0.30%).

Two additional statistics are described in Table 5.13: the correlation of the product with the model variables and the first-order autocorrelation. Both statistics are important in the behavior of business cycles. Likewise, the calculations derived from the model are compared with the empirical evidence. The objective of this is to evaluate if the greater elasticity of the labor supply strengthens the capacity of the model to replicate the data. The correlation and autocorrelation presented in Table 5.13 are described below.

[B] Correlation with GDP In the first place, the correlation of the product with each one of the variables of the model is higher than that observed in the data. Second, this correlation is closer to the empirical evidence as labor supply is more elastic ($\uparrow 1/\gamma_n$). For example, the data suggest that the correlation of the product with consumption is equal to 0.88, while the model infers that this correlation goes from 0.9097 (with $1/\gamma_n = 0.2$) to 0.8834 (with $1/\gamma_n = 5$).

As a third point, the correlation of output with investment, obtained from the model, is not affected by the elasticity of labor supply. As can be seen in Table 5.13, the correlation of output with investment is 0.9856 for any value of $1/\gamma_n$, which is above the value observed in the data (0.8). Fourth, the elasticity of labor supply has little influence on the correlation between output and labor. This is observed in the fact that as the elasticity increases, this correlation only changes in the fourth decimal place (from 0.9730 to 0.9736).

Fifth, the model vastly overestimates the correlation of output with the interest rate and with the real wage. Regarding the interest rate, it is observed that the model infers that said correlation is always positive and close to 1, that is, highly procyclical. However, the data suggest that the interest rate is countercyclical. Regarding the correlation of the product with the real wage, the model captures the qualitative behavior, but not the quantitative one. The data suggest that this correlation is low (0.12); however, the model (for the four values of $1/\gamma_n$) gives correlations greater than 0.9. It is worth mentioning that the elasticity of the labor supply helps to reduce this correlation, but not enough. For example, for a high elasticity ($1/\gamma_n = 5$), the correlation is 0.9351, which is clearly higher than the observed (0.12).

[C] First-order autocorrelation First, a lower elasticity of labor supply helps the model to obtain an autocorrelation of consumption closer to what is observed. For example, for a Frisch elasticity of 0.2, the consumption autocorrelation derived from the model is 0.8093, a figure very close to the observed figure (0.8). Second, the autocorrelation of investment inferred by the model is lower than what was observed (0.84). In addition, the change in the elasticity of labor supply has a marginal impact on this statistic. For example, said statistic goes from 0.7063 to 0.7009, when the elasticity increases from 0.2 to 5. Moreover, a greater elasticity of labor supply causes said autocorrelation to decrease and move further away from the data.

Third, the autocorrelation of the real wage is the one that most react to changes in the elasticity of labor supply. For example, when the elasticity is reduced from 5 to 0.2, said autocorrelation goes from 0.7874 to 0.7388. However, this last value still remains above what was observed (0.66).

5.4 Summary

In this chapter, we have introduced hours worked as an input to the production function and a household decision variable. The result of this exercise is that we are equipped to study the goods and labor markets simultaneously and to ask whether our RBC model can better replicate the stylized facts on the goods market that we discussed in the previous chapter, as well as replicate the facts stylized values associated with wages and hours worked during the business cycle.

As the student should already know, we proceed to present the behavior of households, firms, and the conditions of equilibrium in the market of goods and factors. Since we first introduce the decision to work, we take a closer look at the Frisch elasticity of labor supply and the intertemporal labor substitution elasticity. Both will play an important role as transmission mechanisms in our model.

Then, we proceed to calibrate the model parameters, adding only the Frisch elasticity value as an additional parameter to calibrate. We proceed to find the steady state and log-linearize the model around it. Finally, we solve the linear system with the method of undetermined coefficients and illustrate how we can obtain such a solution with Dynare.

With our model resolved, we proceed to extensively illustrate how the elasticity parameters of the control variables with respect to the state variables depend on the Frisch elasticity, the depreciation value, and the persistence of the shock of productivity. A central result of this section is that the persistence value of the shock will not affect the coefficients associated with capital.

Next, we study the impulse response functions of our fictitious economy when hit by a shock of productivity. The pattern of responses in the goods market remains similar to that studied in the previous chapter; however, now the labor market shows that the wage FIR is hump shaped and employment has an immediate peak and then falls monotonously.

Finally, we compare the theoretical model with the data. We illustrate that to even come close to replicating the stylized facts of interest, we need the productivity shock to have a significant and persistent value, in addition to requiring a relatively high value of the intertemporal elasticity of labor. If we calibrate the model with these characteristics, we obtain the following: (i) all variables in our model are procyclical, while wages are a-cyclical in the data; (ii) the standard deviations have the correct order in the goods market (investment is more volatile than output and consumption is less volatile than output), but we significantly overpredict interest rate volatility relative to of what is in the data. We also reasonably replicate the volatility in labor and real wages found in the data.

After reading this chapter, the student may feel (healthy) skepticism about the scientific value of RBC models: do capitalist economies exhibit such large quarter-to-quarter fluctuations in productivity as these kinds of models suggest? It is precisely in the face of this skepticism that the literature has developed models with a richer variety of *shocks*, one of which we turn to examine in the next chapter. There we will show how we can reconcile an RBC model that replicates the data with moderate values of the shock of productivity.

5.5 Codes

Table 5.14 describes the Matlab and Dynare codes used in this chapter.

Table 5.14 Codes in Matlab and Dynare

Codes	Description
Matlab	
Campbell_Lvariable.m	This m-file contains [1] calibration, [2] calculation of steady state, and [3] calculation of solution coefficients (undetermined coefficients method)
work_ss.m	The objective is to calculate h_{ss} which is expressed in a nonlinear equation
Analysis_sensitivity_irf.m	This m-file plots: [1A] ESI of consumption, [1B] persistence of the shock, [1C] elasticity of Frisch, [2A] (size) shock productivity, [3A] depreciation rate, [4A] Campbell (1994) vs. Long and Plosser (1983) model, and [4B] model only from Campbell (1994) with variable work
Sensitivity_parametros.m	From this m-file, we obtain the simulation of the coefficients of the solution before δ (depreciation rate), α (share of capital in national income), γ_n (Frisch elasticity inverse), and ϕ (persistence of the shock)
Dynare	
Campbell_Lvariable_nonlinear_log1.mod	Campbell (1994) model with variable work. In addition, sensitivity analyses are performed for [A] ESI of consumption ($1/\gamma$), [B] persistence (ϕ) of the shock of productivity, and [C] Frisch elasticity ($1/\gamma_n$)
Campbell_Lvariable_nonlinear_log2.mod	Campbell (1994) model with variable work and different values of shock productivity (σ)
Campbell_Lvariable_nonlinear_log3.mod	Campbell (1994) model with variable labor and different values of the depreciation rate (δ)
Campbell_Lvariable_nonlinear_log4.mod	Long and Plosser (1983) model with Campbell (1994) calibration
Campbell_Lvariable_nonlinear_log5.mod	It is the same model of Campbell (1994) with variable work of "mod1," which is used to build the policy and state function table of this chapter
Campbell_Lvariable_nonlinear_log7.mod	Campbell (1994) model with variable work. The moments of the cyclic component of the variables (HP filter) are analyzed before different values of the shock (σ)
Campbell_Lvariable_nonlinear_log8.mod	Campbell (1994) model with variable work. The moments of the cyclical component of the variables (HP filter) are analyzed before different values of the Frisch elasticity ($1/\gamma_n$)

Appendix

See Figs. 5.15, 5.16, 5.17, 5.18, 5.19, 5.20.

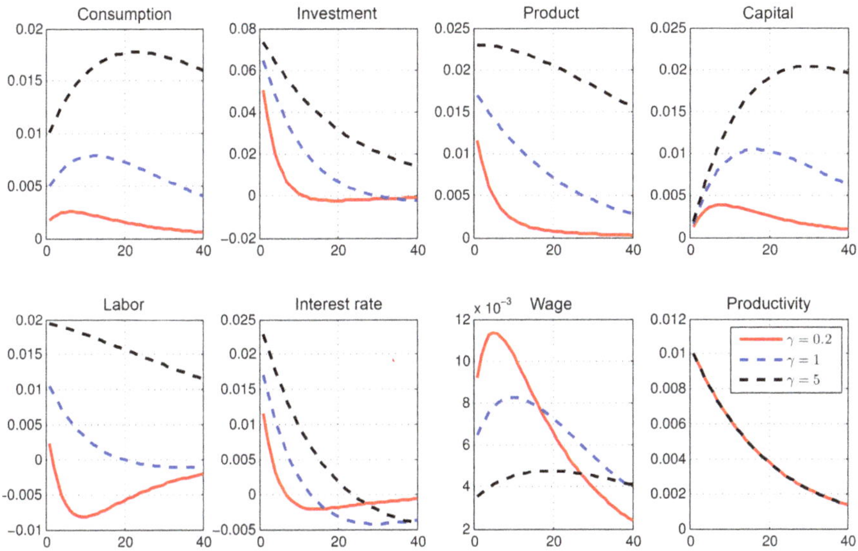

Fig. 5.15 Elasticity of substitution of consumption $(1/\gamma)$

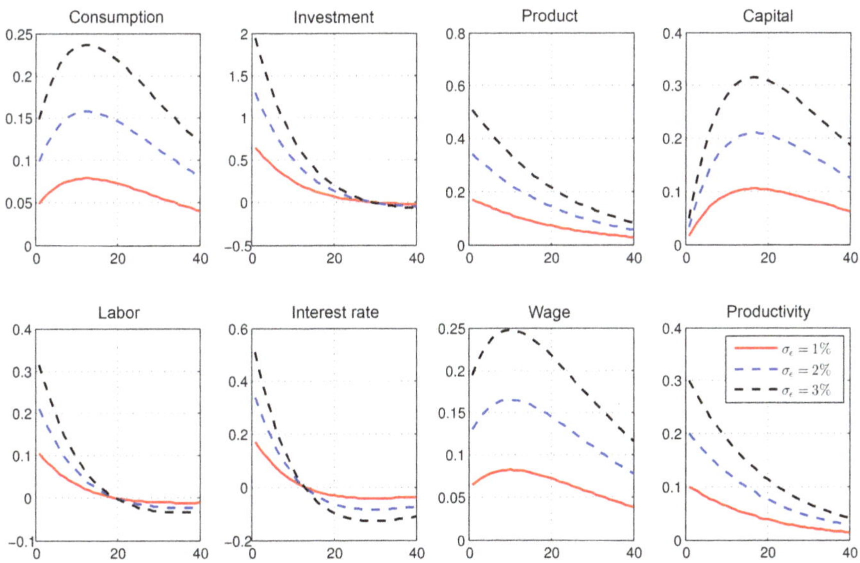

Fig. 5.16 Size (σ_ϵ) of productivity shock

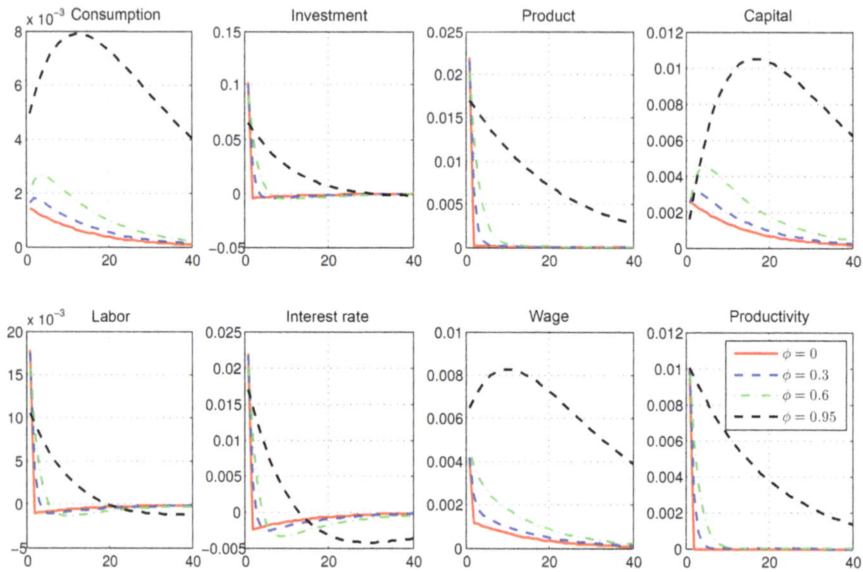

Fig. 5.17 Persistence (ϕ) of productivity shock

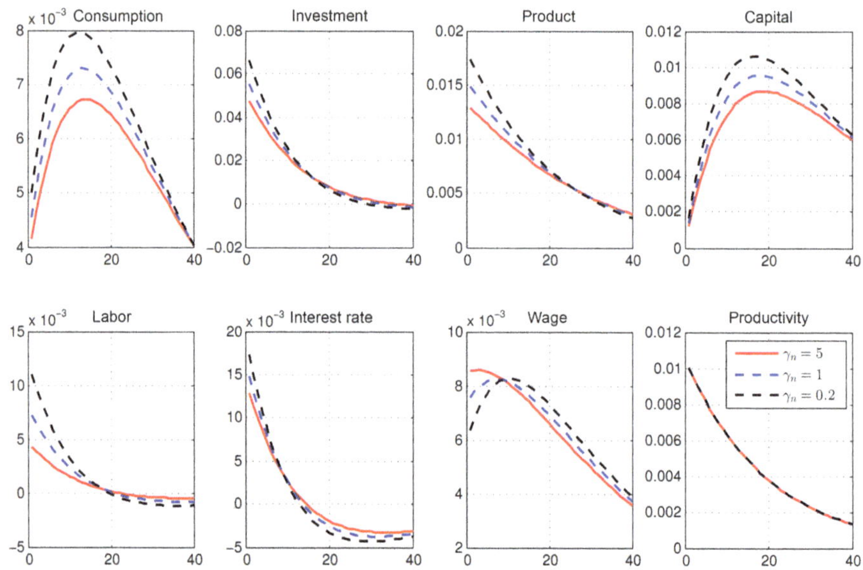

Fig. 5.18 Labor supply elasticity ($1/\gamma_n$)

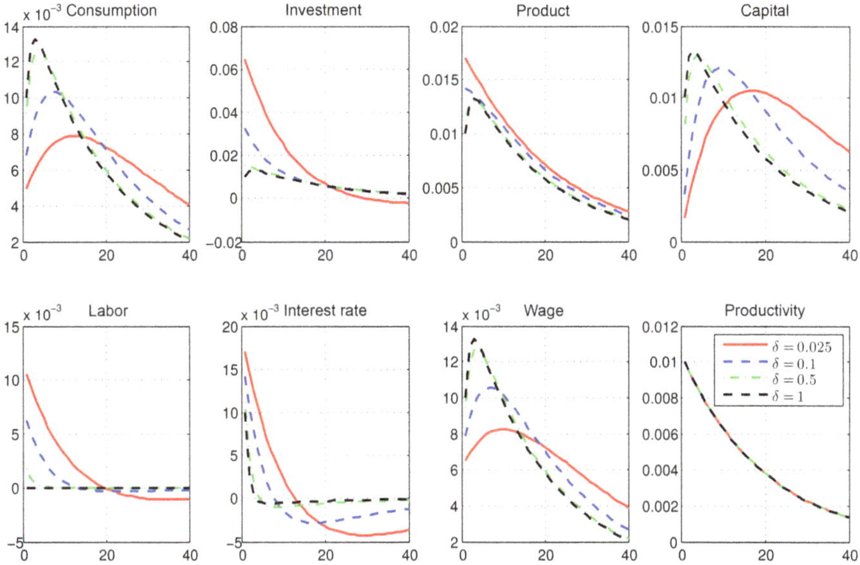

Fig. 5.19 Depreciation rate (δ)

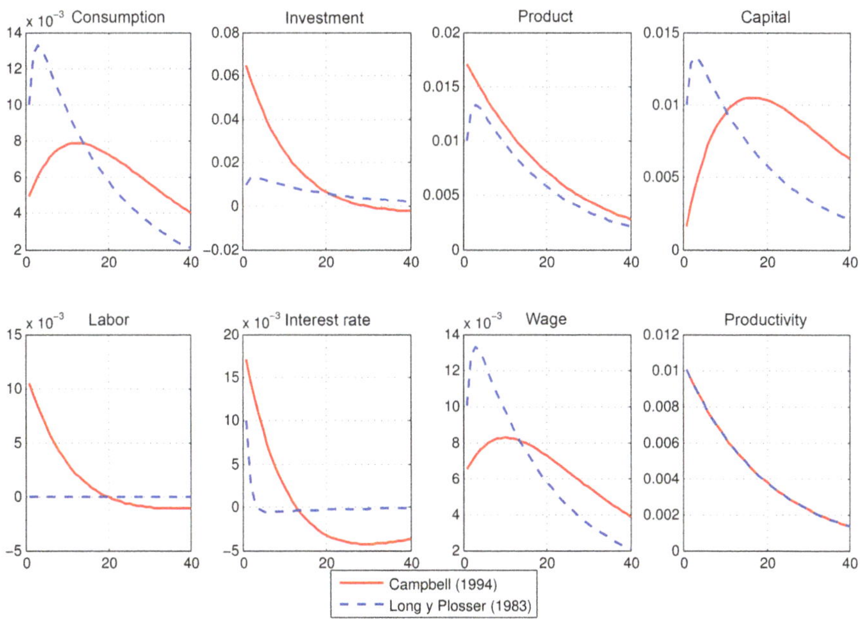

Fig. 5.20 Comparison between the model of Long and Plosser (1983) and Campbell (1994) with variable work

Chapter 6
RBC Model with Shock to Investment and Variable Use of Capital

6.1 Introduction

This chapter analyzes the effects of an investment shock on the endogenous variables, in contrast with the productivity shock analyzed in previous chapters. In the literature, productivity shocks have been widely questioned. One of its main criticisms is that the magnitude and persistence considered in the RBC model exceed those observed in the data. Furthermore, RBC models assume that a recession occurs when productivity is negative, that is, when there is a technological reversal, which is not plausible based on empirical evidence.

Unlike previous chapters, this chapter is based on Keynes's perspective on the sources of business cycles. In particular, Keynes argues that investment is one of the determinants of business cycles. Therefore, in this chapter, we analyze the effect of the shock on investment in the context of the postulates of the RBC school. To this end, the model developed in this chapter follows Greenwood et al. (1988), who postulate the following: an increase in investment efficiency (ϵ_t) increases the formation of new capital (k_{t+1}) and encourages greater use of the capital that is already available (k_t), which accelerates its depreciation (δ_t) (Table 6.1).

This chapter analyzes the effect of an investment shock in two frameworks: in a standard RBC model based on Campbell (1994) and in a model that considers the variable use of capital based on Greenwood et al. (1988). When a shock is incorporated into the marginal efficiency of investment in a standard RBC model, the transmission mechanism is the intertemporal substitution of leisure, which produces countercyclical consumption, which is inconsistent with the empirical evidence. However, by incorporating this shock into a standard RBC model that considers the "variable utilization rate of capital," the model is consistent with the empirical evidence in producing a procyclical consumption. In this case, the transmission mechanism is the "variable capital utilization rate."

H. Galindo Gil et al., *Dynamic Stochastic General Equilibrium Models*, Springer Texts in Business and Economics, https://doi.org/10.1007/978-3-031-58105-2_6

Table 6.1 *Shock* to investment vs. shock to productivity

Standard RBC model Kydland and Prescott (1982), Long and Plosser (1983), Campbell (1994)	A shock of productivity increases production and, therefore, consumption and investment. It follows that "investment reacts to production." This suggests that the shocks must first affect production
Model of Greenwood et al. (1988)	A shock to the marginal efficiency of investment increases tomorrow's capital (k_{t+1}). The latter raises output by $t+1$ (y_{t+1}). So, in this model,"output reacts to investment." This suggests that shocks must first affect investment

6.2 Standard RBC Model and the Investment Shock

The standard RBC model, such as Long and Plosser (1983) and Campbell (1994), usually considers that productivity shock is the main variable that produces business cycles. In this model, the main transmission mechanism is the intertemporal substitution elasticity of leisure in addition to the capital accumulation mechanism. If, in this model, a shock to investment (*demand shock*) is evaluated instead of a shock to productivity (*supply shock*), then the model has problems replicating what is observed in the data. Specifically, the model suggests that consumption decreases while investment increases, generating a negative correlation between these two variables. Furthermore, the model suggests a negative correlation between the output and consumption. These two results are clearly opposite to those observed in the data. In this section, we analyze the model of Campbell (1994) developed in Chap. 5 with a new element: the economy is now subject to an investment shock.

The investment shock is observed in the law of movement of capital:

$$k_{t+1} = (1-\delta)k_t + (1+\epsilon_t)i_t \tag{6.1}$$

The idea behind this shock is that the investment is thus more efficient; that is, if with an investment unit, without a shock, a unit of capital was produced in "t+1," now with the shock, that same investment unit produces ($1+\epsilon_t$) capital units at "t+1." For instance, assuming that the shock equals one ($\epsilon_t = 1$), one unit of investment produces two units of new capital. In contrast, when the shock is absent, the same investment unit produces only one unit of new capital. One of the first effects of this shock is that it increases the *stock* of capital by "t+1"; that is, the supply of capital expands by "t+1."

Given that investment, i_t, is an element of the household's budget constraint, replacing its expression derived from the law of movement of capital allows a shock to investment to influence budget constraints. Furthermore, this constraint plays a role in the optimization in such a way that Euler's equation is also affected by the *investment shock*:

$$\frac{1}{c_t(1+\epsilon_t)} = \beta E_t\left[\frac{1}{c_{t+1}}\left[r_{t+1} + \frac{(1-\delta)}{(1+\epsilon_{t+1})}\right]\right] \tag{6.2}$$

Equation (6.2) shows the Euler equation, modified by an investment shock. Interestingly, investment shock ϵ_t strengthens the intertemporal elasticity of substitution of consumption because it multiplies the interest rate. This strengthening encourages households to reduce their current consumption ($\downarrow c_t$) and increase their future consumption ($\uparrow c_{t+1}$).

In addition, since the productivity shock is eliminated to study only the effect of an investment shock, the production function becomes

$$\text{Standard model} : y_t = a_t k_t^{\alpha} h_t^{1-\alpha}$$
$$\text{Modified model} : y_t = k_t^{\alpha} h_t^{1-\alpha} \tag{6.3}$$

Similarly, the productivity equation $lna_t = \phi lna_{t-1} + \epsilon_t$ is eliminated and replaced by the *investment shock* equation:

$$ln\epsilon_t = \phi ln\epsilon_{t-1} + v_t \tag{6.4}$$

6.2.1 System of Principal Equations

Table 6.2 lists the nonlinear equations of Campbell (1994) model, considering an investment shock. As mentioned, the law of movement of capital, Euler equation, production function, and productivity equation have all been modified to account for the investment shock. The remaining equations are obtained conventionally, as detailed in Chap. 5.

Table 6.2 System of principal nonlinear equations (Campbell 1994 model with *investment shock*)

Equations	Description
$r_t = \alpha \frac{y_t}{k_t}$	Capital demand
$\frac{1}{c_t(1+\epsilon_t)} = \beta E_t \left[\frac{1}{c_{t+1}} [r_{t+1} + \frac{(1-\delta)}{(1+\epsilon_{t+1})}] \right]$	Euler's equation
$\theta(1-h_t)^{-\gamma_n} = \frac{w_t}{c_t}$	Labor supply
$h_t = (1-\alpha)\frac{y_t}{w_t}$	Labor demand
$y_t = k_t^{\alpha} h_t^{1-\alpha}$	Production function
$y_t = c_t + i_t$	Goods market equilibrium
$k_{t+1} = (1-\delta)k_t + (1+\epsilon_t)i_t$	Law of movement of capital
$ln\epsilon_t = \phi ln\epsilon_{t-1} + v_t$	*Shock* to investment

6.2.2 Model Solution

The model represented by the system of equations described in Table 6.2 is written in Dynare to determine the policy and state function (solution). In addition, we use Dynare to compute the theoretical moments (standard deviation, correlation, and autocorrelation) of the cyclical components of the variables. To do this, we write the statement "stoch_simul(order = 1, hp_filter=1600)." This statement tells Dynare to linearize the model, whose variables have been written in logarithms. Specifically, when Dynare linearizes the model, it makes a change of variable as follows:

$$\widehat{x_t} = lnx_t - lnx_{ss}$$

That is, Dynare log-linearizes the model. Additionally, the "hp_filter=1600" option tells Dynare to apply the HP filter to find the cyclical component of each variable. This model is written in the following .mod file "Campbell_Lvariable_nonlinear_log5_inv.mod." Furthermore, the calibration is similar to the model described in Chap. 5.

Table 6.3 shows the solution of the standard RBC model with an *investment shock*. The policy function for consumption is as follows:

$$ln(c_t) = \underbrace{0.1742}_{lnc_{ss}} + 0.5205\widehat{k_t} - 0.2401\widehat{\epsilon}_{t-1} - 0.2528v_t \tag{6.5}$$

$$ln(c_t) = lnc_{ss} + 0.5205\widehat{k_t} - 0.2528\left(\frac{-0.2401}{-0.2528}\widehat{\epsilon}_{t-1} + v_t\right)$$

$$ln(c_t) = lnc_{ss} + 0.5205\widehat{k_t} - 0.2528(0.95\widehat{\epsilon}_{t-1} + v_t)$$

$$ln(c_t) = lnc_{ss} + 0.5205\widehat{k_t} - 0.2528\widehat{\epsilon_t}$$

$$ln(c_t) - lnc_{ss} = 0.5205\widehat{k_t} - 0.2528\widehat{\epsilon_t}$$

$$\widehat{c_t} = 0.5205\widehat{k_t} - 0.2528\widehat{\epsilon_t} \tag{6.6}$$

Equation (6.6) suggests that consumption responds in the opposite direction to the shock and indicates that if the shock to investment is increased by 1% above its steady state, consumption is reduced by 0.2528%. When analyzing how investment

Table 6.3 Policy and state function

	$ln(c_t)$	$ln(i_t)$	$ln(y_t)$	$ln(k_{t+1})$	$ln(h_t)$	$ln(r_t)$	$ln(w_t)$	$ln(\epsilon_t)$
Constant	0.1742	−1.2011	0.3996	3.1810	−0.9890	−3.8810	0.9836	0
$\widehat{k_t}$	0.5205	−1.6972	0.0730	0.9326	−0.3898	−0.9270	0.4628	0
$\widehat{\epsilon}_{t-1}$	−0.2401	2.6000	0.3329	0.0769	0.4991	0.3329	−0.1662	0.95
v_t	−0.2528	2.7368	0.3505	0.0809	0.5254	0.3505	−0.1750	1

Note: The results have been obtained from "Campbell_Lvariable_Dynare_nolinear_log5_inv.mod"

reacts to this shock, the policy function of this variable indicates that investment increases (see Eq. (6.7)). Moreover, a 1% increase in the shock to investment encourages the investment to increase by 2.7368%. This increase in investment is very strong compared to the reduction in consumption:

$$
\begin{aligned}
ln(i_t) &= \underbrace{-1.2011}_{lni_{ss}} -1.6972\widehat{k_t} + 2.6\widehat{\epsilon_{t-1}} + 2.7368v_t \\
ln(i_t) - lni_{ss} &= -1.6972\widehat{k_t} + 2.7368\left(\frac{2.7368}{2.6}\widehat{\epsilon_{t-1}} + v_t\right) \\
\widehat{i_t} &= -1.6972\widehat{k_t} + 2.7368(0.95\widehat{\epsilon_{t-1}} + v_t) \\
\widehat{i_t} &= -1.6972\widehat{k_t} + 2.7368\widehat{\epsilon_t} \qquad (6.7)
\end{aligned}
$$

From the consumption and investment policy functions, we can infer that both variables move in opposite directions in the event of an investment shock, generating a negative correlation, which is contrary to the empirical evidence. This is one of the main shortcomings of the standard RBC model when introducing investment shocks.

Another shortcoming of the model, related to the previous one, is that the consumption moves countercyclically. Looking at the policy function of production, this variable increases when the economy experiences a shock to investment. Therefore, under this shock, we have that at period 't, investment and production increase while consumption decreases.

This behavior leads to a negative correlation between output and consumption, which is not supported by empirical evidence. We then calculate the impulse-response function to evaluate the dynamic effects of the investment shock. The following section details the behavior of endogenous variables in the face of this shock.

6.2.3 Impulse-Response Functions

The continuous-line graphs in Fig. 6.1 show the dynamic response of each variable in the model to a shock to investment. The effects of this shock are described below:

First, the shock to investment strengthens the intertemporal substitution of consumption (SIC) and leads the representative household to reduce its current consumption and increase its future consumption. This effect can be clearly observed in Euler's equation (Eq. (6.8)):

$$
\frac{1}{c_t(1+\epsilon_t)} = \beta E_t\left[\frac{1}{c_{t+1}}\left[r_{t+1} + \frac{(1-\delta)}{(1+\epsilon_{t+1})}\right]\right]
$$

$$\frac{1}{c_t} = \beta E_t\left[\frac{1}{c_{t+1}} \underbrace{(1+\epsilon_t)}_{\text{strengthens SIC}} \underbrace{\left[r_{t+1} + \frac{(1-\delta)}{(1+\epsilon_{t+1})}\right]}_{\text{SIC}}\right] \tag{6.8}$$

Second, given the reduction in current consumption and the fact that production does not move (at least in this step), the goods market equilibrium condition requires investment increases: $y_t =\downarrow c_t + \uparrow i_t$.

The third effect is that both the shock to investment and the increase in the level of investment encourage the creation of new capital k_{t+1}. This is observed in the law of the movement of capital:

$$\begin{aligned} k_{t+1} &= (1-\delta)k_t + (1+\epsilon_t)i_t \\ \uparrow k_{t+1} &\underbrace{=}_{\leftarrow} (1-\delta)k_t + (1+\uparrow\epsilon_t)\uparrow i_t \end{aligned} \tag{6.9}$$

Fourth, the reduction in consumption implies a negative wealth effect on labor supply and encourages households to increase the number of hours worked. Therefore, the labor supply expands (shifts down). This first effect on the labor market, in which labor demand has not yet moved, leads to a decrease in the equilibrium wage and an increase in work.

Fifth, an increase in hours worked encourages greater production ($\uparrow y_t = k_t^{\alpha} h_t^{1-\alpha}$) by firms. This leads to an increase in the marginal productivity of each factor ($\uparrow PMgh_t$ and $\uparrow PMgk_t$); therefore, firms increase their demand for each production factor.

Finally, an increase or shift to the right of $PMgk_t$ raises the current interest rate since the supply of capital is fixed. On the other hand, the increase in labor demand adds an additional positive effect on labor ($\uparrow h_t$) and increases real wage ($\uparrow w_t$), which partially offsets the initial wage reduction. In the net, work increases and real wages decrease.

Consequently, a shock to investment at "t" decreases consumption and the real wage and increases production, capital at "t+1," employment, and the interest rate increase in the same period. Given that the shock loses strength in the following periods but remains above the steady state, consumption progressively recovers as the interest rate declines. This behavior of the variables is similar to that observed in the previously analyzed policy and state functions.

At this point, it is worth asking whether the standard RBC model could improve (obtain an increase in consumption instead of a reduction) if the elasticity of intertemporal labor substitution is greater, that is, if the labor supply is more elastic. With this idea in mind, Fig. 6.1 shows the impulse-response function of the standard RBC model with two different labor supply elasticities. Although the model has a high Frisch elasticity (EF = 4), the model still maintains a drop in consumption in the face of a shock on investment.

In addition, we can observe that the reduction in consumption is very similar in both cases, which indicates that although the usual transmission mechanism of the

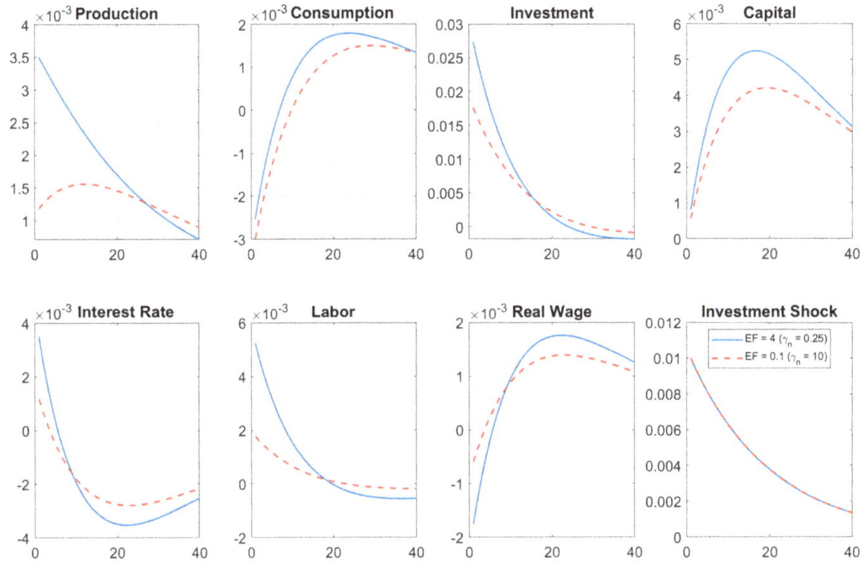

Fig. 6.1 Campbell (1994) model with investment shock. **Note:** "EF" stands for Frisch elasticity ($1/\gamma_n$) or also known as the intertemporal labor substitution elasticity. This figure is obtained from the file "Campbell_Lvariable_nonlinear_log5_inv.mod"

RBC model (intertemporal elasticity of labor) is strengthened, the model continues to show the same weakness (reduction in consumption). Moreover, it is important to mention that these results are obtained by comparing an economy with excessively high elasticity (EF = 4) in contrast to a very small elasticity (EF = 0.1). For intermediate values, there are probably no additional effects on consumption, which is at negative levels (below the steady state).

The second question is whether the elasticity of intertemporal substitution of consumption (EISC) can help improve the model. Figure 6.2 illustrates the effects of a model with low and high EISC. Before analyzing this figure, it is necessary to make some remarks about the utility function so that the EISC remains explicit in the model. Given that the Campbell (1994) model assumes that elasticity is equal to one and, therefore, the utility function is logarithmic in consumption, it is necessary to modify the utility function (more general version) to consider this parameter explicitly. Equation (6.10) shows the Campbell (1994) utility function, whereas Eq. (6.11) shows a general utility function:

$$\text{Campbell's utility function}: u(c_t, h_t) = ln(c_t) + \theta \frac{(1-h_t)^{1-\gamma_n}}{1-\gamma_n} \tag{6.10}$$

$$\text{General utility function}: u(c_t, h_t) = \frac{c_t^{1-\gamma}}{1-\gamma} + \theta \frac{(1-h_t)^{1-\gamma_n}}{1-\gamma_n}, \tag{6.11}$$

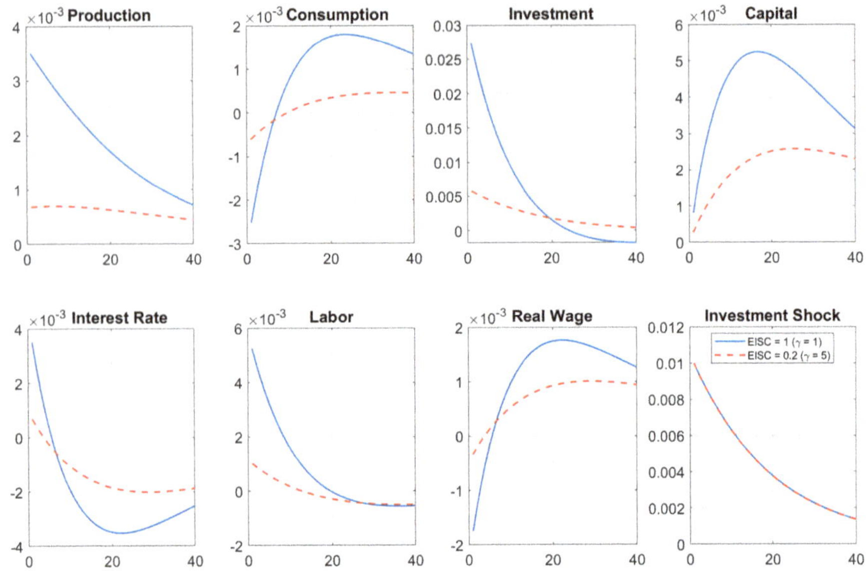

Fig. 6.2 Campbell (1994) model with investment shock. **Note:** "EISC" stands for elasticity of intertemporal substitution of consumption ($1/\gamma$). This figure is obtained from the file "Campbell_Lvariable_nonlinear_log5_inv.mod"

where the parameter γ represents the inverse of the intertemporal elasticity of consumption. Under the utility function described in Eq. (6.11), the following Euler equation is obtained:

$$\frac{1}{c_t^{\gamma}(1+\epsilon_t)} = \beta E_t\left[\frac{1}{c_{t+1}^{\gamma}}\left[r_{t+1} + \frac{(1-\delta)}{(1+\epsilon_{t+1})}\right]\right] \tag{6.12}$$

In Eq. (6.12), we can see how parameter γ controls the elasticity of intertemporal substitution of consumption. This is best observed in the log-linear version of this equation:

$$\widehat{c}_t = E_t\left[\widehat{c}_{t+1} - \frac{1}{\gamma}(A\widehat{r}_{t+1} - \frac{1}{2}(B\widehat{\epsilon}_{t+1} - \widehat{\epsilon}_t))\right] \tag{6.13}$$

$$A = \frac{2r_{ss}}{2r_{ss} + (1-\delta)} \wedge B = \frac{1-\delta}{2r_{ss} + (1-\delta)}$$

Equation (6.13) shows that an increase in the EISC ($1/\gamma$) encourages the household to reduce its current consumption for future consumption. Moreover, it is also observed that said elasticity strengthens or amplifies the effect of the shock to investment, which causes consumption to be further reduced. As mentioned before, the question in this scenario is whether the standard RBC model improves its capacity when a lower EISC is considered so that its effects are not greatly amplified. A priori, it is observed that regardless of the EISC's value, the shock to investment has a negative effect on consumption. The only thing that a lower magnitude of EISC can do is reduce the effect of the shock, but it does not cause consumption to increase. Therefore, since the EISC controls for the substitution effect, which will always be negative for consumption, what is required for consumption to increase in the face of the shock to investment is a significant income effect that completely cancels out this substitution effect, and it is precisely this that is absent in the standard RBC model.

In line with the above, Fig. 6.2 suggests that a lower EISC in the artificial economy reduces the amplification of the shock to investment. This is observed in the fact that the impulse-response function of all variables has a smaller magnitude and returns more quickly to the steady state when the EISC is low. For example, the product reacts three times less in a low EISC model (=0.1) than in a high EISC economy (=1). Likewise, with a low EISC (=0.1), consumption is not reduced as much; however, at equilibrium, it is still below its steady state.

In conclusion, the standard RBC model provides contradictory results to the data when a shock is introduced into the investment. These results hold even when the transmission mechanism via the elasticity of substitution of labor supply increases or when the elasticity of substitution of consumption is reduced. What is missing to improve the model is perhaps a different transmission mechanism and/or a significant income effect, although Barro and King (1984) suggest that the latter is not sufficient.

6.2.4 Comparison of the Model with the Data

This section presents the statistics generated by the model to confirm what was found in the model solution and the impulse-response functions. These statistics are compared to the data to assess the extent to which the model is realistic. Table 6.11 contains three statistics: standard deviation, correlation of GDP with the other macroeconomic variables, and correlation of consumption with the other variables of the model. From this table, the following conclusions can be drawn. First, the correlation between GDP and consumption is positive in the data. However, this model suggests a negative correlation.

Second, the model predicts that the correlation of GDP with real wages is negative; however, the data indicate that it is positive. This suggests that the model lacks some variables that allow the real wage to move procyclically. Although the productivity shock in the standard RBC model does not capture the *quantitative* behavior of the real wage, it does capture its *qualitative* behavior. In other words, the model under a productivity shock implies that the real wage is procyclical but with a value of 0.9423, which is much higher than the observed value (0.12).

Third, the model indicates that the correlations between consumption and investment, product, and labor are negative. That is, consumption moves in the opposite direction to these variables, which contrasts with empirical evidence, which indicates that these variables move in the same direction.

Fourth, the model produces a standard deviation well below that found in the data, except for the interest rate. This suggests that the model requires another transmission mechanism that amplifies the shock to investment more strongly. This flaw in the model is observed even with a high persistence of the shock ($\phi = 0.95$) and a significant value of this shock ($\sigma_v = 0.1$). Under these same parameters, the shock of productivity in the model of Campbell (1994), described in Chap. 5, produces a better model performance. For instance, in the case of consumption, a standard deviation of 0.77% is obtained in contrast to 0.37% for the model with a shock on investment. The same is observed for the output because the model with a shock of productivity obtains a value of 2.22% for the standard deviation compared to the poor performance of the model with an investment shock (0.46%).

All of this confirms what was discussed in the previous sections: the standard RBC model has trouble approaching the data when considering a shock to investment. This is in line with Barro and King (1984), who indicated that in the neoclassical model, a movement in investment demand produces an increase in the interest rate and output but reduces consumption. This behavior does not fit the typical patterns observed in the data. In this scenario, the following question arises: what elements should be considered within the standard RBC model so that it replicates the data in the event of a shock to investment? In 1988, Greenwood et al. (1988) proposed modifications to the standard RBC model, which made it possible to overcome these weaknesses (Table 6.4).

Table 6.4 Comparison of the cyclical behavior of the theoretical model with the empirical data

	Data		Model		
Variable (x_t)	Des. Est. (%)	Corr (PBI, x_t)	Des. Est. (%)	Corr (PBI, x_t)	Corr (c_t, x_t)
Consumption	1.35	0.88	0.37	−0.82	1.00
Investment	5.30	0.80	3.57	0.97	−0.93
Product	1.81	1.00	0.46	1.00	−0.83
Capital			0.36	0.42	0.16
Labor	1.79	0.88	0.69	0.97	−0.94
Interest rate	0.30	−0.35	0.54	0.75	−0.99
Real salary	0.68	0.12	0.27	−0.75	0.99

Note: The empirical values were taken from King and Rebelo (1999), and all the variables are in natural logarithms, except the interest rate. The theoretical values were obtained from a single simulation. These values were obtained from the file "Campbell_Lvariable_nolineal_log5_inv.mod"

6.3 Extended RBC Model: Inclusion of Shock to Investment and Variable Use of Capital

6.3.1 Model Elements

This section closely follows the model proposed by Greenwood et al. (1988). It is worth mentioning that in the original article by these authors, the model is presented from the point of view of the central planner. However, in this chapter, the decentralized version is developed, whose results are similar because of the competitive context in which the model is developed.

On the other hand, the economy in this model is populated by households that live an infinite life and by firms. Both agents develop in a competitive environment in both the goods and factor markets. Likewise, it is assumed that this economy is closed without government presence.

Additionally, this model has three distinctive features with respect to the models studied in previous chapters. First, the utility function eliminates the income effect on labor supply. Second, the firm does not demand capital goods as in the standard RBC models but instead demands "capital services," which represents the producer of the number of hours that capital is used times the number of capital goods. For example, in the previous RBC models, it is considered that the firm demands 100 computers (capital goods). However, in this model, not only the above is considered but also the utilization rate of this capital, which, for example, can be 3 hours a day. Considering both elements, the "capital service" demanded is 300 (100 × 3).

Third, it is assumed that the greater use of capital induces it to depreciate faster. Finally, the shock to investment makes the investment more productive in the generation of new capital goods. This effect is observed in the law of the motion of capital.

Figure 6.3 outlines the relationships between the agents: first, households offer working hours and capital services; second, firms demand both services in the factor market. Finally, the economy is subject to a shock to investment, which initially affects the behavior of households and, hence, firms.

6.3.1.1 Households

[A] Utility Function The utility function of Greenwood et al. (1988) is as follows:

$$\underline{U}(c_t, l_t) = U(c_t - G(l_t)), \tag{6.14}$$

with the following characteristics

$\dot{U} > 0$	$\ddot{U} < 0$	$\dot{G} > 0$	$\ddot{G} > 0$

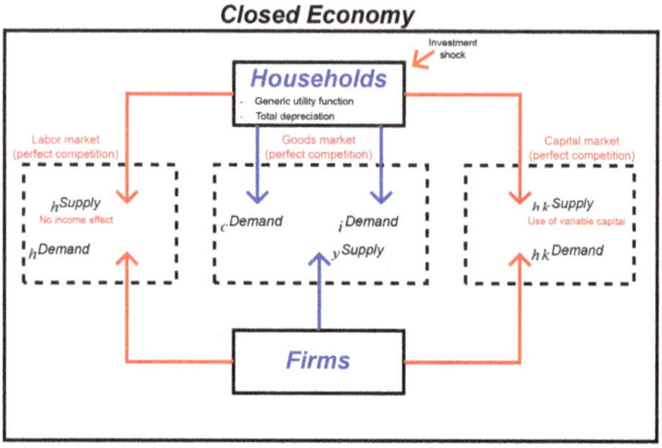

Fig. 6.3 Scheme of the Greenwood et al. (1988) model

In this utility function, we can calculate the marginal utility of consumption ($\underline{U}_1$) and the marginal utility of labor ($\underline{U}_2$), which are expressed as follows:

$$\underline{U}_1 = \frac{\partial \underline{U}}{\partial c_t} = \frac{\partial U(c_t - G(l_t))}{\partial c_t} = \dot{U} \cdot \left(\frac{\partial (c_t - G(l_t))}{\partial c_t} \right) = \dot{U} \tag{6.15}$$

$$\underline{U}_2 = \frac{\partial \underline{U}}{\partial l_t} = \frac{\partial U(c_t - G(l_t))}{\partial l_t} = \dot{U} \cdot \left(\frac{\partial (c_t - G(l_t))}{\partial l_t} \right) = -\dot{U}\dot{G} \tag{6.16}$$

Likewise, the expression of the marginal rate of substitution between consumption and work, which (strictly should be leisure) is represented by

$$TMgS_{c_t,l_t} = -\frac{\underline{U}_2}{\underline{U}_1} = -\frac{-\dot{U}\dot{G}}{\dot{U}} = \dot{G} \tag{6.17}$$

This expression is the main feature of the utility function proposed by Greenwood et al. (1988): the $TMgS_{c_t,l_t}$ only depends on labor l_t and does not depend on consumption c_t. As will be seen later, this is important in the optimization of the household because it allows obtaining a labor supply without the presence of consumption c_t, that is, without the income effect. In other words, the effect of the intertemporal substitution of consumption on l_t is eliminated, and "l_t is determined independently of the intertemporal consumption/saving choice." In addition, this last characteristic is important because it emphasizes the "transmission mechanism" of the shock to investment in this model.

Equation (6.18) is the functional form of the utility function of Greenwood et al. (1988), which is given by

$$\underline{U}(c_t, l_t) = \frac{1}{1-\gamma}\left[\left(c_t - \frac{l_t^{1+\theta}}{1+\theta}\right)^{1-\gamma} - 1\right], \tag{6.18}$$

where the marginal rate of marginal substitution between consumption and labor $TMgS_{c_t,l_t}$ is expressed as follows:

$$TMgS_{c_t,l_t} = l_t^{\theta} \tag{6.19}$$

The expression for the $TMgS_{c_t,l_t}$ derived from the utility function of Greenwood et al. (1988) is different from that of the usual RBC models. For example, Campbell (1994) assumes a utility function of the following form:

$$U(c_t, l_t) = u(c_t) + u(l_t) = lnc_t + \theta \frac{(1 - l_t)^{1-\gamma_n}}{1 - \gamma_n} \tag{6.20}$$

Calculating $TMgS_{c_t,l_t}$ from this utility function, we have

$$TMgS_{c_t,l_t} = -\frac{\mathrm{U}_2}{\mathrm{U}_1} = -\frac{-(1 - l_t)^{-\gamma_n}}{c_t^{-1}} = c_t(1 - l_t)^{-\gamma_n} \tag{6.21}$$

It is clearly observed that the $TMgS_{c_t,l_t}$ of this utility function depends on labor and consumption. Therefore, the wealth effect on labor supply is maintained.

[B] Law of Capital Movement In this model, as previously mentioned, the household not only offers capital goods "k_t" but also the intensity of use of that capital " h_t," which together represent **capital services** $(k_t h_t)$. Likewise, capital evolves according to the law of motion:

$$k_{t+1} = (1 - \delta(h_t))k_t + (1 + \epsilon_t)i_t \tag{6.22}$$

From Eq. (6.22), three observations emerge: the first is that Eq. (6.20) can be seen as a function of production of "new capital' ' (k_{t+1}), which has as "*inputs*" the investment (i_t) and the *stock* of capital (k_t).

The second is that the marginal efficiency of the investment is defined by

$$\frac{\partial k_{t+1}}{\partial i_t} = 1 + \epsilon_t \tag{6.23}$$

This equation indicates that if there is no shock $(\epsilon_t = 0)$, one unit of i_t becomes one unit of k_{t+1}. But if $\epsilon_t > 0$, then one unit of i_t becomes more productive (efficient) because it produces $(1 + \epsilon_t)$ units of k_{t+1}.

The third observation is that $\delta(h_t)$ represents the **endogenous depreciation**, which expresses that greater use of capital (k_t) causes a greater depreciation due to [1] greater deterioration with use and [2] less time for maintenance. The functional form of depreciation considered in the model is as follows:

$$\delta(h_t) = \frac{h_t^{\omega}}{\omega} \tag{6.24}$$

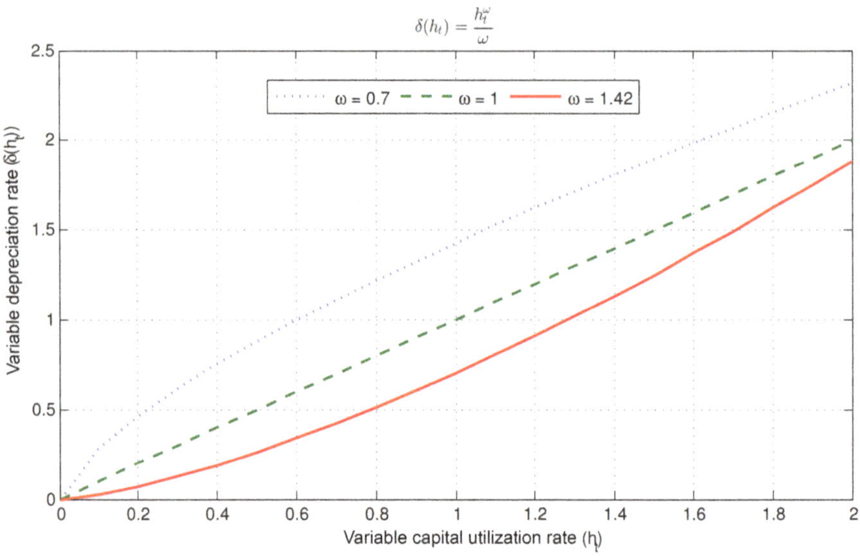

Fig. 6.4 Variable depreciation: dependent on the use of capital

This function has three characteristics. First, it has a positive slope ($\dot{\delta} > 0$), which reflects that greater capital use implies greater depreciation of the *stock* of capital. Second, the second derivative of this function is also positive, $\ddot{\delta} > 0$, which suggests that acceleration in the use (or intensive use) of capital induces the *stock* of capital to depreciate rapidly.

Third, the value of ω must be positive and greater than one so that it satisfies the two aforementioned properties ($\dot{\delta} = h_t^{\omega-1} > 0$ and $\ddot{\delta} = (\omega - 1)h_t^{\omega-2} > 0$). Figure 6.4 shows the depreciation rate δ for three values of ω. Importantly, for values of ω less than or equal to one, the function δ does not meet the aforementioned properties.

In this model, a value of ω (=1.42) is chosen that allows obtaining a steady-state value of depreciation of 0.1 ($\delta_{ss} = 0.1$). In addition, since by definition δ must be less than or equal to one, the value of h_t is limited to values less than 1.3 approximately.

In conclusion, the capital equation of motion is of vital importance in the model because it includes the **push mechanism** "shock to the marginal efficiency of investment (ϵ_t)" and the **propagation mechanism** "the variable use of capital (h_t)."

[C] Budget Constraint The representative household allocates resources for the acquisition of consumer goods (c_t) and investment goods (i_t). Their income is derived from the real salary (w_t), obtained by offering work, and from rental income (r_t^k) from capital services ($k_t h_t$). The equality between income and expenses represents the budget constraint, which is described by Eq. (6.25):

$$c_t + i_t = w_t l_t + r_t (k_t h_t) \tag{6.25}$$

[D] The Optimization Problem The household seeks to maximize its discounted expected utility function $\underline{\mathrm{U}}(c_t, l_t)$, where c_t is the consumption of the only good produced in the economy and l_t is labor. In this model, unlike the standard RBC model, the household also decides on the optimal capital variable utilization rate h_t that it will offer in the capital goods market. This is because the variable h_t influences the household's income $(k_t h_t)$ and affects the consumption-investment decisions of the household. Therefore, there are four control variables: consumption c_t, work l_t, capital utilization rate h_t, and new capital k_{t+1}. With these considerations, the household optimization problem is described as follows:

$$\underset{\{c_t, l_t, h_t, k_{t+1}\}_{t=0}^{\infty}}{\text{Max}} \quad E_0 \sum_{t=0}^{\infty} \beta^t \underline{\mathrm{U}}(c_t, l_t)$$

Subject to the budget constraint and the law of movement of capital

$$c_t + i_t = w_t l_t + r_t(k_t h_t) \tag{6.26}$$

$$k_{t+1} = (1 - \delta(h_t))k_t + (1 + \epsilon_t)i_t, \tag{6.27}$$

where

$$\delta(h_t) = \frac{h_t^{\omega}}{\omega} \text{ and } \underline{\mathrm{U}}(c_t, l_t) = \frac{1}{1-\gamma}\left[\left(c_t - \frac{l_t^{1+\theta}}{1+\theta}\right)^{1-\gamma} - 1\right]$$

These two constraints (Eqs. (6.26) and (6.27)) can be summarized as one by replacing the value of the investment from the law of movement of capital in the budget constraint. Thus, the only restriction is as follows:

$$\underbrace{c_t + \frac{k_{t+1}}{1+\epsilon_t} - (1 - \delta(h_t))\frac{k_t}{1+\epsilon_t}}_{expenses_t} = \underbrace{w_t l_t + r_t(k_t h_t)}_{income_t} \tag{6.28}$$

With the objective function and the only restriction (Eq. (6.28)), the Lagrange function is built as

$$\mathcal{L} = E_0 \sum_{t=0}^{\infty} \beta^t \left[\underline{\mathrm{U}}(c_t, l_t) + \lambda_t[income_t - expenses_t]\right]$$

First-Order Conditions We then proceed to calculate the derivatives of the Lagrange function with respect to each of the control variables (c_t, l_t, h_t, and k_{t+1}).

Derivative with respect to consumption:

$$\frac{\partial \mathcal{L}}{\partial c_t} = 0 \quad \overset{\textbf{ent.}}{\longrightarrow} \quad \underline{\mathrm{U}}_1 + \lambda_t[-1] = 0 \quad \overset{\textbf{ent.}}{\longrightarrow} \quad \underline{\mathrm{U}}_1 = \lambda_t \tag{6.29}$$

where $\underline{\mathrm{U}}_1 = \left(c_t - \frac{l_t^{1+\theta}}{1+\theta}\right)^{-\gamma}$. Therefore

$$\underline{\mathrm{U}}_1 = \left(c_t - \frac{l_t^{1+\theta}}{1+\theta}\right)^{-\gamma} = \lambda_t \tag{6.30}$$

Derivative with respect to labor:

$$\frac{\partial \mathcal{L}}{\partial l_t} = 0 \quad \overset{\textbf{ent.}}{\longrightarrow} \quad \underline{\mathrm{U}}_2 + \lambda_t [w_t] = 0 \quad \overset{\textbf{ent.}}{\longrightarrow} \quad \underline{\mathrm{U}}_2 = -\lambda_t w_t \tag{6.31}$$

where $\underline{\mathrm{U}}_2 = \left(c_t - \frac{l_t^{1+\theta}}{1+\theta}\right)^{-\gamma} (-l_t^{\theta})$. Therefore

$$\underline{\mathrm{U}}_2 = \left(c_t - \frac{l_t^{1+\theta}}{1+\theta}\right)^{-\gamma} (-l_t^{\theta}) = -\lambda_t w_t \tag{6.32}$$

From Eqs. (6.30) and (6.32), we obtain **labor supply**:

$$\frac{\underline{\mathrm{U}}_2}{\underline{\mathrm{U}}_1} = -w_t \tag{6.33}$$

$$\frac{\left(c_t - \frac{l_t^{1+\theta}}{1+\theta}\right)^{-\gamma} (-l_t^{\theta})}{\left(c_t - \frac{l_t^{1+\theta}}{1+\theta}\right)^{-\gamma}} = -w_t$$

$$l_t^{\theta} = w_t \tag{6.34}$$

This labor supply is particular: it does not have an income effect; that is, consumption does not appear in the labor supply function. This is because of the shape of the utility function from which it follows that the marginal rate of substitution between consumption and labor depends only on labor.
Derivative with respect to capital utilization:

$$\frac{\partial \mathcal{L}}{\partial h_t} = 0 \overset{\textbf{then}}{\longrightarrow} \lambda_t \left[r_t k_t - \frac{\dot{\delta}(h_t) k_t}{1 + \epsilon_t} \right] = 0 \tag{6.35}$$

Because λ_t is equal to the marginal utility of consumption $(\partial U(c_t, l_t)/\partial c_t)$, which is positive, the only way for Eq. (6.35) to be fulfilled is for the expression between square brackets to be zero. Therefore, we have the following:

$$\underbrace{r_t k_t = \frac{\dot{\delta}(h_t)k_t}{1+\epsilon_t}}_{\substack{\text{Supply of the (variable)} \\ \text{capital utilization}}} \tag{6.36}$$

Derivative with respect to the new capital:

$$\frac{\partial \mathcal{L}}{\partial k_{t+1}} = 0 \quad \overset{\textbf{ent.}}{\longrightarrow} \quad \lambda_t \left[-\frac{1}{1+\epsilon_t} \right] + E_t \beta \lambda_{t+1} \left[r_{t+1} h_{t+1} + \frac{1-\delta(h_{t+1})}{1+\epsilon_{t+1}} \right] = 0 \tag{6.37}$$

From the above, the optimality condition of the investment is obtained:

$$\lambda_t \left[\frac{1}{1+\epsilon_t} \right] = E_t \beta \lambda_{t+1} \left[r_{t+1} h_{t+1} + \frac{1-\delta(h_{t+1})}{1+\epsilon_{t+1}} \right]$$

$$\left(c_t - \frac{l_t^{1+\theta}}{1+\theta} \right)^{-\gamma} \left[\frac{1}{1+\epsilon_t} \right] =$$

$$\beta E_t \left(c_{t+1} - \frac{l_{t+1}^{1+\theta}}{1+\theta} \right)^{-\gamma} \left[r_{t+1} h_{t+1} + \frac{1-\delta(h_{t+1})}{1+\epsilon_{t+1}} \right] \tag{6.38}$$

6.3.1.2 Firms

On the side of the firms, they seek to maximize their profit function (π_t) in each period subject to their production function, as shown in the following expression:

$$\underset{\{l_t, h_t\}_{t=0}^{\infty}}{\text{Max}} \ \pi_t = y_t - [w_t l_t + r_t (k_t h_t)]$$

Subject to the production function

$$y_t = F(k_t h_t, l_t) \tag{6.39}$$

By inserting the production function into the profit function and differentiating it with respect to the control variables, the following first-order conditions are obtained:

$$\frac{\partial \pi_t}{\partial l_t} = 0 \quad \overset{\textbf{then}}{\longrightarrow} \quad F_2 - w_t = 0 \quad \overset{\textbf{then}}{\longrightarrow} \quad \underbrace{F_2 = w_t}_{\text{Labor demand}} \tag{6.40}$$

$$\frac{\partial \pi_t}{\partial h_t} = 0 \quad \overset{\textbf{then}}{\longrightarrow} \quad F_1 k_t - R_t^k k_t = 0 \quad \overset{\textbf{then}}{\longrightarrow} \quad \underbrace{F_1 = R_t^k}_{\text{Demand for capital services}} \tag{6.41}$$

Considering that the production function has the following specifications:

$$F(k_t h_t, l_t) = (h_t k_t)^\alpha l_t^{1-\alpha} \tag{6.42}$$

Both demands would be expressed as follows:

$$\text{Labor demand} : (1-\alpha)\frac{y_t}{l_t} = w_t \tag{6.43}$$

$$\text{Demand for capital services} : \alpha\frac{y_t}{h_t k_t} = r_t \tag{6.44}$$

6.3.1.3 Market Equilibrium and Definition of Shock

To complete the model, it is necessary to add two equations. The first equation refers to equilibrium in the goods market, which is expressed as follows:

$$y_t = c_t + i_t \tag{6.45}$$

The second equation describes the behavior of the shock to investment, which behaves like an AR(1):

$$\epsilon_t = \rho\epsilon_{t-1} + \nu_t, \quad \nu_t \sim N(0, \sigma_\nu^2) \tag{6.46}$$

Where ν_t is properly the shock to the investment.

6.3.1.4 System of Principal Equations

Table 6.12 shows the equations that describe the optimal behavior of households and firms; likewise, it indicates the equations of market equilibrium and the behavior of the shock to investment. All these equations form a system that represents the RBC model proposed by Greenwood et al. (1988).

6.3.1.5 Calibration

The values associated with the parameters of this model are obtained as follows. To calculate the value of α, we use the annual average of the share of capital in national income between 1948 and 1985. Furthermore, the intertemporal elasticity of labor substitution $1/\theta$ is between 0.3 and 2.2 (Macurdy, 1981; Heckman and Macurdy, 1980). The initially chosen value is 1.7, which allows us to obtain a value of $\theta = 0.6$. However, it is worth conducting a sensitivity analysis for this parameter (Table 6.5).

Two values are proposed for the inverse of the elasticity of intertemporal substitution of consumption (EISC): $\gamma = 1$ and $\gamma = 2$. The simulation of the

Table 6.5 System of principal nonlinear equations

Equations	Description
$\left(c_t - \frac{l_t^{1+\theta}}{1+\theta}\right)^{-\gamma}\left[\frac{1}{1+\epsilon_t}\right] = \beta E_t\left(c_{t+1} - \frac{l_{t+1}^{1+\theta}}{1+\theta}\right)^{-\gamma}\left[r_{t+1}h_{t+1} + \frac{1-\delta_{t+1}}{1+\epsilon_{t+1}}\right]$	Euler's equation
$r_t = \frac{h_t^{\omega-1}}{1+\epsilon_t}$	Capital services offering
$r_t = \alpha\frac{y_t}{h_t k_t}$	Demand for capital services
$l_t^\theta = w_t$	Labor supply
$w_t = (1-\alpha)\frac{y_t}{l_t}$	Labor demand
$y_t = (h_t k_t)^\alpha l_t^{1-\alpha}$	Production function
$y_t = c_t + i_t$	Goods market equilibrium
$k_{t+1} = (1-\delta_t)k_t + (1+\epsilon_t)i_t$	Law of movement of capital
$\delta_t = \frac{h_t^\omega}{\omega}$	Variable depreciation rate
$\epsilon_t = \phi\epsilon_{t-1} + \nu_t$	*Shock* to investment

Table 6.6 Calibration

Parameter	Amount	Observation
β	0.96	Discount factor
α	0.29	Share of capital in national income (annual average between 1950–1985)
θ	0.6	Inverse of the elasticity of labor supply (Frisch elasticity of 1.7)
γ	1–2	Relative coefficient of risk aversion or inverse of the EISC
ω	1.42	Elasticity of depreciation concerning the utilization rate (so that $\delta_{ss} = 0.1$)
σ	0.05–0.0515	Standard deviation of shock to investment ϵ_t
λ	0.47–0.51	First-order autocorrelation coefficient of shock (persistence)

model considers both values to compare the effects of the shock on investment in an economy with a high EISC ($1/\gamma = 1$), in contrast to an economy with a low EISC ($1/\gamma = 1/2$).

Moreover, the elasticity of depreciation for the utilization rate, ω, is calibrated such that the steady-state depreciation rate equals 0.1. Likewise, the two parameters of the behavior of the investment shock, the magnitude of the shock (σ : standard deviation) and the persistence of the shock (ϕ : autocorrelation of first order), are calibrated to reproduce the standard deviation and first-order serial correlation observed in the GDP data. So, for $\gamma = 1$, we have $\sigma = 0.05$ and $\phi = 0.47$, and for $\gamma = 2$, we have $\sigma = 0.0515$ and $\phi = 0.51$. Table 6.6 shows the values associated with each parameter.

6.3.1.6 Stationary State

In Table 6.7, the equations of the model are written in their steady-state representations.

[A] Reducing the Number of Equations (I) First, in *Eq. 10* of Table 6.7, it is considered that in the steady state, the shock takes the value of its mean ($\nu_{ss} = 0$). Therefore, the equation is as follows:

$$\epsilon_{ss} = \phi\epsilon_{ss} + \underbrace{\nu_{ss}}_{=0}$$

From this expression, it follows that the only value of ϵ_{ss} that solves this equation is zero. Therefore, $\epsilon_{ss} = 0$.

Second, from Euler's equation (*Eq. 1*) in Table 6.7, we obtain the following:

$$\left(c_{ss} - \frac{l_{ss}^{1+\theta}}{1+\theta}\right)^{-\gamma}\left[\frac{1}{1+\epsilon_{ss}}\right] = \beta E_t\left(c_{ss} - \frac{l_{ss}^{1+\theta}}{1+\theta}\right)^{-\gamma}\left[r_{ss}h_{ss} + \frac{1-\delta_{ss}}{1+\epsilon_{ss}}\right]$$

$$1 = \beta\left[r_{ss}h_{ss} + \frac{1-\delta_{ss}}{1+\underbrace{\epsilon_{ss}}_{=0}}\right]$$

$$\frac{1}{\beta} = r_{ss}h_{ss} + 1 - \delta_{ss} \tag{6.47}$$

Table 6.7 System of principal nonlinear equations

Equations	Description
1. $\left(c_{ss} - \frac{l_{ss}^{1+\theta}}{1+\theta}\right)^{-\gamma}\left[\frac{1}{1+\epsilon_{ss}}\right] = \beta E_t\left(c_{ss} - \frac{l_{ss}^{1+\theta}}{1+\theta}\right)^{-\gamma}\left[r_{ss}h_{ss} + \frac{1-\delta_{ss}}{1+\epsilon_{ss}}\right]$	Euler's equation
2. $r_{ss} = \frac{h_{ss}^{\omega-1}}{1+\epsilon_{ss}}$	Capital services offering
3. $r_{ss} = \alpha\frac{y_{ss}}{h_{ss}k_{ss}}$	Demand for capital services
4. $l_{ss}^{\theta} = w_{ss}$	Labor supply
5. $w_{ss} = (1-\alpha)\frac{y_{ss}}{l_{ss}}$	Labor demand
6. $y_{ss} = (h_{ss}k_{ss})^{\alpha}l_{ss}^{1-\alpha}$	Production function
7. $y_{ss} = c_{ss} + i_{ss}$	Goods market equilibrium
8. $k_{ss} = (1-\delta_{ss})k_{ss} + (1+\epsilon_{ss})i_{ss}$	Law of movement of capital
9. $\delta_{ss} = \frac{h_{ss}^{\omega}}{\omega}$	Variable depreciation rate
10. $\epsilon_{ss} = \phi\epsilon_{ss} + \nu_{ss}$	*Shock* to investment

Third, considering that $\epsilon_{ss} = 0$, the supply of capital services would be as follows:

$$r_{ss} = \frac{h_{ss}^{\omega-1}}{1+\underbrace{\epsilon_{ss}}_{=0}}$$

$$r_{ss} = h_{ss}^{\omega-1} \tag{6.48}$$

Fourth, the law of movement of capital would be expressed as follows:

$$k_{ss} = (1-\delta_{ss})k_{ss} + (1+\underbrace{\epsilon_{ss}}_{=0})i_{ss}$$

$$\delta_{ss}k_{ss} = i_{ss} \tag{6.49}$$

[B] Reducing the Number of Equations (II) Given that the value of r_{ss} is a function of h_{ss} (Eq. (6.48)) and that, in the same way, δ_{ss} depends on h_{ss} (*Eq. 9* from Table 6.7). Then, substituting both expressions in Eq. (6.47), the value of h_{ss} is obtained based on the model parameters:

$$\frac{1}{\beta} = r_{ss}h_{ss} + 1 - \delta_{ss}$$

$$\frac{1}{\beta} = h_{ss}^{\omega-1}h_{ss} + 1 - \frac{h_{ss}^{\omega}}{\omega}$$

$$\frac{1}{\beta} - 1 = h_{ss}^{\omega} - \frac{h_{ss}^{\omega}}{\omega}$$

$$\frac{1}{\beta} - 1 = h_{ss}^{\omega}\left(1 - \frac{1}{\omega}\right)$$

$$h_{ss} = \left(\frac{\frac{1}{\beta}-1}{1-\frac{1}{\omega}}\right)^{\frac{1}{\omega}} \tag{6.50}$$

Using the value of h_{ss}, it is possible to obtain the values of r_{ss} and δ_{ss}. Thus far, we have the steady-state values of the following variables:

$\epsilon_{ss} = 0$	$h_{ss} = \left(\frac{\frac{1}{\beta}-1}{1-\frac{1}{\omega}}\right)^{\frac{1}{\omega}}$	$r_{ss} = h_{ss}^{\omega-1}$	$\delta_{ss} = \frac{h_{ss}^{\omega}}{\omega}$

[C] Reducing the Number of Equations (III) To obtain the steady-state values of the other variables, we work with ratios. Given that we have the steady-state value of the interest rate, it is useful to start with an equation that contains it, such as the demand for capital services.

$$r_{ss} = \alpha \frac{y_{ss}}{h_{ss}k_{ss}}$$

$$\text{Replacing the production function :}$$

$$r_{ss} = \alpha \frac{(h_{ss}k_{ss})^{\alpha} l_{ss}^{1-\alpha}}{h_{ss}k_{ss}}$$

$$r_{ss} = \alpha \left(\frac{h_{ss}k_{ss}}{l_{ss}}\right)^{\alpha-1}$$

$$\left(\frac{r_{ss}}{\alpha}\right)^{\frac{1}{\alpha-1}} = \frac{h_{ss}k_{ss}}{l_{ss}}$$

$$\frac{k_{ss}}{l_{ss}} = \left(\frac{r_{ss}}{\alpha}\right)^{\frac{1}{\alpha-1}} \frac{1}{h_{ss}} \tag{6.51}$$

Equation (6.51) provides a value for the ratio k_{ss}/l_{ss}. Therefore, it is useful to determine the ratios of the other variables based on this k_{ss}/l_{ss}. First, from the law of movement of capital (Eq. (6.49)), we obtain i_{ss}/l_{ss}:

$$\delta_{ss}k_{ss} = i_{ss}$$

$$\text{Replace the expression of } \delta_{ss} \text{ :}$$

$$\frac{h_{ss}^{\omega}}{\omega} k_{ss} = i_{ss}$$

$$\frac{i_{ss}}{l_{ss}} = \frac{h_{ss}^{\omega}}{\omega} \left[\frac{k_{ss}}{l_{ss}}\right] \tag{6.52}$$

Second, from the production function, we obtain the ratio y_{ss}/l_{ss}:

$$y_{ss} = (h_{ss}k_{ss})^{\alpha} l_{ss}^{1-\alpha}$$

$$\frac{y_{ss}}{l_{ss}} = (h_{ss}k_{ss})^{\alpha} l_{ss}^{-\alpha}$$

$$\frac{y_{ss}}{l_{ss}} = \left(\frac{k_{ss}}{l_{ss}} h_{ss}\right)^{\alpha} \tag{6.53}$$

Third, in goods market equilibrium, the ratio c_{ss}/l_{ss} is obtained:

$$y_{ss} = c_{ss} + i_{ss}$$

$$\frac{y_{ss}}{l_{ss}} = \frac{c_{ss}}{l_{ss}} + \frac{i_{ss}}{l_{ss}}$$

$$\frac{c_{ss}}{l_{ss}} = \frac{y_{ss}}{l_{ss}} - \frac{i_{ss}}{l_{ss}} \tag{6.54}$$

Fourth, the value of w_{ss} is obtained from the labor demand:

$$\begin{aligned} w_{ss} &= (1-\alpha)\frac{y_{ss}}{l_{ss}} \\ w_{ss} &= (1-\alpha)\frac{(h_{ss}k_{ss})^{\alpha} l_{ss}^{1-\alpha}}{l_{ss}} \\ w_{ss} &= (1-\alpha)\left(\frac{h_{ss}k_{ss}}{l_{ss}}\right)^{\alpha} \end{aligned} \tag{6.55}$$

Given that the values of k_{ss}/l_{ss} (Eq. (6.51)) and the value of h_{ss} are known, the real wage in the steady state is defined by Eq. (6.55). Finally, the value of l_{ss} is obtained from labor supply:

$$\begin{aligned} l_{ss}^{\theta} &= w_{ss} \\ l_{ss} &= (w_{ss})^{1/\theta} \end{aligned} \tag{6.56}$$

Working on Eq. (6.56), we have

$$\begin{aligned} l_{ss} &= (\underbrace{w_{ss}}_{\text{Eq. (6.55)}})^{1/\theta} \\ l_{ss} &= \left((1-\alpha)\left(\frac{h_{ss}k_{ss}}{l_{ss}}\right)^{\alpha}\right)^{1/\theta} \\ l_{ss} &= \left((1-\alpha)\left(h_{ss}\underbrace{\frac{k_{ss}}{l_{ss}}}_{\text{Eq. (6.51)}}\right)^{\alpha}\right)^{1/\theta} \\ l_{ss} &= \left((1-\alpha)\left(h_{ss}\left(\frac{r_{ss}}{\alpha}\right)^{\frac{1}{\alpha-1}}\frac{1}{h_{ss}}\right)^{\alpha}\right)^{1/\theta} \\ l_{ss} &= \left((1-\alpha)\left(\frac{r_{ss}}{\alpha}\right)^{\frac{\alpha}{\alpha-1}}\right)^{1/\theta} \end{aligned} \tag{6.57}$$

Given that we have the value of l_{ss}, from the previous equations, we can find capital, investment, product, consumption, and real wages (see Eqs. (6.51)–(6.55)). Table 6.8 shows the expression for the steady state of each variable in the model.

Table 6.8 Steady state

Steady state (recursive form)
$\epsilon_{ss} = 0$
$h_{ss} = \left(\frac{\frac{1}{\beta}-1}{1-\frac{1}{\omega}} \right)^{\frac{1}{\omega}}$
$r_{ss} = h_{ss}^{\omega-1}$
$\delta_{ss} = \frac{h_{ss}^{\omega}}{\omega}$
$l_{ss} = \left((1-\alpha) \left(\frac{r_{ss}}{\alpha} \right)^{\frac{\alpha}{\alpha-1}} \right)^{1/\theta}$
$k_{ss} = l_{ss} \left(\frac{r_{ss}}{\alpha} \right)^{\frac{1}{\alpha-1}} \frac{1}{h_{ss}}$
$i_{ss} = \frac{h_{ss}^{\omega}}{\omega} k_{ss}$
$y_{ss} = (h_{ss}k_{ss})^{\alpha} l_{ss}^{1-\alpha}$
$c_{ss} = y_{ss} - i_{ss}$
$w_{ss} = (1-\alpha)\frac{y_{ss}}{l_{ss}}$

6.3.1.7 Model Solution

Table 6.12 contains ten equations and ten variables of the model. This system of equations is nonlinear. This system can be linearized or log-linearized by Dynare. To log-linearize the system, each variable x should be written in Dynare as $exp(xx)$, where $xx = lnx_t$. For example, the supply of capital services is written in Dynare as follows:

Capital services supply : "in model"

$$r_t = \frac{h_t^{\omega-1}}{1+\epsilon_t}$$

Capital services supply : "in Dynare"

$$exp(rr) = \frac{exp(hh)^{\omega-1}}{1+exp(\epsilon\epsilon)}$$

By implementing this change of variable, Dynare will linearize the model and obtain a variable in log-deviations from its steady state as follows: $\widehat{x_t} = xx_t - xx_{ss} = lnx_t - lnx_{ss}$. Dynare uses the variable $\widehat{x_t}$ to calculate the steady state, policy and state functions, impulse response function, and theoretical moments.

Tables 6.12 and 6.7 show the model's solution (policy and state function) for the two sets of parameter values.

The first table corresponds to the model with $\gamma = 1$, $\phi = 0.47$, and $\sigma_v = 0.05$, whereas the second considers $\gamma = 2$, $\phi = 0.51$, and $\sigma_v = 0.0515$. It is worth mentioning that the important difference between both exercises is the EISC

(γ) because the values of persistence (ϕ) and shock (σ_v) are very similar between exercises. Therefore, the differences between the coefficients in the solution of each endogenous variable respond primarily to γ.

[A] Model 1 ($\gamma = 1$) Table 6.9 shows that the consumption policy function is expressed as

$$lnc_t = -0.7612 + 0.3788\widehat{k_t} - 0.007\widehat{e}_{t-1} - 0.0148\nu_t \tag{6.58}$$

$$lnc_t = lnc_{cc} + 0.3788\widehat{k_t} - 0.0148\left(\frac{0.007}{0.0148}\widehat{e}_{t-1} + \nu_t\right) \tag{6.59}$$

$$lnc_t - lnc_{cc} = 0.3788\widehat{k_t} - 0.0148(0.47\widehat{e}_{t-1} + \nu_t) \tag{6.60}$$

$$\widehat{c_t} = 0.3788\widehat{k_t} - 0.0148\widehat{e_t} \tag{6.61}$$

In the consumption policy function, Eq. (6.61), it is observed that the shock to investment $\widehat{e_t}$ negatively affects consumption during the same period. This indicates that, under a high elasticity of intertemporal substitution of consumption, this variable does not react positively to a shock to investment. By contrast, the policy functions of all other variables, except the interest rate, react positively to the shock to investment, which is consistent with the data. It is worth mentioning that although consumption is reduced, it does so to a lesser extent compared to the model of Campbell (1994). For example, Campbell (1994) model indicates that the elasticity of the consumption shock to investment is −0.25, in contrast to this model of −0.014.

[B] Model 2 ($\gamma = 2$) Table 6.10 shows the policy and state functions of the model under the assumption of $\gamma = 2$. This lower elasticity allows consumption to react positively to the shock to investment (elasticity c_t-e_t is equal to 0.0775) and makes it possible for the correlation between consumption and investment to be positive and procyclical consumption. Similarly, as in the model with $\gamma = 1$, the responses of the other variables have the directions (signs) observed in the data.

6.3.2 *Solution Analysis*

6.3.2.1 Impulse-Response Functions

Next, the response of the endogenous variables in t to a shock to investment in the same period is analyzed.

[A] First Effect First, the shock materializes in period t. Before this period, the variables were at a steady state. For example, shock takes the value of its mean ($\nu_{t-1} = 0$), whereas consumption takes the value of zero ($\widehat{c_t} = 0$). Recall that $\widehat{c_t}$ is the deviation of the logarithm of the variable with respect to the logarithm of its

Table 6.9 Policy and state function (model 1 ($\gamma = 1$))

	lnc_t	lni_t	lny_t	lnk_{t+1}	lnl_t	lnh_t	lnr_t	lnw_t	lnd_t	lne_t
Constante	−0.7612	−2.1213	−0.5327	0.8824	−0.5470	−1.3802	−1.2728	−0.3282	−2.3106	0
$\widehat{k}_t$	0.3788	−0.2828	0.2437	0.9478	0.1523	−0.5326	−0.2237	0.0914	−0.7563	0
$\widehat{e}_{t-1}$	−0.0070	0.6947	0.1363	0.0554	0.0852	0.2615	−0.1252	0.0511	0.3713	0.47
v_t	−0.0148	1.4782	0.2901	0.1179	0.1813	0.5564	−0.2663	0.1088	0.7901	1

Note: The results have been obtained from “modelo_ghh_log1”

Table 6.10 Policy and state function (model 2 ($\gamma = 2$))

	lnc_t	lni_t	lny_t	lnk_{t+1}	lnl_t	lnh_t	lnr_t	lnw_t	lnd_t	lne_t
Constante	−0.7612	−2.1213	−0.5327	0.8824	−0.5470	−1.3802	−1.2728	−0.3282	−2.3106	0
$\widehat{k}_t$	0.3299	−0.0924	0.2437	0.9667	0.1523	−0.5326	−0.2237	0.0914	−0.7563	0
$\widehat{e}_{t-1}$	0.0395	0.5703	0.1479	0.0419	0.0925	0.2838	−0.1358	0.0555	0.4029	0.51
v_t	0.0775	1.1182	0.2901	0.0822	0.1813	0.5564	−0.2663	0.1088	0.7901	1

Nota: The results have been obtained from "model_ghh_log1" steady state, $\widehat{c_t} = lnc_t - lnc_{ss}$. Therefore, $\widehat{c_t} = 0$ implies that $c_t = c_{ss}$; that is, the variable is in its steady state.

Second, an increase in the shock to investment materializes in period t, which means that v_t takes the value of its standard deviation (σ_v) and, thus, it takes $\epsilon_t(\uparrow)$ out of the steady state. This shock has three initial effects: the first is on the Euler equation, the second is on the law of capital movement, and the third is on the supply of capital services.

Euler's Equation The investment shock influences the intertemporal substitution of consumption. An increase in the shock to investment $\uparrow \epsilon_t$ encourages the representative household to substitute its current consumption for future consumption, which is reflected in $\downarrow c_t$ and $\uparrow c_{t+1}$:

$$\left(c_t - \frac{l_t^{1+\theta}}{1+\theta}\right)^{-\gamma}\left[\frac{1}{1+\uparrow \epsilon_t}\right] = \beta E_t\left(c_{t+1} - \frac{l_{t+1}^{1+\theta}}{1+\theta}\right)^{-\gamma}\left[r_{t+1}h_{t+1} + \frac{1-\delta_{t+1}}{1+\epsilon_{t+1}}\right] \tag{6.62}$$

Law of Motion of Capital An increase in the shock to investment $\uparrow \epsilon_t$ encourages the production of new capital at "t+1" to increase:

$$\uparrow k_{t+1} \underbrace{=}_{\leftarrow} (1-\delta_t)k_t + (1+\uparrow \epsilon_t)i_t \tag{6.63}$$

Supply of Capital Services This equation is important in this model. Unlike the standard RBC model, such as that of Campbell (1994), in which there is no difference between the supply of capital and the supply of capital services (both are perfectly inelastic), in the model of Greenwood et al. (1988), both supplies are different. First, the capital supply k_t is perfectly inelastic, as in Campbell (1994) model, because it represents the economy's stock of capital and is a determined variable in t. Second, the supply of capital services $h_t k_t$ has a positive slope (with respect to the interest rate) because an increase in investment encourages households to offer greater use of capital $\uparrow h_t$. This is most clearly observed in the supply of capital services:

$$\begin{aligned} r_t &= \frac{h_t^{\omega-1}}{1+\epsilon_t} \\ (1+\uparrow \epsilon_t)r_t &\underbrace{=}_{\rightarrow} \uparrow h_t^{\omega-1} \end{aligned} \tag{6.64}$$

Thus, a positive investment shock moves the supply of capital services to the right side, that is, a supply expansion (see Fig. 6.5).

[B] Second Effect First, since consumption reduces at "t" and investment is now more productive, the representative household increases investment $\uparrow i_t$. This increase has an additional positive effect on the supply of capital goods at "t+1."

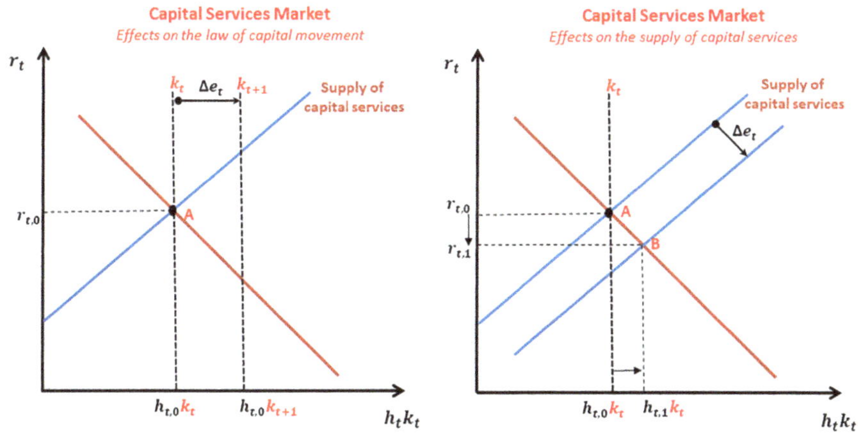

Fig. 6.5 Effects of the investment shock in the capital services market

It should be noted that the reduction in consumption does not have an impact on labor supply, as in the model of Campbell (1994). This is because the utility function considered in Greenwood et al. (1988) eliminates the presence of consumption in the labor supply. As mentioned before, the form of this utility function eliminates the wealth effect on labor supply. The effect of this assumption is that it prevents the real wage from falling.

Second, an increase in the use of capital affects labor demand because both factors are complementary. Unlike the demand for capital services, in which a movement of h_t implies a movement *on the same curve* of the demand for capital (not a shift), in the case of labor demand, a movement of h_t *shifts* that demand.[1] Therefore, a greater use of capital implies an expansion of labor demand, which, in equilibrium, leads to an increase in hours worked $\uparrow l_t$ and real wages $\uparrow w_t$ (see Fig. 6.6).

Third, greater utilization of capital *stock* produces greater depreciation, which negatively affects the accumulation of capital in the following period. Then, it is observed that

$$\uparrow \epsilon_t \rightarrow \uparrow h_t \rightarrow \uparrow \delta_t \rightarrow \downarrow h_{t+1}$$

This can be seen in the law of movement of capital:

$$\downarrow k_{t+1} \underbrace{=}_{\leftarrow} (1 - \uparrow \delta_t) k_t + (1 + \epsilon_t) i_t \tag{6.65}$$

[1] It should be mentioned that these movements are different in the case of a shock of productivity a_t. In it, both demands (labor and capital) expand because a_t does not affect the slope of said curves.

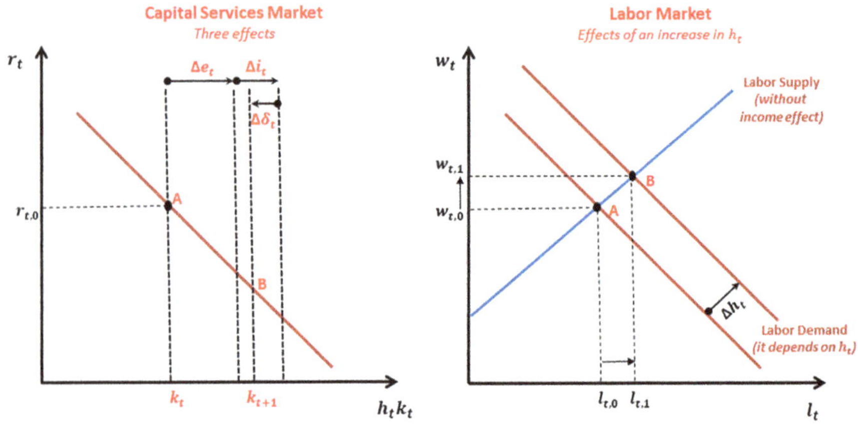

Fig. 6.6 Effects of the investment shock in the supply of capital and the labor market

Therefore, an increase in the shock to productivity has three effects on k_{t+1}:

$$\uparrow \epsilon_t \rightarrow \uparrow k_{t+1} \tag{6.66}$$

$$\uparrow \epsilon_t \rightarrow \uparrow i_t \rightarrow \uparrow k_{t+1} \tag{6.67}$$

$$\uparrow \epsilon_t \rightarrow \uparrow h_t \rightarrow \uparrow \delta_t \rightarrow \downarrow k_{t+1} \tag{6.68}$$

Fourth, the reduction in the interest rate by "t" ($\downarrow r_t$), the increase in capital services ($\uparrow h_t k_t$), and the increase in labor income ($\uparrow w_t l_t$) together produce a positive income effect on the budget constraint of the representative household. These higher incomes increase the consumption ($\uparrow c_t$).

Finally, in period $t + 1$, the effects of the shock are maintained owing to its persistence but with less magnitude. In this period, the interest rate r_{t+1} falls but to a lesser extent than in "t." This reduction in the interest rate produces a substitution effect on current consumption: the household, faced with a reduction in the interest rate by "t+1," reduces its consumption by "t" ($\downarrow c_t$) and increments its consumption by "t+1" ($\downarrow c_{t+1}$). This is because the "gain (r_{t+1})" from parting with a consumption unit in "t" has decreased.

[C] Summary of Effects First, as previously mentioned, the shock to investment has three effects on the *stock* of capital at "t+1 ." The first two increment it ($\uparrow \epsilon_t$ and $\uparrow i_t$) and the third decrement it ($\uparrow \delta_t$). On the net, the *stock* of capital at "t+1" increases.

Second, because there is no income effect on labor supply, real wages and hours worked are higher in equilibrium after the shock to investment. Third, in the capital services market, only supply expands because of the shock to investment, leading to higher utilization of capital. In this market, demand does not shift at "t"; it moves only along the curve. In equilibrium, the real interest rate decreases, and capital utilization increases.

Fourth, investment shock has three effects on current consumption. The first effect is obtained directly from Euler's equation: the shock to investment reduces current consumption ($\downarrow c_t$). This effect can be understood as an "intratemporal substitution effect." The second is obtained through the "wealth effect": income from labor and capital services increases, making the household richer. This wealth effect leads to an increase in current consumption ($\uparrow c_t$). Finally, in period "t+1," the interest rate remains below the steady state, which, through the substitution effect, encourages an increase in consumption in "t" ($\uparrow c_t$). This can be understood as the "intertemporal substitution effect."

[D] Impulse-Response Function Figure 6.7 shows the impulse-response function of the model of Greenwood et al. (1988) for two scenarios. The main difference between the two scenarios is the elasticity of intertemporal substitution of consumption (EISC = $1/\gamma$). These two scenarios also consider different persistence and magnitude of the shock. However, these differences are marginal. The main conclusion of the comparison of these two scenarios is that the lower elasticity of substitution moderates the reduction in consumption in the face of a shock to investment (intratemporal substitution effect). This allows the income effect and intertemporal substitution effect (for a reduction of r_{t+1}) to exceed the reduction in consumption. In the net, consumption increases when EISC is lower.

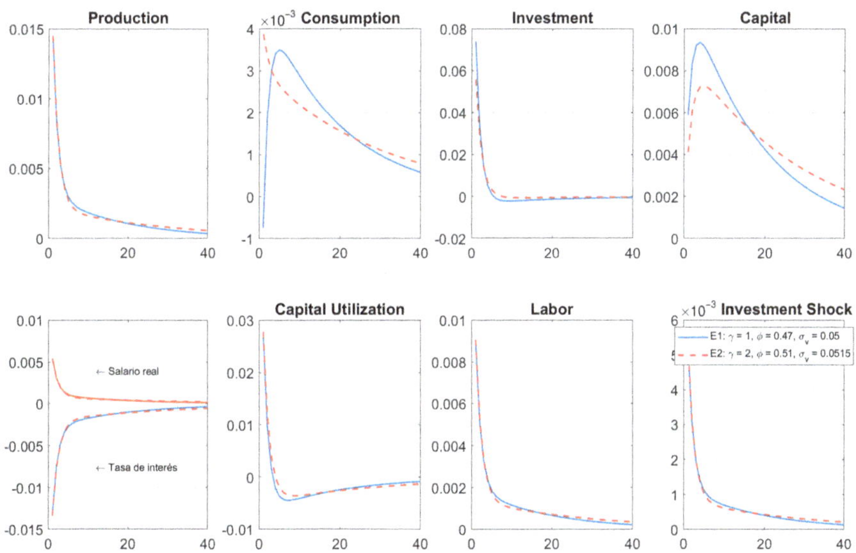

Fig. 6.7 Greenwood et al. (1988)-*shock* to investment. **Remark:** This figure comes from the mod file "modelo_ghh_log1.mod"

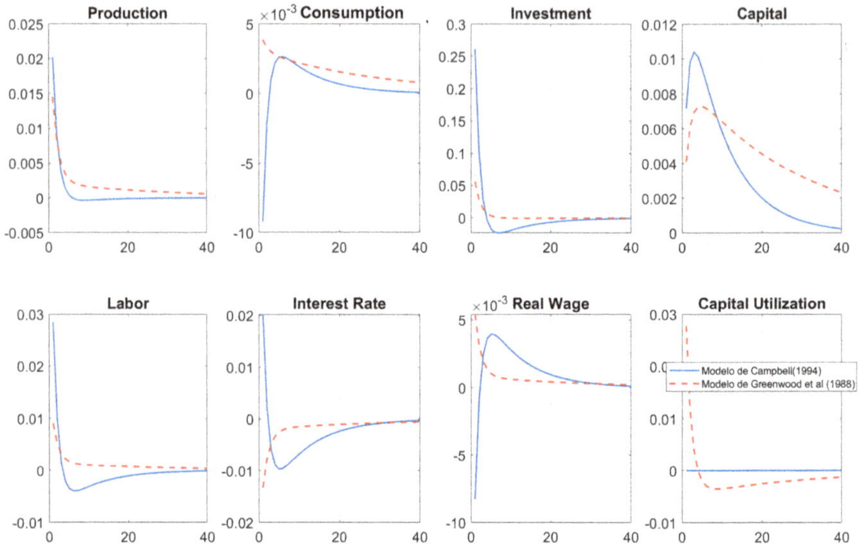

Fig. 6.8 Variable utilization model (Greenwood et al., 1988) vs. fixed use model (Campbell, 1994). **Note:** The Greenwood et al. (1988) model considers $\gamma = 2$, $\phi = 0.51$, and $\sigma_\upsilon = 0.515$. In addition, the Campbell (1994) model maintains the same calibration so that both models are comparable. This graph corresponds to an investment shock. The figure is obtained from the file "Campbell_vs_GHH.m"

On the other hand, when consumption increases in the current period, investment increases but to a lesser extent. This moderate increase in investment has effects on the *stock* of capital at "t+1," which is smaller than that in the higher EISC case. Finally, the other variables were not affected by the EISC.

[E] Comparison of Models Figure 6.8 shows the comparison between the model of Campbell (1994), which considers the use of fixed capital, and the model of Greenwood et al. (1988), which considers the use of variable capital. Both models maintain the same calibration and are subject to an investment shock. The main differences are as follows:

First, the production in the Campbell (1994) model is slightly larger than that in Greenwood et al. (1988) model. This is because, in the first model, the increase in labor is almost three times that in the second. However, this lack of labor response in the second model is offset by an increase in capital use.

Second, consumption in the model of Campbell (1994) shrinks, in contrast to the increase in this variable in the model of Greenwood et al. (1988). In both models, the shock to investment has three effects on current consumption. The first is the intratemporal substitution that allows an increase in consumption, similar in both models. The second is the wealth effect, which also increases current consumption, similar to both models. The third is the intertemporal substitution effect, which differs for each model. In Campbell (1994), the increase in demand for capital, under a perfectly inelastic supply, increases the real interest rate, which remains above the steady state in period "t+1."

This increase in the interest rate at "t+1" induces the household to reduce its consumption in "t." Therefore, the intertemporal substitution effect in Campbell (1994) model reduces consumption. In contrast, in the model of Greenwood et al. (1988), the curve that expands is not the demand for capital but the supply of *services of capital*, which in equilibrium produces an interest rate level below the steady state. This level, but to a lesser extent, is maintained in period "t+1," which induces the household to increase its consumption in "t." Consequently, the intertemporal substitution effect in the model of Greenwood et al. (1988) increases the consumption.

Third, investment increases in both models, although to a lesser extent in the model by Greenwood et al. (1988). This lower volatility responds to the fact that resources are allocated to an increase in consumption, leaving fewer resources for investment. This differs from Campbell (1994) model, in which consumption is reduced by an increase in the interest rate, which makes investment more attractive. This reduction in consumption encourages a shift of resources toward investment. A direct effect of lower investment is lower capital accumulation, as seen in the capital impulse-response function.

Fourth, similarities and differences are observed in the labor market between the model of Campbell (1994) and the model of Greenwood et al. (1988). The main similarity is that the number of hours worked increases in both models, although to a lesser extent in the model by Greenwood et al. (1988) because the labor supply is not subject to the wealth effect (c_t is not present in said offer). The main difference is that the real wage increases in the model of Greenwood et al. (1988) but is reduced in the model of Campbell (1994). The reduction in real wages in Campbell (1994) model is due to the fact that the labor supply expands due to the present wealth effect (given that consumption contracts, the household then decides to work more). This curve movement is absent in the model proposed by Greenwood et al. (1988).

6.3.2.2 Comparison of the Theoretical Model with the Data

To calculate empirical statistics, Greenwood et al. (1988) use annual data from 1948 to 1985. In addition, the extraction process of the cyclical component, both in the data and in the model, is by means of a "linear quadratic trend." This is an important difference from the usual method of separating the trend from RBC models, which use the Hodrick-Prescott filter.

Table 6.11 shows each model variable's empirical and theoretical moments. Given that in previous sections, the policy function and the impulse-response function of two models ($\gamma = 1$ vs. $\gamma = 2$) have been considered, this section shows the moments obtained from each of these models. It is worth mentioning that the theoretical moments derived from the model are obtained from a simulation and without applying any filter. Therefore, the standard deviations are not comparable to the data, but the correlation and autocorrelation are.

Table 6.11 Comparison of the cyclical behavior of the theoretical model with the empirical data

	Data			Model							
				Model 1 ($\gamma = 1$)				Model 2 ($\gamma = 2$)			
Variable (x_t)	(1)[a]	(2)[b]	(3)[c]	(1)[a]	(2)[b]	(3)[c]	(4)[d]	(1)[a]	(2)[b]	(3)[c]	(4)[d]
Consumption	2.20	0.74	0.72	1.27	0.51	0.97	1.00	1.21	0.80	0.95	1.00
Investment	10.50	0.68	0.25	8.27	0.86	0.44	−0.01	6.46	0.90	0.50	0.46
Commodity	3.50	1.00	0.66	1.96	1.00	0.66	0.51	1.96	1.00	0.66	0.80
Stock				3.38	0.71	0.98	0.97	3.20	0.65	0.99	0.97
Labor	2.10	0.81	0.39	1.22	1.00	0.66	0.51	1.23	1.00	0.66	0.80
Usage rate				3.36	0.55	0.48	−0.44	3.42	0.61	0.53	0.01
Real salary interest rate				1.80	−1.00	0.66	−0.51	1.80	−1.00	0.66	−0.80
Real salary	2.20	0.82	0.77	0.73	1.00	0.66	0.51	0.74	1.00	0.66	0.80
Depreciation				4.77	0.55	0.48	−0.44	4.86	0.61	0.53	0.01

Remark: Empirical values were taken from Greenwood et al. (1988), who considered the variables in logarithms and extracted the trend through a linear-quadratic time trend. The theoretical values were obtained from a single simulation, and no filter was applied to obtain the cyclical component of the variables. These values are obtained from the "model_ghh_log1.mod" file

[a] (1) = Standard deviation (%)
[b] (2) = Correlation with the product
[c] (3) = First order autocorrelation
[d] (4) = Correlation with consumption

The main conclusion that emerges from Table 6.11 is that the model with $\gamma = 2$ (lower EISC) allows us to obtain two stylized facts that the standard RBC model could not: the first is that the correlation of consumption with investment is positive, and the second is that consumption is procyclical. The second conclusion is that, in general, the moments inferred by the model were close to those observed in the data. Finally, all these values are obtained considering the persistence of the shock to investment ($\phi = 0.51$) compared with the standard RBC models ($\phi = 0.9$).

6.4 Summary

This chapter presents an RBC model that incorporates two main features: (i) a shock to the marginal efficiency of investment and (ii) the possibility that capital is used in a variable way; that is, there is idle capital in the economy.

The motivation to study such a model serves several purposes. First, we show how RBC models can consider shocks that do not have their origin in technological disturbances. Second, including a shock to investment can reduce the necessary magnitude of the shocks to technology to explain the stylized facts present in the aggregate fluctuations. Finally, it is possible to argue that adding a shock to the marginal efficiency of capital rescues an important part of the spirit of Keynes's General Theory and the role played by investment shocks in explaining macroeconomic fluctuations.

We start by studying a standard RBC model in which we include a shock to investment but assume that capital is fully utilized over the business cycle. After solving the model, we show that the empirical implication of the model is that consumption is countercyclical, whereas it is procyclical in the data. This result is invariant to increasing labor or consumption substitution elasticities in the base model. The rest of the theoretical moments behave in a similar way to the model with the variable labor reviewed in previous chapters.

We then incorporate a new transmission mechanism into the standard RBC model: we allow firms to use a variable fraction of their capital; that is, they have idle capital. Including such a mechanism seems natural, given that capital is never fully utilized during the business cycle.

By incorporating this mechanism into the model, we achieve the following: (i) the countercyclical behavior in consumption disappears, with which we are able to qualitatively replicate all the patterns of comovements in the data that the model with variable work had, and (ii) we managed to reduce the magnitude of the shock to the technology needed to replicate the stylized facts of interest, which has been commonly pointed out as a deficiency in RBC models.

As we wrap up our review of RBC models in the chapters of this book, we should note that substantive progress has been made in bringing the stylized facts of economic fluctuations closer to those predicted by RBC models. However, two stylized facts that we have continually failed to approximate are the countercyclical behavior of the interest rate and the acyclical behavior of wages relative to output. Additionally, the models studied have all been "real," in the sense that the effects of nominal variables such as inflation, money, and the nominal interest rate have not been studied. In the next volume, we review these issues in the framework of neo-Keynesian models.

6.5 Codes

Table 6.12 lists the MATLAB and Dynare codes used in this chapter.

Table 6.12 Codes in Matlab and Dynare

Codes	Description
Matlab	
grafica_depreciacion.m	This *m-file* plots depreciation as a function of capital utilization and three values of ω
Campbell_vs_GHH.m	Plot the impulse-response function of the model of Campbell (1994) vs. Greenwood et al. (1988). Both models have the same calibration proposed by Greenwood et al. (1988)
Dynare	
modelo_ghh_log1.mod	It replicates the model of Greenwood et al. (1988). Furthermore, it simulates the model for two scenarios: E1 ($\gamma = 1, \phi = 0.47$, $\sigma_{\upsilon} = 0.05$) and E2 ($\gamma = 2, \phi = 0.51$, $\sigma_{\upsilon} = 0.0515$)
modelo_ghh_log2.mod	It is the same model as "model_ghh_log1.mod," but with some parameters to reproduce an RBC model with fixed usage
Campbell_Lvariable_nolineal_log5_inv.mod	It is the same "Campbell_Lvariable_nonlinear_log5.mod" mod from Chap. 5, with the only difference being that it has shock on investment when compared to Greenwood et al. (1988) model

Chapter 7
Small Open Economy RBC

7.1 Introduction

This chapter delves into the small open economy RBC model, which is a natural extension of the baseline RBC model that incorporates international trade and cross-border financial flows. The growing pace of globalization and economic integration has increased the importance of studying this setup, as it provides insights into the behavior of macroeconomic aggregates in response to external shocks and the propagation of international disturbances.

The small open economy RBC model is based on the pioneering work of Mendoza (1991). One of the model's main features is its access to international financial markets, allowing domestic agents to separate their savings and investment decisions. This modification enables the model to capture the implications of international capital flows on the economy's aggregate demand, capital accumulation, and welfare. We also consider alternative specifications presented in the literature, aiming to establish a unique steady state. These alternatives are mostly summarized in Schmitt-Grohe and Uribe (2003). Another key feature of the small open economy RBC model is the assumption that the economy is "small" in the sense that the size of the economy is approximated to zero. This assumption implies that domestic shocks do not affect the rest of the world, and therefore, domestic agents take international prices as given.

Furthermore, we explore the model's predictions regarding the dynamics of the economy at business cycle frequencies and compare them with the data. We investigate some of the most frequently used mechanisms to improve the model's fit and offer intuitive explanations for them. In summary, this chapter aims to provide a comprehensive understanding of the small open economy RBC model and its relevance in the domain of international macroeconomic dynamics. Through this analysis, our goal is to enhance our comprehension of the factors influencing the fluctuations of macroeconomic aggregates and the channels through which they operate.

H. Galindo Gil et al., *Dynamic Stochastic General Equilibrium Models*, Springer Texts in Business and Economics, https://doi.org/10.1007/978-3-031-58105-2_7

7.2 Empirics

In this section, we extend the characterization of business cycles discussed in Chap. 1 to a broader set of countries. Our analysis focuses on the cyclical behavior of key variables in international commerce and finance, including output (Y), total private consumption (C), investment (I), public consumption (G), exports (X), imports (M), the trade balance ($TB = X - M$), and the current account (CA), all measured in per capita terms.

One of the main sources of stylized facts about business cycles is the work of Uribe and Schmitt-Grohé (2017). Using the World Bank's World Development Indicators (WDI) database, these authors characterized business cycles around the world over the 1960–2010 period. Their analysis focused on three key criteria: variability, direction, and persistence of the aggregated variables mentioned above. To filter the cyclical component of each series, the authors considered quadratic detrending, HP filtering, and first differences.

Their findings are summarized in Table 7.1, which presents ten stylized facts characterizing business cycles around the world. We build on this work and update the analysis by examining real business cycles around the world over the period 1990–2020, following the methodology proposed by Uribe and Schmitt-Grohé (2017) to calculate the statistics and document the treatment of the data in detail.

As in previous chapters, we focus on certain moments in the data, including the standard deviation related to variability, the cross-correlation with cyclical component of the GDP per capita related to co-movement with the business cycle, and the first-order correlation that provides information on persistence. We also characterize business cycles of countries exhibiting different levels of wealth. We classify countries into these groups using their PPP-converted GDP per capita in US dollars of 2005, and we also categorize them by size using their total population.

To begin, we define the variables used in the analysis and describe in detail the treatment of the variables for analysis through econometric tools. We then present the results using three different filters for the data: (1) Hodrick-Prescott, (2) log-quadratic detrending, and (3) first differences. Finally, we arrive to ten stylized facts characterizing business cycles around the world using updated data, which are similar to those documented by Uribe and Schmitt-Grohé (2017).

7.2.1 *Construction of the Macroeconomic Series*

In order to characterize the business cycles of various countries, it is necessary to obtain macroeconomic time series data. The selected variables are listed in Table 7.2.

The data used in this chapter is from World Bank's World Development Indicators (WDI) database. After obtaining the dataset, we remove the countries that do not report continuous data for every aggregate variable across the period of

Table 7.1 Stylized facts of global macroeconomic fluctuations

Stylized fact	Description
High output volatility	The cross-country average standard deviation of output is twice as large as its US counterpart. This implies that business cycles around the world are generally more volatile than those in the United States
Excess consumption volatility	The average across countries of private consumption including durables is more volatile than output. This suggests that households tend to smooth their consumption less than firms adjust their production in response to macroeconomic shocks
Global ranking of volatilities	The ranking of cross-country average standard deviations from top to bottom is imports, investment, exports, government spending, consumption, and output. This ranking reflects the relative importance of different components of aggregate demand in driving business cycles across countries
Procyclicality of the components of aggregate demand	On average, consumption, investment, exports, and imports are all positively correlated with output. This indicates that the components of aggregate demand tend to move together with overall economic activity
Countercyclicality of the trade balance and the current account	On average across countries, the trade balance, the trade balance to output ratio, the current account, and the current account to output ratio are all negatively correlated with output. This implies that countries tend to run trade surpluses when their economies are weak and deficits when they are strong
Acyclicality of the share of government consumption in GDP	On average across countries, the share of government consumption in output is roughly uncorrelated with output. This suggests that changes in government spending do not play a major role in driving business cycles across countries
Persistence	The components of aggregate supply (output and imports) and aggregate demand (consumption, government spending, investment, and exports) are all positively serially correlated. This means that deviations from trend tend to persist over time in all major components of the economy
Excess volatility of poor and emerging countries	Business cycles in rich countries are about half as volatile as business cycles in emerging or poor countries. This suggests that economic development and financial integration play important roles in determining the level of macroeconomic volatility across countries
Less consumption smoothing in poor and emerging countries	The relative consumption volatility is higher in poor and emerging countries than in rich countries. This implies that households in these countries tend to adjust their consumption more in response to income shocks
The countercyclicality of government spending increases with income	The share of government consumption is countercyclical in rich countries but acyclical in emerging and poor countries. This suggests that the role of government in stabilizing the economy may depend on the level of economic development and the structure of the public sector

Note: This table presents the stylized facts identified by Uribe and Schmitt-Grohé (2017) on global macroeconomic fluctuations. These facts have been distilled from extensive empirical analysis of cross-country data, and they provide important insights into the key features of business cycles around the world

Table 7.2 Variables included in the study

Variable	Description
Y_t	GDP per capita
C_t	Consumption per capita
I_t	Investment per capita
G_t	Government spending per capita
X_t	Exports per capita
M_t	Imports per capita
TB_t	Trade balance per capita
CA_t	Current account per capita

analysis (1990–2020). The Python code for this algorithm is available in the codes document of this book.

For the variables Y_t, C_t, I_t, G_t, X_t, and M_t, we transform the data to natural logarithms. Since logarithms can only transform positive values, this procedure is applied only to the positive-valued variables. For the ratios of interest, i.e., the ratio of government spending to GDP, the ratio of trade balance to GDP, and the ratio of current account to GDP, we do not transform the data to logarithms as deviations already reflect percentage variations.

In macroeconomics, logarithmic transformations of variables are employed to facilitate their interpretation. Specifically, deviations of data in logarithms can be approximated as percentage changes, thereby providing an intuitive and meaningful way to study real-time series. The rationale for interpreting deviations in variables in logarithmic form as percentage changes is explained in the following chart:

Approximation of the subtraction of logarithms

Let X be the percentage change between A and B, where B is different from zero:

$$(A - B)/B = \Delta\%x$$
$$A/B - 1 = \Delta\%x$$
$$A/B = 1 + \Delta\%x \tag{7.1}$$

Now, we take logarithms for both sides of Eq. (7.1) and get

$$ln(A/B) = ln(1 + \Delta\%x)$$
$$ln(A) - ln(B) = ln(1 + \Delta\%x) \tag{7.2}$$

The left side of Eq. (7.2) can be approximated using the Taylor approximation, which consists of approximating the function $f(x)$ around a fixed point a, as follows:

(continued)

$$f(x) \approx f(a) + \frac{f'(a)}{1!}(x-a) + \frac{f''(a)}{2!}(x-a)^2 + \frac{f'''(a)}{3!}(x-a)^3 + ...$$

Let $f(\Delta\%x) = ln(1 + \Delta\%x)$ and $a = 0$ the fixed point. Using the Taylor approximation

$$ln(1 + \Delta\%x) \approx ln(1) + \Delta\%x - \frac{(\Delta\%x)^2}{2} + \frac{(\Delta\%x)^3}{3} + ...$$

For small values of $\Delta\%x$, the terms at the right-hand side of $\Delta\%x$ are very close to zero; therefore, the Taylor expansion stays as a first-order Taylor approximation:

$$ln(1 + \Delta\%x) \approx \Delta\%x \tag{7.3}$$

Finally, using the result on Eq. (7.3), we observe that the subtraction of the logarithm of two values is approximately the percentage variation:

$$ln(A) - ln(B) \approx \Delta\%x$$

The analysis of business cycles extends beyond aggregate variables to include ratios, such as the trade balance to GDP ratio (tb/y). However, treating ratios as aggregate variables can be misleading, and it is crucial to understand the nature of the variables involved. To interpret deviations of an aggregated variable as a percentage variation, it is necessary to transform the data into logarithms. Yet, if the variable is defined as a ratio, the deviation already reflects a percentage variation. Therefore, there is no need to transform the data to logarithms for the ratios of interest, which include the government spending to GDP ratio, the trade balance to GDP ratio, and the current account to GDP ratio:

- Ratio of government spending to GDP
- Ratio of trade balance to GDP
- Ratio of current account to GDP

Finally, there are still aggregate variables, like the trade balance (TB_t) and the current account (CA_t), which fluctuate between positive and negative values throughout the analysis period. In such cases, it is not possible to interpret percentage variation using logarithmic transformation. To address this issue, Uribe and Schmitt-Grohé (2017) propose an alternative approach for aggregate variables with negative values, which involves scaling the variables by the trend component of the GDP series.

Consider a time series denoted by y_t. To analyze fluctuations in the business cycle, we decompose y_t into a trend component, y_t^s, and a cyclical component, y_t^c, as follows:

$$y_t = y_t^s + y_t^c \tag{7.4}$$

The trend component y^s can be estimated using a filter, such as a linear-quadratic filter or a Hodrick-Prescott filter, while the cyclical component y^c represents the deviations from the trend. The way of calculating both trend and cyclical components of a series is explained in the next section. In our case, we scale the variable in the following manner:

$$y_t = \frac{Y_t}{e^{y_t^s}} \tag{7.5}$$

By doing so, deviations from the trend are measured as a percentage of the trend of GDP. Note that y^s is obtained by detrending a logarithmic series, and therefore, it represents the trend component of the series of GDP per capita in logarithms. The exponential function is used to recover the series in levels. Dividing the trade balance TB_t by e^{y^s} yields the ratio that measures the percentage deviations of the trade balance from the trend GDP in levels. This approach is applied to the trade balance and the current account.

Once all the variables are appropriately converted or scaled, they are filtered to extract the cyclical component. The final database comprises the following variables for each country in the sample during the period 1990–2020, with the notation presented below.

7.2.2 *Detrending Techniques for Extraction of the Cyclical Component*

To extract the cyclical component from macroeconomic time series, it is necessary to first obtain the trend component. The method used to detrend the series can have a significant impact on the estimated cyclical component. In this section, we describe three different methods for detrending: log-quadratic detrending, Hodrick-Prescott (HP) filtering, and first differences.

Variable	Description	Unit
y_t	GDP per capita	Logs
c_t	Consumption per capita	Logs
i_t	Investment per capita	Logs
g_t	Government spending per capita	Logs
x_t	Exports per capita	Logs
m_t	Imports per capita	Logs
g/y	Ratio of government spending to GDP	Levels
tb/y_t	Ratio of trade balance to GDP	Levels
ca/y_t	Ratio of current account to GDP	Levels
tb_t	Trade balance	Scaled
ca_t	Current account	Scaled

7.2.2.1 Log-Quadratic Detrending

We begin with log-quadratic detrending, which is used by Uribe and Schmitt-Grohé (2017). To illustrate this method, we use Canadian data and run the following regression for $y_t = \ln(GDP_t)$ on a trend t and the square of the trend t^2:

$$y_t = \alpha + \beta_1 t + \beta_2 t^2 + \epsilon_t$$

where ϵ_t is the perturbation term and α, β_1, and β_2 are the parameters to estimate.

The independent variable t represents the year, which is in the interval [1961–2021]. It is important to note that the units of the independent variable can affect the estimation results. Using years for t instead of a sequential index can prevent a strong correlation between the regressors t and t^2.

After running the regression, we obtain the estimated parameters $\widehat{\alpha}$, $\widehat{\beta_1}$, and $\widehat{\beta_2}$. The trend component of the series y_t is given by the fitted values:

$$\widehat{y_t^s} = \widehat{\alpha} + \widehat{\beta_1} t + \widehat{\beta_2} t^2 \tag{7.6}$$

The cyclical component is given by the estimated errors:

$$\widehat{y_t^c} = y_t - \widehat{y_t^s}$$

The trend component of the series y_t is the vector $\widehat{y_t^s}$, and the cyclical component is $\widehat{y_t^c}$. Intuitively, business cycles are deviations from the trend component of the series. Figure 7.1 shows the detrended series of y_t.

We follow the same procedure for variables c_t and i_t. Figure 7.2 shows the cyclical components of each variable. The method applied to the Canadian data captures some of the key moments of the Canadian economy over the last decades.

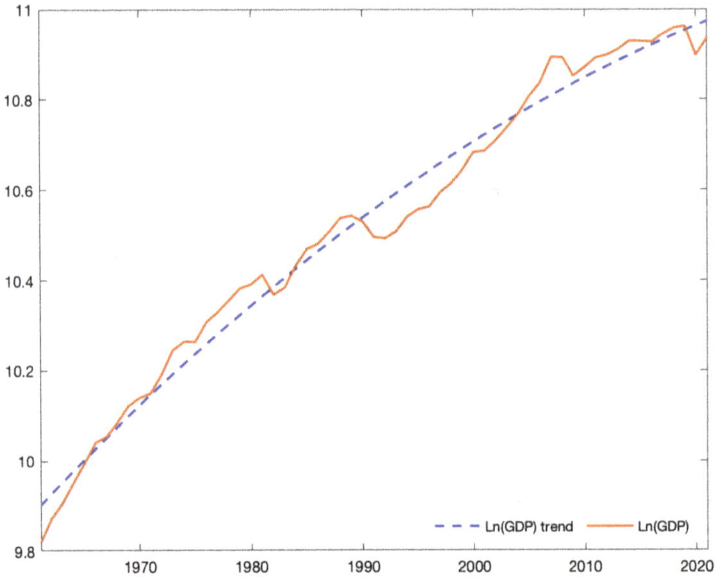

Fig. 7.1 Canada GDP per capita (in logs) and trend component (1961–2021). The trend component has been obtained by log-quadratic detrending the variable

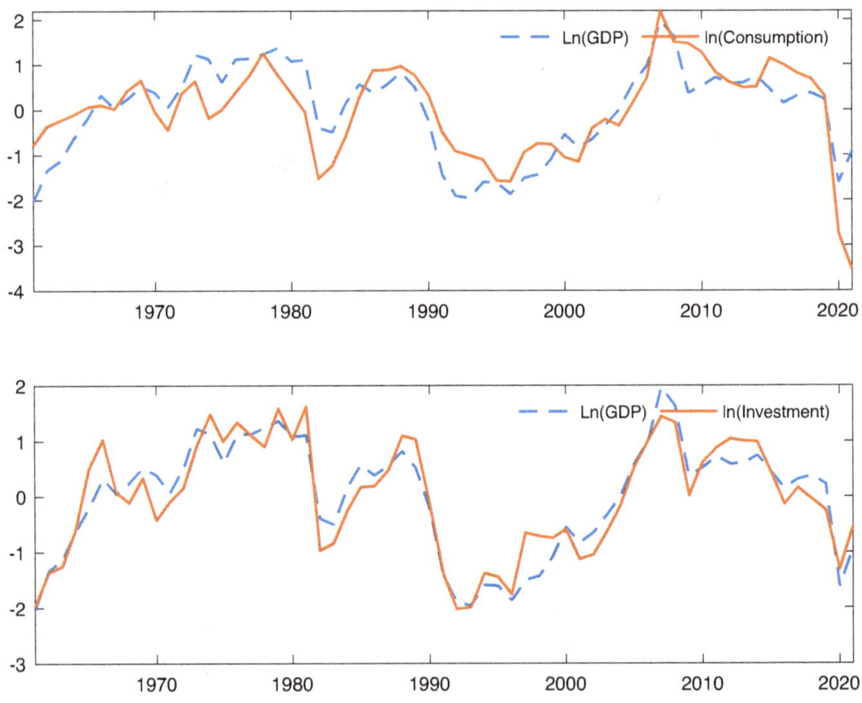

Fig. 7.2 Canada GDP per capita (in logs), consumption and investment (1961–2021)

[Obs1] Despite the global inflation problems, Canada grew considerably during the 1970s, benefiting from the increased oil prices, particularly in the Alberta region.

[Obs2] In the early 1980s, the Canadian economy, as well as other G7 countries, experience a marked slowdown, which is attributed to a weak fiscal position and the increase in global interest rates to combat inflation.

[Obs3] In the early 1990s, Canada experienced a recession, lasting until 1992. The downturn in global demand for Canadian exports and a decline in commodity prices deeply affected the economy.

[Obs4] Finally, the COVID-19 pandemic is captured at the end of the sample, reflecting the downturn experienced due to the severe lockdown and sanitary measures implemented.

In the same way, Fig. 7.3 compares the cyclical components of the ratio trade balance to GDP and the ratio current account to output.

Thus far, we have shown how to apply log-quadratic detrending. The next task is to proceed with the remaining countries in the sample. There are in total 76 countries, each country with 11 variables properly transformed and scaled. The quadratic detrending has to be applied to each variable for every country on the

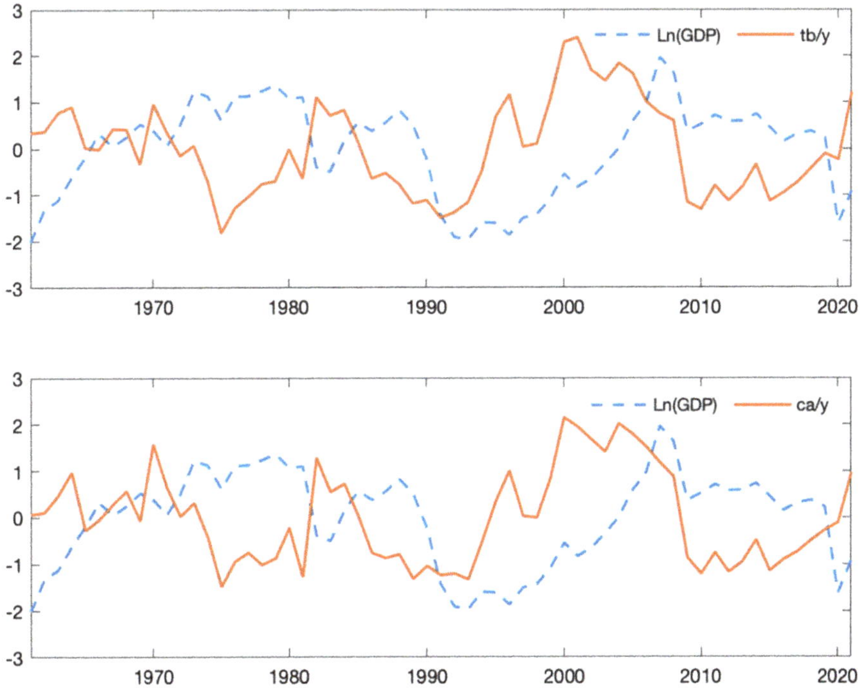

Fig. 7.3 Canada GDP per capita (in logs), trade balance to GDP ratio, and current account to output ratio (1961–2021)

Table 7.3 Log-quadratic detrending (1990–2020)

Statistic	All countries	Poor	Emerging	Rich	Small	Medium	Large
Standard deviations							
σ_y	4.26	3.96	4.81	3.23	4.65	3.92	3.74
σ_c/σ_y	1.36	1.59	1.34	1.26	1.42	1.32	1.22
σ_g/σ_y	2.46	4.08	2.5	1.53	2.36	2.55	2.59
σ_i/σ_y	4	6.05	3.77	3.44	4.11	4.27	3.2
σ_x/σ_y	3.74	5.97	3.6	2.88	3.13	4.23	4.66
σ_m/σ_y	3.6	5.69	3.46	2.8	2.98	4.08	4.51
$\sigma_{tb/y}$	3.45	4.02	3.82	2.35	4.25	2.92	2.09
$\sigma_{ca/y}$	3.31	3.81	3.45	2.74	3.97	2.87	2.14
Correlations with y							
y	1	1	1	1	1	1	1
c	0.62	0.42	0.63	0.69	0.59	0.63	0.69
g/y	−0.27	−0.24	−0.17	−0.5	−0.32	−0.23	−0.21
i	0.65	0.42	0.65	0.76	0.58	0.75	0.66
x	0.36	0.44	0.35	0.35	0.43	0.32	0.22
m	0.51	0.39	0.52	0.55	0.49	0.57	0.46
tb/y	−0.24	−0.09	−0.29	−0.22	−0.13	−0.35	−0.36
tb	−0.26	−0.21	−0.32	−0.17	−0.16	−0.38	−0.36
ca/y	−0.27	−0.13	−0.33	−0.2	−0.2	−0.36	−0.31
ca	−0.29	−0.2	−0.36	−0.19	−0.22	−0.39	−0.31
Serial correlations							
y	0.55	0.54	0.55	0.55	0.56	0.54	0.54
c	0.51	0.47	0.52	0.5	0.52	0.49	0.51
g	0.61	0.48	0.62	0.66	0.59	0.61	0.68
i	0.51	0.44	0.52	0.53	0.48	0.54	0.54
x	0.5	0.52	0.51	0.46	0.46	0.51	0.58
m	0.45	0.51	0.45	0.42	0.43	0.47	0.49
tb/y	0.48	0.41	0.49	0.5	0.46	0.51	0.5
ca/y	0.45	0.35	0.46	0.48	0.39	0.51	0.53

sample. Due to the complexity of database management, the code was written in R, a powerful programming language to deal with large databases.

Our results are presented in Table 7.3. We confirm several of the stylized facts reported by Uribe and Schmitt-Grohé (2017) with subtle variations on the ranking of volatility across variables. The procyclicality of the aggregate demand components and the countercyclicality of the trade balance and current account prevail. Also, emerging and poor countries exhibit higher business cycle volatility and less consumption smoothing than rich countries. Finally, we confirm the relationship between the countercyclicality of government expenditure and income.

Table 7.4 HP filtering (1990–2020)

Statistics	All countries	Poor	Emerging	Rich	Small	Medium	Large
Standard deviations							
σ_y	3	2.73	3.3	2.5	3.29	2.74	2.59
σ_c/σ_y	1.47	1.83	1.48	1.26	1.52	1.45	1.36
σ_g/σ_y	2.58	4.67	2.64	1.34	2.4	2.79	2.7
σ_i/σ_y	4.33	6.56	4.14	3.57	4.61	4.44	3.29
σ_x/σ_y	3.94	6.58	3.76	2.95	3.32	4.48	4.79
σ_m/σ_y	3.88	6.01	3.79	2.95	3.28	4.37	4.73
$\sigma_{tb/y}$	2.79	3.2	3.11	1.89	3.46	2.29	1.75
$\sigma_{ca/y}$	2.7	3.18	2.81	2.22	3.3	2.3	1.69
Correlations with y							
y	1	1	1	1	1	1	1
c	0.62	0.37	0.64	0.7	0.59	0.61	0.72
g/y	−0.33	−0.14	−0.24	−0.62	−0.39	−0.27	−0.25
i	0.62	0.37	0.62	0.74	0.55	0.67	0.71
x	0.36	0.36	0.29	0.51	0.46	0.29	0.2
m	0.49	0.32	0.47	0.64	0.49	0.51	0.48
tb/y	−0.21	−0.02	−0.28	−0.17	−0.1	−0.27	−0.41
tb	−0.23	−0.1	−0.31	−0.13	−0.12	−0.29	−0.42
ca/y	−0.23	−0.06	−0.33	−0.13	−0.16	−0.27	−0.4
ca	−0.25	−0.11	−0.35	−0.12	−0.18	−0.29	−0.4
Serial correlations							
y	0.39	0.34	0.4	0.38	0.39	0.34	0.46
c	0.33	0.3	0.34	0.32	0.34	0.29	0.37
g	0.45	0.32	0.46	0.51	0.42	0.46	0.52
i	0.34	0.21	0.35	0.4	0.32	0.36	0.38
x	0.3	0.33	0.3	0.28	0.27	0.31	0.38
m	0.28	0.31	0.27	0.28	0.25	0.29	0.35
tb/y	0.33	0.24	0.34	0.35	0.3	0.35	0.35
ca/y	0.29	0.17	0.3	0.32	0.23	0.34	0.34

Now, we consider the HP filter detrending method. The results are shown in Table 7.4. All stylized facts prevail. The main difference between the business-cycle facts derived from quadratic detrending and HP filtering is that under the latter detrending method all standard deviations fall by about a third. For example, the average standard deviation of output falls from 6.2 percent under quadratic detrending to 3.8 percent under HP filtering. In all other respects, the log-quadratic and HP filters produce very similar business-cycle facts.

Finally, we present the results of detrending extracting the first differences from the series. Table 7.5 show the results, which confirm the findings under the previous

Table 7.5 First differences (1990–2020)

Statistics	All countries	Poor	Emerging	Rich	Small	Medium	Large
Standard deviations							
$\sigma_{\Delta y}$	3.37	3.39	3.6	2.86	3.69	3.17	2.77
$\sigma_{\Delta c}/\sigma_{\Delta y}$	1.51	1.76	1.55	1.3	1.56	1.48	1.42
$\sigma_{\Delta g}/\sigma_{\Delta y}$	1.51	1.76	1.55	1.3	1.56	1.48	1.42
$\sigma_{\Delta i}/\sigma_{\Delta y}$	4.44	6.67	4.37	3.4	4.88	4.25	3.48
$\sigma_{\Delta x}/\sigma_{\Delta y}$	4.1	5.99	4.08	3.15	3.63	4.38	4.96
$\sigma_{\Delta m}/\sigma_{\Delta y}$	4.11	5.34	4.27	3.12	3.64	4.38	4.97
$\sigma_{tb/y}$	3.45	4.02	3.82	2.35	4.25	2.92	2.09
$\sigma_{ca/y}$	3.31	3.81	3.45	2.74	3.97	2.87	2.14
Correlations with y							
Δy	1	1	1	1	1	1	1
Δc	0.61	0.39	0.62	0.69	0.57	0.64	0.67
g/y	−0.27	−0.24	−0.17	−0.5	−0.32	−0.23	−0.21
Δi	0.59	0.39	0.59	0.68	0.52	0.64	0.67
Δx	0.41	0.32	0.34	0.62	0.54	0.35	0.18
Δm	0.5	0.33	0.47	0.67	0.52	0.51	0.44
tb/y	−0.24	−0.09	−0.29	−0.22	−0.13	−0.35	−0.36
ca/y	−0.27	−0.13	−0.33	−0.2	−0.2	−0.36	−0.31
Serial correlations							
Δy	0.21	0.14	0.23	0.2	0.2	0.18	0.28
Δc	0.05	−0.08	0.04	0.13	0.06	0.02	0.06
Δg	0.11	−0.1	0.09	0.24	0.07	0.11	0.2
Δi	0.01	−0.17	0.01	0.1	−0.04	0.04	0.07
Δx	0.01	−0.01	0	0.04	−0.02	0.04	0.04
Δm	−0.03	−0.05	−0.04	0.02	−0.06	0	0.02
tb/y	0.48	0.41	0.49	0.5	0.46	0.51	0.5
ca/y	0.45	0.35	0.46	0.48	0.39	0.51	0.53

two methods. Following Uribe and Schmitt-Grohé (2017), we also calculate the cyclical stylized facts classifying the countries by income and size. After confirming these stylized facts, we study our baseline model and contrast its results with our findings in the data.

7.3 Model Elements

The open economy presents two fundamental differences from the closed economy case. Firstly, agents can borrow and lend resources from abroad. Consequently, a country is not constrained by its own output level and can utilize foreign resources to finance its growth during a period of high investment opportunities or elevated international demand. Furthermore, domestic agents can benefit from investment opportunities abroad, which can improve the return or risk profile of their portfolios. These aggregate flows are reflected in the balance of payments.

Secondly, even if a country exhibits balanced trade and does not consume or invest more than it produces, it can still gain by specializing in the production of a particular good and trading it for others in the international markets. This chapter and the following one will introduce these features into our model from the perspective of a small open economy.

A small open economy is one in which domestic agents' actions do not affect international prices. For example, if domestic agents increase their savings, the international interest rate will remain unaffected. Although only a few economies should be considered as large economies where domestic dynamics affect world prices, this assumption should be kept in mind when studying long-run dynamics since small economies can become large in the long horizon.

This chapter focuses on the dynamics of an economy where only one good exists, leaving the case of differentiated goods for the next chapter. Here, we examine the dynamics of an economy when domestic agents can use foreign resources to borrow and lend. Although this book focuses on DSGE models, it is useful to begin with the two-period case to gain insights into the dynamics at infinite horizons.

7.3.1 Two-Period Small Open Economy Model

Assuming an economy consisting of households that aim to maximize their lifetime utility, we have the following utility function:

$$U_0 = u(c_1) + \beta u(c_2), \qquad 0 < \beta < 1 \tag{7.7}$$

Here, c_t represents the real consumption in period t, and β denotes the time preference parameter that measures the impatience of agents. The utility function satisfies the standard assumptions: $u'(\cdot) > 0$ and $u''(\cdot) < 0$. Moreover, we assume that

$$\lim_{c \to 0} u'(\cdot) = \infty. \tag{7.8}$$

To simplify the analysis, we assume an endowment economy where households receive y_1 and y_2 units of the consumption good in periods 1 and 2, respectively. This information is known to agents in the first period, and we assume that they have perfect foresight and do not face any uncertainty. This simplification enables us to focus on the forces that determine the equilibrium in a clearer manner.

Since households receive fixed endowments y_1 and y_2, the agent is constrained to consume exactly the amount of those endowments each period. This implies that the level of consumption equals the level of endowment: $c_i = y_i, \forall_{i=1,2}$. However, the agent can allocate his or her resources intertemporally by bringing resources from the future to the present or carrying resources from the present to the future.

If the agent brings resources from the future to the present, it implies that the endowment at period "t = 1" is not sufficient to optimize the level of consumption at the current period c_1. Conversely, if the agent carries resources from the present to the future, it means that the endowment at period "t = 2" is not sufficient to optimize the level of consumption at the following period c_2.

Agents can make this intertemporal decision by changing their stock of financial assets (a_t), which pay an interest rate denoted by r. Therefore, the period budget constraints of the representative household are given by

$$a_1 - a_0 = y_1 - c_1 + ra_0$$

$$a_2 - a_1 = y_2 - c_2 + ra_1.$$

The idea of introducing financial assets in the budget constraint is devolved in detail later on this chapter. Since we consider the two-period deterministic case, we set $a_2 = 0$, which implies that households have no liabilities or assets at the end of the two periods. Moreover, we assume households start with zero assets ($a_0 = 0$). Therefore, they can only use the resources they receive from their endowments in periods 1 and 2.

By replacing these assumptions in the period budget constraints, we can obtain the intertemporal budget constraint:

$$c_1 + \frac{c_2}{1+r} = y_1 + \frac{y_2}{1+r}. \tag{7.9}$$

By allowing the agent to bring resources to the present or carry resources from the present to the future, the agent can achieve higher utility. To show this, Fig. 7.4 plots the intertemporal budget constraint given in Eq. (7.9) on the indifference curves map.

The left graph of Fig. 7.4 illustrates the case where the use of financial assets allows the agent to achieve the optimal path of consumption $\{c_1^*\}$ when $y_1 < c_1$.

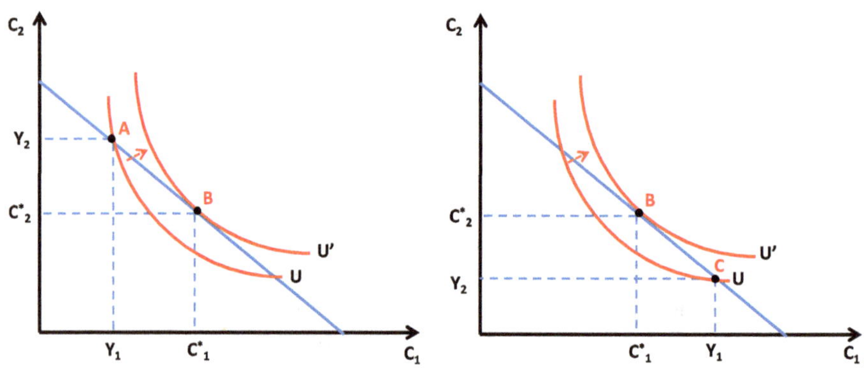

Fig. 7.4 Map of indifference curves

Similarly, the right graph of Fig. 7.4 shows that the agent can attain the optimal level of consumption at period "t = 2" due to the use of financial assets when $y_2 < c_2$. The only scenario in which the use of financial assets does not increase utility is when the endowments are exactly equal to the optimal level of consumption in both periods.

Maximizing the lifetime utility in Eq. (7.7) subject to the intertemporal budget constraint in Eq. (7.9) by choosing the consumption path of c yields

$$u'(c_1) = \beta(1+r)u'(c_2). \tag{7.10}$$

The equilibrium condition in Eq. (7.10) indicates that the consumption pattern depends on the relationship between the subjective discount factor β and the international interest rate r. When domestic agents are relatively more impatient ($\beta < 1/(1+r)$), they consume more in period 1 than in period 2. In contrast, when domestic agents are relatively patient ($\beta > 1/(1+r)$), they consume more in period 2 than in period 1. Thus, we obtain our first result: assuming equal endowments in periods 1 and 2, an economy with relatively impatient households will consume more in period 1 by running a current account deficit. In contrast, an economy with relatively patient households will consume more in period 2 by saving through a current account surplus in period 1.

In the event that $\beta = 1/(1+r)$, we arrive at the *special case* where $c_1 = c_2 = \bar{c}$. Substituting this condition into the intertemporal budget constraint, we obtain

$$\bar{c} = \frac{(1+r)y_1 + y_2}{2+r} \tag{7.11}$$

With this solution for consumption, we can determine the other variables in the model. By aggregating across agents, such that $C_t = \int_0^1 c_t(i)di$, $Y_t = \int_0^1 y_t(i)$, and $B_t = \int_0^1 a_t(i)$, we can calculate the amount the economy borrows from or lends to the foreign economy. Specifically, we obtain the following expressions for the current account balances:

$$CA_1 = B_1 - B_0 = Y_1 - C_1 = Y_1 - \frac{(1+r)Y_1 + Y_2}{2+r}$$

$$CA_2 = B_2 - B_1 = Y_2 - \frac{(1+r)Y_1 + Y_2}{2+r} + r\left(Y_1 - \frac{(1+r)Y_1 + Y_2}{2+r}\right)$$

Further substitutions lead to

$$CA_1 = \frac{Y_1 - Y_2}{2+r} \tag{7.12}$$

$$CA_2 = (1+r)\frac{Y_2 - Y_1}{2+r} + r\frac{Y_1 - Y_2}{2+r} = -\left(\frac{Y_1 - Y_2}{2+r}\right). \tag{7.13}$$

We can draw two conclusions from this result in the *special case* of the two-period endowment model. First, the current account responds to the pattern of endowment income and consumption smoothing, which depends on the relative impatience of domestic agents compared to the foreign interest rate. Specifically, when the endowment in the first period is higher than the endowment in the second period, agents save part of their income for the future to smooth consumption over their lifetime. Conversely, if income is higher in the second period, agents draw resources from period 2 to period 1, leading to a current account deficit in period 1.

Next, we examine the response of the economy to *transitory* and *permanent* changes in income. By increasing the endowment in period 2 by Δ, we obtain the following expressions for the change in the current account balances:

$$\Delta CA_1 = \frac{\Delta}{2+r}$$
$$\Delta CA_2 = -\frac{\Delta}{2+r}.$$

Thus, a positive *transitory* income shock in the first period leads to an increase in consumption in both periods as agents smooth consumption over their lifetime. However, a *permanent* shock has no effect on the current account, as there is no need to shift resources intertemporally. In this case, Y_1 and Y_2 increase in the same magnitude of the shock; therefore, $Y_1 - Y_2 = \Delta$ does not change after the permanent income shock.

In summary, the two-period endowment model highlights that the current account is sensitive to the profile of endowment income and the consumption-smoothing behavior of agents. Transitory income shocks lead to a shift in consumption in both periods, while permanent shocks have no effect on the current account.

The two-period endowment model can be extended to an infinite horizon while maintaining the perfect foresight assumption. The representative household's lifetime discounted utility is given by

$$U_0 = \sum_{t=0}^{\infty} \beta^t u(c_t), \quad 0 < \beta < 1,$$

where c_t represents the real consumption in period t. The time preference parameter is denoted by β and utility is characterized by the properties $u'(\cdot) > 0$, $u''(\cdot) > 0$, and $\lim_{c \to 0} u'(\cdot) = \infty$.

In each period, agents receive an endowment y_t and can save in an asset that yields a return of $1 + r_t$ units of the consumption good in period $t + 1$ ($r_t > 0$). The representative household's maximization problem is given by

$$\max_{\{b_{t+1}, c_t\}} \sum_{t=0}^{\infty} \beta^t u(c_t)$$
$$\text{s.t.} \quad c_t + a_{t+1} = y_t + a_t(1 + r_t), \quad \text{given } b_0, \{y_t\}_{t=0}^{\infty}.$$

The solution to the representative household's problem yields $u'(c_t) = \beta(1 + r_t)u'(c_{t+1})$. When $\beta = \frac{1}{1+r}$, the representative household consumes a constant amount in every period, $c_t = \bar{c}$.

The steady state for net foreign assets, $\bar{a}$, can be obtained assuming convergence in the endowment process and a zero current account in the steady state. By substituting the solution for c_t in the budget constraint and iterating forward

$$\begin{aligned}
a_t(1+r_t) &= \bar{c} - y_t + a_{t+1} \\
&= \bar{c} + \frac{\bar{c}}{1+r} - y_t - \frac{y_{t+1}}{1+r} + a_{t+2} \\
&= \bar{c} + \frac{\bar{c}}{1+r} + \frac{\bar{c}}{(1+r)^2} - y_t - \frac{y_{t+1}}{1+r} - \frac{y_{t+2}}{(1+r)^2} + a_{t+3} \\
&= \dots
\end{aligned}$$

Iterating forward, we obtain the following expression for $a_0(1+r_t)$:

$$a_0(1+r_t) = \bar{c}\sum_{t=0}^{\infty}\frac{1}{(1+r)^t} - \sum_{t=0}^{\infty}\frac{y_t}{(1+r)^t}$$

$$a_0(1+r_t) = \bar{c}\frac{1+r}{r} - \sum_{t=0}^{\infty}\frac{y_t}{(1+r)^t}$$

$$a_0(1+r_t) = \bar{c}\frac{1}{1-\beta} - \sum_{t=0}^{\infty}\frac{y_t}{(1+r)^t}$$

Now, let W be the household's total wealth, represented by the net present value of the stream of all the endowments plus the payment received by the initial position a_0. Recalling that $\beta = \frac{1}{1+r}$, we arrive to

$$a_0(1+r_t) = \frac{1}{1-\beta}\bar{c} - \sum_{t=0}^{\infty}\beta^t y_t$$

$$\frac{1}{1-\beta}\bar{c} = a_0(1+r_t) + \sum_{t=0}^{\infty}\beta^t y_t$$

$$\bar{c} = (1-\beta)\text{W}$$

The steady-state value for $\bar{b}$ is given by

$$\bar{a}(1+r) = \bar{c} - \bar{y} + \bar{b}$$

where $\bar{y}$ is the value to which the endowment process converges. Solving for $\bar{b}$ and taking the solution for $\bar{c}$ yields

$$\bar{a} = \frac{\bar{c} - \bar{y}}{r} = -\frac{\bar{y} - (1 - \beta)\mathrm{W}}{r} = \beta\mathrm{W} - \frac{\bar{y}}{r}$$

Hence, the initial net foreign assets of the economy will determine the steady state. In summary, we find that the steady state of the model is dependent on the initial conditions.

7.3.2 Introducing Stochasticity into the Infinite Horizon Model

In this section, we incorporate stochasticity into the infinite horizon model. In this special case, the two primary equations of the model are as follows:

$$u'(c_t) = u'(c_{t+1}) \tag{7.14}$$

$$a_t(1 + r_t) = a_{t+1} + c_t - y_t \tag{7.15}$$

We log-linearize around the non-stochastic steady state and obtain

$$\hat{c}_t = \hat{c}_{t+1} \tag{7.16}$$

and

$$\bar{C}\hat{c}_t + \bar{\mathrm{W}}\hat{a}_{t+1} = (1 + r)\bar{\mathrm{W}}\hat{a}_t + \bar{\mathrm{W}}\hat{w}_t \tag{7.17}$$

where $\bar{C}$ and $\bar{\mathrm{W}}$ are the steady state of consumption and wealth, respectively.

Solving for $\hat{a}_{t+1}$ and $\hat{c}_t$, we obtain that both follow unit root processes. This result is intuitive, given the consumption smoothing motive and the models reviewed in this chapter. The consumption smoothing motive suggests that agents react to transitory shocks by permanently changing their consumption. In the two-period model, consumption increased or decreased in both periods. In the infinite horizon non-stochastic model, long-run equilibrium values were a function of initial wealth. In the stochastic case, households react to shocks by saving or borrowing, affecting their initial wealth and, consequently, their long-run equilibrium.

The stochasticity in the model presents a problem, as the steady state becomes dependent on initial conditions after every shock, rendering several theoretical moments indeterminate.[1] To address this issue, the literature has proposed various simple mechanisms to induce stationarity of the equilibrium dynamics, including

[1] This limits our capacity to contrast the model predictions with the data. Moreover, it creates problems regarding how to present impulse-response functions.

introducing a variable time-preference term. Schmitt-Grohe and Uribe (2003) present a comprehensive review of these methods.[2]

7.4 Building the Model

This section presents the main components of the model. As in previous chapters, productivity shocks serve as the primary driver of the economy, while the intertemporal elasticity of substitution of leisure and the dynamics of capital accumulation serve as the primary transmission mechanisms. When modeling an open economy, it is important to consider not only the allocation of factors but also their ownership. Although both the international financial market and the goods market will be open to foreign trade, domestic agents will retain ownership of labor and physical capital. These assumptions reflect the segmentation of these markets. Abstraction from international migration flows appears to be a natural choice for labor in an open economy model.[3] For physical capital, market segmentation will be critical.

Since the model considers only one type of good, Mendoza (1991) relates the productivity shock to a shock in terms of trade.[4] The productivity shock reflects that domestic households can produce more goods with the same amount of capital and labor for a period. This triggers an increase in capital through more investment, as in the closed economy case. Unlike the closed economy case, however, agents can use international financial markets to borrow resources from abroad to finance higher investment, which should break the link between aggregate savings and investment. This hypothesis was studied in the seminal work of Feldstein and Horioka (1980), who argued that if economies are financially integrated, the aggregate savings and investment of an individual country should exhibit a low correlation. However, the authors found a high positive correlation between savings and investment rates, a prominent puzzle in international macroeconomics. Limiting the ownership of capital to domestic agents allows us to link the discount factor or interest rate faced by domestic agents with the marginal return of investing in physical capital, which can help the model match the Feldstein-Horioka findings.

The dynamics of the labor market are slightly more complex. The shock creates substitution and income effects. On one hand, higher productivity increases compensation for each hour worked, which in turn increases the incentives to work because it is possible to transform an hour of work into more goods. On the other hand, agents experience a positive wealth effect, which affects their willingness to

[2] Alternatively, it is possible to solve the model using global solution methods and induce stationarity by introducing an occasional binding constraint. For a discussion, see Mendoza (1991).

[3] For an open economy RBC model incorporating migration and remittances flows, see Mandelman and Zlate (2012).

[4] In Chap. 8, we investigate how these two shocks create distinct dynamics within a framework comprising three productive sectors.

sacrifice leisure. In this context, as in the closed economy model, the elasticity of substitution between consumption and leisure becomes crucial for the results. The assumption of segmented international labor markets is also key, as only the workers of the small country experience this productivity shock. To reduce the impact of wealth effects on the supply of labor and wage procyclicality, we follow Greenwood et al. (1988) by using a specific utility function that addresses this dimension.

When formulating an open economy model, it is important to consider several aspects that differentiate it from the closed economy models developed in the previous chapters. Firstly, in closed economy models, the economy's resources available for each period are limited by the output of that period (y_t). This means that the economy is constrained by its own production, and the allocation of consumption (c_t) or investment (i_t) is strictly regulated by the level of output of that period. However, when we "open" the economy, the representative agent can interact with the external sector. Hence, domestic agents can borrow resources from foreign markets and allocate them to consumption or investment. They can also save resources by utilizing international financial markets. In this case, the repayment earned in period $t+1$ will depend on the interest rate of the current period (r_t^f).

Households have two different types of assets at their disposal in the open economy model: capital (k_t) and financial real assets (a_t) in the form of noncontingent bonds. The inclusion of the stock of bonds adds an additional control variable to the households' problem. Similar to previous models, households choose consumption (c_t) and investment (i_t). In addition, they also decide on how much to borrow or lend in international financial markets (Table 7.6).

To express the change in the stock of net foreign assets, we subtract the current stock from the stock of net foreign assets in the next period a_{t+1}. This can be represented by the following equation:

$$\text{Flow of foreign assets at period } t: \Delta a_{t+1} = a_{t+1} - a_t$$

If $\Delta a_{t+1} > 0$, households accumulate new foreign assets by lending to the rest of the world. If $\Delta a_{t+1} < 0$, the agent decreases their foreign assets by borrowing from the rest of the world. If $\Delta a_{t+1} = 0$, households maintain their net foreign assets position.

As a result, households' budget constraint in an open economy incorporates a_t as domestic households interact with the rest of the world. This budget constraint can be expressed as

Table 7.6 Net financial assets

Stock	Description
$a_t > 0$	In aggregate, the economy has a net positive position with respect to the rest of the world. The foreign assets are greater than the foreign liabilities
$a_t = 0$	In aggregate, the economy has a positive position with respect to the rest of the world. The foreign assets equal the foreign liabilities
$a_t < 0$	In aggregate, the economy has a net negative position with respect to the rest of the world. The foreign assets are fewer than the foreign liabilities

$$c_t + i_t + a_{t+1} = y_t + \left(1 + r_{t-1}^f\right) a_t \tag{7.18}$$

The left-hand side of Eq. (7.18) shows the allocation of resources by agents. They can either consume c_t, invest in physical capital i_t, or hold foreign assets a_{t+1}. The right-hand side contains the sources of income of the domestic agents, which are the output y_t and the foreign assets from the previous period, including any interest paid or received ($r_{t-1}^f a_t$).

7.4.1 Households

[A] Preferences The economy consists of infinite-lived households who derive utility from consumption (c_t) and disutility from labor (h_t). The functional form of the utility function is given by (Greenwood et al. 1988):

$$U(c_t, h_t) = \frac{(c_t - \frac{h_t^\omega}{\omega})^{1-\gamma} - 1}{1-\gamma} \tag{7.19}$$

This functional form of the utility function was also used in Chap. 6 to eliminate the income effect, which is the effect of the intertemporal substitution of consumption on labor. This assumption helps the model replicate the behavior of wages, which exhibit weak procyclicality.

[B] Law of movement of capital We assume that only domestic households own physical capital in the economy. Hence, they have to invest i_t to supply capital in period "t+1." The law of motion of capital is given by

$$k_{t+1} = (1-\delta)k_t + i_t \tag{7.20}$$

Here, $\delta \in [0, 1)$ represents the capital depreciation rate.

[C] Budget constraint The representative household allocates resources to consumption (c_t), investment in physical capital (i_t), accumulation of foreign assets a_{t+1}, and paying the adjustment cost of physical capital $\Phi(k_{t+1} - k_t)$. Households' income is derived from the real salary (w_t) obtained by offering labor, rental income (r_t^k) of the physical capital they own, and financial return on their foreign assets (r_{t-1}^f). These terms form the budget constraint:

$$c_t + i_t + a_{t+1} + \Phi(k_{t+1} - k_t) \leq w_t l_t + r_t k_t + \left(1 + r_{t-1}^f\right) a_t \tag{7.21}$$

Here, the function $\Phi(\cdot)$ has the following form:

$$\Phi(k_{t+1} - k_t) = \frac{\phi}{2}(k_{t+1} - k_t)^2 \tag{7.22}$$

The function Φ satisfies the following conditions: $\Phi(0) = \Phi'(0) = 0$. The parameter ϕ measures the cost of adjusting the level of capital stock in one unit and will be instrumental in characterizing the dynamics of investment in the business cycle. The quadratic term suggests that the more abrupt the change in the stock of capital, the higher the costs. Evaluating the first and second derivatives of the function yields

$$\Phi' = \phi(k_{t+1} - k_t) \tag{7.23}$$

$$\Phi'' = \phi \tag{7.24}$$

[D] Closing the model To induce stationarity, we assume that the interest rate is elastic to the level of net foreign assets, following Schmitt-Grohe and Uribe (2003). That is, as a_t falls below its long-run level $\bar{a}$, the risk premium component of the interest rate increases. We can express this relationship as follows:

$$r_t^f = r^*(\exp(\varepsilon_t^n)) + rp_t \tag{7.25}$$

where ε_t^n represents the transitory deviations of the international interest rate and rp_t is the risk premium, defined as follows:

$$rp_t = \chi(\exp(-a_t - \bar{d}) - 1), \tag{7.26}$$

where $\chi > 0$ and $\bar{d}$ is the exogenous level of steady-state debt.[5]

[E] The optimization problem The households' problem consists of maximizing the expected discounted utility stream by choosing optimal sequences of consumption (c_t), labor supply (h_t), capital stock (k_{t+1}), and noncontingent one-period real bonds (a_{t+1}):

$$\underset{\{c_t, h_t, a_{t+1}, k_{t+1}\}}{\text{Max}} E_0 \left[\sum_{k=0}^{\infty} \beta^t \left(\frac{(c_t - \frac{h_t^\omega}{\omega})^{1-\gamma} - 1}{1-\gamma} \right) \right]$$

subject to the sequence of budget constraints and the law of motion of capital

$$c_t + i_t + a_{t+1} + \Phi(k_{t+1} - k_t) = w_t h_t + r_t^k k_t + (1 + r_{t-1}^f) a_t + \Gamma_t, \ \forall_t \tag{7.27}$$

$$k_{t+1} = (1 - \delta) k_t + i_t, \tag{7.28}$$

[5] For simplicity, we assume that households take the interest rate, r^f, as given. Relaxing this assumption does not alter the main results of the model.

and the no-Ponzi condition

$$\lim_{j\to\infty} E_t \frac{a_{t+j}}{\Pi_{s=1}^{j}(1+r_s)} \geq 0.$$

where the time discount factor $\beta \in [0, 1]$ and Γ_t represents the profits from production firms.

We can summarize the first two constraints by replacing the value of investment from the law of motion of capital into the budget constraint. Also, we can replace the expression for the function Φ from Eq. (7.22). Then, we can rewrite the budget constraint as follows:

$$c_t + k_{t+1} - (1-\delta)k_t + \frac{\phi}{2}(k_{t+1} - k_t)^2 + a_{t+1} = w_t h_t + r_t^k k_t + (1 + r_{t-1}^f)a_t + \Gamma_t.$$

The Lagrangian then is defined by the following expression:

$$\mathcal{L} = E_0 \left\{ \sum_{t=0}^{\infty} \beta^t \left[\frac{(c_t - \frac{h_t^{\omega}}{\omega})^{1-\gamma} - 1}{1-\gamma} + \right.\right.$$

$$\left.\left. + \lambda_t \left(w_t h_t + r_t^k k_t + (1 + r_{t-1}^f)a_t + \Gamma_t - c_t - k_{t+1} + (1-\delta)k_t - \frac{\phi}{2}(k_{t+1} - k_t)^2 - a_{t+1} \right) \right] \right\}$$

The optimality conditions of the households' problem are given by

$$\{c_t\} : \left(c_t - \frac{h_t^{\omega}}{\omega} \right)^{-\gamma} = \lambda_t \tag{7.29}$$

$$\{h_t\} : \left(c_t - \frac{h_t^{\omega}}{\omega} \right)^{-\gamma} h_t^{\omega-1} = \lambda_t (w_t) \tag{7.30}$$

$$\{k_{t+1}\} : \lambda_t(1+\phi(k_{t+1}-k_t)) = \beta E_t\left[\lambda_{t+1}(r_{t+1}^k+1-\delta+\phi(k_{t+2}-k_{t+1}))\right] \tag{7.31}$$

$$\{a_{t+1}\} : \lambda_t = E_t\left[\beta\lambda_{t+1}(1 + r_t^f)\right] \tag{7.32}$$

$$\{\lambda_t\} : c_t + k_{t+1} - (1-\delta)k_t + \frac{\phi}{2}(k_{t+1}-k_t)^2 + a_{t+1} = w_t h_t + r_t^k k_t + (1+r_{t-1}^f)a_t + \Gamma_t$$

The intratemporal condition, which represents labor supply, is obtained by substituting λ_t from Eq. (7.29) into Eq. (7.30):

$$h_t^{\omega-1} = w_t \tag{7.33}$$

The intertemporal condition, which indicates the optimal consumption path given the interest rate, is represented by the Euler equation and is obtained from Eq. (7.29) and (7.32):

$$\left(c_t - \frac{h_t^\omega}{\omega}\right)^{-\gamma} = \beta E_t\left[(1+r_t^f)\left(c_{t+1} - \frac{h_{t+1}^\omega}{\omega}\right)^{-\gamma}\right] \tag{7.34}$$

The physical capital supply is obtained by combining Eqs. (7.29) and (7.31), which yields

$$U_{c_t}(1+\phi(k_{t+1}-k_t)) = \beta E_t\left[U_{c_{t+1}}\left(r_{t+1}^k + 1 - \delta + \phi\left(k_{t+2}-k_{t+1}\right)\right)\right] \tag{7.35}$$

Here, $U_{c_t} = \frac{\partial U(c_t,h_t)}{\partial c_t} = \left(c_t - \frac{h_t^\omega}{\omega}\right)^{-\gamma}$.

Equation (7.35) determines the investment decisions of agents. The intertemporal decision takes into account the presence of adjustment costs to investment, which results in a relative price between consumption and investment goods that is no longer unity. A higher value of ϕ leads to agents placing more emphasis on smoothing the dynamics of capital.

7.4.2 Firms

We assume perfect competition in both goods and factor markets. Firms demand capital and labor and treat the final good price, wage, and rental rate of capital as exogenous. The representative firm maximizes profits as follows:

$$\underset{\{k_t,h_t\}}{\text{Max}}\, \Gamma_t = y_t - w_t h_t - r_t^k k_t$$

The production function is given by

$$y_t = \exp(\varepsilon_t^e) k_t^\alpha h_t^{1-\alpha} \tag{7.36}$$

where $\exp(\varepsilon_t^e)$ is an exogenous and stochastic productivity shock. The first-order conditions are

$$\begin{aligned} \{h_t\} : (1-\alpha)\exp(\varepsilon_t^e) k_t^\alpha h_t^{-\alpha} &= w_t \\ \{k_t\} : \alpha \exp(\varepsilon_t^e) k_t^{\alpha-1} h_t^{1-\alpha} &= r_t^k \end{aligned}$$

The labor demand and capital demand equations are

$$\alpha \frac{y_t}{h_t} = w_t \quad \text{(Labor demand)} \tag{7.37}$$

$$(1-\alpha)\frac{y_t}{k_t} = r_t^k \quad \text{(Capital demand)} \tag{7.38}$$

7.4.3 The External Sector

In an open economy, it is necessary to keep track of the international financial position through the balance of payments, which tracks the international transactions made by the residents of the country. In our model, the balance of payments should give us the identity between the current account and the combined capital and financial accounts. Specifically, we define

$$\begin{aligned} ca_t &= y_t - \Phi(k_{t+1} - k_t) - c_t - i_t + r_{t-1}^f a_t \\ &= tb_t + r_{t-1}^f a_t \end{aligned} \tag{7.39}$$

where we define the trade balance tb_t as the output minus the net capital adjustment costs minus domestic absorption. Using this definition, we can derive from the households' budget constraint:

$$ca_t = a_{t+1} - a_t \tag{7.40}$$

This equation tells us that the change in the financial and capital account should yield the total change in net foreign assets. Furthermore, these identities allow us to define the trade balance. Resources flowing out of the economy are exports (x_t), while resources flowing into the economy are imports (m_t). At the end of each period, the net flow of resources is the difference between exports and imports ($x_t - m_t$) or the trade balance tb_t.

To write down the model, the external sector is represented by the ratios of current account to output and trade balance to output. Therefore, we can define the following variables based on the definitions provided in Eqs. (7.39) and (7.40):

$$\frac{ca_t}{y_t} = \frac{a_{t+1} - a_t}{y_t} \tag{7.41}$$

$$\frac{tb_t}{y_t} = \frac{ca_t - r_{t-1}^f a_t}{y_t} \tag{7.42}$$

Define s_t as the savings of the economy at period "t," which is the sum of the current account and the investment:

$$s_t = ca_t + i_t$$

7.4.4 Market Equilibrium and Shock Definition

In this model, aggregate savings will define the change in the net asset position of residents and the balance of payments. Any goods not consumed or invested will be traded to foreign economies. As a result, the market-clearing condition for domestic goods can be expressed as follows:

$$c_t + i_t + tb_t + \frac{\phi}{2}(k_{t+1} - k_t)^2 = y_t \tag{7.43}$$

Again, to work with the ratio tb_t/y_t, divide (7.43) by y_t and it obtains

$$\frac{c_t + i_t}{y_t} + \frac{tb_t}{y_t} + \frac{1}{y_t}\frac{\phi}{2}(k_{t+1} - k_t)^2 = 1 \tag{7.44}$$

Since the economy is subject to shocks, we aim to describe the dynamics of the small open economy after productivity shocks, assuming they behave as an AR(1) process:

$$\varepsilon_t^e = \rho_e \varepsilon_{t-1}^e + v_t^e, \quad v_t^e \sim N(0, \sigma_{\epsilon^e}^2) \tag{7.45}$$

Here, v_t^e is referred to as the total factor productivity shock.

Furthermore, we are interested in assessing the impact of international financial shocks on the small open economy, particularly a shock to the foreign interest rate. We assume that the behavior of the foreign interest rate also follows an AR(1) process:

$$\varepsilon_t^n = \rho_n \varepsilon_{t-1}^n + v_t^n, \quad v_t^n \sim N(0, \sigma_{\epsilon^n}^2) \tag{7.46}$$

Here, v_t^n is referred to as the foreign interest rate shock.

7.4.5 System of Main Equations

Table 7.7 displays the primary equations describing the optimal behaviors of households and firms. It also indicates the market-clearing conditions, total factor productivity behavior, and the definitions of the external interest rate and risk premium level. This set of equations forms a system representing the small open economy RBC model with variable labor, in line with Mendoza (1991).

7.5 Parametrization

Parametrization corresponds to the values in Mendoza (1991). Table 7.8 shows the values associated with the model parameters.

Table 7.7 Nonlinear system of equations on the model

Equations
[1] Euler equation for consumption $(c_t - \frac{h_t^{\omega}}{\omega})^{-\gamma} = E[\beta(1 + r_t^f)(c_{t+1} - \frac{h_{t+1}^{\omega}}{\omega})^{-\gamma}]$
[2] Euler equation for investment $U_{c_t}(1 + \phi(k_{t+1} - k_t)) = \beta E_t U_{c_{t+1}}\left[\left(r_{t+1}^k + 1 - \delta + \phi\left(k_{t+2} - k_{t+1}\right)\right)\right]$
[3] Labor supply $h_t^{\omega-1} = w_t$
[4] Law of motion for capital $k_{t+1} = (1 - \delta)k_t + i_t$
[5] Labor demand $(1 - \alpha)\frac{y_t}{h_t} = w_t$
[6] Capital demand $\alpha\frac{y_t}{k_t} = r_t^k$
[7] Production function $y_t = \exp(\varepsilon_t^e)k_t^{\alpha}h_t^{1-\alpha}$
[8] Ratio of current account to output $\frac{ca_t}{y_t} = \frac{a_{t+1} - a_t}{y_t}$
[9] Ratio of trade balance to output $\frac{tb_t}{y_t} = \frac{ca_t - r_{t-1}^f a_t}{y_t}$
[10] Savings $s_t = ca_t + i_t$
[11] Real interest rate $r_t^f = r^*(\exp(\varepsilon_t^n)) + rp_t$
[12] Risk premium level $rp_t = \chi(e^{(-a_t - \bar{d})} - 1)$
[13] Market clearing $\frac{c_t + i_t}{y_t} + \frac{tb_t}{y_t} + \frac{1}{y_t}\frac{\phi}{2}(k_{t+1} - k_t)^2 = 1$
[14] Productivity shock $\varepsilon_t^e = \rho_e \varepsilon_{t-1}^e + v_t^e$
[15] External interest rate shock $\varepsilon_t^n = \rho_n \varepsilon_{t-1}^n + v_t^n$

Table 7.8 Parametrization

Parameter	Definition
$\gamma = 2$	Risk aversion
$\omega = 1.455$	Frisch elasticity
$\chi = 0.000742$	Debt elasticity
$\alpha = 0.32$	Capital share in income
$\phi = 0.028$	Capital adjustment costs
$r^{*} = 0.04$	External interest rate
$\delta = 0.1$	Depreciation rate
$\rho = 0.42$	Shock persistence
$\bar{d} = 0.7442$	Average level of debt
$\upsilon^{e} = 0.01$	Productivity shock

7.6 Steady State

Before log-linearization, it is necessary to determine the non-stochastic steady-state equilibrium of the model. In this equilibrium, all variables in the model remain constant ($\Delta x_t = 0$), and the productivity shock (ε_t^e) is eliminated. The steady state serves as a reference point for approximating the stochastic model using perturbation techniques. The equations representing the steady-state version of the model are listed in Table 7.9. Finding the steady state is a crucial step in the model's analysis.

- From the productivity shock in Eq. (7.45)

$$\begin{aligned}\varepsilon_{ss}^{e} &= \rho_e \varepsilon_{ss}^{e}\\ \varepsilon_{ss}^{e} &= 0\end{aligned} \tag{7.47}$$

- From the external interest rate shock in Eq. (7.46)

$$\begin{aligned}\varepsilon_{ss}^{n} &= \rho_e \varepsilon_{ss}^{n}\\ \varepsilon_{ss}^{n} &= 0\end{aligned} \tag{7.48}$$

- From the risk premium level definition in Eq. (7.26):

$$\begin{aligned}rp_{ss} &= \chi\left(e^{-a_{ss}-\bar{d}} - 1\right)\\ rp_{ss} &= \chi\left(e^{\bar{d}-\bar{d}} - 1\right)\\ rp_{ss} &= 0\end{aligned} \tag{7.49}$$

- From the real interest rate definition in Eqs. (7.25) and (7.49)

Table 7.9 Steady state

Steady state
$\varepsilon^e_{ss} = 0$
$\varepsilon^n_{ss} = 0$
$\beta = 1/(1+r^*)$
$a_{ss} = -\bar{d}$
$rp_{ss} = 0$
$r^f_{ss} = 1/\beta - 1$
$r^k_{ss} = 1/\beta - 1 + \delta$
$h_{ss} = ((1-\alpha)(\frac{\beta^{-1}-1+\delta}{\alpha})^{\alpha/(\alpha-1)})^{1/(\omega-1)}$
$k_{ss} = h_{ss}(\frac{\beta^{-1}-1+\delta}{\alpha})^{1/(\alpha-1)}$
$y_{ss} = k^{\alpha}_{ss} h^{1-\alpha}_{ss}$
$w_{ss} = \alpha y_{ss}/h_{ss}$
$i_{ss} = \delta k_{ss}$
$tb_{ss} = -a_{ss} r^f_{ss}$
$c_{ss} = y_{ss} - i_{ss} - tb_{ss}$
$ca_{ss} = 0$

$$r^f_{ss} = r^* + rp_{ss}$$

$$r^f_{ss} = r^* + \chi\left(e^{-a_{ss}-\bar{d}} - 1\right) \tag{7.50}$$

- From the Euler equation for consumption in Eq. (7.34) and using Eq. (7.50)

$$\left(c_{ss} - \frac{h^{\omega}_{ss}}{\omega}\right)^{-\gamma} = \beta(1+r^f_{ss})\left(c_{ss} - \frac{h^{\omega}_{ss}}{\omega}\right)^{-\gamma}$$

$$1 = \beta(1+r^f_{ss})$$

$$1 = \beta\left(1 + r^* + \chi\left(e^{-a_{ss}-\bar{d}} - 1\right)\right) \tag{7.51}$$

- We assume $1 = \beta(1+r^*)$. Since $r^* = 0.04$, this yields the impatience discount factor to take the value $\beta = 0.962$. From Eq. (7.51)

$$1 = \beta\left(1 + r^* + \chi\left(e^{-a_{ss}-\bar{d}} - 1\right)\right)$$

$$1 = \beta(1+r^*) + \beta\left(\chi\left(e^{-a_{ss}-\bar{d}} - 1\right)\right)$$

$$\chi(e^{-a_{ss}-\bar{d}} - 1) = 0$$

$$e^{-a_{ss}-\bar{d}} = 1$$

$$-a_{ss} = \bar{d} \tag{7.52}$$

- From the capital demand in Eq. (7.38)

$$\alpha \frac{y_{ss}}{k_{ss}} = r_{ss}^k \tag{7.53}$$

- From the production function in Eq. (7.36)

$$\begin{aligned} y_{ss} &= \exp(\varepsilon_{ss}^e) k_{ss}^\alpha h_{ss}^{1-\alpha} \\ y_{ss} &= k_{ss}^\alpha h_{ss}^{1-\alpha} \end{aligned} \tag{7.54}$$

- From the optimality condition for investment in Eq. (7.31)

$$\begin{aligned} 1 + \phi(k_{ss} - k_{ss}) &= \beta \frac{U_{c_{ss}}}{U_{c_{ss}}} \left(r_{ss}^k + 1 - \delta + \phi\left(k_{ss} - k_{ss}\right) \right) \\ 1 + \phi(0) &= \beta \left(r_{ss}^k + 1 - \delta + \phi(0) \right)) \\ 1 &= \beta (r_{ss}^k + 1 - \delta) \end{aligned} \tag{7.55}$$

- From Eqs. (7.53) and (7.55)

$$1 = \beta \left(\alpha \frac{y_{ss}}{k_{ss}} + 1 - \delta \right) \tag{7.56}$$

- Using Eq. (7.54) in Eq. (7.56)

$$\begin{aligned} 1 &= \beta \left(\alpha \frac{k_{ss}^\alpha h_{ss}^{1-\alpha}}{k_t} + 1 - \delta \right) \\ 1 &= \beta \left(\alpha \left(\frac{h_{ss}}{k_{ss}} \right)^{1-\alpha} + 1 - \delta \right) \\ \frac{k_{ss}}{h_{ss}} &= \left(\frac{\beta^{-1} - 1 + \delta}{\alpha} \right)^{1/(\alpha-1)} \\ k_{ss} &= h_{ss} \left(\frac{\beta^{-1} - 1 + \delta}{\alpha} \right)^{1/(\alpha-1)} \end{aligned} \tag{7.57}$$

- From the labor demand in Eq. (7.37)

$$w_{ss} = (1 - \alpha) \frac{y_{ss}}{h_{ss}}$$

$$
\begin{aligned}
w_{ss} &= (1-\alpha)\frac{k_{ss}^{\alpha}h_{ss}^{1-\alpha}}{h_{ss}} \\
w_{ss} &= (1-\alpha)\left(\frac{k_{ss}}{h_{ss}}\right)^{\alpha} \\
w_{ss} &= (1-\alpha)\left(\frac{\beta^{-1}-1+\delta}{\alpha}\right)^{\alpha/(\alpha-1)}
\end{aligned} \tag{7.58}
$$

- From the labor supply in Eq. (7.30) and using Eq. (7.58)

$$
\begin{aligned}
h_{ss}^{\omega-1} &= w_{ss} \\
h_{ss} &= w_{ss}^{1/(\omega-1)} \\
h_{ss} &= \left((1-\alpha)\left(\frac{\beta^{-1}-1+\delta}{\alpha}\right)^{\alpha/(\alpha-1)}\right)^{1/(\omega-1)}
\end{aligned} \tag{7.59}
$$

- From the law of motion for capital in Eq. (7.28)

$$
\begin{aligned}
k_{ss} &= (1-\delta)k_{ss} + i_{ss} \\
i_{ss} &= \delta k_{ss}
\end{aligned} \tag{7.60}
$$

- From the goods market equilibrium in Eq. (7.44), the current account definition in Eq. (7.41) and the trade balance definition in Eq. (7.42)

$$
c_{ss} = y_{ss} - i_{ss} + a_{ss}r_{ss}^{f} \tag{7.61}
$$

$$
tb_{ss} = -a_{ss}r_{ss}^{f} \tag{7.62}
$$

$$
ca_{ss} = tb_{ss} + a_{ss}r_{ss}^{f} = 0 \tag{7.63}
$$

In Table 7.9, we present the steady-state values of the model variables.

7.6.1 Model Solution

Table 7.7 presents the 14 nonlinear equations and variables of the model, constituting a nonlinear system. To facilitate log-linearization, each variable is expressed in Dynare as $exp(xx)$, where $xx = \ln x_t$. However, for ease of interpretation, the variables for capital rent (r_t^k), real interest rate (r_t^f), risk premium (rp_t), trade balance to output (tb_t), foreign assets (a_t), and current account-output (ca_t) are denoted in Dynare as x. For example, the capital demand and current account to output ratio equations are represented in Dynare as

Table 7.10 Policy and state functions

	lny_t	lnc_t	lnk_{t+1}	lni_t	lnh_t	lnw_t	lnr_t^k
Constant	0.396	0.111	1.223	−1.080	0.007	0.003	0.140
rf(−1)	0.000	−0.028	−0.005	−0.047	0.000	0.000	0.000
a(−1)	0.000	0.039	0.007	0.066	0.000	0.000	0.000
e(−1)	0.789	0.529	0.282	2.823	0.542	0.247	0.110
n(−1)	0.000	−0.006	−0.101	−1.006	0.000	0.000	0.000
kk(−1)	0.601	0.506	0.500	−3.997	0.413	0.188	−0.056
e_e	1.877	1.260	0.672	6.721	1.290	0.587	0.263
e_r	0.000	−0.013	−0.239	−2.394	0.000	0.000	0.000
	r_t^f	rp_t	a_{t+1}	tb_t/y_t	ca_t/y_t	ε_t^e	ε_t^e
Constant	0.040	0.000	−0.744	0.020	0.000	0.000	0.000
rf(−1)	0.001	0.001	−0.697	0.032	−0.469	0.000	0.000
a(−1)	−0.001	−0.001	0.974	−0.045	−0.018	0.000	0.000
e(−1)	0.000	0.000	−0.378	−0.270	−0.255	0.420	0.000
n(−1)	0.017	−0.000	0.348	0.234	0.234	0.000	0.420
kk(−1)	−0.001	−0.001	1.685	1.122	1.134	0.000	0.000
e_e	0.001	0.001	−0.901	−0.644	−0.606	1.000	0.000
e_r	0.039	−0.001	0.828	0.557	0.557	0.000	1.000

Capital demand : in model

$$r_t^k = \alpha \frac{y_{t+1}}{k_t}$$

Capital demand : in Dynare

$$rk = \alpha \frac{exp(yy)}{exp(kk(-1))}$$

Current account to output ratio : in model

$$\frac{ca_t}{y_t} = \frac{a_{t+1} - a_t}{y_t}$$

Current account to output ratio : in Dynare

$$ca\_y = (a - a(-1))/exp(yy) \tag{7.64}$$

Dynare performs linearization of variables expressed in logarithms and levels to obtain variables in log deviations and deviations from their steady state, respectively. Specifically, Dynare expresses the log-deviation variable as $\widehat{x}_t = \ln x_t - \ln x_{ss}$, where x_t is the variable in question and x_{ss} is its steady-state value. Similarly, the deviation variable is expressed as $\widetilde{x}_t = x_t - x_{ss}$. These variables are used by Dynare to calculate the steady state, policy and state functions, impulse-response functions, and theoretical moments.

Table 7.10 shows the model solution (policy and state function)

7.7 Impulse-Response Functions

This section shows the optimal behavior of agents in response to an exogenous shock. In the model developed in this chapter, two shocks are present: the productivity shock (v_t^e) and the external interest rate shock (v_t^n).

7.7.1 *Impulse-Response Functions to Total Factor Productivity Shock*

Here, we study the behavior of the economy predicted by the model in response to an exogenous productivity shock. Figure 7.5 illustrates the response of the endogenous variables to the shock occurring in period "t = 1."

Firstly, all variables are in their steady state before this period. For instance, the shock takes the value of its mean ($v_0^e = 0$), and consumption is set to zero ($\widehat{c_0} = 0$). It's important to note that $\widehat{c_0}$ represents the deviation of the natural logarithm of the variable from the natural logarithm of its steady state, where $\widehat{c_0} = \ln c_0 - \ln c_{ss}$.

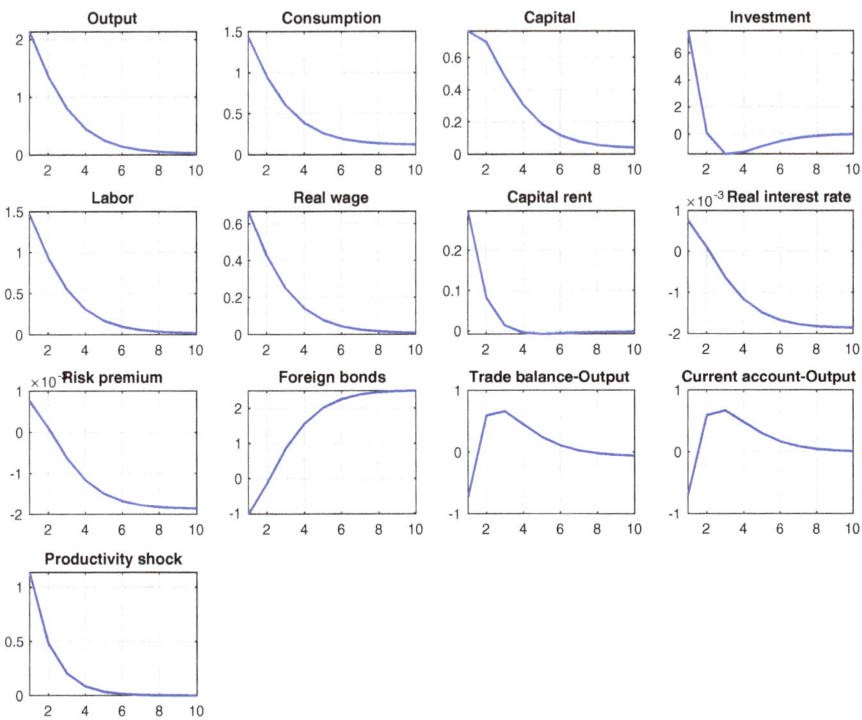

Fig. 7.5 Effects of a productivity shock ($v_t^e = 1.29$)

Therefore, when $\widehat{c}_0 = 0$, it implies that $c_0 = c_{ss}$, indicating that the variable is in its steady state. This applies to every variable.

Period $t = 1$ Now, an increase in the productivity shock in period "t = 1" means that v_1^e takes the value of its standard deviation ($\sigma_\varepsilon = 1.29$), which takes $\varepsilon_1^e(\uparrow)$ out of the steady state. This shock affects both firms' and households' decisions.

Effects on firms The increase in productivity has a positive impact on output:

$$y_1 = exp(\varepsilon_1)k_1^\alpha h_1^{1-\alpha} \tag{7.65}$$

The shock also positively affects the marginal product of both capital and labor, leading to an increase in the demand for both factors of production:

$$w_1 = (1-\alpha)\frac{y_1}{h_1}$$

$$r_1^k = \alpha\frac{y_1}{k_1}$$

Effects on households The representative household is indirectly impacted by the productivity shock through the factors market. In response to the change in conditions, the household adjusts its equilibrium labor and capital supply. The increase in labor demand responds to the increase in real wages, leading to more work in equilibrium. Since the utility function used in this model does not account for an income effect, labor supply is not reduced. Therefore, the substitution effect results in higher labor in equilibrium:

$$h_1^{\omega-1} =\uparrow w_1$$

As the supply of capital in period "t = 1" is determined in period "t = 0," capital remains at its steady state in period "t = 1," despite the increase in r_1^k. The increase in productivity generates an "income effect" as the economy can produce more goods at a lower real cost. Households allocate the higher production to consumption $\widehat{c}_1$, investment $\widehat{i}_1$, and savings in bonds $\widetilde{a}_{t+1}$:

$$c_1 + i_1 + \frac{\phi}{2}(k_{t+1} - k_1) + a_{t+1} = \uparrow w_1 h_1 + \uparrow r_1^k k_1 + (1 + r_{t-1}^f)a_1$$

The determination of capital supply for period "t = 2" occurs in period "t = 1." Consequently, households take into account the expected capital return rate in period "t = 2" to supply physical capital. Therefore, the persistence of the shock (ρ) must be closely examined because it significantly impacts the expected future capital rate (r_2^k). A positive shock in productivity in period "t = 1" has a positive influence on the marginal product of capital in period "t = 2" due to the shock's persistence. Thus, the more persistent the shocks, the greater the rewards of an additional unit of capital today, leading to households postponing consumption. This is determined by the

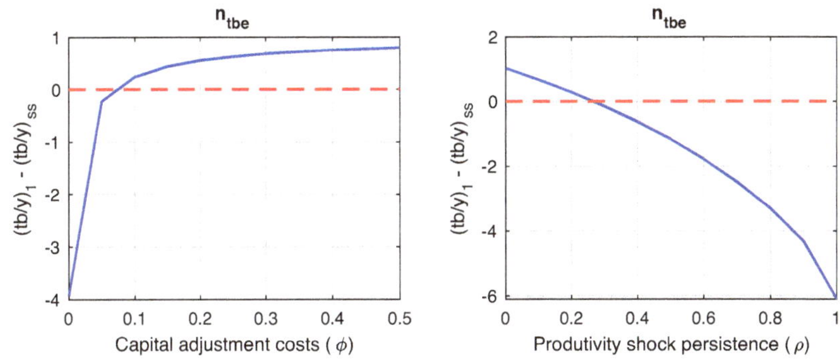

Fig. 7.6 Impact response of trade balance to productivity shock $v_t^e = 1.29$

optimality condition for investment, as shown in the equation below:

$$U_{c_1}(1+\phi(k_2-k_1)) = \beta E_1\left[U_{c_2}\left(\uparrow r_2^k - \delta + 1 + \phi\,(k_3-k_2)\right)\right]$$

The parameter for capital adjustment costs, ϕ, plays a crucial role in the households' investment decision. If ϕ is too high, allocating a unit to investment becomes more resource consuming. Even when the agent wants to take advantage of the persistence of the productivity shock, they also have to consider the price of investment. In this intertemporal decision, two forces are at play: (1) the expected rate of return of capital relative to the stochastic discount factor and (2) the capital smoothing motive, akin to the adjustment cost of investment. When the adjustment cost increases, the second force creates a smoother path for capital. When it is smaller, the rental rate of capital gets closer to the one-period bond rate, meaning a rapid adjustment for capital to its optimal level.

To illustrate this point, Fig. 7.6 displays the impact of a productivity shock on the trade balance-output relationship for a range of values of the parameters ϕ and ρ. The left panel of the figure presents the initial effect of the shock on the trade balance for values of $\phi \in (0, 0.5)$ while holding the initial values of other parameters constant. Similarly, the right panel displays the initial response of the trade balance to the shock for values of $\rho \in (0, 1)$ while keeping ϕ fixed.

When we vary only the value of ϕ, we find that the countercyclical behavior of the trade balance to output is achievable only for values of ϕ less than approximately 0.5. Moreover, for values of ϕ above approximately 0.1, the response of the trade balance to changes in ϕ is less sensitive. However, for values of ϕ below 0.5, the initial response of the trade balance is very sensitive to changes in ϕ.

Similarly, when we change only the value of ρ (with ϕ fixed at 0.028), countercyclical behavior of the trade balance to output is achievable only for values of ρ higher than approximately 0.3. Unlike the right panel of the figure, the sensitivity of the trade balance to changes in persistence is approximately equal at all levels.

In this model, the parametrization of the persistence and capital adjustment cost parameters plays a crucial role in the investment dynamics. The model is calibrated with $\rho = 0.42$ and $\phi = 0.028$. This ensures that households not only postpone consumption to invest but also take a negative financial position with respect to the world to finance investment. Even when output increases, these additional resources are not sufficient to finance the desired level of investment. Therefore, the economy issues bonds, reducing the stock of financial assets held until the following period (a_{t+1}):

$$c_1 + \uparrow i_1 + \frac{\phi}{2}(k_{t+1} - k_1) + \downarrow a_{t+1} = \uparrow y_1 + (1 + r_{t-1}^f)a_1$$

As households in the economy start issuing bonds to finance investment, both the current account and the trade balance account go into deficit. The stock of financial assets decreases since a_{t+1} becomes negative and a_1 remains constant because it was determined in the previous period. This is reflected in the current account equation:

$$ca = \downarrow a_{t+1} - a_1 \longrightarrow \Delta a_{t+1} < 0$$

The trade balance follows a similar dynamic. Since there is a negative variation in financial assets and both the real interest rate of the previous period and the stock of capital held until the current period remain constant, we have

$$tb = \downarrow a_{t+1} - a_1 + (1 + r_{t-1}^f)a_1$$

This model assumes an elastic debt interest rate. When the economy incurs debt through bond issuance, the risk premium imposed on the economy increases, leading to a corresponding rise in the interest rate faced by agents:

$$\uparrow rp = \chi(e^{-\downarrow a_{t+1} - \bar{a}})$$
$$r_1^f = r^* + \uparrow rp_1$$

The change in the interest rate affects the intertemporal consumption decisions of agents. According to the Euler equation of consumption, an increase in the interest rate encourages households to delay consumption, aligning with the investment decisions of agents:

$$U_{c_1} = \beta E_t \left[(1 + \uparrow r_t^f)U_{c_2}\right]$$

Period $t = 2$ We focus on the variables that are relevant for the dynamics of an open economy, namely, y_t, c_t, i_t, k_{t+1}, a_{t+1}, $tb - t$, and ca_t.

In both the closed economy case and the path to equilibrium, there is noticeable persistence. This is influenced by two main factors: (1) the exogenous persistence of the assumed productivity shock (ρ) and (2) the endogenous persistence channel, which operates through the capital accumulation of the economy.

Throughout the path to equilibrium, output and consumption remain above their steady-state levels. The utility function exhibits a high elasticity of substitution between consumption and leisure. The increased productivity alters the relative price between consumption and leisure, prompting agents to increase consumption and reduce leisure. As productivity gradually returns to its steady state, households adjust by decreasing consumption and increasing leisure accordingly.

After adapting to the "surprise" component of the shock in period "t = 0" through a significant surge in investment, the pace of capital adjustment slows from period "t = 1" onward. It is of interest to analyze what happens to investment and capital beyond period "t = 2." Figure 7.5 illustrates that investment in period "t = 3," denoted as i_3, falls below its stationary state level. This implies that desired capital decreases more rapidly than the depreciation rate, even after accounting for the adjustment costs that smooth the path of capital. Reduced investment results in an overall reduction in the economy's absorption, leading to a positive trade balance and an increase in foreign bonds. With the interest rate being debt elastic, this variable declines, creating a sustained trajectory for consumption. The consumption above equilibrium, in conjunction with the reduced risk premium and interest rate, will gradually restore foreign bonds and all other variables back to their equilibrium levels.

Figure 7.7 depicts the model's dynamics under different adjustment cost scenarios, which encompass three scenarios: the first being the absence of capital adjustment costs ($\phi = 0$), the second representing the baseline value ($\phi = 0.028$), and the third indicating a higher capital adjustment cost value ($\phi = 5$).

Table 7.11 offers a comprehensive view of the theoretical moments observed in these three models. It is worth noting that modest adjustment costs effectively discourage agents from making swift changes to the capital stock, resulting in a significant reduction in investment volatility. Another crucial aspect influenced by capital adjustment costs is the dynamics of the trade balance. In the baseline parametrization, capital adjustment costs contribute to a deceleration in the economy's absorption, as investment experiences only a modest increase after the shock. This leads to a moderate trade deficit and some persistence in the behavior of the trade balance. In the case of high capital adjustment costs, the reaction of investment to the shock is minimal. Consequently, the economy manages to produce more with the same level of capital. Since the domestic economy doesn't rely on importing factors to finance investment, the trade balance turns positive after the shock. This dynamic plays a crucial role in explaining a significant stylized fact observed in the data: the countercyclical behavior of the trade balance.

Note that both labor and output have perfect correlation. The specification of GHH utility function eliminates the income effect from the labor supply. Therefore, in presence of the productivity shock, the new equilibrium in the labor market is determined by the shock though the demand for labor, because the labor supply curve does not change.

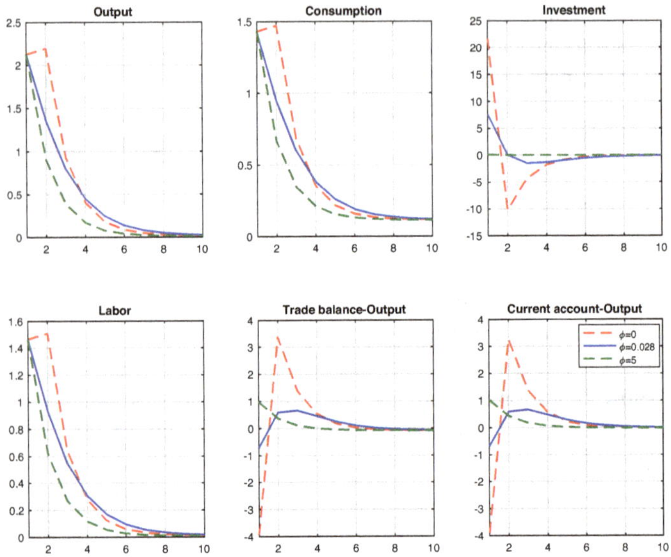

Fig. 7.7 Effects of the *shock* to productivity. Capital adjustment costs (ϕ)

Table 7.11 Model generated moments for alternative model economies

	Model 1 ($\phi = 0$)			Model 2 ($\phi = 0.028$)			Model 3 ($\phi = 5$)		
Variable (x_t)	σ_{x_t}	ρ_{y_t,x_t}	$\rho_{x_t,x_{t-1}}$	σ_{x_t}	ρ_{y_t,x_t}	$\rho_{x_t,x_{t-1}}$	σ_{x_t}	ρ_{y_t,x_t}	$\rho_{x_t,x_{t-1}}$
yy	3.243	1.000	0.692	2.714	1.000	0.617	2.369	1.000	0.432
cc	2.644	0.874	0.800	2.383	0.844	0.782	2.192	0.811	0.713
ii	24.403	0.240	−0.283	7.959	0.669	0.069	0.439	0.437	0.950
hh	2.229	1.000	0.692	1.865	1.000	0.617	1.628	1.000	0.432
tb_y	5.476	0.019	−0.232	1.566	−0.044	0.509	1.415	0.666	0.642
ca_y	5.301	0.024	−0.260	1.279	0.050	0.322	1.131	0.986	0.417
Corr(s,ii)	0.316			0.711			0.356		

Next, we delve into the impact of the persistence of productivity shocks. Figure 7.8 displays the impulse-response functions for three different values of this parameter, enabling a comparison of the effects of the productivity shock between the baseline and the alternative cases. In these alternative parametrizations, ρ is set to two distinct values: 0.05 and 0.9. Table 7.12 shows the theoretical moment across the models with different values for ρ.

When the productivity shock is transitory (with a low persistence of $\rho = 0.05$), the shock's effects are short-lived. In this scenario, there isn't much incentive for agents to invest in capital. However, the economy experiences increased output with the existing capital. This leads to a positive balance of trade and current account, resulting in an accumulation of foreign assets. Lower interest rates, which

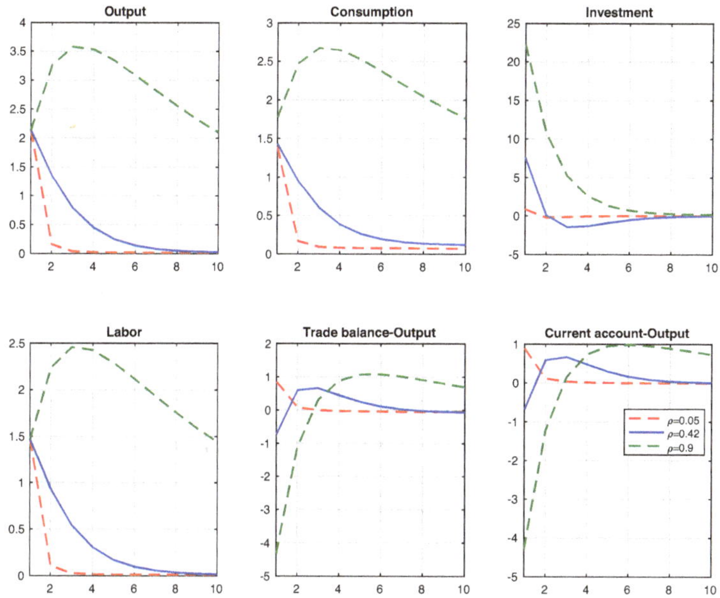

Fig. 7.8 Effects of the *shock* to productivity. Persistence of the shock (ρ)

Table 7.12 Moments generated across models

	Model 1 ($\rho = 0.05$)			Model 2 ($\rho = 0.42$)			Model 3 ($\rho = 0.9$)		
Variable (x_t)	σ_{x_t}	ρ_{y_t,x_t}	$\rho_{x_t,x_{t-1}}$	σ_{x_t}	ρ_{y_t,x_t}	$\rho_{x_t,x_{t-1}}$	σ_{x_t}	ρ_{y_t,x_t}	$\rho_{x_t,x_{t-1}}$
yy	2.145	1.000	0.080	2.714	1.000	0.617	10.332	1.000	0.970
cc	1.679	0.874	0.387	2.383	0.844	0.782	10.498	0.864	0.982
ii	0.918	0.918	−0.097	7.959	0.669	0.069	25.496	0.470	0.486
hh	1.474	1.000	0.080	1.865	1.000	0.617	7.101	1.000	0.970
tb_y	1.036	0.778	0.384	1.566	−0.044	0.509	6.473	0.088	0.623
ca_y	0.902	0.991	0.138	1.279	0.050	0.322	5.247	0.203	0.453
Corr(s,ii)	0.908			0.711			0.472		

are associated with higher international assets, cause consumption to slowly move toward a steady state.

In the case of a highly persistent productivity shock ($\rho = 0.9$), there's a strong incentive for capital accumulation due to the prolonged duration of the shock. However, capital adjustment costs slightly slow down the process. This results in a hump-shaped pattern of output, labor, and consumption. After reaching its peak, the dynamics become similar to the baseline case as the productivity shock wanes, investment declines, and the economy experiences a positive trade balance. The debt-elastic interest rate, aimed at inducing convergence to a unique steady state, will drive all variables back to this equilibrium.

7.7.2 Impulse-Response Functions to External Interest Rate Shock

In this section, we investigate the economy's response to an increase in the external interest rate r^*. Figure 7.9 depicts the reaction of the endogenous variables to this external interest rate shock, which occurs in period "t = 1." As in the previous section, we examine how the variables behave in response to this exogenous shock.

As in the case of the productivity shock, all variables are in their steady state before the period when the shock occurs. For instance, the shock takes the value of its mean ($v_0^e = 0$), and consumption is at its steady state ($\widehat{c}_0 = 0$).

Period $t = 1$ An increase in the interest rate in period "t = 1" means that v_1^n takes the value of 1.29, which pushes $\varepsilon_1^n(\uparrow)$ out of the steady state.

Effects on firms The shock to the external interest rate will not affect firm decisions on impact since agents cannot change the level of capital immediately. With the same level of capital and overall productivity of labor, output does not shift on impact.

Effects on households The shock affects investment for the next period's level of capital. The increased interest rates create a higher opportunity cost for investing

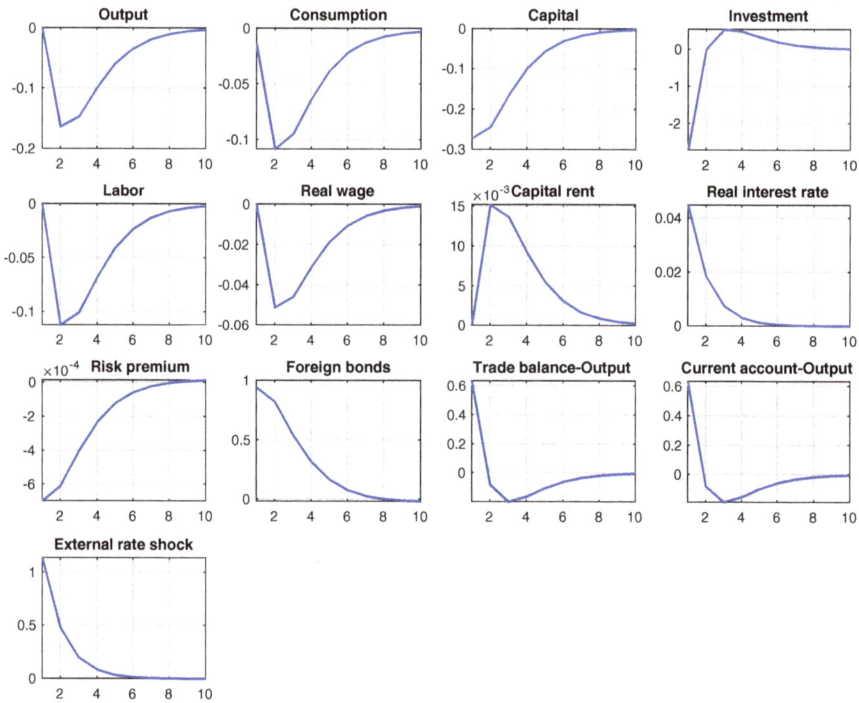

Fig. 7.9 Effects of an external interest rate shock ($v_t^n = 1.29$)

in physical capital, leading agents to reduce the amount of capital until the point at which the marginal return, taking adjustment costs into account, matches the international interest rate:

$$(1+\phi(k_2-k_1)) = \frac{\mathrm{E}_t\left[r_2^k+1-\delta+\phi(k_3-k_2)\right]}{1+r_1^f}$$

$$(1+\phi(k_2-k_1)) = \frac{\mathrm{E}_t\left[\mathrm{MP}_{k_2}+1-\delta+\phi(k_3-k_2)\right]}{1+r_1^f}$$

$$\underbrace{(1+\phi(k_2-k_1))}_{\text{cost of capital}} = \underbrace{\frac{\mathrm{E}_t\left[\mathrm{MP}_{k_2}+1-\delta\right]}{1+\uparrow r_1^f}}_{\text{flow of marginal productivity}} + \underbrace{\frac{\mathrm{E}_t\left[\phi(k_3-k_2)\right]}{1+\uparrow r_1^f}}_{\text{capital smoothing benefits}}$$

The overall decrease in absorption leads to an increase in foreign assets. As a result, the risk premium of the real interest rate decreases. However, the initial shock to the external interest rate pushes the real interest rate up by more than this decline. Overall, the real interest rate faced by domestic agents increases to a lesser extent than the shock initially caused:

$$\uparrow U_{c_1} = \beta E_t\left[(1+\uparrow r_t^f)U_{c_2}\right]$$

Period $t=2$

Effects on firms The interest rate increase leads households to reduce the level of capital and raise the rental rate. Since a smaller amount of capital was chosen in period "t = 1" to be available in period "t = 2," there is less capital accessible to firms in this period, which in turn affects output:

$$\uparrow r_2^k = \alpha\frac{y_1}{k_1} = \uparrow \mathrm{MP}_{k_2}$$

With fewer available capital for production, the marginal productivity of labor declines, resulting in a decrease in the real wage:

$$\downarrow w_2 = (1-\alpha)\frac{y_2}{h_2} = \downarrow \mathrm{MP}_{l_2}$$

As previously mentioned, a salary reduction leads to a decrease in labor. In equilibrium, firms operate with less capital and less labor, consequently leading to a decrease in output:

$$\downarrow y_t = \downarrow {k_2}^{\alpha} \downarrow {h_2}^{(1-\alpha)}$$

Effects on households The representative household is also affected by this shock through the Euler equation of consumption. An important feature of the model is that agents can easily substitute consumption with leisure. As the price of leisure falls and the price of present consumption increases, agents reduce consumption and increase leisure, thereby smoothing their utility across periods.

The net effect of lower output, reduced consumption, and decreased capital results in a positive trade balance and an accumulation of foreign assets. In short, agents substitute domestic capital with foreign assets until their return rates equalize. On the path back to equilibrium, the foreign interest rate falls, and domestic agents gradually restore their level of physical capital.

7.7.3 Comparison of the Model with the Data

In this section, we compare the simulations conducted with the model to actual data. Following the approach of Mendoza (1991), we use Canadian data. We present the results from the baseline model, which assumes values for the parameters governing capital adjustment costs (ϕ) and shock persistence (ρ) of 0.028 and 0.42, respectively. Table 7.13 presents the results.

The model exhibits several significant attributes. It successfully approximates the variability of economic variables, as indicated by their standard deviations. Additionally, it replicates a procyclical pattern in key economic factors such as consumption, savings, investment, employment, and productivity. Moreover, the model generates first-order autocorrelation coefficients for essential variables, including output, consumption, labor, and trade balance.

The results also illustrate the presence of some anomalies. In particular, the variability of investment and output is underestimated. Also, the positive co-movement between these two variables is larger in the data. The co-movement between labor and output is grossly underestimated. This is a feature of the model that generates a perfect correlation between these two variables.

A notable characteristic of this model is its challenge in replicating the negative correlation between the current account and GDP observed in Canadian data.

Table 7.13 Comparison of the cyclical behavior of the theoretic model with the empirical data

	Canadian data			Model		
Variable (x_t)	σ_{x_t}	ρ_{y_t,x_t}	$\rho_{x_t,x_{t-1}}$	σ_{x_t}	ρ_{y_t,x_t}	$\rho_{x_t,x_{t-1}}$
Output (y)	4.223	1.000	0.849	2.714	1.000	0.617
Consumption (c)	2.430	0.822	0.780	2.383	0.844	0.782
Investment (i)	11.478	0.938	0.759	7.958	0.669	0.069
Labor (h)	2.262	0.452	0.696	1.865	1.000	0.617
Trade balance (tb_y)	1.748	−0.215	0.797	1.566	−0.044	0.509
Current account (ca_y)	1.822	−0.135	0.751	1.279	0.050	0.322
Corr(savings,investment)	0.7758			0.7110		

A similar issue is also evident in the behavior of the trade balance. However, as previously discussed, through a meticulous parametrization of capital adjustment costs, the model manages to obtain a negative correlation between these variables, even though it may be relatively weak.

Finally, the model demonstrates its capacity to explain the strong correlation observed in the data between investment and savings, a phenomenon previously explored by Feldstein and Horioka (1980). This correlation in the data is often linked to the concept of imperfect international markets and barriers to capital mobility. Within this model, the persistence of the productivity shock plays a crucial role in capturing this specific stylized fact. Permanent (nonstationary) shocks fail to generate positive saving responses, and highly transitory ones don't lead to significant investment responses, underscoring the importance of shock persistence in modeling these dynamics.

7.8 Summary

This chapter develops the standard model of a small open economy and introduces capital adjustment costs as shown by Mendoza (1991). The moments generated by the model are consistent with two key empirical regularities typical of open economies: a strong positive correlation between savings and investment and the countercyclicality of the trade balance.

In this economy, agents have access to international financial markets and can accumulate foreign financial assets. These assets either pay or charge a debt-elastic interest rate. This interest rate is determined by the external interest rate and the risk premium of the economy, which in turn depends on the deviation of debt from its long-run level. The use of a debt-elastic interest rate on debt induces stationarity in the model, following Schmitt-Grohe and Uribe (2003). Additionally, the economy is subject to shocks in productivity and the external interest rate.

The instantaneous utility function is specified as a GHH function. As a result, the marginal rate of substitution depends solely on the levels of labor, but not on consumption. Therefore, labor supply depends only on the real wage.

The persistence of the productivity shock is crucial in establishing a positive correlation between savings and investment. When the shock is not persistent enough, the investment necessary to equalize expected returns is not sufficient to generate a strong correlation between savings and investment.

Furthermore, the introduction of capital adjustment costs discourages agents from making rapid changes in capital stock, leading to a significant reduction in investment volatility. This feature moderates the trade balance deficit because investment experiences only a modest increase after the productivity shock. The dynamics of the model are also analyzed with a shock to the external interest rate.

7.9 Codes

The solution of the model as well as the impulse-response functions have been developed directly in Matlab (by building several *m-file*) and also through Dynare (by building a *mod-file*). The result of both paths is the same, but the advantage of directly building an m-file is that many details can be made explicit in the solution and simulation of the model, which is already programmed in Dynare. In addition, both the R and Python scripts for working with the database have been uploaded to the webpage (Table 7.14).

Table 7.14 Codes in Matlab and Dynare

Codes	Description
Matlab	
Mendoza91.m	This *m-file* plots the impulse-response functions of the model from alternative parametrizations of ϕ and ρ
Parameter_sensibility.m	This *m-file* computes and plots the impact response of the trade balance to the productivity shock according different values of ϕ and ρ
series_canada.m	This *m-file* plots various series of aggregated variables of Canada for comparison
Dynare	
Mendoza91_log.mod	This mod file contains the nonlinear model with logarithmic variables and is what Dynare uses to solve the model. Also, it contains the IRF graphs for alternative parametrizations of ϕ and ρ
Mendoza91_log_loop.mod	This mod file should be used along with the *m-file* Mendoza91.m to run models with different parametrizations

Chapter 8
Nontradable Goods in a Small Open Economy RBC

8.1 Introduction

This chapter extends the groundwork laid by the small open economy RBC model introduced in Chap. 7. While the single-good small open economy RBC model by Mendoza (1991) provided valuable insights into various stylized data patterns, its limitations became apparent when addressing broader questions in international trade and finance. One such question revolves around the impact of terms of trade—a metric quantifying the ratio of a country's export price index to its import price index—on business cycles.

Incorporating relative prices provides a means to investigate the behavior of the real exchange rate, which reflects the relative price of domestic and foreign consumption baskets. A pivotal aspect in comprehending the dynamics of this relative price lies in distinguishing between tradable and nontradable goods. This differentiation holds significance because tradable goods (i.e., those that can be purchased far from their point of origin) maintain similar prices globally, while the prices of nontradable goods (i.e., those only accessible in proximity to their production source) depend more on local market dynamics. Consequently, nontradable prices play a pivotal role in shaping the fluctuations of the real exchange rate.

This leads us to a second crucial question: the procyclicality of the real exchange rate. Replicating this stylized fact with a productivity shock in the single-good small open economy model discussed in the preceding chapter presents a significant challenge. The reason for this challenge lies in the fact that productivity shocks drive output expansions alongside cheaper domestic goods, making it challenging to reproduce the observation that domestic prices, and consequently the real exchange rate, rise during economic expansions.

This chapter is dedicated to studying the pivotal role played by terms of trade and their contribution to business cycle fluctuations. Our intent is to delve deeper into the fundamental determinants that drive the fluctuations observed in macroeconomic aggregates in small open economies under the presence of nontradables. Notably,

H. Galindo Gil et al., *Dynamic Stochastic General Equilibrium Models*, Springer Texts in Business and Economics, https://doi.org/10.1007/978-3-031-58105-2_8

Mendoza (1995) was a pioneering study that quantitatively examined the potency of terms of trade shocks in steering business cycles through a dynamic stochastic model of a small open economy. Our approach closely aligns with this framework.

8.2 Empirics

In examining the empirical aspects of this chapter, we utilize data from 48 emerging and low-income economies. The primary variables under consideration include output, consumption, investment, trade balance, terms of trade, and the real exchange rate. It is important to note that output, consumption, investment, and trade balance are measured in current dollars. Therefore, these variables are expressed in nominal terms, as opposed to the real (deflated) terms used for the variables discussed in earlier chapters. This approach is highly relevant as it streamlines the subsequent deflation of the variables and their presentation in units that align with our chosen framework.

8.2.1 Construction of the Macroeconomic Series

The model introduced in this chapter employs the methodology developed in Uribe and Schmitt-Grohé (2017) to incorporate variables sourced from the data, setting it apart from the preceding models. The previous models source all their variables from the data in real terms (constant local currency) since they articulate the variables within the model in relation to final goods, thus eliminating the need to introduce dedicated deflators. In contrast, the model adopted for this chapter constructs all variables in reference to units of importables. Consequently, it becomes essential to deflate all nominal-term variables, ensuring their alignment with units of import-related variables.

To analyze business cycles across various countries, we collected time series data on the variables presented in Table 8.1. The data used in this chapter has been sourced from the World Bank's World Development Indicators (WDI). After obtaining the dataset, we initiated a process to exclude countries that do not offer consistent data for each aggregate variable throughout the specified analysis period

Table 8.1 Variables included in the study

Variable	Description
Y_t	GDP per capita
C_t	Consumption per capita
I_t	Investment per capita
TB_t	Trade balance per capita
tot_t	Terms of trade
RER_t	Real exchange rate

(1980–2020). The Python code outlining this algorithm is available in the code documentation accompanying this book. As a result, the final sample size comprises 48 countries.

For maintaining consistency between the data and the units in the model, it is indispensable to adhere to the following criteria: key variables such as output, consumption, investment, and trade balance are expressed in current dollars, reflecting their nominal character. To convert these variables into units associated with importable goods, it is necessary to divide them by the import price index. For this purpose, a practical estimate for this index, as suggested by the WEO, is the import unit value, denominated in dollars and specifically employed for terms of trade calculations.

Before proceeding further, it is crucial to formally define several important variables for the analysis. Firstly, we define the terms of trade, denoted as tot, which measures the relative price of exports in relation to imports. This variable is expressed as follows:

$$tot_t = \frac{p_t^x}{p_t^m}.$$

When calculating a specific country's terms of trade, the World Development Indicators (WDI) utilize trade-weighted export and import unit value indices. The empirical quantification of the real exchange rate, denoted by RER_t, involves the bilateral US dollar real exchange rate, which is defined as

$$RER_t = \frac{p_t}{\xi_t p_t^{\text{US}}},$$

where ξ_t represents the nominal exchange rate in dollars, indicating the domestic-currency price of one US dollar. Additionally, p_t^{US} signifies the US consumer price index, while p_t denotes the domestic consumer price index. The real exchange rate RER_t measures how expensive the foreign country is in relation to the local country: it indicates the relative price of a consumption basket in the local country in terms of consumption baskets in the foreign country. An increase in this indicator means that the country experiences a real appreciation.

The data variables are denoted in current dollars as follows: output is represented by $p_t^y Y_t$, consumption by $p_t^c C_t$, investment by $p_t^i I_t$, and the trade balance by $p_t^x X_t - p_t^m M_t$. To align them with import prices, they are divided by the import unit value, which serves as an approximation to the importables price index p_t^m.

8.2.2 Business Cycle Properties

Once the appropriate metrics have been established within the database, the subsequent phase entails the computation of statistical moments. Given our central

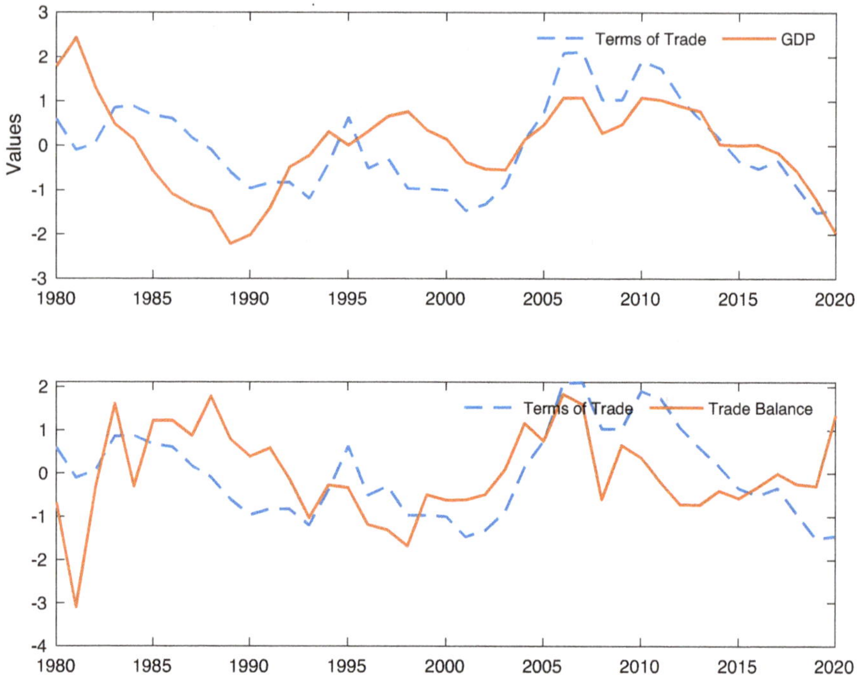

Fig. 8.1 Series of Chile

emphasis on the influence of terms of trade on aggregate variables, our analysis proceeds to evaluate both the relative standard deviation and covariance of these variables vis-à-vis the terms of trade.

To illustrate the potential influence of the terms of trade on aggregate variables, we conduct an analysis for Chile, a small open economy notably influenced by metal prices. In Fig. 8.1, we compare GDP and trade balance as a percentage of GDP cycles with the terms of trade cycle. The series has been detrended using a logarithmic quadratic detrending method. The results capture significant economic developments in Chile over the past few decades.

[Obs1] The economic crisis that began in 1982, during Augusto Pinochet's regime, is attributed to the rise in global interest rates and lower copper prices. By late 1983, unemployment had surged to over 30% of the labor force, and the proportion of the population living in absolute poverty had increased to around 55% from about 30% in 1981. The crisis also led to the collapse of several banks.

[Obs2] The "second economic miracle" occurred between 1988 and 1998 as a result of the second wave of reforms initiated in 1985 and the return to democracy. This period came to an end with the Asian economic crises of 1998–1999.

Table 8.2 Business cycle properties (1980–2020)

	$\sigma_x/\sigma_{\text{tot}}$	$\rho_{xt,xt-1}$	$\rho_{yt,xt}$	$\rho_{\text{tot},xt}$
GDP (y_t)	1.32	0.63	1	0.42
Consumption (c_t)	1.4	0.63	0.88	0.29
Investment (i_t)	2.14	0.59	0.71	0.29
Trade balance (tb_t)	0.56	0.55	−0.1	0.17
Terms of trade (tot_t)	1	0.66	0.42	1
Real exchange rate (RER_t)	0.97	0.64	0.57	0.19

Note: The countries considered in the database were Algeria, Bolivia, Botswana, Brazil, Cameroon, Central African Republic, Chile, China, Colombia, Comoros, Congo Rep., Costa Rica, Dominican Republic, Egypt, Arab Rep., El Salvador, Guatemala, Honduras, India, Kenya, Korea, Rep., Madagascar, Malaysia, Mauritania, Mauritius, Mexico, Morocco, Namibia, Pakistan, Paraguay, Peru, Rwanda, Senegal, South Africa, Sudan, Thailand, Tunisia, Turkey, and Zimbabwe. Statistics regarding RER, the countries considered, given the availability of the data, were Algeria, Bolivia, Brazil, Cameroon, Central African Republic, Chile, China, Colombia, Costa Rica, Dominican Republic, Malaysia, Mexico, Pakistan, Paraguay, South Africa, and Tunisia

[Obs3] The "mineral super-cycle" took place between 2003 and 2012, witnessing a significant surge in commodity prices that drove several Latin-American economies into a phase of high growth rates and positive trade balances. This episode was briefly interrupted by the global financial crisis of 2008–2009, but capital flows quickly recovered.

To examine the characteristics of business cycles related to the terms of trade in aggregate variables, we compute statistics for the detrended series to evaluate their volatility, persistence, and cyclicality. Table 8.2 provides the statistical data for 42 countries, covering the period from 1980 to 2020.

We can observe that the stylized facts reviewed in the previous chapter are also evident in Table 8.2, including the countercyclicality of the current account with respect to output, the procyclicality of consumption and investment, and the high volatility of investment.

It is worth noting that terms of trade show a relatively weak correlation with macroeconomic aggregate variables. This observation aligns with the findings of Schmitt-Grohé and Uribe (2018), who utilized a structural vector autoregressive (SVAR) methodology to gauge the significance of terms of trade. Their research indicated that, on average, terms of trade shocks contribute to approximately 10% of the variability in output, consumption, investment, and the trade balance and 14% of the variability in the real exchange rate. These estimates were based on annual data from 38 emerging and impoverished countries, covering the period from 1980 to 2011.

Furthermore, Fernández et al. (2017) investigated the impact of disaggregated world prices on business cycles using an SVAR model. The model incorporates various world prices, including commodity prices such as agricultural, metal, and fuel prices, as well as the world interest rate. Their results indicate that world price shocks, on average, account for approximately 34% of the variance in output, 21% in consumption and investment, and 15% in the trade balance to output ratio. Additionally, the study reveals that not all world prices affect all macroeconomic indicators uniformly, suggesting that a specific commodity price acts as the primary transmitter of world shocks to one macroeconomic indicator but not to others. These estimates were derived from annual data spanning 138 countries over the period from 1960 to 2015.

8.3 Model Elements

In this section, we discuss some key features of the model. First, we allow for three different consumption goods: (1) importables, (2) exportables, and (3) nontradables. Firms will produce importable and exportable goods, but exportable goods price (p^x) will be affected by an exogenous shock, which constitutes a terms of trade shock. In this manner, it is possible to study the impact of terms of trade shocks in the economy. In particular, significant interest has been paid to the relationship between terms of trade and the trade balance. There are two effects that have been amply discussed in the literature:

[A] The Harberger-Laursen-Metzler Effect
The Harberger-Laursen-Metzler (HLM) effect posits that an exogenous adverse shock to the terms of trade of a small economy results in a decline in its current account balance. A reduction in the terms of trade leads to a decrease in "real income," subsequently causing diminished savings when measured in terms of exportable goods. Assuming investment remains unchanged and there is no government deficit, the change in savings is identical to the change in the current account surplus.

[B] The Obstfeld-Razin-Svensson Effect
The Obstfeld-Razin-Svensson (ORS) effect challenges the HLM result and emphasizes the importance of the persistence of terms of trade shocks in the outcomes. Specifically, a temporary negative terms of trade shock, resulting in a decrease in real income and a change in the real interest rate, leads to reduced savings and a deteriorated trade balance. Furthermore, a decline in the real interest rate contributes to a worsening current account. In contrast, a permanent deterioration in terms of trade may either improve or worsen the real trade balance, depending on various factors, such as the impact on the real interest rate or the behavior of the discount factor, which is linked to the assumptions regarding the stationarity of equilibrium. Therefore, under the ORS effect, we can anticipate that the positive relationship between terms of trade and the trade balance diminishes as the persistence of terms of trade shocks increases.

8.4 Building the Model

This section presents the main components of the model, with particular emphasis on terms of trade shocks. A critical aspect of this model is the incorporation of nontradable goods. For these goods, the quantities used for consumption and investment must be sourced locally. Positive wealth effects, which promote increased consumption, tend to shift resources toward the nontradable sector. This shift is expected to manifest in the prices of nontradable goods, impacting the consumer price index (p^c). Consequently, the relative price of the domestic consumption basket is anticipated to rise in comparison to the foreign one, leading to an appreciation of the real exchange rate. This mechanism allows the model to align with the cyclical behavior of the real exchange rate, as the dynamics resulting from productivity shocks yield distinct empirical predictions.

8.4.1 Households

[A] Preferences The economy is composed of infinitely lived households deriving utility from consumption denoted as c_t and leisure represented by l_t. The immediate utility function employed in this chapter is as follows:

$$u(c_t, l_t) = \frac{(c_t l_t^{\omega})^{1-\gamma}}{1-\gamma}$$

where ω is the labor supply elasticity and γ is the intertemporal inverse elasticity of substitution in consumption.

Aggregated consumption, denoted as c_t, is an index composed of the consumption of tradables, denoted as c_t^T, and nontradables, denoted as c_t^n. This index is expressed in the form of a constant elasticity of substitution (CES) function:

$$c_t = \left[(c_t^T)^{-\mu} + (c_t^n)^{-\mu}\right]^{-\frac{1}{\mu}} \tag{8.1}$$

where $1/(1+\mu)$ is the elasticity of substitution between tradables and nontradables.

The consumption of tradable goods considers both exportable goods (c^x) and importable goods (c^m), which are expressed in a Cobb-Douglas form with unitary elasticity:

$$c_t^T = (c_t^x)^a (c_t^m)^{1-a} \tag{8.2}$$

where a represents the share of expenditure in exportable goods (c_t^x) in the total expenditure on tradable goods.

Table 8.3 Supply of households to firms

Variables	Name	Sector
k^f	Capital for importable-producing firms	Tradable sector
k^x	Capital for exportable-producing firms	
h^f	Labor for importable-producing firms	
h^x	Labor for exportable-producing firms	
k^n	Capital for nontradable- producing firms	Nontradable sector
h^n	Labor for nontradable-producing firms	

[B] Production Factors The model outlines the involvement of households in two distinct sectors: the tradable sector and the nontradable sector. The tradable sector further encompasses two key industries: the exportables industry and the importables industry. Conversely, the nontradable sector is solely represented by the domestic industry, which is responsible for producing nontradables. In each sector, a continuum of representative firms operates with the goal of maximizing their profits. Households possess dedicated capital and workforce for each industry, ensuring that both capital and labor are exclusively directed to firms within the relevant sector. Table 8.3 illustrates the factors supplied by households across the economy.

We also consider some specific simplifying assumptions. The model in Mendoza (1995) assumes an inelastic supply of labor for the tradable sector (h^x and h^m) and capital for the nontradable sector (k^n). In essence, these variables remain constant over time, without any fluctuations, as they do not reflect decisions taken by agents. Since that model is solved in a centralized manner, there is no need to account for the equilibrium price of these factors. In our case, we solve the model in a decentralized manner. This assumption will not affect the main predictions of the model. Households will choose the levels allocated to firms for k_t^f, k_t^x, and h_t^n, while h^f, h^x, and k^n remain unchanged.

Capital is homogeneous in the tradable sector; therefore, k_t^T is defined as the sum of both stocks of capital for exportable- and importable-producing firms. Therefore, k_t^T, the level of capital stock in the tradables sector, follows:

$$k_t^T = k_t^x + k_t^m. \tag{8.3}$$

[C] Law of Motion for Capital It is assumed that only families in the home country own the capital within the economy. Domestic households invest in period t to supply capital in period $t+1$. Households choose how much capital is supplied to exportable- and importable-producing firms by choosing investment i_t^T. Since k^n is fixed over time, the level of investment in capital for nontradable-producing firms i^n should also be fixed. The laws of motion for capital in the tradable and nontradable sectors are

$$k_{t+1}^T = (1-\delta)k_t^T + i_t^T \tag{8.4}$$

$$k^n = (1 - \delta)k^n + i^n \tag{8.5}$$

where $\delta \in [0, 1)$ represents the capital depreciation rate. Again, k^n does not have the subscript t because it is inelastically supplied and therefore is time invariant.

[D] Time and Budget Constraints Households are bound by a time constraint, with a fixed amount of available time, denoted as H, in each period t. The endowment of time, subtracted by the fixed hours supplied to the tradable sector, h^x and h^m, is allocated to labor hours h_t^n or to leisure l_t. Consequently, the labor supplied to each industry conforms to the following equation:

$$l_t + h_t^n + h^x + h^m = H \tag{8.6}$$

In turn, the households' budget constraint is given by

$$\begin{aligned} &p_t^c c_t + i^n + k_{t+1}^T + (1-\delta)k_t^T + B_{t+1} + \Phi(k_{t+1}^T - k_t^T) \\ &= w_t h_t^n + r_t^k k_t^T + w_t^x h^x + w_t^n h^m + r_t^{kn} k^n + (1 + r_{t-1}^f)B_t + \Pi_t^x + \Pi_t^m + \Pi_t^n \end{aligned} \tag{8.7}$$

where $w_t h_t^n$ represents the real wage income and $r_t^k k_t^T$ stands for the real capital rent received from the tradable sector (importables and exportable-producing firms). The payments received from the production factors with fixed supply are given by $w_t^x h^x$, $w_t^n h^m$, and $r_t^{kn} k^n$. The payoffs from the bonds acquired in the previous period are represented by $(1 + r_{t-1}^f)B_t$. As usual, c_t and i_t^T represent consumption and investment in the tradable sector, respectively. Finally, $\Phi(k_{t+1}^T - k_t^T)$ represents the capital adjustment costs.

By consolidating all components into a single equation, we derive the expression for the household budget constraint. The variable i_t^T can be substituted using the capital law of motion from Eq. (8.4).

[E] Closing the Model As in the previous chapter, to induce stationarity, we assume that the interest rate is elastic to the level of net foreign assets, following Schmitt-Grohe and Uribe (2003). That is, as B_t falls below its long-run level $\bar{B}$, the risk premium component of the interest rate increases. We can express this relationship as follows:

$$r_t^f = r^* + rp_t \tag{8.8}$$

where rp_t is the risk premium, defined as

$$rp_t = \chi(\exp(\bar{B} - B_t) - 1),$$

where $\chi > 0$ and $\bar{B}$ is the exogenous level of steady-state net foreign assets.[1]

[F] Optimization Problem The objective of households is to maximize their expected discounted utility stream by determining the optimal trajectory for consumption c_t, leisure l_t, capital in the tradable sector k_t^T, and noncontingent bonds B_{t+1} which yield an interest rate of r_t^f in the subsequent period:

$$\underset{\{c_t,l_t,k_{t+1}^T,B_{t+1}\}_{t=0}^{\infty}}{\text{Max}} \quad E_0\left[\sum_{k=0}^{\infty}\beta^t\frac{(c_t l_t^{\omega})^{1-\gamma}}{1-\gamma}\right]$$

subject to the time and private budget constraints from Eqs. (8.6) and (8.7).

In order to streamline the problem, Eq. (8.6) can be employed within Eq. (8.7) to substitute h_t^n. Consequently, the corresponding Lagrangian takes the form:

$$\begin{aligned}\mathcal{L} = E_0\Bigg\{\sum_{t=0}^{\infty}\beta^t\Bigg[&\frac{(c_t l_t^{\omega})^{1-\gamma}}{1-\gamma} + \lambda_t\Bigg(w_t(H - l_t - h_t^x - h_t^m) + r_t^k k_t + w_t^x h^x \\ &+ w_t^n h^m + r_t^{kn} k^n + (1 + r_{t-1}^f)B_t - p_t^c c_t - k_{t+1}^T + (1-\delta)k_t^T \\ &- B_{t+1} - \Phi(k_{t+1}^T - k_t^T)\Bigg)\Bigg]\Bigg\}\end{aligned}$$

The first-order conditions (FOCs) for period "t" are

$$\{c_t\}: \quad (c_t l_t^{\omega})^{-\gamma} l_t^{\omega} = \lambda_t p_t^c$$

$$\{l_t\}: \quad (c_t l_t^{\omega})^{-\gamma} c_t \omega l_t^{\omega-1} = \lambda_t w_t$$

$$\{B_{t+1}\}: \quad \lambda_t = \beta E_t\left[\lambda_{t+1}(1 + r_t^f)\right]$$

$$\{k_{t+1}^T\}: \quad \lambda_t(1 + \phi(k_{t+1}^T - k_t^T)) = \beta E_t\left[\lambda_{t+1}(r_{t+1}^k + (1-\delta) + \phi(k_{t+2}^T - k_{t+1}^T))\right]$$

From the FOCs of c_t and B_{t+1}, the Euler equation for consumption is expressed as

$$\frac{(c_t l_t^{\omega})^{-\gamma} l_t^{\omega}}{p_t^c} = \beta E_t\left[(1 + r_t^f)\frac{(c_{t+1} l_{t+1}^{\omega})^{-\gamma} l_{t+1}^{\omega}}{p_{t+1}^c}\right] \tag{8.9}$$

Similarly, from FOCs of l_t and c_t, we obtain the labor supply:

$$\frac{c_t}{l_t} = \frac{w_t}{p_t^c} \tag{8.10}$$

[1] For simplicity, we assume that households take the interest rate, r^f, as given. Relaxing this assumption does not alter the main results of the model.

Denote the marginal utility of consumption as $U_{c_t} = \frac{(c_t l_t^{\omega})^{-\gamma} l_t^{\omega}}{p_t^c}$. Then, U_{c_t} is equal to λ_t from the FOC of c_t. Therefore, from the FOCs of k_{t+1}^T and B_{t+1}, we arrive to the optimality condition for investment:

$$\lambda_t(1+\phi(k_{t+1}^T - k_t^T)) = \beta E_t\left[\lambda_{t+1}(r_{t+1}^k + (1-\delta) + \phi(k_{t+2}^T - k_{t+1}^T))\right]$$

$$\frac{U_{c_t}}{p_t^c}(1+\phi(k_{t+1}^T - k_t^T)) = \beta E_t\left[\frac{U_{c_{t+1}}}{p_{t+1}^c}(r_{t+1}^k + (1-\delta) + \phi(k_{t+2}^T - k_{t+1}^T))\right] \tag{8.11}$$

[G] Expenditure Minimization Problems In order to derive the demand for nontradables in relation to tradables, we formulate the expenditure minimization problem. The objective of this problem is to minimize the expenditure on the consumption of goods c_t^T and c_t^n, subject to the definition of c_t as specified in Eq. (8.1). Since the model is defined in units of importables, the relative prices of tradables and nontradables are p_t^T and p_t^n:

$$\underset{\{c_t^T, c_t^n\}}{\text{Min}} \quad p_t^T c_t^T + p_t^n c_t^n \quad \text{subject to} \quad c_t = \left[(c_t^T)^{-\mu} + (c_t^n)^{-\mu}\right]^{-\frac{1}{\mu}}$$

The Lagrangian of the problem is as follows:

$$\mathcal{L} = p_t^T c_t^T + p_t^n c_t^n + \lambda\left(c_t - \left[(c_t^T)^{-\mu} + (c_t^n)^{-\mu}\right]^{-\frac{1}{\mu}}\right)$$

The first-order conditions are

$$\{c_t^T\}: \quad p_t^T = \lambda\left(\frac{1}{\mu}\left[(c_t^T)^{-\mu} + (c_t^n)^{-\mu}\right]^{-\frac{1}{\mu}-1}(-\mu)(c_t^T)^{-\mu-1}\right)$$

$$\{c_t^n\}: \quad p_t^n = \lambda\left(\frac{1}{\mu}\left[(c_t^T)^{-\mu} + (c_t^n)^{-\mu}\right]^{-\frac{1}{\mu}-1}(-\mu)(c_t^n)^{-\mu-1}\right)$$

The way the optimization was stated allows the Lagrange multiplier to be interpreted as the price of c_t. This implies that $\lambda = p_t^c$. Then, from the FOC of c_t^T

$$p_t^T = p_t^c\left(\left[(c_t^T)^{-\mu} + (c_t^n)^{-\mu}\right]^{\frac{-1}{\mu}(1+\mu)}(c_t^T)^{-\mu-1}\right)$$

$$p_t^T = p_t^c\left({c_t}^{1+\mu}(c_t^T)^{-\mu-1}\right)$$

$$p_t^T = p_t^c \frac{c_t^{1+\mu}}{(c_t^T)^{1+\mu}}$$

$$\frac{c_t}{c_t^T} = \left(\frac{p_t^T}{p_t^c}\right)^{\frac{1}{1+\mu}} \tag{8.12}$$

This problem is symmetric, so an analogous result is obtained when working with the FOC of c_t^n:

$$\frac{c_t}{c_t^n} = \left(\frac{p_t^n}{p_t^c}\right)^{\frac{1}{1+\mu}} \tag{8.13}$$

The same procedure is applied to obtain the relative demands for exportable (c_t^x) and importable (c_t^m) goods. In this case, the objective function is the expenditure on consumption of goods c_t^x and c_t^m in units of importable goods subject to the definition of c_t^T, provided in Eq. (8.2). Since the model is defined in units of importables, the relative price of exportables is p_t^x; therefore, it reflects the terms of trade. The stochastic process for this price will be specified later on the chapter:

$$\underset{\{c_t^x, c_t^m\}}{\text{Min}} \quad p_t^x c_t^x + c_t^m \quad \text{subject to} \quad c_t^T = (c_t^x)^a (c_t^m)^{1-a}$$

The Lagrangian of the problem is as follows:

$$\mathcal{L} = p_t^x c_t^x + c_t^m + \lambda \left(c_t^T - (c_t^x)^a (c_t^m)^{1-a}\right)$$

The first-order conditions are

$$\{c_t^x\}: \quad p_t^x = \lambda \left(a(c_t^x)^{a-1}(c_t^m)^{1-a}\right)$$

$$\{c_t^m\}: \quad 1 = \lambda \left((1-a)(c_t^x)^a (c_t^m)^{-a}\right)$$

The way the optimization was stated allows the Lagrange multiplier to be interpreted as the price of c_t^T. Then, from equation the FOC of c_t^x

$$p_t^x = p_t^T \left(a(c_t^x)^{a-1}(c_t^m)^{1-a}\right)$$

$$\frac{c_t^T}{c_t^x} = \frac{1}{a}\frac{p_t^x}{p_t^T} \tag{8.14}$$

This problem is also symmetric; therefore, for c_t^m, we obtain

$$\frac{c_t^T}{c_t^m} = \frac{1}{1-a}\frac{1}{p_t^T} \tag{8.15}$$

Table 8.4 Household equations

Description
1. Law of motion for capital: $k_{t+1}^T = (1-\delta)k_t^T + i_t$
2. Tradable capital: $k_t^T = k_t^x + k_t^m$
3. Time constraint: $l_t + h_t^n + h^x + h^m = H$
4. Real interest rate: $r_t^f = r^* + rp_t$
5. Risk premium: $rp_t = \chi(e^{\bar{B}-B_t} - 1)$
6. Euler equation for consumption: $\frac{(c_t l_t^{\omega})^{-\gamma} l_t^{\omega}}{p_t^c} = \beta E_t \left[(1+r_t^f) \frac{(c_{t+1} l_{t+1}^{\omega})^{-\gamma} l_{t+1}^{\omega}}{p_{t+1}^c} \right]$
7. Euler equation for investment: $\frac{U_{c_t}}{p_t^c}(1+\phi(k_{t+1}^T - k_t^T)) = \beta E_t \left[\frac{U_{c_{t+1}}}{p_{t+1}^c}(r_{t+1}^k + (1-\delta) + \phi(k_{t+2}^T - k_{t+1}^T)) \right]$
8. Labor supply: $\frac{c_t}{l_t} = \frac{w_t}{p_t^c}$
9. Demand for c_t^T: $\frac{c_t}{c_t^T} = \left(\frac{p_t^T}{p_t^c}\right)^{\frac{1}{1+\mu}}$
10. Demand for c_t^n: $\frac{c_t}{c_t^n} = \left(\frac{p_t^N}{p_t^c}\right)^{\frac{1}{1+\mu}}$
11. Demand for c_t^x: $\frac{c_t^T}{c_t^x} = \frac{1}{a}\frac{p_t^x}{p_t^T}$
12. Demand for c_t^m: $\frac{c_t^T}{c_t^m} = \frac{1}{1-a}\frac{1}{p_t^T}$

Table 8.4 summarizes the main equations that describe the household's behavior represented by Eqs. (8.4), (8.6), (8.9), (8.10), (8.11), (8.12), (8.13), (8.14), and (8.15).

8.4.2 Firms

There are three types of firms in this economy: [A] exportable-, [B] importabl, and [C] nontradable-producing firms. Since households supply homogeneous capital for the tradable sector, the optimal allocation of capital across firms in this sector is determined by the equalization of the marginal products of k_t^x and k_t^m. As shown below, the marginal productivity of capital is equal to the marginal cost of capital. Therefore, both exportable- and importable-producing firms will pay the same capital rental rate, denoted as r_t^k.

[A] Exportable-Producing Firms These firms decide the level of labor h_t^x and capital k_t^x employed in the production process. The profits of the firm are given by

$$\Pi_t^x = p_t^x Q A_t^x (k_t^x)^{1-\alpha^x} (h_t^x)^{\alpha^x} - r_t^k k_t^x - w_t^x h_t^x$$

where A_t^x is an exogenous and stochastic productivity shock, Q is a parameter that scales total factor productivity, and $0 < \alpha^x < 1$. The labor and capital factor prices are w_t^x and r_t^k, respectively. The firms choose the levels of labor h_t^x and capital k_t^x that maximize its profits. The first-order conditions are

$$\frac{\partial \Pi_t^x}{\partial h_t^x} \Longrightarrow \alpha^x p_t^x Q A_t^x (k_t^x)^{1-\alpha^x} (h_t^x)^{\alpha^x - 1} - w_t^x = 0$$

$$\alpha^x p_t^x Q A_t^x (k_t^x)^{1-\alpha^x} (h_t^x)^{\alpha^x - 1} = w_t^x$$

$$\frac{\partial \Pi_t^x}{\partial k_t^x} \Longrightarrow (1-\alpha^x) p_t^x Q A_t^x (k_t^x)^{-\alpha^x} (h_t^x)^{\alpha^x} - r_t^k = 0$$

$$(1-\alpha^x) p_t^x Q A_t^x (k_t^x)^{-\alpha^x} (h_t^x)^{\alpha^x} = r_t^k$$

[B] Importable-Producing Firms These firms decide the level of labor h_t^m and capital k_t^m employed in the production process. The profits of the firms are given by

$$\Pi_t^m = p_t^m Q A_t^m (k_t^m)^{1-\alpha^x} (h_t^m)^{\alpha^m} - r_t^k k_t^m - w_t^m h_t^m \tag{8.16}$$

where A_t^m is an exogenous and stochastic productivity shock. The firms choose the level of labor h_t^m and capital k_t^m that maximizes its profits. The first-order conditions are

$$\frac{\partial \Pi_t^m}{\partial h_t^m} \Longrightarrow \alpha^m p_t^m Q A_t^m (k_t^m)^{1-\alpha^m} (h_t^m)^{\alpha^m - 1} - w_t^m = 0$$

$$\alpha^m p_t^m Q A_t^m (k_t^m)^{1-\alpha^m} (h_t^m)^{\alpha^m - 1} = w_t^m$$

$$\frac{\partial \Pi_t^m}{\partial k_t^m} \Longrightarrow (1-\alpha^m) p_t^m Q A_t^m (k_t^m)^{-\alpha^m} (h_t^m)^{\alpha^m} - r_t^k = 0$$

$$(1-\alpha^m)p_t^m QA_t^m(k_t^m)^{-\alpha^m}(h_t^m)^{\alpha^m} = r_t^k \tag{8.17}$$

where we have used the assumption that $p^m = 1$, as we express all series in terms of importables.

[C] Nontradable-Producing Firms These firms decide the level of labor h_t^n and capital k_t^n employed in the production process. The profits of the firm are given by

$$\Pi_t^n = p_t^n QA_t^n(k_t^n)^{1-\alpha^n}(h_t^n)^{\alpha^n} - w_t h_t^n - r_t^{kn} k_t^n$$

where A_t^n is an exogenous and stochastic productivity shock. The firms choose the level of labor h_t^n and capital k_t^n that maximizes their profits. The first-order conditions are

$$\frac{\partial \Pi_t^n}{\partial h_t^n} \Longrightarrow \alpha^n p_t^n QA_t^n(k_t^n)^{1-\alpha^n}(h_t^n)^{\alpha^n-1} - w_t = 0$$

$$\alpha^n p_t^n QA_t^n(k_t^n)^{1-\alpha^n}(h^n)^{\alpha^n-1} = w_t$$

$$\frac{\partial \Pi_t^n}{\partial k_t^n} \Longrightarrow (1-\alpha^n)p_t^n QA_t^n(k_t^n)^{-\alpha^n}(h_t^n)^{\alpha^n} - r_t^{kn} = 0$$

$$(1-\alpha^n)p_t^n QA_t^n(k_t^n)^{-\alpha^n}(h_t^n)^{\alpha^n} = r_t^{kn} \tag{8.18}$$

Turning to market equilibrium, the labor market in the tradable sector and the capital market in the nontradable sector exhibit perfectly inelastic supply curves. Consequently, equilibrium prices in these markets are determined by the factor demands. We define the production functions of the firms as

$$y_t^x = QA_t^x(k_t^x)^{1-\alpha^x}(h^x)^{\alpha^x} \tag{8.19}$$

$$y_t^m = QA_t^m(k_t^m)^{1-\alpha^m}(h^m)^{\alpha^m} \tag{8.20}$$

$$y_t^n = QA_t^n(k^n)^{1-\alpha^n}(h_t^n)^{\alpha^n} \tag{8.21}$$

where y_t^x, y_t^m, and y_t^n are the exportable, importable, and nontradable production, respectively.

With the production technologies, we can express the factors' demand as

$$\alpha^x p_t^x \frac{y_t^x}{h^x} = w_t^x \tag{8.22}$$

$$(1-\alpha^x)\frac{p_t^x y_t^x}{k_t^x} = r_t^k \tag{8.23}$$

$$\alpha^m \frac{y_t^m}{h^m} = w_t^m \tag{8.24}$$

Table 8.5 Firms equations

Description
13. Exportables' production function: $y_t^x = QA_t^x (k_t^x)^{1-\alpha^x} (h^x)^{\alpha^x}$
14. Capital demand from exportable-producing firms: $(1-\alpha^x)\frac{p_t^x y_t^x}{k_t^x} = r_t^k$
15. Labor demand from exportable-producing firms: $\alpha^x \frac{p_t^x y_t^x}{h^x} = w_t^x$
16. Importables' production function: $y_t^m = QA_t^m (k_t^m)^{1-\alpha^m} (h^m)^{\alpha^m}$
17. Capital demand from importable-producing firms: $(1-\alpha^m)\frac{y_t^m}{k_t^m} = r_t^k$
18. Labor demand from importable-producing firms: $\alpha^m \frac{y_t^m}{h^m} = w_t^m$
19. Nontradables' production function: $y_t^n = QA_t^n (k^n)^{1-\alpha^n} (h_t^n)^{\alpha^n}$
20. Capital demand from nontradable-producing firms: $(1-\alpha^n)\frac{p_t^n y_t^n}{k^n} = r_t^{kn}$
21. Labor demand from nontradable-producing firms: $\alpha^n \frac{p_t^n y_t^n}{h_t^n} = w_t$

$$(1-\alpha^m)\frac{y_t^m}{k_t^m} = r_t^k \tag{8.25}$$

$$\alpha^n p_t^n \frac{y_t^n}{h_t^n} = w_t \tag{8.26}$$

$$(1-\alpha^n) p_t^n \frac{y_n^t}{k_n} = r_t^{kn} \tag{8.27}$$

Table 8.5 summarizes the Eqs. (8.19)–(8.27) from the firms' problem.

8.4.3 *Market Clearing and Shock Definitions*

The resource constraint for the tradable sector, which includes the importable and exportables sectors, is expressed in units of importables:

$$p_t^x c_t^x + c_t^m + i_t^T + \frac{\phi}{2}(k_{t+1}^T - k_t^T)^2 + B_{t+1} = p_t^x y_t^x + y_t^m + (1 + r_{t-1}^f)B_t \tag{8.28}$$

For the nontradable sector, the resource constraint is as follows:

$$c_t^n + k^n - (1 - \delta)k^n = y_t^n \tag{8.29}$$

It is essential to construct a GDP measure that is comparable to conventional real GDP and consistent with the concept of aggregated Cobb-Douglas technology. In this case, the sectoral Cobb-Douglas production functions for tradables are constructed as follows:

$$y_t^T = (y_t^x)^a (y_t^m)^{1-a} \tag{8.30}$$

And the aggregate Cobb-Douglas function is then defined as

$$y_t = (y_t^T)^\kappa (y_t^n)^{1-\kappa} \tag{8.31}$$

where κ represents the weight of tradables in the final goods production.

In this economy, the shocks affecting the economy are the shock to terms of trade, ϵ_t^p, and the shock to productivity in tradable sector, ϵ_t^T. The stochastic processes are the following:

$$\ln(p_t^x) = \rho \ln(p_{t-1}^x) + \epsilon_t^p, \quad \epsilon_t^p \sim N(0, \sigma_{\epsilon_t^p}^2) \tag{8.32}$$

$$\ln(A_t^x) = \rho \ln(A_{t-1}^x) + \rho^T \epsilon_t^p + \epsilon_t^T, \quad \epsilon^T \sim N(0, \sigma_{\epsilon_t^T}^2) \tag{8.33}$$

$$\ln(A_t^m) = \rho \ln(A_{t-1}^m) + \rho^T \epsilon_t^p + \epsilon_t^T \tag{8.34}$$

$$\ln(A_t^n) = \rho \ln(A_{t-1}^n) + \rho^N (\rho^T \epsilon_t^p + \epsilon_t^T) \tag{8.35}$$

The parameters ρ, ρ^T, and ρ^N stand for the persistence of the shocks, the correlation between the terms of trade and productivity in the tradable sector, and the correlation between the productivity of the tradable sector and the nontradable sector, respectively.

8.4.4 Expressing Variables at Import Prices

Since the data moments were reported at import prices, all variables under analysis need to be expressed in the same unit of measure to maintain consistency with the data. In the model, both the investment in the tradable sector i_t^T and the ratio of the trade balance to output $\frac{tb_t}{y_t}$ are already measured at import prices. However, variables like consumption c_t and aggregated output y_t are measured in units of each variable (they are essentially composite or other variables). Therefore, it is necessary to construct both a relative price of consumption p_t^c and a relative price of aggregated output p_t^y, to express these variables in units of import prices.

For this purpose, we employ the same strategy, which involves formulating an expenditure minimization problem. This time, it pertains to exportables and importables in the context of tradables; therefore, the problem is

$$\underset{\{y_t^x, y_t^m\}}{\text{Min}} \quad p_t^x y_t^x + y_t^m \quad \text{subject to} \quad (y_t^x)^a (y_t^m)^{1-a} = y_t^T$$

The Lagrange of the problem is as follows:

$$\mathcal{L} = p_t^x y_t^x + y_t^m + \lambda \left(y_t^T - (y_t^x)^a (y_t^m)^{1-a} \right)$$

The first-order conditions are

$$\begin{aligned} \{y_t^x\}: \quad & p_t^x = \lambda \left(a (y_t^x)^{a-1} (y_t^m)^{1-a} \right) \\ \{y_t^m\}: \quad & 1 = \lambda \left((1-a)(y_t^x)^a (y_t^m)^{-a} \right) \end{aligned}$$

The way the optimization was stated allows the Lagrange multiplier to be interpreted as the price of y_t^T. This implies that $\lambda = p_t^T$. Then, from the FOC of y_t^x, it is elaborated:

$$\begin{aligned} p_t^x &= a p_t^T (y_t^x)^{a-1} (y_t^m)^{1-a} \\ p_t^x &= a p_t^T \frac{y_t^T}{y_t^x} \end{aligned} \tag{8.36}$$

This problem is symmetric; therefore, working with equation the FOC of y_t^m

$$1 = (1-a) p_t^T \frac{y_t^T}{y_t^m} \tag{8.37}$$

Up to this point, it is possible to find an expression for p_t. The definition of output from tradable sector is $y_t^T = (y_t^x)^a (y_t^m)^{1-a}$; then, Eqs. (8.36) and (8.37) are replaced in this expression as follows:

$$\begin{aligned} y_t^T &= \left(a y_t^T \frac{p_t^T}{p_t^x} \right)^a \left((1-a) y_t^T p_t^T \right)^{1-a} \\ y_t^T &= p_t^T y_t^T a^a (p_t^x)^a (1-a)^{1-a} \\ p_t^T &= a^{-a} (p_t^x)^a (1-a)^{-(1-a)}. \end{aligned} \tag{8.38}$$

Notice that p_t^T is expressed in terms of parameters and p_t^x, which is useful for defining its steady-state value.

It is also necessary to find the price of output at import prices. Here, the expenditure minimization problem is

$$\underset{\{y_t^T, y_t^n\}}{\text{Min}} \quad p_t^T y_t^T + p_t^n y_t^n \quad \text{subject to} \quad y_t = (y_t^T)^a (y_t^n)^{1-a}$$

The Lagrangian of the problem is as follows:

$$\mathcal{L} = p_t^T y_t^T + p_t^n y_t^n + \lambda \left(y_t - (y_t^T)^a (y_t^n)^{1-a} \right)$$

The first-order conditions are

$$\{y_t^T\}: \quad p_t^T = \lambda \left(a (y_t^T)^{a-1} (y_t^n)^{1-a} \right)$$

$$\{y_t^n\}: \quad p_t^n = \lambda \left((1-a) (y_t^T)^a (y_t^n)^{-a} \right)$$

The way the optimization was stated allows the Lagrange multiplier to be interpreted as the price of y_t. This implies that $\lambda = p_t^y$. From the FOC of y_t^T

$$p_t^T = a p_t^y \left(\frac{(y_t^T)^a (y_t^n)^{1-a}}{y_t^T} \right)$$

$$p_t^T = a p_t^y \frac{y_t}{y_t^T} \tag{8.39}$$

This problem is symmetric; thus, a similar result is obtained when working with the FOC of y_t^n:

$$p_t^n = (1-a) p_t^y \frac{y_t}{y_t^n} \tag{8.40}$$

Output is defined as an aggregate production function, using a weighted geometric average of sectoral production functions. This implies $y_t = (y_t^T)^\kappa (y_n)^{1-\kappa}$. In order to obtain the price level of output y_t in terms of import goods, we replace the Eqs. (8.39) and (8.40) as follows:

$$y_t = \left(\kappa y_t \frac{p_t^y}{p_t^T} \right)^\kappa \left((1-\kappa) y_t \frac{p_t^y}{p_t^n} \right)^{1-\kappa}$$

$$1 = p_t^y \left(\frac{\kappa}{a^{-a} (p_t^x)^a (1-a)^{-(1-a)}} \right)^\kappa \left(\frac{(1-\kappa)}{p_t^n} \right)^{1-\kappa}$$

$$p_t^y = \left(\left(\frac{p_t^x}{\kappa a}\right)^a \left(\frac{1}{\kappa(1-a)}\right)^{1-a}\right)^\kappa \left(\frac{p_t^n}{1-\kappa}\right)^{1-\kappa}$$

To obtain the price of consumption in terms of import goods p_t^c, we need to use the demands of each type of consumption derived in the minimization problem in the section above; these are

$$\frac{c_t}{c_t^T} = \left(\frac{p_t^T}{p_t^c}\right)^{\frac{1}{1+\mu}}$$

$$\frac{c_t}{c_t^n} = \left(\frac{p_t^N}{p_t^c}\right)^{\frac{1}{1+\mu}}$$

$$\frac{c_t^x}{c_t^T} = a\frac{p_t^T}{p_t^x}$$

$$\frac{c_t^m}{c_t^T} = (1-a)p_t^T$$

Recall the definition from consumption $c_t = \left[(c_t^T)^{-\mu} + (c_t^n)^{-\mu}\right]^{-\frac{1}{\mu}}$. Then, it follows that

$$c_t = \left[\left(c_t\left(\frac{p_t^c}{p_t^T}\right)^{\frac{1}{1+\mu}}\right)^{-\mu} + \left(c_t\left(\frac{p_t^c}{p_t^n}\right)^{\frac{1}{1+\mu}}\right)^{-\mu}\right]^{-\frac{1}{\mu}}$$

$$c_t = c_t(p_t^c)^{\frac{1}{1+\mu}}\left[\left(\left(\frac{1}{p_t^T}\right)^{\frac{1}{1+\mu}}\right)^{-\mu} + \left(\left(\frac{1}{p_t^n}\right)^{\frac{1}{1+\mu}}\right)^{-\mu}\right]^{-\frac{1}{\mu}}$$

$$p_t^c = \left[\left(a^{-a}(1-a)^{-(1-a)}(p_t^x)^a\right)^{\frac{\mu}{1+\mu}} + (p_t^n)^{\frac{\mu}{1+\mu}}\right]^{\frac{1+\mu}{\mu}} \tag{8.41}$$

This expression for p_t^c represents the consumer price index (CPI) of the model.

To ensure that the analysis of the model's variables aligns with the data, we consider the aggregated variables of output and consumption at import prices. As a result, the deflators obtained in this section convert these variables from their unit of measurement to import prices. Consequently, we define output at import prices (y_t^{imp}) and consumption at import prices (c_t^{imp}) as follows:

$$y_t^{imp} = p_t^y y_t \tag{8.42}$$

$$c_t^{imp} = p_t^c c_t \tag{8.43}$$

8.4.5 External Sector

One of the objectives of the model is to study the relationship between terms of trade and international variables, such as trade balance and real exchange rate. The trade balance is defined as in the previous chapter:

$$(tb/y)_t = \frac{B_{t+1} - (1 + r^f_{t-1})B_t}{y_t}; \tag{8.44}$$

The real exchange rate bears varying interpretations within equilibrium models. In particular, in three-good models, a more accurate measurement of the real exchange rate is achieved by employing the domestic relative price of aggregate consumption p^c_t–a metric which is a function of both p^n_t and p^x_t. The real exchange rate indicates the relative price of the consumption basket in the home country in terms of the consumption basket in the foreign country:

$$RER_t = \left[\left(a^{-a}(1-a)^{-(1-a)}(p^x_t)^a \right)^{\frac{\mu}{1+\mu}} + (p^n_t)^{\frac{\mu}{1+\mu}} \right]^{\frac{1+\mu}{\mu}}$$

Finally, the interest rate differential is measured as follows:

$$int\_diff = \frac{p^c_t}{p^c_{t-1}}(1 + r^*) - (1 + r^*)$$

Table 8.6 summarizes the main equations from the sections above. Together with Tables 8.4 and 8.5, it contains all the remaining equations needed to solve the model.

8.4.6 Parametrization

Parametrization corresponds to the values in Mendoza (1995). Table 8.7 shows the values associated with the model parameters.

8.4.7 Steady State

Calculating the steady state analytically presents a challenge due to the intricate nature of the involved nonlinear equations.

First, the ratio of expenditure on nontradables to expenditure on tradables, $\frac{p^n_t c^n_t}{p^T_t c^T_t}$, is established at 0.87. Furthermore, the allocation of time follows this distribution: 10% is allocated to the tradable sector, with 5% allocated to each industry within it,

Table 8.6 Rest of the model

Description
22. Resource constraint for the tradable sector:
$p_t^x c_t^x + c_t^m + i_t^T + \frac{\phi}{2}(k_{t+1}^T - k_t^T)^2 + B_{t+1} = p_t^x y_t^x + y_t^m + (1+r_{t-1}^f)B_t$
23. Resource constraint for the nontradable sector:
$c_t^n + k^n - (1-\delta)k^n = y_t^n$
24. Tradable Cobb-Douglas production function:
$y^T = (y_t^x)^a (y_t^m)^{1-a}$
25. Aggregate Cobb-Douglas production function:
$y_t = (y_t^T)^\kappa (y_t^n)^{1-\kappa}$
26. Terms of trade :
$\ln(p_t^x) = \rho \ln(p_{t-1}^x) + \epsilon_t^p$
27. Exportables firms productivity:
$\ln(A_t^x) = \rho \ln(A_{t-1}^x) + \rho^T$
28. Importables firms productivity:
$\ln(A_t^m) = \rho \ln(A_{t-1}^m) + \rho^T \epsilon_t^p + \epsilon_t^T$
29. Nontradables firms productivity:
$\ln(A_t^n) = \rho \ln(A_{t-1}^n) + \rho^N(\rho^T \epsilon_t^p + \epsilon_t^T)$
30. Price index for aggregate Cobb-Douglas production function:
$p_t^y = \left(\left(\frac{p_t^x}{\kappa a}\right)^a \left(\frac{1}{\kappa(1-a)}\right)^{1-a}\right)^\kappa \left(\frac{p_t^n}{1-\kappa}\right)^{1-\kappa}$
31. Output at import prices:
$y_t^{imp} = p_t^y y_t$
32. Consumption at import prices:
$c_t^{imp} = p_t^c c_t$
33. Ratio trade balance to output:
$(tb/y)_t = \frac{B_{t+1} - (1+r_{t-1}^f)B_t}{y_t}$
34. Real exchange rate:
$RER_t = \left[\left(a^{-a}(1-a)^{-(1-a)}(p_t^x)^a\right)^{\frac{\mu}{1+\mu}} + (p_t^n)^{\frac{\mu}{1+\mu}}\right]^{\frac{1+\mu}{\mu}}$
35. Interest rate differential:
$int\_diff = \frac{p_t^c}{p_{t-1}^c}(1+r^*) - (1+r^*)$

Table 8.7 Parametrization

Parameter	Value	Description
H	100	Total time available for leisure or labor
exp_share	0.87	Ratio of expenditure on nontradables to expenditure on tradables
Q	1	Scale parameter for total factor productivity
κ	0.5	Share of exportables in total tradable consumption
ρ	0.414	Shock persistence
ρ^T	0.165	Correlation between p^x and A^x,A^m
ρ^N	0.95	Correlation between A^x,A^m and A^n
r^*	0.04	Steady-state foreign interest rate
α^x	0.51	Labor share in income from exportables
α^m	0.73	Labor share in income from importables
α^n	0.56	Labor share in income from nontradables
δ	0.1	Depreciation rate uniform across sectors
ϕ	0.028	Capital adjustment costs
γ	1.5	Intertemporal inverse elasticity
μ	0.35	Elasticity of subs. between tradables and nontradables
a	0.3	Share of expenditure in exportable goods
ω	2.08	Labor supply elasticity
σ_p	0.019	Terms of trade shock
σ_T	0.019	Productivity shock in the tradable sector

and an additional 11,39% is allocated to the nontradable sector. As a result, the time-invariant variables representing labor for exportables and importable-producing firms both assume a value of 5 ($h^x = 5, h^m = 5$), while leisure during the steady-state l_{ss} is 78.61. Additionally, a value of 15 is imposed on the time-invariant capital in the nontradable sector k^n.

From the time constraint, Eq. (8.6), the available time allocated in leisure in steady state is given by

$$\begin{aligned} l_{ss} &= H - h^n_{ss} - h^x - h^m \\ l_{ss} &= 100 - 11.39 - 5 - 5 \\ l_{ss} &= 78.61 \end{aligned} \tag{8.45}$$

From the definition of the risk premium, Eq. (8.9)

$$\begin{aligned} rp_{ss} &= \chi(e^{\bar{B}-B_t} - 1) \\ rp_{ss} &= \chi(e^{\bar{B}-\bar{B}} - 1) \\ rp_{ss} &= 0 \end{aligned} \tag{8.46}$$

From the definition of the real interest rate, given the value of rp_{ss}

$$r^f_{ss} = r^* + rp_{ss}$$
$$r^f_{ss} = r^* \tag{8.47}$$

From the Euler equation for consumption, we obtain

$$\frac{(c_{ss}l^{\omega}_{ss})^{-\gamma}l^{\omega}_{ss}}{p^c_{ss}} = \beta(1+r^f_{ss})\frac{(c_{ss}l^{\omega}_{ss})^{-\gamma}l^{\omega}_{ss}}{p^c_{ss}}$$
$$1 = \beta(1+r^f_{ss})$$
$$\beta = \frac{1}{1+r^f_{ss}}$$
$$\beta = \frac{1}{1+r^*} \tag{8.48}$$

From the optimality condition for investment, we obtain

$$(1+\phi(k_{ss}-k_{ss}) = \beta\frac{U_{c_{ss}}}{U_{c_{ss}}}\frac{p^c_{ss}}{p^c_{ss}}(r^k_{ss} + (1-\delta) + \phi(k_{ss}-k_{ss}))$$
$$1 = \beta(r^k_{ss} + (1-\delta))$$
$$r^k_{ss} = \frac{1}{\beta} - (1-\delta) \tag{8.49}$$

Using the capital demands from the firms of the tradable sector, Eqs. (8.23) and (8.25), and the fact that $k^T_t = k^x_t + k^m_t$, we obtain k^m_{ss}, k^m_{ss}, and k^T_{ss}:

$$k^m_{ss} = \left(\frac{r^k_{ss}}{Q(1-\alpha^m)}\right)^{-1/\alpha^m} h^m \tag{8.50}$$
$$k^x_{ss} = \left(\frac{r^k_{ss}}{Q(1-\alpha^x)}\right)^{-1/\alpha^x} h^x \tag{8.51}$$
$$k^T_{ss} = k^m_{ss} + k^x_{ss} \tag{8.52}$$

From the production function for each sector in Eqs. (8.19), (8.20), and (8.21), we obtain the levels of y^x_{ss}, y^m_{ss}, and y^n_{ss}:

$$y^x_{ss} = Q(k^x_{ss})^{1-\alpha^x}(h^x)^{\alpha^x} \tag{8.53}$$
$$y^m_{ss} = Q(k^m_{ss})^{1-\alpha^m}(h^m)^{\alpha^m} \tag{8.54}$$
$$y^n_{ss} = Q(k^n)^{1-\alpha^n}(h^n_{ss})^{\alpha^n} \tag{8.55}$$

The measure for domestic GDP, Eq. (8.31), defines the steady state of aggregated output:

$$y_{ss} = \left((y^x_{ss})^a (y^m_{ss})^{1-a} \right)^\kappa (y^n_{ss})^{1-\kappa} \tag{8.56}$$

From the law of motion for capital, Eq. (8.4), we obtain the level of i^T_{ss}:

$$i^T_{ss} = k^T_{ss} - (1-\delta)k^T_{ss} = \delta k^T_{ss} \tag{8.57}$$

From the market-clearing condition, Eq. (8.29), we obtain the level of c^n_{ss}:

$$c^n_{ss} = y^n_{ss} - \delta k^n \tag{8.58}$$

The definition of the price of tradables, Eq. (8.38), obtained in the expenditure minimization problem defines the steady-state level of p^T_t:

$$p^T_{ss} = a^{-a}(1-a)^{-(1-a)} \tag{8.59}$$

From the relative demands for c^T_t and c^n_t, we divide the terms in Eqs. (8.12) and (8.13) and arrive to

$$\frac{\frac{c_{ss}}{c^T_{ss}}}{\frac{c_{ss}}{c^n_{ss}}} = \frac{\left(\frac{p^T_{ss}}{p^c_{ss}}\right)^{\frac{1}{1+\mu}}}{\left(\frac{p^N_{ss}}{p^c_{ss}}\right)^{\frac{1}{1+\mu}}}$$

If we work with this equation further, we can obtain the expenditure share, defined as $\frac{c^T_{ss} p^T_{ss}}{c^n_{ss} p^n_{ss}}$, and the level of p^n_{ss}:

$$p^n_{ss} = \left(\frac{c^T_{ss} p^T_{ss}}{c^n_{ss} p^n_{ss}} \right)^{(1+\mu)/\mu} p^T_{ss} = (0.87)^{(1+\mu)/\mu} p^T_{ss} \tag{8.60}$$

From the CPI definition, Eq. (8.41), the steady state level of p^c_t is:

$$p^c_{ss} = \left((p^T_{ss})^{\mu/(1+\mu)} + (p^n_{ss})^{\mu/(1+\mu)} \right)^{(1+\mu)/\mu} \tag{8.61}$$

From the relative demand for c^m_t, Eq (8.15), we obtain the level of c^m_{ss}:

$$\frac{1}{p^T_{ss}} \frac{c^m_{ss}}{c^T_{ss}} = 1 - a$$

$$c^m_{ss} = (1-a) c^T_{ss} p^T_{ss} \frac{c^n_{ss} p^n_{ss}}{c^n_{ss} p^n_{ss}}$$

$$c^m_{ss} = (1-a)\frac{c^n_{ss}p^n_{ss}}{(c^n_{ss}p^n_{ss})/(c^T_{ss}p^T_{ss})}$$

$$c^m_{ss} = (1-a)\frac{c^n_{ss}p^n_{ss}}{0.87} \tag{8.62}$$

The level of c^x_{ss} is obtained straightforward, using Eq. (8.14):

$$c^x_{ss} = \frac{a}{1-a}c^m_{ss} \tag{8.63}$$

From Eq. (8.1), we obtain the level of c_{ss}:

$$c_{ss} = \left((c^T_{ss})^{-\mu} + (c^n_{ss})^{-\mu}\right)^{-1/\mu} \tag{8.64}$$

From the demand for labor from the exportable-, importable-, and nontradable-producing firms and the demand for capital from the nontradable-producing firms, we obtain an expression for the levels of w_{ss}, w^x_{ss}, w^m_{ss}, and r^{kn}_{ss}:

$$w_{ss} = \alpha^n p^n_{ss}\frac{y^n_{ss}}{h^n_{ss}} \tag{8.65}$$

$$w^x_{ss} = \alpha^x p^x_{ss}\frac{y^x_{ss}}{h^x} \tag{8.66}$$

$$w^m_{ss} = \alpha^m \frac{y^m_{ss}}{h^m} \tag{8.67}$$

$$r^{kn}_{ss} = (1-\alpha^n)Q(p^n_{ss})(h^n_{ss})^{\alpha^n}(k^n)^{-\alpha^n} \tag{8.68}$$

Equations (8.45)–(8.68) define the steady state of the entire model.

8.4.8 Model Solution

Tables 8.4, 8.5, and 8.6 present the 35 nonlinear equations and variables of the model, constituting a nonlinear system. For ease of log-linearization, each variable is expressed in Dynare as $exp(xx)$, where $xx = \ln x_t$. However, the following variables are denoted in Dynare as x: foreign assets (B_t), terms of trade disturbance (p^x_t), labor for nontradable-producing firms (h^n_t), leisure (l_t), capital rent in the tradable sector (r^k_t), capital rent for nontradable-producing firms (r^{kn}_t), productivity disturbances across sectors (A^x_t, A^m_t, A^n_t), real interest rate (r^f_t), risk premium (rp_t), interest differential (int_diff), trade balance to output ratio $(tb/y)_t$, and current account to output ratio $(ca/y)_t$.

Dynare conducts linearization of variables represented in logarithms and levels to derive variables in log deviations and deviations from their steady state, respectively. Specifically, Dynare expresses the log-deviation variable as $\widehat{xt} = \ln x_t - \ln xss$, where x_t represents the variable of interest and x_{ss} denotes its steady-state value. Similarly, the deviation variable is expressed as $\widetilde{xt} = x_t - xss$. These variables are utilized by Dynare to compute steady states, policy and state functions, impulse-response functions, and theoretical moments.

8.5 Impulse-Response Analysis

This section examines the impulse-response functions of the model variables induced by a terms of trade shock and a uniform productivity shock across sectors.

8.5.1 Impulse-Response Functions to Terms of Trade Shock

Figure 8.2 plots the response of the aggregated variables measured at import prices.

Firstly, an improvement in the terms of trade induces to shift capital from importables to exportables industry. Because capital is homogeneous, firms allocate more capital to the exportables sector and less capital in the importables sector until returns on capital from both industries equalize, given a stock of capital available to tradable sector. This capital reallocation over time from the importables sector to the exportables sector is depicted in Fig. 8.3.

Indeed, with reference to Eqs. (8.23) and (8.25), the marginal productivity of capital remains equal across the tradable industries. Hence, employing the definitions of output for exports and imports, we can derive the following relationship:

$$\frac{y_t^m}{k_t^m} = \frac{p_t^x y_t^x}{k_t^m}$$

$$QA_t^x (k_t^x)^{-\alpha^x} (h^x)^{\alpha^x} = p_t^x QA_t^m (k_t^m)^{-\alpha^m} (h^m)^{\alpha^m}$$

Turning to the optimality condition for investment, a terms of trade shock prompts an economic expansion. This occurs because the expected returns from capital in the tradable sector increase, leading households to reallocate resources toward accumulating capital for the production of exportables in the subsequent period, as shown in Fig. 8.2.

When the price of exportable goods rises due to the expenditure switching effect, households tend to consume more importable goods and fewer exportable goods within the basket of tradable goods. This causes a shift in production from importable to exportable goods, while consumption shifts from exportables to

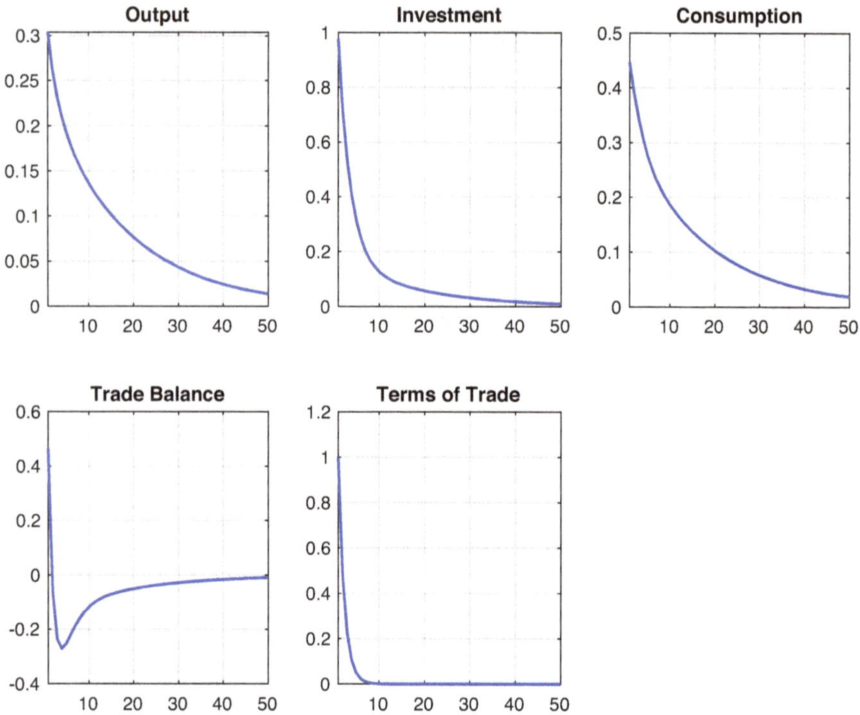

Fig. 8.2 Effects of a terms of trade shock

importables. Understanding these dynamics requires considering the "price effects" as pivotal. As illustrated in Fig. 8.2, the increase in real output is proportionally smaller than the increase in consumption and investment. These dynamics typically signal a deterioration in the trade balance. However, as output shifts toward the production of exportable goods and consumption moves toward importable goods, the economy achieves a positive trade balance and accumulates net foreign assets in terms of value. Consequently, output at import prices experiences a significant increase, primarily due to the direct positive impact of the terms of trade on purchasing power, as depicted in Fig. 8.4.

Consumption of nontradables also increases. Given this increment, total consumption at import prices increases after the shock. Figure 8.4 plots the response of the composite goods and the relative prices. This result aligns with the Harberger-Laursen-Metzler (HLM) effect.

Figure 8.4 also illustrates that both p_t^n and RER_t increase in response to the terms of trade shock, triggering a real appreciation. The increase in p_t^n underscores the fact that the increased demand for nontradables is met with a nearly unaltered

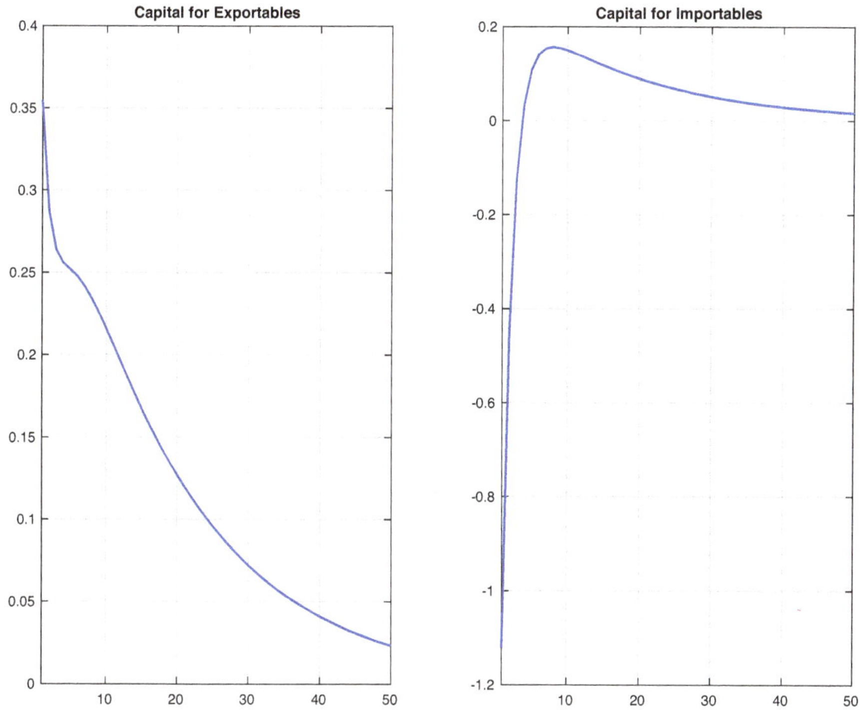

Fig. 8.3 Effects of a terms of trade shock on capital allocations

supply, which yields a rise in p_t^n. Given the structure of the consumer price index (CPI), which contains p_t^x, the shock results in an appreciation of the real exchange rate.

For this reason, a positive real interest rate differential increases alongside the real appreciation. Consequently, the anticipated realignment of the real exchange rate results in a negative interest rate differential. As the terms of trade shock gradually diminishes, less capital needs to be allocated to the exportables sector compared to the importables sector to equalize returns between both sectors. The growth rate of output at import prices slows down, reflecting the declining purchasing power of exports and the return of capital k_t^T to its initial level. This convergence follows a monotonic path toward equilibrium.

Similarly, consumption c_t^{imp} follows a monotonically convergent trajectory, albeit at a slower pace. This slower pace is attributed to trade surpluses in earlier periods that finance subsequent deficits. Likewise, the ratio of the trade balance to output $(tb/y)_t$ requires time to fully return to its initial equilibrium. Thus, surpluses from earlier periods are offset by deficits over multiple future periods.

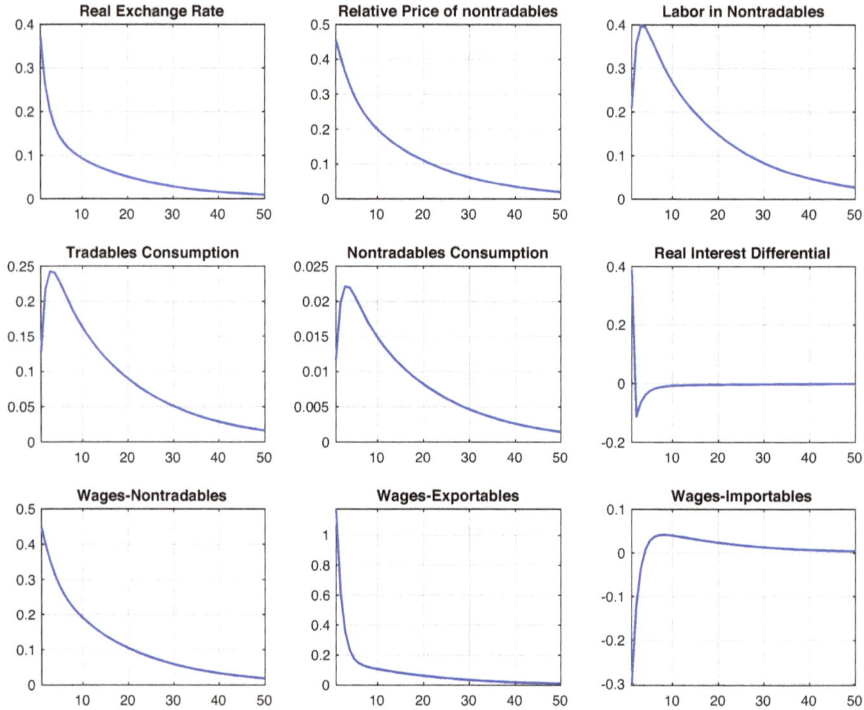

Fig. 8.4 Effects of a terms of trade shock

8.5.2 *Impulse-Response Functions to Productivity Shock Across Sectors*

Figure 8.5 depicts the response of aggregated variables measured at import prices.

The dynamics caused by productivity shocks exhibit distinct differences compared to those induced by a terms of trade (TOT) shock. First and foremost, the productivity shock triggers a more robust surge in net exports. This outcome materializes due to the uniform enhancement in productivity across both tradable and nontradable sectors, generating a potent wealth effect that prompts households to amplify their savings. Given that capital remains fixed in the nontradeable sector, these heightened savings predominantly find allocation in foreign assets. Additionally, the variance-covariance and autocorrelation structures of the shocks curtail significant deviations in the anticipated, risk-adjusted differentials between domestic marginal products of capital in the tradable sector and r^*. Consequently, the substantial variance of the trade balance in the G-7 benchmark can be attributed to the estimated size of productivity shocks and their positive correlation with TOT shocks.

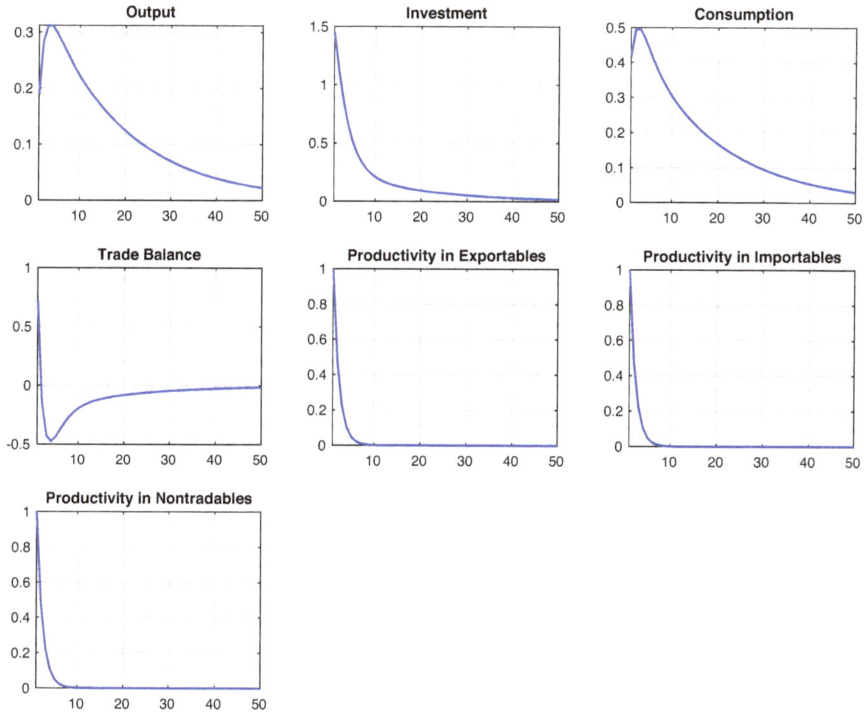

Fig. 8.5 Effects of a productivity shock across sectors

Moreover, the responses of the real exchange rate, the relative price of nontradables, and the real interest rate differential exhibit their own distinctive patterns. In the context of the productivity shock, both tradables and nontradables undergo a substantial supply response, albeit with a slight decline in h_t^n due to a wealth-induced leisure effect. This decline contributes to a reduction in p_t^n in order to attain market equilibrium, consequently resulting in a depreciation of the real exchange rate. Importantly, given that the terms of trade remain unaltered, the magnitude of real depreciation is smaller than the decline in the price of nontradables p_t^n.

Furthermore, the real interest differential shifts into the negative territory following the real exchange rate appreciation. Subsequently, an anticipated appreciation prompts a change in the direction of the interest differential (Fig. 8.6).

8.5.3 Comparison of Data and Theoretical Moments

Finally, we compare the simulations conducted with the model to actual data. In this case, we use data of the 42 countries studied in this chapter. We focus on the moments related to terms of trade and the real exchange rate. The model

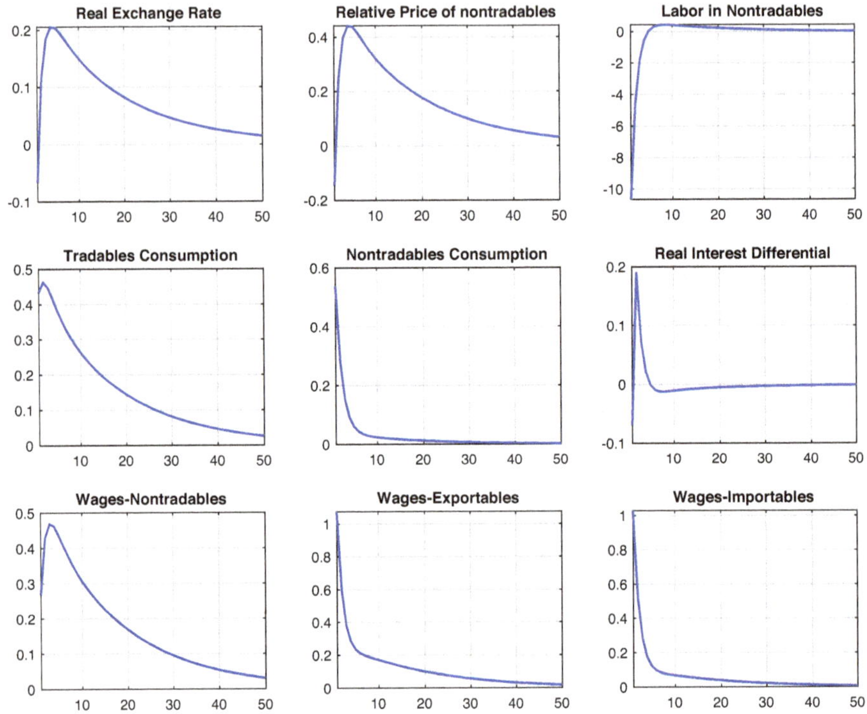

Fig. 8.6 Effects of a productivity shock across sectors

Table 8.8 Comparison of the cyclical behavior of the theoretic model with the empirical data

	Data			Model		
Variable (x_t)	$\rho_{x_t, y_{\text{imp}}}$	ρ_{x_t, p^x}	$\rho_{x_t, x_{t-1}}$	$\rho_{x_t, y_{\text{imp}}}$	ρ_{x_t, p^x}	$\rho_{x_t, x_{t-1}}$
y_{imp}	1.000	0.420	0.630	1.000	0.526	0.925
c_{imp}	0.880	0.290	0.630	0.999	0.545	0.923
$investment$	0.710	0.290	0.590	0.883	0.766	0.768
$trade\ balance$	−0.100	0.170	0.550	−0.490	0.316	0.588
p^x	0.420	1.000	0.660	0.526	1.000	0.473
RER	0.570	0.190	0.640	0.968	0.694	0.857

overestimates the procyclicality of real exchange rate and its relationship with the terms of trade. The model is also capable of obtaining a stronger negative correlation between the balance of trade and the business cycle, although the data in the sample of countries considered shows a weaker one (Table 8.8).

8.6 Summary

This chapter presents a small open economy RBC model that incorporates three main features: (i) a nontradable sector, (ii) a tradable sector composed of exportable- and importable-producing goods, and (iii) a terms of trade shock that affects the relative price of exports.

The motivation to study such a model serves several purposes. First, terms of trade shocks are considered one of the key drivers of business cycles, especially in small open economies with sizable commodity export sectors. Second, it permits to study the factors behind the reaction of the balance of trade to terms of trade shocks and disentangle the reasons for the presence of a Harberger-Laursen-Metzler (HLM) effect or a Obstfeld-Razin-Svensson (ORS) effect. Finally, the presence of nontradables allows for the study of the business cycle properties of the real exchange rate, which exhibit a procyclical behavior in the data, a stylized fact hard to replicate by productivity shocks.

We start by examining the stylized facts linking terms of trade, real exchange rates, and business cycles in the data. We study a sample of 42 countries covering the period from 1980 to 2020. The findings confirm the procyclical behavior observed in the real exchange rate and the positive correlation between terms of trade and GDP.

We then proceed to introduce the model, closely following Mendoza (1995) and solve it. We confirm the capacity of the model to match these two stylized facts. Under positive productivity shocks, output expansion occurs in conjunction with a fall in nontradable prices. Since importables' prices are determined by world markets, this generates a fall in nontradable prices relative to tradable prices on impact. Since the price of the foreign basket is unaffected, the cheaper domestic basket represents a real depreciation.

By contrast, a terms of trade shock increases the price of exportables. The shift on relative prices creates important sectoral dynamics as production shifts to exportables, while consumption shifts to importables. This reallocation contributes to the positive wealth effect, also increasing the demand for nontradable goods. Given the higher demand and low elasticity of supply, the price of nontradable goods augments. The higher nontradables' prices represent a real exchange rate appreciation, which helps obtaining a positive correlation between the real exchange rate and the business cycle.

8.7 Codes

The model's solution, along with the impulse-response functions, has been directly developed in Matlab by creating several *m-files* and also in Dynare by constructing a *mod-file*. The results from both approaches are consistent. However, the advantage of creating an m-file directly is that it allows for the explicit handling of many details in the model's solution and simulation. Additionally, both the R and Python scripts for working with the database have been uploaded to the book's companion website (Table 8.9).

Table 8.9 Codes in Matlab and Dynare

Codes	Description
Matlab	
Graphs.m	This *m-file* plots the impulse-response functions of the model to terms of trade shock and productivity shock across sectors. It use the mod file Mendoza95_irf.mod
series_chile.m	This *m-file* plots various series of aggregated variables of Chile for comparison
Dynare	
Mendoza95.mod	This mod file contains the nonlinear model and is solved in Dynare
Mendoza95_irf.mod	This mod file provides the impulse-response functions for both the terms of trade and productivity shocks

Appendix A
Dynamic Optimization

A.1 Introduction

This appendix describes the mathematical elements needed in dynamic programming. Each of the models described in the book can be approached by this method, which is widely used in macroeconomics.

This appendix has two parts. The first contains some concepts of real analysis and the second contains the main elements of dynamic programming. The objective of the first part is to emphasize the necessary concepts in this technique; therefore, we have only focused on some issues of real analysis. In the second part, we have tried to be explicit in the hypotheses, propositions, and theorems that underlie dynamic programming so that the reader has a clear overview of this technique. Finally, we have described an application step by step so that the reader can observe how to use the technique, and we have left an exercise so that the reader is free to apply what has been learned.

A.2 Fundamentals of Real Analysis

A.2.1 What Mathematical Concepts Do We Need?

To define what mathematical concepts we need in dynamic programming, it is useful to start with one of its main theorems called **fixed-point theorem for (Banach's) contractions**.

This theorem indicates the following: let $C_a(X)$ the set of continuous and bounded functions with the norm of the supremum $\|\cdot\|$ (complete normed vector space), and then the operator "**T**," defined in $C_a(X)$, is an application of this space on itself; that is, T: $C_a(X) \rightarrow C_a(X)$, defined as

H. Galindo Gil et al., *Dynamic Stochastic General Equilibrium Models*, Springer Texts in Business and Economics, https://doi.org/10.1007/978-3-031-58105-2

$$T[V](x) = sup\left\{r(x_t, u_t) + \beta V(g(x_t, u_t))\right\} \tag{A.1}$$

subject to, $u_t \in \Gamma(x_t)$, **satisfies:**

1. $T[V] \in C_a(X)$
2. "T" has a single fixed-point "V": $T[V] = V$
3. For any $V_0 \in C_a(X)$, it has

$$\|T^n(V_0) - V\| \leq \beta^n \|V_0 - V\|$$

Particularly

$$\lim_{n\to\infty} T^n(V_0) = V$$

This theorem contains three major concepts, which we will develop here:

1. A space of functions $C_a(X)$. To understand this space, it is worth reviewing the definition of a vector space, a metric space, a normed space, and a complete space.
2. Contraction $T[V]$. In particular, we are interested in finding the sufficient conditions for an operator to be considered a "contraction."
3. Fixed point (of a contraction). Similarly to the case of contraction, we are interested in finding some conditions for a contraction to have a "fixed point."

A.2.2 Concepts (Part I): Spaces

A.2.2.1 Vectorial Space

A (real) vector space "X" is a set of elements (vectors) with two operations:

1. **Addition.** For two vectors $x, y \in X$, addition gives a vector "$x + y$" $\in X$.
2. **Scalar multiplication.** For a vector $x \in X$ and a real number $\alpha \in \mathbf{R}$, scalar multiplication gives a vector "αx" $\in X$.

Furthermore, such operations obey the usual laws of algebra; that is, for everything $x, y, z \in X$, and $\alpha, \beta \in \mathbf{R}$:

- $x + y = y + x$
- $(x + y) + z = x + (y + z)$
- $\alpha(x + y) = \alpha x + \alpha y$
- $(\alpha + \beta)x = \alpha x + \beta x$
- $(\alpha\beta)x = \alpha(\beta x)$

In addition, there exists a vector "0" $\in X$ that has the following properties:

- $x + 0 = x$

- $0x = 0$
  Finally
- $1x = x$

The following two examples illustrate the properties of a vector space:

Example A.1 (The Cartesian Plane R^2) This plane, whose elements have the following form (x, y) with $x, y \in R$, is a real vector space with the following operations:

- Addition

$$(x_1, y_1) + (x_2, y_2) = (x_1 + x_2, y_1 + y_2)$$

- Scalar multiplication

$$a.(x, y) = (ax, ay)$$

Where "$a \in R$"

Example A.2 (Set of Functions) Let X be a non-empty set. The set R^X of all functions from X to R is a real vector space with the following operations:

- Addition

$$(f + g)(x) = f(x) + g(x)$$

- Scalar multiplication

$$a.f(x) = af(x)$$

$\forall x \in X, \forall a \in R$

- If $X = R$, then the space of all real functions of real variable is obtained.
- If X is an open interval, say (a, b) or R, and $C(X)$ is the set of continuous functions of X on R, then $C(X)$ is a real vector space.

Vector Space with Additional Structure Although vector spaces *ad hoc* represent an important conceptual element in real analysis, they do not offer a framework for analyzing whether a *sequence of functions converges to another function*. Furthermore, it is not adapted to deal with *infinite series*, since the sum only allows a finite number of terms.

Both themes are fundamental in mathematical analysis. For this reason, new structures are required, such as metric spaces and normed spaces, which are important in dynamic programming. Before addressing these new structures, it is worth mentioning that the normed space is a vector space; however, a metric space may or may not be a vector space.

A.2.2.2 Metric Space

What Is a Metric? A metric (or distance) is a function "d," defined as

$$d : SxS \rightarrow \mathbf{R}$$

Such that for all $x, y, z \in S$, the following holds:

(a) $d(x, y) \geq 0$, with equality if and only if $x = y$ nonnegativity
(b) $d(x, y) = d(y, x)$ (symmetry)
(c) $d(x, z) \leq d(x, y) + d(y, z)$ (triangle inequality)

The definition of "metric" summarizes the four basic properties of Euclidean distance:

1. The distance between different points is strictly positive.
2. The distance of a point from itself is zero.
3. The distance is symmetric.
4. The triangle inequality holds.

What Is a Metric Space? A metric space is a set "S" on which a metric "d" has been defined. Usually, the pair (S, d) is called a metric space. This concept is illustrated below with two examples:

Example A.3 (*R* as a Metric Space) R is a metric space with a distance function $d(x, y) = |x - y|$. So, (R, d) is a metric space.

Example A.4 (Space of Functions) The set of functions $C[a, b]$ (continuous functions of the closed interval $[a, b]$ on R) is a metric space with a distance function (metrics):

$$d_\infty : C[a, b]xC[a, b] \rightarrow R$$

Defined by

$$d_\infty(f, g) = \sup_{t \in [a,b]} |f(t) - g(t)|$$

Then, $(C[a, b], d_\infty)$ is a metric space.

Why Is the Concept of a Metric Space Useful? Metric spaces have four properties:

- **Connexed:** If a space can be separated into two open sets with empty intersection, then the space is not connected.
- **Separability:** Related to countable sets.
- **Compactness:** A space can be described by a finite number of open sets.
- **Completeness:** Allows us to analyze whether a sequence is convergent without the need to know its limit.

The last two properties (compactness and completeness) are essential in real analysis and in optimization theory. In addition, in metric spaces, you can study open sets, closed sets, and interior points, among other concepts of sets.

A.2.2.3 Normed (Vector) Space

What Is a Norm? A norm is a function that gives the notion of "length" of a vector. The norma "$\|\cdot\|$" is defined as

$$\|\cdot\| : S \to \mathbf{R}$$

Such that for everything $x, y, z \in S$ and $\alpha \in \mathbf{R}$ it holds that:

(a) $\|\cdot\| \geq 0$, with equality if and only if $x = 0$
(b) $\|\alpha x\| =| \alpha | \|x\|$
(c) $\|x + y\| \leq \|x\| + \|y\|$ (triangle inequality)

For example, the norm of the supremo is defined as follows:

$$\|f\| = \sup\{|f(x)|\} \tag{A.2}$$

What Is a Normed Space? A normed space is a vector space "S" in which a standard has been defined "$\|\cdot\|$." The usual notation is as follows: $(S, \|\cdot\|)$ it is called a normed space.

Likewise, any normed space $(S, \|\cdot\|)$ is a metric space with the metric given by

$$d(x, y) = \|x - y\|$$

This metric is called "metric induced by the norm $\|\cdot\|$." Furthermore, all the concepts defined for metric spaces apply to normed spaces.

A.2.2.4 Complete Space

Convergence of a Sequence A sequence $\{x_n\}_{n=0}^{\infty}$ in S converges to $x \in S$, if for every $\epsilon > 0$, exists N_ϵ such that

$$d(x_n, x) < \epsilon, \text{ for all} n \geq N_\epsilon \tag{A.3}$$

Therefore, a sequence $\{x_n\}_{n=0}^{\infty}$ in a metric space (S, d) converges to $x \in S$ if and only if the sequence of distances $\{d(x_n, x)\}$, a sequence in $\mathbf{R}_+$, converges to zero. In this case, it is written

$$x_n \longrightarrow x \Longleftrightarrow d(x_n, x) \longrightarrow 0$$

Cauchy Sequence A sequence $\{x_n\}_{n=0}^{\infty}$ in S is a Cauchy sequence (*satisfies the Cauchy criterion*) if for each $\epsilon > 0$, there exists N_ϵ such that

$$d(x_n, x_m) < \epsilon, \text{ for all} n, m \geq N_\epsilon \tag{A.4}$$

Therefore, a sequence is Cauchy if the points are getting closer to each other. The advantage of the Cauchy criterion, compared to (A.3), is that (A.4) can be checked only knowing the sequence $\{x_n\}_{n=0}^{\infty}$. However, for the Cauchy criterion to be useful, it is necessary to work in spaces where it (the space) implies the existence of a limit point. So, when can it be affirmed that a Cauchy sequence implies convergence (of said sequence)? This can be confirmed when we work in complete spaces.

Complete (Metric) Space A metric space (S, d) is complete if every Cauchy sequence in S converges to an element in S. In a complete space, verifying that a sequence satisfies the Cauchy criterion is one way to verify the existence of a limit point in S. It is worth mentioning that a complete normed vector space is called Banach space.

Complete Normed Space Let $X \subseteq R^l$, and let $C_a(X)$ be the set of continuous and bounded functions $f : X \to R$ with the norm of the supremum, $\|f\| = \sup_{x \in X} \|f(x)\|$; then

$$C_a(X) \text{ is a complete normed vector space.}$$

In this space, the defined metric is $d(x, y) = \|x - y\|$, where x, y are functions.

A.2.3 *Concepts (Part II): Contractions*

A.2.3.1 Contraction (Contractive Application)

What Is a Contraction? Let (X, d) be a metric space. An application (function) on itself $T : S \to S$ is called contraction (with modulo β) if $\forall x, y \in S$, there exists some $\beta \in (0, 1)$ such that

$$d(T(x), T(y)) \leq \beta d(x, y)$$

That is, the distance between the images of the two points is less than the distance between these points. Every contraction has the following properties:

- A contraction has at least one fixed point.
- The Banach fixed-point theorem states that every contraction over a complete metric space has a unique fixed point, and therefore, for each x of S, the iterative sequence $x, f(x), f(f(x)), f(f(f(x))), \ldots$ converges to the fixed point.
- Every contraction T in a metric space (S, d) is continuous.

A.2.3.2 Blackwell's Conditions

Blackwell provides conditions for an operator T to be considered a contraction.

Sufficient Blackwell Conditions for Contractions Let $X \subseteq R^l$, and let $B(X)$ be the space of bounded functions defined on X, $f : X \to R$, with the norm of the supreme. Let $T : B(X) \to B(X)$ be an operator that satisfies

1. (Monotonicity) $f, g \in B(X)$ y $f(x) \leq g(x)$, for all $x \in X$, implies

$$T[f](x) \leq T[g](x), \text{ for all } x \in X$$

2. (Discount) is there any $\beta \in (0, 1)$ such that

$$T[f + a](x) \leq T[f](x) + \beta a, \text{ for all } f \in B(X), a \geq 0, x \in X$$

Where $(f + a)(x)$ is the function defined by $(f + a)(x) = f(x) + a$

So, "T" is a contraction with module β.

A.2.4 *Concepts (Part III): Fixed Point*

A.2.4.1 What Is a Fixed Point?

The fixed points of T are the elements of S that satisfy

$$T(x) = x$$

That is, they are the intersections with the 45 line. In this context, the question that arises is: under what circumstances can it be ensured that a contraction has a fixed point? under the conditions of Banach's theorem.

A.2.4.2 Contractive Application Theorem

If (S, d) is a complete metric space and $T : S \to S$ is a contractive mapping with module β, **then:**

(a) T has only one fixed-point $v \in S$
(b) For any $v_0 \in S, \quad d(T^n, v_0, v) \leq \beta^n d(v_0, v), n = 0, 1, 2 \ldots$

This theorem suggests two important issues:

- To ensure that the operator T has a unique fixed point, two things are required: [1] That the workspace (set of functions) is a complete metric space and [2] T is a contraction.

- Will converge to that fixed point regardless of where we start to iterate the operator. This follows from the expression "for any $v_0 \in S$" in item "b."

A.3 Dynamic Programming

Dynamic programming is one of the main mathematical tools in macroeconomics. Its usefulness lies in the fact that it facilitates the solution of recursive models, common in macroeconomics, by means of Bellman's "principle of optimality" (Bellman, 1957). This principle indicates that we can start solving the model from the last period, considering as given the solution of the previous period. This recursive process is performed period by period up to the initial period. An excellent book that explains in greater detail the concepts related to dynamic programming is that of Stokey and Lucas (1989).

A.3.1 Outlook

In this section, we define what problem we want to solve. In dynamic macroeconomics, usually the problem is defined in *sequential* terms. This means that the solution consists of a set of sequences such as the "consumption sequence" $\{c_t\}_{t=0}^{\infty}$, which in extended form is $c_0, c_1, c_2, c_3 ... c_i ...$ where each consumption value in each period is the (optimal) equilibrium value that the representative consumer chooses as a solution to the dynamic optimization problem he/she faces. The interesting thing about the dynamic programming method is that it transforms this sequential problem into a functional problem, which is the simplest to solve under certain conditions. Likewise, in this section, the value function, the Bellman equation, and the functional problem are defined.

A.3.1.1 What Kind of Problem Do We Want to Solve?

We want to solve a "*dynamic optimization*" problem, which we will call sequential problem (SP):

$$\sup_{\{u_t\}} \sum_{t=0}^{\infty} \beta^t r(x_t, u_t) \tag{A.5}$$

$$s.a :$$

$$x_{t+1} = g(x_t, u_t)$$

$$u_t \in \Gamma(x_t), \quad t = 0, 1, 2, ...$$

$$x_0 \in X \quad \text{given}$$

Where:

1. $\mathbf{r(x_t, u_t)}$: return function (instantaneous)

$$r(x_t, u_t) : XxR^m \rightarrow R$$

2. $\boldsymbol{\beta}$ **:** discount factor, $\beta \in [0, \infty)$
3. $\mathbf{x_t}$: state variables vector ($x_t \in R^n$)
4. $\mathbf{u_t}$: control variables vector ($u_t \in R^m$)
5. $\mathbf{g(x_t, u_t)}$: function that describes the evolution of the state variables (function of transition or movement law)

$$g(x_t, u_t) : XxR^m \rightarrow X$$

6. $\boldsymbol{\Gamma}(\mathbf{x_t})$: is a **correspondence** that describes the possibilities of the control variable when the economy is in the state "x_t"

$$\Gamma : X \rightrightarrows R^m$$

7. $\mathbf{X}$: is the space of the values that the state variable can take ($X \subset R^n$)
8. $\mathbf{x_0}$: the initial value of the state variable (initial state)

Example (Brock and Mirman (1972)) The basic growth model is described by the following problem (in general terms):

$$\underset{\{c_t, k_{t+1}\}_{t=0}^{\infty}}{\text{Max}} \sum_{t=0}^{\infty} \beta^t lnc_t$$

s.t.:

$$k_{t+1} = (1 - \delta)k_t + i_t$$

$$c_t + i_t = f(k_t)$$

$$c_t, k_t \geq 0 \forall t$$

We call this problem the sequential problem (SP). Considering the following functional forms: $u(c_t) = lnc_t$, $f(k_t) = k_t^{\alpha}$. In addition to the following assumptions, $\alpha \in (0, 1)$, $\delta = 1$, and k_0 given, if you have the following:

$$\underset{\{c_t,k_{t+1}\}_{t=0}^{\infty}}{\text{Max}} \sum_{t=0}^{\infty} \beta^t lnc_t$$

s.a:

$$k_{t+1} = k_t^{\alpha} - c_t$$

$$c_t, k_t \geq 0$$

There are three ways to solve this type of problem:

1. **Method of successive approximations**. This method starts from an initial value of the solution and *successively* we approach the solution.
2. **Dynamic programming**. This method solves a dynamic optimization problem through the analysis of functional equations.
3. **Lagrange method**. Method that we have used throughout the book and that is an extension of the Lagrange technique applied to the static model.

A.3.1.2 Function Valor

Bellman (1974) indicates that SP has a recursive property, which allows transforming SP into a functional problem (FP). In this context, a "function value $V(x_0)$" is defined which indicates the maximum value of the objective function for each $x_0 \geqslant 0$:

$$V(x_0) = \max_{\{u_t\}}\left\{\sum_{t=0}^{\infty} \beta^t r(x_t, u_t)\right\} \tag{A.6}$$

For example, in $t = 1$, if you have x_1

$$V(x_1) = \max_{\{u_t\}}\left\{\sum_{t=1}^{\infty} \beta^{t-1} r(x_t, u_t)\right\} \tag{A.7}$$

A.3.1.3 Bellman Equation

Bellman (1974) transforms the objective function of SP into a functional equation:

$$\begin{aligned} V(x_0) &= \max_{\{u_t\}}\left\{\sum_{t=0}^{\infty} \beta^t r(x_t, u_t)\right\} \\ &= \max_{\{u_t\}}\left\{r(x_0, u_0) + \beta r(x_1, u_1) + \beta^2 r(x_2, u_2)\ldots\right\} \end{aligned}$$

$$= \max_{\{u_t\}} \left\{ r(x_0, u_0) + \beta \big[\underbrace{r(x_1, u_1) + \beta^2 r(x_2, u_2) \ldots}_{V(x_1)} \big] \right\}$$

$$V(x_0) = \max_{\{u_t\}} \left\{ r(x_0, u_0) + \beta V(x_1) \right\}$$

This last equation is known as the Bellman equation. This is a functional equation; that is, it is an equation whose solution is a function (function value).

A.3.1.4 Functional Problem

Substituting the Bellman equation into the SP, we get the FP (for t):

$$V(x_t) = \max_{\{u_t\}} \left\{ r(x_0, u_0) + \beta V(g(x_t, u_t)) \right\} \tag{A.8}$$

$$\begin{aligned} &s.a\ : \\ &u_t \in \Gamma(x_t), \quad t = 0, 1, 2, \ldots \\ &x_0 \in X \quad \text{dado} \end{aligned}$$

This FP deserves three comments:

1. The problem of infinite periods (SP) has become a problem of two periods.
2. SP recursion is being used (exploited).
3. Now the problem consists of finding the function that solves the FP; that is, the function value.

A.3.1.5 From SP to FP

Figure A.1 describes the transformation process from SP to FP and how this problem is solved. The process is as follows: first, the SP is transformed into a FP, whose solution consists of a function called function value. Second, the FP becomes a fixed-point problem, which is easier to solve under the "fixed-point" theorem. The interesting thing about this "new" problem is that the fixed-point theorem suggests a way to find the solution (function) by iterating the value function. After finding this function, we proceed to find the policy function that describes the behavior of the control variables as a function of the state variables; then, the optimal plan of the control variables is found. Finally, this solution of the fixed-point problem is the solution of the FP, which by means of the equivalence theorem is the solution of the SP.

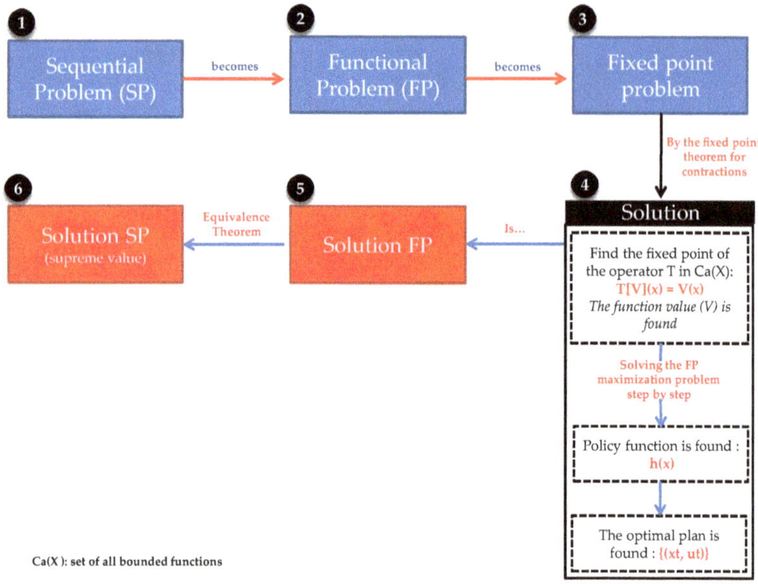

Fig. A.1 From SP to FP and its solution process

A.3.2 Details

In the previous section, we have defined the SP, the FP, and the relationship between them. Moreover, we have seen how we can transform the SP to a FP. However, we have not been explicit in the assumptions behind said relationship nor have we obtained said relationship formally. In this section, we will detail how to go from SP to FP and what are the hypotheses we need to obtain said relationship.

Hypotheses that Support the Propositions and Theorems In Fig. A.2, the hypotheses that support the propositions and theorems for the SP and FP are described. In dynamic programming, there are three main theorems: the first is the *equivalence theorem*, which allows transforming SP to FP; the second is the *fixe- point theorem*, which allows us to transform the FP into a fixed-point problem. Finally, the third theorem is about the *differentiability of the value function*, which allows us to obtain the solution of the FP by exploiting the properties of the value function.

Each of these theorems are based on a set of hypotheses (or assumptions). For example, the first theorem is based on four propositions, which, in turn, are based on three hypotheses (H1–H3). Likewise, the second theorem is based on two hypotheses (H4 and H5). Finally, the third theorem is based on eight hypotheses (H4, H5, and H7–H12). All these hypotheses will be described later in the appendix.

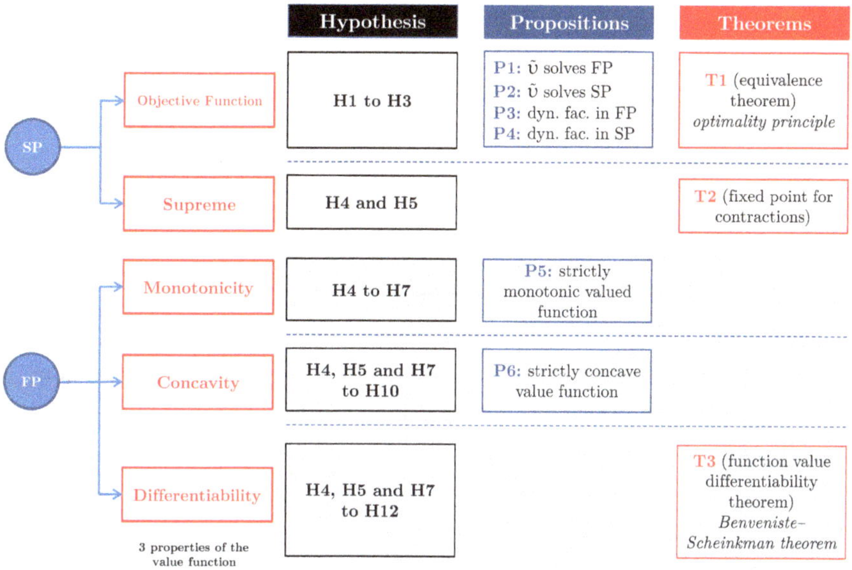

Fig. A.2 Three main theorems in dynamic programming (and their relationship with their hypotheses and propositions)

A.3.2.1 Optimality Principle

Bellman (1974) proposed a principle, which allowed finding a relationship between the solution of the SP and the FP. This principle is known as the "principle of optimality."

Theorem A.1 (Optimality Principle) *The solution V of the FP, evaluated at x_0, gives the value of the supremum in the SP when the initial state is x_0. Furthermore, a sequence $\{u_t\}_{t=0}^{\infty}$ reaches the supremum if and only if this sequence satisfies (A.9)*

$$V(x_t) = r(x_t, u_t) + \beta V(x_{t+1}) \tag{A.9}$$

The question that arises is **under what conditions does the principle of optimality hold?** Four propositions together establish the conditions that allow the solution of the SP and the FP to coincide exactly and that make it possible for the optimal policies to be those that satisfy (A.9). These propositions are detailed below (see Fig. A.2):

1. **Proposition 1.** Establishes that the function of the supremum $\widetilde{V}$ for the SP satisfies the FP (from SP to FP). However, the functional equation (besides $\widetilde{V}$) can have other solutions.
2. **Proposition 2.** Establishes the inverse partially (from FP to SP). It is partial because a bounding condition is imposed. This proposition prevents the func-

tional equation from having other solutions because they do not satisfy the strong transversality condition. The only solution that satisfies this condition is $\widetilde{V}$.

3. **Proposition 3.** Shows that if $\{u_t\}_{t=0}^{\infty}$ is a sequence that reaches the supremum in the SP, then it satisfies (A.9) for

$$\underbrace{V}_{\text{sol. FP}} = \underbrace{\widetilde{V}}_{\text{sol. SP}}$$

4. **Proposition 4.** States that any sequence $\{u_t\}_{t=0}^{\infty}$ that satisfies (A.9) for $V = \widetilde{V}$ and that also satisfies a bounding condition, then it also reaches the supremum in SP.

Definitions Before analyzing the hypotheses that support the four propositions, it is important to mention some definitions:

1. **Dynamic feasible from** x_0. Is a succession of states and controls $\{(x_t, u_t)\}_{t=0}^{\infty}$ in XxR^m for the SP if $u_t \in \Gamma(x_t)$ y $x_{t+1} = g(x_t, u_t)$ for all $t = 0, 1, 2....$
2. $\Pi(x_0)$: Set of all feasible dynamics from x_0

$$\Pi(x_0) : \left\{\{(x_t, u_t)\}_{t=0}^{\infty} \text{ such that } u_t \in \Gamma(x_t), \forall t = 0, 1, 2...\right\}$$

3. **Feasible plan from** x_0. It is a sequence of controls $\{(u_t)\}_{t=0}^{\infty}$.
4. **Optimal plan from** x_0. Is a feasible plan $\{(u_t^*)\}_{t=0}^{\infty}$ that allows you to reach the supreme SP.

It is worth mentioning that a feasible plan uniquely determines a feasible dynamic. Therefore, an optimal plan $\{(u_t)\}_{t=0}^{\infty}$ determines an optimal dynamic $\{(x_t^*, u_t^*)\}_{t=0}^{\infty}$.

Hypothesis A.1 ($\Gamma(x) \neq \phi$ **for all** $x \in X$)

- Hypothesis A.1 ensures that $\Pi(x_0)$ (set of feasible dynamics from x_0) is not empty $\forall x_0 \in X$. This indicates that all feasible plans can be evaluated using $r(x, u)$ and β.
- In the SP, $\sum_{t=0}^{\infty} \beta^t r(x_t, u_t)$ could take three values: a finite number, $+\infty$, or $-\infty$. We want this objective function to be bounded; that is, that the infinite summation has a finite value.

Hypothesis A.2 (Objective Function) For all $x_0 \in X$, $\exists M_{x_0} \in R$, such that $\sum_{t=0}^{\infty} \beta^t r(x_t, u_t) \leq M_{x_0}$ for **all** feasible dynamics $\{(x_t, u_t)\}_{t=0,1,2...}$ from x_0.

- Hypothesis A.2 eliminates the possibility that $\sum_{t=0}^{\infty} \beta^t r(x_t, u_t)$ is $+\infty$. To do this, the set of feasible dynamics is restricted in such a way that said sum is bounded (superiorly).
- However, the objective function (infinite sum) can still take, for sure feasible dynamics, the value of $-\infty$. Hypothesis A.3 seeks to delimit said dynamics.

Hypothesis A.3 (Objective Function) For all $x_0 \in X$, $\exists$ **a** dynamically feasible $\{(x_t, u_t)\}_{t=0,1,2...}$ since x_0 and a $m_{x_0} \in R$, such that the sequence of partial sums $\{S_n\}_{t=0,1,2...} S_n = \sum_{t=0}^{n} \beta^t r(x_t, u_t)$ satisfies $m_{x_0} \leq S_n$.

- Therefore, hypotheses 2 and 3 have the sole purpose of guaranteeing the existence of a finite value for the supreme of the SP; that is, that the objective function is well defined for each feasible dynamic $\{(x_t, u_t)\} \in \Gamma(x_0)$.
- Based on the above conditions, we can define the "supreme function" $\widetilde{V} : X \to R$ to be the supreme value of SP:

$$\widetilde{V}(x_0) = \sup_{\{(x_t,u_t)\}\in\Pi(x_0)} \sum_{t=0}^{\infty} \beta^t r(x_t, u_t) \tag{A.10}$$

Where $\widetilde{V}(x_0)$ is the supreme value of the SP. This function $\widetilde{V}$ is called a "value function."

Supreme Function By definition, the function supreme $\widetilde{V} : X \to \overline{R}$ is unique and satisfies three conditions (considering a generic objective function $\mu(x)$):

$$\widetilde{V}(x_0) = \sup_{x\in\Pi(x_0)} \mu(x)$$

1. Si $|\widetilde{V}(x_0)| < \infty$, then:
   - $\widetilde{V}(x_0) \geq \mu(x)$, $\forall$(for all) $x \in \Pi(x_0)$
   - For any $\epsilon > 0$: $\widetilde{V}(x_0) \leq \mu(x) + \epsilon$, for some $x \in \Pi(x_0)$
2. If $|\widetilde{V}(x_0)| = +\infty$, then there exists a sequence $\{x^k\}$ in $\Pi(x_0)$ such that

$$\operatorname{Lim}_{k\to\infty} \mu(x^k) = +\infty$$

3. If $|\widetilde{V}(x_0)| = -\infty$, then $\mu(x) = -\infty$, for all $x \in \Pi(x_0)$

Next, the four propositions that support the principle of optimality are described in detail.

Proposition A.1 *Under hypotheses 1, 2, and 3, $\widetilde{V}$ solves the FP.*

Proof The proof strategy has two steps. The first is to find the relationship between the supreme function $\widetilde{V}$ and the functional equation for two different initial values x_1 and x_0; the second is to join the result of step 1 for x_1 and x_0.

1. Evaluating at x_1: Let $\epsilon > 0$, $u_0 \in \Gamma(x_0)$, and $x_1 = g(x_0, u_0)$
   - Since $\widetilde{V}(x_1)$ is the supreme value of SP with initial value $x_1 (t = 1)$, **then** $\exists$ a feasible dynamic from x_1, $\{(x_1, u_1), (x_2, u_2), ...\}$, such that (by the property of the supreme)

$$\sum_{t=1}^{\infty} \beta^{t-1} r(x_t, u_t) \geq \widetilde{V}(x_1) - \epsilon \tag{A.11}$$

- It is known that $\{(x_0, u_0), (x_1, u_1), ...\} \in \Pi(x_0)$ and that by the property of the supreme

$$\begin{aligned}
\widetilde{V}(x_0) &\geq \sum_{t=0}^{\infty} \beta^t r(x_t, u_t) \\
&\geq r(x_0, u_0) + \beta \sum_{t=1}^{\infty} \beta^{t-1} r(x_t, u_t) \\
&\geq r(x_0, u_0) + \beta \widetilde{V}(x_1) - \beta\epsilon \\
\widetilde{V}(x_0) &\geq r(x_0, u_0) + \beta \widetilde{V}(g(x_0, u_0)) - \beta\epsilon
\end{aligned}$$

  To go from the second to the third line, Eq. (A.11) is used.
- As the last equation is true for all $\epsilon > 0$ and u_0 in any element of $\Gamma(x_0)$, then we have that

$$\widetilde{V}(x_0) \geq r(x_0, u_0) + \beta \widetilde{V}(g(x_0, u_0)), \qquad \forall u_0 \in \Gamma(x_0)$$

- Since the previous equation is true for all u_0, then

$$\widetilde{V}(x_0) \geq \sup_{u_0 \in \Gamma(x_0)} \left\{ r(x_0, u_0) + \beta \widetilde{V}(g(x_0, u_0)) \right\}$$

- Generalizing for all "t"

$$\widetilde{V}(x) \geq \sup_{u \in \Gamma(x)} \left\{ r(x, u) + \beta \widetilde{V}(g(x, u)) \right\} \tag{A.12}$$

2. Evaluating at x_0: Let $\epsilon > 0$, then by definition of supremum, $\exists$ a feasible dynamic from x_0 $\{(x_0, u_0), (x_1, u_1), ...\}$, such that

$$\begin{aligned}
\widetilde{V}(x_0) &\leq \sum_{t=0}^{\infty} \beta^t r(x_t, u_t) + \epsilon \\
\widetilde{V}(x_0) &\leq r(x_0, u_0) + \beta \widetilde{V}(x_1) + \epsilon
\end{aligned}$$

- Since ϵ is arbitrary, then

$$\widetilde{V}(x_0) \leq r(x_0, u_0) + \beta\widetilde{V}(g(x_0, u_0))$$

$$\widetilde{V}(x_0) \leq \sup_{u_0 \in \Gamma(x_0)} \left\{ r(x_0, u_0) + \beta\widetilde{V}(g(x_0, u_0)) \right\}$$

- Generalizing for all "t"

$$\widetilde{V}(x) \leq \sup_{u \in \Gamma(x)} \left\{ r(x, u) + \beta\widetilde{V}(g(x, u)) \right\} \tag{A.13}$$

3. Joining results: By joining the Eqs. (A.12) and (A.13), we have

$$\sup_{u \in \Gamma(x)} \left\{ r(x, u) + \beta\widetilde{V}(g(x, u)) \right\} \leq \widetilde{V}(x) \leq \sup_{u \in \Gamma(x)} \left\{ r(x, u) + \beta\widetilde{V}(g(x, u)) \right\}$$

4. Therefore

$$\widetilde{V}(x) = \sup_{u \in \Gamma(x)} \left\{ r(x, u) + \beta\widetilde{V}(g(x, u)) \right\} \tag{A.14}$$

   Which indicates that the supreme function (or value function) is a solution of the functional equation (FP).
5. Proposition 1 indicates that $\widetilde{V}$ is a solution of the FP, but it does not indicate that it is the only one. In order to ensure that this is the only solution of the FP, an additional constraint is imposed: "strong transversality condition." Proposition 2 ensures the above.

Proposition A.2 *According to hypotheses 1, 2, and 3, V solves the FP, and if the strong transversality condition is also met*

$$\underset{t\to\infty}{Lim} \beta^t V(x_t) = 0$$

for all $x_0 \in X$ and dynamically feasible $\{(x_t, u_t)\}$ from x_0, then $\widetilde{V} = V$ (i.e., V solves for the SP).

Proof In this case, we must prove that V is the supreme function $\widetilde{V}$. The proof strategy has two steps: the first is to show that for all feasible dynamics from x_0 it is true that $V(x_0) \geq \sum_{t=0}^{\infty} \beta^t r(x_t, u_t)$; the second is to show that for every $\epsilon > 0$, $\exists$ a dynamically feasible $\{(x_t, u_t)\}$ from x_0, such that $V(x_0) \leq \sum_{t=0}^{\infty} \beta^t r(x_t, u_t) + \epsilon$. Both steps ensure that V is the supreme function (or value function).

1. **Step 1a.** Since V is a solution of the FP, then $\forall$ feasible dynamics $\{(x_t, u_t)\} \in \Pi(x_0)$, we have

$$V(x_0) \geq r(x_0, u_0) + \beta V(x_1)_{\text{(BY SUPREME PROPERTY)}}$$

$$V(x_1) \geq r(x_1, u_1) + \beta V(x_2)_{(\text{FOR } x_1)}$$

$$r(x_0, u_0) + \beta V(x_1) \geq r(x_0, u_0) + \beta r(x_1, u_1) + \beta\big[\beta V(x_2)\big]$$

BY TRANSITIVITY IN THE 1ST INEQUALITY:

$$V(x_0) \geq r(x_0, u_0) + \beta r(x_1, u_1) + \beta^2 V(x_2)$$

$$V(x_0) \geq \sum_{t=0}^{1} \beta^t r(x_t, u_t) + \beta^2 V(x_2) \text{ (IN COMPACT FORM)}$$

BY INDUCTION (K STEPS):

$$V(x_0) \geq \sum_{t=0}^{k} \beta^t r(x_t, u_t) + \beta^{k+1} V(x_{k+1}) \tag{A.15}$$

2. **Step 1b.** Making $k \to \infty$ and using the strong transversality condition

$$V(x_0) \geq \underset{k\to\infty}{Lim}\left\{\sum_{t=0}^{k} \beta^t r(x_t, u_t) + \beta^{k+1} V(x_{k+1})\right\}$$

$$V(x_0) \geq \underset{k\to\infty}{Lim}\left\{\sum_{t=0}^{k} \beta^t r(x_t, u_t)\right\} + \underset{k\to\infty}{Lim}\left\{\beta^{k+1} V(x_{k+1})\right\}$$

FOR STRONG TRANSVERSALITY CONDITION:

$$V(x_0) \geq \sum_{t=0}^{\infty} \beta^t r(x_t, u_t) + 0$$

$$V(x_0) \geq \sum_{t=0}^{\infty} \beta^t r(x_t, u_t) \tag{A.16}$$

3. **Step 2a.** Let $\epsilon > 0$ and $\{\delta_t\}_{t=0,1,2...}$ be a sequence of positive real numbers, such that

$$\sum_{t=0}^{\infty} \delta_t \beta^t \leq \epsilon \tag{A.17}$$

Step 2b. Since V resolves the FP, then $\exists u_0 \in \Gamma(x_0)$ such that

(BY SUPREME PROPERTY)

$$V(x_0) \leq r(x_0, u_0) + \beta V(x_1) + \delta_0$$

THERE ALSO EXISTS $u_1 \in \Gamma(x_1)$ SUCH THAT:

$$V(x_1) \leq r(x_1, u_1) + \beta V(x_2) + \delta_1$$

$$r(x_0, u_0) + \beta V(x_1) \leq r(x_0, u_0) + \beta r(x_1, u_1) + \beta\big[\beta V(x_2)\big] + \beta\delta_1$$

BY TRANSITIVITY IN THE 1ST INEQUALITY:

$$V(x_0) \leq r(x_0, u_0) + \beta r(x_1, u_1) + \beta^2 V(x_2) + \beta\delta_1$$

(IN COMPACT FORM)

$$V(x_0) \leq \sum_{t=0}^{1} \beta^t r(x_t, u_t) + \beta^2 V(x_2) + \sum_{t=1}^{1} \beta^t \delta_t$$

4. **Step 2c.** By induction (k steps)

$$V(x_0) \leq \sum_{t=0}^{k} \beta^t r(x_t, u_t) + \beta^{k+1} V(x_{k+1}) + \sum_{t=1}^{k} \beta^t \delta_t$$

5. **Step 2d.** Making $k \to \infty$ and using Expression (A.17)

$$V(x_0) \leq \underset{k\to\infty}{Lim}\left\{ \sum_{t=0}^{k} \beta^t r(x_t, u_t) + \beta^{k+1} V(x_{k+1}) + \sum_{t=1}^{k} \beta^t \delta_t \right\}$$

$$V(x_0) \leq \underset{k\to\infty}{Lim}\left\{ \sum_{t=0}^{k} \beta^t r(x_t, u_t) \right\} + \underset{k\to\infty}{Lim}\left\{ \beta^{k+1} V(x_{k+1}) \right\} + \underset{k\to\infty}{Lim}\left\{ \sum_{t=1}^{k} \beta^t \delta_t \right\}$$

BY CONDITION OF STRONG TRANSVERSALITY AND (A.17):

$$V(x_0) \leq \sum_{t=0}^{\infty} \beta^t r(x_t, u_t) + 0 + \epsilon$$

$$V(x_0) \leq \sum_{t=0}^{\infty} \beta^t r(x_t, u_t) + \epsilon \tag{A.18}$$

6. From relations (A.16) and (A.18), it is concluded that V is the supreme function (value function).
7. The FP can have many solutions, but proposition 2 shows that these solutions (except $\widetilde{V}$) violate the strong transversality condition and the only one that satisfies said condition is $\widetilde{V}$. Therefore, $V = \widetilde{V}$.

Proposition A.3 *Under hypotheses A.1, A.2, and A.3, let $\{(x_t^*, u_t^*)\}$ be a feasible dynamic from x_0^* that allows reaching the supreme of SP, if then said feasible dynamics satisfies (A.9)*

$$\widetilde{V}(x_t^*) = r(x_t^*, u_t^*) + \beta \widetilde{V}(x_{t+1}^*) \tag{A.19}$$

That is, it allows one to reach the supreme in the FP.

Proof The proof strategy has two steps: first we prove that Eq. (A.19) holds for $t = 0$; then, we extend this result for all $t = 1, 2, 3$ (by induction).

1. **Step 1a**. Because $\{(x_t^*, u_t^*)\}$ is a feasible dynamic from x_0^* that allows reaching the supremum of SP, then it is true:

$$\widetilde{V}(x_0^*) = \sum_{t=0}^{\infty} \beta^t r(x_t^*, u_t^*)$$

$$\sum_{t=0}^{\infty} \beta^t r(x_t^*, u_t^*) = r(x_0^*, u_0^*) + \beta \sum_{t=0}^{\infty} \beta^t r(x_{t+1}^*, u_{t+1}^*) \tag{A.20}$$

2. **Step 1b**. For all feasible dynamics $\{(x_1^*, u_1), (x_2, u_2), (x_3, u_3), ...\} \in \Pi(x_1^*)$, by the definition of the supreme, it is fulfilled:

$$\sum_{t=0}^{\infty} \beta^t r(x_t^*, u_t^*) \geq r(x_0^*, u_0^*) + \beta \sum_{t=0}^{\infty} \beta^t r(x_{t+1}, u_{t+1}) \tag{A.21}$$

Therefore, from Expressions (A.20) and (A.21), we have that

$$\sum_{t=0}^{\infty} \beta^t r(x_{t+1}^*, u_{t+1}^*) \geq \sum_{t=0}^{\infty} \beta^t r(x_{t+1}, u_{t+1}) \tag{A.22}$$

3. **Step 1c**. Furthermore, as the feasible dynamics $\{(x_1^*, u_1^*), (x_2^*, u_2^*), (x_3^*, u_3^*), ...\} \in \Pi(x_1^*)$, then it is fulfilled that $\sum_{t=0}^{\infty} \beta^t r(x_{t+1}^*, u_{t+1}^*)$ has to be the supreme value with initial value in x_1^*:

$$\widetilde{V}(x_1^*) = \sum_{t=0}^{\infty} \beta^t r(x_{t+1}^*, u_{t+1}^*) \tag{A.23}$$

4. **Step 1d**. Replacing Expressions (A.23) in (A.20), we have

$$\widetilde{V}(x_0^*) = r(x_0^*, u_0^*) + \beta \widetilde{V}(x_1^*) \tag{A.24}$$

5. **Step 2a**. It was proved that

$$\widetilde{V}(x_0^*) = r(x_0^*, u_0^*) + \beta \widetilde{V}(x_1^*)$$

$$\widetilde{V}(x_1^*) = \sum_{t=0}^{\infty} \beta^t r(x_{t+1}^*, u_{t+1}^*)$$

6. **Step 2b**. The inductive hypothesis is proposed:

$$\widetilde{V}(x_k^*) = r(x_k^*, u_k^*) + \beta \widetilde{V}(x_{k+1}^*) \tag{A.25}$$

Where $\widetilde{V}(x_k^*) \forall k \in N$ is defined as

$$\widetilde{V}(x_k^*) = \sum_{t=0}^{\infty} \beta^t r(x_{t+k}^*, u_{t+k}^*) \tag{A.26}$$

If the hypothesis (Eq. (A.25)) holds for "$k+1$," then the hypothesis is true.

7. **Step 2c**. Reviewing for "$k+1$"

$$r(x_k^*, u_k^*) + \beta\widetilde{V}(x_{k+1}^*) \overset{\text{FROM (A.25) AND (A.26)}}{=} \widetilde{V}(x_k^*) = \sum_{t=0}^{\infty} \beta^t r(x_{t+k}^*, u_{t+k}^*)$$

$$r(x_k^*, u_k^*) + \beta\widetilde{V}(x_{k+1}^*) = r(x_k^*, u_k^*) + \beta \sum_{t=0}^{\infty} \beta^t r(x_{t+(k+1)}^*, u_{t+(k+1)}^*)$$

$$\widetilde{V}(x_{k+1}^*) = \sum_{t=0}^{\infty} \beta^t r(x_{t+(k+1)}^*, u_{t+(k+1)}^*)$$

$$\widetilde{V}(x_{k+1}^*) = r(x_{k+1}^*, u_{k+1}^*) + \beta \sum_{t=0}^{\infty} \beta^t r(x_{t+(k+2)}^*, u_{t+(k+2)}^*)$$

$$\widetilde{V}(x_{k+1}^*) = r(x_{k+1}^*, u_{k+1}^*) + \beta\widetilde{V}(x_{k+2}^*) \tag{A.27}$$

Therefore, the inductive hypothesis is true and generalizable for all "t=0, 1, 2, ..."

Proposition A.4 *Under hypotheses 1, 2, and 3, if $\{(x_t^*, u_t^*)\}$ a feasible dynamic from x_0^* that satisfies (A.19) and the weak transversality condition is fulfilled*

$$\lim_{t\to\infty} \beta^t V(x_t) \leq 0,$$

then *$\{(x_t^*, u_t^*)\}$ solves the SP.*

Proof The strategy is as follows: if $\{(x_t^*, u_t^*)\}$ solves the SP, this means that it allows to reach the supreme: $\widetilde{V}(x_0) = \sup_{\{u_t\}}\{\sum_{t=0}^{\infty} \beta^t r(x_t, u_t)\}$; i.e., $\widetilde{V}(x_0^*) = \sum_{t=0}^{\infty} \beta^t r(x_t^*, u_t^*)$. This last is what we have to prove.

1. **Step 1.** Since $\{(x_t^*, u_t^*)\}$ is a feasible dynamic from x_0, then

$$\widetilde{V}(x_0^*) \geq \sum_{t=0}^{\infty} \beta^t r(x_t^*, u_t^*) \tag{A.28}$$

2. **Step 2.** Also, $\{(x_t^*, u_t^*)\}$ satisfies (A.19); that is, it allows to reach the supreme in the FP:

$$\widetilde{V}(x_t^*) = r(x_t^*, u_t^*) + \beta \widetilde{V}(x_{t+1}^*)$$

$$\forall t = 0, 1, 2, \ldots :$$

$$\widetilde{V}(x_0^*) = r(x_0^*, u_0^*) + \beta \widetilde{V}(x_1^*)$$
$$\widetilde{V}(x_1^*) = r(x_1^*, u_1^*) + \beta \widetilde{V}(x_2^*)$$
$$\widetilde{V}(x_2^*) = r(x_2^*, u_2^*) + \beta \widetilde{V}(x_3^*)$$
$$\ldots$$
$$\widetilde{V}(x_k^*) = r(x_k^*, u_k^*) + \beta \widetilde{V}(x_{k+1}^*)$$

3. **Step 3.** Substituting $\widetilde{V}(x_2^*)$ in $\widetilde{V}(x_1^*)$

$$\widetilde{V}(x_2^*) = r(x_2^*, u_2^*) + \beta \widetilde{V}(x_3^*)$$
$$\widetilde{V}(x_1^*) = r(x_1^*, u_1^*) + \beta \left[r(x_2^*, u_2^*) + \beta \widetilde{V}(x_3^*) \right]$$

REPLACING $\widetilde{V}(x_1^*)$ IN $\widetilde{V}(x_0^*)$:

$$\widetilde{V}(x_0^*) = r(x_0^*, u_0^*) + \beta \left[r(x_1^*, u_1^*) + \beta r(x_2^*, u_2^*) + \beta^2 \widetilde{V}(x_3^*) \right]$$

COMPACTLY:

$$\widetilde{V}(x_0^*) = \sum_{t=0}^{2} \beta^t r(x_t^*, u_t^*) + \beta^3 \widetilde{V}(x_3^*)$$

BY INDUCTION (K STEPS):

$$\widetilde{V}(x_0^*) = \sum_{t=0}^{k} \beta^t r(x_t^*, u_t^*) + \beta^{k+1} \widetilde{V}(x_{k+1}^*) \tag{A.29}$$

4. **Step 4.** Taking $k \to \infty$ into Eq. (A.29)

$$\widetilde{V}(x_0^*) = \lim_{k\to\infty} \left[\sum_{t=0}^{k} \beta^t r(x_t^*, u_t^*) + \beta^{k+1} \widetilde{V}(x_{k+1}^*) \right]$$
$$\widetilde{V}(x_0^*) = \sum_{t=0}^{\infty} \beta^t r(x_t^*, u_t^*) + \lim_{k\to\infty} \left[\beta^{k+1} \widetilde{V}(x_{k+1}^*) \right]$$

FOR WEAK TRANSVERSALITY CONDITION: $\lim_{t\to\infty} \beta^t V(x_t) \leq 0$

$$\widetilde{V}(x_0^*) \leq \sum_{t=0}^{\infty} \beta^t r(x_t^*, u_t^*) \tag{A.30}$$

5. **Step 5.** From Relations (A.28) and (A.30), we have

$$\sum_{t=0}^{\infty} \beta^t r(x_t^*, u_t^*) \leq \widetilde{V}(x_0^*) \leq \sum_{t=0}^{\infty} \beta^t r(x_t^*, u_t^*) \tag{A.31}$$

Therefore

$$\widetilde{V}(x_0^*) = \sum_{t=0}^{\infty} \beta^t r(x_t^*, u_t^*) \tag{A.32}$$

Which indicates that the feasible dynamics $\{(x_t^*, u_t^*)\}$ solve the SP.

Conclusion Propositions 1 to 4 imply that (under hypotheses 1, 2, and 3) the solution to Eq. (A.9): $V(x_t) = r(x_t, u_t) + \beta V(x_{t+1})$ (FP) coincides exactly (in terms of optimal values and plans) with the solution of SP; that is, the principle of optimality holds.

A.3.2.2 Method to Solve the FP

So far, the relationship between the SP and the FP has been studied, but no method has been presented to solve the FP. The interesting thing about dynamic programming is that it offers several FP solution methods: theoretical and numerical methods. The main method is to consider the FP as a fixed-point problem. For this, we need two additional hypotheses: about the correspondence $\Gamma(x)$ and the return function $r(x, u)$.

Hypotheses that allow considering the PF as a fixed point:

Hypothesis A.4 $\Gamma : X \rightrightarrows X$ is a compact-valued mapping (i.e., $\Gamma(x)$ is compact for all x), continuous and $\Gamma(x) \neq \phi$ for all x.

Hypothesis A.5 $\beta \in (0, 1)$ y $r(x_t, u_t)$ is bounded and continuous on the graph of Γ. Where

$$\text{graph of} \Gamma : \left\{(x, u) \in XxR^m \text{ such that } u \in \Gamma(x)\right\}$$

- Hypotheses A.4 and A.5 imply hypotheses 1, 2, and 3. Thus, propositions 1 through 4 hold and hence the principle of optimality.
- By hypothesis A.5, $\widetilde{V}$ (and, consequently, "V" by the optimality principle), which is a real function, is also bounded and continuous.
- Let's define $C_a(X)$: Space of real, continuous, and bounded functions. So:$\widetilde{V} = V \in C_a(X)$.
- We define an operator T: $C_a(X) \rightarrow C_a(X)$ of FP:

$$T[V](x) = \sup_{\{u\} \in \Gamma(x)} \left\{ r(x, u) + \beta V(g(x, u)) \right\} \quad \text{(A.33)}$$

- From the FP, we know

$$V(x) = \sup_{\{u\} \in \Gamma(x)} \left\{ r(x, u) + \beta V(g(x, u)) \right\} \quad \text{(A.34)}$$

- From (A.33) and (A.34), the FP becomes a "fixed-point problem (fixed point)":

$$T[V](x) = V(x) \quad \text{(A.35)}$$

  Where the function V is the fixed point. If we find the function V that solves (A.35) (fixed point), then we will have the solution of the FP, and by the *principle of optimality*, we will have the solution of the SP.
- Since we have the function value, we can find the optimal plan:
  - Form 1: solving step by step the problem of the maximum that appears in the FP (i.e., finding the policy function)
  - Form 2: solving the system of equations

$$V(x_t^*) = r(x_t^*, u_t^*) + \beta V(x_{t+1}^*), \quad t = 0, 1, 2, 3...$$

We need a theorem that ensures that the operator "$T : C_a(X) \to C_a(X)$" has a unique fixed point and, therefore, a solution to (A.35) (fixed point) . The fixed-point theorem for contractions ensures this.

Theorem A.2 (Fixed-Point Theorem) *Under hypotheses A.4 and A.5, let $C_a(X)$ (space of real, continuous, and bounded functions on X) with the norm of supremum $\|\cdot\|$, then the operator "**T**" defined on $C_a(X)$ is an application of this space on itself, T: $C_a(X) \to C_a(X)$, defined as*

$$T[V](x) = sup \left\{ r(x_t, u_t) + \beta V(g(x_t, u_t)) \right\} \quad \text{(A.36)}$$

*subject to, $u_t \in \Gamma(x_t)$, **satisfies:***

1. *$T[V] \in C_a(X)$*
2. *"T" has a unique fixed-point "V": $T[V] = V$*
3. *For any $V_0 \in C_a(X)$, it has:*

$$\|T^n(V_0) - V\| \leq \beta^n \|V_0 - V\|$$

Particularly

$$\underset{n \to \infty}{Lim}\, T^n(V_0) = V$$

Note: The norm of supremum $\| \cdot \|$ *is defined as*

$$\|f\| = sup\{|f(x)|\} \tag{A.37}$$

The fixed-point theorem offers a method of solving the PF: "the convergence of successive iterations of a contractive function to the fixed point," which consists of the sequence of functions $\{V_n\}_{n=0}^{\infty}$, defined as

$$V_n = T[V_{n-1}], \quad n \geq 1 \tag{A.38}$$

Which converges to the fixed point (V) of the contraction T; that is to say

$$\underset{n \to \infty}{\text{Lim}}\, V_n = V \tag{A.39}$$

Proof

1. **Step 1.** Under hypotheses 4, 5, and 8, we have that for each $f \in C_a(X) \wedge x \in X$, the fixed-point problem

$$T[f](x) = \max_{u_t \in \Gamma(X)} \left\{ r(x_t, u_t) + \beta f(u_t) \right\} \tag{A.40}$$

   It reduces to maximizing the continuous function:

$$\left\{ r(x_t, \cdot) + \beta f(\cdot) \right\} \tag{A.41}$$

   About the compact set $\Gamma(X)$. This allows you to reach the maximum.
   One question we have to answer is: is $T[f]$ bounded and continuous? His/her domain is known to be.
2. **Step 2a**. Since $r(x_t, u_t)$ and $f(u_t)$ are bounded, then

$$T[f], \text{ is also bounded.}$$

3. **Step 2b**. Since $r(x_t, u_t)$ and $f(u_t)$ are continuous, and $\Gamma(X)$ is compact, then by the maximum theorem, $T[f]$ is keep going.
   Therefore, from step 2a and 2b we have that $T[f]$ is continuous and bounded, and since T was defined (domain) in $C_a(X)$, then it is obtained that the operator $T[f]$ is

$$T[f] : C_a(X) \to C_a(X)$$

4. **Step 4**. T is a contraction?
   If this is because the operator T satisfies the Blackwell conditions.

5. **Step 5**. Does T have a unique fixed point?
   Yeah. Since $C_a(X)$ is a Banach space, then by the "contractive mapping" theorem, T has a unique fixed point $V \in C_a(X)$ and it holds that

$$\|T^n(V_0) - V\| \leq \beta^n \|V_0 - V\|$$

With these tools in our hands, let's move on to solve some examples.

Example Brock and Mirman model (1972)

The basic growth model is described by the following problem (in general terms):

$$\underset{\{c_t,k_{t+1}\}_{t=0}^{\infty}}{\text{Max}} \sum_{t=0}^{\infty} \beta^t lnc_t$$

s.t.:

$$k_{t+1} = (1 - \delta)k_t + i_t$$

$$c_t + i_t = f(k_t)$$

$$c_t, k_t \geq 0 \forall t$$

We call this problem a sequential problem (SP). Considering the following functional forms $\left(u(c_t)lnc_t,\ f(k_t) = k_t^{\alpha}\ \right)$ and assumptions $\left(\alpha \in (0, 1)\ , \delta = 1\right.$ and k_0 given $\left.\right)$, we have

$$\underset{\{c_t,k_{t+1}\}_{t=0}^{\infty}}{\text{Max}} \sum_{t=0}^{\infty} \beta^t lnc_t$$

s.t.:

$$k_{t+1} = k_t^{\alpha} - c_t$$

$$c_t, k_t \geq 0$$

The functional (or Bellman) equation is

$$V(k_t) = \underset{\{c_t,k_{t+1}\}_{t=0}^{\infty}}{\text{Max}} \left\{lnc_t + \beta V(k_{t+1})\right\}$$

By replacing the constraint in the Bellman equation $k_{t+1} = k_t^{\alpha} - c_t$, the associated functional problem is described as follows:

$$V(k_t) = \underset{\{c_t\}_{t=0}^{\infty}}{\text{Max}} \left\{lnc_t + \beta V(k_t^{\alpha} - c_t)\right\}$$

$$0 \leq c_t \leq k_t^{\alpha}$$

1. To solve the PF, we will use the value function iteration method (proposed by the fixed-point theorem for contractions), Expression (A.38):

$$V_n = T[V_{n-1}], \quad n \geq 1 \tag{A.42}$$

   It starts with the simplest function: $V_0 = 0$
2. Finding V_1

$$\begin{aligned} V_1 &= T[V_0] \\ &\downarrow \\ &= \underset{\{c_t\}_{t=0}^{\infty}}{\text{Max}} \left\{lnc_t + \beta \underbrace{V_0(k_t^{\alpha} - c_t)}_{=0}\right\} \\ &= \underset{\{c_t\}_{t=0}^{\infty}}{\text{Max}} \left\{lnc_t\right\} \end{aligned} \tag{A.43}$$

   (a) At this stage, the first-order condition applies

$$\frac{\partial \text{ Objective Function}}{\partial c_t} = 0$$

   However, in this case, since "ln" is monotone, then the maximum value is reached when $c_t = k_t^{\alpha}$ (see the FP constraint).

   (b) Replacing c_t that maximizes the objective function in (A.73), we obtain $T[V_0]$ and, therefore, V_1

$$\begin{aligned} V_1 &= T[V_0] = ln\left[k_t^{\alpha}\right] \\ V_1 &= \alpha lnk_t \end{aligned} \tag{A.44}$$

3. Finding V_2

$$\begin{aligned} V_2 &= T[V_1] \\ &\downarrow \\ &= \underset{\{c_t\}_{t=0}^{\infty}}{\text{Max}} \left\{lnc_t + \beta \underbrace{V_1(k_t^{\alpha} - c_t)}_{=\alpha ln(k_t^{\alpha} - c_t)}\right\} \end{aligned}$$

$$= \underset{\{c_t\}_{t=0}^{\infty}}{\text{Max}} \left\{lnc_t + \beta\alpha ln(k_t^{\alpha} - c_t)\right\} \tag{A.45}$$

- (*a*) At this stage, the first-order condition applies

$$\frac{\partial \text{ objective function}}{\partial c_t} = 0$$

$$c_t = \frac{k_t^{\alpha}}{1 + \beta\alpha} \tag{A.46}$$

- (*b*) Replacing c_t that maximizes the objective function in (A.75) gives $T[V_1]$ and, therefore, V_2

$$V_2 = T[V_1] = \alpha(1 + \beta\alpha)lnk_t + \beta\alpha ln\left[\frac{\beta\alpha}{1 + \beta\alpha}\right] - ln(1 + \beta\alpha)$$

$$V_2 = \alpha(1 + \beta\alpha)lnk_t + \beta\alpha ln\left[\frac{\beta\alpha}{1 + \beta\alpha}\right] - ln(1 + \beta\alpha) \tag{A.47}$$

4. In the same way, we can do for V_3 and then, in general, we see that

$$V_n(k_t) = A_n + \left(\alpha \sum_{i=0}^{n-1} (\beta\alpha)^i lnk_t\right) \tag{A.48}$$

Where we make $n \to \infty$ for the property (A.39)

$$\underset{n \to \infty}{\text{Lim}}\, V_n = V$$

$$\underset{n \to \infty}{\text{Lim}}\, V_n(k_t) = \underset{n \to \infty}{\text{Lim}}\, A_n + \underset{n \to \infty}{\text{Lim}} \left(\alpha \sum_{i=0}^{n-1} (\beta\alpha)^i lnk_t\right)$$

$$V = A + \left(\alpha \sum_{i=0}^{\infty} (\beta\alpha)^i lnk_t\right)$$

$$V = A + \frac{\alpha}{1 - \beta\alpha} lnk_t \tag{A.49}$$

The constant "A" can be found by replacing "V" and we can find the optimal dynamics in the Bellman equation. After this, we move on to finding the policy function. With this end in mind, since we already know the value function (V), we plug it into the Bellman PF equation.

1. Replacing the function value in the FP

$$V(k_t) = \underset{\{c_t\}_{t=0}^{\infty}}{\text{Max}} \left\{lnc_t + \beta\left[ln(k_t^{\alpha} - c_t)\right]\right\}$$

$$0 \leq c_t \leq k_t^{\alpha}$$

The functional problem becomes a standard optimization problem (in "t"), to which first-order conditions (FOC) can be applied.

Applying FOC

$$\frac{\partial \text{Objective Function}}{\partial c_t} = 0$$

We find the policy function: $c_t = h(k_t)$

$$c_t = (1 - \alpha\beta)k_t^{\alpha} \tag{A.50}$$

2. Finding the constant "A": We plug the value function and the policy function into the Bellman equation (the maximum disappears because the policy function allows it to be reached):

$$A + \frac{\alpha}{1 - \beta\alpha} lnk_t = ln(h(k_t)) + \beta\left[ln(k_t^{\alpha} - h(k_t))\right]$$

Solving and equating the coefficients of like terms

$$A = \left[\frac{1}{1 - \beta}\right](ln(1 - \alpha\beta) + \frac{\alpha\beta}{1 - \alpha\beta} ln\alpha\beta)$$

Finally, we find the optimal dynamics:

1. The optimal dynamics is the sequence $\{c_t, k_t\}_{t=0}^{\infty}$ described by this system of equations (with k_0 given):

STATE VARIABLE EVOLUTION EQUATION

$$k_{t+1} = k_t^{\alpha} - (1 - \alpha\beta)k_t^{\alpha} = \alpha\beta k_t^{\alpha} \tag{A.51}$$

POLICY FUNCTION

$$c_t = (1 - \alpha\beta)k_t^{\alpha} \tag{A.52}$$

The following exercise is left to the reader. The way to solve it is by following the steps in the example.

Exercise model with consumption habits

$$\underset{\{c_t,k_{t+1}\}_{t=0}^{\infty}}{\text{Max}} \sum_{t=0}^{\infty} \beta^t (lnc_t + \gamma lnc_{t-1})$$

subject to

$$c_t + k_{t+1} \leq Ak_t^{\alpha}$$

Where $\beta \in (0, 1)$, $\gamma < 0$, $A > 0$ y $\alpha \in (0, 1)$. k_0 y c_{-1} given.

1. Write the Bellman equation.
2. Show that the solution of the said equation has the following form:

$$v(k_t, c_{t-1}) = E + Flnk_t + Glnc_{t-1}$$

3. Show that the optimal dynamics of capital has this form:

$$lnk_{t+1} = I + Hlnk_t$$

Where E, F, G, H, and I are constants. Give explicit formulas for these constants in terms of the parameters of the problem.

A.3.2.3 Differential Calculus Method to Solve the PF

In order to apply the methods of differential calculus in the solution of dynamic optimization problems, it is required that the value function has three important properties: monotonicity, concavity, and differentiability.

[1] Monotonicity of $V(x_t)$ To ensure the monotonicity of the value function, we need two additional hypotheses (H6 and H7).

Hipotesis A.6 ($r(x, u)$ **y** $g(x, u)$) For each $u \in R^m$, the functions

$$r(x_t, u) : X \rightarrow R \text{ is strictly increasing}$$
$$g(x_t, u) : X \rightarrow X \text{ is increasing}$$

Hypothesis A.7 ($\Gamma(x)$) Γ is monotone (i.e., if $x' > x \rightarrow \Gamma(x') \supseteq \Gamma(x)$)

With these two additional hypotheses, we have the following proposition that ensures the monotonicity of the function value:

Proposition A.5 (Monotonicity of $V(x)$) *Under hypotheses A.4 to A.7, the value function is strictly increasing.*

Proof The strategy has two steps. The first is to prove that "T[f]" is a strictly increasing function; the second step is to consider the "fixed-point problem" and from there derive that "V" is also strictly increasing.

1. We know:
   - $C_a(X)$ is the space of real, continuous, and bounded functions with the norm of the supremum.
   - $C_c(X) \subset C_a(X)$ is the space of real, continuous, bounded, and increasing functions.
   - It is observed that $C_c(X)$ is a closed subspace in $C_a(X)$, and therefore, it is a complete space in the norm of the supremum.
2. Step 1. Let's prove that "if $f \in C_a(X)$ is increasing, then $T[f]$ is a strictly increasing function."
3. Step 1a. By hypothesis A.6, if $x' \geq x$, then $g(x', u) \geq g(x, u) \quad \forall u$:

SINCE F IS INCREASING:

$$f(g(x', u)) \geq f(g(x, u))$$

$$r(x', u) + \beta f(g(x', u)) \geq r(x', u) + \beta f(g(x, u))$$

BY HYPOTHESIS A.6 $r(x, u)$ IS INCREASING:

$r(x', u) \geq r(x, u)$, THEN:

$$r(x', u) + \beta f(g(x', u)) > r(x, u) + \beta f(g(x, u)) \tag{A.53}$$

4. Step 1b. Applying "**max**" on the relation (A.53)

$$\max_{u \in \Gamma(x)} \left\{ r(x', u) + \beta f(g(x', u)) \right\} > \max_{u \in \Gamma(x)} \left\{ r(x, u) + \beta f(g(x, u)) \right\} \tag{A.54}$$

5. Step 1c. By hypothesis A.7, we have that "if $x' \geq x \Rightarrow \Gamma(x') \supseteq \Gamma(x)$"

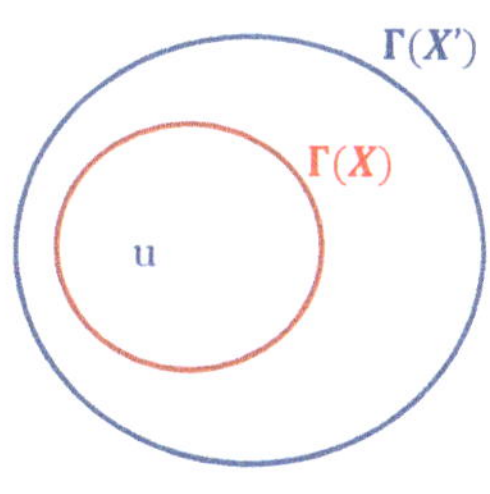

Where $u \in \Gamma(x)$, then $u \in \Gamma(x')$. Replacing this result in (A.54), we have

$$\max_{u \in \Gamma(x')} \left\{ r(x', u) + \beta f(g(x', u)) \right\} > \max_{u \in \Gamma(x)} \left\{ r(x, u) + \beta f(g(x, u)) \right\} \tag{A.55}$$

6. Step 1d. By the definition of the operator "T" for any function "f"

$$T[f](x) = \sup_{\{u\} \in \Gamma(x)} \left\{ r(x, u) + \beta f(g(x, u)) \right\}$$

Expression (A.55) becomes

$$T[f](x') > T[f](x) \tag{A.56}$$

That is, $T[f]$ is strictly increasing.
Conclusion 1
What we wanted to test in step 1 is fulfilled: "If $f \in C_a(X)$ is increasing, then $T[f]$ is a strictly increasing function."
7. Step 2. Since $C_c(X)$ is a closed subspace of $C_a(X)$, **then** the function value "V" is in $C_c(X)$:

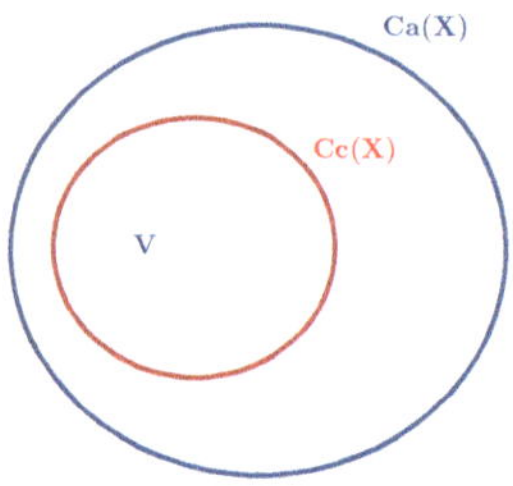

Also, since $T[V] = V$, and T is strictly increasing, **then** "V" is also strictly increasing.
Conclusion 2
The function value (V) is strictly increasing.

[2] Concavity of $V(x_t)$ To ensure the concavity of the value function, three additional hypotheses are required: the first is related to the set X, the second, with the functions $r(\cdot)$ and $g(\cdot)$, and the third, with $\Gamma(x)$.

Hypothesis A.8 (X) X is a convex subset of R^n.

It should be remembered that the set "X" is convex if, for two elements of said set x and y, the linear combination (with $t \in [0, 1]$) also lies within a said set. That is, $\forall x \wedge y \in X$ y $\forall t \in [0, 1]$ it is true that $[(1-t)x + ty] \in X$.

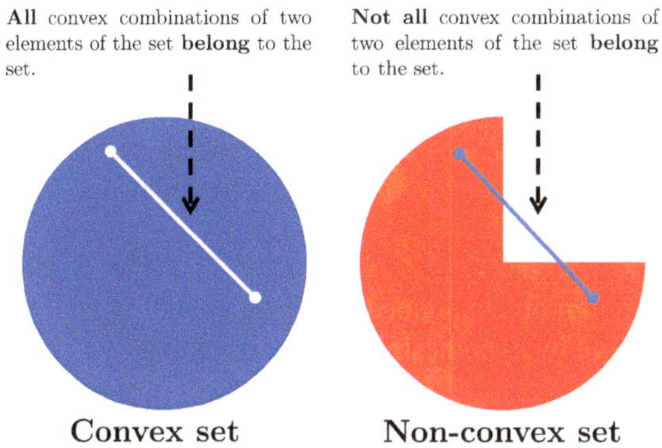

Hypothesis A.9 ($r(x, u)$ **y** $g(x, u)$) $r(x_t, u_t)$ is strictly concave and $g(x_t, u_t)$ is concave.

Let us remember that a real function, defined in a convex set (domain), is concave if for any two points x and y defined in their domain, and for any $t \in [0, 1]$, it is fulfilled:

$f(tx + (1-t)y) \geq tf(x) + (1-t)f(y)$.

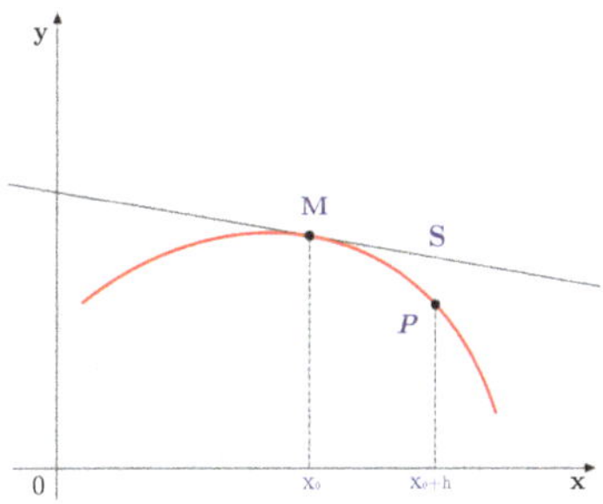

Hypothesis A.10 ($\Gamma(x)$) $\Gamma(x_t)$ is convex; that is to say

1. $\Gamma(x)$ is a convex set for all $x \in X$.
2. Given $\lambda \in [0, 1]$, $x, x' \in X$ and $x \neq x'$, **then** if $u \in \Gamma(x)$ y $u' \in \Gamma(x')$ implies that

$$\lambda u + (1-\lambda)u' \in \Gamma(\lambda x + (1-\lambda)x')$$

With these additional assumptions, the concavity of the value function is assured, which is expressed in the following proposition:

Proposition A.6 (Concavity of $V(x)$**)** *According to hypotheses 4, 5, 8, 9, and 10, the value function is strictly concave and the policy correspondence is a continuous function.*

Proof The strategy is to first prove that "T[f]" is an increasing and strictly concave function; then, it is to consider the "fixed-point problem" and from there derive that "V" is also increasing and strictly concave.

1. Step 1. Let's prove that "if $f \in C_a(X)$ is increasing and concave, **then** $T[f]$ is an increasing and strictly concave function." (We know that it is increasing from *proposition 5*.)
2. Step 1a. Given $\lambda \in [0, 1]$, $x, x' \in X$ and $x \neq x'$, and let u, u' be such that they solve the maximum problem defined by $T[f](x)$ and $T[f](x')$, respectively.
3. Step 1b. In addition, by hypothesis A.10, we have that

$$\lambda u + (1-\lambda)u' \in \Gamma(\lambda x + (1-\lambda)x')$$

Then, we have that (by the definition of the supreme)

$$T[f](\widetilde{x}) \geq r(\widetilde{x}, \widetilde{u}) + \beta f(g(\widetilde{x}, \widetilde{u})) \tag{A.57}$$

Where

$$\widetilde{x} = \lambda x + (1-\lambda)x'$$
$$\widetilde{u} = u + (1-\lambda)u'$$

4. Step 1c. But $r(\cdot,\cdot)$ is strictly concave (hypothesis A.9); then, for $r(\widetilde{x}, \widetilde{u})$ which is equal to $r(\lambda x + (1-\lambda)x', u + (1-\lambda)u')$, you have to

$$r(\lambda x + (1-\lambda)x', u + (1-\lambda)u') > \lambda r(x, u) + (1-\lambda)r(x', u') \tag{A.58}$$

5. Step 1d. Also, since $g(\cdot,\cdot)$ is concave (hypothesis A.9), then we have

$$g(\widetilde{x}, \widetilde{u}) \geq \lambda g(x, u) + (1-\lambda)g(x', u') \tag{A.59}$$

And since f is increasing, then applying "f" to the previous equation (Eq. A.59)

$$f(g(\widetilde{x}, \widetilde{u})) \geq f(\lambda g(x, u) + (1-\lambda)g(x', u')) \tag{A.60}$$

And since f is concave

$$f(\lambda g(x, u) + (1-\lambda)g(x', u')) \geq \lambda f(g(x, u)) + (1-\lambda)f(g(x', u')) \tag{A.61}$$

6. Step 1e. Introducing Expressions (A.58) and (A.61) (multiplied by β) in the initial expression (A.57), we have

$$\begin{aligned} T[f](\widetilde{x}) &\geq r(\widetilde{x}, \widetilde{u}) + \beta f(g(\widetilde{x}, \widetilde{u})) \\ &> \lambda r(x, u) + (1-\lambda)r(x', u') + \beta[\lambda f(g(x, u)) + (1-\lambda)f(g(x', u'))] \end{aligned}$$

$$> \left[\lambda r(x,u) + \lambda\beta f(g(x,u))\right]$$
$$+\left[(1-\lambda)r(x',u') + (1-\lambda)\beta f(g(x',u'))\right]$$
$$> \lambda\Big[\underbrace{r(x,u) + \beta f(g(x,u))}_{T[f](x)}\Big] + (1-\lambda)\Big[\underbrace{r(x',u') + \beta f(g(x',u'))}_{T[f](x')}\Big]$$

$$T[f](\widetilde{x}) > \lambda T[f](x) + (1-\lambda)T[f](x')$$

Conclusion 1: What we wanted to prove in step 1 is fulfilled:

"If $f \in C_a(X)$ is increasing and concave, **then** $T[f]$ is an increasing and strictly concave function."

7. Step 2. Since $C_c(X)$ (bounded for strictly concave functions) is a closed subspace of $C_a(X)$, **then** the function value "V" is in $C_c(X)$ (bounded for strictly concave functions):

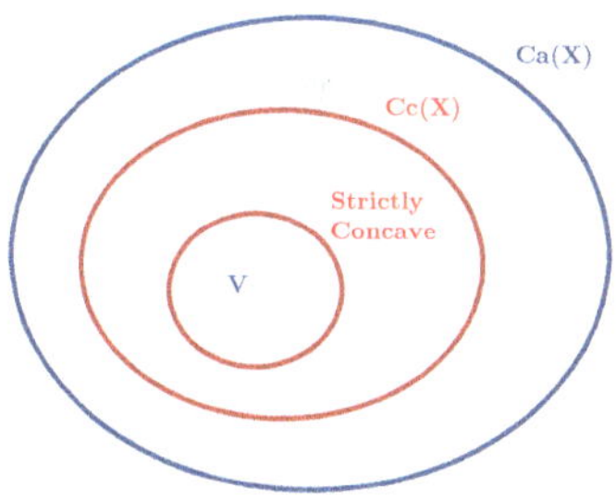

Also, since $T[V] = V$, and T is strictly concave, **so** "V" is too.
Conclusion 2: The function value (V) is strictly concave.

[3] Differentiability of $V(x_t)$ In the same way as in the two previous properties of the value function, for it to be differentiable, two additional hypotheses are required.

Hypothesis A.11 ($r(x,u)$ **and** $g(x,u)$) $r(x_t,u_t)$ and $g(x_t,u_t)$ are continuously differentiable inside the graph of $\Gamma(x_t)$.

Hypothesis A.12 (Differentiability) Let (x^*, u^*) be in the interior of the graph of Γ, such that $\exists$ a differentiable function "τ" defined in an open neighborhood **V** of x^* such that

$$\tau : V \to U$$

And for everything $x \in V : \tau(x) \in \Gamma(x)$ y $g(x, \tau(x)) = g(x^*, u^*)$

With these two additional hypotheses, two very useful theorems in dynamic programming are obtained. The first corresponds to the differentiability of the value function, and the second is a practical way of obtaining the first-order conditions directly from differentiating the value function. Both theorems come from Benveniste-Scheinkman; the latter is known as the *envelope theorem*.

Theorem A.3A (Differentiability of the Value Function (Benveniste-Scheinkman)) *Under hypotheses A.4, A.5, A.8, A.9, A.10, A.11, and A.12; if $x_0 \in Int(X)$ and $h(x_0) \in Int(\Gamma(x_0))$, then the function value is continuously differentiable at x_0, and its derivative is given by*

$$\frac{\partial V(x_0)}{\partial x_0} = \frac{\partial r(x_0, h(x_0))}{\partial x_0} + \beta \frac{\partial V(g(x_0, h(x_0)))}{\partial x_0} \tag{A.62}$$

This is generalized for all t.

This theorem is a previous step to proving the envelope theorem. Also, said theorem requires that the policy function $h(x)$ be introduced into the Bellman equation (in addition to the equation of motion of the state variable $g(x, h(x))$). It should be noted that the hypotheses described ensure that the value function is twice differentiable (Stokey and Lucas, 1989 p. 84), which ensures that the policy function $h(x)$ is differentiable. This property is collected in the theorem of 3A and 3B.

Theorem A.4A (Theorem of the Envelope (Benveniste-Scheinkman)) *Under hypotheses A.4, A.5, A.8, A.9, A.10, A.11, and A.12; if $x_0 \in Int(X)$ and $h(x_0) \in Int(\Gamma(x_0))$, and fulfilling theorem 3A, then for x, u it is true:*

$$\frac{\partial V(x_0)}{\partial x_0} = \frac{\partial r(x_0, u_0)}{\partial u_0} \tag{A.63}$$

This is generalized for all t.

This theorem ensures a relationship between the value function and the utility function.

Steps to use the Benveniste-Scheinkman method

1. In the Bellman equation applies the FOC; that is, derive the right-hand side of the said equation with respect to the control variable.
2. Apply the envelope theorem. Remember that the differentiability theorem is only to prove the envelope theorem.

It should be noted that this method (BS theorem) explicitly provides the FOC without the need to know the value function; however, it does not provide the solution to the problem, that is, it does not specify the policy function.

Example Application of the envelope theorem. A typical example of the consumer problem

$$\underset{\{c_t, w_{t+1}\}_{t=0}^{\infty}}{\text{Max}} \sum_{t=0}^{\infty} \beta^t u(c_t)$$

subject to

$$w_{t+1} = (1+r)(w_t + c_t)$$

Where $\beta \in (0, 1)$, w_t is the wealth of the individual and w_0 given.

Solution Bellman equation is

$$V(w_t) = \underset{\{c_t\}_{t=0}^{\infty}}{\text{Max}} \left\{ u(c_t) + \beta V(w_{t+1}) \right\}$$

Introducing the equation of the state variable

$$V(w_t) = \underset{\{c_t\}_{t=0}^{\infty}}{\text{Max}} \left\{ u(c_t) + \beta V((1+r)(w_t + c_t)) \right\} \tag{A.64}$$

The first-order conditions are obtained by differentiating the right-hand side of the Bellman equation with respect to the control variable c_t:

$$\frac{\partial u(c_t)}{\partial c_t} + \beta \frac{\partial V(w_{t+1})}{\partial w_{t+1}} \frac{\partial [(1+r)(w_t + c_t)]}{\partial c_t} = 0$$

$$\frac{\partial u(c_t)}{\partial c_t} + \beta \frac{\partial V(w_{t+1})}{\partial w_{t+1}} (-1)(1+r) = 0$$

$$\frac{\partial u(c_t)}{\partial c_t} = \beta (1+r) \frac{\partial V(w_{t+1})}{\partial w_{t+1}} \tag{A.65}$$

The envelope theorem states

$$\frac{\partial V(w_t)}{\partial w_t} = \frac{\partial u(c_t)}{\partial c_t} \tag{A.66}$$

One period forward

$$\frac{\partial V(w_{t+1})}{\partial w_{t+1}} = \frac{\partial u(c_{t+1})}{\partial c_{t+1}} \tag{A.67}$$

Introducing Eq. (A.67) (envelope theorem) in Eq. (A.68) (FOC), we have Euler's equation:

$$\frac{\partial u(c_t)}{\partial c_t} = \beta (1+r) \frac{\partial V(w_{t+1})}{\partial w_{t+1}}$$

$$\frac{\partial u(c_t)}{\partial c_t} = \beta (1+r) \frac{\partial u(c_{t+1})}{\partial c_{t+1}} \tag{A.68}$$

A.3.3 Applications

A.3.3.1 Growth with Human Capital

Preliminaries

1. This model holds that there is a *trade off* between the time spent working (n_t) and training (accumulating human capital (h_t)). The more time spent working, the less time will be dedicated to training: "to accumulate human capital, you have to dedicate time to study/train, which implies stopping working for a bit":

$$\uparrow n_t \rightarrow \downarrow h_t$$

2. The dynamic described is captured by this expression:

$$h_{t+1} = h_t \Psi(n_t) \tag{A.69}$$

Where $\Psi(n_t)$ is a function of [0, 1] in R_+

$$\Psi(n_t) : [0, 1] \rightarrow R_+$$

: In addition, it is assumed that $\Psi(n_t)$ fulfills the following properties:

- Continue
- Strictly concave
- Strictly decreasing
- $\Psi(0) = 1 + \lambda$, which indicates that if the representative agent dedicates all his/her time to training, then the accumulation of human capital will grow at a constant rate (λ):

$$h_{t+1} = h_t(1 + \lambda)$$

- $\Psi(1) = 1 - \delta$, which indicates that if the representative agent dedicates all his/her time to work, then the accumulation of human capital will decrease at a constant rate (δ):

$$h_{t+1} = h_t(1 - \delta)$$

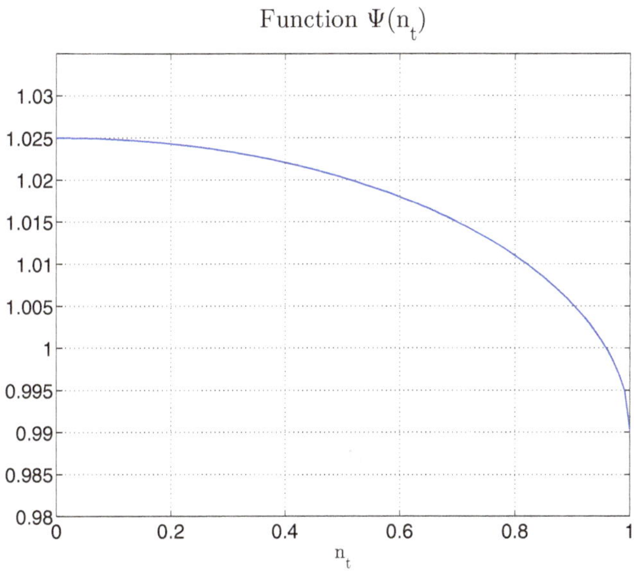

Statement

$$\underset{\{c_t, n_t\}_{t=0}^{\infty}}{\text{Max}} \sum_{t=0}^{\infty} \beta^t \left[\frac{c_t^{\sigma}}{\sigma} \right]$$

subject to

$$c_t = f(h_t n_t) = (h_t n_t)^{\alpha}$$

$$h_{t+1} = h_t \Psi(n_t)$$

$\Psi(n_t) = (\lambda + \delta)\sqrt{1 - n_t^2} + (1 - \delta)$, $\beta \in (0, 1)$, $\gamma \in (0, 1)$, $\alpha \in (0, 1)$ y h_0 given.

You are prompted for the following:

1. Set up the sequential problem.
2. Find the Bellman equation and state the functional problem.
3. Prove that the function value (V) has the form $A h_t^{\alpha\sigma}$.
4. Prove that the policy function is constant (i.e., find the optimal job) (n) and the constant A of the function value, considering the values of the parameters: $\sigma = 0.5$, $\beta = 0.95$, $\lambda = 0.025$, $\delta = 0.01$, $\alpha = 0.8$. In this case, build a code in Matlab to solve the nonlinear system.

Solution
[1] Sequential Problem

$$\underset{\{n_t\}_{t=0}^{\infty}}{\text{Max}} \sum_{t=0}^{\infty} \beta^t \left[\frac{[h_t n_t]^{\alpha\sigma}}{\sigma}\right]$$

subject to

$$h_{t+1} = h_t \Psi(n_t)$$

[2] Bellman Equation

$$V(h_t) = \underset{\{n_t\}_{t=0}^{\infty}}{\text{Max}} \left\{\frac{[h_t n_t]^{\alpha\sigma}}{\sigma} + \beta V(h_{t+1})\right\} \tag{A.70}$$

[3] Functional Problem

Introducing the equation of the state variable in the Bellman equation

$$V(h_t) = \underset{\{n_t\}_{t=0}^{\infty}}{\text{Max}} \left\{\frac{[h_t n_t]^{\alpha\sigma}}{\sigma} + \beta V(h_t \Psi(n_t))\right\} \tag{A.71}$$

subject to

$$0 \le n_t \le 1$$

[4] Iteration of the Value Function

1. To solve the FP, we will use the value function iteration method (proposed by the fixed-point theorem for contractions):

$$V_n = T[V_{n-1}], \quad n \ge 1 \tag{A.72}$$

   It starts with the simplest function: $V_0 = 0$
2. Finding V_1

$$\begin{aligned} V_1 &= T[V_0] \\ &\downarrow \\ &= \underset{\{n_t\}_{t=0}^{\infty}}{\text{Max}} \left\{\frac{[h_t n_t]^{\alpha\sigma}}{\sigma} + \beta \underbrace{V_0(h_t \Psi(n_t))}_{=0}\right\} \\ &= \underset{\{n_t\}_{t=0}^{\infty}}{\text{Max}} \left\{\frac{[h_t n_t]^{\alpha\sigma}}{\sigma}\right\} \end{aligned} \tag{A.73}$$

- (*a*) At this stage, the first-order condition applies:

$$\frac{\partial \text{ objective function}}{\partial n_t} = 0$$

However, in this case, the objective function takes its maximum value when $n_t = 1$ (see the FP restriction).

- (*b*) Replacing n_t that maximizes the objective function at (A.73), it obtains $T[V_0]$ and, therefore, V_1:

$$V_1 = T[V_0] = \frac{[h_t]^{\alpha\sigma}}{\sigma}$$

$$V_1 = \frac{[h_t]^{\alpha\sigma}}{\sigma} \tag{A.74}$$

3. Finding V_2

$$V_2 = T[V_1]$$

$$\downarrow$$

$$= \underset{\{n_t\}_{t=0}^{\infty}}{\text{Max}} \left\{ \frac{[h_t n_t]^{\alpha\sigma}}{\sigma} + \beta \underbrace{V_1(h_t \Psi(n_t))}_{= \frac{[h_t \Psi(n_t)]^{\alpha\sigma}}{\sigma}} \right\}$$

$$= \underset{\{n_t\}_{t=0}^{\infty}}{\text{Max}} \left\{ \frac{[h_t n_t]^{\alpha\sigma}}{\sigma} + \beta \frac{[h_t \Psi(n_t)]^{\alpha\sigma}}{\sigma} \right\} \tag{A.75}$$

(a) At this stage, the first-order condition applies:

$$\frac{\partial \text{ objective function}}{\partial c_t} = 0$$

However, it can be seen that the maximization of the objective function does not depend on h_t. This indicates that when deriving said objective function with respect to the control variable (n_t), it will only depend on the parameters of the model (constant values) and, therefore, $n_t = \text{constant}$. Consequently, in the value function, it could be considered as a constant A.

Factoring $\left\{ \frac{[h_t]^{\alpha\sigma}}{\sigma} \right\}$

$$V_2 = \left\{ \frac{[h_t]^{\alpha\sigma}}{\sigma} \right\} \underset{\{n_t\}_{t=0}^{\infty}}{\text{Max}} \left\{ \underbrace{[n_t]^{\alpha\sigma} + \beta[\Psi(n_t)]^{\alpha\sigma}}_{\text{Does not depend on} h_t} \right\} \tag{A.76}$$

From the FOC, it obtains

$$n_t = \text{constant depending on the parameters} = n \tag{A.77}$$

(b) Replacing $n_t = n$ that maximizes the objective function in (A.75), we obtain $T[V_1]$ and, therefore, V_2:

$$V_2 = T[V_1] = A(n)\left\{\frac{[h_t]^{\alpha\sigma}}{\sigma}\right\}$$

$$V_2 = A(n)\left\{\frac{[h_t]^{\alpha\sigma}}{\sigma}\right\} \tag{A.78}$$

Where $A(n)$ is a constant, which we just call A.

4. We can generalize the above equation:

$$V(h_t) = A\left\{\frac{[h_t]^{\alpha\sigma}}{\sigma}\right\} \tag{A.79}$$

The constant "A" can be found by substituting "V" and the optimal dynamics into Bellman equation.

[5] Finding the Policy Function

Substituting the value function (V) into the Bellman equation

$$V(h_t) = \underset{\{n_t\}_{t=0}^{\infty}}{\text{Max}}\left\{\frac{[h_t n_t]^{\alpha\sigma}}{\sigma} + \beta\,\underbrace{V(h_t\Psi(n_t))}_{=A\frac{[h_t\Psi(n_t)]^{\alpha\sigma}}{\sigma}}\right\}$$

$$= \underset{\{n_t\}_{t=0}^{\infty}}{\text{Max}}\left\{\frac{[h_t n_t]^{\alpha\sigma}}{\sigma} + \beta A\frac{[h_t\Psi(n_t)]^{\alpha\sigma}}{\sigma}\right\} \tag{A.80}$$

Factoring $\left\{\frac{[h_t]^{\alpha\sigma}}{\sigma}\right\}$

$$V(h_t) = \left\{\frac{[h_t]^{\alpha\sigma}}{\sigma}\right\}\underset{\{n_t\}_{t=0}^{\infty}}{\text{Max}}\left\{[n_t]^{\alpha\sigma} + \beta A[\Psi(n_t)]^{\alpha\sigma}\right\} \tag{A.81}$$

Applying FOC (derivative with respect to the control variable), we have

$$n_t^{\alpha\sigma-1} = -\beta A(\Psi(n_t))^{\alpha\sigma-1}\dot{\Psi}(n_t) \tag{A.82}$$

The solution of this nonlinear equation is the following:

$$n_t = n^*$$

The policy function is a constant; that is, it does not matter what the level of human capital (h_t) is, since the agent always chooses to work n^*. To know the value of n^*, we have to find the constant A and define the function $\Psi(n_t)$.

[6] Finding the Constant A

Substituting the value function and the policy function in the Bellman equation, we have

$$A\frac{[h_t]^{\alpha\sigma}}{\sigma} = \left\{\frac{[h_t]^{\alpha\sigma}}{\sigma}\right\}\left\{[n^*]^{\alpha\sigma} + \beta A[\Psi(n^*)]^{\alpha\sigma}\right\}$$

Therefore

$$A = [n^*]^{\alpha\sigma} + \beta A[\Psi(n^*)]^{\alpha\sigma} \tag{A.83}$$

Then

$$A = A(n^*)$$

Equations (A.82) and (A.83) form a system of nonlinear equations in (n^*, A):

$$n^{*\alpha\sigma-1} = -\beta A(\Psi(n^*))^{\alpha\sigma-1}\dot{\Psi}(n^*) \tag{A.84}$$

$$A = [n^*]^{\alpha\sigma} + \beta A[\Psi(n^*)]^{\alpha\sigma} \tag{A.85}$$

Where

$$\Psi(n_t) = (\lambda + \delta)\sqrt{1 - n_t^2} + (1 - \delta)$$

The question that arises is the following: How do we solve a system of nonlinear equations in Matlab? The "fsolve" function will help us in this task.

Solution of Systems of Nonlinear Equations (Matlab) This function solves systems of nonlinear equations; that is, finding the roots of the system. For this, the system has to be specified like this:

$$F(x) = 0$$

The goal is to find the value of the vector x that makes $F(x)$ equal to zero. The syntax

$$x = fsolve(fun, x0)$$

Where "fun" is a function containing the nonlinear system of equations ($F(x)$) and $x0$ is the initial value for the vector x.

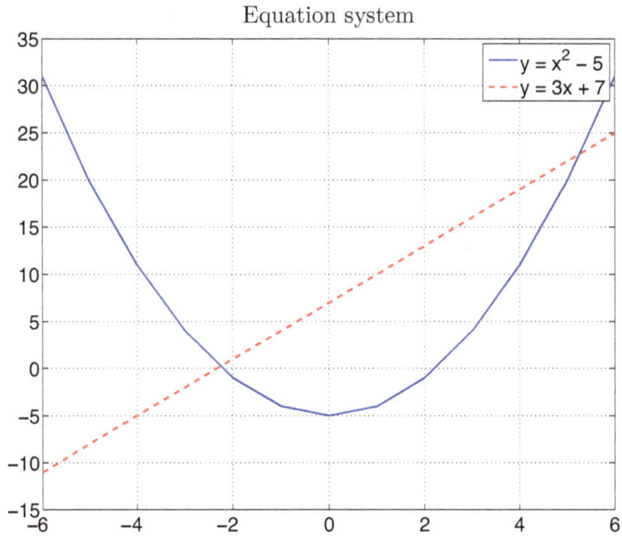

Fig. A.3 Solution of a system of nonlinear equations (see the function "system_na.m")

Example Consider the following system of nonlinear equations:

$$y = x^2 - 5 \tag{A.86}$$

$$y = 3x + 7 \tag{A.87}$$

We can rewrite the system as

$$F_1 = y - x^2 + 5 = 0 \tag{A.88}$$

$$F_2 = y - 3x - 7 = 0 \tag{A.89}$$

Then

$$F(x) = [F_1, F_2]$$

Assuming that $z = [z(1), z(2)] = [x, y]$, we write a function in Matlab that captures the nonlinear system (see example_function.m and sol_example_function.m) (Fig. A.3).

A.3.3.2 Hercowitz and Sampson (1991) Model

This model is left as an exercise for the reader. To solve it, following the steps described in the first application is suggested. Consider the basic growth model with these data:

$$u(c_t, l_t) = ln(c_t - an_t^{\gamma})$$
$$y_t = k_t{}^{\alpha} n_t{}^{1-\alpha}$$
$$k_{t+1} = k_t \left(\frac{i_t}{k_t}\right)^{1-\delta} = k_t{}^{\delta} i_t{}^{1-\delta}$$

Considering that $a > 0$ and $\gamma > 1$, the following is requested:

1. Set up the SP, the Bellman equation, and the FP.
2. Prove that the function value has the following form:

$$V(k_t) = D_0 + D_1 lnk_t$$

   Where D_i are constants.
3. Prove that the policy function has the following form:

$$c_t = \Pi_1 k_t^{\Psi_1}$$
$$n_t = \Pi_2 k_t^{\Psi_2}$$

   Where $\Psi_2 = \frac{\alpha}{-1+\gamma+\alpha}$
4. Show that the optimal dynamics of capital are

$$k_{t+1} = \Pi_3 k_t^{\Psi_3}$$

   Where Π_i are constants.

References

Abel, A.B., and B.S. Bernanke. 2001. *Macroeconomics*, 4th ed. New York: Addison-Wesley.

Ahmadi, Pooyan Amir, and Harald Uhlig. 2015. Sign Restrictions in Bayesian FaVARs with an application to monetary policy shocks, Technical Report, National Bureau of Economic Research.

Aiyagari, S. Rao, Lawrence J. Christiano ,and Martin Eichenbaum. 1992. The output, employment, and interest rate effects of government consumption. *Journal of Monetary Economics* 30(1): 73–86.

Arroyo Abad, Leticia, and Kareem Khalifa. 2015. What are stylized facts? *Journal of Economic Methodology* 22(2): 143–156.

Barro, Robert J. 1981. Output effects of government purchases. *Journal of Political Economy* 89(6): 1086–1121.

Barro, R.J. 1983. Inflationary finance under discretion and rules. *The Canadian Journal of Economics/Revue Canadienne d'Economique* 16(1): 1–16.

Barro, Robert J. 1987. Government spending, interest rates, prices, and budget deficits in the United Kingdom, 1701–1918. *Journal of Monetary Economics* 20(2): 221–247.

Barro, Robert J., and Robert G. King. 1984. Time-separable preferences and intertemporal-substitution models of business cycles. *The Quarterly Journal of Economics* 99(4): 817–839.

Barro, Robert J., Xavier Sala-i-Martin, Robert Andrew Robinson, and José Ramón de Espinoza. 2009. *Crecimiento Económico*, Reverté.

Baxter, Marianne, and Robert G. King. 1993. Fiscal policy in general equilibrium. *The American Economic Review* 83: 315–334.

Baxter, Marianne, and Robert G. King. 1999. Measuring business cycles: Approximate band-pass filters for economic time series. *Review of Economics and Statistics* 81(4): 575–593.

Bellman, Richard. 1957. *Dynamic Programming*, 1st ed. Princeton, NJ: Princeton University Press.

Benhabib, Jess, Richard Rogerson, and Randall Wright. 1991. Homework in macroeconomics: Household production and aggregate fluctuations. *Journal of Political Economy* 99(6): 1166–1187.

Bernanke, Ben S., and Alan S. Blinder. 1992. The federal funds rate and the channels of monetary transmission. *The American Economic Review* 82: 901–921.

Bernanke, Ben S., Jean Boivin, and Piotr Eliasz. 2005. Measuring the effects of monetary policy: A factor-augmented vector autoregressive (FAVAR) approach. *The Quarterly Journal of Economics* 120(1): 387–422.

Blanchard, Olivier Jean, and Charles M. Kahn. 1980. The solution of linear difference models under rational expectations. *Econometrica: Journal of the Econometric Society* 48: 1305–1311.

Blanchard, Olivier, and Roberto Perotti. 1999. *An empirical characterization of the dynamic effects of changes in government spending and taxes on output NBER Working Paper, 7269.*

Blanchard, Olivier, and Roberto Perotti. 2002. An empirical characterization of the dynamic effects of changes in government spending and taxes on output. *The Quarterly Journal of Economics* 117(4): 1329–1368.

Boldrin, Michele, Lawrence J. Christiano, and Jonas D.M. Fisher. 2001. Habit persistence, asset returns, and the business cycle. *American Economic Review* 91(1): 149–166.

Burns, Arthur F., and W.C. Mitchell. 1946. *Measuring Business Cycles*. Nber Books.

Burnside, C., and M. Eichenbaum. 1996. Factor-hoarding and the propagation of business-cycle shocks. *American Economic Review* 86(5): 1154–1174.

Burnside, A. Craig, Martin S. Eichenbaum, and Sergio T. Rebelo. 1996. Sectoral solow residuals. *European Economic Review* 40(3–5): 861–869.

Burnside, Craig, Martin Eichenbaum, and Jonas D. M. Fisher. 2000. Assessing the effects of fiscal shocks, Technical Report, National Bureau of Economic Research.

Calvo, Guillermo A. 1983. Staggered prices in a utility-maximizing framework. *Journal of Monetary Economics* 12(3): 383–398.

Campbell, John Y. 1994. Inspecting the mechanism: An analytical approach to the stochastic growth model. *Journal of Monetary Economics* 33(3): 463–506.

Christiano, Lawrence J. 1991. Modeling the liquidity effect of a money shock. *Federal Reserve Bank of Minneapolis. Quarterly Review-Federal Reserve Bank of Minneapolis* 15(1): 3.

Christiano, Lawrence J., and Martin Eichenbaum. 1992a. Current real-business-cycle theories and aggregate labor-market fluctuations. *The American Economic Review* 82(3): 430–450.

Christiano, Lawrence J., and Martin Eichenbaum. 1992b. Liquidity effects and the monetary transmission mechanism, Technical Report, National Bureau of Economic Research.

Christiano, L., and T. Fitzgerald. 1999. The band pass filter. Federal reserve bank of cleveland, Technical Report, Working Paper 9906.

Chudik, Alexander, and Michael Fidora. 2011. Using the global dimension to identify shocks with sign restrictions. *Working Paper Series, No 1013, European Central Bank.*

Cogley, Timothy, and James M. Nason. 1995. Output dynamics in real-business-cycle models. *The American Economic Review* 85(3): 492–511.

Coibion, Olivier. 2012. Are the effects of monetary policy shocks big or small? *American Economic Journal: Macroeconomics* 4(2): 1–32.

Cooley, Thomas F., and Gary D. Hansen. 1989. The inflation tax in a real business cycle model. *The American Economic Review* 79(4): 733–748.

Cooley, Thomas F., and Gary D. Hansen. 1991. The welfare costs of moderate inflations. *Journal of Money, Credit and Banking* 23(3): 483–503.
Cooley, Thomas F., and Gary D. Hansen. 1992. Tax distortions in a neoclassical monetary economy. *Journal of Economic Theory* 58(2): 290–316.
Cooley, Thomas F., and Edward C. Prescott. 1995. Economic growth and business cycles. *Frontiers of Business Cycle Research* 1: 1–38.
Cooper, Russell W. 1998. Business cycles: Theory, evidence and policy implications. *The Scandinavian Journal of Economics* 100(1): 213–237.
Davis, Steven J., and James A. Kahn. 2008. Interpreting the great moderation: Changes in the volatility of economic activity at the macro and micro levels. *Journal of Economic Perspectives* 22(4): 155–80.
DeJong, David N., and Chetan Dave. 2007. *Structural Macroeconometrics*. Princeton: Princeton University Press.
DeJong, David N., and Chetan Dave. 2011. *Structural Macroeconometrics*. Princeton: Princeton University Press.
Eichenbaum, M. 1992. Comments: Interpreting the macroeconomic time series facts: The effects of monetary policy. *European Economic Review* 36(5): 1001–1011.
Eichenbaum, Martin, and Kenneth J. Singleton, 1986. Do equilibrium real business cycle theories explain postwar U. S. business cycles? *NBER Macroeconomics Annual* 1: 91–135.
Eisner, Robert. 1988. Extended accounts for national income and product. *Journal of Economic Literature* 26(4): 1611–1684.
Farmer, Roger E. A. 1997. Money in a real business cycle model. *Journal of Money, Credit and Banking* 29(4): 568–611.
Fatás, Antonio, and Ilian Mihov. 2001. The effects of fiscal policy on consumption and employment: Theory and evidence. *CEPR Discussion Paper No. 2770.*
Faust, Jon, and Dale W. Henderson. 2004. Is inflation targeting best-practice monetary policy? *International Finance Discussion Papers, No. 807, Board of Governors of the Federal Reserve System.*
Feldstein, Martin, and Charles Horioka. 1980. Domestic saving and international capital flows. *Economic Journal* 90(358): 314–29. https://EconPapers.repec.org/RePEc:ecj:econjl:v:90:y:1980:i:358:p:314-29
Fernald, John G., and J. Christina Wang. 2016. Why has the cyclicality of productivity changed? What does it mean? *Annual Review of Economics* 8: 465–496.
Fernández, Andrés, Stephanie Schmitt-Grohe, and Martín Uribe. 2017. World shocks, world prices, and business cycles: An empirical investigation. *Journal of International Economics* 108(S1): S2–S14. https://EconPapers.repec.org/RePEc:eee:inecon:v:108:y:2017:i:s1:p:s2-s14
Finn, Mary G. 1998. Cyclical effects of government's employment and goods purchases. *International Economic Review* 39: 635–657.
Fisher, Jonas D.M. 2006. The dynamic effects of neutral and investment-specific technology shocks. *Journal of political Economy* 114(3): 413–451.
Friedman, M., and Schwartz, A.J. 1963. *A Monetary History of the United States, 1867–1960.* Princeton University Press.
Frisch, Ragnar. 1933. *Propagation Problems and Impulse Problems in Dynamic Economics.* London: G. Allen & Unwin.
Gali, J., and T. van Rens. 2010. The vanishing procyclicality of labor productivity. *Economics Working Papers 1230, Department of Economics and Business, Universitat Pompeu Fabra.*
Galí, Jordi, J. David López-Salido, and Javier Vallés. 2007. Understanding the effects of government spending on consumption. *Journal of the European Economic Association* 5(1): 227–270.
Goodfriend, Marvin, and Robert G. King. 1997. The new neoclassical synthesis and the role of monetary policy. *NBER Macroeconomics Annual* 12: 231–283.
Gordon, Robert J. 1982. Price inertia and policy ineffectiveness in the United States, 1890–1980. *Journal of Political Economy* 90(6): 1087–1117.

Greenwald, Bruce C., Joseph E. Stiglitz, Robert E. Hall, and Stanley Fischer 1988. Examining alternative macroeconomic theories. *Brookings Papers on Economic Activity* 1988(1): 207–270.

Greenwood, Jeremy, and Gregory W. Huffman 1987. A dynamic equilibrium model of inflation and unemployment. *Journal of Monetary Economics* 19(2): 203–228.

Greenwood, Jeremy, Zvi Hercowitz, and Gregory W. Huffman. 1988. Investment, capacity utilization, and the real business cycle. *The American Economic Review* 78(3): 402–417.

Guerrieri, L., D. Henderson, and J. Kim. 2010. Interpreting investment-specifictechnology shocks. *Board of Governors of the Federal Reserve System, International Finance Discussion Papers 1000.*

Hall, Robert E. 1986. Liquidity constraints, fiscal policy, and consumption. *Brookings Papers on Economic Activity* 1986(1): 1–59.

Hall, Robert E., and Frederic S. Mishkin. 1980. The sensitivity of consumption to transitory income: Estimates from panel data on households. *NBER Working Papers 0505, National Bureau of Economic Research, Inc.*

Hansen, Alvin H. 1949. *Monetary Theory and Fiscal Policy*. London: Mcgraw-Hill Kogakusha, Ltd.

Hansen, Alvin Harvey. 1953. *A Guide to Keynes*. New York: McGraw-Hill.

Hansen, Gary D. 1985. Indivisible labor and the business cycle. *Journal of Monetary Economics* 16(3): 309–327.

Hartley, James, Kevin Hoover, and Kevin Salyer. 1998. A user's guide to solving real business cycle models. In *Real Business Cycle: A Reader*. London: Routledge.

Heckman, James. 1984. Comments on the Ashenfelter and Kydland papers. *Carnegie-Rochester Conference Series on Public Policy, Elsevier* 21(1): 209–224.

Heckman, James, J., and Thomas Macurdy. 1980. A life-cycle model of female labor supply. *Review of Economic Studies* 47: 47–74.

Heer, Burkhard, and Alfred Maussner. 2009. *Dynamic General Equilibrium Modeling: Computational Methods and Applications*. Cham: Springer Science & Business Media.

Hicks, John R. 1937. Mr. Keynes and the "classics": A suggested interpretation. *Econometrica: Journal of the Econometric Society* 5: 147–159.

Hodrick, Robert J., and Edward Prescott. 1981. Post-war U.S. business cycles: An empirical investigation. *Discussion Papers 451, Northwestern University, Center for Mathematical Studies in Economics and Management Science.*

Hoover, Kevin D. 1995. Facts and artifacts: Calibration and the empirical assessment of real-business-cycle models. *Oxford Economic Papers* 47(1): 24–44.

Jones, Charles I. 2016. The facts of economic growth. In *Handbook of Macroeconomics*, vol. 2, 3–69. Amsterdam: Elsevier.

Judd, Kenneth L., and Sy-Ming Guu. 1993. Perturbation solution methods for economic growth models. In *Economic and Financial Modeling with Mathematica*. New York: Springer.

Justiniano, Alejandro, and Giorgio E. Primiceri. 2008. The time-varying volatility of macroeconomic fluctuations. *American Economic Review* 98(3): 604–41.

Kaldor, Nicholas. 1957. A model of economic growth. *The Economic Journal* 67(268): 591–624.

Kaldor, Nicholas. 1961. Capital accumulation and economic growth. In *The Theory of Capital*, 177–222. Berlin: Springer.

Kaldor, N. 1963. *Capital Accumulation and Economic Growth*. London: MacMillan.

Kelley, C. T. 2003. *Solving Nonlinear Equations with Newton's Method*. Series: Fundamentals of Algorithms. Philadelphia: Society for Industrial and Applied Mathematics.

King, Robert G., and Sergio T. Rebelo. 1999. Resuscitating real business cycles. *Handbook of Macroeconomics* 1: 927–1007.

King, R.G., Plosser, C.I., Stock, J.H., and Watson, M.W. 1991. Stochastic trends and economic fluctuations. *The American Economic Review* 81(4): 819–840.

King, Robert G., Charles I. Plosser, and Sergio T. Rebelo. 1988a. Production, growth and business cycles: I. The basic neoclassical model. *Journal of Monetary Economics* 21(2–3): 195–232.

King, Robert G., Charles I. Plosser, and Sergio T. Rebelo. 1988b. Production, growth and business cycles: II. New directions. *Journal of Monetary Economics* 21(2–3): 309–341.

King, Robert G., Charles I. Plosser, and Sergio T. Rebelo. 2002. Production, growth and business cycles: Technical appendix. *Computational Economics* 20(1): 87–116.

Klein, Paul. 2000. Using the generalized Schur form to solve a multivariate linear rational expectations model. *Journal of Economic Dynamics and Control* 24(10): 1405–1423.

Kydland, Finn E. 1995. Business cycles and aggregate labor market fluctuations. In *Frontiers of Business Cycle Research*, 126–156. Princeton: Princeton University Press.

Kydland, Finn E., and Edward C. Prescott. 1982. Time to build and aggregate fluctuations. *Econometrica: Journal of the Econometric Society* 50: 1345–1370.

Kydland, Finn E., and Edward C. Prescott. 1990. Business cycles: Real facts and a monetary myth. *Real Business Cycles: A Reader* 383: 3–18.

Lau, Morten, I., Andreas Pahlke, and Thomas, F. Rutherford. 2002. Approximating infinite-horizon models in a complementarity format: A primer in dynamic general equilibrium analysis. *Journal of Economic Dynamics and Control* 26(4): 577–609.

Leeper, Eric M. 1997. Narrative and VAR approaches to monetary policy: Common identification problems. *Journal of Monetary Economics* 40(3): 641–657.

Levy, Daniel, and Haiwei Chen. 1994. Estimates of the aggregate quarterly capital sotck for the post-war US economy. *Review of Income and Wealth* 40(3): 317–349.

Long, John B., and Charles I. Plosser. 1983. Real business cycles. *Journal of Political Economy* 91(1): 39–69.

Lucas, Robert E. 1972. Expectations and the neutrality of money. *Journal of Economic Theory* 4(2): 103–124.

Lucas, Robert E. 1973. Some international evidence on output-inflation tradeoffs. *The American Economic Review* 63(3): 326–334.

Lucas, Robert E. 1977. Understanding business cycles. In *Carnegie-Rochester Conference Series on Public Policy*, vol. 5, 7–29. Amsterdam: Elsevier.

Lucas, Robert E. 1980. Methods and problems in business cycle theory. *Journal of Money, Credit and banking* 12(4): 696–715.

Lucas, Robert E., and Nancy L. Stokey. 1983. Optimal fiscal and monetary policy in an economy without capital. *Journal of Monetary Economics* 12(1): 55–93.

Lucas, Robert E., and Nancy L. Stokey. 1987. Money and interest in a cash-in-advance economy. *Econometrica: Journal of the Econometric Society* 55: 491–513.

Ludvigson, Sydney. 1996. The macroeconomic effects of government debt in a stochastic growth model. *Journal of Monetary Economics* 38(1): 25–45.

Macurdy, Thomas. 1981. An empirical model of labor supply in a life-cycle setting. *Journal of Political Economy* 89: 1059–85.

Mandelman, Federico S., and Andrei Zlate. 2012. Immigration, remittances and business cycles. *Journal of Monetary Economics* 59(2): 196–213. https://ideas.repec.org/a/eee/moneco/v59y2012i2p196-213.html

McConnell, Margaret M., and Gabriel Perez-Quiros. 2000. Output fluctuations in the United States: What has changed since the early 1980's? *The American Economic Review* 90(5): 13.

Mehra, Rajnish, and Edward C. Prescott. 1985. The equity premium: A puzzle. *Journal of Monetary Economics* 15(2): 145–161.

Mendoza, Enrique G. 1991. Real business cycles in a small open economy. *The American Economic Review* 81(4): 797–818.

Mendoza, Enrique G. 1995. The terms of trade, the real exchange rate, and economic fluctuations. *International Economic Review* 36: 101–137.

Mountford, Andrew, and Harald Uhlig. 2009. What are the effects of fiscal policy shocks? *Journal of Applied Econometrics* 24(6): 960–992.

Pappa, Evi. 2009. The effects of fiscal shocks on employment and the real wage. *International Economic Review* 50(1): 217–244.

Perotti, Roberto. 2005.'Estimating the effects of fiscal policy in OECD countries. *CEPR Discussion Paper No. 4842*.

Plosser, Charles I. 1989. Understanding real business cycles. *The Journal of Economic Perspectives* 3(3): 51–77.

Prescott, Edward C. 1986. Theory ahead of business-cycle measurement. In *Carnegie-Rochester Conference Series on Public Policy*, vol. 25, 11–44. Amsterdam: Elsevier.

Ramey, Valerie A. 2011. Can government purchases stimulate the economy? *Journal of Economic Literature* 49(3): 673–85.

Ramey, Valerie A. 2016. Macroeconomic shocks and their propagation. In *Handbook of Macroeconomics*, vol. 2, 71–162. Amsterdam: Elsevier.

Ramey, Valerie A., and Matthew D. Shapiro. 1998. Costly capital reallocation and the effects of government spending. In *Carnegie-Rochester Conference Series on Public Policy*, vol. 48, 145–194. Amsterdam: Elsevier.

Rebelo, Sergio. 2005. Real business cycle models: Past, present and future. *The Scandinavian Journal of Economics* 107(2): 217–238.

Romer, Christina D., and David H. Romer. 1989. Does monetary policy matter? A new test in the spirit of Friedman and Schwartz. *NBER Macroeconomics Annual* 4: 121–170.

Romer, Christina D., and David H. Romer. 2010. The macroeconomic effects of tax changes: Estimates based on a new measure of fiscal shocks. *American Economic Review* 100(3): 763–801.

Rotemberg, Julio J., and Michael Woodford. 1992. Oligopolistic pricing and the effects of aggregate demand on economic activity. *Journal of Political Economy* 100(6): 1153–1207.

Rotemberg, Julio J., and Michael Woodford. 1993. Dynamic general equilibrium models with imperfectly competitive product markets, Technical Report, National Bureau of Economic Research.

Rotemberg, Julio J., and Michael Woodford. 1996. Real-business-cycle models and the forecastable movements in output, hours, and consumption. *The American Economic Review* 86(1): 71–89.

Rouwenhorst, K. Geert. 1991. Time to build and aggregate fluctuations: A reconsideration. *Journal of Monetary Economics* 27(2): 241–254.

Samuelson, P.A. 1955. *Economics*, 3rd ed. New York: McGraw-Hill.

Schmitt-Grohe, Stephanie, and Martin Uribe. 2003. Closing small open economy models. *Journal of International Economics* 61(1): 163–185. https://ideas.repec.org/a/eee/inecon/v61y2003i1p163-185.html

Schmitt-Grohé, Stephanie, and Martín Uribe. 2018. How important are terms-of-trade shocks? *International Economic Review* 59(1): 85–111. http://www.jstor.org/stable/45018885

Shapiro, Matthew D. 1994. Federal Reserve policy: Cause and effect. In *Monetary Policy*, 307–334. Chicago: The University of Chicago Press.

Sims, Christopher A. 2002. Solving linear rational expectations models. *Computational Economics* 20(1): 1–20.

Slutsky, E.E. 1937. Qualche proposizione relativa alla teoria delle funzioni aleatorie. *Giorn Ist Ital Attuari* 8: 183–199.

Smets, Frank, and Rafael Wouters. 2007. Shocks and frictions in US business cycles: A Bayesian DSGE approach. *American Economic Review* 97(3): 586–606.

Snowdon, Brian, and Howard R. Vane. 2005. *Modern Macroeconomics: Its Origins, Development and Current State*. Cheltenham: Edward Elgar Publishing.

Stadler, George W. 1994. Real business cycles. *Journal of Economic Literature* 32(4): 1750–1783.

Stiroh, Kevin J. 2009. Volatility accounting: As production perspective on increased economic stability. *Journal of the European Economic Association* 7(4): 671–696.

Stock, James H., and Mark W. Watson. 1999. Business cycle fluctuations in US macroeconomic time series. *Handbook of Macroeconomics* 1: 3–64.

Stock, James H., and Mark W. Watson. 2002. Has the business cycle changed and why? *NBER Macroeconomics Annual* 17: 159–218.

Stoker, Thomas M. 1993. Empirical approaches to the problem of aggregation over individuals. *Journal of Economic Literature* 31(4): 1827–1874.

Stokey, Nancy, Edward Prescott, and Robert E. Lucas. 1989. *Recursive Methods in Economic Dynamics*. Cambridge: Harvard University Press.

Svensson, Lars E.O. 1985. Money and asset prices in a cash-in-advance economy. *Journal of Political Economy* 93(5): 919–944.

Taylor, John B. 1980. Aggregate dynamics and staggered contracts. *Journal of Political Economy* 88(1): 1–23.

Uhlig, Harald. 1995. A toolkit for analyzing nonlinear dynamic stochastic models easily. *Discussion Paper 1995-97, Tilburg University, Center for Economic Research* .

Uhlig, H. 1999. A toolkit for analyzing nonlinear dynamic stochastic models easily. In *Computational Methods for the Study of Dynamic Economies*, ed. Ramon Marimon and Andrew Scott, 30–61. Oxford: Oxford University Press.

Uribe, M., and S. Schmitt-Grohé. 2017. *Open Economy Macroeconomics*. Princeton: Princeton University Press. https://books.google.com.pe/books?id=kHptDQAAQBAJ

Woitek, Ulrich. 1998. A note on the baxter-king filter. *Working Papers 9813, Business School - Economics, University of Glasgow*.

Index

B

Business cycles, 1–23, 25–27, 29–40, 47, 50–53, 177, 229, 279, 280, 287, 321, 323–325, 327, 329, 332, 333, 367–372, 398, 399

C

Calibration, 11, 12, 30, 37, 56, 63, 77, 78, 101, 112, 115–116, 120, 183, 184, 229, 235–236, 282, 290, 304–305, 318, 322

Closed economy, 47, 54, 55, 109, 178, 213, 334, 341, 342, 358

G

General equilibrium, 8, 27, 34, 50, 55, 75, 106, 184, 246

L

Log-linearization, 57, 116, 121–135, 187–200, 229, 236, 240–246, 350, 353, 392

O

Open economy, 24, 33, 36, 37, 323–400

R

RBC models, 1–59, 105–175, 177–227, 229–285, 287–323, 341, 348, 367, 399

S

Steady state, vii, 12, 45, 46, 53, 55, 57, 61, 63, 65–67, 69–72, 74, 76–78, 83–86, 88–92, 95, 103, 105, 116–122, 126–129, 131, 137, 159–163, 165–167, 169, 170, 175, 177, 183–188, 212, 214, 216–221, 225–227, 229, 236–242, 246, 258, 282, 290, 292, 295, 305–307, 309–311, 314, 317, 319, 323, 339, 340, 344, 350–356, 359, 361, 362, 376, 385, 387–393

H. Galindo Gil et al., *Dynamic Stochastic General Equilibrium Models*, Springer Texts in Business and Economics, https://doi.org/10.1007/978-3-031-58105-2

Printed in the USA
CPSIA information can be obtained
at www.ICGtesting.com
CBHW061853131024
15794CB00003B/113

9 783031 581045